Reading Greek
TEXT AND VOCABULARY

SECOND EDITION

First published in 1978, *Reading Greek* has become a best-selling one-year introductory course in ancient Greek for students and adults. It combines the best of modern and traditional language-learning techniques and is used widely in schools, summer schools and universities across the world. It has also been translated into several foreign languages. This volume contains a narrative adapted entirely from ancient authors, including Herodotus, Euripides, Aristophanes and Demosthenes, in order to encourage students rapidly to develop their reading skills. Generous support is provided with vocabulary. At the same time, through the texts and numerous illustrations, students will receive a good introduction to Greek culture, and especially that of Classical Athens. The accompanying *Grammar and Exercises* volume provides full grammatical support together with numerous exercises at different levels, Greek–English and English–Greek vocabularies, a substantial reference grammar and language surveys.

THE JOINT ASSOCIATION OF CLASSICAL TEACHERS' GREEK COURSE

Reading Greek

TEXT AND VOCABULARY

SECOND EDITION

CAMBRIDGE
UNIVERSITY PRESS

CAMBRIDGE UNIVERSITY PRESS
Cambridge, New York, Melbourne, Madrid, Cape Town, Singapore, São Paulo

Cambridge University Press
The Edinburgh Building, Cambridge CB2 8RU, UK

Published in the United States of America by Cambridge University Press, New York

www.cambridge.org
Information on this title: www.cambridge.org/9780521698511

First edition published 1978
Twenty-seventh reprint 2007
Second edition published 2007

Printed in the United Kingdom at the University Press, Cambridge

A catalogue record for this publication is available from the British Library

ISBN 978-0-521-69851-1 paperback

Contents

Foreword

There is one criterion, and one only, by which a course for the learners of a language no longer spoken should be judged: the efficiency and speed with which it brings them to the stage of reading texts in the original language with precision, understanding and enjoyment. The setting-up of the Greek Project by the Joint Association of Classical Teachers was the product of a conviction that it was possible to compose an Ancient Greek course which would satisfy that criterion substantially better than any course already existing.

There would have been little point in such a project if the current decline of Greek in schools had clearly reflected a general, growing and irreversible failure on the part of modern society to respond aesthetically and intellectually to Greek culture; but there has been no such failure of response, for the popularity of Greek literature in translation and of courses in Greek art and history has continued to increase. It seemed to the Joint Association that there was a gap waiting for a bridge. Bridges cost money, and when an appeal for £40,000 was launched at the beginning of 1974 by Dr Michael Ramsey and others it was legitimate to wonder how the cause of Greek would fare in competition with louder claims. But the optimists were justified: by November £63,000 had been contributed, a sum which more than compensated for the effect of inflation after the original costing of the project, and in 1976 an appeal for the money required for a fourth and final year of work brought in more than £15,000. Gratitude is due to hundreds of individuals, to many schools, colleges, institutions and trusts, and in particular to the Leverhulme Trust Fund, the Ernest Cook Trust and the Cambridge University Faculty of Classics.

It would not have been difficult to compile yet another systematic descriptive grammar of Greek and interleave it with exercises which would test the learner's progress through grammar stage by stage. Nor would it have been difficult to confront the learner with an anthology of Greek literature, translate most of it for him, offer from time to time some grammatical rules-of-thumb and inspire him with the hope that he would get the hang of the language and eventually pick up the 'gist' or the 'essentials' of any Greek text.

Anyone who learns Greek by the first of those two ways will take a very long time to reach the point of reading a genuine Greek text; on the way he will have acquired much more grammatical knowledge than he needs and much less knowledge than he needs of Greek thought and feeling. The technique of compiling a descriptive grammar for reference purposes and the technique of introducing a learner to a language are utterly different, as teachers of modern languages know.

The notion that one can get the gist of alien texts simply by reading a lot of them with the help of translations but without careful linguistic guidance is equally illusory. We can indeed hope to understand much of what is said to us in a modern language if we are put into an environment in which we hear it all day; but our progress depends on our being an ingredient of the situation in which the words are uttered and on the readiness of the native speaker to repeat, simplify, slow down and supplement language by signs and gestures. Our relationship to Greek authors is different; if we tackle Platonic argument or tragic dialogue with only a hazy idea of grammar the chances of misunderstanding – not marginal, but total misunderstanding – are very high.

The Project course has been composed and scrutinised by people who care most about what works best and do not use 'traditional' or 'modern' as complimentary or derogatory terms. In the earlier sections the commonest words and constructions preponderate, and the sentences are short; but the sentence-structure has not been anglicised, and the test of frequency has not been so rigorously applied to the admission of vocabulary and idiom as to bleach all colour out of the language. At the start the Greek text is modern composition, though its subject-matter is derived from Greek sources, but the voices of Plato and Aristophanes soon begin to be heard, and thereafter modern composers are edged out as the ancient authors, progressively less rewritten to suit the beginner's limitations, take over. The content of the text is determined as seldom as possible by linguistic tidiness and as often as possible by the need to acquaint the adult and near-adult learner directly with the characteristic features of Greek culture.

Not everyone thinks that it is right to make up Greek or to adapt original texts. There is nothing, in any language course, that everyone thinks is right. The Project Team, the Steering Committee and the Advisory Panel have been compelled repeatedly to take decisions – sometimes against the judgment of a minority, but never without patient and friendly discussion – which will incur criticism. Critics are asked to reflect that the combined class-room, lecture-room and tutorial experience of Team, Committee and Panel is not only considerable but also very varied; that successive drafts, having been tested in the JACT Summer School and elsewhere, in this country and in the United States, have been constantly revised in the light of what emerged from the testing; and that in language-learning occasions may arise on which one man's succulent meat is another man's cold cabbage. The Team has been from first to last imaginative and resourceful, prompt and cheerful in response to criticism and unfailingly resilient in the face of technical difficulties. They have produced a course which they have many good reasons to believe will prove, for the majority of learners, a straighter and shorter path than any other into Greek literature as the Greeks themselves knew it.

K.J. Dover

Preface to the second edition

The Joint Association of Classical Teachers' Greek Course *Reading Greek* has been written for beginners in the upper school, at university and in adult education. Its aim is to enable students to read fifth- and fourth-century Attic Greek, Homer and Herodotus, with some fluency and intelligence in one to two years. It consists of a continuous, graded Greek text, adapted from original sources (contained in *Reading Greek* [*Text*, with vocabularies]), coupled with a grammar book (*Reading Greek* [*Grammar and Exercises*]) which runs in phase with the text.

Method

The two books are to be used in conjunction.

Stage One (using the *Text* and running vocabularies) With the help of the teacher and accompanying vocabularies, read and translate the Greek in the *Text* up to the point in the *Grammar* book where grammatical explanations for those sections begin. The text has been written to encourage beginners to read with increasing fluency and confidence. The running vocabularies are so written as to enable students to read ahead out of class once the main grammatical principles have been established. It is vital to encourage students to do this.

Stage Two Ensure that the learning vocabularies have been mastered.

Stage Three Turn to the running Grammar, which lays out and explains clearly and practically the relevant grammar which should now be learnt.

Stage Four Do as many of the Exercises as the teacher considers necessary to clarify and reinforce the grammar. When all this has been done, the student should be able to tackle successfully the Test Exercise as an unseen.

Then return to the *Text* and repeat the process. As the student progresses, adaptation of the *Text* lessens until wholly unadapted Greek is being read.

At the back of the *Grammar* is a Reference Grammar which summarises the material in the running Grammar, Language Surveys which review and expand upon the features met in the running Grammar, Vocabularies and various indices.

The use of the Course

It is essential that students should be encouraged to read the *Text* with as much speed – consonant with accurate understanding – as possible. The amount of reading given, its controlled gradient and the very full vocabulary help should all further this end. The Grammar and Exercises contain the detailed linguistic work needed to clinch the grammatical lessons of the *Text*.

The design of the Course makes it ideal for students who can spend only a short time with their teachers each week. Because there is a great deal of carefully graded reading, supported by full vocabulary help, such students will find plenty of reading which they can do on their own.

Independent learners

Students working on their own will be helped through the course by *An Independent Study Guide to Reading Greek* (second edition, 2008).

Further help

Peter Jones, *Learn Ancient Greek* (Duckworth/Barnes and Noble, 1998) is a very simple self-teach introduction to the basics of ancient Greek which has proved a useful 'starter' course for *Reading Greek*.

The following two inexpensive Oxford paperbacks are highly recommended.

James Morwood and John Taylor (eds.), *Pocket Oxford Classical Greek Dictionary* (Oxford 2002).

James Morwood, *Oxford Grammar of Classical Greek* (Oxford 2001).

After *Reading Greek*

Reading Greek prepares students to read mainstream fifth- and fourth-century Attic, Homer and Herodotus.

The second part of the Course consists of three volumes - two texts (fully illustrated) and a vocabulary - again published by Cambridge University Press under the general rubric of 'The Joint Association of Classical Teachers' Greek Course' series. Each text consists of 600-900 line selections from major classical authors, with facing-page vocabulary and notes:

A World of Heroes (1979): Homer, Herodotus, and Sophocles.

The Intellectual Revolution (1980): Euripides, Thucydides and Plato.

Greek Vocabulary (1980): this slim volume contains all the vocabulary not glossed on the facing pages of the above texts.

The success of *Reading Greek* has generated demand for further texts in the series, all with notes and facing-page vocabularies, and fully illustrated. These too are designed to follow on immediately after *Reading Greek*:

The Triumph of Odysseus (1996): Homer's *Odyssey* 21–22 (complete).

New Testament Greek: A Reader (2001).

A Greek Anthology (2002): extracts from over a thousand years of Greek literature.

The World of Athens (second edition, 2008)

Published in 1984 and now completely revised in the light of recent scholarship by Professor Robin Osborne (King's College Cambridge), *The World of Athens* provides an up-to-date, fully illustrated and clearly-written introduction to the history, culture and society of classical Athens. It deals with all the issues raised in the *Text* of *Reading Greek*. Cross-references to *The World of Athens* (second edition) will be found throughout the *Text*. From time to time we also quote extracts from *WoA*^{ii}, adjusted to fit the context or with additional relevant material. WoAii's conventions of spelling have been brought into line with RG's in these casts.

Acknowledgements to the original edition of *Reading Greek* (1978)

Reading Greek was developed by a Project Team (Dr P.V. Jones, Dr K.C. Sidwell and Miss F.E. Corrie) under the guidance of a Steering Committee and Advisory Panel made up as follows:

Steering Committee: Professor J.P.A. Gould (Bristol University) (Chairman); M.G. Balme (Harrow School); R.M. Griffin (Manchester Grammar School); Dr J.T. Killen (Joint Treasurer, Jesus College, Cambridge); Sir Desmond Lee (Joint Treasurer, President, Hughes Hall, Cambridge); A.C.F. Verity (Headmaster, Leeds Grammar School); Miss E.P. Story (Hughes Hall, Cambridge).

Advisory Panel: G.L. Cawkwell (University College, Oxford); Dr J. Chadwick (Downing College, Cambridge); Professor A. Morpurgo Davies (Somerville College, Oxford); Sir Kenneth Dover (President, Corpus Christi College, Oxford); Professor E.W. Handley (University College, London); B.W. Kay (HMI); Dr A.H. Sommerstein (Nottingham University); Dr B. Sparkes (Southampton University); G. Suggitt (Headmaster, Stratton School); A.F. Turberfield (HMI). The Committee and Panel met in full session three times a year during the period 1974-8 while the Course was being developed, but also divided up into sub-committees to give specific help to the Project Team on certain aspects of the Course, as follows:

Text: K.J.D.; E.W.H.

Grammar: J.C.; A.M.D.; A.H.S. (who, with K.J.D., have kindly made individual contributions to the Reference Grammar and Language Surveys).

Exercises: M.G.B.; R.M.G.; A.C.F.V.

Background: G.L.C.; J.P.A.G.; B.S.

Dissemination: B.W.K.; H.D.P.L.; E.P.S.; G.S.; A.F.T.

We have also been guided by a number of overseas scholars who have used, or given advice on, the Course, as follows:

J.A. Barsby (Dunedin, New Zealand); S. Ebbesen (Copenhagen, Denmark); B. Gollan (Queensland, Australia); Professor A.S. Henry (Monash, Australia); Drs D. Sieswerda (Holland); Professor H.A. Thompson (Princeton, U.S.A.).

We would like to stress the immense debt of gratitude which we all owe to the Steering Committee, Advisory Panel and our overseas advisers. But we would also like to make it clear that the final decisions about every aspect of the Course and any errors of omission and commission are the sole responsibility of the Team.

We gratefully acknowledge the help and advice of Professor D. W. Packard (Chapel Hill, N. Carolina, U.S.A.) on the use of the computer in analysing and printing Greek; and of Dr John Dawson of the Cambridge University Literary and Linguistic Computing Laboratory, who made available to us the resources of the Computer Centre for printing and analysing draft material in the early stages of the Project.

We have learnt a great deal from members of the Team who produced the Cambridge Latin Course, and are extremely grateful to them for help, especially in the early stages of the Project. If we have produced a Course which takes a more traditional view of language-learning, our debt to many of the principles and much of the practice which the C.L.C. first advocated is still very great.

Finally, our best thanks go to all the teachers in schools, universities and adult education centres both in the U.K. and overseas who used and criticised draft materials. We owe an especial debt of thanks to the organisers of the J.A.C.T. Greek Summer School in Cheltenham, who allowed us to use our material at the School for the three years while the Course was being developed.

Peter V. Jones (Director)
Keith C. Sidwell (Second Writer)
Frances E. Corrie (Research Assistant)

The second edition of *Reading Greek* (2007)

The main features of the revised course

Reading Greek was originally written on the assumption that its users would know Latin. *Tempora mutantur* – it has now been revised on the assumption that they do not, and in the light of the experiences of those using the course over nearly thirty years. While the overall structure of the course and its reading matter remain the same, the most important changes are:

Text

1. The running and learning vocabularies are now in the *Text*, on the same pages as the Greek to which they refer. The *Text* also has the total Greek-English Learning Vocabulary at the back, as does the *Grammar*.
2. There are indications throughout the *Text* of what grammatical material is being introduced and at what point; and there are cross-references to the sections of *The World of Athens* (second edition) relevant to the story-line and issues under discussion.

   As a result of these changes, the Text *can now act as a stand-alone 'revision' reader for anyone who has a basic grasp of ancient Greek, whatever beginners' course they have used. The second half of the* Text *in particular, starting with its carefully adapted extracts from the extremely important legal speech against the woman Neaira and leading on to Plato and an introduction to the dialects of Herodotus and Homer, makes an ideal introduction to some superb literature and central social, cultural, historical and philosophical issues relating to the ancient Greek world.*

3. Various aspects of the cultural and historical background of the *Text* are discussed from time to time *in situ*.
4. The original Section Five has been split into two sections, Five and Six. As a result, there are now twenty sections to the course.

Grammar

The *Grammar* has been completely re-written and re–designed. The aim has been to make its lay-out and content more user-friendly:

1. There is an introduction to some basics of English grammar and its terminology, and its relation to ancient Greek.
2. Explanations are clearer and fuller, composed for those who have never learnt an inflected language, and the lay-out more generous on the eye.
3. Brief, usually one-word, *Exercises* accompany the explanations of each new item of grammar. *If the teacher so chooses*, these can be used to provide instant feed-back on the student's grasp of the new material.
4. Declensions go down, not across, the page and the 'shading' of cases has been abandoned.

Acknowledgements

The revision was conducted under the aegis of a sub-committee of the Joint Association of Classical Teachers' Greek Committee, the body that invented the idea of the Project and oversaw it from its inception in 1974. The sub-committee consisted of Professor David Langslow (University of Manchester, chairman), Dr Peter Jones (Course Director), Dr Andrew Morrison (University of Manchester), James Morwood (Wadham College, Oxford), Dr James Robson (Open University), Dr John Taylor (Tonbridge School), Dr Naoko Yamagata (Open University), Dr James Clackson (Jesus College, Cambridge) and Adrian Spooner (Management Consultant).

The sub-committee met roughly once a term for two years and took decisions that affected every aspect of the second edition. It concentrated particularly on the *Grammar*. Sections 1–2 were revised in the first instance by Dr Andrew Morrison, Sections 3–9 by Dr James Robson and Sections 10–20 by Dr Peter Jones, while the Language Surveys were revised by Professor David Langslow. Members of the sub-committee read and commented on virtually everything. Professor Brian Sparkes (University of Southampton) again advised on the illustrations. We are grateful to the students and tutors at the 2006 JACT Greek Summer School in Bryanston for giving a thorough testing to the first half of the revised course in draft form, especially to Anthony Bowen (Jesus College, Cambridge); and to Dr Janet Watson for work on the proofs.

Cambridge University Press has given its full backing to the revision. Dr Michael Sharp patiently discussed and met with most of our requests, Peter

Ducker solved the complicated design problems with elegance and ingenuity and Dr Caroline Murray expertly oversaw the computerisation of the text.

Dr Peter Jones as Director carries final responsibility for this second edition.

Peter Jones
Newcastle on Tyne
September 2006

Notes on illustrations

p. 3 *top*	Map showing the route from Byzantium to Athens.
p. 3 *bottom*	View of the Acropolis of Athens from the south-west. On the left are the Propylaia and small Nike temple; over the brow in the centre is the Erekhtheion with the Parthenon standing out at the southern edge. Photo: Alison Frantz (AT 71). Courtesy of the American School of Classical Studies at Athens.
p. 5	Detail of a merchant vessel taken from the same cup depicted on p. 7.
p. 7	Attic black-figure cup depicting a merchant vessel on the left and a two-level warship on the right. The merchant vessel is round and capacious and powered by sails; the warship is sleek and low and propelled by oars or sail. Late sixth century BC. London, British Museum (B 436). © The Trustees of the British Museum.
p. 11 *left*	Detail of an Attic red-figure Nolan amphora, attributed to the Oionokles Painter, showing Herakles destroying the house of Syleus; he puts his axe to a fallen capital. Syleus of Lydia usually forced passing strangers to dig his vineyard; Herakles uprooted his vines and/or tore down his house. Second quarter of the fifth century BC. Paris, Louvre (G 210). Photo: RMN – Hervé Lewandowski.
p. 11 *right*	Detail of an Attic black-figure oinokhoe, attributed to the Keyside Class, showing a ship with one man standing on the prow and others in the forepart of the ship – the subject is uncertain. That the ship is not coming to land is shown by the raised mast and sail and by the fact that ships were beached stern first. Late sixth century BC. London, British Museum (B 508). © The Trustees of the British Museum.
p. 16	Attic red-figure amphora of Panathenaic shape, attributed to the Kleophrades Painter, depicting Poseidon with some of the attributes of his realm: a trident and a fish. Poseidon is depicted as a mature man with beard and long hair. Early fifth century BC. © bpk, Berlin, 2006/Antikensammlung, SMB (F 2164)/ Jutta Tietz-Glagow.
p. 19	Attic red-figure neck-amphora, attributed to the Kleophrades Painter, depicting an rhapsode on a platform. He stands with

his staff held prominently in front of him, and the painter has added words in front of his mouth – 'Once upon a time in Tyrins [*sic*] …' – most likely the beginning of an epic in hexameters. Early fifth century BC. London, British Museum (E 270). © The Trustees of the British Museum.

p. 22 *left*   Attic red-figure skyphos, attributed to a follower of Douris, depicting a Persian seated on a rock, his right hand stretched out to his large wicker shield. He wears an outfit that is furnished with trousers and long sleeves, and has a soft hat (*tiara*) on his head. This is one of a number of representations of Persians that seem to have been influenced by the contacts of the early fifth century. Mid-fifth century BC. © bpk, Berlin, 2006/Antikensammlung, SMB (VI 3156).

p. 22 *right*   Interior design of an Attic red-figure cup, attributed to the Triptolemos Painter, depicting a fight between a Greek and a Persian. A contrast is made between the outfit of the Greek warrior (bronze helmet, greaves and breast-plate) and the Persian trouser-suit. Both warriors wield curved swords, but the Greek has a shield and the Persian a bow and quiver. First quarter of the fifth century BC. Edinburgh, National Museums of Scotland (1887.213). © The Trustees of the National Museums of Scotland.

p. 24   Carved frieze from the 'Treasury' of the Palace at Persepolis. On a platform in the centre sits Dareios enthroned with Xerxes behind him. He is giving an audience to a Median official who is making a gesture of respect; in front of him are two incense burners. The poles of the now missing baldacchino separate the armed guards from the central characters. Behind Xerxes stand two high court officials. Much of the architecture and sculpture of the palace at Persepolis betrays the influence and the hand of Greek craftsmen. Early fifth century BC. Teheran, Archaeological Museum. Photo copyright The Oriental Institute Museum, Chicago, all rights reserved.

p. 26   Design on an Attic black-figure plate, attributed to Psiax, depicting a trumpeter, hand on hip, trumpet held high, blowing a summons. The trumpeter is dressed in armour. Last quarter of the sixth century BC. London, British Museum (B 590). © The Trustees of the British Museum.

p. 28   Map of Athens and Salamis.

p. 32   Interior design of an Attic red-figure cup depicting a warrior wearing a loin-cloth and greaves and carrying a shield, helmet and spear. The warrior runs to the right but looks left; is he fleeing from the fight? The painter, Skythes ('Skythian'), tends to have a humourous view on life. Last quarter of the sixth century BC. Paris, Louvre (CA 1527). Photo: RMN.

p. 38 *left* Map of Athens and the harbours at Periaieus

p. 38 *right* Detail of an Attic red-figure oinokhoe depicting a young man in front of an altar pouring a libation from a shallow bowl.First quarter of the fifth century BC. Antikenmuseum Basel und Sammlung Ludwig, Inv. Kä 423. Photo: Andreas F. Vögelin and Claire Niggli.

p. 40 Bronze figurine of Zeus making ready to hurl his thunderbolt. The workmanship is most likely Corinthian. Second quarter of the fifth century BC. © bpk, Berlin, 2006/Antikensammlung, SMB (10561)/Christa Begall.

p. 42 Detail of Attic black-figure one-handled kantharos showing a man lying on his bier. The woman (painted white) had the duty of preparing the body for burial, and the men now come to pay their respects and to join in the lamentation. London, British Museum (1899.7-21.1). © The Trustees of the British Museum.

p. 46 Drawing of the sanctuary of the Twelve Gods in the centre of Athens. Situated near the northern edge of the Agora, this sanctuary, consisting of an altar within a fenced area, was a place of refuge and the point from which distances to other parts of Greece were measured. The sanctuary was founded by the younger Peisistratos in the year of his archonship, 522/1 BC.

p. 52 *left* Attic red-figure skyphos, attributed to the Euaion Painter, depicting Theseus in a cloak and traveling hat. He carries two spears. Sinis, the pine-bender, is shown on the other side of the skyphos, seated under a tree and holding a club. This is one of Theseus' adventures on his way from Troizen to Athens. Mid-fifth century BC. © bpk, Berlin, 2006/Antikensammlung, SMB (F 2580)/Jutta Tietz-Glagow.

p. 52 *right* Detail of an Attic red-figure pelike, attributed to a painter who is a bad imitation of the Chicago Painter, showing Telephos, king of the Mysians, who has seized the infant Orestes as hostage and has taken refuge on an altar as a suppliant. His bandaged left thigh indicates the place of the wound inflicted by Achilles' spear. Agamemnon (not shown) faces him on the left. Second quarter of the fifth century BC. London, British Museum (E 382). © The Trustees of the British Museum.

p. 53 *left* Bronze figurine of a horse, part of a chariot team of four. The harness is particularly clear, showing the bit with curved cheek-piece and the collar to which the traces were fastened. Second quarter of the fifth century BC. Olympia, Museum. Photo: DAI Athen (Olympia 1808).

p. 53 *right* A selection of Athenian silver coins of various denominations. Cambridge, Fitzwilliam Museum. Reproduced by permission of the Syndics of the Fitzwilliam Museum.

p. 57   A clay lamp with lighted wick. This small container for oil could supply light for 2-3 hours and burn brighter than a candle. Athens, Agora Museum (L 4137). Photo courtesy of the American School of Classical Studies at Athens, Agora Excavations.

p. 61   These two oven-bells were pre-heated and placed over already prepared dough; they were also used as fire extinguishers. C. 500 BC (left) and c. 400 BC (right). Athens, Agora Museum (P 8862 and P 10133). Photo courtesy of the American School of Classical Studies at Athens, Agora Excavations.

p. 64 *left*   A pair of model clay travelling boots found in an Early Geometric cremation grave of a woman. Athens, Agora Museum (P 19429). Photo courtesy of the American School of Classical Studies at Athens, Agora Excavations.

p. 64 *right*   Detail of an Attic red-figure amphora, attributed to the Painter of the Munich Amphora, depicting a pair of boots on a small footstool under a table; above the table a man reclines on a couch. Early fifth century BC. Munich, Antikensammlung (2303). Photo: Hirmer Fotoarchiv.

p. 72   View of Delphi facing south-east. The fourth-century version of Apollo's temple lies beyond the theatre in the foreground. Photo: Alison Frantz (ST 1b). Courtesy of the American School of Classical Studies at Athens.

p. 73   Detail of an Attic red-figure volute-krater, attributed to the Kleophon Painter and found at Spina in Italy, depicting a procession to Apollo at Delphi. Apollo is seated at the right on a throne raised on a platform. The setting is a temple represented by four columns of the Doric order. Apollo's attributes consist of a laurel branch and crown, and a quiver and bow on the wall; the Delphic location is given by the naval stone and tripod in front of the columns. An official waits for the procession to arrive; it is headed by a young girl in festal robe carrying a sacrificial basket (*kanoun*) on her head. Third quarter of the fifth century BC. Museo Archeologico Nazionale di Ferrara (T 57C VP).

p. 76 *left*   The pedestal of an Attic marble votive relief showing a cobbler's shop with men and a child at work. The inscription which starts below this scene indicates that the dedication is by a cobbler Dionysios and his children to the hero Kallistephanos. The main relief above the pedestal is not preserved. Mid-fourth century BC. Athens, Agora Museum (I 7396). Photo courtesy of the American School of Classical Studies at Athens, Agora Excavations.

p. 76 *right*   East Greek (Samian?) rock crystal with an intaglio design of a helmet-maker seated on a stool tapping the crown of the helmet with a small hammer. It is a popular motif in gem carving. Late sixth century BC. Munich, Staatliche Münzsammlung (36246).

who is seated with a lyre. Above their heads is the inscription 'The boy is handsome' (*kalos*), a popular comment whether in this general form or with a particular name substituted. Second quarter of the fifth century BC. Hamburg, Museum für Kunst und Gewerbe (1900.164).

p. 105 *left*   Interior design of an Attic red-figure cup, attributed to the Antiphon Painter, depicting a she-ass with a wooden-framed pack saddle. The ass, which was the usual pack animal, has no bit or mouthpiece. C. 480 BC. Boston, Museum of Fine Arts (10.199). James Fund and Museum purchase with funds donated by contributors. Photograph © 2006, Museum of Fine Arts, Boston.

p. 105 *right*   Attic red-figure pelike, attributed to a painter near the Göttingen Painter, depicting Odysseus escaping under a ram. He is in armour and wields a sword; he clings on but the lines across the animal make allusion to the tying of his comrades. No Cyclops is shown; the story was so well known and distinctive that it could be presented in extract. C. 490-480 BC. Boston, Museum of Fine Arts (61.384). Anonymous gift in memory of Laccy D. Caskey. Photograph © 2006, Museum of Fine Arts, Boston.

p. 110 *left*   Modern replicas of an Athenian water-clock (*klepsydra*) used for timing speeches in the lawcourts. A plug in the bronze tube at the base of the bowl was released at the start of a speech. The two *khis* indicate that the bowl held two *khoes* (6.4 litres), and the bowl was emptied in six minutes. The name *Antiokhidos*, meaning 'belonging to the Antiokhis tribe', may indicate that this bowl was used when the tribe was presiding in the Council chamber (*Bouleuterion*). Athens, Agora Museum (P 2084). Photo courtesy of the American School of Classical Studies at Athens, Agora Excavations.

p. 110 *right*   Interior design of an Attic red-figure cup, attributed to the Foundry Painter, depicting a reveller, with a scarf around his head, a cloak over his shoulders and a stick under his armpit, relieving himself into a jug. First quarter of the fifth century BC. © bpk, Berlin, 2006/Antikensammlung, SMB (VI 3198).

p. 111 *left*   Interior design of an Attic red-figure cup, attributed to Onesimos, depicting a balding man picking his way along with a basket and stick in his left hand and a bucket (*kados*), most likely of bronze, in his right. The garland round his temples proclaims him as a reveller. First quarter of the fifth century BC. Boston, Museum of Fine Arts (95.29). Catharine Page Perkins Fund. Photograph © 2006, Museum of Fine Arts, Boston.

p. 111 *right*   A clay bucket (*kados*) used for drawing water from the well, as opposed to the water-jar (hydria) which was used at the fountain. On the shoulder of this bucket the words 'I am a kados' have been scratched; it is usual for objects to be given the power of speech in such inscriptions. The word *kalos* has also been scratched, as though the bucket were calling itself 'handsome'. Late sixth century BC. Photo: DAI Athen (Kerameikos 7357).

p. 112   The trial of Labes from a modern Greek production of Aristophanes' *Wasps*. Courtesy of D. H. Harrisiades and the National Tourism Organisation of Greece.

p. 114   A selection of ordinary Athenian kitchen equipment: a casserole on a deep firebox, a barrel cooker and a brazier. Fifth and fourth centuries BC. Athens, Agora Museum (P 2306 on 16521, P 16512 on 16520, P 2362). Photo courtesy of the American School of Classical Studies at Athens, Agora Excavations.

p. 117   Boiotian terracotta figurine of a woman grating stuff into a mixing bowl. Early fifth century BC. Boston, Museum of Fine Arts (01.7783). Museum purchase with funds donated by contributors. Photograph © 2006, Museum of Fine Arts, Boston.

p. 126   Detail of an Attic red-figure skyphos, attributed to the Brygos Painter, depicting a reveler and a courtesan (*hetaira*). Early fifth century BC. Paris, Louvre (G 156). Photo: RMN – Chuzeville.

p. 128 *left*   Interior of an Attic red-figure cup, attributed to Onesimos, depicting a balding man at a party inviting a courtesan (*hetaira*) to disrobe. The man wears shoes and holds his walking stick; a basket and a lyre are in the background. First quarter of the fifth century BC. London, British Museum (E 44). © The Trustees of the British Museum.

p. 128 *right*   Detail of an Attic red-figure cup, attributed to Makron, with a reveler and a courtesan (*hetaira*) together on a couch. First quarter of the fifth century BC. New York, The Metropolitan Museum of Art, Rogers Fund, 1920 (20.246). Image © The Metropolitan Museum of Art.

p. 130   Drawing of the Athenian Agora from the north-west.

p. 133   Attic red-figure plate, attributed to Epiktetos, depicting an archer drawing a bow from his quiver as he turns his head to the right to face his unseen pursuer. He wears an 'Oriental' suit with long sleeves and trousers and a high-crowned Scythian cap. Last quarter of the sixth century BC. London, British Museum (E 135). © The Trustees of the British Museum.

p. 136   Interior of an Attic red-figure cup, in the manner of the Antiphon Painter, depicting a youth holding a cup in his left hand and a ladle in his right. Behind him stands a mixing-bowl with a wine-cooler set inside. The garland in his hair is a further indication that this is an extract from a party. First quarter of the fifth century BC. Compiègne, Musée Vivenel (inv. 1102).

p. 138   Attic red-figure cup, attributed to the Amphitrite Painter, depicting a bridegroom leading his bride towards their home. The bride, who is as usual veiled, is followed by a woman with a torch, whilst on the left the house is represented by a door and a column within which stands the groom's mother also holding torches. A young man serenades the couple on the lyre. This may be a version of the wedding of Peleus and Thetis. Second quarter of the fifth century BC. © bpk, Berlin, 2006/ Antikensammlung, SMB (F 2530)/Jutta Tietz-Glagow.

p. 144   The agora area of Athens, with the 'Hephaisteion' on the far left and the Acropolis on the far right. The long building in the centre is the recently rebuilt Stoa of Attalos, originally erected in the middle of the second century BC; it then formed the east side of the agora. The west side was below the hill on which the 'Hephaisteion' stood. The lawcourts lay in and around this area. In the middle distance rises the peak of Lykabettos and on the right the range of Hymettos. Photo: DAI Athen.

p. 148   Reconstructed drawing of the monument of the Eponymous Heroes. This consisted of a row of statues of the 'patrons' of the ten tribes into which Athens and Attica were divided by Kleisthenes at the close of the sixth century BC. The base of the monument was used for the display of drafts of proposed new laws, notices of lawsuits and lists for military service. Courtesy of the American School of Classical Studies at Athens.

p. 152   Detail of an Attic red-figure plaque, found at Eleusis, showing extracts from the Eleusinian cult. Precise interpretation of the scenes is not sure, but Demeter may be represented twice at the right side with Persephone by her side in the upper level and Iakkhos facing her with torches on the lower level. The figures on the left may be initiates approaching. An inscription on the plaque says that it was dedicated to the goddesses by Niinnion, perhaps the courtesan Nannion of that period. Mid-fourth century BC. Athens, National Archaeological Museum (inv. 11036).

p. 155   Official voting discs found in the Athenian Agora. Each juror was given two discs, one with solid hub (for acquittal), one with hollow hub (for condemnation); by placing thumb and forefinger over the hubs the juror could make his vote without revealing his preference. Some discs carry the inscription 'Official ballot', some a letter in relief, perhaps to indicate the jury-section. A less sophisticated system of pebbles (*psephoi*) was in operation before the fourth century BC. Athens, Agora Museum (B 1056, 146, 728, 1058, 1055). Photo courtesy of the American School of Classical Studies at Athens, Agora Excavations.

p. 156   Attic red-figure cup, attributed to the Brygos Painter, depicting a symposium in progress. The men recline on couches; one girl plays the pipes while another prepares to give a cup of wine to one of the men. A youth holds a lyre by a column, an indication of an indoor scene. Baskets hang on the wall. First quarter of the fifth century BC. London, British Museum (E 68). © The Trustees of the British Museum.

p. 162   Detail of rolled-out drawing of Attic black-figure lekythos, attributed to the Amasis Painter, depicting women at work spinning, preparing wool and weaving. The lekythos may have been a wedding present to a bride. Mid-sixth century BC. New York, The Metropolitan Museum of Art, Fletcher Fund, 1931 (31.11.10). Image © The Metropolitan Museum of Art.

p. 174   The side-reliefs of a marble altar frame (?), the so-called Ludovisi Throne. A contrast is made between the veiled woman at the incense-burner and the naked flute-girl. The purpose, meaning and place of manufacture are all in doubt. Second quarter of the fifth century BC. Rome, Museo Nazionale Romano (inv. 8670). Photo: Alinari Archives, Florence.

p. 183   Detail of an Attic red-figure onos (used in wool-working), attributed to the Eretria Painter, depicting preparations for the wedding of Alkestis (on the right). She is pictured at the entrance to her bridal chamber, and her friends fill a loutrophoros with myrtle (centre) and lebetes gamikoi with sprigs (left), both types of vase connected with the wedding ceremony. Two other friends play with a pet bird. The object may have been a wedding present to a bride. Third quarter of the fifth century BC. Athens, National Archaeological Museum (inv. 1629).

p. 187   Detail of an Apulian red-figure loutrophoros depicting Alkestis surrounded by her children and with her husband Admetos on the left. The white-haired woman on the right may be Admetos' mother or nurse; the old man is the children's tutor (*paidagogos*). This is one of the finest of the South Italian treatments of tragic themes. Mid-fourth century BC. Antikenmuseum Basel und Sammlung Ludwig, Inv. S 21. Photo: Andreas F. Vögelin and Claire Niggli.

p. 189   Attic red-figure cup, attributed to the Panaitios Painter, depicting a brawl between revellers. C. 480 BC. The State Hermitage Museum, St Petersburg (B-2100).

p. 204   Drawn reconstruction of a country house near Vari in Attica. From *Annual of the British School at Athens* 68 (1973), 355-452.

p. 205   A bronze hydria. Third quarter of the fifth century BC. Cambridge, Mass., Fogg Museum (1949.89). Reproduced courtesy of the Trustees of the Harvard University Art Museums.

Notes to the second edition

1   Running and learning vocabularies accompany the *Text*. Grammar and exercises, written to run in step with the *Text*, are to be found in the companion volume *Reading Greek* (*Grammar and Exercises*).

2   A linking-device (⌢) is used in places in the *Text*. Its purpose is to show words or groups of words which should be taken together either because they agree or because they make a phrase. When the words to be linked are separated by intervening words, the linking device takes the shape ⌐ ¬. They are phased out as the grammar that underpins them is learnt.

    Look up such linked phrases in the vocabulary *under the first word*.

3   The sources quoted on the title-page of each Part are the major (though by no means exclusive) sources for the whole Part.

4   The title-page of each Part carries time recommendations for that Part. They are based on a three to four-session week, and assume preparation by students (particularly by reading ahead on their own, with the help of the vocabularies). If the recommendations are followed, *Reading Greek* will be completed in 37 weeks.

    There are 118 sub-sections (i.e. sections marked A, B, C, etc.)

5   Transcriptions of proper names into English:

  (a) Generally, proper names are transcribed from Greek into English in accordance with the transcriptions given in the *Grammar and Exercises*, **342**. Note that the transcription will not distinguish between ε and η, ο and ω, or other long and short vowels.

  (b) There are, however, some 'privileged' names, so common in their received form that to alter them by the principles of transcription that we generally adopt would be off-putting. You will find, for example, 'Athens', not 'Athenai' (Ἀθῆναι), 'Homer', not 'Homeros' (Ὅμηρος), and 'Plato', not 'Platon' (Πλάτων).

  (c) All proper names met in the *Text* are transcribed either in the running vocabulary or in the List of Proper Names in the *Grammar and Exercises* book. (Most Greek words have, traditionally, been transcribed according to Latin principles, and the most important of these are given in *Grammar and Exercises*, **454**).

6   All dates are B.C., except where otherwise stated.

Introduction

Dikaiopolis sails towards the harbour of Athens, Peiraieus. On board ship a criminal plot is foiled, and then the story of the naval battle of Salamis is recalled while the ship passes the island. As the ship comes into port, the Spartans launch a surprise attack.

The scene is set during the early part of the Peloponnesian War, which began in 431.

Sources

Demosthenes, *Orations* 32
Plato, *Ion* 540eff.
A comic fragment, *Com.*
  Adespot. 340 (Edmonds)
Lysias, *Funeral Speech* 27ff.
Herodotus, *Histories* 8.83ff.
Homer, *Iliad (passim)*

Aeschylus, *Persians* 353ff.
Thucydides, *Histories* 2.93–4,
  1.142, 6.32
Xenophon, *Hellenika* 5.i. 19–23
Aristophanes, *Akharnians*
  393ff.
Euripides, *Helen* 1577ff.

Time to be taken

Five weeks (= twenty sessions at four sessions a week)

Important note on the accompanying vocabulary-lists

1. Each vocabulary-list appears in *alphabetical order*.
2. Many phrases in the text are joined by the linking devices ⌢ and ⌐ ⌐ , e.g. the first sentence τὸ‿πλοῖόν ἐστιν ἐν‿Βυζαντίῳ. ἐν⌐ δὲ ⌐Βυζαντίῳ … . Such phrases will be listed in the running vocabularies *under the **first** word of the phrase*. Thus τὸ‿πλοῖόν will appear under τὸ; ἐν⌐ δὲ ⌐Βυζαντίῳ will appear under ἐν; and so on. Links are phased out as noun-types and cases are learnt.

3. At the end of each running vocabulary-list, and elsewhere in the accompanying *Grammar* explanations, you will find lists of *words to be learnt*. These words will not be repeated in the running vocabulary lists but are grouped together in the *Grammar* from time to time (e.g. p. 23). All such vocabulary will be found in the *Total Greek-English Learning Vocabulary* at the back of both the *Text* volume and the *Grammar* volume.

4. Accents in the running vocabularies are printed as they appear in the text.

5. Macra – indicating a vowel pronounced long – are marked *only* in *Learning Vocabularies* and the *Total Vocabulary* at the back.

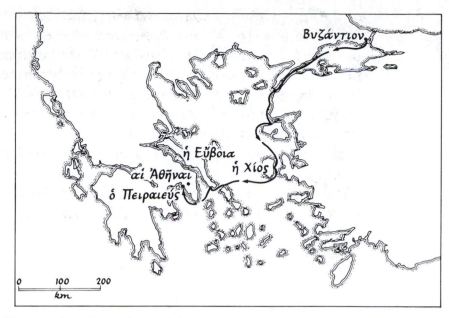

The route from Byzantium to Athens

ὁ Ζηνόθεμις ὁρᾷ τήν τε ἀκρόπολιν καὶ τὸν Παρθενῶνα

Section One A–J: The insurance scam

A

*Hegestratos and Sdenothemis are partners in the corn-shipping
business. They have insured the load of grain on board their ship
for far more than it is worth and plan to 'lose' it in an 'accident',
thus making a healthy profit. They embark in Byzantium, with
grain, captain and crew. The ship sails to Khios (where a
rhapsode boards) and Euboia (where Dikaiopolis gets on), and
eventually comes into sight of Athens and its harbour, Peiraieus
(modern Piraeus). While Sdenothemis engages the passengers'
attention with an appreciation of the sights, a strange noise is
heard below ...*

In *World of Athens*: ships and sailing 2.4, 19; rhapsodes 3.44; grain
trade 6.65–9; loans on ships 5.59; Peiraieus 1.32, 2.23–5, 32, 5.58; the
Parthenon 1.51, 2.34, 8.92–9.

τὸ‿πλοῖόν ἐστιν ἐν‿Βυζαντίῳ. ἐν⌐ δὲ ⌐Βυζαντίῳ, ὁ‿Ἡγέστρατος
βαίνει εἰς‿τὸ‿πλοῖον, ἔπειτα ὁ‿Ζηνόθεμις βαίνει εἰς‿τὸ‿πλοῖον,
τέλος δὲ ὁ‿κυβερνήτης καὶ οἱ‿ναῦται εἰσβαίνουσιν εἰς‿τὸ‿πλοῖον.
τὸ⌐ δὲ ⌐πλοῖον πλεῖ εἰς‿Χίον. ἐν⌐ δὲ ⌐Χίῳ, ὁ‿ῥαψῳδὸς εἰσβαίνει.
ἔπειτα δὲ πλεῖ τὸ‿πλοῖον εἰς‿Εὔβοιαν. ἐν⌐ δὲ ⌐Εὐβοίᾳ, εἰσβαίνει   5
ὁ‿Δικαιόπολις. τέλος δὲ πρὸς‿τὰς‿ Ἀθήνας πλεῖ τὸ‿πλοῖον καὶ
πρὸς‿τὸν‿Πειραιᾶ.
    τὸ⌐ μὲν οὖν ⌐πλοῖον πλεῖ, ὁ⌐ δὲ ⌐Ζηνόθεμις πρὸς‿τὴν‿γῆν βλέπει.
τί ὁρᾷ ὁ‿Ζηνόθεμις; ὁ‿Ζηνόθεμις ὁρᾷ τήν⌐ τε ⌐ἀκρόπολιν καὶ
τὸν‿Παρθενῶνα. ἔπειτα δὲ ὅ⌐ τε ⌐Δικαιόπολις καὶ ὁ‿κυβερνήτης   10
πρὸς‿τὴν‿γῆν βλέπουσιν. τί ὁρῶσιν ὁ‿Δικαιόπολις καὶ
ὁ‿κυβερνήτης; καὶ ὁ‿Δικαιόπολις καὶ ὁ‿κυβερνήτης τήν⌐ τε
⌐ἀκρόπολιν ὁρῶσι καὶ τὸν‿Παρθενῶνα. ἐξαίφνης ὅ⌐ τε ⌐Δικαιόπολις
καὶ ὁ‿κυβερνήτης ψόφον ἀκούουσιν.

Vocabulary for Section One A

> Grammar for 1A–B
> - The definite article 'the', ὁ ἡ τό
> - The principle of 'agreement'
> - Adjectives like καλός καλή καλόν
> - The vocative case

ἀκού-ουσι(ν) (they) hear
βαίν-ει (he) goes
βλέπ-ει (he) looks
βλέπ-ουσι(ν) (they) look
δὲ and; but
εἰς to, into
εἰς Εὔβοιαν to Euboia
εἰς τὸ πλοῖ-ον onto the ship
εἰς Χί-ον to Chios
εἰσ-βαίν-ει (he) embarks
εἰσ-βαίν-ουσι(ν) (they) embark
ἐν in, on
ἐν Βυζαντίῳ in Byzantium
ἐν Εὐβοίᾳ in Euboia
ἐξαίφνης suddenly
ἔπειτα then, next
ἐστι(ν) (it/there) is
καὶ and
καὶ . . . καὶ both . . . and

μὲν . . . δὲ on the one hand .
  . . on the other
ὁ the
ὁ Δικαιόπολις Dikaiopolis
ὁ Ζηνόθεμις Sdenothemis
ὁ Ἡγέστρατ-ος Hegestratos
ὁ κυβερνήτης the captain
ὁ ῥαψῳδ-ός the rhapsode
οἱ the
οἱ ναῦται the sailors, crew
ὁρ-ᾷ (he) sees
ὁρ-ῶσι(ν) (they) see
οὖν so, really, therefore
πλ-εῖ (it) sails
πρὸς towards
πρὸς τὰς Ἀθήνας towards
  Athens
πρὸς τὴν γῆν towards the land
πρὸς τὸν Πειραιᾶ towards
  the Peiraieus

τε . . . καὶ both . . . and
τέλος finally
τὴν the
τὴν ἀκρόπολιν the
  Acropolis
τί; what?
τὸν the
τὸν Παρθενῶνα the
  Parthenon
τὸ the
τὸ πλοῖ-ον the ship, vessel
ψόφ-ον a noise

Vocabulary to be learnt
δέ *and; but*
ἔπειτα *then, next*
καί *and*
τε . . . καί *A and B, both A*
  and B

τὸ πλοῖον

B

ΖΗΝΟΘΕΜΙΣ (*pointing to the land*)
δεῦρο ἐλθέ, ὦ Δικαιόπολι, καὶ βλέπε. ἐγὼ γὰρ
τὴν ἀκρόπολιν ὁρῶ. ἆρα καὶ σὺ τὴν ἀκρόπολιν ὁρᾷς;
ΔΙΚΑΙΟΠΟΛΙΣ (*peering towards the land*)
ποῦ ἐστιν ἡ ἀκρόπολις; ἐγὼ γὰρ τὴν ἀκρόπολιν οὐχ ὁρῶ.   5
ΖΗΝ.   δεῦρο ἐλθέ, καὶ βλέπε. ἆρα οὐχ ὁρᾷς σὺ τὸν Παρθενῶνα;
ΔΙΚ.   ναί. νῦν γὰρ τὴν ἀκρόπολιν ὁρῶ καὶ ἐγώ.
ΖΗΝ.   ὦ Ζεῦ. ὡς καλός ἐστιν ὁ Παρθενών, καλὴ δὲ ἡ ἀκρόπολις.
ΚΥΒΕΡΝΗΤΗΣ (*agreeing*)
ἀληθῆ σὺ λέγεις, ὦ Ζηνόθεμι.   10
(*with a sudden start*)
ἄκουε, ψόφος. ἆρα ἀκούεις; τίς ἐστιν ὁ ψόφος; ἆρα
ἀκούεις καὶ σὺ τὸν ψόφον, ὦ Ζηνόθεμι;
ΖΗΝ.   (*hurriedly dismissing the subject*)
οὐ μὰ Δία, οὐδὲν ἀκούω ἐγώ, ὦ κυβερνῆτα. μὴ φρόντιζε.   15
ἀλλὰ δεῦρο ἐλθὲ καὶ βλέπε. ἐγὼ γὰρ τὸ νεώριον ὁρῶ καὶ
τὸν Πειραιᾶ. ἆρα ὁρᾷς καὶ σὺ τὸ νεώριον;
ΚΥΒ.   ναί.
ΖΗΝ.   ὦ Ζεῦ, ὡς καλόν ἐστι τὸ νεώριον, καλὸς δὲ ὁ Πειραιεύς.
ΚΥΒ.   (*agreeing impatiently*)   20
ἀληθῆ λέγεις, ὦ Ζηνόθεμι. ἰδού, ψόφος. αὖθις γὰρ
τὸν ψόφον ἀκούω ἔγωγε.
ΔΙΚ.   καὶ ἐγὼ τὸν ψόφον αὖθις ἀκούω, ὦ κυβερνῆτα, σαφῶς.
ἐγὼ οὖν καὶ σὺ ἀκούομεν τὸν ψόφον.

Vocabulary for Section One B

ἀκού-ω I hear
ἀκού-εις you (s.) hear
ἀκού-ομεν we hear
ἄκου-ε listen! (s.)
ἀληθῆ the truth
ἀλλά but
ἆρα = *question*
αὖθις again
βλέπ-ε look! (s.)
γὰρ for

δεῦρο here, over here
Δικαιόπολι Dikaiopolis
ἐγὼ I
ἔγωγε I at least
ἐλθ-έ come! (s.)
ἐστι(ν) (it) is
Ζεῦ Zeus
Ζηνόθεμι Sdenothemis
ἡ ἀκρόπολις the Acropolis
ἡμεῖς we

ἰδού here! hey! look! (s.)
καὶ also
καλ-ός beautiful
καλ-ή beautiful
καλ-όν beautiful
κυβερνῆτα captain
κυβερνήτης captain
λέγ-εις you (s.) are speak-
     ing
μὰ Δία by Zeus

μὴ don't
ναί yes
νῦν now
ὁ Παρθενών the Parthenon
ὁ Πειραιεύς the Peiraieus
ὁρ-ῶ I see
ὁρ-ᾷς you (s.) see
οὐ no
οὐδὲν nothing
οὖν so, really, therefore
οὐχ not
ὁ ψόφ-ος the noise
ποῦ; where?
σαφ-ῶς clearly

σὺ you (s.)
τὴν ἀκρόπολιν the
   Acropolis
τίς; what?
τὸ νεώρι-ον the naval
   dockyard
τὸν Παρθενῶνα the
   Parthenon
τὸν Πειραιᾶ the
   Peiraieus
τὸν ψόφ-ον the noise
φρόντιζ-ε worry! (s.)
   (sc. 'about it')
ψόφ-ος a noise

ὦ O
ὡς how!

Vocabulary to be learnt
ἆρα *indicates question*
δεῦρο *here, over here*
ἐγώ *I*
καί *also*
σύ *you (s.)*
τίς; *what? who?*
ὦ O *(addressing
   someone)*

A merchantman and a warship

C

ZHN.   (*more frantically*)
  ἐγὼ δὲ οὐκ ἀκούω, ὦ φίλοι. μὴ φροντίζετε. ἀλλὰ δεῦρο
  ἔλθετε καὶ βλέπετε, δεῦρο. ὁρῶ γὰρ τὰ ἐμπόρια καὶ
  τὰς ὁλκάδας ἔγωγε. ἆρα ὁρᾶτε τὰ ἐμπόρια καὶ ὑμεῖς;
ΚΥΒ. καὶ ΔΙΚ. ὁρῶμεν καὶ ἡμεῖς. τί μήν;   5
ZHN.   (*waxing lyrical*)
  ὦ Πόσειδον, ὡς καλαί εἰσιν αἱ ὁλκάδες, ὡς καλά ἐστι
  τὰ ἐμπόρια. ἀλλὰ δεῦρο βλέπετε, ὦ φίλοι.
ΚΥΒ.   ἄκουε, ὦ Ζηνόθεμι, καὶ μὴ λέγε 'ὡς καλά ἐστι τὰ ἐμπόρια.'
  ἡμεῖς γὰρ τὸν ψόφον σαφῶς ἀκούομεν.   10
ΔΙΚ.   ἀλλὰ πόθεν ὁ ψόφος;
ΚΥΒ.   (*pointing down below*)
  κάτωθεν, ὦ Δικαιόπολι. διὰ τί οὐ καταβαίνομεν ἡμεῖς;
  ἐλθέ, ὦ Δικαιόπολι –
ZHN.   (*by now quite desperate*)   15
  ποῖ βαίνετε ὑμεῖς; ποῖ βαίνετε; διὰ τί οὐ μένετε, ὦ φίλοι; μὴ
  φροντίζετε. ὁρῶ γὰρ ἐγώ –

Vocabulary for Section One C

> Grammar for 1C–D
> * Verbs ending in –ω (present 'tense', indicative 'mood', active 'voice')
> * The concept of tense, mood, voice, person and number
> * Compound verbs (with prefixes)
> * The imperative [command/order] 'mood'
> * The vocative case

αἱ the
αἱ ὁλκάδες the merchant
 ships
ἀκού-ω I hear
ἀκού-ομεν we hear
ἄκου-ε listen! (s.)
ἀλλά but
βαίν-ετε you (pl.) are going
βλέπ-ετε look! (pl.)
γὰρ for

διὰ τί; why?
Δικαιόπολι Dikaiopolis
ἔγωγε I; I for my part
εἰσι(ν) (they) are
ἐλθ-έ come! (s.)
ἔλθ-ετε come! (pl.)
ἐστι(ν) (they) are
Ζηνόθεμι Sdenothemis
ἡμεῖς we
καλ-αί beautiful, fine

καλ-ά beautiful, fine
κατα-βαίν-ομεν we go
 down
κάτωθεν from below
λέγ-ε say! (s.)
μέν-ετε you (pl.) stay
μὴ don't
ὁρ-ῶ I see
ὁρ-ῶμεν (we) see
ὁρ-ᾶτε you (pl.) see

οὐκ not
ὁ ψόφ-ος the noise
πόθεν; from where?
ποῖ; where to?
Πόσειδον Poseidon (god of the sea)
σαφ-ῶς clearly
τὰ the
τὰ ἐμπόρι-α the markets

τὰς the
τὰς ὁλκάδας the merchant ships
τί μήν; so what?; of course
τὸν ψόφ-ον the noise
ὑμεῖς you (pl.)
φίλ-οι friends
φροντίζ-ετε worry! (pl.) (sc. 'about it')

ὡς how!

Vocabulary to be learnt
ἀλλά but
γάρ for
ἡμεῖς we
μή don't
οὐ, οὐκ, οὐχ no; not
ὡς how!

Transporting heavy goods

Before the development of the steam engine or of properly surfaced and maintained roads, or in the absence of camels (rightly called the 'ships of the desert'), transport of heavy goods long distances overland was effectively impossible. The main means of heavy overland haulage was the bullock, at 2mph, whose carts lacked swivel-axles to negotiate corners. Ships were the only answer when it came to transporting heavy cargoes any distance (like grain in this story), which is why most large ancient towns are sited on or near a coast or navigable river.

In the fifth and fourth centuries Athens was strongly dependent upon what was brought in by sea, not simply because the quantity of cereals grown within Attica was insufficient for the urban population but because a reputation for being the place to which one came to find goods from all parts of the Greek world was vital to the thriving life of the town of Athens and the Peiraieus. Few voyages would have been taken for pleasure, as pirates were a constant source of danger until the Athenians cleared them from the Aegean in the 470s. Nor was a sea voyage possible at all times of the year. The islands lying within the Aegean basin enable sailors to chart their course by reference to fixed points, but traders did not avoid the open sea. The slow, broad cargo-ships depended on sail and wind, and travelled at an average speed of five knots. Nelson's *Victory*, a much larger and heavier warship with sails, averaged seven knots. Ships powered by oars were swifter than sailing ships, but their lighter bulk and the presence of the rowers fitted them for use mainly in time of war. The trireme, with 170 rowers, was the fastest and the finest man-of-war in the classical period, and could reach a speed of seven to eight knots with a continuous power output, or even up to thirteen knots for a short burst of ten to twenty minutes. Greek cargo-ships, with their small number of crew and their heavy loads, had no reason for rationing the supply of food and water, and so could sail for many days and nights without putting in to land; warships, with their complement of about two hundred and their need to be as light as possible, carried few provisions and had to put in frequently to enable the rowers to rest and eat.

World of Athens (second edition), 2.19

D

The captain goes into the hold followed by Dikaiopolis and the crew. There they come upon Hegestratos, the author of the mysterious noise.

In *World of Athens*: helmsman 7.34–7.

καταβαίνει μὲν οὖν ὁ⌢κυβερνήτης, καταβαίνουσι δὲ ὅ⌐ τε
⌐Δικαιόπολις καὶ οἱ⌢ναῦται. κάτωθεν γὰρ ὁ⌢ψόφος. κάτω δὲ
τὸν⌢Ἡγέστρατον ὁρῶσιν ὅ⌐ τε ⌐κυβερνήτης καὶ οἱ⌢ναῦται. ὁ⌐ δὲ
⌐Ἡγέστρατος τὸν⌢ψόφον ποιεῖ κάτω.

5

ΚΥΒ.	οὗτος, τί ποιεῖς;
	(*suddenly realising it is Hegestratos*)
	ἀλλὰ τί ποιεῖς σύ, ὦ Ἡγέστρατε; τίς ὁ⌢ψόφος;
ΗΓΕΣΤΡΑΤΟΣ (*innocently*)
	οὐδὲν ποιῶ ἔγωγε, ὦ κυβερνῆτα, οὐδὲ ψόφον⌢οὐδένα 10
	ἀκούω. μὴ φρόντιζε.
ΔΙΚ.	(*looking behind Hegestratos' back*)
	δεῦρο ἐλθὲ καὶ βλέπε, ὦ κυβερνῆτα. ἔχει γάρ τι ἐν⌢τῇ⌢δεξιᾷ
	ὁ⌢Ἡγέστρατος.
ΚΥΒ.	τί ἔχεις ἐν⌢τῇ⌢δεξιᾷ, ὦ Ἡγέστρατε; 15
ΗΓ.	(*desperately trying to cover up*)
	οὐδὲν ἔχω ἔγωγε, ὦ φίλε.
ΔΙΚ.	ὦ Ζεῦ. οὐ γὰρ ἀληθῆ λέγει ὁ⌢Ἡγέστρατος. πέλεκυν γὰρ
	ἔχει ἐν⌢τῇ⌢δεξιᾷ ὁ⌢Ἡγέστρατος. ὁ⌢ἄνθρωπος τὸ⌢πλοῖον
	καταδύει. 20
ΚΥΒ.	(*shocked*)
	τί λέγεις, ὦ Δικαιόπολι; δύει τὸ⌢πλοῖον ὁ⌢Ἡγέστρατος;
	(*calling to the crew*)
	ἀλλὰ διὰ⌢τί οὐ λαμβάνετε ὑμεῖς τὸν⌢ἄνθρωπον, ὦ ναῦται;
	δεῦρο, δεῦρο. 25
ΗΓ.	οἴμοι, φεύγω ἔγωγε, καὶ ῥίπτω ἐμαυτὸν ἐκ⌢τοῦ⌢πλοίου.
ΚΥΒ.	(*urging the crew to help*)
	βοηθεῖτε, ὦ ναῦται, βοηθεῖτε καὶ διώκετε.

πέλεκυν γὰρ ἔχει

ῥίπτω ἐμαυτὸν ἐκ τοῦ πλοίου

Vocabulary for Section One D

ἀκού-ω I hear
ἀληθῆ the truth
βλέπ-ε look! (s.)
βοηθ-εῖτε help! (pl.)
διὰ τί; why?
Δικαιόπολι Dikaiopolis
διώκ-ετε give chase! (pl.)
δύ-ει (he) is sinking
ἔγωγε I; I at least
ἐκ out of, from
ἐκ τοῦ πλοίου from the ship
ἐλθέ come! (s.)
ἐμαυτ-ὸν myself
ἐν τῇ δεξιᾷ in (his/your)
    right hand
ἔχ-ω (I) have/am holding
ἔχ-εις you (s.) have/are
    holding
ἔχ-ει (he) has/is holding
Ζεῦ Zeus
Ἡγέστρατ-ε Hegestratos
κατα-βαίν-ει (he) goes down
κατα-βαίν-ομεν we go down
κατα-βαίν-ουσι(ν) (they) go
    down
κατα-δύ-ει (he) is sinking

κάτω below
κάτωθεν from below
κυβερνῆτα captain
λαμβάν-ετε you (pl.) catch/
    seize
λέγ-εις you (s.) are saying
λέγ-ει (he) is telling
μὲν . . . δὲ on one hand . . .
    on the other
ναῦται sailors
ὁ ἄνθρωπ-ος the fellow
ὁ Δικαιόπολις Dikaiopolis
ὁ Ἡγέστρατ-ος Hegestratos
οἴμοι oh dear!
οἱ ναῦται the sailors, crew
ὁ κυβερνήτης the captain
ὁρ-ᾶτε you (pl.) see
ὁρ-ῶσι(ν) (they) see
οὐδὲ and . . . not
οὐδὲν nothing
οὖν so, then, therefore
οὗτος hey, you!
ὁ ψόφ-ος the noise
πέλεκυς axe (nom.)
πέλεκυν axe (acc.)
ποι-ῶ (I) am doing

ποι-εῖς you (s.) are doing
ποι-εῖ (he) is making
ῥίπτ-ω I am throwing
    (going to throw)
τί; what?
τι something
τὸν ἄνθρωπ-ον the fellow
τὸν Ἡγέστρατ-ον
    Hegestratos
τὸν ψόφ-ον the noise
τὸ πλοῖ-ον the ship
ὑμεῖς you (pl.)
φεύγ-ω (I) am off
φίλ-ε friend
φρόντιζ-ε worry! (sc. 'about it')
ψόφ-ον οὐδένα any noise

Vocabulary to be learnt
ἀληθῆ *the truth*
ἔγωγε I; *I at least/for my
    part*
οὐδέν *nothing*
οὖν *so, then, really, therefore*
τί; *what?*
ὑμεῖς *you (pl.)*

E

ὁ˻ μὲν ˥Ἡγέστρατος φεύγει κάτωθεν, οἱˍ δὲ ˥ναῦται βοηθοῦσι καὶ τὸν˘
Ἡγέστρατον διώκουσιν. ἄνω μένει ὁ˘Ζηνόθεμις. ὁˍ μὲν ˥Ἡγέστρατος
πρὸς˘τὸν˘Ζηνόθεμιν βλέπει, ὁˍ δὲ ˥Ζηνόθεμις πρὸς˘τοὺς˘ναύτας.
ἀναβαίνουσι γὰρ οἱ˘ναῦται καὶ διώκουσιν.

5

ΖΗΝ.	ἀλλὰ τί ποιεῖς, ὦ Ἡγέστρατε;
ΗΓ.	(*running up to Sdenothemis*)
	ἰδού, διώκουσί με οἱ˘ναῦται, ὦ Ζηνόθεμι. ἐγὼ δὲ
	φεύγω. μὴ μένε, ἀλλὰ φεῦγε καὶ σύ, καὶ ῥῖπτε σεαυτὸν
	ἐκ˘τοῦ˘πλοίου. ἀναβαίνουσι γαρ ἤδη οἱ˘ἄνδρες.

10

ΖΗΝ.	(*with a glance at the pursuing crew*)
	οἴμοι. τοὺςˍ γὰρ ˥ναύτας ἤδη˘γε σαφῶς ὁρῶ. σὺ δὲ ποῖ
	φεύγεις;
ΗΓ.	φεύγω εἰς˘τὴν˘θάλατταν ἔγωγε. ὁˍ γὰρ ˥λέμβος
	ἐν˘τῇ˘θαλάττῃ ἐστίν. ἄγε δὴ σύ, σῷζε σεαυτόν. ῥῖπτε

15

σεαυτὸν εἰς˘τὴν˘θάλατταν, καὶ μὴ μένε.

Vocabulary for Section One E

> **Grammar for 1E–F**
> - 'Contract' verbs (-άω, -έω, -όω): present tense and imperative
> - Rules of 'contract'
> - Adverbs (' –ly')

ἄγε come on! (s.)
ἀνα-βαίν-ουσι (they) are coming up
ἄνω above
βλέπ-ει (he) looks
βοηθ-οῦσι (they) help
δή then; now (stressing)
διώκ-ουσι(ν) (they) pursue/ (give) chase
εἰς τὴν θάλατταν into the sea
ἐκ τοῦ πλοίου out of the ship
ἐν τῇ θαλάττῃ on the sea

ἐστί(ν) (it) is
Ζηνόθεμι Sdenothemis
ἤδη now; already
ἤδη γε yes, already
ἰδού look! (s.)
κάτωθεν from below
με me
μὲν ... δὲ on the one hand ... on the other
μέν-ει (he) stays/is waiting
μέν-ε stay! (s.)
ὁ Ζηνόθεμις Sdenothemis
ὁ Ἡγέστρατ-ος Hegestratos
οἱ ἄνδρες the men

οἴμοι oh dear!
οἱ ναῦται the sailors/crew
ὁ λέμβ-ος the life-boat
ὁρ-ῶ I see
ποῖ; where . . . to?
ποι-εῖς you (s.) are doing
πρὸς τὸν Ζηνόθεμιν towards Sdenothemis
πρὸς τοὺς ναύτας towards the sailors
ῥῖπτ-ε throw! (s.)
σαφῶς clearly
σεαυτ-ὸν yourself (s.)
σῷζ-ε save! (s.)

τῇ θαλάττῃ the sea
τὸν Ἡγέστρατ-ον
  Hegestratos
τοὺς the
τοὺς ναύτας the sailors/
  crew

φεύγ-ω (I) am off
φεύγ-εις you (s.) are off/
  running away
φεύγ-ει (he) runs off
φεῦγ-ε run away! be off!
  (s.)

Vocabulary to be learnt
μέν . . . δέ *on the one*
  hand . . . on the other
ποῖ; *where to?*
σεαυτόν *yourself (s.)*

Triremes

The trireme carried masts, and on a long voyage it was possible to exploit a favourable wind. Nor did all the rowers row all the time, except in battle. There was no room on board for eating or sleeping, and little room for supplies (a crew would need about 300 kg of grain and 500 litres of water a day). The trireme, generally speaking, had to be beached at night for crews to acquire provisions, eat and sleep. The account given by Xenophon of the voyage of Iphikrates round the Peloponnese illuminates normal practice; Iphikrates was in a hurry and wanted to train his crews at the same time, but one can infer what was normal from Xenophon's account:

'When Iphikrates began his voyage round the Peloponnese, he took with him all the equipment he needed for a naval battle. He left his large sails at home, as if he was sailing to battle, and made very little use of his small sails even when the wind was favourable. By proceeding under oars in this way he made his crews fitter and his ships faster. And when the expedition was due for its morning or evening meal at any particular place, he would order the leading ships back, turn the line round again to face the land and make them race at a signal for the shore… Again, if they were taking a meal on hostile territory, he set the usual sentries on land but he also raised his ships' masts and had men keeping watch from the top of them. They had a far wider view from their point of vantage than they would have had from ground level… On daylight voyages he trained them to form line ahead or line abreast at a signal, so that in the course of their voyage they had practised and become skilled at the manoeuvres needed in a naval battle before they reached the area of sea which they supposed to be in enemy control.' (Xenophon, *Hellênika* 6.2.27–30)

One point, which does not emerge from this account, was of great importance: the trireme was so light that it could not be used in really rough weather. This meant that naval operations were, generally speaking, not possible in winter, nor in the bad weather caused by the Etesian winds. Weather was a constant limiting factor in naval strategy.

The World of Athens (second edition), 7.35

F

Hegestratos and Sdenothemis leap into the waves and head for the life-boat. But the captain has other ideas.

In *World of Athens*: friends and enemies 4.2, 14–16; prayers 3.34, 8.13; sacrifice 3.28–32.

ὁ Ἡγέστρατος καὶ Ζηνόθεμις οὐ μένουσιν ἀλλὰ φεύγουσιν. εἰς τὴν
γὰρ θάλατταν ῥίπτουσιν ἑαυτοὺς οἱ ἄνθρωποι, καὶ τὸν λέμβον
ζητοῦσιν. καὶ οἱ μὲν ναῦται ἀπὸ τοῦ πλοίου τὴν φυγὴν σαφῶς
ὁρῶσιν, ὁ δὲ κυβερνήτης τὸν λέμβον ἀπολύει. ὁ δὲ λέμβος
ἀπὸ τοῦ πλοίου ἀποχωρεῖ.   5

ZHN.   (*thrashing around in the waves*)
        οἴμοι, ποῦ ὁ λέμβος; ποῦ ἐστιν, ὦ Ἡγέστρατε;
ΗΓ.   ἐγὼ τὸν λέμβον οὐχ ὁρῶ, ὦ Ζηνόθεμι – οἴμοι.
ZHN.   ἀποθνήσκομεν, ὦ Ἡγέστρατε. βοηθεῖτε, ὦ ναῦται,   10
        βοηθεῖτε.
ΗΓ.   ἀποθνήσκω –
ΔΙΚ.   ἆρα τοὺς ἀνθρώπους ὁρᾷς σύ, ὦ κυβερνῆτα; ἀποθνήσκουσι
        γὰρ οἱ ἄνθρωποι. ὁ γὰρ λέμβος ἀπὸ τοῦ πλοίου σαφῶς
        ἀποχωρεῖ.   15
ΚΥΒ.   μὴ φρόντιζε· κακοὶ γάρ εἰσιν οἱ ἄνθρωποι, ὦ Δικαιόπολι,
        καὶ κακῶς ἀποθνήσκουσιν.

Vocabulary for Section One F

ἀπὸ from
ἀπὸ τοῦ πλοίου from the ship
ἀπο-θνήσκ-ω I am dying
ἀπο-θνήσκ-ομεν we are dying
ἀπο-θνήσκ-ουσι(ν) (they) are dying
ἀπο-λύ-ει (he) lets go/ releases
ἀπο-χωρ-εῖ (it) goes away
βοηθ-εῖτε help! (pl.)

Δικαιόπολι Dikaiopolis
ἑαυτ-οὺς themselves
εἰς τὴν θάλατταν into the sea
εἰσι(ν) (they) are
ἐστι(ν) it is
Ζηνόθεμι Sdenothemis
ζητ-οῦσι(ν) they look for
Ἡγέστρατ-ε Hegestratos
κακ-οί bad
κακ-ῶς badly (tr. 'a bad death')

κυβερνῆτα captain
μέν-ουσι(ν) (they) wait
ναῦται sailors
ὁ Ἡγέστρατος Hegestratos
οἱ ἄνθρωπ-οι the fellows
οἴμοι alas! oh dear!
οἱ ναῦται the sailors/crew
ὁ κυβερνήτης the captain
ὁ λέμβ-ος the life-boat
ὁρ-ῶ I see
ὁρ-ᾷς you (s.) see
ὁρ-ῶσι(ν) (they) see

ποῦ; where?
ῥίπτ-ουσι(ν) (they) throw
σαφῶς clearly
τὴν φυγὴν their flight
τὸν λέμβ-ον the life-boat

τοὺς ἀνθρώπ-ους the
  fellows
φεύγ-ουσι(ν) they run away
φρόντιζ-ε worry! (s.) (sc.
  'about it')

Vocabulary to be learnt
οἴμοι *alas! oh dear!*
ποῦ; *where?*

Peiraieus

The harbour town of Peiraieus, 7–8 km south-west of Athens, was created only in the fifth century. Up until that time the Athenians relied on beaching ships in Phaleron Bay, but the creation of an enlarged navy and increased commercial activity led to the establishment of the port of Peiraieus on and around the neighbouring promontory of Akte. There were three harbours: Kantharos on the west, which was the main harbour and commercial emporium with a market on the east side and the *deigma*, a place for displaying goods; and the smaller harbours of Zea and Mounykhia on the east for warships. All three were noted for their splendid ship-sheds. The town itself was laid out on a regular grid pattern of streets by Hippodamos, a native of the Greek city of Miletos on the west coast of Asia Minor where a similar street plan was also used. In contrast to Athens, notorious for narrow and winding streets, the harbour town must have looked rigidly organised, with straight streets, well placed houses and open public areas. Besides the naval installations, the town boasted many of the amenities that Athens had, including a set of fortifications that were necessary to protect Athens' trade and a theatre. By the middle of the fifth century the harbour was linked to Athens by Long Walls, no mean feat of construction given the distance covered and the marshy character of the terrain at the Peiraieus end. The population of Peiraieus was mixed, for not only did foreign traders lodge there temporarily but many of Athens' resident aliens (*metoikoi*) lived at the port, some of whom were responsible for Athens' trade and ran businesses such as armouries and banking; the *metoikoi* might also be grain-dealers or carry on such trades as fulling and baking.

This mixture of population meant that the shrines and sanctuaries that dotted the harbour town boasted a greater variety of worship than places less accessible to foreign influence, and such non-Greek deities as Bendis and Kybele had shrines there. These religious novelties attracted the curiosity of Athenians, and it was a festival of the Thracian goddess Bendis that occasioned the visit of Socrates and Glaukon to the Peiraieus at the beginning of Plato's *Republic* (2.46):

I went down yesterday to the Peiraieus with Glaukon, son of Ariston. I wanted to say a prayer to the Goddess and also to see what they would make of the festival, as this was the first time they were holding it. I must say that I thought that the local contribution to the procession was splendid…

The World of Athens (second edition), 2.23-4

G

(*suddenly realising the danger*)

ΚΥΒ.   ἀλλὰ ἆρά ἐστι σῶον τὸ ἡμέτερον πλοῖον, σῶοι δὲ καὶ
ἡμεῖς; διὰ τί ἐγὼ οὐ καταβαίνω καὶ περισκοπῶ ἀκριβῶς;
ἐγὼ γὰρ ὁ κυβερνήτης· ἐμὸν οὖν τὸ ἔργον, καὶ ἐν ἐμοὶ ἡ
ἡμετέρα σωτηρία.

(καταβαίνει ὁ κυβερνήτης καὶ σκοπεῖ. ὁ δὲ Δικαιόπολις ἄνω μένει.)   5

ΔΙΚ.   (*praying fervently*)

νῦν, ὦ Πόσειδον, σῷζε ἡμᾶς εἰς τὸν λιμένα. ἡμεῖς μὲν γὰρ
ἀεί σοι θυσίας θύομεν, σὺ δὲ ἀεὶ σῴζεις τοὺς ἀνθρώπους
ἐκ τῆς θαλάττης. ἡμεῖς δὲ νῦν κακῶς ἀποθνῄσκομεν·   10
τὸ μὲν γὰρ ἡμέτερον πλοῖον σαφῶς καταδύνει
εἰς τὴν θάλατταν, ὁ δὲ ἡμέτερος λέμβος σαφῶς
ἀποχωρεῖ, καὶ οὐ βεβαία ἡ ἡμετέρα σωτηρία.

(ἀναβαίνει ὁ κυβερνήτης.)

ΚΥΒ.   (*with relief*)   15

σιώπα, ὦ Δικαιόπολι. σῶον μὲν γὰρ τὸ ἡμέτερον πλοῖον, σῶοι
δὲ καὶ ἡμεῖς. ἐν κινδύνῳ οὖν ἡμεῖς οὔκ ἐσμεν. καὶ δὴ καὶ
ἐγγύς ἐστιν ὁ λιμήν. βεβαία οὖν ἡ ἡμετέρα σωτηρία.

ὁ Ποσειδῶν

Vocabulary for Section One G

> **Grammar for 1G**
> - Nouns like ἄνθρωπος ('man', 2a) and ἔργον ('work', 2b)
> - The concept of 'declension'
> - Neuter nouns as subject or object
> - Adjectives like ἡμέτερος ἡμετέρα ἡμέτερον
> - Prepositions like 'towards', 'from', 'in'
> - Particles and their position; enclitics

ἀεί always
ἀκριβ-ῶς closely; in detail
ἀνα-βαίν-ει (he) comes up (on deck)
ἄνω above (on deck)
ἀπο-θνῄσκ-ομεν we are dying
ἀπο-χωρ-εῖ (it) goes away
βεβαία assured
διὰ τί; why?
Δικαιόπολι Dikaiopolis
ἐγγύς nearby
εἰς τὴν θάλατταν into the sea
εἰς τὸν λιμένα to the harbour
ἐκ τῆς θαλάττης out of the sea
ἐμ-όν mine
ἐν ἐμοὶ in my hands (lit. 'in me')

ἐν κινδύνῳ in danger
ἐσμέν we are
ἔστι(ν) (it) is
ἡ ἡμετέρ-α σωτηρί-α [the] our safety
ἡμᾶς us
θύ-ομεν we sacrifice
θυσίας sacrifices
καὶ δὴ καί and moreover
κακ-ῶς badly (tr. 'a bad death')
κατα-βαίν-ω (I) go down
κατα-βαίν-ει (he) goes down
κατα-δύν-ει (it) is sinking
μέν-ει (he) remains
νῦν now
ὁ Δικαιόπολις Dikaiopolis
ὁ κυβερνήτης the captain
ὁ ἡμέτερ-ος λέμβ-ος [the] our life-boat

ὁ λιμήν the harbour
περι-σκοπ-ῶ (I) look around
Πόσειδον Poseidon (*god of the sea*)
σιώπα be quiet! (s.)
σκοπ-εῖ (he) makes an examination, looks
σοι to you (s.)
σῷζ-ε save! (s.)
σῴζ-εις you (s.) save
σῶ-οι safe
σῶ-ον safe
τὸ ἔργ-ον the task
τὸ ἡμέτερ-ον πλοῖ-ον [the] our ship
τοὺς ἀνθρώπ-ους men

Vocabulary to be learnt
διὰ τί; *why?*
νῦν *now*

Prayers

Prayers, like sacrifices, were more or less fixed in their general shape … The god is invoked by name or titles, which are often numerous; he is reminded of past kindnesses, then the request is made. Without some reference to the ties binding a god to his worshippers there was no ground for expecting divine aid, for the basic assumption was one of reciprocity. A prayer was made to the Olympians standing, with hands raised, to the underworld with hands lowered towards the earth.

The World of Athens (second edition), 3.34

H

The captain brings the ship towards harbour. By now it has become dark. A rhapsode, who insists on quoting Homer on every possible occasion, is submitted to a Socratic style of inquiry about his art by Dikaiopolis.

In *World of Athens*: Homer 8.1; Socrates 8.33–6; words and argument 8.18–21.

ὁ οὖν κυβερνήτης τὸ πλοῖον κυβερνᾷ πρὸς⌐τὸν⌐λιμένα. ναύτης⌐ δέ
⌐τις τὸν⌐κυβερνήτην ἐρωτᾷ ποῦ εἰσιν. ὁ γὰρ ναύτης οὐ σαφῶς οἶδε
ποῦ εἰσι· νὺξ γάρ ἐστιν. ὁ οὖν κυβερνήτης λέγει ὅτι εἰς⌐τὸν⌐λιμένα
πλέουσιν. ἔστι δὲ ἐν τῷ⌐πλοίῳ ῥαψῳδός⌐τις. ὁ δὲ ῥαψῳδὸς ἀεὶ
ὁμηρίζει. ὁ δὲ Δικαιόπολις παίζει πρὸς τὸν ῥαψῳδὸν ὥσπερ   5
ὁ⌐Σωκράτης πρὸς τοὺς⌐μαθητάς.

ΝΑΥΤΗΣ   ποῦ ἐσμεν ἡμεῖς, ὦ κυβερνῆτα; ἆρα οἶσθα σύ; οὐ γὰρ σαφῶς
                οἶδα ἔγωγε. ἐγὼ γὰρ οὐδὲν ὁρῶ διὰ τὴν⌐νύκτα, καὶ οὐκ
                οἶδα ποῦ ἐσμεν.   10
ΚΥΒΕΡΝΗΤΗΣ οἶδα σαφῶς. πλέομεν γὰρ πρὸς τὸν⌐λιμένα, ὦ ναῦτα.
ΡΑΨΩΙΔΟΣ   *(butting into the conversation with a Homeric phrase)*
                ‘πλέομεν δ’ ἐπὶ οἴνοπα⌐πόντον.’
ΝΑΥ.   τί λέγει ὁ ἄνθρωπος;
ΔΙΚ.   δῆλόν ἐστιν ὅτι ὁμηρίζει ὁ ἄνθρωπος. ῥαψῳδὸς οὖν ἐστίν.   15
ΡΑΨ.   ἀληθῆ λέγεις, ὦ τᾶν·
                ‘πλέομεν δ’ ἐν νηὶ⌐μελαίνῃ.’
ΔΙΚ.   τί λέγεις, ὦ ῥαψῳδέ; τί⌐τὸ ‘ἐν νηὶ⌐μελαίνῃ’; οὐ γὰρ
                μέλαινα ἡ ἡμετέρα ναῦς. δῆλόν ἐστιν ὅτι μῶρος εἶ σύ, καὶ
                οὐκ οἶσθα οὐδέν, ἀλλὰ παίζεις πρὸς ἡμᾶς.   20
ΡΑΨ.   σιώπα. ‘ἐν νηὶ⌐θοῇ’ πλέομεν, ‘κοίλῃ⌐ἐνὶ⌐νηί.’
ΔΙΚ.   ἆρα ἀκούετε, ὦ ναῦται; δεῦρο ἔλθετε καὶ ἀκούετε. δῆλόν
                ἐστιν ὅτι μῶρος ὁ ἡμέτερος ῥαψῳδός. οὐ γὰρ οἶδεν οὐδέν
                ἀκριβῶς ὁ ἄνθρωπος, ἀλλὰ παίζει πρὸς ἡμᾶς.

Vocabulary for Section One H

Grammar for 1H–J
- Verbs εἰμί 'I am' and οἶδα 'I know'
- Complement and ellipse with εἰμί
- Adjectives used as nouns
- More particles

ἀεί always
ἀκριβ-ῶς closely
δῆλόν ἐστι(ν) it is clear
διά (+acc.) because of
εἶ you (s.) are
ἐστι(ν) he/there/it is
ἐσμεν (we) are
εἰσι(ν) (they) are
ἐπί (+ acc.) over
ἐρωτά-ω ask
ἡμᾶς us
ἡ ναῦς the ship
κοίλη ἐνὶ νηί in a hollow
    ship
κυβερνά-ω steer
κυβερνῆτα captain (voc.)
μέλαινα black (nom.)
μῶρ-ος -α -ον stupid
ναῦτα sailor (voc.)
ναῦται sailors (voc.)

ναύτης τις a sailor (nom.)
νηὶ θοῇ a swift ship
νηὶ μελαίνη a black ship
νύξ night (nom.)
οἴνοπα πόντον the wine-
    faced sea (acc.)
ὁ ναύτης the sailor
ὁ Σωκράτης Socrates
οἶδα I know
οἶσθα you (s.) know
οἶδε(ν) (he) knows
ὁμηρίζ-ω quote Homer
ὅτι that
παίζ-ω (πρός + acc.) joke
    (at)
πλέομεν/πλέουσιν: εε +
    εει are the only forms of
    πλέω that are contracted
    in Attic Greek
ῥαψῳδ-ός, ὁ rhapsode (2a)

ῥαψῳδ-ός τις a rhapsode
σαφ-ῶς clearly
σιωπά-ω be quiet
τᾶν my dear chap
    (condescendingly)
τὴν νύκτα the night/dark
τί τὸ what's this?
τὸν κυβερνήτην the captain
τὸν λιμένα the harbour
τοὺς μαθητάς the/his
    students
τῷ πλοίῳ the ship
ὥσπερ like

Vocabulary to be learnt
δῆλος η ον *clear; obvious*
ὅτι *that*
παίζω (πρός + acc.) *play;*
    joke (at)

ὁ ῥαψῳδός

Rhapsodes

Where we read books, Athenians would more normally listen to live recitations, when a poet or historian or scientist would stand up and address an audience (in public or private) … Athenians probably heard the *Iliad* and *Odyssey* performed by rhapsodes [professional reciters of poetry] … much more often than they actually sat down and *read* Homer.

The World of Athens (second edition), 8.17

PAΨ.   ἀλλὰ ἐγὼ μῶρος μὲν οὐκ εἰμί, πολλὰ δὲ γιγνώσκω.

ΔΙΚ.   πῶς σὺ πολλὰ γιγνώσκεις; δῆλον μὲν οὖν ὅτι ἀπαίδευτος
εἶ, ὦ ῥαψῳδέ. οὐ γὰρ οἶσθα σὺ πότερον 'μέλαινα' ἡ ἡμετέρα
ναῦς ἢ 'θοὴ' ἢ 'κοίλη'.

PAΨ.   οὐ μὰ Δία, οὐκ ἀπαίδευτός εἰμι ἐγὼ περὶ Ὁμήρου. πολλὰ   5
γὰρ γιγνώσκω διότι πολλὰ γιγνώσκει Ὅμηρος. γιγνώσκει
γὰρ Ὅμηρος τά τε πολεμικὰ ἔργα καὶ τὰ ναυτικὰ καὶ τὰ
στρατιωτικὰ καὶ τὰ στρατηγικά –

ΔΙΚ.   γιγνώσκεις οὖν καὶ σὺ τὰ στρατηγικὰ ἔργα;

PAΨ.   πῶς γὰρ οὔ; ἐμὸν γὰρ τὸ ἔργον.   10

ΔΙΚ.   τί δέ; ἆρα ἔμπειρος εἶ περὶ τὰ στρατηγικά, ὦ ῥαψῳδέ;

PAΨ.   ναί. ἔμπειρος μὲν γὰρ περὶ τὰ στρατηγικὰ ἔργα ἐστὶν
Ὅμηρος, ἔμπειρος δέ εἰμι καὶ ἐγώ.

Vocabulary for Section One I

ἀπαίδευτ-ος -ον an
  ignoramus
γιγνώσκ-ω know
διότι because
εἰμι I am
εἶ you (s.) are
ἐστὶ(ν) (he) is
ἐμ-ός -ή -όν my
ἔμπειρ-ος -ον experienced
ἡ ναῦς the ship
ἤ or
θο-ός –ή -όν swift
κοῖλ-ος -η -ον hollow
μὰ Δία by Zeus
μέλαινα black (nom.)
μὲν οὖν no, rather
μῶρ-ος -α -ον stupid

ναί yes
ναυτικ-ά, τά naval matters
  (2b)
οἶσθα you (s.) know
Ὅμηρ-ος, ὁ Homer (2a)
  (epic poet, author of the
  Iliad and *Odyssey*)
περί (+ acc.) about, with
  regard to
περὶ Ὁμήρου about Homer
πολεμικ-ός -ή -όν of war
πολλά many things (acc.)
πότερον... ἤ whether... or
πῶς how?
πῶς γὰρ οὔ; of course
στρατηγικ-ά, τά generalship
  (2b)

στρατηγικ-ός -ή -όν of a
  general
στρατιωτικ-ά, τά soldiering
  (2b)
τί δέ; what next?

Vocabulary to be learnt
γιγνώσκω (γνο-) *know;*
  perceive; resolve
ἔμπειρος ον *skilled,*
  experienced
μῶρος ᾱ ον *stupid; foolish*
περί *(+ acc.) about*
πολλά *many things (acc.)*
ναί *yes*

J

ΔΙΚ.	μία᷉ οὖν ᷉τέχνη ἥ᷉ τε ᷉ῥαψῳδικὴ καὶ ἡ᷉στρατηγική;
ΡΑΨ.	μία᷉τέχνη, ὦ Δικαιόπολι.
ΔΙΚ.	οὔκουν οἱ ἀγαθοὶ ῥαψῳδοί εἰσιν ἅμα καὶ στρατηγοὶ ἀγαθοί;
ΡΑΨ.	ναί, ὦ Δικαιόπολι.
ΔΙΚ.	καὶ σὺ ἄριστος ῥαψῳδὸς εἶ τῶν᷉ Ἑλλήνων;
ΡΑΨ.	μάλιστα, ὦ Δικαιόπολι.
ΔΙΚ.	σὺ οὖν, ὦ ῥαψῳδέ, στρατηγὸς ἄριστος εἶ τῶν᷉ Ἑλλήνων;
ΡΑΨ.	πῶς γὰρ οὔ;
ΔΙΚ.	τί λέγετε, ὦ ναῦται; ἆρα μῶρος ὁ ῥαψῳδὸς ἢ οὔ;
ΝΑΥ.	μῶρος μέντοι νὴ᷉ Δία ὁ ῥαψῳδός, ὦ Δικαιόπολι. στρατηγὸς μὲν γὰρ δήπου ἄριστος τῶν᷉ Ἑλλήνων ἐστὶν ὁ ἄνθρωπος, ἀλλὰ οὐκ οἶδεν ἀκριβῶς πότερον 'μέλαινα' ἢ 'θοὴ' ἢ 'κοίλη' ἡ᷉ναῦς. μῶρός οὖν ἐστιν ὁ ἄριστος τῶν᷉ Ἑλλήνων στρατηγός.
ΡΑΨ.	δῆλόν ἐστιν, ὦ Δικαιόπολι, ὅτι Σωκρατεῖς καὶ παίζεις πρός᷉ἐμέ. ὁ᷉ γὰρ ᷉Σωκράτης οὕτως ἀεὶ πρὸς τοὺς μαθητὰς παίζει.
ΔΙΚ.	ναί. οἱ᷉ Ἕλληνες ἀεὶ παῖδές εἰσιν.

5

10

15

Vocabulary for Section One J

ἀγαθ-ός -ή -όν good
ἀεί always
ἅμα at the same time
ἄριστ-ος -η -ον best
δήπου of course
εἶ you (s.) are
ἐστι(ν) (he/it) is
εἰσι(ν) (they) are
ἐμέ me
ἡ ναῦς the ship
ἡ ῥαψῳδική the rhapsode's
  skill
ἡ στρατηγική the general's
  skill
ἢ or
θο-ός -ή -όν swift
κοῖλ-ος -η -ον hollow

μάλιστα yes, indeed
μέλαινα black (nom.)
μέντοι yes indeed
μία τέχνη one and the same
  skill (nom.)
ναῦται sailors (voc.)
νὴ Δία by Zeus
οἱ Ἕλληνες the Greeks
οἶδε(ν) (he) knows
ὁ Σωκράτης Socrates
οὔκουν not. . . therefore
οὕτως thus, in this way
παῖδες children (nom.)
πότερον . . . ἢ whether ... or
πρὸς ἐμέ at/with me
πῶς γὰρ οὔ; of course
στρατηγ-ός, ὁ general (2a)

Σωκρατέ-ω play Socrates
τοὺς μαθητὰς the/his
  students
τῶν Ἑλλήνων of the
  Greeks

Vocabulary to be learnt
ἀεί *always*
ἄριστος η ον *best; very
  good*
εἰμί *I am* (= verb 'to be')
Ἕλλην, ὁ *Greek*
ἤ *or*
ναῦς, ἡ *ship*
οἶδα *know*
πῶς γὰρ οὔ; *of course*
στρατηγός, ὁ *general (2a)*

Section Two A–D: The glorious past

A

The ship is now passing the island of Salamis. The rhapsode is invited to show his skill by narrating the great naval battle of 480, fought in these straits between the Greeks and Persians.

In *World of Athens*: the Persian Wars 1.27–39; rhetoric and style 8.21; supplication 3.35–6; *hubris* 4.17.

ἡ μὲν ναῦς πρὸς τὸν ⸢Πειραιᾶ βραδέως ἔρχεται. ὁ δὲ Δικαιόπολις
καὶ οἱ ⸢ναῦται καὶ ὁ κυβερνήτης καὶ ὁ ῥαψῳδὸς πρὸς ἀλλήλους
ἡδέως διαλέγονται. ἔρχεται δὲ ἡ ναῦς ἤδη παρὰ τὴν ⸢Σαλαμῖνα καὶ ὁ
κυβερνήτης λέγει 'διὰ τί ὁ ῥαψῳδὸς οὐ διέρχεται τὴν⸢ περὶ Σαλαμῖνα
⸢ναυμαχίαν, καὶ διὰ τί οὐ λέγει τί γίγνεται ἐν τοῖς ⸢Μηδικοῖς καὶ πῶς   5
μάχονται οἱ ⸢Ἕλληνες καὶ οἱ Μῆδοι, καὶ τίνα ⸢ἔργα τολμῶσι, καὶ
ὁπόσοι πίπτουσιν;' ὁ δὲ ῥαψῳδὸς τὴν ⸢ναυμαχίαν ἡδέως διέρχεται.

ΚΥΒ.   σὺ δέ, ὦ ῥαψῳδέ, πολλὰ γιγνώσκεις περὶ ⸢Ὁμήρου. πολλὰ
         οὖν γιγνώσκεις καὶ περὶ τὰ ῥητορικά (ῥητορικὸς γὰρ Ὅμηρος·   10
         οὐ ⸢γάρ;) ἄγε δή, δεῦρο ἐλθὲ καὶ λέγε ἡμῖν τὰ⸢ περὶ Σαλαμῖνα

Πέρσης τις

μάχονται οἱ Ἕλληνες καὶ οἱ Μῆδοι

⌐πράγματα. ἐκεῖ μὲν γὰρ Σαλαμὶς ἡ νῆσος, ἐρχόμεθα δὲ
ἡμεῖς βραδέως παρὰ Σαλαμῖνα πρὸς τὰς⌐ Ἀθήνας. λέγε
οὖν ἡμῖν τά τε Μηδικὰ καὶ τὴν⌐ περὶ Σαλαμῖνα ⌐ναυμαχίαν
καὶ τὴν⌐ἡμετέραν⌐τόλμαν καὶ τὴν⌐νίκην. οὐ γὰρ νικῶσιν   15
ἡμᾶς οἱ Πέρσαι, οὐδὲ δουλοῦνται. λέγε ἡμῖν τί γίγνεται
ἐν τοῖς⌐Μηδικοῖς καὶ πῶς μάχονται οἱ⌐Ἕλληνες καὶ οἱ
βάρβαροι, καὶ ὁπόσοι πίπτουσι. σὺ γάρ, ὦ φίλε, οἶσθα σαφῶς
τὰ⌐ περὶ Σαλαμῖνα⌐πράγματα, οἱ⌐ δε ⌐ναῦται οὐδὲν ἴσασιν.

ΝΑΥ.   ναί. οὐδὲν ἴσμεν ἀκριβῶς ἡμεῖς οἱ⌐ναῦται. ἡδέως οὖν ἀκούομεν.   20
         ἀλλὰ λέγε, ὦ ῥαψῳδέ, καὶ κάλλιστον ποίει τὸν λόγον.

ΡΑΨ.   μάλιστα. ἐγὼ γὰρ ἀεὶ τοὺς λόγους καλλίστους ποιῶ.
         ἡσυχάζετε οὖν, ὦ ναῦται, καὶ ἀκούετε.

Vocabulary for Section Two A

> Grammar for 2A–D
> - 'Middle' verbs in -ομαι (middle 'voice': present and imperative)
> - 'Contract' middle verbs in -άομαι, -έομαι, -όομαι (present and imperative)
> - Nouns like βοή (1a), ἀπορίᾱ (1b), τόλμα (1c), ναύτης (1d)
> - The genitive case, 'of'
> - 'Sandwich' and 'repeated article' constructions
> - Prepositions governing accusative and dative cases

ἄγε come! (s.)
ἀλλήλ-ους one another (acc.)
βάρβαρ-ος, ὁ barbarian,
   Persian (2a)
βραδ-έως slowly
γίγν-εται (it) happens
δή now, then (with imperative)
δια-λέγ-ονται (they) converse
δι-έρχ-εται (he) relates
δουλ-οῦνται (they) enslave
ἐκεῖ there
ἔρχ-εται (it) is going
ἐρχ-όμεθα (we) are going
ἡδέ-ως gladly, with
   pleasure
ἤδη now
ἡμᾶς us (acc.)
ἡμῖν to us
ἡσυχάζ-ω keep quiet

κάλλιστ-ος -η -ον very,
   most beautiful
λόγ-ος, ὁ story (2a)
μάλιστα yes, indeed; very well
μάχ-ονται (they) fight
Μηδικ-ά, τά the Persian
   Wars (2b)
Μῆδ-ος, ὁ Persian (2a)
ναῦτ-αι sailors
νῆσ-ος, ἡ island (2a)
οἱ Ἕλληνες the Greeks
οἱ ναῦτ-αι the sailors, crew
ὁπόσ-οι -αι -α how many?
οὐ γάρ; is he not?
οὐδὲ and not
παρὰ (+ acc.) past, along
περὶ Ὁμήρου about Homer
πίπτ-ω fall, die
ῥητορικ-ά, τά rhetoric (2b)

ῥητορικ-ός - ή -όν rhetorical
Σαλαμῖνα Salamis (acc.)
τὰ πράγματα events
τὰς Ἀθήν-ας Athens
τὴν ἡμετέρ-αν τόλμ-αν our
   courage
τὴν ναυμαχί-αν the naval
   battle
τὴν νίκ-ην the/our victory
τὴν Σαλαμῖνα Salamis
τίνα ἔργα what deeds (acc.)
τοῖς Μηδικοῖς the Persian Wars
τολμά-ω dare, undertake
τὸν Πειραιᾶ the Peiraieus

Vocabulary to be learnt
ἡδέως *with pleasure, happily*
ἤδη *by now, now, already*
παρά *(+ acc.) along, beside*

B

ΡΑΨ. 'μῆνιν⌐ ἄειδε, Θεά, Ξέρξου⌒θείου⌒βασιλῆος ⌐οὐλομένην'
οἱ μὲν οὖν βάρβαροι βραδέως προσέρχονται πρὸς
τὴν⌒πόλιν, οἱ δὲ Ἀθηναῖοι ἀποροῦσι καὶ φοβοῦνται. πολλὴ
μὲν γὰρ ἡ⌐ τῶν⌒Περσῶν ⌐στρατιά, ὀλίγοι δὲ οἱ Ἀθηναῖοι.
καὶ πολλαὶ μὲν αἱ⌐ τῶν⌒Περσῶν ⌐νῆες, ὀλίγαι δὲ αἱ⌒νῆες   5
αἱ⌒τῶν⌒ Ἀθηναίων. πολὺς μὲν οὖν ὁ τῶν⌒ Ἀθηναίων
κίνδυνος, πολλὴ δὲ ἡ⌒ἀπορία, πολὺς δὲ καὶ ὁ φόβος.
τὰς⌐ μὲν οὖν ⌐θυσίας τοῖς⌒θεοῖς θύουσιν οἱ Ἀθηναῖοι καὶ
πολλὰ⌒εὔχονται, εἰσβαίνουσι δὲ ταχέως εἰς τὰς⌒ναῦς καὶ
ὑπὲρ⌒τῆς⌒ἐλευθερίας μάχονται. ἀγαθὸν γὰρ ἡ⌒ἐλευθερία.   10
τέλος δὲ ἀφικνοῦνται οἱ Πέρσαι, μάχονται δὲ οἱ⌒ Ἕλληνες.
πολλὴ γὰρ ἡ⌒τόλμα ἡ τῶν⌐ τε ⌐Ἑλλήνων καὶ τῶν⌒στρατηγῶν.
καὶ ἐν τῇ⌒ναυμαχίᾳ ὅσαι εἰσὶν αἱ⌒βοαί, ὅσαι αἱ⌒ἀπορίαι, ὅσαι
αἱ⌐ τῶν⌒θεῶν ⌐ἱκετεῖαι. τέλος δὲ νικῶσι μὲν τὸ τῶν⌒Περσῶν
ναυτικὸν οἱ Ἀθηναῖοι, πίπτουσι δὲ οἱ⌒ Πέρσαι, καὶ οὐ   15
δουλοῦνται τοὺς Ἀθηναιούς. καὶ τὴν⌒ Ἑλλάδα ἐλευθεροῦσιν
οἱ Ἀθηναῖοι καὶ τὴν⌒πατρίδα σῴζουσι διὰ τὴν⌒τόλμαν. ἡ⌐ γὰρ
⌐ἀρετὴ καὶ ἡ⌒τόλμα τήν⌐ τε ⌐ὕβριν καὶ τὸ⌒πλῆθος ἀεὶ νικῶσιν.
οὕτως οὖν βεβαία γίγνεται ἡ⌐ τῶν⌒ Ἑλλήνων ⌐σωτηρία.

ὁ τῶν Περσῶν βασιλεύς

Vocabulary for Section Two B

ἀγαθ-ός -ή -όν good
ἄειδ-ε sing! (s.)
Ἀθηναῖ-ος, ὁ Athenian (2a)
αἱ ἀπορί-αι the perplexities,
   distress
αἱ βο-αί the shouts
αἱ ἱκετεῖ-αι the
   supplications
αἱ νῆες the ships
αἱ τῶν Ἀθηναί-ων the
   (ships) of the Athenians
ἀπορέ-ω be at a loss, be
   perplexed
ἀφ-ικν-οῦνται (they) arrive
βάρβαρ-ος, ὁ Persian,
   barbarian (2a)
βέβαι-ος -α -ον secure
βραδέ-ως slowly
γίγν-εται (it) becomes
διά (+acc.) on account of
δουλ-οῦνται (they) enslave
εἰσ-βαίν-ω embark
ἐλευθερ-οῦσι(ν) (they) set
   free
ἡ ἀπορί-α the perplexity,
   distress
ἡ ἀρετ-ή (the) courage,
   excellence
ἡ ἐλευθερί-α (the) freedom
ἡ στρατι-ά the army
ἡ τόλμ-α (the) courage
ἡ τῶν Ἑλλήνων the
   (courage) of the Greeks

Θε-ά goddess (voc.)
θύ-ω (make a) sacrifice
κίνδυν-ος, ὁ danger (2a)
μάχ-ονται (they) fight
μῆνιν οὐλομένην
   destructive wrath (acc.)
ναυτικ-όν, τό the navy (2b)
νικά-ω defeat, win
Ξέρξου θείου βασιλῆος of
   Xerxes, the god-like king
οἱ Ἕλληνες the Greeks
οἱ Πέρσ-αι the Persians
ὀλίγ-οι –αι -α few
ὅσ-οι –αι -α how many!
οὕτως thus, so
πίπτ-ω fall, die
πολλ-αί many (nom.)
πολλ-ή much (nom.)
πολ-ὺς much, great (nom.)
πολλὰ εὔχ-ονται they make
   many prayers
προσ-έρχ-εται (it) advances
προσ-έρχ-ονται (they)
   advance
τὰς θυσί-ας the sacrifices
τὰς ναῦς their ships
ταχέ-ως quickly
τέλος finally
τῇ ναυμαχί-ᾳ the naval
   battle
τὴν Ἑλλάδα Greece
τὴν πατρίδα the(ir)
   fatherland

τὴν πόλιν the city
τὴν τόλμ-αν their courage
τὴν ὕβριν the aggression
τοῖς θεοῖς to the gods
τὸ πλῆθος superior numbers
τῶν Ἀθηναί-ων of the
   Athenians
τῶν Ἑλλήνων of the
   Greeks
τῶν θε-ῶν of the gods
τῶν Περσ-ῶν of the
   Persians
τῶν στρατηγ-ῶν of their
   generals
ὑπὲρ τῆς ἐλευθερί-ας for
   freedom
φόβ-ος, ὁ fear (2a)
φοβ-οῦνται (they) fear

Vocabulary to be learnt

ἀγαθός ή όν *good, noble,*
   courageous
Ἀθηναῖος, ὁ *Athenian (2a)*
ἀπορέ-ω *be at a loss; have*
   no resources
βέβαιος ᾱ ον *secure*
βραδέως *slowly*
νῑκάω *win, defeat*
ὅσος η ον *how great!*
πίπτω (πεσ-) *fall, die*
τέλος *in the end, finally*

The Persian wars

The Persian Wars featured four great encounters: Marathon (491), when the Athenians repelled the first Persian invasion, Thermopylae (480), when Spartans tried to hold up the second invasion, Salamis (480), when the Persian fleet was destroyed and Plataea (479), when the Persian army was finally defeated. In our text the rhapsode produces a flowery account of Salamis based on a funeral speech by Lysias, full of emotional repetitions but lacking substance,. The captain bases his version on our two most important sources, Herodotus 8.83ff and Aeschylus' *Persians* 353ff.

C

The captain is not impressed, and proceeds to give his grandfather's first-hand version of the battle.

In *World of Athens*: Herodotus 8.40–1, 93; Aeschylus' *Persians* 8.49, 60; patriotism 5.83; divine intervention 3.7–9; sea-battles 7.39; Greek (dis)unity 1.55–6.

σιωπᾷ ὁ ῥαψῳδός. ὁ δὲ κυβερνήτης λέγει ὅτι οὐδὲν λέγει ὁ ῥαψῳδός. ἔπειτα δὲ καὶ ὁ κυβερνήτης λέγει τὰ⌜ περὶ Σαλαμῖνα ⌝πράγματα.

ΚΥΒ.	οὐδὲν‿λέγεις, ὦ φίλε, καὶ οὐκ οἶσθα οὐδέν. οὔκουν
	κάλλιστον τὸν λόγον ποιεῖς. 5
ΡΑΨ.	τί φής; διὰ τί οὐ κάλλιστον ποιῶ τὸν λόγον;
ΚΥΒ.	σκόπει δή. ἡμεῖς μὲν γὰρ τὰ‿ἀληθῆ ζητοῦμεν, σὺ δὲ ψευδῆ
	λέγεις.
ΡΑΨ.	σὺ δὲ πῶς οἶσθα πότερον τὰ‿ἀληθῆ λέγω ἢ ψευδῆ;
ΚΥΒ.	ἄκουε, ὦ φίλε. ὁ γὰρ πάππος ὁ ἐμὸς Σαλαμινομάχης, 10
	καὶ πολλάκις τὰ⌜ περὶ Σαλαμῖνα ⌝πράγματα ἀληθῶς μοι
	λέγει, ἀλλὰ οὐχ ὥσπερ σύ, ψευδῶς. σὺ μὲν γὰρ ἴσως
	καλόν‿τινα‿λόγον ἡμῖν λέγεις, ὁ δὲ πάππος τὰ‿πράγματα.
	ἡσυχίαν⌜οὖν ⌝ἔχετε, καὶ ἀκούετε αὖθις, ὦ ναῦται, τὰ καλὰ
	ἔργα τὰ τῶν‿Ἑλλήνων. ὧδε γὰρ τὰ‿πράγματα τὰ‿περὶ 15
	Σαλαμῖνα λέγει ὁ πάππος.

(ἡσυχίαν‿ἔχουσιν οἱ ναῦται)

ἡ σάλπιγξ ἠχεῖ

ἀφικνεῖται μὲν γὰρ τὸ τῶν ͜Περσῶν ναυτικόν,
καὶ ἐγγὺς ͜Σαλαμῖνος μένει, ἡμεῖς δὲ οἱ ͜Ἕλληνες
ἡσυχίαν ͜ἔχομεν. ἐπειδὴ δὲ νὺξ γίγνεται, ἔνθα ͜καὶ ͜ἔνθα   20
πλέουσι βραδέως αἱ⌈ τῶν ͜Περσῶν ⌉νῆες. ἀλλὰ ἅμα ͜ἔῳ
βοή ͜τις γίγνεται, καὶ ἐπειδὴ ἡ ͜σάλπιγξ ἠχεῖ ἐκ
τῶν ͜πετρῶν, φόβος ἅμα γίγνεται ἐν τοῖς ͜βαρβάροις.
ἀκούουσι γὰρ ἤδη σαφῶς τὴν ͜βοήν·
      'ὦ παῖδες Ἑλλήνων ἴτε,   25
ἐλευθεροῦτε πατρίδ', ἐλευθεροῦτε δὲ
παῖδας, γυναῖκας· νῦν ὑπὲρ ͜πάντων ἀγών.'

Vocabulary for Section Two C

ἀγών the contest (nom.)
αἱ νῆες the ships
ἀληθῶς truthfully
ἅμα at the same time
ἅμα ἔῳ at daybreak
αὖθις again
ἀφ-ικν-εῖται (it) arrives
βο-ή τις a shout
γίγν-εται there is, it becomes
γυναῖκας your wives (acc.)
δή then, now (stressing)
ἐγγὺς Σαλαμῖνος near Salamis
ἐλευθερ-οῦτε free! (pl.)
Ἑλλήνων of the Greeks
ἐμ-ός -ή -όν my
ἔνθα καὶ ἔνθα this way and
   that
ἐν τοῖς βαρβάροις among
   the barbarians
ἐπειδή when
ζητέ-ω seek, look for
ἤδη now, already
ἡμῖν to us
ἡ σάλπιγξ trumpet
ἡσυχί-αν ἔχ-ω keep quiet
ἠχέ-ω echo
ἴσως perhaps
ἴτε come! (pl.)
κάλλιστ-ος -η -ον very fine,
   most lovely

καλόν τινα λόγον a fine tale
λόγ-ος, ὁ story, tale (2a)
μοι to me
ναῦτ-αι sailors (voc.)
ναυτικ-όν, τό navy (2b)
νὺξ night
οἱ Ἕλληνες the Greeks
οὐδὲν λέγ-ω speak
   nonsense
οὔκουν not . . . therefore
παῖδες children (voc.)
παῖδας your children (acc.)
πάππ-ος, ὁ grandfather (2a)
πατρίδ'= πατρίδα fatherland
   (acc.)
πολλάκις often
πότερον . . . ἢ whether
   . . . or
Σαλαμῖνα Salamis (acc.)
Σαλαμινομάχ-ης a soldier at
   Salamis
σιωπά-ω be quiet
σκοπέ-ω look
τὰ ἀληθῆ the truth
τὰ πράγματα the events
τὰ περί . . . (the events)
   around
τὰ τῶν Ἑλλήνων the (fine
   deeds) of the Greeks
τὴν βο-ὴν the shout

τοῖς βαρβάροις the
   barbarians
τὸ ποίημα the poem
τῶν Ἑλλήνων of the Greeks
τῶν Περσ-ῶν of the
   Persians
τῶν πετρ-ῶν the rocks
ὑπὲρ πάντων for everything
φής you (s.) say
φόβ-ος, ὁ fear (2a)
ψευδῆ lies (acc.)
ψευδ-ῶς falsely
ὧδε as follows, thus
ὥσπερ like

Vocabulary to be learnt
ἅμα *at the same time*
αὖθις *again*
βάρβαρος, ὁ *barbarian,*
   foreigner (2a)
ἐμός ή όν *my; mine*
ἡσυχάζω *be quiet, keep*
   quiet
κάλλιστος η ον *most/very*
   fine/beautiful/good
λόγος, ὁ *story, tale (2a)*
πότερον . . . ἢ *whether . . . or*
σιωπά-ω *be silent*
σκοπέ-ω *look (at), consider*
ψευδῶς *falsely*

D

KYB. προσέρχονται μὲν οὖν ταχέως οἱ πολέμιοι ἐπὶ ναυμαχίαν
      (θεᾶται δὲ ἡδέως τὴν ναυμαχίαν Ξέρξης ὁ βασιλεύς),
      ἐγὼ δὲ ἀναχωρῶ· καὶ ἀναχωροῦσιν οἱ ἄλλοι Ἕλληνες.
      ἐξαίφνης δὲ φαίνεται φάσμα τι γυναικεῖον, μάλα δεινόν.
      ἐγὼ δὲ τὸ φάσμα φοβοῦμαι. ἀλλὰ λέγει τὸ φάσμα· 'ὦ   5
      φίλοι, διὰ τί ἔτι ἀναχωρεῖτε; μὴ φοβεῖσθε τοὺς Μήδους
      ἀλλὰ βοηθεῖτε καὶ τολμᾶτε.' καὶ ἐγὼ μὲν ταχέως ἐπιπλέω τε
      καὶ οὐκέτι φοβοῦμαι, ἐπιπλέουσι δὲ καὶ οἱ ἄλλοι Ἕλληνες
      ταχέως καὶ ἐπὶ τοὺς Μήδους ἐπέρχονται. νῦν δὲ κόσμῳ
      μαχόμεθα ἡμεῖς καὶ κατὰ τάξιν, ἀκόσμως δὲ καὶ ἀτάκτως   10
      μάχονται οἱ βάρβαροι, ἐπειδὴ οὐ τολμῶσιν ὥσπερ ἡμεῖς.
          τέλος δὲ τῶν Περσῶν οἱ μὲν φεύγουσι, οἱ δὲ μένουσι
      καὶ πίπτουσι. καὶ τῶν Ἑλλήνων οἱ μὲν διώκουσι τοὺς
      Πέρσας, οἱ δὲ λαμβάνουσι τὰς ναῦς καὶ τοὺς ναύτας.
      ἐπειδὴ δὲ διώκουσιν οἱ Ἀθηναῖοι τοὺς Πέρσας, φεύγει   15
      καὶ ὁ Ξέρξης καὶ τὴν ναυμαχίαν οὐκέτι θεᾶται. ἐλεύθεροι
      οὖν γίγνονται οἱ Ἕλληνες διὰ τὴν ἀρετήν. οὕτως οὖν
      οἱ θεοὶ κολάζουσι τὴν τῶν Περσῶν ὕβριν καὶ σῴζουσι
      τὴν πόλιν. καὶ οὐ δουλοῦνται τοὺς Ἀθηναίους οἱ Πέρσαι.
ΔΙΚ. εὖ λέγεις, ὦ κυβερνῆτα. νῦν δὲ σαφῶς καὶ ἀκριβῶς ἴσμεν   20
      περὶ τὰ Μηδικά. ἀλλὰ πολλὴ νῦν ἐστιν ἡ τῶν πραγμάτων
      μεταβολή· τότε μὲν γὰρ φίλοι ἀλλήλοις οἱ Ἕλληνες, νῦν
      δὲ οὐκέτι ὁμονοοῦσιν, ἀλλὰ μισοῦσιν ἀλλήλους διὰ τὸν
      πόλεμον. τότε μὲν ὁμόνοια ἐν τοῖς Ἕλλησι, νῦν δὲ μῖσος.
      φεῦ φεῦ τῶν Ἑλλήνων, φεῦ τοῦ πολέμου.   25

Salamis

Vocabulary for Section Two D

ἀκόσμ-ως in disorder
ἀλλήλοις to one another
ἀλλήλ-ους one another
   (acc.)
ἄλλ-ος -η -ο other, rest of
ἀνα-χωρέ-ω retreat
ἀτάκτ-ως out of rank
γίγν-ονται (they) become
δειν-ός -ή -όν terrible, dire
διά (+acc.) because of
δουλ-οῦνται (they) enslave
ἐλεύθερ-ος -α -ον free
ἐξαίφνης suddenly, out of
   the blue
ἐπειδὴ when, since, because
ἐπ-έρχ-ονται they advance
   against
ἐπὶ (+acc.) to, against,
   towards
ἐπι-πλέ-ω sail forward,
   attack
ἔτι still
εὖ well
ἡ μεταβολ-ή the change
θε-ᾶται (he) watches, gazes
   at
θε-ός, ὁ god (2a)
κατὰ (+acc.) by, in,
   according to
κολάζ-ω punish
κόσμῳ in order
κυβερνῆτα captain
λαμβάν-ω capture, take
μάλα very
μαχ-όμεθα (we) fight
μάχ-ονται (they) fight
Μηδικ-ά, τά the
   PersianWars (2b)

Μῆδ-ος, ὁ Persian (2a)
μισέ-ω hate
μῖσος hatred (nom.)
ναυμαχί-αν a naval battle
   (acc.)
Ξέρξ-ης Xerxes (nom.)
ὁ βασιλεὺς the king
οἱ δὲ (with οἱ μὲν) others
οἱ μὲν (with οἱ δὲ) some
ὁμονοέ-ω be of one mind,
   agree
ὁμόνοι-α agreement
   (nom.)
ὁ Ξέρξης Xerxes
οὐκέτι no longer
οὕτως in this way
πολέμι-οι, οἱ the enemy
   (2a)
πόλεμ-ος, ὁ war (2a)
πολλ-ὴ much, great (nom.)
προσ-έρχ-ονται (they)
   advance
τάξιν rank (acc.)
τὰς ναῦς the ships
ταχέ-ως quickly
τὴν ἀρετ-ὴν their courage
τὴν ναυμαχί-αν the naval
   battle
τὴν πόλιν the city
τὴν ὕβριν the aggression
τι a (nom.)
τοῖς Ἕλλησι the Greeks
τολμά-ω be daring
τότε then
τὸ φάσμα the phantom,
   apparition
τοὺς ναύτ-ας the sailors
τοὺς Πέρσ-ας the Persians

τῶν Περσ-ῶν of the
   Persians
τῶν πραγμάτων of/in
   things, affairs
φαίν-εται (it) appears
φάσμα τι γυναικεῖον a
   phantom in female form
   (nom. n.)
φεῦ alas!
φεῦ τοῦ πολέμου alas for
   the war!
φεῦ τῶν Ἑλλήνων alas for
   the Greeks!
φοβ-οῦμαι (I) fear
φοβ-εῖσθε be afraid of! (pl.)
ὥσπερ like, as

Vocabulary to be learnt
ἀναχωρέω *retreat*
διά *(+acc.) because of*
ἐλεύθερος ᾱ ον *free*
ἐπειδή *when*
ἐπί *(+ acc.) against, at, to,*
   to get
οὐκέτι *no longer*
οὕτω(ς) *thus, so, in this*
   way
πολέμιοι, οἱ *the enemy*
   (2a)
πολέμιος ᾱ ον *hostile,*
   enemy
πόλεμος, ὁ *war (2a)*
ταχέως *quickly*
τι *a, something*
τολμάω *dare, be daring,*
   undertake
ὥσπερ *like, as*

Section Three A–E: Athens and Sparta

A

As the ship enters the harbour, Dikaiopolis sees a light shining from Salamis. The reaction of the captain is abrupt.

In *World of Athens*: Peloponnesian War 1.56–81.

οὕτως οὖν ἡ ναῦς πρὸς τὸν⁀λιμένα βραδέως χωρεῖ. ὁ δὲ Δικαιόπολις
λαμπάδα τινὰ ὁρᾷ ἐν Σαλαμῖνι. ἐρωτᾷ οὖν ὁ κυβερνήτης πόθεν
ἡ⁀λαμπάς· ἐπειδὴ δὲ ὁρᾷ, εὐθὺς σπεύδει πρὸς τὸν⁀λιμένα.

ΚΥΒ.	*(pointing towards the harbour)*	5

ΚΥΒ. *(pointing towards the harbour)*   5
      δεῦρο ἐλθὲ σὺ καὶ βλέπε. πρὸς γὰρ τὸν⁀λιμένα
      ἀφικνούμεθα ἤδη.
ΔΙΚ. (βλέπει πρὸς τὴν⁀Σαλαμῖνα)
      ἰδού, ὦ κυβερνῆτα. λαμπάδα⁀τινὰ ὁρῶ ἐγὼ ἐν τῇ⁀νήσῳ.
ΚΥΒ. τί φής; πόθεν ἡ⁀λαμπάς;   10
ΔΙΚ. ὁπόθεν; ἰδού.
ΚΥΒ. (βλέπει πρὸς τὴν νῆσον καὶ ὁ κυβερνήτης)
      ὦ Ζεῦ. λαμπάδα γὰρ οὐχ ὁρᾷς, ἀλλὰ τὰ πυρά.
ΝΑΥΤΗΣ τί φής; τὰ πυρὰ λέγεις; ὦ Ζεῦ. ἄγε δή, ὦ κυβερνῆτα, σπεῦδε,
      σπεῦδε καὶ σῷζε ἡμᾶς εἰς τὸν⁀λιμένα.   15
ΚΥΒ. *(impatiently)*
      ἀλλὰ σῴζω ὑμᾶς ἔγωγε. μὴ φοβεῖσθε· σπεύδω γάρ, καὶ
      ἐπιστρέφει ἤδη ἡ ναῦς εἰς τὸν⁀λιμένα.
ΔΙΚ. ἀλλὰ διὰ τί σπεύδομεν; ἆρα κίνδυνός⁀τίς ἐστιν ἡμῖν;
ΝΑΥ. νὴ⁀τὸν⁀Δία· ἐν κινδύνῳ ἡμεῖς ἐσμέν, ὦ Δικαιόπολι, εὖ οἶδα   20
      ὅτι. σπεύδομεν διότι τὰ πυρὰ δηλοῖ τι⁀δεινόν.
ΔΙΚ. τί δηλοῖ τὰ πυρά;
ΝΑΥ. σαφῶς δηλοῖ ὅτι αἱ⁀πολέμιαι⁀νῆες ἐπὶ ἡμᾶς ἐπέρχονται.

Vocabulary for Section Three A

> **Grammar for 3A–B**
> - Type 3a nouns: λιμήν and νύξ (3a)
> - Personal pronouns: ἐγώ, σύ, ἡμεῖς, ὑμεῖς

ἄγε come! (s.)
αἱ πολέμιαι νῆες the enemy
  ships
ἀφ-ικνέ-ομαι arrive, come
δειν-ός -ή -όν dire, terrible
δή then (with imper.)
διότι because
ἐπι-στρέφ-ω turn round
ἐρωτά-ω ask
εὖ well
εὐθὺς immediately
Ζεῦ Zeus
ἡ λαμπάς the torch
ἡμᾶς us
ἡμῖν for/to us
ἡ πόλις the city
ἰδού look! (s.)

κίνδυνός τις some danger
  (nom.)
κινδύνῳ danger
λαμπάδ-α a torch (acc.)
λαμπάδ-α τινὰ a torch
  (acc.)
νὴ τὸν Δί-α yes, by Zeus
νῆσ-ος, ἡ island (2a)
ὁπόθεν where from?
πόθεν from where?
πυρ-ά, τά fire-signal (2b)
Σαλαμῖνι Salamis
σπεύδ-ω hurry
τῇ νήσῳ the island
τὴν Σαλαμῖνα Salamis
τι δεινόν something terrible
τὸν λιμέν-α the harbour

ὑμᾶς you (acc. pl)
φής you (s.) say
χωρέ-ω come, go

Vocabulary to be learnt
ἄγε *come!*
ἀφικνέομαι (ἀφῖκ-) *arrive,
  come*
ἐρωτάω (ἐρ-) *ask*
ἰδού *look! here! hey!*
κίνδῡνος, ὁ *danger (2a)*
νῆσος, ἡ *island (2a)*
πόθεν; *from where?*
πυρά, τά *fire-signal (2b)*
σπεύδω *hurry*
χωρέω *go, come*

The attack on Peiraieus

Since Peiraieus was so vital for Athens' prosperity and safety, there was a system for early warning in the case of attack. Here Thucydides describes a surprise attack by sea on Peiraieus early on during the Peloponnesian War in 429, which, had it been successful, might have brought the war to an end at once:

'Knemos and Brasidas and the others in command of the Peloponnesian fleet decided on the advice of the Megarians to make an attempt on Peiraieus, the port of Athens, which the Athenians, reasonably enough because of their superiority at sea, had left open and unguarded. The plan was that each sailor should take his oar, cushion and oar-loop, and that they should then proceed on foot to the sea on the Athenian side, make for Megara as quickly as they could and launch from the docks at Nisaia [Megara's port] forty ships which happened to be there and then sail straight to Peiraieus… They arrived by night, launched the ships from Nisaia and sailed, not for Peiraieus as they had originally intended, thinking it too risky (and because the wind was unfavourable, it was said later) but to the promontory of Salamis that fronts Megara… Meanwhile beacons were lit to warn Athens of the attack, and the biggest panic of the war ensued.' (*World of Athens*, 2.25)

B

The scene on shore is one of utter confusion. Polos comes out of his house to find out what is going on. There he meets his neighbour Protarchos who, as an armed soldier on a trireme, is running to get his weapons.

In *World of Athens*: ships and hoplites 7.34; manning triremes 7.44–5.

ἐπειδὴ δὲ οἱ ἐν τῷ Πειραιεῖ ταῦτα τὰ πυρὰ ὁρῶσι, πολὺς γίγνεται ἐν τῷ λιμένι θόρυβος, πολλαὶ δὲ αἱ βοαί, οὐδαμοῦ δὲ κόσμος. νὺξ γάρ ἐστι, καὶ πολλοὶ ἄνδρες φαίνονται ἐν ταῖς ὁδοῖς καὶ τὰ πυρὰ θεῶνται. Πρώταρχος καὶ Πῶλος ὁ γείτων ὁρῶσι τοὺς ἄνδρας.

5

ΠΩΛΟΣ　(ἔξω θεῖ ἐκ τῆς οἰκίας)
　　　　εἰπέ μοι, τίς ἡ βοὴ αὕτη; τίς ὁ θόρυβος οὗτος, ὦ γεῖτον;
　　　　ἆρα οἶσθα; μέγας μὲν γὰρ ὁ θόρυβος, μεγάλη δὲ ἡ βοὴ ἡ ἐν τῷ λιμένι.
ΠΡΩΤΑΡΧΟΣ (θεῖ οἴκαδε)　　　　　　　　　　　　　　　　　　　　　　　10
　　　　δεῦρο ἐλθέ, ὦ γεῖτον, καὶ ἐκεῖσε βλέπε. ἆρα οὐχ ὁρᾷς
　　　　ἐκεῖνα τὰ πυρά; ἰδού. δῆλον γὰρ ὅτι ἐν κινδύνῳ ἐστὶν ἡ Σαλαμίς.
ΠΩΛΟΣ　εἰπέ μοι, ὦ γεῖτον, ποῖ τρέχεις;
ΠΡΩΤ.　οἴκαδε τρέχω ἔγωγε ἐπὶ τὰ ὅπλα. εἶτα δὲ εἰς τὴν ναῦν　　　15
　　　　ταχέως πορεύομαι. δεινὸς γὰρ οὗτος ὁ κίνδυνος καὶ μέγας.
　　　　ἀλλὰ διὰ τί σὺ οὐ μετὰ ἐμοῦ πορεύῃ;
ΠΩΛΟΣ　καὶ δὴ μετὰ σοῦ πορεύομαι. ἀλλὰ μένε, ὦ φίλε.
ΠΡΩΤ.　ἀλλὰ ποῖ σὺ τρέχεις;

τὰ ὅπλα

ΠΩΛΟΣ   εἰς τὴν οἰκίαν ἔγωγε, ἐπὶ τὸν⌐τροπωτῆρα καὶ τὸ ὑπηρέσιον.   20
δῆλον γὰρ ὅτι ἐπὶ ναυμαχίαν πορευόμεθα.

οὕτως οὖν ἐκφέρει ὁ μὲν Πῶλος τόν⌐ τε ⌐τροπωτῆρα καὶ τὸ
ὑπηρέσιον, ὁ⌐ δὲ τοῦ⌐Πρωτάρχου⌐παῖς τά τε ὅπλα καὶ τὴν⌐λαμπάδα
ἐκφέρει. ἔπειτα πορεύονται οἱ⌐ἄνδρες πρὸς τὸν⌐λιμένα.   25

Vocabulary for Section Three B

αὕτ-η this (with βο-ή)
  (*nom.*)
γεῖτον neighbour (voc.)
δειν-ός -ή -όν terrible
εἰπ-έ speak! tell (me)!
εἶτα then
ἐκεῖν-α τά those (acc.)
ἐκεῖσε there, over there
ἐκ-φέρ-ω carry out
ἔξω outside
εὖ well
ἡ Σαλαμίς Salamis
ἡμῖν for/to us
θεά-ομαι watch, gaze at
θέ-ω run
θόρυβ-ος, ὁ din, hustle and
  bustle (2a)
καὶ δὴ yes (I am . . .)
κινδύνῳ danger
κόσμ-ος, ὁ order (2a)
μέγας great (nom.)
μεγάλη great (nom.)
μετὰ ἐμοῦ with me
μετὰ σοῦ with you
μοι to me
νὺξ night
ὁ γείτων his neighbour
οἱ ἄνδρ-ες the men

οἴκαδε home(wards)
οἰκί-α, ἡ house (1b)
ὁ παῖς the slave
ὅπλ-α, τά weapons (2b)
οὐδαμοῦ nowhere
οὗτ-ος ὁ this (nom.)
οὗτ-ος this (with θόρυβος)
  (nom.)
πολλ-αὶ many (nom.)
πολλ-οὶ ἄνδρ-ες many men
  (nom.)
πολ-ὺς much, a lot of
  (nom.)
πορεύ-ομαι journey, come,
  go
Πρώταρχ-ος, ὁ Protarchos
  (2a) (*an armed soldier on
  a trireme*)
Πῶλ-ος, ὁ Polos (2a) (*a
  rower*)
ταῖς ὁδοῖς the streets
ταῦτ-α τά these (acc.)
τὴν λαμπάδ-α the torch
τὴν ναῦν the ship
τῆς οἰκίας the house
τὸν λιμέν-α the harbour
τὸν τροπωτῆρ-α the/his
  oar-loop

τοῦ Πώλου Polos'
τοὺς ἄνδρ-ας the men
τρέχ-ω run
τῷ λιμένι the harbour
τῷ Πειραιεῖ the Peiraieus
ὑπηρέσι-ον, τό cushion
  (2b)
φαίν-ομαι appear

Vocabulary to be learnt
δεινός ἡ όν *terrible, dire,
  clever*
ἐγώ 1
εὖ *well*
ἡμεῖς *we*
θεάομαι *watch, gaze at*
θόρυβος, ὁ *noise, din, hustle
  and bustle (2a)*
οἰκίᾱ, ἡ *house (1b)*
οἴκαδε *homewards*
ὅπλα, τά *weapons, arms
  (2b)*
πορεύομαι *march, journey,
  go*
σύ *you (s.)*
ὑμεῖς *you (pl.)*
φαίνομαι (φαν-) *appear,
  seem*

C

Back on the ship, the rhapsode is terrified, but the crew assures him all will be well.

In *World of Athens*: Sparta 1.24, 7.11; Periclean policy 1.57; Athenian sea-power and empire 6.70–4.

ἐν⌐ δὲ ⌐τούτῳ ὅ τε Δικαιόπολις καὶ οἱ ναῦται ἔτι πρὸς ἀλλήλους διαλέγονται.

ΔΙΚ.	ὦ Ζεῦ. δεινὸς γὰρ ὁ ἐν Σαλαμῖνι κίνδυνος ἡμῖν καὶ μέγας.
	ἰδού, ὦ ῥαψῳδέ· ἀλλὰ ποῦ ἐστιν ὁ⌢ἀνήρ; οὐ γὰρ ὁρῶ 5
	ἐκεῖνον⌢τὸν⌢ἄνδρα.
ΝΑΥ.	ἰδού, 'πτώσσει' οὗτος⌢ὁ ῥαψῳδὸς ἐν τῇ⌢νηί, 'ὥσπερ Ἀχαιὸς
	ὑφ'⌢⌢Ἕκτορι'. φοβεῖται γὰρ τοὺς Λακεδαιμονίους.
ΔΙΚ.	εἰπέ μοι, ὦ ῥαψῳδέ, τί ποιεῖς; τίς φόβος λαμβάνει σε;
	σὺ γὰρ στρατηγὸς εἶ τῶν Ἑλλήνων ἄριστος. μὴ ποίει 10
	τοῦτο μηδὲ φοβοῦ τοὺς Λακεδαιμονίους τούτους. ἰδού,
	ἐγγὺς⌢τοῦ⌢λιμένος ἐσμὲν ἤδη. μὴ οὖν φοβοῦ.
ΡΑΨ.	(*still shaking with fear*)
	τί φής; ἆρα ἀφικνοῦνται οἱ Λακεδαιμόνιοι; φοβοῦμαι γὰρ
	τοὺς Λακεδαιμονίους ἔγωγε. τοὺς γὰρ ναύτας λαμβάνουσιν 15
	ἐκεῖνοι καὶ ἀποκτείνουσιν.
ΝΑΥ.	ἀλλὰ οὐδεμία⌢ναῦς ἔρχεται, ὦ τᾶν, καὶ δῆλον ὅτι οὐκ
	ἀφικνεῖται Λακεδαιμόνιος⌢οὐδείς, οὐδὲ λαμβάνει οὐδένα,
	οὐδὲ ἀποκτείνει οὔτε ἡμᾶς οὔτε ὑμᾶς. σὺ δὲ οὐ μιμνήσκῃ
	τοὺς τοῦ⌢Περικλέους λόγους; 20
ΡΑΨ.	τίνες οἱ λόγοι; λέγε μοι· οὐ γὰρ μιμνήσκομαι.
ΝΑΥ.	ἄκουε οὖν τί λέγει ὁ Περικλῆς ἐν τῇ⌢ἐκκλησίᾳ περὶ⌢τοῦ⌢
	πολέμου⌢καὶ⌢τῶν⌢ναυτικῶν· 'μὴ φοβεῖσθε, ὦ ἄνδρες
	Ἀθηναῖοι, τοὺς Λακεδαιμονίους. ἐκεῖνοι μὲν γὰρ κρατοῦσι
	κατὰ γῆν, ἡμεῖς δὲ κατὰ θάλατταν. ἀλλὰ καὶ ἡμεῖς ἔχομεν 25
	ἐμπειρίαν⌢τινὰ κατὰ γῆν, ἐκεῖνοι δὲ οὐδεμίαν⌐ ἔχουσιν εἰς
	τὰ ναυτικὰ ⌐ἐμπειρίαν.

Vocabulary Section Three C

> **Grammar for 3C–E**
> - Adjectives/pronouns: οὗτος, ἐκεῖνος
> - Adjectives: πολύς, μέγας
> - Irregular nouns: ναῦς, Ζεύς
> - Negatives

ἀλλήλ-ους one another (acc.)
ἀπο-κτείν-ω kill
Ἀχαι-ός, ὁ Akhaian (2a) (*Homer's word for 'Greek'*)
γῆ, ἡ land (1a)
δια-λέγ-ομαι converse
ἐγγὺς τοῦ λιμένος near the harbour
εἰπ-έ speak! tell me!
ἐκεῖν-οι οἱ those (nom.)
ἐκεῖν-οι they, those men (nom.)
ἐκεῖν-ον τὸν ἄνδρ-α that man
ἐμπειρί-αν τινά some experience
ἐν τούτῳ meanwhile
ἔτι still
Ζεῦ Zeus
κατά (+acc.) on, by
κρατέ-ω hold sway, power
Λακεδαιμόνι-ος, ὁ Spartan (2a)
Λακεδαιμόνι-ος οὐδείς no Spartan (at all)
λαμβάν-ω take, capture
λόγ-ος, ὁ word (2a)
μηδέ and don't
μιμνήσκ-ομαι remember

μοι to me
ναυτικ-ός -ή -όν naval
ναυτικά, τά naval matters (2b)
ὁ ἀνήρ the man
ὁ Περικλῆς Pericles
οὐδαμ-ῶς in no way, not at all
οὐδὲ and not
οὐδεμί-α ναῦς no ship (nom.)
οὐδεμί-αν ἐμπειρί-αν no experience (acc.)
οὐδέν-α any one at all (acc.)
οὗτ-ος ὁ this
περὶ τοῦ πολέμου καὶ τῶν ναυτικῶν about the war and naval matters
πτώσσ-ω crouch, cower
Σαλαμῖνι Salamis
σε you (s.) (acc.)
τᾶν my dear chap (*condescending*)
τῇ ἐκκλησίᾳ the Assembly of the people (*where all political decisions were made*)
τῇ νηί the ship
τίνες what? (nom.)
τις someone, one (nom.)
τοῦ Περικλέους Pericles'

τοῦτ-ο this (acc.)
τούτ-ους these (with τοὺς Λακεδαιμονίους)
ὑμῶν of you
ὑφ' Ἕκτορι at Hektor's mercy (*Hektor: Trojan hero killed by Akhilleus*)
φής you (s.) say
φόβ-ος, ὁ fear (2a)

Vocabulary to be learnt
ἀλλήλους *each other, one another (2a)*
ἄλλος η ο *other, the rest of*
ἐγγύς *(+gen.) near, nearby*
εἰπέ *speak! tell me!*
ἐπειδή *when, since, because*
κατά *(+acc.) in, on, by, according to*
Λακεδαιμόνιος, ὁ *Spartan (2a)*
λαμβάνω (λαβ-) *take, capture*
λόγος, ὁ *word, speech; story, tale (2a)*
μανθάνω (μαθ-) *learn, understand*
ναυτικός ή ον *naval*
οὐδέ *and not, not even*
τέχνη, ἡ *skill, art, expertise (1a)*

καὶ δὴ καὶ οὐ ῥαδίως μανθάνουσιν οἱ Λακεδαιμόνιοι τὰ
ναυτικά, εὖ οἶδα ὅτι, ἐπειδὴ γεωργοί εἰσι καὶ οὐ θαλάττιοι.
τὸ δὲ ναυτικὸν τέχνη ἐστί· καὶ ταύτην μανθάνουσιν οἱ   30
ἄνθρωποι διὰ τὴν μελετήν, ὥσπερ καὶ τὰς ἄλλας τέχνας,
ἄλλως δὲ οὐδαμῶς. ὑμεῖς γὰρ δὴ εὖ ἴστε ὅτι οὐ ῥαδίως,
ἀλλὰ χαλεπῶς καὶ μετὰ πολλῆς μελετῆς, μανθάνετε
ταύτην τὴν τέχνην. – "ἀλλὰ οἱ Λακεδαιμόνιοι" – φησί τις
ὑμῶν – "ἆρα οὐ μελετῶσιν;" – ἐγὼ δὲ ἀποκρίνομαι "οὔκ,   35
ἀλλὰ ἡμεῖς, ἐπειδὴ κρατοῦμεν κατὰ θάλατταν, κωλύομεν."'

ΔΙΚ.   (comfortingly)
καὶ μὴν ὁρᾶτε τὸν λιμένα. ὅσαι αἱ λαμπάδες, ὅσαι αἱ νῆες,
ὅσος ὁ θόρυβος, ὅσοι οἱ ἄνδρες. ἰδού· ὥσπερ γὰρ μύρμηκες,
οὕτω συνέρχονται ἐκεῖνοι οἱ ναῦται εἰς τὸν λιμένα. μέγα   40
γὰρ ἡμῖν τὸ πλῆθος τὸ τῶν τε νεῶν καὶ τῶν τριηράρχων.

αἱ λαμπάδ-ες the torches	καὶ μὴν pay attention! See!	οἱ ἄνδρ-ες the men
αἱ νῆ-ες the ships	κατά (+acc.) on, by	οὕτω = οὕτως
ἄλλ-ος -η -ο other, rest of	κρατέ-ω hold sway, power	ῥᾳδί-ως easily
ἄλλ-ως otherwise	κωλύ-ω prevent, stop	συν-έρχ-ομαι assemble,
ἀπο-κρίν-ομαι answer	Λακεδαιμόνι-ος, ὁ Spartan	come together, swarm
γὰρ δὴ really, I assure you	(2a)	ταύτ-ην it, this (acc.)
γεωργ-ός, ὁ farmer (2a)	μανθάν-ω learn	ταύτ-ην τὴν this (acc.)
ἐκεῖν-οι οἱ those (nom.)	μέγα great (nom.)	τέχν-η, ἡ skill (1a)
ἐκεῖν-οι they, those men	μελετά-ω practice	τὸν λιμέν-α the harbour
(nom.)	μελετ-ή, ἡ practice (1a)	τὸ πλῆθος the number
ἐπειδή since, because	μετὰ πολλῆς μελετῆς with	τριήραρχ-ος, ὁ trierarch (2a)
ἡμῖν to/for us	much practice	τῶν νεῶν of the ships
θαλάττι-ος -α -ον sea, of	μύρμηκ-ες ants (nom.)	φησί (he) says
the sea	ναυτικά, τά naval matters (2b)	χαλεπ-ῶς with difficulty
καὶ δὴ καὶ and moreover	ναυτικόν, τό navigation (2b)	

D

*Dikaiopolis disembarks and observes the chaos. Polos is sent off
to rouse the ship's trierarch (master) by an agitated boatswain.*

In *World of Athens*: trierarchs 7.43–6; deme-names 5.12.

ἐπειδὴ οὖν ὁ Δικαιόπολις καὶ ὁ ῥαψῳδὸς εἰς τὴν γῆν ἀφικνοῦνται,
θόρυβος γίγνεται πολύς. οἱ δὲ ἄνδρες ἡσυχάζουσι καὶ τὴν θέαν
θεῶνται. ἐγγὺς δὲ τῆς νεώς ἐστι κελευστής τις, βοᾷ δὲ οὗτος.

ΚΕΛΕΥΣΤΗΣ εἰπέ μοι, ποῦ ὁ τριήραρχος ὁ ἡμέτερος;   5
ΠΩΛΟΣ   δῆλον ὅτι οἴκοι, ὦ κελευστά. καθεύδει γάρ⁀που.
ΚΕΛ.   οἴμοι. δεινὸς μὲν ὁ τῶν Ἀθηναίων κίνδυνος, ἀλλὰ ἐκεῖνος
         οἴκοι καθεύδει. σπεῦδε οὖν, ὦ Πῶλε, καὶ ζήτει τὸν τριήραρχον
         καὶ λέγε περὶ⁀τούτου⁀τοῦ⌐ ἐν Σαλαμῖνι ⌐κινδύνου.
ΠΩΛΟΣ   μάλιστά⁀γε, ὦ κελευστά.   10
(οὕτως οὖν τρέχει ταχέως πρὸς τὸν τριήραρχον ὁ Πῶλος. τέλος δὲ
εἰς τὴν θύραν ἀφικνεῖται.)
ΠΩΛΟΣ   (knocks on the door)
         παῖ, παῖ. τί ποιεῖς; ἆρα καθεύδει ὁ⁀παῖς; παῖ, παῖ.
ΠΑΙΣ   (blearily)   15
         τίς ἐστι; τίς βοᾷ;
         (opens the door)
         διὰ τί καλεῖς με; τίνα ζητεῖς;
ΠΩΛΟΣ   εἰπέ μοι, ἆρα ἔνδον ἐστὶν ὁ τριήραρχος; ἢ οὐχ οὕτως;
ΠΑΙΣ   οὕτως⁀γε.   20
ΠΩΛΟΣ   φέρε, ὦ παῖ, διὰ τί ἔτι μένεις καὶ οὐ καλεῖς τὸν δεσπότην;
         ζητῶ γὰρ ἐκεῖνον.
ΠΑΙΣ   ἀλλὰ ἀδύνατον· καθεύδει γὰρ ὁ δεσπότης ἥσυχος.
         (shuts the door)
ΠΩΛΟΣ   τί φῄς; ἀδύνατον; βάλλε⁀εἰς⁀κόρακας· μὴ παῖζε πρὸς ἐμέ.   25
         (he approaches the door)
         διὰ τί οὐ κόπτω ταύτην τὴν θύραν; τριήραρχε, τριήραρχε·
         σὲ γὰρ βοῶ.

Vocabulary for Section Three D

ἀ-δύνατ-ος -ον impossible
βάλλε εἰς κόρακ-ας go to
   hell! (lit. 'to the crows')
βοά-ω shout (for)
γάρ που of course, no need
   to say
δεσπότ-ης, ὁ master (1d)
ἐκεῖν-ον him (acc.)
ἐκεῖν-ος he (nom.)
ἐμέ me (acc.)
ἔνδον inside
ἔτι still
ζητέ-ω seek, look for
ἥσυχ-ος -ον quiet, quietly
θέ-α, ἡ sight (1b)

θύρ-α, ἡ door (1b)
καθεύδ-ω sleep
καλέ-ω call, summon
κελευστ-ής, ὁ boatswain (1d)
κελευστ-ής τις a boatswain
   (he gave the time to the
   rowers)
κόπτ-ω knock
μάλιστά γε yes, all right
με me (acc.)
μοι to me
οἱ ἄνδρ-ες the men
οἴκοι at home
ὁ παῖς the slave
οὗτ-ος he, the latter (nom.)

οὕτως γε yes, he is
παῖ slave!
περὶ τούτ-ου τοῦ κινδύνου
   about this danger
πολ-ύς much (nom.)
Σαλαμῖνι Salamis
σὲ you (acc. s.)
ταύτ-ην τὴν this (acc.)
τῆς νεώς the ship
τίνα whom? (acc.)
τρέχ-ω run
τριήραρχ-ος, ὁ trierarch,
   master (2a)
φέρ-ε come now!
φῄς you (s.) say, mean

ΤΡΙΗΡΑΡΧΟΣ βάλλε‿εἰς‿κόρακας. ἀλλὰ τίς κόπτει τὴν θύραν; τί
τοῦτο‿τὸ‿πρᾶγμά ἐστι; τίς καλεῖ με; τίς βοᾷ;   30
ΠΩΛΟΣ   Πῶλος καλεῖ σε, ὁ‿Κυδαθηναιεύς, ἐγώ.
ΤΡΙ.   ἀλλὰ καθεύδω ἥσυχος –
ΠΩΛΟΣ   ἀλλὰ μὴ κάθευδε, ὦ τριήραρχε· ἐν κινδύνῳ γὰρ ἡ‿Σαλαμίς.
    ἐλθὲ καὶ βλέπε ἐκεῖσε. ἆρα οὐχ ὁρᾷς ἐκεῖνα‿τὰ πυρά;
ΤΡΙ.   τί φής; ἆρα παίζεις πρὸς ἐμέ;   35
(ὁρᾷ τὰ πυρὰ τὰ ἐν τῇ‿νήσῳ)
    οἴμοι. μένε, ὦ Πῶλε. ταχὺ γὰρ ἔρχομαι.

βοά-ω shout (for)
ἐκεῖν-α τὰ those (acc.)
ἐκεῖσε there
ἡ Σαλαμίς Salamis
ἥσυχ-ος -ον quiet,
    quietly
θύρ-α, ἡ door (1b)
καθεύδ-ω sleep
καλέ-ω call, summon
κινδύνῳ danger
κόπτ-ω knock

οἱ ἄνδρ-ες the men
ὁ Κυδαθηναιεὺς the
    member of Kydathene
    deme (*a district of*
    Athens)
ταχύ quickly
τῇ νήσῳ the island
τοῦτ-ο τὸ πρᾶγμα this
    business (nom.)
φής you (s.) say, mean

Vocabulary to be learnt
βοάω *shout (for)*
ἔτι *still, yet*
ζητέω *look for, seek*
θύρᾱ, ἡ *door (1b)*
καθεύδω *sleep*
καλέω *call, summon*
κελευστής, ὁ *boatswain (1d)*
οἴκοι *at home*
τρέχω (δραμ-) *run*
τριήραρχος, ὁ *trierarch (2a)*

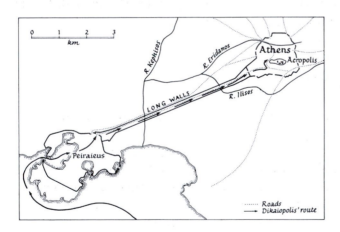

Athens and the harbours of Peiraieus

τὴν σπονδὴν σπένδει

E

Captain and crew finally embark on their trireme. Ritual prayers accompany their departure.

In *World of Athens*: libations 3.28.

τέλος δὲ ἐμβαίνουσι μὲν εἰς τὰς ναῦς οἱ ναῦται καὶ ὁ κελευστής, ἐμβαίνει δὲ καὶ ὁ τριήραρχος. καὶ ἐπειδὴ ἐκεῖνος κελεύει, ἡ ναῦς ἀποπλεῖ.

ΤΡΙ.	κατακέλευε δή, ὦ κελευστά.	5
ΚΕΛ.	ὠὸπ ὄπ ὠὸπ ὄπ.	
ΤΡΙ.	εὖ γε. νῦν γὰρ σπονδὴν τοῖς θεοῖς σπένδω καὶ τὰς εὐχὰς εὔχομαι.	

(τὰς εὐχὰς εὔχεται)

ὦναξ Πόσειδον – σὺ μὲν γὰρ σωτὴρ ἄριστος τῶν ναυτῶν,   10
ἡμεῖς δὲ πολλάκις ὑπὲρ τῆς σωτηρίας σοι θυσίας θύομεν
– σῷζε ἡμᾶς ἐπὶ τὴν πατρίδα πάλιν.

(τὴν σπονδὴν σπένδει)

νῦν δὲ κατακέλευε αὖθις, ὦ κελευστά.

ΚΕΛ.	ὠὸπ ὄπ ὠὸπ ὄπ. εὖ γε, ὦνδρες. ἀποπλεῖ γὰρ ἡ ἡμετέρα ναῦς.	15
ΤΡΙ.	ταχέως νῦν, ὦ κελευστά· κατακέλευε δή.	
ΚΕΛ.	ὠὸπ ὄπ, ὠὸπ ὄπ, ὠὸπ ὄπ.	

Vocabulary for Section Three E

ἀπο-πλέ-ω sail off
δή then, now
ἐκεῖν-ος the former (nom.)
ἐμ-βαίν-ω embark
εὖ γε well done!
εὐχ-ή, ἡ prayer (1a)
εὔχ-ομαι pray
θυσί-α, ἡ sacrifice (1b)
θύ-ω sacrifice
κατα-κελεύ-ω give the time
κελεύ-ω order, give orders
πάλιν back, again
πολλάκις often

Πόσειδον Poseidon *(sea god)* (voc.)
σοι to you (s.)
σπένδ-ω make a libation
σπονδ- ή, ἡ libation (1a)
σωτήρ saviour (nom.)
τὰς ναῦς the ships
τὴν πατρίδ-α our fatherland
τοῖς θεοῖς to the gods
ὑπὲρ τῆς σωτηρίας for our safety
ὦναξ=ὦ ἄναξ O lord!
ὦνδρες=ὦ ἄνδρ-ες men!

ὠὸπ ὄπ in ... out... in ... out

Vocabulary to be learnt
δή *then, indeed*
ἐμβαίνω (ἐμβα-) *embark*
εὐχή, ἡ *prayer (1a)*
εὔχομαι *pray*
θυσίᾱ, ἡ *a sacrifice (1b)*
θύω *sacrifice*
κελεύω *order*
σπένδω *pour a libation*
σπονδή, ἡ *a libation (1a)*

Ζεύς

Introduction

The later part of the fifth century was a time when many traditional values were shaken by new ideas. As Dikaiopolis and the rhapsode make their way towards Athens, a city torn by war and plague, they see examples of the breakdown of conventional respect for law and the gods.

The changing attitude to traditional values is explored further through consideration of the influence of Socrates (Σωκράτης) and the sophists as seen by both the comic poet Aristophanes (Ἀριστοφάνης) and the philosopher Plato (Πλάτων).

Contemporary interest in the comparison of behaviour in different societies will be illustrated by a story from the historian Herodotus (Ἡρόδοτος), before we return to Dikaiopolis and the immediate problems of the war.

Sources

Thucydides, *Histories* 2.13–17, 51–3, 66–7; 3.83
Pindar, *Pythian* 8.135
Euripides, *Alkestis* 780ff.
Xenophon, *Hellenika* 2.iii. 52ff.

Solon, *Elegies* 4.31–2 (West)
Aristophanes, *Clouds* 1–246, 694–791
Plato, *Apology* 20c–23b
Euthydemos 275–277c
Herodotus, *Histories* 4.110–16

Time to be taken

Seven weeks

Section Four A–D: Lawlessness in Athenian life

A

Dikaiopolis and the rhapsode walk up towards the city between the Long Walls, through an area crowded with makeshift dwellings, where Dikaiopolis has now made his home. All around are funeral pyres, ready to receive their dead; one belongs to a neighbour of Dikaiopolis.

In *World of Athens*: walls of Athens 1.41, 2.23, 32; Pericles 1.57; farmers 2.14, 5.51; sea-power 7.3; the plague 1.57, 3.7, 5.82.

ΡΑΨ.   ὦ Ἡράκλεις. ὅσον⌐ ἀνθρώπων ⌐πλῆθος. πλέα γὰρ
φαίνεται τὰ⌐τείχη. διὰ τί τοσοῦτον⌐πλῆθος ἔχει ἡ⌐πόλις,
ὦ Δικαιόπολι; οἴμοι, τί τοῦτο; πυράς τινας ὁρῶ. εἰπέ μοι,
πρὸς⌐τῶν⌐θεῶν, τίς ἡ αἰτία; ἦ⌐που δῆλον ὅτι δαίμων τις
κακὸς κολάζει τὴν⌐πόλιν.   5

ΔΙΚ.   κακοδαίμων νὴ Δία ἡ⌐πόλις ἐστίν, ὦ ῥαψῳδέ, κακόδαιμον
δὲ τὸ⌐πλῆθος, κακοδαίμονες δὲ οἱ γεωργοὶ μάλιστα. αἴτιος
δὲ πρῶτον μὲν ὁ πόλεμος, ἔπειτα δὲ καὶ ὁ⌐Περικλῆς.

ΡΑΨ.   ἀλλὰ στρατηγὸς ἄριστος ὁ⌐Περικλῆς. ὁ γὰρ ναύτης –

ΔΙΚ.   ἀλλὰ δῆλόν ἐστιν ὅτι φιλεῖ τὸν⌐Περικλέα ἐκεῖνος, ναύτης   10
ὤν. ἐγὼ δὲ ναύτης οὔκ εἰμι, ἀλλὰ γεωργός. καὶ γεωργὸς ὤν

ὀλοφύρομαι τὸν ἐμὸν υἱόν, οὐκέτ᾽ ὄντα

Περικλέα αἴτιον νομίζω. φησὶ γάρ – 'ἡμεῖς μὲν κρατοῦμεν
κατὰ θάλατταν, Λακεδαιμόνιοι δὲ κατὰ γῆν. καταλείπετε
οὖν, ὦ γεωργοί, τὰς οἰκίας καὶ τὴν γῆν, καὶ εἰσκομίζεσθε
εἰς τὸ ἄστυ τὰ⌜ ὑμέτερα ⌝σκεύη. καὶ μὴ φροντίζετε. πόλις   15
γὰρ οὐκ οἰκήσεις ἢ γῆ, ἀλλὰ ἄνδρες.'
     οὕτω μὲν οὖν πείθει ἡμᾶς ὁ Περικλῆς, ῥήτωρ ὢν
πιθανός. ἡμεῖς δὲ εἰσκομιζόμεθα ἐκ τῶν ἀγρῶν τοὺς παῖδας
καὶ τὰς γυναῖκας καὶ τὰ⌜ ἄλλα ⌝σκεύη. τὰ δὲ πρόβατα εἰς
τὴν Εὔβοιαν διαπεμπόμεθα.   20

Vocabulary for Section Four A

Grammar for 4A–B
- Types 3b, c, e, f nouns: πρᾶγμα, πλῆθος, πόλις, πρέσβυς, ἄστυ
- Adjectives: εὔφρων
- Adjectives/pronouns: τις, τίς, οὐδείς
- Present participles: ὤν

ἀγρ-ός, ὁ field (pl. country) (2a)
αἰτί-ᾱ, ἡ reason, cause (1b)
αἴτι-ος -ᾱ -ον responsible
γεωργ-ός, ὁ farmer (2a)
δαίμων (δαιμον-), ὁ god, daimon (3a)
δια-πέμπ-ομαι send across
εἰσ-κομίζ-ομαι bring in
Εὔβοι-α, ἡ Euboia (1b)
ἡ πόλις city
ἦ που surely
Ἡράκλεις Herakles!
κακο-δαίμων wretched, unlucky (nom.)
κακό-δαιμον wretched, unlucky (nom.)
κακο-δαίμον-ες wretched, unlucky (nom.)

κατα-λείπ-ω leave behind
κολάζ-ω punish
κρατέ-ω hold sway
μάλιστα particularly
νὴ (+ acc.) by . . .!
νομίζ-ω think x (acc.) to be Y (acc.)
οἰκήσ-εις dwellings (nom., acc.)
ὁ Περικλῆς Pericles
ὅσον πλῆθος what a lot! (nom.)
πείθ-ω persuade
πιθαν-ός -ή -όν persuasive
πλέ-ως -α -ων full
πόλ-ις city (nom.)
πρόβατ-α, τά sheep (2b)
πρὸς τῶν θε-ῶν in the name of the gods

πρῶτον (μὲν) first
πυρ-ά, ἡ funeral pyre (1b)
ῥήτωρ (ῥητορ-), ὁ politician, orator (3a)
τὰ σκεύ-η equipment, furniture
τὰ τείχ-η the walls (of the city)
τὴν πόλ-ιν the city
τινας some (acc.)
τὸ ἄστ-υ the city (of Athens)
τὸν Περικλέ-α Pericles
τοσ-οῦτ-ον πλῆθος so great a number
φησὶ he says
φιλέ-ω love, be well disposed to
ὢν being (nom.)

ἐπειδὴ δὲ ἡμεῖς, πολλοὶ ὄντες, ἀφικνούμεθα εἰς τὸ ἄστυ,
χαλεπὸν γίγνεται τὸ πρᾶγμα. τὰς⌐ μὲν γὰρ ⌐οἰκήσεις, ὀλίγας
οὔσας, ἔχουσιν οἱ ἀστοί, ἡμεῖς δὲ πρῶτον μὲν τὰ⌐ μακρὰ
⌐τείχη, ἔπειτα δὲ τὰ ἱερὰ οἰκοῦμεν. μετὰ δὲ ταῦτα ἡ νόσος
ἐπιγίγνεται, καὶ δεινὴ οὖσα πολλοὺς ἄνδρας διαφθείρει   25
καὶ πολλὰς γυναῖκας καὶ πολλὰ παιδία. διαφθείρει δὲ καὶ
τοὺς ἐμοὺς οἰκείους ἡ νόσος. ὀλοφύρομαι γὰρ ἔτι καὶ νῦν
τὸν ἐμὸν υἱόν, οὐκέτ' ὄντα, καὶ τὴν ἐμὴν γυναῖκα,
οὐκέτ' οὖσαν. ἔχεις τὸ πρᾶγμα. ἐμὲ οὖν ὁρᾷς, ὦ ῥαψῳδέ,
κακοδαίμονα ὄντα. τὴν⌐ δὲ ⌐πόλιν ὁρᾷς κακοδαίμονα δὴ   30
οὖσαν. τοὺς δ' ἐν τῇ πόλει ὁρᾷς κακοδαίμονας ὄντας.

ἀστ-ός, ὁ townsman (2a)
γυνή (γυναικ-), ἡ wife, woman (3a)
δ'=δέ
δια-φθείρ-ω kill, destroy
ἐπι-γίγν-ομαι occur, follow
ἔτι καὶ νῦν even now
ἱερ-όν, τό sanctuary (2b)
κακο-δαίμον-α wretched, unlucky (acc.)
κακο-δαίμον-ας wretched, unlucky (acc.)
μακρ-ός -ά -όν long
μετά (+ acc.) after
μοι to me
νόσ-ος, ἡ plague (2a)
οἰκέ-ω dwell in, reside in
οἰκήσ-εις dwellings (nom., acc.)

οἰκεῖ-ος, ὁ member of family (2a)
ὀλίγ-οι -αι -α few
ὀλοφύρ-ομαι lament, mourn for
ὄντ-α (acc.)
ὄντ-ες (nom.) } being
ὄντ-ας (acc.)
οὐκέτ'=οὐκέτι
οὖσ-α (nom.)
οὖσ-αν (acc.) } being
οὖσ-ας (acc.)
παιδί-ον, τό child (2b)
Περικλέ-α Pericles (acc.)
πόλ-ις city (nom.)
τὰς οἰκήσ-εις the dwellings
τὴν πόλ-ιν the city
τῇ πόλει the city
τὸ ἄστ-υ the city (of Athens)
τὸ πλῆθος the people

τὸ πρᾶγμα the matter
υἱ-ός, ὁ son (2a)
ὑμέτερ-ος -α - ον your (where 'you'=more than one)
χαλεπ-ός -ή -όν difficult

Vocabulary to be learnt
γεωργός, ὁ *farmer (2a)*
γυνή (γυναικ-), ἡ *woman, wife (3a)*
δαίμων (δαιμον-), ὁ *god, daimon (3a)*
ἔτι καὶ νῦν *even now, still now*
κρατέω *hold sway, power (over)*
νή *(+acc.) by . . .!*
ὀλίγος η ον *small, few*

The plague of Athens

'All the usual funerary rituals were turned upside down, and they buried the dead as best they could. Because so many died, people ran out of the necessary means of burial and took refuge in disgraceful methods. They would commandeer a funeral pyre made for others, put their own dead on it and set it alight; or throw the corpse they were carrying onto an already burning pyre and make off.' (Thucydides, *Peloponnesian War* 2.52)

B

At this moment a young man approaches, followed at a distance by his slave, who is labouring under a heavy weight.

In *World of Athens*: death and burial 5.78–83; *hubris* 4.17; relations between gods and men 3.22–7.

ΝΕΑΝΙΑΣ ἰδού, πυρά. δεῦρ᾽ ἐλθέ, ὦ παῖ, ταχέως.
ΔΟΥΛΟΣ μένε, ὦ δέσποτα, μένε καὶ μὴ σπεῦδε. βαρὺς γάρ ἐστιν ὁ
            νεκρὸς οὗτος, βαρὺν δ᾽ ὄντα βραδέως δὴ φέρω ἔγωγε.
ΔΙΚ. (*overhearing*)
            τί φής; νεκρόν τινα φέρεις;   5
ΝΕΑΝ. (*ignoring Dikaiopolis*)
            ἄγε νυν, ὦ παῖ, ἐπίβαλλε τὸν νεκρὸν ἐπὶ τὴν πυρὰν ταύτην.
ΔΙΚ. (*shocked, comes forward*)
            ἀλλὰ τί ποιεῖτε; μὴ ποιεῖτε τοῦτο, πρὸς θεῶν. παύεσθε.
ΝΕΑΝ. (*turns angrily on Dikaiopolis and hits him*)   10
            μὴ κώλυε, ὦ ᾽νθρωπε.
ΔΙΚ. ὦ μίαρε, τύπτεις ἐμὲ πολίτην ὄντα; ὦ τῆς ὕβρεως. μὴ τύπτε.
ΓΕΡΩΝ (*comes out of his shack*)
            τί τὸ πρᾶγμα; τίνες αἱ βοαί; οὗτος, τί ποιεῖς; τύπτεις
            πολίτην; ὦ τῆς ἀνομίας. παῦε. οἴμοι, τί τοῦτο; νεκρὸν   15
            ἐπιβάλλεις ἐπ᾽ ἐκείνην τὴν πυράν; ὦ τῆς ἀσεβείας. παῦε –
ΝΕΑΝ. (*threateningly*)
            μὴ κώλυε, ὦ γέρον.

Vocabulary for Section Four B

βαρ-ὺς (nom.) ⎫
βαρ-ὺν (acc.) ⎬ heavy
δεσπότ-ης, ὁ master (1d)
δεῦρ᾽=δεῦρο
ἐπι-βάλλ-ω throw onto
κωλύ-ω prevent, stop
μιαρ-ός -ά -όν foul, polluted
νεκρ-ός, ὁ corpse (2a)
νεκρ-όν τιν-α a corpse
   (acc.)

᾽νθρωπε=ἄνθρωπε
ὄντ-α (acc.) being
οὗτος, hey, you!
παύ-ομαι stop
παῦ-ε stop!
πολίτ-ης, ὁ citizen (1d)
πρὸς θε-ῶν in the name of
   the gods!
πυρ-ά, ἡ funeral pyre
   (1b)

τὸ πρᾶγμα the matter
τύπτ-ω strike
φέρ-ω carry
φής you (s.) say
ὦ τῆς ἀνομίας what
   lawlessness!
ὦ τῆς ἀσεβείας what
   irreverence!
ὦ τῆς ὕβρεως what
   aggressive behaviour!

ΓΕΡ.   ἀλλὰ θάπτω τήμερον τὸν ἐμὸν υἱόν, καὶ ἐμὴ ἡ πυρά.
ΝΕΑΝ.   οὐ φροντίζω ἔγωγε.   20
ΓΕΡ.   ἆρ' οὐ σέβῃ τοὺς θεούς; ἆρ' οὐ τιμᾷς τοὺς τῶν ἀνθρώπων
        νόμους; ἀλλ' οὐδὲν κωλύει σε, οὔτε θεῶν φόβος οὔτε
        ἀνθρώπων νόμος;
ΝΕΑΝ.   τί φής; νεκροὶ ἐπὶ‿νεκροῖς πίπτουσιν, ἀποθνήσκουσι
        δ' οἱ ἄνθρωποι ὥσπερ πρόβατα ἐν ταῖς‿οἰκίαις καὶ ἐν   25
        τοῖς‿ἱεροῖς. σὺ δέ μοι θεοὺς λέγεις καὶ νόμους; ὦ μῶρε σύ
        – οἱ γὰρ θεοὶ ἢ οὐκ εἰσὶν ἢ οὐ φροντίζουσιν ἡμῶν, ἐπειδὴ ἡ
        νόσος διαφθείρει τούς⌐ τε ⌐εὐσεβεῖς ἅμα καὶ τοὺς‿ἀσεβεῖς.
        ποῦ γὰρ ἡ ἐμὴ μήτηρ καὶ ὁ πατήρ, εὐσεβοῦντες ἀεί; νῦν δὲ
        ποῦ ἐστιν ὁ ἀδελφός, εὐσεβέστατος ἀνθρώπων ὤν; ἰδού.   30
        (*points to the corpse*)
        καὶ μή μοι λέγε περὶ‿νόμων‿καὶ‿ὕβρεως. οὐ γὰρ φοβοῦμαι
        τὴν‿κόλασιν. ἢ οὐκ οἶσθα ὅτι ἐφήμεροι οἱ ἄνθρωποι; τί δ'
        ἐσμέν; τί δ' οὐκ ἐσμέν;
                    'σκιᾶς ὄναρ ἄνθρωπος'.   35
        (*sets light to the pyre*)
ΓΕΡ.   παῦε, παῦε. ἀτιμάζεις γὰρ τοὺς θεούς, θνητὸς ὤν.
ΝΕΑΝ.   ἀλλ' οὐκ ἀτιμάζω τοὺς θεοὺς ἔγωγε. τιμῶ γὰρ μάλιστα τὴν
        Ἀφροδίτην. καλὴ γὰρ καὶ εὔφρων ἡ θεός. καλὴ γὰρ καὶ

τὸ ἱερόν

εὔφρων οὖσα ἡ θεός, εὐδαίμονα ποιεῖ τὸν βίον. ἐγὼ οὖν   40
πρὸς Ἀφροδίτην τρέπομαι καὶ τὴν ἡδονήν, καλὰς οὔσας.
He goes off, helped by the slave. The old man looks on.
ΔΙΚ.   ἆρα θαυμάζεις, ὦ ῥαψῳδέ, ὅτι τὸ ἄστυ μισῶ, γεωργὸς ὤν, καὶ
τὸν ἐμὸν δῆμον ποθῶ; ἐν γὰρ τῇ πόλει οὐδὲν ἄλλο ἢ ἀνομία
καὶ ἀσέβεια καὶ νόσος καὶ πολὺ τῶν νεκρῶν πλῆθος.   45

ἀδελφ-ός, ὁ brother (2a)
ἀλλ'=ἀλλά
ἀ-νομί-α, ἡ lawlessness (1b)
ἆρ'=ἆρα
ἀ-σέβει-α, ἡ disrespect
   towards the gods, impiety
   (1b)
ἀ-τιμάζ-ω hold in dishonour
Ἀφροδίτ-η, ἡ Aphrodite
   (1a) *(goddess of love and*
   sexual pleasure)
βί-ος, ὁ life (2a)
γέρων (γεροντ-), ὁ old man
   (3a)
δ'=δέ
δῆμ-ος, ὁ deme (2a) *(local*
   districts into which Attica
   was divided)
δια-φθείρ-ω kill
δοῦλ-ος, ὁ slave (2a)
ἐπ'=ἐπί
ἐπὶ νεκροῖς on top of
   corpses
εὐ-δαίμον-α fortunate
   (ruled by a benevolent
   daimon) (acc.)
εὐ-σεβέστατ-ος -η -ον most
   respectful of the gods
   (nom.)
εὐ-σεβοῦντες respecting the
   gods (nom.)
εὔ-φρων well-disposed
ἐφ-ήμερ-ος -ον ephemeral,
   short-lived
ἤ than
ἤ ... ἤ either ... or

ἡδον-ή, ἡ pleasure (1a)
θάπτ-ω bury
θαυμάζ-ω wonder
θε-ός, ὁ/ἡ god(-dess) (2a)
θνητ-ός -ή -όν mortal
κωλύ-ω prevent, stop
μάλιστα very much
μήτηρ (μητερ-), ἡ mother
   (3a)
μισέ-ω hate
μοι to me
νεανί-ας, ὁ young man (1d)
νεκρ-όν τιν-α a corpse
   (acc.)
νόμ-ος, ὁ law, convention
   (2a)
νόσ-ος, ἡ plague (2a)
νυν now then
ὄναρ a dream (nom.)
οὖσ-α (nom.)
οὖσ-ας (acc.) } being
οὔτε ... οὔτε neither ...
   nor
πατήρ (πατερ-), ὁ father
   (3a)
παῦ-ε stop!
περὶ νόμων καὶ ὕβρεως
   about laws and aggression
ποθέ-ω desire, long for
πολὺ πλῆθος a great
   number (nom.)
πρόβατ-α, τά sheep (2b)
πυρ-ά, ἡ funeral pyre (1b)
σέβ-ομαι show respect for
σκιᾶς of a shadow
ταῖς οἰκίαις the houses

τῇ πόλει the city
τήμερον today
τὴν κόλασ-ιν punishment
τιμά-ω honour
τίν-ες; what? (nom.)
τοῖς ἱεροῖς the sanctuaries
τοὺς ἀ-σεβεῖς those who are
   disrespectful of the gods
τοὺς εὐ-σεβεῖς those who
   respect the gods
τρέπ-ομαι turn (oneself)
υἱ-ός, ὁ son (2a)
φής you (s.) say
φόβ-ος, ὁ fear (2a)
ὤν being (nom.)

Vocabulary to be learnt
ἀτῑμάζω *dishonour, hold in*
   dishonour
δεσπότης, ὁ *master (1d)*
διαφθείρω (διαφθειρα-)
   destroy, kill
θεός, ὁ/ἡ *god(-dess) (2a)*
θνητός ή όν *mortal*
κωλύω *prevent, stop*
μάλιστα *especially;*
   particularly; yes
νεκρός, ὁ *corpse (2a)*
νόμος, ὁ *law, convention*
   (2a)
νόσος, ἡ *plague, disease (2a)*
πυρά, ἡ *funeral pyre (1b)*
τῑμάω *honour*
τύπτω *strike, hit*
φέρω (ἐνεγκ-) *carry, bear*
φόβος, ὁ *fear (2a)*

C

In *World of Athens*: altar of the Twelve Gods 2.28; supplication 3.35–6; the Eleven 6.31; *hupēretēs* 5.63; sanctuary 3.38.

Δικαιόπολις καὶ ὁ ῥαψῳδὸς πορεύονται εἰς τὸ ἄστυ. ἐξαίφνης δ’ ἀνήρ τις τρέχει πρὸς αὐτούς.

ΔΙΚ.	εἰπέ μοι, ὦ ῥαψῳδέ, τίς ὁ θόρυβος; τίνες αἱ βοαί; τί γίγνεται;
ΡΑΨ.	ἰδού, ὦ Δικαιόπολι, ἄνθρωπός τις δεῦρο τρέχει. ἆρ’ ὁρᾷς 5
	τὸν ἄνδρα; ἢ λανθάνει σε ὁ ἀνὴρ δεῦρο τρέχων;
ΔΙΚ.	οὐ μὰ Δία. ὁρῶ γὰρ αὐτὸν προστρέχοντα. ἀλλ’ ἄτοπον τὸ
	πρᾶγμα. τίς πότ’ ἐστιν;
ΡΑΨ.	ἴσως δοῦλός τίς ἐστι καὶ ἀποφεύγων τυγχάνει.
ΔΙΚ.	ἀλλὰ δοῦλος μὲν οὔκ ἐστιν, ὁδοιπόρος δὲ ὢν φαίνεται. ἢ 10
	λανθάνει σε ὁ ἀνὴρ χλαμύδα ἔχων;
ΡΑΨ.	ὀρθῶς λέγεις, ὦ Δικαιόπολι. ἀλλ’ ἴσως ξένος ἐστίν.
ΔΙΚ.	ἰδού. τρέχει γὰρ ὁ ἀνὴρ εἰς τὸ Ἡράκλειον ἱερόν. ἀλλὰ τί
	πάσχει, φεύγων εἰς τὸ ἱερόν;
ΡΑΨ.	δῆλον ὅτι ἐφ’ ἱκετείαν τρέπεται. καὶ μὴν προσέρχονται 15
	ἄνδρες τινές. καὶ δῆλοί εἰσι διώκοντες τὸν ἄνδρα.
ΔΙΚ.	ἀλλὰ τί τοῦτο τὸ πρᾶγμα; προσέρχεται γὰρ κῆρυξ καὶ
	– οἱ ἕνδεκα καὶ οἱ ὑπηρέται. ἀλλὰ ὁ ἀνὴρ φθάνει
	τοὺς ἕνδεκα εἰς τὸ ἱερὸν τρέχων.

The leader of the Eleven, Satyros, approaches.   20
ΣΑΤΥΡΟΣ ποῖ φεύγει ὁ Λακεδαιμόνιος; ποῦ ἐστιν;
  (*turns to the rhapsode*)
    οὗτος, ἆρ’ οἶσθα ποῦ ἐστιν ὁ φεύγων; ἢ λανθάνει σε ὁ
    ἀνὴρ φεύγων;

ΡΑΨ.	οὐ λανθάνει ἐμέ. ἀλλ’ ἐν ἐκείνῳ τῷ ἱερῷ ἐστιν, ἱκέτης ὤν. 25
ΣΑΤ.	δεῦρ’ ἔλθετε, ὦ ὑπηρέται, εἰς ἐκεῖνο τὸ ἱερόν. ἀπάγετε
	ταχέως τὸν ξένον, Λακεδαιμόνιον ὄντα.
ΔΙΚ.	μὴ ἄπαγε τὸν φεύγοντα, ὦ κῆρυξ, καίπερ Λακεδαιμόνιον
	ὄντα. ἱκέτης γὰρ τυγχάνει ὢν ὁ ξένος, καὶ φθάνει ὑμᾶς εἰς
	τὸ ἱερὸν τρέχων. ἱκέτης δ’ ὤν, ὅσιός ἐστιν. 30
ΡΑΨ.	῾πρὸς῾ γὰρ ⌐Διός εἰσιν ἅπαντες
	ξεῖνοι.’

The herald intervenes.

ΚΗΡΥΞ   μὴ φροντίζετε, ὦ ὑπηρέται, ἀλλ' ἀπάγετε τὸν ἄνδρα.

ΔΙΚ.   ὦ˘τῆς˘ἀνομίας. δυστυχὴς δὴ φαίνεται ὢν ὁ ξένος.   35

Vocabulary for Section Four C

Grammar for 4C–D
- Present participles, active and middle: παύων, παυόμενος
- Uses of participles; expressions using participles
- 3g nouns: βασιλεύς
- Elision and crasis

ἀπ-άγ-ω lead away
ἅπαντες all (nom.)
ἀπο-φεύγ-ων escaping (nom.)
ἄ-τοπ-ος -ον strange
αὐτ-ὸν him (acc.)
αὐτ-οὺς them (acc.)
δῆλ-ος clear(ly)
διώκ-οντ-ες pursuing (nom.)
δοῦλ-ος, ὁ slave (2a)
δυσ-τυχής unfortunate (nom.)
ἐκείνῳ τῷ ἱερῷ that sanctuary
ἐξαίφνης suddenly
ἐφ'=ἐπί
ἔχ-ων having, wearing (nom.)
Ἡράκλει-ος -α -ον of Herakles
ἱερ-όν, τό sanctuary (2b)
ἱκετεί-α, ἡ supplication (1b)
ἱκέτ-ης, ὁ suppliant (1d)
ἴσως perhaps
καὶ μήν look!
καίπερ despite -ing, although
κῆρυξ (κηρυκ-), ὁ herald (3a)
λανθάν-ω escape the notice of x (acc) in -ing

μὰ (+acc.) by . . .! (*usually,* 'no, by . . .!')
μοι to me
ξέν-ος, ὁ (or ξεῖν-ος, ὁ) stranger, foreigner (2a)
ὁδοι-πόρ-ος, ὁ traveller (2a)
οἱ ἕνδεκα the Eleven (*a body of eleven magistrates responsible for the prisons and for summary justice*)
ὀρθ-ῶς correctly
ὅσι-ος -α -ον sanctified
οὗτος, hey, you!
ὁ φεύγ-ων the man running off
πάσχ-ω suffer, experience, undergo
ποτε ever
πρὸς Διός under Zeus' protection
προσ-τρέχ-οντ-α running towards (acc.)
Σάτυρ-ος, ὁ Satyros (2a)
τὸν φεύγ-οντ-α the man running off
τοὺς ἕνδεκα the Eleven
τρέπ-ομαι turn (oneself)
τρέχ-ων running (nom.)

τυγχάν-ω happen to be -ing, be actually –ing
ὑπηρέτ-ης, ὁ public slave (1d)
φαίν-ομαι appear to be (-ing)
φεύγ-οντ-α (acc.) } running
φεύγ-ων (nom.)   } off
φθάν-ω anticipate x (acc.) by -ing
χλαμύς (χλαμυδ-), ἡ short cloak, travelling cloak (3a)
ὦ τῆς ἀνομίας what lawlessness!

Vocabulary to be learnt
ἀνομίᾱ, ἡ *lawlessness (1b)*
ἀπάγω (ἀπαγαγ-) *lead/take away*
ἀποφεύγω (ἀποφυγ-) *escape, run off*
δοῦλος, ὁ *slave (2a)*
ἱερόν, τό *sanctuary (2b)*
ἱκέτης, ὁ *suppliant (1d)*
μὰ (+*acc.*) *by. . . !*
ξένος/ξεῖνος, ὁ *foreigner, guest, host (2a)*
ὀρθός ή όν *straight, correct, right*

D

(looks inside the sanctuary)

ΔΙΚ.   ἰδού, ὦ ῥαψῳδέ, ἆρ' ὁρᾷς; ὦ τῆς ἀσεβείας. καθίζεται γὰρ
ἐπὶ τοῦ βωμοῦ ὁ δυστυχὴς ξένος, ἱκέτης ὤν, ἀλλ' ἀφέλκουσι
μὲν αὐτὸν οἱ ὑπηρέται, λαμβάνεται δὲ τοῦ βωμοῦ ὁ ξένος
καὶ ἐπικαλεῖται τοὺς θεούς. ὦ πόλις, πόλις.   5
(watches what happens inside)

ΣΑΤ.   ἀφέλκετε τὸν ἄνδρα τοῦτον, Λακεδαιμόνιον ὄντα, ἀπὸ
τοῦ βωμοῦ.

ΞΕΝΟΣ   ἐπικαλοῦμαι τοὺς θεούς –

ΥΠΗΡΕΤΗΣ ΤΙΣ ἀλλὰ λαμβάνεται ὁ ξένος τοῦ βωμοῦ, ὦ Σάτυρε.   10

ΣΑΤ.   ἀπόκοπτε τὰς χεῖρας.

ΞΕΝΟΣ   *(sees Dikaiopolis and the rhapsode)*
ἐπικαλοῦμαι ὑμᾶς, ὤνδρες.

ΔΙΚ.   ἐπικαλεῖται ἡμᾶς ὁ ξένος, ὦ ῥαψῳδέ, καὶ οὐ παύεται
ἐπικαλούμενος.   15

ΡΑΨ.   (ἡσυχάζει ὁ ῥαψῳδός. τέλος δὲ λέγει)
ἀλλ' ὅμως ἡσύχαζε καὶ σύ, ὦ Δικαιόπολι, καὶ παῦε
ὀλοφυρόμενος, καὶ μὴ ποίει μηδέν. ἆρ' οὐχ ὁρᾷς ἐκείνους
τοὺς ὑπηρέτας, τοὺς⌐ τὰ ἐγχειρίδια ⌐ἔχοντας;

ΞΕΝΟΣ   (οὐ παύεται ἐπικαλούμενος τοὺς θεούς)   20
ὦ θεοί, καθορᾶτε τί πάσχω. καθορᾶτε τοὺς⌐ περὶ Δία
ἱκέσιον καὶ ξένιον ⌐ἀσεβοῦντας.

(ἀφέλκουσιν ἀπὸ τοῦ βωμοῦ οἱ ὑπηρέται τὸν⌐ τοὺς θεοὺς ⌐ἐπικαλούμενον)

ΣΑΤ.   παῦε, ὦ, νθρωπε, τοὺς θεοὺς ἐπικαλούμενος. ὑμεῖς δέ,
ὦ ὑπηρέται, ἀπάγετε τὸν ἄνθρωπον πρὸς τοὺς ἄλλους   25
Λακεδαιμονίους.

ΞΕΝΟΣ   ἆρ' ὑμεῖς, ὦ Ἀθηναῖοι, ἀφέλκετε τοὺς⌐ εἰς τὰ ἱερὰ
⌐φεύγοντας; ἆρ' ἀποκτείνετε τοὺς⌐ ἐφ' ἱκετείαν
⌐τρεπομένους; ἀλλά, ναὶ τὼ σιώ, δῆλοί ἐστε περὶ
ἀνθρώπους ἄδικοι ὄντες καὶ περὶ θεοὺς ἀσεβεῖς.   30

ΔΙΚ.   ἀλλὰ τίς ἐστιν ὁ ξένος ἐκεῖνος;

ΣΑΤ.   πρεσβευτής τις ὢν τυγχάνει –

ΔΙΚ.   τί φῄς; πρεσβευτής; ὦ τῆς ἀνομίας. ἆρ' ἀποκτείνεις τοὺς
πρέσβεις;

ΣΑΤ.   πρεσβευτής τις, καὶ πορευόμενος τυγχάνει πρὸς   35
βασιλέα τὸν μέγαν. σὺ δὲ δῆλος εἶ φιλῶν τοὺς

        Λακεδαιμονίους. σιώπα οὖν καὶ παῦε ὀλοφυρόμενος τὸν
        Λακεδαιμόνιον.
(οἱ μὲν ὑπηρέται ἀπάγουσι τὸν Λακεδαιμόνιον πρὸς τὴν ἀγοράν. ὁ
δὲ ξένος οὐ παύεται βοῶν καὶ δηλῶν τί πάσχει ὑπὸ˘τῶν˘Ἀθηναίων.)   40
ΔΙΚ.   δῆλόν ἐστιν ὅτι μισοῦσι τὸν ἄνδρα οἱ θεοί. ἀποκτείνουσι
        γὰρ αὐτόν, καίπερ πρεσβευτὴν καὶ ἱκέτην ὄντα. ἦ˘που
        νέμεσις μεγάλη ἐκ θεῶν λαμβάνει αὐτὸν διὰ τοὺς
        προγόνους καὶ τὴν τῶν προγόνων ὕβριν.

          ἀλλὰ τί πάσχει ἡ πόλις ἡ ἡμετέρα; τί γίγνεται; βίαιος   45
        διδάσκαλος φαίνεται ὢν ὁ πόλεμος, ὦ ῥαψῳδέ. ἐν γὰρ
        εἰρήνῃ οὐ γίγνεται ταῦτα. ἐν μὲν γὰρ εἰρήνῃ εὐνομία καὶ
        εὐπορία ἐν τῇ˘πόλει. ἐν δὲ τῷ πολέμῳ ἀνομία καὶ ἀπορία.
ΡΑΨ.   'ὡς κακὰ πλεῖστα πόλει Δυσνομία παρέχει,
        Εὐνομία δ' εὔκοσμα καὶ ἄρτια πάντ' ἀποφαίνει.'   50

Vocabulary for Section Four D

ἀγορ-ά, ἡ agora, market-
   place (1b)
ἄ-δικ-ος -ον unjust
ἀπο-κόπτ-ω cut off
ἀπο-κτείν-ω kill
ἀπο-φαίν-ω make to appear
ἄρτι-ος -α -ον perfect
ἀ-σεβεῖς irreverent (nom.)
αὐτ-ὸν him (acc.)
ἀφ-έλκ-ω drag away
βασιλέ-α τὸν μέγαν the
   Great King (of Persia)
βίαι-ος -α -ον violent
βο-ῶν shouting (nom.)
δῆλ-ος clear(ly)
δηλ-ῶν showing, making
   clear (nom.)
διδάσκαλ-ος, ὁ teacher (2a)
Δυσνομί-α, ἡ bad
   government (1b)
δυσ-τυχὴς unfortunate
   (nom.)
ἐγ-χειρ-ίδι-ον, τό dagger
   (2b)

εἰρήνη peace
ἐπὶ τοῦ βωμοῦ on the altar
ἐπι-καλέ-ομαι call upon (to
   witness)
ἐπι-καλ-ούμεν-ος calling
   upon (nom.)
εὔ-κοσμ-ος -ον in good
   order
εὐ-νομί-α, ἡ good
   government (1b)
εὐ-πορί-α, ἡ solution of
   difficulties; plenty (1b)
ἐφ'=ἐπί
ἦ που surely
ἱκέσι-ος –α -ον of
   suppliants (*title of Zeus*)
ἱκετεί-α, ἡ supplication (1b)
καθ-ίζ-ομαι sit down
καθ-ορά-ω look down upon,
   see clearly
καίπερ despite, although
κῆρυξ (κηρυκ-), ὁ herald
   (3a)
λαμβάν-ομαι take hold of

μηδείς μηδεμί-α μηδέν no
   one, no
μισέ-ω hate
ναὶ τὼ σιώ by the two gods
   (Castor and Pollux) (a
   typical Spartan oath)
νέμεσ-ις, ἡ nemesis,
   retribution (3e)
ξένι-ος -α -ον of guests/
   strangers (*title of Zeus*)
ὀλοφυρ-όμεν-ος lamenting
   (for) (nom.)
ὅμως nevertheless
πάντ'=πάντα
παρ-έχ-ω give, provide
πάσχ-ω experience, suffer
παύ-ομαι stop (–ing)
παῦ-ε stop! (s.) (–ing)
πλεῖστ-ος -η -ον very many
πόλει to the city
πορευ-όμεν-ος travelling
   (nom.)
πρέσβ-εις, οἱ ambassadors
   (3e)

πρεσβευτ-ής, ὁ ambassador (1d)

πρό-γον-ος, ὁ ancestor (2a)

Σάτυρ-ος, ὁ Satyros (2a)

τῇ πόλει the city

τὸν ἐπι-καλ-ούμεν-ον the one calling on (acc.)

τοῦ βωμοῦ the altar

τοὺς ἀ-σεβ-οῦντ-ας those who are being irreverent

τοὺς ἔχ-οντ-ας the ones who have

τοὺς τρεπ-ομέν-ους the ones turning

τοὺς φεύγ-οντ-ας the ones running off

τυγχάν-ω happen to be, be actually (-ing)

τῷ πολέμῳ (the) war

ὕβρ-ις, ἡ aggression (3e)

ὑπηρέτ-ης, ὁ public slave (1d)

ὑπὸ τῶν Ἀθηναί-ων at the hands of the Athenians

φαίν-ομαι appear to be (–ing)

φής you (s.) say

φιλ-ῶν being well-disposed to (nom.)

χείρ (χειρ-), ἡ hand (3a)

ὢ τῆς ἀνομίας what lawlessness!

ὢ τῆς ἀσεβείας what irreverence!

Vocabulary to be learnt

ἀποκτείνω (ἀποκτεινα-) *kill*

ἀσέβεια, ἡ *irreverence to the gods (1b)*

αὐτόν ἥν ὅ *him, her, it, them*

ἀφέλκω (ἀφελκυσα-) *drag off*

βασιλεύς, ὁ *king (3g)*

βωμός, ὁ *altar (2a)*

ἐπικαλέομαι *call upon (to witness)*

κῆρυξ (κηρυκ-), ὁ *herald (3a)*

λανθάνω (λαθ-) *escape notice of X (acc.) in –ing (part.)*

μῑσέω hate

ὀλοφύρομαι *lament, mourn for*

πάσχω (παθ-) *suffer, experience, undergo*

παύομαι *stop*

πρεσβευτής, ὁ *ambassador (1d)*

πρέσβεις, οἱ *ambassadors (3e)*

τρέπομαι (τραπ-) *turn, turn in flight*

τυγχάνω (τυχ-) *happen to be -ing, be actually –ing (+ nom. part.)*

ὕβρις, ἡ *aggression, violence (3e)*

ὑπηρέτης, ὁ *servant, slave (1d)*

φαίνομαι (φαν-) *seem to be, appear to be (+part.)*

φθάνω *anticipate X (acc.) in -ing (nom. part.)*

ὢ *what . . . ! (+gen.)*

χλαμύδα ἔχει   καθίζεται ἐπὶ τοῦ βωμοῦ ὁ ξένος, ἱκέτης ὤν

Sections Five A–D and Six A–D: 'Socrates corrupts the young'

Introduction

The questioning of traditional morality, which could be seen either as a new humanism or as moral degeneracy, was popularly associated with the influence of people like Socrates and the sophists. Socrates had a profound influence on Greek thought of his time, and the philosopher Plato, from whose writings we derive much of our idea of Socrates, was one of his most ardent disciples. Others, however, regarded him as a pernicious influence on Athenian society, and the claims that he 'corrupted the young' and 'believed in strange gods' led to his trial and execution in 399.

In his portayal of Socrates in his comedy *Clouds* (423), Aristophanes exploits all the humorous possibilities of popular prejudice against 'intellectuals' with their 'new-fangled' ideas and their arguments which are 'too clever by half'.

In *World of Athens*: Greek comedy 8.67–80; festivals 8.45, cf. 3.44; Socrates 8.33.

Note

The Greek you have been reading so far has been adapted very heavily from original sources. The ideas and original vocabulary have been kept, but the sentence construction has been noticeably different.

From now on, you will, for the most part, be reading continuous extracts from single works (rather than collations of sources), and the Greek of the text will approximate more and more closely to the original. For example, Strepsiades' first ten words in this extract are the actual opening of the *Clouds*, though it must be emphasized that Aristophanes was a poet and composed in verse, not (as would appear from these extracts) prose.

Each of Aristophanes' comedies – text, facing-page translation and commentary on the translation – has been translated and edited by Alan Sommerstein and published by Aris and Phillips/Oxbow Books.

ἵππος τις

τὰ χρήματα

A

Strepsiades, an old man, is deep in debt because of his son's expensive tastes and cannot sleep because of his worries.

In *World of Athens*: rich and poor 4.21, 5.26; horses 2.16, 4.9; women and marriage 5.17ff.; town and city 2.21–2.

ὁ Στρεψιάδης ὀλοφυρόμενος τυγχάνει διότι πολλὰ χρήματα ὀφείλει. ὁ γὰρ υἱός, ἱππομανὴς ὤν, πολλὰ χρήματα ἀεὶ λαμβάνει. νῦν δὲ τυγχάνει βαθέως καθεύδων ὁ υἱός, ὕπνος δ' οὐκ ἔχει τὸν πατέρα.

ΣΤΡΕΨΙΑΔΗΣ (*yawning and groaning*)   5
      ἰοὺ ἰού. ὦ Ζεῦ βασιλεῦ. τὸ χρῆμα τῶν νυκτῶν, ὅσον ἐστί· καὶ οὐδέπω
      ἡμέρα γίγνεται.
      (*turns round as he hears some loud snores*)
      ἰδού, βαθέως καθεύδει ὁ υἱὸς καὶ οὐ παύεται καθεύδων.
      (*lies down again to try to sleep*)   10
      οἴμοι τάλας. ἀλλ' ὕπνος βαθὺς οὐδέπω μ' ἔχει. ἄγρυπνος δ' εἰμὶ
      ὁ δυστυχής. ἄγρυπνον δ' ὄντα με δάκνει τὰ χρέα βαρέα ὄντα. χρήματα
      γὰρ πολλὰ ὀφείλω διὰ τὸν υἱὸν τουτονί, ὀφείλοντα δέ με διώκουσιν οἱ
      χρῆσται καὶ δίκην λαμβάνουσιν ἀεί.
      (*again tries to sleep*)   15
      ἀλλ' ἔτι ἄγρυπνός εἰμι, καὶ ἀπορῶ. καὶ χθὲς ἄγρυπνος ἦ ἐγώ,
      σχεδὸν ὅλην τὴν νύκτα. ὀλίγον γάρ τινα χρόνον ἐκάθευδον ἐγώ.
      ἀλλ' ὅτε ἐκάθευδον, τότε ἐν τοῖς ὀνείροις ἐδίωκόν με οἱ χρῆσται καὶ
      δίκην ἐλάμβανον διὰ τὸν ἐμὸν υἱόν. καὶ ἐν ἀπορίᾳ μ' ὄντα οὐδεὶς
      ἔσῳζεν, ἀλλ' ἐγὼ μὲν ὅλην τὴν νύκτα τὰς δίκας ταύτας ἀεὶ ἔφευγον, ὁ δ'   20
      υἱὸς οὑτοσὶ χρήματα πολλὰ ἀεὶ ἐλάμβανεν, ἱππομανὴς ὤν. καὶ δὴ καὶ
      καθεύδων ὀνειροπολεῖ ὁ νεανίας ἵππους. καὶ γὰρ ἔτι παῖς ὢν
      ὠνειροπόλει τοὺς ἵππους. οἴμοι. τίς αἴτιος ἦν; αἰτία ἡ γυνή, εὖ οἶδ' ὅτι.
      ἐκείνη γὰρ ἀεὶ τὸν υἱὸν ἐλάμβανε καὶ δι-ελέγετο περὶ τῶν ἵππων. ὁ οὖν
      υἱὸς ἀεὶ περὶ ἵππων ἤκουε καὶ ἐμάνθανεν.   25
      (*a loud snore is heard from his son*)
      σὺ δέ, ὥσπερ ἔχεις, βαθέως κάθευδε· τὰ γὰρ χρέα, εὖ οἶσθ' ὅτι, εἰς τὴν
      κεφαλὴν τὴν ἐμὴν τρέπεται, οἴμοι. οὐ γὰρ ἐπαυόμεθα οὐδέποτ' ἐγώ
      τε καὶ ἡ γυνὴ περὶ τοῦ παιδὸς λοιδορούμενοι· ἀεὶ γὰρ ἐλοιδορούμεθα.
      ἀλλ' ὦ Ζεῦ βασιλεῦ, διὰ τί τοὺς γάμους οὕτω πικροὺς ποιεῖς; ἀεὶ γὰρ   30
      πικρὸν ποιεῖ τὸν ἐμὸν βίον ἡ γυνή. ἀλλ' ὡς ἡδὺς ἦν ὁ ἄγροικος βίος. ὁ δὲ
      γάμος ὡς πικρός. ἡ γὰρ γυνὴ ἡ ἐμὴ ἐξ ἄστεως οὖσα τυγχάνει καί, ἀστικὴ
      οὖσα, πολλὴν τὴν δαπάνην εἰσ-έφερεν. αὕτη δ' ἡ δαπάνη τότ' ἤδη με δι-
      έφθειρεν. καὶ ἔτι καὶ νῦν διαφθείρει.

Vocabulary for Section Five A

> **Grammar for 5A–B**
> - Imperfect indicative, active and middle: ἔπαυον, ἐπαυόμην
> - Augments
> - Position of adjectives

ἄγρ-οικ-ος -ον from the country
ἄγρ-υπν-ος -ον sleepless
αἴτι-ος -α -ον responsible, to blame
ἀπορία perplexity
ἄστεως the city (of Athens)
ἀστικ-ός -ή -όν from the city
βαθύς deep (nom.)
βαθέ-ως deeply
βαρέα heavy (nom.)
βί-ος, ὁ life (2a)
γάμ-ος, ὁ marriage (2a)
δάκν-ω bite, worry
δαπάν-η, ἡ expense (1a)
δια-φθείρ-ω ruin
δι-ε-λέγ-ετο she used to converse (δια-λέγ-ομαι)
δι-έ-φθειρ-εν (it) was ruining (δια-φθείρ-ω)
δίκ-η, ἡ lawsuit (1a)
δίκ-ην λαμβάν-ω exact one's due
δίκ-ην ἐ-λάμβαν-ον they kept trying to exact their due
διότι because
ἐ-δίωκ-ον (they) kept on pursuing (διώκ-ω)
εἰσ-έ-φερ-ε(ν) (she) started to bring in/cause (εἰσ-φέρ-ω)
ἐ-κάθευδ-ον I was sleeping (καθεύδ-ω)
ἐ-λάμβαν-ε(ν) (she/he) used to take, kept taking (λαμβάν-ω)
ἐ-λοιδορ-ούμεθα we kept arguing (λοιδορέ-ομαι)
ἐ-μάνθαν-ε(ν) (he) used to learn (μανθάν-ω)
ἐξ=ἐκ
ἐ-παυ-όμεθα (we) used to stop (παύ-ομαι)

ἔ-σῳζ-ε(ν) (he) was saving (σῴζ-ω)
ἔ-φευγ-ον (I) was running away from (φεύγ-ω)
ἡδύς sweet (nom.)
ἤκουε (he) used to hear (ἄκούω)
ἦ I was
ἡμέρ-α, ἡ day (1b)
ἦν (she/it) was
ἰού alas!
ἱππο-μανής horse-mad (nom.)
ἵππ-ος, ὁ horse (2a)
καὶ γὰρ yes, certainly
καὶ δὴ καὶ and moreover
κεφαλ-ή, ἡ head (1a)
λοιδορέ-ομαι argue
νεανί-ας, ὁ young man (1d)
ὁ δυσ-τυχής the unlucky one
ὅλ-ος -η -ον (ὁ) all of
ὀνειρο-πολέ-ω dream (of)
ὅτε when
οὐδέποτε never
οὐδέπω not yet
οὑτοσί αὑτηί τουτοί this here (pointing)
ὀφείλ-ω owe
πατήρ (πατερ-), ὁ father (3a)
περὶ τοῦ παιδὸς about the child
περὶ τῶν ἵππ-ων about horses
πικρ-ός -ά -όν bitter
Στρεψιάδ-ης, ὁ Strepsiades (1d)
σχεδὸν nearly
τάλας unhappy me!
τοῖς ὀνείροις my dreams
τότε then
υἱ-ός, ὁ son (2a)
ὕπν-ος, ὁ sleep (2a)
χθὲς yesterday

χρέ-α, τά debts (3c uncontr.)
χρῆμα (χρηματ-), τό thing; size; length (3b)
χρήματ-α, τά money (3b)
χρήστ-ης, ὁ creditor (1d)
χρόν-ος, ὁ time (2a)
ὠνειρο-πόλ-ει he used to dream of (ὀνειρο-πολέ-ω)
ὥσπερ ἔχεις just as you are

Vocabulary to be learnt

αἴτιος ᾱ ον *responsible (for), guilty (of)*
βαθύς *deep*
βαρύς *heavy*
βίος, ὁ *life, means, livelihood (2a)*
γάμος, ὁ *marriage (2a)*
διαλέγομαι *converse*
δίκη, ἡ *lawsuit; penalty; justice (1a)*
δίκην λαμβάνω (λαβ-) *exact one's due; punish (παρά + gen.)*
διότι *because*
δυστυχής *unlucky*
εἰσφέρω (εἰσενεγκ-) *bring in, carry in*
ἡδύς *sweet, pleasant*
ἵππος, ὁ *horse (2a)*
ὅλος η ον *whole of*
οὐδέπω/οὔπω *not yet*
ὀφείλω *owe*
πατήρ (πατ(ε)ρ-), ὁ *father (3a)*
σχεδόν *near, nearly; almost*
τότε *then*
υἱός, ὁ *son (2a)*
χρήματα, τά *money (3b)*

B

In *World of Athens*: olives 2.9–14, 5.51–2; slaves 5.61ff.; rhetoric and education 5.45, 8.17–21.

ΣΤΡΕΨ.   (*suddenly decides to check on his debts*)
ἀλλὰ τί ὀφείλω; παῖ, δεῦρ' ἐλθέ· ἅπτε λύχνον. νῦν γὰρ οὐχ ὁρῶ οὐδέν·
νὺξ γάρ ἐστι βαθεῖα.
ΘΕΡΑΠΩΝ πῶς οὖν λύχνον ἅπτω, ὦ δέσποτα; ἰδού· ἔλαιον οὐκ ἔνεστιν ἐν τῷ λύχνῳ.
ΣΤΡΕΨ.   τί φῄς; ἔλαιον οὐκ ἔχει ὁ λύχνος; οἴμοι τάλας. δεῦρ' ἐλθὲ καὶ κλαῖε.   5
(*lifts his hand to strike, but checks himself*)
ὡς κακός ἐσθ' ὁ πόλεμος. τοὺς γὰρ οἰκέτας οὐ κολάζω οὐκέτι, καίπερ
ἀργοὺς ὄντας. ὁ γὰρ πόλεμος κωλύει. οἴμοι τῶν κακῶν. νῦν γὰρ ἡμεῖς
μὲν κελεύομεν, ἐκεῖνοι δ' οὐ πείθονται. ἀλλ' ὅτε νέοι ἦμεν ἡμεῖς, τότε
οἱ γέροντες ἀεὶ ἐκόλαζον τοὺς οἰκέτας. ἀργοὶ οὖν οὐκ ἦσαν ἐκεῖνοι,   10
οὐδὲ τοὺς δεσπότας κακὰ ἐποίουν, ἦσαν δὲ χρηστοὶ καὶ ἀεὶ ἐπείθοντο.
ἐφοβοῦντο γὰρ τὴν κόλασιν.
(*with determination*)
ἀλλὰ διὰ τί οὐ σῴζω ἐμαυτὸν καὶ τὸν υἱὸν ἐκ τῶν χρεῶν; διὰ τί οὐ ζητῶ
γνώμην τινά, καὶ παύω τὰ χρέα ταῦτα;   15
(*thinks furiously*)
νῦν οὖν, ὦ Στρεψιάδη, σῷζε σεαυτόν.
(*in triumph*)
ἰοὺ ἰού. γνώμην τινὰ ἔχω. νῦν δὲ διὰ τί οὐ παύω καθεύδοντα τοῦτον τὸν
νεανίαν;   20

Vocabulary for Section Five B

ἅπτ-ω light
ἀργ-ός -ή –όν lazy
βαθεῖα deep (nom.)
γέρων (γεροντ-), ὁ old man (3a)
γνώμ-η, ἡ plan (1a)
ἐ-κόλαζ-ον (they) used to punish (κολάζ-ω)
ἔλαι-ον, τό olive-oil (2b)
ἐμαυτ-όν myself
ἔν-ειμι be in
ἐ-πείθ-οντο they would obey (πείθ-ομαι)
ἐ-φοβ-οῦντο they were afraid of (φοβέ-ομαι)
ἦμεν (we) were
ἦσαν (they) were
ἰού hurrah!
καίπερ despite, although (+ part.)
κακὰ ἐ-ποί-ουν they would treat badly (κακὰ ποιέ-ω)

κλαί-ω weep, be punished
κολάζ-ω punish
κόλασ-ις, ἡ punishment (3e)
λύχν-ος, ὁ oil-lamp (2a)
νεανί-ας, ὁ young man (1d)
νέ-ος -α -ον young
οἰκέτ-ης, ὁ house-slave (1d)
οἴμοι τῶν κακ-ῶν alas for my troubles!
ὅτε when
παύ-ω stop x (acc.) –ing (acc. part.)
πείθ-ομαι obey
τάλας unhappy me!
τῷ λύχνῳ the oil-lamp
φῄς you (s.) say
χρέ-α, τά debts (3c uncontr., gen. pl. χρε-ῶν)
χρηστ-ός -ή -όν good, fine

Vocabulary to be learnt
ἅπτω *light; fasten, fix*
ἔνειμι *be in*
κακά }
κακῶς } ποιέω *treat badly; do harm to*
κολάζω *punish*
νεᾱνίᾱς, ὁ *young man (1d)*
νέος ᾱ ον *young*
οἰκέτης, ὁ *house-slave (1d)*
παύω *stop*
πείθομαι (πιθ-) *trust, obey (+dat.)*
φῄς *you (s.) say*
χρέα, τά *debts (3c uncontr.)*
χρηστός ή όν *good, fine, serviceable*

ὁ λυχνός

The importance of the sophists

Athens' radical democracy gave every Athenian male citizen over 18 the chance to make his views heard at the weekly ἐκκλησία, which took all decisions that governments take in the modern world. But a man's influence depended on his ability to speak effectively in public. As a result, many leading intellectuals came to Athens because of the opportunities which its large and wealthy community offered for earning money from teaching such skills. These teachers were generally lumped together under the title of 'sophists'. Many of them were men of the highest intellectual distinction, though Plato hated them, and drew a strong distinction between them and Socrates, who never taught formally or charged fees (Plato's influence has given sophists a bad name). Sophists developed and taught their own specialities and grappled in their own way with many major philosophical questions. It is their questions, along with those of Socrates, which provided the background and basis for the dialogues of Plato and so for the whole development of western philosophy…

Socrates never wrote a word, but he was the key figure in changing the direction of Greek philosophy away from cosmology to man's position in the world. We have to reconstruct what Socrates said from the testimony of three main witnesses, none of them impartial and all with tendencies to reinterpret Socrates according to their own interests. These are Plato, Xenophon, and Aristophanes. Socrates was part of the same intellectual movement which produced the sophists, and Aristophanes' treatment of him in *Clouds* suggests that many Athenians thought of him as a sophist. The Socrates of *Clouds* is a composite figure—all 'modern' movements rolled into one—but one element is the sophist. Plato, who drew a sharp contrast between Socrates and the sophists, nevertheless represented Socrates in discussion with them. As far as Plato was concerned, the sophists were interested in success, in giving their pupils techniques, especially in the art of speaking, that would enable them to get on in the world, whereas Socrates was interested in morals, in what one must do to be good. Xenophon confirms this moral preoccupation, and Aristotle characterises Socrates as 'concerned with the moral virtues'. (*World of Athens*, 8.22, 33)

C

Strepsiades' plan involves his son, Pheidippides, taking a course of higher education, but this is a subject which must be broached gently to the horse-mad youth.

ΣΤΡΕΨ.	Φειδιππίδη, Φειδιππίδιον.
ΦΕΙΔΙΠΠΙΔΗΣ	τί, ὦ πάτερ;
ΣΤΡΕΨ.	εἰπέ μοι, ὦ υἱέ, ἆρα φιλεῖς με;
ΦΕΙΔ.	ἔγωγε, καὶ οὐ παύομαι οὐδέποτε.
ΣΤΡΕΨ.	ἆρ' αὔριον φιλήσεις με; 5
ΦΕΙΔ.	νὴ τὸν Ποσειδῶ τουτονὶ τὸν ἵππιον, αὔριόν σε φιλήσω, καὶ οὐ παύσομαι οὐδέποτε.
ΣΤΡΕΨ.	μὴ λέγε μηδαμῶς 'τοῦτον τὸν ἵππιον', ὦ παῖ – τῶν γὰρ κακῶν τῶν ἐμῶν ἐκεῖνος τὴν αἰτίαν ἔχει – ἀλλ' ἄκουε, καὶ πείθου.
ΦΕΙΔ.	ἰδού, ἀκούω, καὶ πείθομαι καὶ πείσομαι ἀεί. σὺ δὲ λέγε δή. τί κελεύεις; 10
ΣΤΡΕΨ.	σμικρόν τι κελεύσω, ὦ παῖ, πάνυ σμικρόν τι. ἔχω γὰρ διάνοιάν τινα, καὶ διανοοῦμαί τι· ἀλλὰ πείσῃ;
ΦΕΙΔ.	πείσομαι, νὴ τὸν Διόνυσον· μὴ φρόντιζε, πάτερ. *(immediately falls asleep)*
ΣΤΡΕΨ.	ἆρ' ἤκουες; ἢ οὐκ ἤκουες; ἢ μάτην λέγω; παύσω σε καθεύδοντα. 15
ΦΕΙΔ.	*(wakes up again)*
	ναί. ἤκουον ἐγὼ καὶ ἀκούω ἐγὼ νυνὶ καὶ ἀκούσομαι. ἀλλὰ τί μοι ἔλεγες;
ΣΤΡΕΨ.	ἔλεγόν σοι ὅτι διάνοιάν τινα ἔχω.
ΦΕΙΔ.	ἀλλὰ τίς ἡ διάνοια; τί ἐν νῷ ἔχεις, καὶ τί διανοῇ; ἆρ' ἔλεγες;
ΣΤΡΕΨ.	οὐχί, ἀλλά σοι λέξω. ἴσως γὰρ αὕτη ἡ διάνοια ἡμᾶς παύσει πως ἐκ τῶν 20 χρεῶν. μέγα γάρ τι διανοοῦμαι.
ΦΕΙΔ.	εἰπὲ δή. τίς ἡ σὴ διάνοια, ὦ πάτερ; τί κελεύσεις; πῶς ἡ διάνοια σώσει ἡμᾶς; πῶς παυσόμεθα ἐκ τῶν χρεῶν;
ΣΤΡΕΨ.	σὺ δὲ ποιήσεις;
ΦΕΙΔ.	ποιήσω νὴ τὸν Διόνυσον. 25

Vocabulary for Section Five C

Grammar for 5C–D
- Future indicative, active and middle: παύσω, παύσομαι
- Future of 'to be' and 'to go': ἔσομαι, εἶμι

αἰτί-α, ἡ responsibility (1b)
ἀκούσ-ομαι I shall listen (ἀκού-ω)
αὔριον tomorrow
δια-νοέ-ομαι intend, have in mind

διά-νοι-α, ἡ plan (1b)
Διόνυσ-ος, ὁ Dionysos (2a) (*god of nature, esp. wine*)
ἤκου-ον ⎫
ἤκου-ες ⎭ imperfect of ἀκού-ω
ἵππι-ος -α -ον of horses, horsey

ἴσως perhaps
κελεύσ-ω I shall order (κελεύ-ω)
κελεύσ-εις you (s.) will order (κελεύ-ω)
λέξ-ω I shall tell (λέγ-ω)
μάτην in vain, to no purpose

μηδαμ-ῶς in no way, not at all
μοι to me
νυνὶ =νῦν
νῷ mind
οὐδέποτε never
οὐχί=οὐκ
πάνυ very
παύσ-ομαι I shall stop/cease
  (παύ-ομαι)
παυσ-όμεθα we shall stop, cease
  (παύ-ομαι)
παύσ-ω I shall stop (παύ-ω)
παύσ-ει (it) will stop (παύ-ω)
πείσ-ομαι I shall obey
  (πείθ-ομαι)
πείσ-ῃ you (s.) will obey
  (πείθ-ομαι)

ποιήσ-ω I shall do (ποιέ-ω)
ποιήσ-εις you will do (ποιέ-ω)
Ποσειδῶν (Ποσειδων-), ὁ
  Poseidon (3a)
πως somehow
σμικρ-ός -ά -όν small
σοι to you
σ-ός σ-ή σ-όν your
σώσ-ει (it) will save (σῴζ-ω)
Φειδιππίδ-ης, ὁ Pheidippides (1d)
Φειδιππίδι-ον dear little
  Pheidippides (2b)
φιλέ-ω love
φιλήσ-ω I shall love (φιλέ-ω)
φιλήσ-εις you (s.) will love
  (φιλέ-ω)

Vocabulary to be learnt
αἰτίᾱ, ἡ *reason, cause,*
  responsibility (1b)
διανοέομαι *intend, plan*
διάνοια, ἡ *intention, plan (1b)*
νοῦς, ὁ (νόος *contr.*) *mind, sense*
  (2a)
οὐδέποτε *never*
Ποσειδῶν (Ποσειδων-), ὁ
  Poseidon (god of sea) (3a)
  (*voc.* Πόσειδον; *acc.* Ποσειδῶ)
πως *somehow*
φιλέω *love, kiss*

Horses

Horses were a sign of a rich man, who would use them for hunting and racing (the disabled client of Lysias, 24.11–12 defends himself against the allegation that he was getting above himself by hiring a horse while claiming a pension). They were expensive to keep, as they needed grain as feed to maintain them in good condition, and grain was usually required for human consumption. Their harness was rudimentary and, if the horse put his head down to pull, soon choked him. The horse was therefore unsuitable for heavy draught work either on farm or road, while the absence of stirrups limited its usefulness in war (stirrup-less riders being easily unseated). It was only in the lusher parts of northern Greece (Thessaly and beyond) that horses were raised in any numbers…

[Here Alcibiades argues that he should lead the huge military expedition to Sicily in 415BC. To support his claim, he boasts of the victories he won with his chariots at the Olympic Games. See Thucydides, *Peloponnesian War* 6.16]:

'Athenians, … let me begin by saying that I have a better claim to command than others and believe that I am qualified for it. Indeed the very things for which I am criticised in fact bring honour to my ancestors and myself and benefit our country. For, after thinking the war had ruined our city, the Greek world came to overestimate our power because of the magnificent showing I made at the Olympic games. I entered seven chariots for the chariot race (a larger number than any private individual before), took first, second and fourth place, and did everything in suitably grand style. Custom honours such successes, and at the same time they give an impression of power…' (*World of Athens*, 2.16, 4.9)

D

In *World of Athens*: Socrates and sophists 8.33–6; intellectuals and argument 8.6–14.

ΣΤΡΕΨ.   (*takes him outside and points to a building across the road*)
          δεῦρό νυν ἀπόβλεπε. ὁρᾷς τὸ θύριον τοῦτο καὶ τὸ οἰκίδιον;
ΦΕΙΔ.   ὁρῶ. τί οὖν τοῦτό ἐστιν, ὦ πάτερ;
ΣΤΡΕΨ.   ψυχῶν σοφῶν τοῦτό ἐστι φροντιστήριον. ἔνδον ἐνοικοῦσιν ἄνδρες
          σοφοί, λέγοντες δὲ πείθουσι τοὺς μαθητὰς ὡς ὁ οὐρανός ἐστι πνιγεύς,
          καὶ ἔστιν ὁ πνιγεὺς οὗτος περὶ ἡμᾶς, ἡμεῖς δ' οἱ ἄνθρακές ἐσμεν.   5
          πείθουσι τοὺς μαθητὰς οἱ ἄνδρες οὗτοι, διδάσκοντες ἀεὶ καὶ χρήματα
          πολλὰ δεχόμενοι. καὶ νὴ Δία οὐ παύσεται οὐδεὶς αὐτῶν χρήματα πολλὰ
          δεχόμενος παρὰ⌢ τῶν⌢ μαθητῶν.
ΦΕΙΔ.   ἀλλὰ τί διδάσκουσιν οἱ ἄνδρες; τί μαθήσονται οἱ νεανίαι, μαθηταὶ ὄντες;
ΣΤΡΕΨ.   λόγους μαθήσονται οἱ μαθηταί.   10
ΦΕΙΔ.   τίνας λόγους λέγεις, ὦ πάτερ;
ΣΤΡΕΨ.   τίνας; τὸν δίκαιον καὶ τὸν ἄδικον λόγον λέγω.
ΦΕΙΔ.   τούτους οὖν τοὺς λόγους μαθήσονται οἱ μαθηταί;
ΣΤΡΕΨ.   νὴ τὸν Δία. καὶ⌢ δὴ⌢ καὶ ἐν ταῖς⌢ δίκαις τοὺς ἀντιδίκους νικήσουσιν ἀεί.
ΦΕΙΔ.   εἰσὶν δὲ τίνες οἱ ἄνδρες οὗτοι; τί τὸ ὄνομα τῶν ἀνδρῶν;   15
ΣΤΡΕΨ.   οὐκ οἶδα τὸ ὄνομα. σοφισταὶ δέ εἰσι καλοί⌢ τε⌢ κἀγαθοί.
ΦΕΙΔ.   (*in disgust*)
          αἰβοῖ. πονηροί γ', οἶδα. τούς τε ὠχροὺς καὶ ἀνυποδήτους λέγεις, τὸν⌐
          κακοδαίμονα ⌐Σωκράτη καὶ Χαιρεφῶντα.
ΣΤΡΕΨ.   (*desperately silencing him*)   20
          ἤ⌢ ἤ σιώπα. ἀλλ' οὐκ ἀκούσῃ;
ΦΕΙΔ.   ἀκούσομαι. ἀλλὰ τί μοι λέξεις;
ΣΤΡΕΨ.   ἀλλ' ὥσπερ ἔλεγον, δύο ἔχουσι τοὺς λόγους οἱ ἔνδον, τὸν δίκαιον καὶ τὸν
          ἄδικον. σὺ δὲ διὰ τί οὐκ εἰσέρχῃ μαθητής; οὕτω γὰρ παυσόμεθα ἐκ τῶν
          χρεῶν.   25
ΦΕΙΔ.   ἀλλὰ τί μαθήσομαι;
ΣΤΡΕΨ.   τὸν ἄδικον λόγον. ὁ μὲν γὰρ ἄδικος λόγος διαφθερεῖ τὰ χρέα, ὁ δὲ
          δίκαιος οὐχί. σὺ δὲ μάνθανε· οὕτως οὖν οἱ χρῆσται οὐ λήψονται οὐδὲν
          τούτων τῶν χρεῶν. διὰ τί οὐκ εἰσέρχῃ σὺ εἰς τὸ φροντιστήριον, ὦ ἄριστε
          ἀνθρώπων;   30
ΦΕΙΔ.   τί φῄς; ἐγὼ εἰς τὸ φροντιστήριον; μὰ τὸν Ποσειδῶ τὸν ἵππιον οὐ ποιήσω
          τοῦτό γε. οὔτε τήμερον εἰσέρχομαι οὔτε αὔριον εἴσειμι οὔτε ποιήσω
          τοῦτο οὐδαμῶς. τοὺς μὲν γὰρ ἵππους φιλῶ ἐγώ, τοὺς δὲ σοφιστὰς οὔ.
ΣΤΡΕΨ.   οὔκουν πείσῃ, οὐδὲ ποιήσεις;
ΦΕΙΔ.   οὐ πείσομαι ἔγωγε, οὐδὲ ποιήσω. ὠχρὸς γὰρ γενήσομαι, μαθητὴς ὤν.   35
ΣΤΡΕΨ.   ἀλλ' εἰ σὺ μὴ εἴσει, τίς εἴσεισι;
          (*makes one last effort to engage Pheidippides*)
          ἆρ' εἴσιμεν ἅμα σύ τε κἀγώ;

Vocabulary for Section Five D

ἄ-δικ-ος -ον unjust
αἰβοῖ uggghh!
ἀκούσ-ομαι I shall listen (ἀκού-ω)
ἀκούσ-ῃ you (s.) will listen (ἀκού-ω)
ἄνθραξ (ἀνθρακ-), ὁ charcoal (3a)
ἀντί-δικ-ος, -ου adversary (in court) (2a)
ἀν-υπό-δητ-ος -ον unshod, barefoot
ἀπο-βλέπ-ω gaze at, observe closely
αὔριον tomorrow
γε at least; yes, and
γενήσ-ομαι I shall become (γίγν-ομαι)
δέχ-ομαι receive
δια-φθερ-εῖ (it) will get rid of (δια-φθείρ-ω)
διδάσκ-ω teach
δίκαι-ος -α -ον just
δύο two (acc.)
εἰσ-έρχ-ομαι enter
εἴσ-ειμι I shall enter (εἰσ-έρχ-ομαι)

εἴσ-ει (you) (s.) will enter (εἰσ-έρχ-ομαι)
εἴσ-εισι(ν) (he) will enter (εἰσ-έρχ-ομαι)
εἴσ-ιμεν we will enter (εἰσ-έρχ-ομαι)
ἔνδον inside
ἐν-οικέ-ω live (in)
ἤ ἤ tut tut!
θύρι-ον, τό little door (2b)
ἵππι-ος -α -ον of horses, horsey
κἀγώ=καὶ ἐγώ
καὶ δὴ καὶ and moreover
καλοί τε κἀγαθοί jolly good chaps, real gentlemen
λέξ-εις you (s.) will say (λέγ-ω)
λόγ-ος, ὁ argument (2a)
μαθήσ-ομαι I shall learn (μανθάν-ω)
μαθήσ-ονται they shall learn (μανθάν-ω)
μαθητ-ής, ὁ student (1d)
μὴ not
νικήσ-ουσι(ν) they will defeat (νικά-ω)
νυν then

οἰκίδι-ον, τό little house (2b)
ὄνομα (ὀνοματ-), τό name (3b)
οὐδαμ-ῶς no way, not at all
οὔκουν not . . . therefore
οὐραν-ός, ὁ sky (2a)
οὔτε . . . οὔτε neither . . . nor
παρὰ τῶν μαθητῶν from the students
παύσ-εται (he) will stop (παύ-ομαι)
παυσ-όμεθα we shall cease (παύ-ομαι)
παύσ-ω I shall stop (παύ-ω)
πείθ-ω persuade
πείσ-ομαι I shall obey (πείθ-ομαι)
πείσ-ῃ you (s.) will obey (πείθ-ομαι)
πνιγεύς, ὁ oven (3g)
ποιήσ-ω I shall do (ποιέ-ω)
ποιήσ-εις you (s.) will do (ποιέ-ω)
πονηρ-ός -ά -όν wicked, nasty
σοφιστ-ής, ὁ sophist (1d)
σοφ-ός -ή -όν wise, clever
ταῖς δίκαις their lawsuits

δύο πνιγεῖς

ΦΕΙΔ.   οὐκ ἔγωγε.

ΣΤΡΕΨ.   (*in a rage*)   40
          ἀλλὰ διώξω σε ἐκ τῆς⌢ οἰκίας καὶ ἐκβαλῶ εἰς⌢ κόρακας.

ΦΕΙΔ.   κἀγὼ δὴ φεύξομαι.
          (*turns to leave*)
          ἀλλ' εἴσειμι εἰς τὴν οἰκίαν, ἀλλ' οὐκ εἰς τὸ τῶν σοφιστῶν φροντιστήριον.

ΣΤΡΕΨ.   τί δῆτα ποιήσω;   45
          (*with determination*)
          οὐ γὰρ νικήσει Φειδιππίδης, ἀλλ' ἐγὼ νικηφόρος γενήσομαι.
          (*has a sudden idea*)
          ἀλλ' οἶδ' ἔγωγε. ἐγὼ γὰρ αὐτὸς εἴσειμι εἰς τὸ φροντιστήριον, μαθητὴς δὲ
          τῶν σοφιστῶν γενήσομαι καὶ γνώσομαι τὸν ἄδικον λόγον. οὕτως οὖν   50
          τοὺς χρήστας ἐκείνους παύσω ἔγωγε λαμβάνοντας τὰ χρήματα.
          (*a wave of despair hits him*)
          πῶς οὖν γέρων ὢν καὶ βραδὺς περὶ τοὺς λόγους τοὺς ἀκριβεῖς τὴν
          φιλοσοφίαν μαθήσομαι; ὅμως εἴσειμι. ἀλλὰ διὰ τί οὐ κόπτω τὴν θύραν
          ταύτην καὶ βοῶ;   55
          (*with a deep breath*)
          ἀλλὰ ποιήσω τοῦτο καὶ κόψω τὴν θύραν καὶ βοήσομαι.

ἄ-δικ-ος -ον unjust
ἀκριβεῖς exact, accurate (acc.)
αὐτ-ός myself (nom.)
βοήσ-ομαι I shall shout (βοά -ω)
βραδὺς slow (nom.)
γενήσ-ομαι I shall become
  (γίγν-ομαι)
γέρων (γεροντ-), ὁ old man (3a)
γνώσ-ομαι I shall get to know
  (γιγνώσκ-ω)
δῆτα then
διώξ-ω I shall chase (διώκ-ω)
εἰ (μὴ) if (not)
εἴσ-ειμι I shall enter
  (εἰσ-έρχ-ομαι)
εἰς κόρακας to hell! (lit. 'to the
  crows')
ἐκ-βαλ-ῶ I shall throw out
  (ἐκ-βάλλ-ω)
εὔξ-ομαι I shall offer prayers
  (εὔχ-ομαι)
κἀγώ=καὶ ἐγώ
κόπτ-ω knock (on)
κόψ-ω I shall knock (on)
  (κόπτ-ω)
λήψ-ονται (they) will get
  (λαμβάν-ω)

λόγ-ος, ὁ argument (2a)
μαθήσ-ομαι I shall learn
  (μανθάν-ω)
μαθητ-ής, ὁ student (1d)
μοι to me
νικήσ-ει (he) will win (νικά-ω)
νικη-φόρ-ος -ον victorious
ὅμως nevertheless
παύσ-εται (he) will stop
  (παύ-ομαι)
παυσ-όμεθα we shall cease
  (παύ-ομαι)
παύσ-ω I shall stop (παύ-ω)
πείθ-ω persuade
πείσ-ομαι I shall obey (πείθ-ομαι)
πείσ-ῃ you (s.) will obey
  (πείθ-ομαι)
πνιγεύς, ὁ oven (3g)
ποιήσ-ω I shall do (ποιέ-ω)
σοφιστ-ής, ὁ sophist (1d)
τῆς οἰκίας the house
τήμερον today
τὸν Σωκράτη Socrates
φεύξ-ομαι I shall run off
  (φεύγ-ω)
φιλο-σοφί-α, ἡ philosophy
  (1b)

φροντιστήρι-ον, τό think-tank,
  mental institute (2b)
Χαιρεφῶν (Χαιρεφωντ-),
  ὁ Khairephon (3a)
χρήστ-ης, ὁ creditor (1d)
ψυχ-ή, ἡ soul (1a)
ὡς that
ὠχρ-ός -ά -όν pale

Vocabulary to be learnt
ἄδικος ον *unjust*
αὔριον *tomorrow*
γε *at least (denotes some sort of*
  reservation)
δέχομαι *receive*
διδάσκω *teach*
δίκαιος ᾱ ον *just*
εἰσέρχομαι (εἰσελθ-) *enter*
ἔνδον *inside*
καὶ δὴ καί *moreover*
κόπτω *knock (on), cut*
λόγος, ὁ *argument; word,*
  speech; story, tale; reason (2a)
μαθητής, ὁ *student (1d)*
οὔτε … οὔτε *neither … nor*
πείθω *persuade*
σοφός ή όν *wise, clever*

Section Six A–D

Introduction

A student at Socrates 'Think-Tank' introduces Strepsiades to the 'new thought' and describes how fleas' feet are used to measure distance. Further technical 'wonders' are revealed inside the institution, when Socrates enters, suspended in a basket in the air. A bewildered but impressed Strepsiades informs Socrates that he wants to learn the 'wrong' arguments in order to escape his debts, but turns out to be a hopeless student.

In *World of Athens*: physical speculation 8.7–9; mathematics 8.25; Thales 8.7.

A

(Στρεψιάδης κόπτει τὴν θύραν καὶ βοᾷ)
ΣΤΡΕΨ.　παῖ, παιδίον.
ΜΑΘΗΤΗΣ (*comes out of the* phrontisterion)
　　　βάλλ᾿ εἰς κόρακας. τίς ἔκοψε τὴν θύραν; τίς ἐβόησεν;
ΣΤΡΕΨ.　ἔγωγε ἔκοψα τὴν θύραν καὶ ἐβόησα.
ΜΑΘ.　τίς ὢν σὺ τοῦτο ἐποίησας; ἀμαθής τις, εὖ οἶδα.　　　　　　　5
ΣΤΡΕΨ.　Στρεψιάδης Κικυννόθεν.
ΜΑΘ.　εἰς κόρακας αὖθις.
　　　(*goes back into the* phrontisterion)
ΣΤΡΕΨ.　οἴμοι, τί ποιήσω; ἀλλ᾿ αὖθις κόψω.
(αὖθις κόπτει τὴν θύραν)　　　　　　　　　　　　　　　　　　　10
ΜΑΘ.　τίς ὁ κόπτων; διὰ τί οὗτος οὐκ ἐπαύσατο κόπτων ὁ ἄνθρωπος, ἐπεὶ
　　　ἐκέλευσα ἐγώ;

Vocabulary for Section Six A

Grammar for 6A–B
- First aorist indicative, active and middle: ἔπαυσα, ἐπαυσάμην
- Aspect
- Type 3h nouns: ὀφρύς

ἀ-μαθής ignoramus (nom.)
βάλλ᾿ εἰς κόρακας go to hell!
ἐ-βόησ-α I shouted (βοά -ω)
ἐ-βόησ-ε(ν) (he) shouted (βοάω)
εἰς κόρακας to hell!

ἐ-κέλευσ-α (I) gave the order
　(κελεύ-ω)
ἔ-κοψ-α (I) knocked at (κόπτ-ω)
ἔ-κοψ-ε (he) knocked at
　(κόπτ-ω)

ἐ-παύσ-ατο he stopped (παύ-ομαι)
ἐ-ποίησ-ας (you) (s.) did (ποιέ-ω)
Κικυννόθεν from the deme
　Kikynna
παιδί-ον, τό slave, slave dear (2b)

(re-appears, annoyed)

διὰ τί σὺ πάλιν κόπτεις; τί ἐν νῷ ἔχεις; τὴν γὰρ ἐμὴν φροντίδα ἀπ-   15
έκοψας, ποιῶν τοῦτο.

ΣΤΡΕΨ.   ἀλλ' ἄρτι ἐπαυσάμην, ὦ 'γαθέ. ἐκέλευσας γὰρ σύ. μὴ οὖν ἔκβαλλέ με,
καίπερ ἄγροικον ὄντα καὶ ἀμαθῆ. ἀλλὰ τίς ἡ φροντίς, εἰπὲ δή.

ΜΑΘ.   ἀλλ' οὐ θέμις. μόνοι γὰρ μανθάνουσι τὰς τῶν σοφιστῶν φροντίδας
ταύτας οἱ μαθηταί.   20

ΣΤΡΕΨ.   εἰπέ μοι οὖν. ἥκω γὰρ ἐγὼ μαθητὴς τῶν σοφιστῶν εἰς τὸ φροντιστήριον.

ΜΑΘ.   λέξω σοι· ψύλλα γάρ τις δάκνει τὴν⌜ Χαιρεφῶντος ⌝ὀφρῦν. ὅτε δὲ πηδᾷ
ἐπὶ τὴν κεφαλὴν τὴν Σωκράτους, οὕτω διαλέγονται οἱ ἄνδρες.

'ΣΩΚΡΑΤΗΣ   ὅρα, ὦ Χαιρεφῶν. οὐ γὰρ λανθάνει με ἡ ψύλλα ἀξία οὖσα
τοῦ⌒ Ὀλυμπίκου⌒ στεφάνου. ἀλλὰ λέγε, ὁπόσους⌒ τοὺς⌒ ἑαυ-   25
τῆς⌒ πόδας ἐπήδησεν ἡ ψύλλα.

ΧΑΙΡΕΦΩΝ   οὐκ οἶδα, ὦ Σώκρατες. ἀλλὰ διὰ τί οὐ μετροῦμεν τὸ
χωρίον;

ΣΩΚ.   ἀλλὰ πῶς μετρήσομεν, ὦ Χαιρεφῶν;

ΧΑΙ.   ἰδού. πρῶτον μὲν γὰρ κηρὸν λαμβάνω, εἶτα τὸν κηρὸν   30
θερμὸν ποιῶ. τέλος δὲ τοὺς τῆς⌒ ψύλλης πόδας εἰς τὸν
κηρὸν τίθημι.

ΣΩΚ.   τί⌒ δέ;

ΧΑΙ.   νῦν ὁ κηρὸς ψυχρὸς γίγνεται. ἰδού, ὦ Σώκρατες. ἡ γὰρ
ψύλλα ἐμβάδας ἔχει.   35

ΣΩΚ.   ἀλλὰ τί νῦν ποιεῖς;

ΧΑΙ.   νῦν δὲ τὰς ἐμβάδας λύω. ἰδού.'

ΣΤΡΕΨ.   ὦ Ζεῦ βασιλεῦ. ὦ τῆς⌒ σοφίας τῶν ἀνδρῶν.

(admiration fades into bewilderment)

ἀλλ' εἰπέ μοι, τί ποτ' ἐποίησαν οἱ ἄνδρες, ὦ μαθητά;   40

ΜΑΘ.   οὐ λανθάνεις με ἄγροικος ὤν, ὦ Στρεψιάδη, οὐ μανθάνων οὐδέν.
ἀλλ' ὡς ἔλεγον, πρῶτον μὲν θερμὸν ἐποίησαν τὸν κηρόν. ἔπειτα τοὺς
τῆς⌒ ψύλλης πόδας ἔθεσαν εἰς τὸν κηρόν. τέλος δὲ τὰς ἐμβάδας ἔλυσαν
καὶ ἐμέτρησαν – πῶς γὰρ οὔ; – τὸ χωρίον.

ἐμβάδες

ΣΤΡΕΨ.   ὦ Ζεῦ βασιλεῦ· σοφοὶ δὴ φαίνονται ὄντες οἱ ἄνδρες. τί δῆτ' ἐκεῖνον τὸν   45
Θαλῆν θαυμάζομεν; ἦ ῥᾳδίως φεύξομαι τὴν δίκην. γνώσομαι γὰρ τὸ
ψύλλης πήδημα.
(*shouts*)
ἀλλ' ἄνοιγε, ἄνοιγε τὴν θύραν.

ἄγρ-οικ-ος -ον from the country
ἀ-μαθῆ ignorant (acc.)
ἄνοιγε open!
ἄξι-ος -α -ον worthy of
ἀπ-έ-κοψ-ας you (s.) cut off
   (ἀπο-κόπτ-ω)
ἄρτι recently, just now
δάκν-ω bite, worry
ἐ-βόησ-ας you (s.) shouted
   (βοάω)
ἔ-θε-σαν they placed (τίθημι)
εἶτα then
ἐκ-βάλλ-ω throw out
ἐ-κέλευσ-ας you (s.) gave the
   order (κελεύ-ω)
ἔ-λυσ-αν they undid (λύ-ω)
ἐμβάς (ἐμβαδ-), ἡ slipper (3a)
ἐ-μέτρησ-αν they measured
   (μετρέ-ω)
ἐ-παυσ-άμην I stopped
   (παύ-ομαι)
ἐπεὶ when
ἐ-πήδησ-ε(ν) (it) leapt
   (πηδά-ω)
ἐ-ποίησ-αν (they) did (ποιέ-ω)
ἦ truly
ἥκ-ω I have come
Θαλ-ῆς, ὁ Thales (1d) *(early
   Greek scientist and inventor, a
   by-word for cleverness)*
θαυμάζ-ω wonder (at)

θέμις, ἡ right, lawful (lit. law
   sanctioned by the gods) (3a)
θερμ-ός -ή -όν hot
καίπερ despite, although (+part.)
κεφαλ-ή, ἡ head (1a)
κηρ-ός, ὁ wax (2a)
λύ-ω release, undo
μετρέ-ω measure (fut. μετρήσ-ω)
μοι to me
μόν-ος -η -ον alone
νῷ mind
ὁπόσους τοὺς ἑαυτῆς πόδας how
   many of its own foot lengths
οὗτος hey, you!
πάλιν again
πηδά-ω leap
πήδημα (πηδηματ-), τό a leap
   (3b)
πόδας *see* πούς
ποτε ever
πούς (ποδ-), ὁ foot (3a)
πρῶτον first
ῥᾳδί-ως easily
σοι to you
Σωκράτους Socrates'
τὴν ὀφρ-ῦν the eyebrow
τῆς σοφίας the cleverness!
τῆς ψύλλης of the flea
τί δέ; what next?
τί δῆτ' why then …?
τίθημι I place, put

τοῦ Ὀλυμπικοῦ στεφάνου the
   Olympic crown
φροντίς (φροντιδ-), ἡ thought
   (3a)
φροντιστήρι-ον, τό think-tank,
   mental institute (2b)
Χαιρεφῶντος Khairephon's
χωρί-ον, τό space, distance (2b)
ψύλλ-α, ἡ flea (1c)
ψύλλης flea's
ψυχρ-ός -ά -όν cold
ὡς as

Vocabulary to be learnt
ἄγροικος ον *from the country,
   boorish*
βάλλ' εἰς κόρακας *go to hell!*
δάκνω (δακ-) *bite, worry*
ἐκβάλλω (ἐκβαλ-) *throw out*
ἐν νῷ ἔχω *intend, have in mind*
καίπερ *despite, although (+part.)*
κεφαλή, ἡ *head (1a)*
λύω *release*
ὅτε *when*
ὀφρῦς (ὀφρυ-), ἡ *eyebrow (3h)*
πούς (ποδ-), ὁ *foot (3a)*
ῥᾴδι-ος ᾱ ον *easy*
ῥᾳδίως *easily*
φροντίς (φροντιδ-), ἡ *thought,
   care, concern (3a)*
ὡς *as*

B

The door opens and Strepsiades starts back in horror.

In *World of Athens*: Athens' intellectual achievements 8.14–15, 22; technical work 8.24.

ΣΤΡΕΨ.	ὦ Ἡράκλεις, τίνα ταῦτα τὰ θηρία;
ΜΑΘ.	οὗτος, διὰ τί ἐθαύμασας; διὰ τί αὖθις ἐβόησας; ἆρα τοὺς μαθητὰς τούτους θαυμάζεις;
ΣΤΡΕΨ.	ναὶ μὰ Δία θαυμάζω. ἀλλὰ τί ποιοῦσιν οὗτοι οἱ εἰς τὴν γῆν βλέποντες;
ΜΑΘ.	ζητοῦσιν οὗτοι τὰ κατὰ γῆς.

ΣΤΡΕΨ.   βολβοὺς ἄρα ζητοῦσι. μὴ νῦν τοῦτό γ' ἔτι φροντίζετε, ὦ θηρία· ἐγὼ γὰρ
         οἶδα ὅπου εἰσὶ μεγάλοι καὶ καλοί. ἀλλὰ τίς οὑτοσί; διὰ τί ὁ πρωκτὸς εἰς
         τὸν οὐρανὸν βλέπει;

ΜΑΘ.   διότι ἀστρονομεῖ ὁ πρωκτός.

ΣΤΡΕΨ.   (*points to one of the strange devices cluttering up the* phrontisterion)   10
         ἰδού· τί δ' ἐστὶ τοῦτο; δίδασκέ με.

ΜΑΘ.   ἀστρονομία μὲν αὕτη.

ΣΤΡΕΨ.   (*points to another device*)
         τοῦτο δὲ τί;

ΜΑΘ.   γεωμετρία.   15

ΣΤΡΕΨ.   καὶ εἰς τί χρήσιμον αὕτη; δίδασκε.

ΜΑΘ.   ταύτῃ τὴν γῆν ἀναμετροῦμεν.
         (*picks up a map*)
         αὕτη δ' ἐστὶ γῆς περίοδος.
         (*points at the map*)   20
         ὁρᾷς; αὗται μὲν Ἀθῆναι.

ΣΤΡΕΨ.   (*in disbelief*)
         τί σὺ λέγεις; οὐ πείθομαι, ἐπεὶ τῶν δικαστῶν οὐχ ὁρῶ οὐδὲ ἕνα
         καθιζόμενον. ποῦ δ' ἐσθ' ὁ ἐμὸς δῆμος;

ΜΑΘ.   (*points at the map*)   25
         ἐνταῦθα ἔνεστιν. τὴν δ' Εὔβοιαν ὁρᾷς;

ΣΤΡΕΨ.   ὁρῶ. ἀλλ' ἡ Λακεδαίμων ποῦ τυγχάνει οὖσα;

ΜΑΘ.   ὅπου; αὕτη.

ΣΤΡΕΨ.   (*taken aback*)
         παπαῖ. ἄπελθε, ἄπελθε. ὡς ἐγγὺς ἡμῶν ἡ Λακεδαίμων. ἀλλὰ διὰ τί οὐκ   30
         ἀπάγεις ταύτην ἀφ' ἡμῶν πόρρω πάνυ;

ΜΑΘ.   ἀλλ' ἀδύνατον.

ΣΤΡΕΨ.   νὴ Δία ὀλοφυρεῖσθ' ἄρα.
         (*looks up and sees Socrates hanging in a basket*)
         ἀλλ' εἰπέ μοι, τίς οὗτος ὁ ἐπὶ τῆς κρεμάθρας ὤν;   35

ΜΑΘ.   αὐτός.

ΣΤΡΕΨ.   τίς αὐτός;

ΜΑΘ.   Σωκράτης.

Vocabulary for Section Six B

ἀ-δύνατ-ος -ον impossible
Ἀθῆν-αι, αἱ Athens (1a)
ἀνα-μετρέ-ω measure up
ἄπ-ελθε go away!
ἄρα then, in that case
ἀστρο-νομέ-ω observe the stars
ἀστρο-νομί-α, ἡ astronomy (1b)
αὐτ-ός Himself, the Master
   (nom.)
βολβ-ός, ὁ truffle (2a)
γεωμετρί-α, ἡ geometry (1b)
γῆς of the earth
δῆμ-ος, ὁ deme (2a)
δικαστ-ής, ὁ dikast, juror (1d)
ἐ-βόησ-ας you (s.) shouted
   (βοά-ω)
ἐγγὺς ἡμῶν near to us
ἐ-θαύμασ-ας you (s.) were
   amazed (θαυμάζ-ω)

ἐνταῦθα here
ἐπεὶ since
ἐπὶ τῆς κρεμάθρας in the
   basket
Εὔβοι-α, ἡ Euboia (1b)
Ἡράκλεις Herakles!
θαυμάζ-ω be amazed
θηρί-ον, τό beast (2b)
καθ-ίζομαι sit down
κατὰ γῆς below the earth
Λακεδαίμων (Λακεδαιμον-), ἡ
   Sparta (3a)
μοι to me
ὀλοφυρ-εῖσθ' = 2nd pl. fut.
   (contr.) of ὀλοφύρ-ομαι
ὅπου where?
οὐραν-ός, ὁ sky (2a)
πάνυ very
παπαῖ good heavens!

πείθ-ομαι believe
περί-οδ-ος, ἡ map (2a)
πόρρω far
πρωκτ-ός, ὁ rump (2a)
ταύτῃ with this
χρήσιμ-ος -η -ον useful

Vocabulary to be learnt
ἀδύνατος ον *impossible*
Ἀθῆναι, αἱ *Athens (1a)*
δῆμος, ὁ *deme (2a)*
θαυμάζω *wonder at, be*
   amazed at
ὅπου *where? where*
οὐρανός, ὁ *sky, heavens (2a)*
πείθομαι (πιθ-) *believe, trust,*
   obey

The range of sophists' work

[See note on the sophists on p. 57]

The sophists both helped to create a demand for education, and also came when there was an unfulfilled need for it. They taught a vast variety of subjects—from astronomy and law through to mathematics and rhetoric. It is in large measure due to the sophists that subjects such as grammar, logic, ethics, politics, physics and metaphysics first emerged as separate entities. The sophists were at the head of a movement to make man, not the physical world, the centre of intellectual debate. If their main preoccupation was to describe how man could be most successful in life, rather than with questions of right and wrong of the sort that Socrates and Plato insisted upon, this does not undermine their intellectual importance.

Much work was going on in other fields at this time too. If our sources can be trusted, technical manuals were written by Sophocles on tragedy, by Iktinos on the Parthenon, by Polykleitos on the symmetry of the human body, and by Hippodamos (who designed the layout of the Peiraeus) on town planning and social engineering. Rudimentary experimental work in sciences may also have been going on, if we wish so to interpret the evidence of Aristophanes' *Clouds*. When the rustic Strepsiades is introduced into Socrates' private school (φροντιστήριον or 'think tank'), he finds all sorts of extraordinary devices cluttering up the place … These cosmic models (celestial globes? star maps? compasses? maps?) are an important feature of the play, where the association between the new thought and its various trappings is constantly being made. It suggests that the use of models and apparatus, generally seen as a later, post-Aristotelian device, was understood well enough in fifth-century Athens to be made the subject of comic humour. (*World of Athens*, 8.23–4)

C

(ἀπέρχεται ὁ μαθητής. ὁ Στρεψιάδης τὸν Σωκράτη καλεῖ.)

ΣΤΡΕΨ.	ὦ Σώκρατες, ὦ Σωκρατίδιον, δεῦρ᾽ ἐλθέ.
ΣΩΚ.	τίς ἐβόησε; τίς ἐβιάσατο εἰς τὸ φροντιστήριον τὸ τῶν σοφιστῶν;
ΣΤΡΕΨ.	ἐβόησα ἐγώ, Στρεψιάδης Κικυννόθεν. ἀλλ᾽ οὐκ ἐβιασάμην εἰς τὸ
	φροντιστήριον.
ΣΩΚ.	τί με καλεῖς, ὦ ἐφήμερε; ἦλθες δὲ σὺ κατὰ⌢τί;
ΣΤΡΕΨ.	ἦλθον μαθητὴς εἰς τὸ φροντιστήριον. ἤδη γάρ σε ἤκουσα ὡς εἶ σοφός.
ΣΩΚ.	εἰπέ μοι, τίς εἶπε τοῦτο; πῶς δ᾽ ἤκουσάς με ὡς σοφός εἰμι;
ΣΤΡΕΨ.	εἶπε τοῦτο τῶν μαθητῶν τις.
ΣΩΚ.	τί δ᾽ εἶπεν ὁ μαθητής; λέγε.
ΣΤΡΕΨ.	εἶπε γάρ ὁ μαθητὴς ὡς ψύλλα τις ἔδακε τὴν Χαιρεφῶντος ὀφρῦν. εἶτα ἐπὶ
	τὴν σὴν κεφαλὴν ἐπήδησε. σὺ δὲ τὸν Χαιρεφῶντα ἤρου ὁπόσους⌢τοὺς⌢ἐ
	αὐτῆς⌢πόδας ἐπήδησεν ἡ ψύλλα. ἀν-εμετρήσατε δ᾽ ὑμεῖς οὕτως· πρῶτον
	μὲν γὰρ τὴν ψύλλαν ἐλάβετε καὶ ἔθετε εἰς κηρὸν θερμόν. ἐπειδὴ δὲ ψυχρὸς
	ἐγένετο ὁ κηρός, ἡ ψύλλα ἔσχεν ἐμβάδας τινὰς Περσικάς. εἶτα δὲ ἀν-
	εμετρήσατε τὸ χωρίον.
	(*with an admiring glance*)
	οὐδέποτε εἶδον ἔγωγε πρᾶγμα οὕτω σοφόν.
ΣΩΚ.	οὐδέποτε εἶδες σύ γε πρᾶγμα οὕτω σοφόν; ἀλλὰ πόθεν ὢν
	τυγχάνεις;
ΣΤΡΕΨ.	Κικυννόθεν.
ΣΩΚ.	οὐ γὰρ ἔλαθές με ἄγροικος ὤν, καὶ ἀμαθής.
ΣΤΡΕΨ.	μὴ μέμφου μοι. ἀλλ᾽ εἰπέ, τί δρᾷς ἐπὶ⌢ταύτης⌢τῆς⌢κρεμάθρας ὤν, ὦ
	Σώκρατες;
ΣΩΚ.	(*solemnly*)
	ἀεροβατῶ καὶ περιφρονῶ τὸν ἥλιον.
ΣΤΡΕΨ.	τί δ᾽ ἀπὸ κρεμάθρας τοῦτο δρᾷς, ἀλλ᾽ οὐκ ἀπὸ τῆς⌢γῆς; τί ἐξευρίσκεις ἢ τί
	μανθάνεις, ἐπὶ⌢κρεμάθρας ὤν;
ΣΩΚ.	οὐδέποτε γὰρ ἐξηῦρον ἐγώ τὰ μετέωρα πράγματα οὐδ᾽ ἔμαθον οὐδέν, ἀπὸ
	τῆς⌢γῆς σκοπῶν. ἡ γὰρ γῆ ἔτυχε κωλύουσα τὴν φροντίδα.

5

10

15

20

25

30

Vocabulary for Section Six C

> **Grammar for 6C–D**
> - Second aorist indicative, active and middle: ἔλαβον, ἐλαβόμην
> - Interrogatives: τί
> - Indirect speech

ἀερο-βατέ-ω tread the air	βιάζ-ομαι use force, force one's	ἔ-δακ-ε (it) bit (δάκν-ω)
ἀ-μαθής ignorant (nom.)	way	ἔ-θε-τε you (pl.) put (τίθημι)
ἀνα-μετρέ-ω measure up	δρά-ω do	εἶδ-ον (I) saw (ὁρά-ω)
ἀπ-έρχ-ομαι depart	ἐ-γέν-ετο (it) became (γίγν-ομαι)	εἶδ-ες (you) (s.) saw (ὁρά-ω)

εἶπ-ε (he) said (λέγ-ω)
εἶτα then, next
ἐ-λάβ-ετε you (pl.) took
   (λαμβάν-ω)
ἔ-λαθ-ες you (s.) escaped the
   notice of (λανθάν-ω)
ἔ-μαθ-ον (I) learnt (μανθάν-ω)
ἐμβάς (ἐμβαδ-), ἡ slipper (3a)
ἐξ-ευρίσκ-ω (ἐξευρ-) find out,
   discover
ἐξ-ηῦρ-ον (I) found out,
   discovered (ἐξ-ευρίσκ-ω)
ἐπὶ κρεμάθρας in a basket
ἐπὶ ταύτης τῆς κρεμάθρας in this
   basket
ἔ-σχ-ε(ν) (it) had (ἔχ-ω)
ἔ-τυχ-ε (it) happened to, actually
   was (τυγχάν-ω)
ἐφ-ήμερ-ος -ον lasting a day,
   creature of a day
ἦλθ-ον I came (ἔρχ-ομαι)
ἦλθ-ες (you) (s.) came
   (ἔρχ-ομαι)
ἥλι-ος, ὁ sun (2a)
ἤρ-ου you (s.) asked (ἐρωτά-ω)

θερμ-ός -ή -όν hot
κατὰ τί ; for what?
κηρ-ός, ὁ wax (2a)
Κικυννόθεν from the deme
   Kikynna
κρεμάθρας a basket
μέμφ-ομαι blame, find fault with
μετέωρ-ος -ον in the air
μοι me
ὁπόσους τοὺς ἑαυτῆς πόδας how
   many of its own foot lengths
οὐδὲν λέγ-ω speak nonsense
οὐδέποτε never
περι-φρονέ-ω surround with
   thought, circumcontemplate
Περσικ-ός -ή -όν Persian
πηδά-ω leap
πρῶτον first
σ-ός σ-ή σ-όν your
Σωκρατίδι-ον dear Socrates (2b)
τῆς γῆς the earth
τί; why?
φροντιστήρι-ον, τό think-tank,
   mental institute (2b)
Χαιρεφῶντος of Khairephon

χωρί-ον, τό space, distance (2b)
ψύλλ-α, ἡ flea (1c)
ψυχρ-ός -ά -όν cold
ὡς that

Vocabulary to be learnt

ἀπέρχομαι (ἀπελθ-) *depart, go
   away*
βιάζομαι *use force*
εἶτα *then, next*
ἐξευρίσκω (ἐξευρ-) *find out*
ἥλιος, ὁ *sun (2a)*
ὁπόσος η ον *how many, much*
πηδάω *leap, jump*
πόρρω *far, far off*
πρῶτος η ον *first*
πρῶτον *first, at first*
Σωκράτης, ὁ *Socrates (3d)*
τί; *why?*
(τίθημι) θε- *put, place*
χωρίον, τό *place, space, region
   (2b)*

Misrepresenting intellectuals

As we have already observed, the Socrates of *Clouds* bears little relationship to the real Socrates (see p. 57). The reason for Aristophanes' portrayal of him in this fashion is probably that, since Aristophanes was a comic poet aiming to win first prize at the comic festival, he had to appeal to the prejudices of his audience. In the same way that 'professors' today are popularly caricatured as 'mad', with their heads in the clouds (an image as old as Aristophanes) and wholly divorced from 'real life', so in Aristophanic Athens it was typical of comic poets to present 'intellectuals' as dotty in one sense or another. After all, the story was told of one of the most famous intellectuals of all, Thales (*Text* 6A, l.45–6), that he spent so much time contemplating the heavens that he did not spot the well in front of him and promptly fell in. Further, the Greek man-in-the-street seems to have found it very hard to swallow the idea that men who tried to think rationally and 'scientifically' about the cosmos were not somehow subverting traditional religious beliefs and therefore conventional piety. Thus intellectuals, whatever they actually believed, were fair game to be mocked, and in the streets of Athens Socrates was probably the most famous intellectual of them all.

D

ΣΤΡΕΨ.	ἀλλ᾽ ὦ Σωκρατίδιον, τί οὐ καταβαίνεις; ἦλθον γὰρ ἐγὼ εἰς τὸ φροντιστήριον διότι, χρήματα πολλὰ ὀφείλων, ὑπόχρεώς εἰμι.
ΣΩΚ.	ἀλλὰ πῶς σὺ ὑπόχρεως ἐγένου; πῶς τοῦτο πάσχεις;
ΣΤΡΕΨ.	ἔλαθον ἐμαυτὸν ἱππομανῆ τὸν υἱὸν ἔχων. ὑπόχρεως οὖν ἐγενόμην.

καὶ τοῦτο ἔπαθον διὰ τὴν ἱππικὴν καὶ διὰ τὸν ἐμὸν υἱόν. ἀεὶ γὰρ δίκας   5
λαμβάνουσιν οἱ χρῆσται, καὶ εἰ μή τι ποιήσω, εἰς ἀεὶ λήψονται. δίδασκε
οὖν με τὸν ἕτερον τῶν σῶν λόγων.

ΣΩΚ.	τὸν ἕτερον τῶν ἐμῶν λόγων; πότερον λέγεις; τὸν κρείττονα ἢ τὸν ἥττονα;
ΣΤΡΕΨ.	τὸν ἄδικον λέγω, τὸν ἥττονα, τὸν τὰ χρέα παύοντα. οὗτος γὰρ ὁ λόγος

τὰς δίκας νικήσει, ὁ κρείττων δ᾽ οὔ. τί δράσω;   10

ΣΩΚ.	(*points to a couch*)

ὅ τι; πρῶτον μὲν κατακλίνηθι ἐπὶ‿τῆς‿κλίνης. ἔπειτα ἐκφρόντιζέ τι τῶν
σεαυτοῦ πραγμάτων.

ΣΤΡΕΨ.	(*sees the bugs*)

κακοδαίμων ἐγώ. δίκην γὰρ λήψονται οἱ κόρεις τήμερον.   15

He lies down. There is a long pause. Eventually . . .

ΣΩΚ.	οὗτος, τί ποιεῖς; οὐχὶ φροντίζεις;
ΣΤΡΕΨ.	ἐγώ; νή τὸν Ποσειδῶ.
ΣΩΚ.	καὶ τί δῆτ᾽ ἐφρόντισας;
ΣΤΡΕΨ.	εἰ‿ἄρα λήσω τοὺς κόρεις, τοὺς δάκνοντας ἐμὲ δεινῶς. 20
ΣΩΚ.	(*with annoyance*)

οὐδὲν‿λέγεις.

(*another long pause*)

ἀλλὰ σιγᾷ ὁ ἄνθρωπος. τί δρᾷ οὗτος;   25

(τὸν Στρεψιάδη προσαγορεύει)

οὗτος, καθεύδεις;

ΣΤΡΕΨ.	μὰ τὸν Ἀπόλλω, ἐγὼ μὲν οὔ.
ΣΩΚ.	ἔχεις τι;
ΣΤΡΕΨ.	μὰ Δι᾽ οὐ δῆτ᾽ ἔγωγε.
ΣΩΚ.	οὐδὲν πάνυ; 30
ΣΤΡΕΨ.	τὸ πέος ἔχω ἐν τῇ‿δεξιᾷ.
ΣΩΚ.	εἰς κόρακας. μὴ παῖζε, ὦ ᾽νθρωπε.

(*after a long pause*)

ΣΤΡΕΨ.	ὦ Σωκρατίδιον.
ΣΩΚ.	τί, ὦ γέρον; 35
ΣΤΡΕΨ.	ἔχω γνώμην τινά.
ΣΩΚ.	λέγε τὴν γνώμην.
ΣΤΡΕΨ.	λήψομαι γυναῖκα φαρμακίδα καὶ κλέψω ἐν νυκτὶ τὴν σελήνην.
ΣΩΚ.	(*puzzled*)

τί φής; κλέψεις τὴν σελήνην; εἰπὲ δή – πῶς τοῦτο χρήσιμον;   40

ΣΤΡΕΨ.   ὅπως; ἄκουε. οἱ γὰρ χρῆσται δανείζουσι τὰ χρήματα κατὰ μῆνα. ἐγὼ
μὲν οὖν κλέψω τὴν σελήνην. ἡ δὲ σελήνη οὐκέτι ἀνατελεῖ. πῶς οὖν τὰ
χρήματα λήψονται οἱ χρῆσται;

ΣΩΚ.   (*very annoyed*)
βάλλ᾽ εἰς κόρακας. ἄγροικος εἶ καὶ ἀμαθής. οὐ διδάξω σ᾽ οὐκέτι, ἀμαθῆ   45
δὴ ὄντα.

Strepsiades goes back out into the street, and sadly contemplates his fate.

Vocabulary for Section Six D

ἀ-μαθής ignorant (nom.)
ἀ-μαθῆ ignorant (acc.)
ἀνα-τελ-εῖ (it) will rise (fut. of
   ἀνα-τέλλ-ω)
Ἀπόλλων (Ἀπολλων-), ὁ Apollo
   (3a) (acc. Ἀπόλλω)
γέρων (γεροντ-), ὁ old man (3a)
γνώμ-η, ἡ plan (1a)
δανείζ-ω lend (money)
δῆτα then; indeed
δρά-ω (δρασ-) do, act
ἐ-γεν-όμην I became (γίγν-ομαι)
ἐ-γέν-ου (you) (s.) became
   (γίγν-ομαι)
εἰ if
εἰ ἄρα whether, indeed
ἐκφροντίζ-ω think out
ἔ-λαθ-ον I escaped notice
   (λανθάν-ω)
ἐμαυτ-ὸν myself (acc)
ἔ-παθ-ον I experienced, suffered
   (πάσχ-ω)
ἐπὶ τῆς κλίνης on the couch
ἕτερ-ος -α -ον the one (of 2)
ἦλθ-ον (I) came (ἔρχ-ομαι)
ἥττων ἧττον (ἡττον-) weaker,
   lesser
ἱππικ-ή, ἡ horse-fever (1a)
ἱππο-μανῆ horse-mad (acc.)
κατα-κλίνηθι lie down! (s.)

κλέπτω steal
κόρ-ις, ὁ bug (3e)
κρείττων κρεῖττον (κρειττον-)
   stronger, greater
λήσ-ω I shall escape notice
   (fut. of λανθάν-ω)
μὴ not
μὴν (μην-), ὁ month (3a)
νυκτὶ at night
ὅπως; how?
ὅτι; what?
οὗτος, hey, you!
πάνυ at all
πέ-ος, τό penis (3c)
πότερ-ος -α -ον which (of two)?
προσ-αγορεύ-ω address
σεαυτοῦ your own
σελήν-η, ἡ moon (1a)
σιγά-ω be quiet
σ-ός σ-ή σ-όν your
Σωκρατίδι-ον dear Socrates (2b)
τῇ δεξιᾷ right hand
τήμερον today
ὑπο-χρέ-ως -ων in debt
φαρμακίς (φαρμακιδ-), ἡ witch,
   sorceress (3a)
φροντιστήρι-ον, τό think-tank,
   mental institute (2b)
χρήσιμ-ος -η -ον useful
χρήστ-ης, ὁ creditor (1d)

Vocabulary to be learnt
ἀμαθής *ignorant*
ἄρα *then, in that case*
   (inferring)
γέρων (γεροντ-), ὁ *old man*
   (3a)
γνώμη, ἡ *mind, purpose,*
   judgment, plan (1a)
δεξιός ά όν *right*
δεξιά, ἡ *right hand (1b)*
δῆτα *then*
δράω (δρᾶσ-) *do, act*
εἰ *if, whether*
ἐμαυτόν *myself*
ἕτερος ᾱ ον *one (or the other)*
   of two
ἥττων ἧττον (ἡττον-) *lesser,*
   weaker
κλέπτω *steal*
κρείττων κρεῖττον (κρειττον-)
   stronger, greater
οὗτος, *hey there! hey you!*
πάνυ *very (much); at all*
πότερος ᾱ ον *which (of two)*
σελήνη, ἡ *moon (1a)*
σός σή σόν *your (when 'you' are*
   one person)
τήμερον *today*
χρήσιμος η ον *useful,*
   profitable

Section Seven A–H: Socrates and intellectual inquiry

Introduction

Plato's picture of Socrates is quite different from Aristophanes'. The following passage is based on Plato's account of Socrates' defence when he was on trial for his life (399 BC) on a charge of corrupting the young and introducing new gods. This famous speech is known as 'The Apology': Greek ἀπολογία, 'defence'.

In *World of Athens*: lawcourts 6.39ff.; Delphi and the oracle 3.17–19; speeches 8.17–21; Socratic 'ignorance' 8.35; Socrates' contribution to philosophy 8.34.

Δελφοί

ὁ θεὸς ὁ ἐν Δελφοῖς

Socrates

Socrates emerges from all the descriptions as a great arguer, concerned with both clarity and precision of thought. Aristotle attributes to him the systematic use of 'inductive argument and general definition'. One must beware of the modern associations of the word 'induction', and 'argument from example' is a better translation. The argument 'leads you on' (the literal meaning of the Greek word for 'induction') by observation of particular instances of e.g. 'goodness' to understand the general characteristics of that quality – and so to a 'general definition'. Socrates was looking for precision and definite standards. If you want to be good or brave you must first know what goodness or bravery is; so, in a sense, goodness is knowledge, and it should be possible to be as *precise* about moral virtue as a carpenter is about what makes a good chair. Socrates pursued his general definition in *dialogue* with others, and the word 'dialectic' (which Plato was to use as a term for philosophy) is derived from the Greek word for dialogue. Plato portrays Socrates arguing against the relativism and scepticism, which characterised much of sophistic thought, and looking for a precision about definitions of moral virtues of the sort that existed in the technical world. Plato's Socrates is looking for some kind of stable reality and standard behind the confusion of perceptions and standards in the world of common experience. (*World of Athens*, 8.34–5)

A

Socrates addresses the dikasts (jurors) at his trial and tells them the reason for his methods of inquiry and the causes of his unpopularity. He first puts a question into the mouths of the dikasts which he will proceed to answer.

ἐρωτῶσιν οὖν τινες· 'ἀλλ', ὦ Σώκρατες, διὰ τί διαβάλλουσί σε οὗτοι οἱ ἄνδρες; τί ἐν νῷ ἔχουσιν; πόθεν γίγνονται αὗται αἱ διαβολαὶ καὶ ἡ δόξα ἡ σή; λέγε οὖν, καὶ δίδασκε ἡμᾶς. ἡμεῖς γὰρ οὐ βουλόμεθα διαβάλλειν σε.' βούλομαι οὖν διδάσκειν ὑμᾶς καὶ λέγειν διὰ τί διέβαλόν με οὗτοι οἱ ἄνδρες καὶ πόθεν ἐγένοντο αἱ διαβολαὶ καὶ ἡ δόξα. ἀκούετε δή. καὶ εὖ ἴστε ὅτι οὐ βούλομαι παίζειν πρὸς ὑμᾶς. ἴσως μὲν γὰρ   5
φανοῦμαι παίζειν, εὖ μέντοι ἴστε ὅτι οὐδὲν ἄλλο ἢ τὴν ἀλήθειαν λέγειν βούλομαι.

ἐγὼ γάρ, ὦ ἄνδρες Ἀθηναῖοι, διὰ σοφίαν τινὰ τυγχάνω ἔχων τὴν δόξαν ταύτην. ἆρα βούλεσθε εἰδέναι τίς ἐστιν ἡ σοφία αὕτη; ὡς μάρτυρα βούλομαι παρέχεσθαι τὸν θεὸν τὸν ἐν Δελφοῖς. ὁ γὰρ θεὸς ὁ ἐν Δελφοῖς μαρτυρήσει τὴν σοφίαν τὴν ἐμήν. καὶ μὴν ἀνάγκη ἐστὶ τὸν θεὸν λέγειν τὴν ἀλήθειαν.   10

Χαιρεφῶντα γὰρ ἴστε που. οὗτος γὰρ ἐμὸς ἑταῖρος ἦν ἐκ νέου. καὶ ἴστε δή, ὡς σφοδρὸς ἦν ὁ Χαιρεφῶν περὶ πάντα. καὶ ὁ Χαιρεφῶν οὕτως ποτὲ ἐλογίζετο πρὸς ἑαυτόν. 'ὅτι Σωκράτης σοφός ἐστιν, εὖ οἶδα. βούλομαι δ' εἰδέναι εἴ τίς ἐστι σοφώτερος ἢ Σωκράτης. ἴσως γὰρ Σωκράτης σοφώτατός ἐστιν ἀνθρώπων. τί οὖν ποιεῖν με δεῖ; δῆλον ὅτι δεῖ με εἰς Δελφοὺς ἰέναι, καὶ μαντεύεσθαι. πολλὴ γὰρ   15
ἀνάγκη ἐστὶ τὸν θεὸν τὴν ἀλήθειαν λέγειν.'

ᾔει οὖν ὁ Χαιρεφῶν εἰς Δελφούς, καὶ ταύτην τὴν μαντείαν ἐμαντεύσατο παρὰ τῷ θεῷ. καὶ μὴ θορυβεῖτε, ὦνδρες. ἤρετο γὰρ δὴ εἴ τίς ἐστι σοφώτερος ἢ Σωκράτης, ἀπεκρίνατο δ' ἡ Πυθία ὅτι οὐδείς ἐστι σοφώτερος.

Vocabulary for Section Seven A

> **Grammar for 7A–C**
> - Present infinitives, active and middle: παύειν, παύεσθαι
> - Irregular present infinitives: εἶναι, ἰέναι, εἰδέναι
> - Verbs taking infinitives (e.g. βούλομαι, δεῖ, δοκέω)
> - Comparative and superlative adjectives, regular and irregular
> - Past of εἶμι: ᾖα 'I went'

ἀλήθει-α, ἡ truth (1b)
ἀνάγκ-η, ἡ necessity (1a)
ἀνάγκ-η ἐστί it is obligatory for x (acc.) to – (inf.)
ἀπο-κρίν-ομαι (ἀποκριν-) answer
βούλ-ομαι wish, want
γὰρ δή I assure you; indeed
γὰρ . . . που of course (no need to ask)

δεῖ it is necessary for x (acc.) to – (inf.)
Δελφ-οί, οἱ Delphi (2a) *(site of Apollo's oracle)*
Δελφοῖς Delphi
δια-βάλλ-ειν to slander
δια-βάλλ-ω (διαβαλ-) slander
δια-βολ-ή, ἡ a slander (1a)
διδάσκ-ειν to teach

δι-έ-βαλ-ον they slandered (aor. of διαβάλλ-ω)
δόξ-α, ἡ reputation (1c)
ἑαυτ-όν himself
εἰδέναι to know (οἶδα)
ἑταῖρ-ος, ὁ friend (2a)
ἤ than
ἤ-ει (he) went (impf. of ἔρχ-ομαι/εἶμι)
θορυβέ-ω make a din

ἰέναι to go (ἔρχ-ομαι/εἶμι)
ἴσως perhaps
καὶ μὴν moreover
λέγ-ειν to speak, say, tell
    (λέγ-ω)
λογίζ-ομαι reckon, consider
μαντεί-α, ἡ answer,
    pronouncement (1b)
μαντεύ-εσθαι to consult the
    oracle
μαντεύ-ομαι get from the
    oracle
μαρτυρέ-ω bear witness
μάρτυς (μαρτυρ-), ὁ witness
    (3a)
μέντοι however
νέου youth

παίζ-ειν to joke, to poke fun at
    (παίζ-ω)
πάντα everything (acc.)
παρὰ τῷ θεῷ in the god's
    presence
παρ-έχ-εσθαι to present
    (παρ-έχ-ομαι)
ποι-εῖν to do (ποιέ-ω)
ποτέ once
Πυθί-α, ἡ the Pythian priestess
    (1b) (who sat on a tripod and
    delivered Apollo's oracle
    to the priest, who interpreted
    it)
σοφί-α, ἡ wisdom (1b)
σοφώτατ-ος -η -ον wisest
    (σοφ-ός)

σοφώτερ-ος -α -ον wiser
    (σοφ-ός)
σφοδρ-ός -ά -όν impetuous
φαν-οῦμαι I shall appear (fut. of
    φαίν-ομαι)

Vocabulary to be learnt
ἀλήθεια, ἡ *truth (1b)*
βούλομαι *wish, want*
διαβάλλω (διαβαλ-) *slander*
δόξα, ἡ *reputation, opinion
    (1c)*
ἑαυτόν *himself*
ἤ *than*
ἴσως *perhaps*
σοφίᾱ, ἡ *wisdom (1b)*

The oracle at Delphi

When states as well as individuals needed advice or help, not just in times of national emergency but to cope with everyday occurrences, they would send to an oracle. The Sanctuary of Apollo at Delphi was home to the most influential oracle … It is important to stress that the function of an oracle was not to foretell the future, but to advise. It is inevitable that, if the advice was good, the oracle would get the reputation for being *able* to foretell the future, but that was not its function. What oracles offered was insight into the will of the gods; and the regular form of consultation involved asking the god which choice of possible policies was better, or what appropriate rituals should attend it. Generally speaking (and discounting for the moment myth and legend), the oracle at, for example, Delphi, spoke directly to questioners in perfectly plain and simple terms. There is no good evidence that in the fifth century the Delphic prophetess (Pythia) was in a state of babbling ecstasy … That said, there was a strong *literary* tradition, in both myth and the early history of Greece, that oracles were opaque and tended to deceive (the philosopher Herakleitos said 'The lord whose oracle is in Delphi does not speak and does not conceal: instead, he sends a sign'). Herodotos tells of the oracle given to the Athenians as the Persians advanced on the city that Zeus would grant them a wooden wall as a stronghold for themselves and their children. But what did that mean? The oracle had to be given to special readers of oracles to interpret; and it is notable that the religious experts were in the end ignored when the people were persuaded by the politician Themistokles that wooden walls meant the fleet. The question of what to do was a *political* question, and it was settled in a political forum by the political expert. (*World of Athens*, 3.17–19)

B

ἐγὼ δέ, ἐπεὶ ἤκουσα, ἐλογιζόμην οὑτωσὶ πρὸς ἐμαυτόν· 'τί ποτε βούλεται λέγειν ὁ
θεός; ἐγὼ γὰρ δὴ οἶδα ὅτι σοφὸς οὔκ εἰμι. τί οὖν ποτε λέγει ὁ θεός, λέγων ὡς ἐγὼ
σοφώτατός εἰμι, καὶ ὡς οὐδεὶς σοφώτερος; οὐ γὰρ δήπου ψεύδεταί γε· οὐ γὰρ
θέμις αὐτῷ. ἀνάγκη γάρ ἐστι τὸν θεὸν οὐδὲν ἄλλο ἢ τὴν ἀλήθειαν λέγειν.' καὶ
πολὺν μὲν χρόνον ἠπόρουν τί ποτε λέγει, ἔπειτα δὲ ἐπὶ ζήτησιν ἐτραπόμην πότερον   5
ἀληθῆ λέγει ὁ θεός, ἢ οὔ. οὐ γὰρ ἐβουλόμην ἐν ἀπορίᾳ εἶναι περὶ τὸ μαντεῖον.

ἦλθον οὖν ἐπὶ σοφόν τινα (ἐδόκει γοῦν σοφὸς εἶναι). ἐβουλόμην γὰρ ἐλέγχειν τὸ
μαντεῖον καὶ ἀποφαίνειν ὅτι 'σὺ μέν, ὦ Ἄπολλον, ἔλεγες ὅτι ἐγὼ σοφώτατος, οὗτος δὲ
σοφώτερός ἐστιν.' διελεγόμην οὖν ἐγὼ πρὸς τοῦτον τὸν σοφόν, πολιτικόν τινα ὄντα. ὁ
δ' ἀνήρ, ὡς ἐγὼ ᾤμην, ἔδοξέ γε σοφὸς εἶναι, οὐκ ὤν. καὶ ἐπειδὴ ἐπειρώμην ἀποφαίνειν   10
αὐτὸν δοκοῦντα σοφὸν εἶναι, οὐκ ὄντα, οὗτος καὶ πολλοὶ τῶν παρόντων ἐμίσουν με.
πρὸς ἐμαυτὸν οὖν οὕτως ἐλογιζόμην, ὅτι 'ἐγὼ σοφώτερός εἰμι ἢ οὗτος. οὗτος μὲν γὰρ
δοκεῖ τι εἰδέναι, οὐδὲν εἰδώς, ἐγὼ δέ, οὐδὲν εἰδώς, οὐδὲ δοκῶ εἰδέναι.' ἐντεῦθεν ἐπ'
ἄλλον τινὰ σοφὸν ᾖα, καὶ ἐδόκει καὶ ἐκεῖνός τι εἰδέναι, οὐκ εἰδώς. ἐντεῦθεν δὲ καὶ
ἐκεῖνος καὶ ἄλλοι τῶν παρόντων ἐμίσουν με.   15

μετὰ ταῦτα οὖν ᾖα ἐπὶ τοὺς ἄλλους τοὺς δοκοῦντάς τι εἰδέναι. καὶ νὴ τὸν κύνα,
οἱ μὲν δοκοῦντές τι εἰδέναι ἦσαν μωρότεροι, ὡς ἐγὼ ᾤμην, οἱ δ' οὐδὲν δοκοῦντες
εἰδέναι σοφώτεροι. μετὰ γὰρ τοὺς πολιτικοὺς ᾖα ἐπὶ τοὺς ποιητάς. αἰσχύνομαι δὲ
λέγειν τὴν ἀλήθειαν, ὦνδρες, ὅμως δὲ λέγειν με δεῖ. οὐ γὰρ διὰ σοφίαν ποιοῦσιν οἱ
ποιηταὶ τὰ ποιήματα, ἀλλὰ διὰ φύσιν καὶ ἐνθουσιασμόν, ὥσπερ οἱ θεομάντεις καὶ   20
οἱ χρησμῳδοί. καὶ γὰρ οὗτοι λέγουσι μὲν πολλὰ καὶ καλά, τοὺς δὲ λόγους τούτους
οὐκ ἴσασιν ὅ τι νοοῦσιν. καὶ ἅμα ἐδόκουν οἱ ποιηταὶ διὰ τὴν ποίησιν εἰδέναι τι, οὐκ
εἰδότες, καὶ σοφώτατοι εἶναι ἀνθρώπων, οὐκ ὄντες. ἀπῇα οὖν καὶ ἐγὼ ἐντεῦθεν,
σοφώτερος δοκῶν εἶναι ἢ οἱ ποιηταί.

χειροτέχναι

Vocabulary for Section Seven B

αἰσχύν-ομαι be ashamed
ἀνάγκ-η ἐστὶ it is obligatory for
  x (acc.) to – (inf.)
ἀπ-ῇ-α I went off (impf. of
  ἀπ-έρχ-ομαι/ἄπειμι)
Ἀπόλλων (Ἀπόλλων-), ὁ Apollo
  (3a) (acc. Ἀπόλλω)
ἀπορίᾳ perplexity
ἀποφαίν-ειν to reveal, to show
  (ἀπο-φαίν-ω)
αὐτῷ for him
γὰρ δή I am positive; really
γοῦν at any rate
δεῖ it is necessary for x (acc.) to
  – (inf.)
δοκέ-ω seem; consider oneself
  to – (+inf.)
εἰδέναι to know (οἶδα)
εἰδότ-ες knowing (nom.)
  (οἶδα)
εἰδ-ώς knowing (nom.) (οἶδα)
εἶναι to be (εἰμί)
ἐλέγχ-ειν to refute (ἐλέγχ-ω)
ἐν-θουσιασμ-ός, ὁ inspiration
  (2a)
ἐντεῦθεν from that point, from
  there
ἐπεὶ when

ᾖ-α I went (impf. of ἔρχ-ομαι/
  εἶμι)
ζήτησ-ις, ἡ inquiry (3e)
θέμις lawful (lit. θέμις, ἡ law of
  the gods [3a])
θεό-μαντ-ις, ὁ prophet (3e)
καὶ γὰρ for really
κύων (κυν-), ὁ dog (3a)
λέγ-ειν to say, to tell (λέγ-ω)
λογίζ-ομαι reckon, consider
μαντεῖ-ον, τό oracle (2b)
μετὰ (+acc.) after
μωρότερ-ος -α -ον more stupid
νοέ-ω mean
ὅμως nevertheless
ὅτι what
οὐ γὰρ δήπου . . . γε it can't be
  that. . .
οὑτωσὶ as follows
παρ-όντ-ες present (part. of
  πάρ-ειμι)
πειρά-ομαι try
ποίημα (ποιηματ-), τό poem (3b)
ποίησ-ις, ἡ poetry (3e)
ποιητ-ής, ὁ poet (1d)
πολιτικ-ός -ή -όν concerned
  with the city
ποτε ever

σοφώτατ-ος -η -ον wisest
  (σοφ-ός)
σοφώτερ-ος -α -ον wiser
  (σοφ-ός)
χρησμ-ῳδ-ός, ὁ soothsayer (2a)
χρόν-ος, ὁ time (2a)
φύσ-ις, ἡ nature (3e)
ψεύδ-ομαι tell lies
ᾤμην I thought (οἶμαι)
ὡς that

Vocabulary to be learnt
ἀνάγκη ἐστί it is obligatory (for
  X [acc. or dat].) to – (inf.)
ἀνάγκη, ἡ necessity (1a)
ἀποφαίνω reveal, show
γὰρ δή really; I assure you
δεῖ it is necessary for X (acc.) to
  – (inf.)
ἐντεῦθεν from then, from there
λογίζομαι reckon, calculate,
  consider
νοέω think, notice, mean,
  intend
πάρειμι be present, be at hand
ποιητής, ὁ poet (1d)
ποτε once, ever
ὡς that

The Socratic method – described by Socrates

Socrates always proclaimed himself ignorant. So here he likens what capacities
he has to those of a midwife - helping to bring ideas into the light:

'My art of midwifery is concerned with men and not women, and I am concerned with minds in labour, not bodies … And there is another point which I
have in common with the mid-wives—I cannot myself give birth to wisdom, and
the criticism which has so often been made of me, that though I ask questions of
others I have no contribution to make myself because I have no wisdom in me, is
quite true. The reason is that the god compels me to be midwife but forbids me to
give birth. So I am myself quite without wisdom nor has my mind produced any
original thought; but those who keep my company, though at first some of them
may appear quite ignorant, in due course will, if the god wills it, make what both
they and others think is marvellous progress. This is clearly not because of anything they have learned from me, but because they have made many marvellous
discoveries of themselves and given birth to them. But the delivery of them is my
work and the god's…' (Plato, *Theaitetos* 150b)

C

τέλος δ' ἐπὶ τοὺς χειροτέχνας ᾖα. ἤδη γὰρ ὅτι οὐδὲν οἶδα καὶ ὅτι οἱ χειροτέχναι
πολλὰ καὶ καλὰ ἴσασιν. πολλὰ οὖν εἰδότες, σοφώτεροι ἦσαν οἱ χειροτέχναι ἢ ἐγώ.
ἀλλ' ἔδοξαν, ὡς ἐγὼ ᾤμην, διὰ τὴν τέχνην σοφώτατοι εἶναι περὶ ἄλλα πολλά, οὐκ
ὄντες. τοιοῦτον⌐ οὖν ⌐πάθος ἐφαίνοντο καὶ οἱ ποιηταὶ καὶ οἱ χειροτέχναι πάσχοντες.
    ἐκ ταυτησὶ⌐ δὴ ⌐τῆς ζητήσεως, ὦ ἄνδρες Ἀθηναῖοι, ἐγένοντο αἱ ἐμαὶ διαβολαί,   5
βαρεῖαι δὴ οὖσαι, καὶ ἡ δόξα. καὶ δὴ καὶ οἱ νεανίαι, οἵ γε πλούσιοι ὄντες καὶ μάλιστα
σχολὴν ἔχοντες, ἥδονται ἀκούοντες τοὺς ἐμοὺς λόγους καὶ πολλάκις πειρῶνται
ἄλλους ἐξετάζειν, ὥσπερ ἐγώ. ὑβρισταὶ γὰρ οἱ νεανίαι καὶ μάλιστα ἥδονται
ἐξετάζοντες τοὺς πρεσβυτέρους. καί, ὡς ἐγὼ οἶμαι, ἐξετάζοντες εὑρίσκουσι πολὺ
πλῆθος τῶν δοκούντων μέν τι εἰδέναι, εἰδότων δ' ὀλίγα ἢ οὐδέν. ἐντεῦθεν οὖν οἱ   10
δοκοῦντές τι εἰδέναι ὀργίζονται καὶ λέγουσιν ὅτι 'Σωκράτης τίς ἐστι μιαρώτατος
καὶ διαφθείρει τοὺς νέους.' ἀλλ' ἐγὼ ἐρωτᾶν βούλομαι 'πῶς διαφθείρει τοὺς νέους
ὁ Σωκράτης; τί ποιῶν, ἢ τί διδάσκων, διαφθείρει αὐτούς;' ἔχουσι μὲν οὐδὲν λέγειν
ἐκεῖνοι, οὐ μέντοι βουλόμενοι δοκεῖν ἀπορεῖν, λέγουσιν ὅτι, ὥσπερ οἱ ἄλλοι
φιλόσοφοι, διδάσκει Σωκράτης 'τὰ μετέωρα καὶ τὰ ὑπὸ γῆς' καὶ 'θεοὺς μὴ νομίζειν'   15
καὶ 'τὸν ἥττονα λόγον κρείττονα ποιεῖν'. οὐ γὰρ βούλονται, ὡς ἐγὼ οἶμαι, τἀληθῆ
λέγειν, ὅτι κατάδηλοι γίγνονται δοκοῦντες μέν τι εἰδέναι, εἰδότες δ' οὐδέν.

Vocabulary for Section Seven C

ἀπορ-εῖν to be at a loss (ἀπορέ-ω)
βαρεῖ-αι serious (nom.)
δια-βολ-ή, ἡ slander (1a)
δια-φθείρ-ω corrupt
δοκ-εῖν to seem (δοκέ-ω)
δοκέ-ω seem; consider oneself
    to –
εἰδέναι to know (οἶδα)
εἰδότ-ες knowing (nom.) (οἶδα)
εἰδότ-ων knowing (gen.) (οἶδα)
εἶναι to be (εἰμί)
ἐξ-ετάζ-ειν to question closely
    (ἐξ-ετάζ-ω)
ἐξ-ετάζ-ω question closely
ἐρωτ-ᾶν to ask (ἐρωτά-ω)
εὑρίσκ-ω find, discover
ᾖ-α I went, came (impf. of
    ἔρχ-ομαι/εἶμι)
ἤδ-η I knew (past of οἶδα)
ἤδ-ομαι enjoy
κατά-δηλ-ος -ον obvious
λέγ-ειν to say, tell (λέγ-ω)
μέντοι however, but

μετέωρ-α, τά things in the air
    (2b)
μὴ not
μιαρώτατ-ος -η -ον most
    abominable (person)
    (μιαρ-ός)
νομίζ-ειν to acknowledge
    (νομίζ-ω)
οἶμαι think
ὀργίζ-ομαι get angry
πάθ-ος, τό experience (3c)
πειρά-ομαι try
πλούσι-ος -α -ον rich
ποι-εῖν to make (ποιέ-ω)
πολλάκις often
πρεσβύτερ-ος, ὁ older man (2a)
σοφώτατ-ος -η -ον wisest
    (σοφ-ός)
σοφώτερ-ος -α -ον wiser
    (σοφ-ός)
σχολ-ή, ἡ leisure (1a)
ταυτησὶ τῆς ζητήσεως this
    inquiry

τοιοῦτος τοιούτη τοιοῦτο(ν) . . .
    καί the same sort of . . . as
ὑβριστ-ής, ὁ bully (1d)
ὑπὸ γῆς beneath the earth
φιλό-σοφ-ος, ὁ philosopher (2a)
χειρο-τέχν-ης, ὁ craftsman (1d)
ᾤμην I thought (impf. of οἶμαι)

Vocabulary to be learnt
διαβολή, ἡ *slander (1a)*
διαφθείρω (διαφθειρα-) *corrupt;*
    kill; destroy
δοκέω *seem; consider oneself to –*
εἰδώς εἰδυῖα εἰδός (εἰδοτ-)
    knowing (part. of οἶδα)
εἶμι, *I shall go;* ἰέναι *to go;* ᾖα
    I went
ἐξετάζω *question closely*
εὑρίσκω (εὑρ-) *find, come upon*
μή *not; don't! (with imper.)*
οἶμαι *think (impf.* ᾤμην)
πειράομαι (πειρᾶσα-) *try, test*
πολλάκις *often*

D

Introduction

According to Plato, Socrates did not claim to teach, nor did he take fees for teaching, even though he was popularly linked, as we have seen from Aristophanes, with the sophists, who *were* professional teachers. One of the most important lessons offered by the sophists in their courses of higher education was the art of speaking with equal persuasion on both sides of a question, a facility which could be used unscrupulously. In the following incident Plato shows how empty such verbal dexterity could be.

In *World of Athens*: arguing both sides of the case 8.30; dissatisfaction with sophistic quibbling 5.47–9.

Socrates relates to his friend Kriton how he asked two sophists, Euthydemos and his brother Dionysodoros, to help a young man called Kleinias in his search for the truth. But Kleinias fell victim to Euthydemos' verbal trickery.

ἦλθον χθὲς εἰς τὸ Λύκειον, ὦ Κρίτων, καὶ κατέλαβον Εὐθύδημόν τε καὶ Διονυσόδωρον διαλεγομένους μετ᾽ ἄλλων πολλῶν. καὶ οἶσθα σύ γε ἀμφοτέρους τοὺς ἄνδρας, ὅτι καλὴν δόξαν ἔχουσι, προτρέποντες εἰς φιλοσοφίαν τοὺς ἀνθρώπους. ἐγὼ οὖν τοὺς ἐκείνων λόγους ἀκούειν βουλόμενος,

'ὑμεῖς ἄρα', ἦν δ᾽ ἐγώ, 'ὦ Διονυσόδωρε, δόξαν ἔχετε ὅτι προτρέπετε τοὺς   5
ἀνθρώπους εἰς φιλοσοφίαν καὶ ἀρετὴν ἢ οὔ;'
'δοκοῦμέν γε δή, ὦ Σώκρατες', ἦ δ᾽ ὅς.

Vocabulary for Section Seven D

> **Grammar for 7D–F**
> - First aorist participles, active and middle: παύσας, παυσάμενος
> - Aspect in participles
> - Past of οἶδα: ᾔδη 'I knew'
> - Present and past of φημί 'I say'

ἀμφότερ-οι -αι -α both
ἀρετ-ή, ἡ excellence, virtue (1a)
Διονυσόδωρ-ος, ὁ Dionysodoros (2a)
ἦν δ᾽ ἐγώ I said
ἦ δ᾽ ὅς he said

κατα-λαμβάν-ω (κατα-λαβ-) come upon
Λύκει-ον, τό Lykeion (2b) (*a training ground, where young and old met*)

μετ(ὰ) ἄλλων πολλῶν with many others
προ-τρέπ-ω urge, impel
φιλοσοφί-α, ἡ philosophy (1b)
χθές yesterday

‘εἶεν’, ἦν δ᾽ ἐγώ. ‘δεῖ οὖν ὑμᾶς προτρέπειν τουτονὶ τὸν νεανίσκον εἰς
φιλοσοφίαν καὶ ἀρετήν. καλοῦσι δ᾽ αὐτὸν Κλεινίαν. ἔστι δὲ νέος. ἀλλὰ διὰ τί οὐκ
ἐξετάζετε τὸν νεανίσκον, διαλεγόμενοι ἐνθάδε ἐναντίον ἡμῶν;’   10
    ὁ δ᾽ Εὐθύδημος εὐθὺς ἀνδρείως ἀπεκρίνατο·
‘βουλόμεθα δὴ ἐνθάδε διαλέγεσθαι, ὦ Σώκρατες. ἀλλὰ δεῖ τὸν νεανίσκον
ἀποκρίνεσθαι.’
    ‘ἀλλὰ μὲν δή⌐’, ἔφην ἐγώ, ‘ὅ γε Κλεινίας ἥδεται ἀποκρινόμενος. πολλάκις γὰρ
πρὸς αὐτὸν προσέρχονται οἱ φίλοι ἐρωτῶντες καὶ διαλεγόμενοι, ἀεὶ δὲ λέγοντα   15
αὐτὸν καὶ ἀποκρινόμενον ἐξετάζουσιν.’
    καὶ ὁ Εὐθύδημος, ‘ἄκουε οὖν, ὦ Κλεινία’, ἦ δ᾽ ὅς, ‘ἀκούσας δέ, ἀποκρίνου.’
    ὁ δὲ Κλεινίας, ‘ποιήσω τοῦτο’, ἦ δ᾽ ὅς, ‘καὶ ἀποκρινοῦμαι. ἥδομαι γὰρ ἔγωγε
ἀποκρινόμενος. λέγε οὖν, ὦ Εὐθύδημε, καὶ ἐξέταζε. λέγων γὰρ δήπου καὶ ἐξετάζων
ὁ σοφιστὴς προτρέπει τοὺς μαθητὰς εἰς ἀρετήν.’   20
    καὶ ὁ Εὐθύδημος ‘εἰπὲ οὖν’, ἔφη, ‘πότεροί εἰσιν οἱ μανθάνοντες, οἱ σοφοὶ ἢ οἱ
ἀμαθεῖς;’
    καὶ ὁ νεανίσκος – μέγα γὰρ ἔτυχεν ὂν τὸ ἐρώτημα – ἠπόρησεν. ἀπορήσας δ᾽
ἔβλεπεν εἰς ἐμέ, καὶ ἠρυθρίασεν.
    ἐγὼ δ᾽ ἐρυθριῶντα αὐτὸν ὁρῶν ‘μὴ φρόντιζε’, ἔφην, ‘μηδὲ φοβοῦ, ἀλλ᾽ ἀνδρείως   25
ἀποκρίνου.’
    καὶ ἐν τούτῳ ὁ Διονυσόδωρος ἐγέλασεν, γελάσας δέ,
‘καὶ μήν’, ἦ δ᾽ ὅς, ‘εὖ οἶδ᾽ ὅτι Εὐθύδημος αὐτὸν νικήσει λέγων.’
    καὶ ἐγὼ οὐκ ἀπεκρινάμην. ὁ γὰρ Κλεινίας, ἕως ταῦτα ἔλεγεν ὁ Διονυσόδωρος,
ἀποκρινάμενος ἔτυχεν ὅτι οἱ σοφοί εἰσιν οἱ μανθάνοντες.   30

ἀκούσ-ας upon hearing
    (nom. s. m.) (ἀκού-ω)
ἀλλὰ μὲν δὴ . . . γε but the fact
    is that. . .
ἀμαθεῖς ignorant (nom.)
ἀνδρεί-ως bravely
ἀπο-κρίν-ομαι answer (fut.
    ἀπο-κριν-οῦμαι)
ἀπο-κριν-άμεν-ος in answer,
    answering (ἀπο-κρίν-ομαι)
ἀπορήσ-ας on being at a loss
    (nom. s. m.) (ἀπορέ-ω)
ἀρετ-ή, ἡ excellence, virtue (1a)
γὰρ δήπου of course
γε δὴ certainly
γελά-ω (γελασ-) laugh
γελάσ-ας on laughing, with a
    laugh (nom. s. m.) (γελά-ω)

Διονυσόδωρ-ος, ὁ Dionysodoros
    (2a)
εἶεν well, all right then!
ἐναντίον ἡμῶν in front of us
ἐνθάδε here
ἐρυθριά-ω blush
ἐρώτημα (ἐρωτηματ-), τό
    question (3b)
Εὐθύδημ-ος, ὁ Euthydemos (2a)
εὐθύς at once
ἔ-φην (I) said (φημί)
ἔ-φη (he) said (φημί)
ἕως while
ἥδ-ομαι enjoy
ἦ δ᾽ ὅς he said
ἠρυθρίασ-εν see ἐρυθριά-ω
καὶ μὴν look here
Κλεινί-ας, ὁ Kleinias (1d)

Κρίτων (Κριτων-), ὁ Kriton (3a)
μηδὲ and don't
νεανίσκ-ος, ὁ young man (2a)
προ-τρέπ-ω urge, impel
τούτῳ this [interval of time]
φιλοσοφί-α, ἡ philosophy (1b)

Vocabulary to be learnt
ἀνδρεῖος ᾱ ον brave, manly
ἀποκρίνομαι (ἀποκρῑνα-) answer
ἀρετή, ἡ virtue, excellence (1a)
δήπου of course, surely
ἥδομαι enjoy, be pleased
ἦν δ᾽ ἐγώ I said
ἦ δ᾽ ὅς he said
νεανίσκος, ὁ young man (2a)
προτρέπω urge on, impel
φιλοσοφίᾱ, ἡ philosophy (1b)

E

Kleinias has answered that it is the clever who learn. But Euthydemos now exploits an ambiguity in the terms 'clever', 'ignorant', 'learner': a man may be clever either because he has learnt something, or because he is able to learn it. The same word covers both cases, and this gives Euthydemos room to manoeuvre.

καὶ ὁ Εὐθύδημος, 'ἀλλὰ τίς διδάσκει τοὺς μανθάνοντας', ἔφη, 'ὁ διδάσκαλος, ἢ ἄλλος τις;'
  ὡμολόγει ὅτι ὁ διδάσκαλος τοὺς μανθάνοντας διδάσκει.
  'καὶ ὅτε ὁ διδάσκαλος ἐδίδασκεν ὑμᾶς παῖδας ὄντας, ὑμεῖς μαθηταὶ ἦτε;'
  ὡμολόγει.   5
  'καὶ ὅτε μαθηταὶ ἦτε, οὐδὲν ᾖστέ πω;'
  'οὐ μὰ Δία. μαθηταὶ γὰρ ὄντες, οὐδὲν ᾖσμεν.'
  'ἆρ' οὖν σοφοὶ ἦτε, οὐκ εἰδότες οὐδέν;'
  'οὐ δῆτα σοφοὶ ἦμεν', ἦ δ' ὃς ὁ Κλεινίας, 'ἐπειδὴ οὐκ ᾖσμεν οὐδέν.'
  'οὐκοῦν εἰ μὴ σοφοί, ἀμαθεῖς;'   10
  'πάνυ γε.'
  'ὑμεῖς ἄρα, μαθηταὶ ὄντες, οὐκ ᾖστε οὐδέν, ἀλλ' ἀμαθεῖς ὄντες ἐμανθάνετε;'
  ὡμολόγει τὸ μειράκιον.
  'οἱ ἀμαθεῖς ἄρα μανθάνουσιν, ὦ Κλεινία, ἀλλ' οὐχὶ οἱ σοφοί, ὡς σὺ οἴῃ.'

ὁ διδάσκαλος τὸν μανθάνοντα διδάσκει

Vocabulary for Section Seven E

ἀμαθεῖς ignorant (nom.)
διδάσκαλ-ος, ὁ teacher (2a)
ἔ-φη (he) said (φημί)
ᾖσ-μεν we knew (past of οἶδα)
ᾖσ-τε you (pl.) knew (past of οἶδα)
μειράκι-ον, τό youth (2b)

πάνυ γε yes indeed
πω yet
ὡμο-λόγ-ει (he) agreed (ὁμο-λογέ-ω)

Vocabulary to be learnt
διδάσκαλος, ὁ *teacher (2a)*

ὁμολογέω *agree*
οὐκοῦν *therefore*
οὔκουν *not. . . therefore*

It is left for Dionysodoros to confuse Kleinias further, by turning the argument on its head.

ταῦτ' οὖν εἶπεν ὁ Εὐθύδημος. οἱ δὲ μαθηταί, ἅμα θορυβήσαντές τε καὶ γελάσαντες, τὴν σοφίαν ταύτην ἐπήνεσαν. καὶ ὥσπερ σφαῖραν εὐθὺς ἐξεδέξατο τὸν λόγον ὁ Διονυσόδωρος, ἐκδεξάμενος δέ,
   'τί δέ, ὦ Κλεινία;' ἔφη. 'καὶ δὴ λέγει ὁ διδάσκαλος λόγους τινάς. πότεροι μανθάνουσι τοὺς λόγους, οἱ σοφοὶ ἢ οἱ ἀμαθεῖς;'   5
   'οἱ σοφοί', ἦ δ' ὃς ὁ Κλεινίας.
   'οἱ σοφοὶ ἄρα μανθάνουσιν, ἀλλ' οὐχὶ οἱ ἀμαθεῖς, καὶ οὐκ εὖ σὺ ἄρτι ἀπεκρίνω.'
   ἐνταῦθα δὴ καὶ πάνυ γελάσαντές τε καὶ θορυβήσαντες, οἱ μαθηταὶ τὴν σοφίαν ταύτην εὐθὺς ἐπήνεσαν. ἡμεῖς δ' ἐν ἀπορίᾳ ἐμπίπτοντες, ἐσιωπῶμεν.

Vocabulary for Section Seven F

ἀμαθεῖς ignorant (nom.)	ἐνταῦθα at this point	**Vocabulary to be learnt**
ἀπορίᾳ perplexity	ἐπ-αινέ-ω praise (aor.	γελάω (γελασα-) *laugh*
ἄρτι just now	ἐπ-ήνεσ-α)	ἐκδέχομαι *receive in turn*
γελάσ-αντ-ες laughing, with	εὐθὺς at once	ἐμπίπτω (ἐμπεσ-) *fall into, on*
laughs (nom. pl. m.)	ἔ-φη (he) said (φημί)	(+ἐν or εἰς)
(γελά-ω)	θορυβήσ-αντ-ες making a	ἐπαινέω (ἐπαινεσα-) *praise*
ἐκ-δεξ-άμεν-ος receiving in turn	din, with a din (nom. pl. m.)	εὐθύς *at once, straightaway*
(ἐκ-δέχ-ομαι)	(θορυβέ-ω)	φημί/ἔφην *I say/I said*
ἐκ-δέχ-ομαι take up, receive in	καὶ δὴ let's suppose	
turn	σφαῖρ-α, ἡ ball (1b)	
ἐμ-πίπτ-ω fall into		

G

Introduction

The traditional view of universal standards relating to human behaviour and sanctioned by the gods was challenged by the ability of the sophists to present cogent arguments for both sides of a moral issue. It was also shaken as the Greeks became aware that other nations behaved and thought in ways entirely different from themselves. This interest is particularly reflected in the work of the Greek historian Herodotus (Ἡρόδοτος), from whose *Histories* the following story is taken. Herodotus assiduously collected stories of the different habits of foreign peoples and related them within the context of his main theme, the history of the Greek and Persian peoples that culminated in the Persian Wars.

In *World of Athens*: Herodotus 8.41, 9.3; *nomos-physis* 8.32, 9.7; Greek views of women 3.12, 4.22–4, 5.23–9; Greeks and barbarians 9.2ff.

*Although the Greeks conquer the Amazons in battle, their Amazon prisoners
take them by surprise on the voyage home.*

ὅτε δ' οἱ Ἕλληνες εἰσπεσόντες εἰς τὰς Ἀμαζόνας ἐμάχοντο, τότε δὴ οἱ Ἕλληνες
ἐνίκησαν αὐτὰς ἐν τῇ͜ μάχῃ. νικήσαντες δέ, τὰς Ἀμαζόνας τὰς ἐκ τῆς͜ μάχης
περιούσας ἔλαβον. λαβόντες δ' αὐτάς, ἀπῆλθον ἐν τρισὶ͜ πλοίοις· οὐ μέντοι
ἀφίκοντο εἰς τὴν πατρίδα. ἐν γὰρ τῇ͜ θαλάττῃ ὄντες οὐκ ἐφύλαξαν τὰς Ἀμαζόνας. αἱ

οἱ Σκύθαι

Vocabulary for Section Seven G

> **Grammar for 7G–H**
> - Second aorist participles, active and middle: λαβών, γενόμενος
> - Pronouns: αὐτός, ὁ αὐτός, αὐτόν; ἐμαυτόν, σεαυτόν, ἑαυτόν/αὐτόν
> - δύναμαι

Ἀμαζών (Ἀμαζον-), ἡ Amazon
  (3a)
ἀφ-ικ-όμεν-αι arriving (nom. pl.
  f.) (ἀφ-ικνέ-ομαι/
  ἀφ-ικ-όμην)
εἰσ-πεσ-όντ-ες attacking, falling
  upon (nom. pl. m.)
  (εἰσ-πίπτ-ω/εἰσ-έ-πεσ-ον)

ἰδ-οῦσ-αι upon seeing (nom.
  pl.f.) (ὁρά-ω/εἶδ-ον)
λαβ-όντ-ες upon taking (nom.
  pl. m.) (λαμβάν-ω/ἔ-λαβ-ον)
μάχ-η, ἡ fight, battle (1a)
μέντοι however, but
περι-ούσ-ας surviving (part. of
  περί-ειμι)

τῇ θαλάττῃ the sea
τρισὶ πλοίοις three ships
φυλάττ-ω guard

δ' Ἀμαζόνες, ἰδοῦσαι τοὺς ἄνδρας οὐ φυλάττοντας, ἀπέκτειναν. ἀλλ' οὐκ ἔμπειροι   5
ἦσαν περὶ τὰ ναυτικὰ αἱ Ἀμαζόνες. ἀποκτείνασαι οὖν τοὺς ἄνδρας ἔπλεον ἧπερ
ἔφερεν ὁ ἄνεμος.

τέλος δ' εἰς τὴν τῶν Σκυθῶν γῆν ἀφικόμεναι καὶ ἀποβᾶσαι ἀπὸ τῶν πλοίων,
ηὗρον ἱπποφόρβιον, καὶ τοὺς ἵππους λαβοῦσαι διήρπασαν τὴν τῶν Σκυθῶν γῆν.
οἱ δὲ Σκύθαι, οὐ γιγνώσκοντες τὴν φωνήν, καὶ ἄνδρας νομίζοντες τὰς Ἀμαζόνας,   10
ἐμπεσόντες καὶ μαχεσάμενοι τοὺς νεκροὺς ἀνεῖλον. οὕτως οὖν ἔγνωσαν γυναῖκας
οὔσας, ἀνελόντες τοὺς νεκρούς.

γνόντες δὲ ταῦτα, καὶ οὐ βουλόμενοι ἀποκτείνειν ἔτι, ἀλλὰ ἐξ αὐτῶν παιδοποιεῖσθαι,
τοὺς ἑαυτῶν νεανίσκους ἀπέπεμψαν εἰς αὐτάς, κελεύοντες μάχεσθαι μὲν μή, ἕπεσθαι
δὲ καὶ στρατοπεδεύεσθαι πλησίον τῶν Ἀμαζόνων. πλησίον οὖν ἐλθόντες εἵποντο οἱ   15
νεανίσκοι, καὶ ἐστρατοπεδεύσαντο. καὶ πρῶτον μὲν ἀπῆλθον αἱ Ἀμαζόνες, ἀπελθοῦσαι
δ' εἶδον τοὺς ἄνδρας ἑπομένους. αἱ μὲν οὖν Ἀμαζόνες ἐδίωκον, οἱ δ' ἄνδρες ἔφευγον.
ἰδοῦσαι οὖν φεύγοντας τοὺς ἄνδρας, ἡσύχαζον αἱ Ἀμαζόνες. οὕτως οὖν, μαθοῦσαι τοὺς
ἄνδρας οὐ πολεμίους ὄντας, οὐκέτι ἐφρόντιζον αὐτῶν.

ἡμεῖς τοξεύομεν καὶ ἱππαζόμεθα

ἀν-εῖλ-ον they took up (aor. of ἀν-αιρέ-ω)

ἀν-ελ-όντ-ες on taking up (nom. pl. m.) (ἀναιρέ-ω/ἀν-εῖλ-ον)

ἄνεμ-ος, ὁ wind (2a)

ἀπ-ελθ-οῦσ-αι upon going away (nom. pl. f.) (ἀπ-έρχ-ομαι/ἀπ-ῆλθ-ον)

ἀπο-βᾶσ-αι upon disembarking (nom. pl. f.) (ἀπο-βαίν-ω/ἀπ-έ-βην)

ἀπο-πέμπ-ω send off

ἀφ-ίκ-οντο they arrived (aor. of ἀφ-ικνέ-ομαι)

γν-όντ-ες knowing, realizing (nom. pl. m.) (γιγνώσκ-ω/ἔ-γνω-ν)

δι-αρπάζ-ω lay waste

ἔ-γνω-σαν they recognized (them) (aor. of γιγνώσκ-ω)

ἐμ-πεσ-όντ-ες attacking, falling upon (nom. pl. m.) (ἐμ-πίπτ-ω/ἐν-έ-πεσ-ον)

ἐλθ-όντ-ες upon coming (nom. pl. m.) (ἔρχ-ομαι/ἦλθ-ον)

ἕπ-ομαι follow

ἥπερ where

ηὗρ-ον they came upon (aor. of εὑρίσκ-ω)

ἱππο-φόρβι-ον, τό herd of horses (2b)

λαβ-οῦσ-αι upon taking (nom. pl. f.) (λαμβάν-ω/ἔ-λαβ-ον)

μαθ-οῦσ-αι upon understanding (nom. pl. f.) (μανθάν-ω/ἔ-μαθ-ον)

νομίζ-ω think x (acc.) to be y (acc.)

παιδο-ποιέ-ομαι beget children

πλησίον nearby, near (+ gen.)

Σκύθ-ης, ὁ Scythian (1d)

στρατοπεδεύ-ομαι make camp

τῇ μάχῃ the battle

τῆς μάχης the battle

φων-ή, ἡ language, speech (1a)

Vocabulary to be learnt

ἀναιρέω (ἀνελ-) *pick up*

ἀποβαίνω (ἀποβα-) *leave, depart*

ἕπομαι (ἑσπ-) *follow*

μάχη, ἡ *fight, battle (1a)*

μέντοι *however, but*

νομίζω *think, acknowledge*

φυλάττω *guard*

The 'threat' of alternative life-styles

Greeks endlessly debated subjects the nature of justice and the relationship between it and written law; the nature of right and wrong, and where expediency fitted in; the nature of power, and the rights that the stronger held over the weaker; and, most famous of all, the relationship between *nomos* ('custom', 'law', 'culture') and *phusis* ('nature') and the question 'Is there an absolute right and wrong in any situation, or does it depend on the circumstances?' Herodotos was fascinated by this issue, and puts it at its sharpest in the following story:

'If anyone were to offer men the opportunity to make from all the customs in the world what seemed to them the best selection, everyone would after careful consideration choose his own; for everyone considers his own customs far the best … A particular piece of evidence is this: when Dareios was King of Persia, he summoned certain Greeks who were at his court and asked them how much he would have to pay them to eat the bodies of their dead fathers. They replied that there was no sum for which they would do such a thing. Later he summoned certain Indians of a tribe called Callatians, who do eat their parents' bodies, and asked them in the presence of the Greeks, through an interpreter so that the Greeks understood what was being said, how much they would have to be paid to burn their fathers' dead bodies. They cried aloud and told him not to utter such blasphemy. Such is custom, and Pindar was in my opinion right when he wrote that "Custom is King of all".' (Herodotos, *Histories* 3.38)

… These questions can easily seem, and seemed to many Athenians, to strike at the very heart of morality, and set the stage for the long and at times bitter intellectual debate which rages still today. (*World of Athens*, 8.32)

H

The Scythians track the Amazons, and notice that, at midday, they disperse in ones and twos. An enterprising Scythian follows one, and . . .

οὕτως οὖν νεανίσκος τις Ἀμαζόνα τινὰ μόνην οὖσαν καταλαβών, εὐθὺς ἐχρῆτο. καὶ
ἡ Ἀμαζὼν οὐκ ἐκώλυσεν. καὶ φωνεῖν μὲν οὐκ ἐδύνατο, διὰ⌈ δὲ ⌉σημείου ἐκέλευε
τὸν νεανίαν εἰς τὴν ὑστεραίαν ἰέναι εἰς τὸ‿ αὐτὸ χωρίον καὶ ἕτερον νεανίαν ἄγειν,
σημαίνουσα ὅτι αὐτὴ τὸ‿ αὐτὸ ποιήσει καὶ ἑτέραν Ἀμαζόνα ἄξει. ὁ δὲ νεανίας
ἀπελθὼν εἶπε ταῦτα πρὸς τοὺς λοιπούς, τῇ⌈ δ' ⌉ὑστεραίᾳ ἐλθὼν αὐτὸς εἰς τὸ‿ αὐτὸ   5
χωρίον, ἕτερον ἄγων νεανίαν, τὴν Ἀμαζόνα αὐτὴν ηὗρεν, ἑτέραν ἀγαγοῦσαν
Ἀμαζόνα. οἱ δὲ δύο νεανίαι, εὑρόντες τὰς Ἀμαζόνας καὶ χρησάμενοι, ἀπῆλθον. οἱ δὲ
λοιποὶ τῶν νεανιῶν, μαθόντες τὰ γενόμενα, ἐποίουν τὸ‿ αὐτὸ καὶ αὐτοί.
    μετὰ δὲ ταῦτα συνῴκουν ὁμοῦ οἵ τε Σκύθαι καὶ αἱ Ἀμαζόνες. τὴν δὲ φωνὴν τὴν
μὲν τῶν Ἀμαζόνων οἱ ἄνδρες οὐκ ἐδύναντο μανθάνειν, τὴν δὲ τῶν Σκυθῶν αἱ   10
γυναῖκες ἔμαθον. τέλος δὲ εἶπον πρὸς αὐτὰς οἱ νεανίαι· 'τοκέας καὶ κτήματα ἔχομεν
ἡμεῖς. διὰ τί οὖν οὐκ ἀπερχόμεθα εἰς τὸ ἡμέτερον πλῆθος; γυναῖκας δ' ἕξομεν
ὑμᾶς καὶ οὐδεμίας ἄλλας.' αἱ‿ δὲ πρὸς ταῦτα 'ἡμεῖς', ἔφασαν, 'οὐ δυνάμεθα οἰκεῖν
μετὰ‿ τῶν‿ ὑμετέρων‿ γυναικῶν. οὐ γὰρ οἱ‿ αὐτοὶ οἵ τε ἡμέτεροι νόμοι καὶ οἱ τῶν
Σκυθῶν. ἡμεῖς μὲν γὰρ τοξεύομεν καὶ ἱππαζόμεθα, ἔργα δὲ γυναικεῖα οὐκ ἐμάθομεν.   15
αἱ δ' ὑμέτεραι γυναῖκες οὐδὲν τούτων ποιοῦσιν, ἀλλ' ἔργα γυναικεῖα ἐργάζονται,
μένουσαι ἐν ταῖς‿ ἁμάξαις καὶ οὐ τοξεύουσαι οὐδ' ἱππαζόμεναι. ἀλλ' εἰ βούλεσθε
γυναῖκας ἔχειν ἡμᾶς, ἐλθόντας εἰς τοὺς τοκέας δεῖ ὑμᾶς ἀπολαγχάνειν τὸ τῶν‿
κτημάτων μέρος, καὶ ἔπειτα ἐπανελθόντας συνοικεῖν μεθ'‿ ἡμῶν.'
    ταῦτα δ' εἰποῦσαι ἔπεισαν τοὺς νεανίσκους. ἀπολαχόντες οὖν οἱ νεανίσκοι   20
τὸ τῶν κτημάτων μέρος, ἐπανῆλθον πάλιν παρὰ τὰς Ἀμαζόνας. εἶπον οὖν πρὸς
αὐτοὺς αἱ Ἀμαζόνες· 'ἀλλ' ἡμᾶς ἔχει φόβος τις μέγας. οὐ γὰρ δυνάμεθα οἰκεῖν ἐν
τούτῳ‿ τῷ‿ χώρῳ, διαρπάσασαι τὴν γῆν. ἀλλ' εἰ βούλεσθε ἡμᾶς γυναῖκας ἔχειν, διὰ
τί οὐκ ἐξανιστάμεθα ἐκ τῆς‿ γῆς‿ ταύτης καὶ τὸν Τάναϊν ποταμὸν διαβάντες ἐκεῖ
οἰκοῦμεν;' καὶ ἐπείθοντο καὶ ταῦτα οἱ νεανίαι. ἐξαναστάντες οὖν καὶ ἀφικόμενοι   25
πρὸς τὸν χῶρον, ᾤκησαν αὐτόν.

Vocabulary for Section Seven H

ἀγαγ-οῦσ-αν bringing
    (acc. s. f.) (ἄγ-ω/ἤγαγ-ον)
ἄγ-ω (ἀγαγ-) lead, bring
αἱ δὲ but they
Ἀμαζών (Ἀμαζον-), ἡ Amazon (3a)
ἀπ-ελθ-ών going away (nom. s.
    m.) (ἀπ-έρχ-ομαι /ἀπ-ῆλθ-ον)
ἀπο-λαγχάν-ω (ἀπο-λαχ-)
    obtain by lot
ἀπο-λαχ-όντ-ες upon obtaining
    (nom. pl. m.) (ἀπο-λαγχάν-ω/
    ἀπ-έ-λαχ-ον)

αὐτ-ὴν herself
αὐτ-ὴ she herself
αὐτ-οί they themselves
αὐτ-ὸς he himself
ἀφ-ικ-όμεν-οι upon arriving
    (nom. pl. m.) (ἀφ-ικνέ-ομαι/
    ἀφ-ικ-όμην)
γεν-όμεν-α, τά what had
    happened, the
    happenings (γίγν-ομαι/
    ἐ-γεν-όμην)
γυναικεῖ-ος -α -ον woman's

διὰ σημείου by means of sign-
    language
δια-βάντ-ες crossing, once
    across (nom. pl. m.)
    (δια-βαίν-ω/δι-έ-βην)
δι-αρπάζ-ω lay waste
δυν-άμεθα (we) are able
δύο two (nom.)
ἐ-δύν-ατο she was able
    (δύν-αμαι)
ἐ-δύν-αντο they were able
    (δύν-αμαι)

εἰπ-οῦσ-αι saying (nom. pl. f.)
(λέγ-ω/εἶπ-ον)

ἐκεῖ there

ἐλθ-όντ-ας on going (acc. pl. m.)
(ἔρχ-ομαι/ἦλθ-ον)

ἐλθ-ών upon coming (nom.
s. m.) (ἔρχ-ομαι/ἦλθ-ον)

ἐξ-ανα-στά-ντ-ες upon getting
up and going off (nom. pl. m.)
(ἐξ-αν-ίστα-μαι/
ἐξ-αν-έ-στη-ν)

ἐξ-αν-ιστά-μεθα we get up and
go off

ἕξ-ομεν we shall have (fut. of
ἔχ-ω)

ἐπ-αν-ελθ-όντ-ας upon returning
(acc. pl. m.) (ἐπ-αν-έρχ-ομαι/
ἐπ-αν-ῆλθ-ον)

ἐπ-αν-έρχ-ομαι (ἐπ-αν-ελθ-)
return

ἐργάζ-ομαι perform, do

εὑρ-όντ-ες on finding (nom. pl.
m.) (εὑρίσκ-ω/ηὗρ-ον)

ἱππάζ-ομαι ride horses

κατα-λαβ-ών on coming across
(nom. s. m.) (κατα-λαμβάν-ω/
κατ-έ-λαβ-ον)

κατα-λαμβάν-ω (κατα-λαβ-)
come across

κτῆμα (κτηματ-), τό possession
(3b)

λοιπ-ός -ή -όν other, rest of

μαθ-όντ-ες on learning (nom. pl.
m.) (μανθάν-ω/ἔ-μαθ-ον)

μεθ' ἡμῶν with us

μέρ-ος, τό share, portion (3c)

μετὰ τῶν ὑμετέρων γυναικῶν
with your women

μετά (+acc.) after

μόν-ος -η -ον alone

νόμ-ος, ὁ custom, usage (2a)

οἱ αὐτοί the same

οἰκέ-ω dwell in

ὁμοῦ together

πάλιν back, again

ποταμ-ός, ὁ river (2a)

σημαίν-ω give a sign

Σκύθ-ης, ὁ Scythian (1d)

συν-οικέ-ω live together

ταῖς ἁμάξαις their waggons
(Scythians were nomads)

Τάνα-ις, ὁ Tanais (3e) (the river
Don)

τῇ ὑστεραίᾳ on the next day

τῆς γῆς ταύτης this land

τὸ αὐτ-ό the same

τοκ-ῆς, οἱ parents (3g)

τοξεύ-ω use bows and arrows

τούτῳ τῷ χώρῳ this land

ὑστεραί-α, ἡ next day (1b)

φωνέ-ω speak, converse

φων-ή, ἡ language (1a)

χρά-ομαι use, have sex with

χῶρ-ος, ὁ place, region (2a)

Vocabulary to be learnt

ἄγω (ἀγαγ-) *lead, bring*

αὐτός ἡ ό *self*

διαβαίνω (διαβα-) *cross*

δύναμαι *be able*

δύο *two*

ἐπανέρχομαι (ἐπανελθ-)
return

καταλαμβάνω (καταλαβ-)
come across, overtake

κτῆμα (κτηματ-), τό
possession (3b)

μετά (+acc.) after

ὁ αὐτός *the same*

οἰκέω *dwell (in), live*

πάλιν *back, again*

ποταμός, ὁ *river (2a)*

σημεῖον, τό *sign, signal (2b)*

ὑμέτερος ᾱ ον *your*

φωνέω *speak, utter*

φωνή, ἡ *voice, language,
speech (1a)*

Comic actors

Part Three Athens through the comic poet's eyes

Introduction

The narrative returns to Dikaiopolis, who continues on his way through the city with the rhapsode. They meet Euelpides and Peisetairos, two friends who plan to escape from Athens and its troubles and found a new city, Cloudcuckooland (Νεφελοκοκκυγία), a Utopia in the sky with the birds (Section 8). 'Utopia' (a word confected in 1516 by Sir Thomas More to describe an ideal society) = οὐ τόπος 'no place' – or should that be εὖ τόπος (Eutopia)?

We have already seen some of the troubles they want to escape – the war, the plague, increasing lawlessness and disrespect for the gods and human institutions, the collapse of morality and the challenge of the sophists – but Euelpides mentions another, the Athenian obsession with law-suits, a theme which is comically explored in scenes from Aristophanes' *Wasps* (Section 9).

Peisetairos and Euelpides have already decided on their plan of escape, but Aristophanes provides two other possible comic solutions: in *Lysistrata* (Section 10) the women of Athens stage a sex-strike to end the war, and in *Akharnians* (Section 11) Dikaiopolis finally finds his own solution to the problems of Athens at war.

Sources

Aristophanes, *Birds* 32–48 *Knights* 303–7, 752–3
Homer, *Odyssey* 1.267
Homeric Hymn to Demeter 216–17
Philemon (fragment – Kock 71)
Plato, Gorgias 515*b*–516*a* Republic 327*b*
Aristophanes, *Wasps* 1, 54, 67–213, 760–862, 891–1008

Aristophanes, *Lysistrata* 120–80, 240–6, 829–955
Akharnians 19–61, 129–32, 175–203
Plato, *Republic* 557*e*–558*c*, 563*c*–*e*
  Alkibiades 1, 134*b*
Aristophanes, *Knights* 1111–30
(Xenophon), *Constitution of Athens* 1.6–8, 3.1–2

In *World of Athens*: Aristophanes and politics 8.78–9.

Time to be taken

Seven weeks

Section Eight A–C: Aristophanes' *Birds* and visions of Utopia

A

Dikaiopolis and the rhapsode walk on through Athens, leaving the Spartan ambassador to his fate. On the way Dikaiopolis meets his old friends, Peisetairos and Euelpides, who are leaving Athens. They explain their dissatisfaction with Athens, and particularly the politicians, and in the course of this Dikaiopolis determines to make peace somehow. The rhapsode is not eager to involve himself, and takes a different course.

In *World of Athens*: the *agora* 2.29ff.; *kuria ekklesia* 6.10ff. Cf. 2.24, 1.25–6.

θεασάμενος τὴν τῶν ἔνδεκα ἀνομίαν ὁ Δικαιόπολις, καὶ ἀκούσας τοὺς
τοῦ ἱκέτου λόγους, ἀπέρχεται διὰ τοῦ τῶν πολιτῶν πλήθους πρὸς τὴν ἀγορὰν
μετὰ τοῦ ῥαψῳδοῦ. καὶ Εὐελπίδης, ὁ τοῦ Πολεμάρχου υἱός, καθορᾷ αὐτὸν πρὸς
τὴν ἀγορὰν ἀπιόντα μετὰ τοῦ ῥαψῳδοῦ, κατιδὼν δὲ πέμπει πρὸς αὐτοὺς τὸν παῖδα.
προσέρχεται οὖν ὁ παῖς ὁ τοῦ Εὐελπίδου ὡς τὸν Δικαιόπολιν, προσιὼν δὲ βοᾷ.   5

ΠΑΙΣ   μένε, ὦ Δικαιόπολι, μένε.
ΔΙΚ.   τίς ἡ βοή; τίς αἴτιός ἐστι τῆς βοῆς ἐκείνης;
(ὁ παῖς προσελθὼν λαμβάνεται τοῦ ἱματίου)

παῖς τις κανοῦν ἔχων

ΠΑΙΣ	ἐγὼ αἴτιος τῆς βοῆς.	10
ΔΙΚ.	τίς ὢν σύ γε τοῦ ἐμοῦ ἱματίου λαμβάνῃ, ὦ ἄνθρωπε;	
ΠΑΙΣ	παῖς εἰμι.	
ΔΙΚ.	ἀλλὰ τίνος ἀνθρώπου παῖς ὢν τυγχάνεις; τίς σε ἔπεμψεν;	
ΠΑΙΣ	εἰμὶ ἐγὼ τοῦ Εὐελπίδου παῖς, καὶ ἔτυχε πέμψας με ἐκεῖνος. ἀσπάζεται	
	γάρ σε Εὐελπίδης, ὁ τοῦ Πολεμάρχου.	15
ΔΙΚ.	ἀλλὰ ποῦ ἐστιν αὐτός;	
ΠΑΙΣ	οὗτος ὄπισθεν προσέρχεται. ἆρ' οὐχ ὁρᾶτε αὐτὸν τρέχοντα διὰ τοῦ	
	τῶν πολιτῶν πλήθους; καὶ μετ' αὐτοῦ ἑταῖρός τις ἕπεται, Πεισέταιρος,	
	ὁ Στιλβωνίδου. δῆλον ὅτι ὑμῶν ἕνεκα τρέχει. ἀλλὰ περιμένετε.	
ΔΙΚ.	ἀλλὰ περιμενοῦμεν.	20

(ὁ Εὐελπίδης προστρέχει, κανοῦν ἔχων ἐν τῇ χειρί. προσδραμὼν δὲ φθάνει τὸν
Πεισέταιρον, καὶ τῆς χειρὸς τῆς τοῦ Δικαιοπόλεως λαβόμενος ἀσπάζεται)

ΕΥΕΛΠΙΔΗΣ	χαῖρε, ὦ φίλε Δικαιόπολι. ποῖ δὴ καὶ πόθεν;	
ΔΙΚ.	ἐκ τοῦ Πειραιῶς, ὦ βέλτιστε. προσιὼν δὲ τυγχάνω πρὸς τὴν ἐκκλησίαν.	
	κυρία γὰρ ἐκκλησία γενήσεται τήμερον.	25

Vocabulary for Section Eight A

> **Grammar for 8A–C**
> - The genitive case and its uses
> - Further comparative and superlative adjectives
> - Mood
> - Present optative, active and middle: παύοιμι, παυοίμην
> - ἀνίσταμαι 'I get up and go'

ἀγορ-ά, ἡ market-place, agora (1b)
αἴτι-ος -α -ον responsible for
ἀπ-ιόντ-α going off (acc. s. m.)
 (part. of ἀπ-έρχ-ομαι/ἄπ-ειμι)
ἀσπάζ-ομαι greet
βέλτιστ-ε my very good friend
διὰ τοῦ πλήθ-ους through the
 crowd
ἐκκλησί-α, ἡ assembly, ekklesia
 (1b)
ἑταῖρ-ος, ὁ friend, companion (2a)
Εὐελπίδ-ης, ὁ Euelpides (1d)
 ('Son of great hopes')
καθ-οράω (κατ-ιδ-) see, notice
καν-οῦν, τό basket (2b έ-ον
 contr.) *(holding sacrificial
 meal and knife)*
κύρι-ος -α -ον with power,
 sovereign
λαμβάν-ομαι (λαβ-) take hold of
μετ' αὐτ-οῦ with him

μετὰ τοῦ ῥαψῳδ-οῦ with the
 rhapsode
ὄπισθεν behind
ὁ Στιλβωνίδ-ου Stilbonides'
 son
ὁ τοῦ Πολεμάρχ-ου
 Polemarkhos' son
Πεισ-έταιρ-ος, ὁ Peisetairos (2a)
 ('Persuasive-friend')
πέμπ-ω send
περι-μέν-ω wait around (fut.
 περι-μενέ-ω)
προσ-δραμ-ών *see* προσ-τρέχ-ω
προσ-ιών approaching (nom.
 s. m.) (part. of προσ-έρχ-ομαι/
 πρόσ-ειμι)
προσ-τρέχ-ω (προσδραμ-) run
 towards
τῇ χειρί his hand
τῆς βο-ῆς ἐκείν-ης that shout
 (*after* αἴτιος)

τῆς τοῦ Δικαιοπόλ-εως (the
 hand) of Dikaiopolis
τῆς χειρ-ὸς the hand (*after*
 λαβ-όμενος)
τίν-ος ἀνθρώπ-ου; of which
 man? whose?
τοῦ ἐμ-οῦ ἱματί-ου my cloak
 (*after* λαμβάνῃ)
τοῦ Εὐελπίδ-ου of Euelpides
τοῦ ἱκέτ-ου of the suppliant
τοῦ ἱματί-ου his cloak (*after*
 λαμβάν-εται)
τοῦ Πειραι-ῶς the Piraeus
τοῦ Πολεμάρχ-ου of
 Polemarkhos
τῶν ἕνδεκα of the Eleven
ὑμ-ῶν ἕνεκα for your sake,
 because of you
χαῖρ-ε hello! greetings!
ὡς (+acc.) to

(ἐν⌐ δὲ ⌐τούτῳ τυγχάνει προσιὼν Πεισέταιρος, κόρακα ἔχων ἐπὶ⌢ τῇ⌢ χειρί)

ΔΙΚ.   χαῖρε καὶ σύ γε, ὦ Πεισέταιρε. ποῖ δὴ μετ'⌐ἐκείνου⌢ τοῦ⌢ κόρακος; μῶν εἰς
        κόρακας;

ΠΕΙΣΕΤΑΙΡΟΣ πῶς δ' οὔ; ἀνιστάμεθα γὰρ ἐκ τῆς⌢ πατρίδος.

ΔΙΚ.   ἀλλὰ τί βουλόμενοι οὕτως ἀνίστασθε, ὦ φίλοι; λέγοιτε⌢ ἄν. ἐγὼ γὰρ πάνυ   30
        ἡδέως ἂν⌢ ἀκούοιμι τὴν αἰτίαν.

ΕΥ.   λέγοιμι⌢ ἄν. ζητοῦμεν γὰρ ἡμεῖς τόπον τινὰ ἀπράγμονα. ἐκεῖσε δ' ἴμεν,
        ἐλθόντες δὲ πόλιν ἀπράγμονα οἰκιοῦμεν.

ΔΙΚ.   ἀλλὰ τί βουλόμενος ἐκεῖνον τὸν κόρακα ἔχεις ἐπὶ⌢ τῇ⌢ χειρί;

ΠΕΙΣ.   οὗτος μὲν ὁ κόραξ ἡγεῖται, ἡμεῖς δὲ ἑπόμεθα. τίς γὰρ ἡγεμὼν βελτίων εἰς   35
        κόρακας ἢ κόραξ;

ΡΑΨ.   ἡγεμὼν βέλτιστος δή.

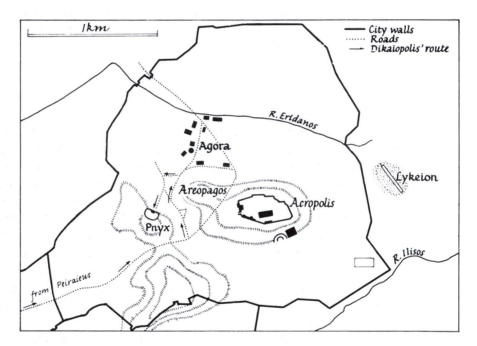

A sketch plan of Athens about 425. The agora was the town centre and market place, where the main civic buildings were. The assembly (ἐκκλησία) met on the hill of the Pnyx, and the Lykeion sports ground (γυμνάσιον) was a place for the men of the city to meet, exercise and discuss.

The Areopagus was the hill of Ares, where the Council of 400 met.

ἄν ἀκού-οιμι I would listen to

ἀν-ίστα-μαι get up and leave, emigrate

ἀ-πράγμων ἄ-πραγμον (ἀπραγμον-) free from trouble

βέλτιστ-ος -η -ον best

βελτίων βέλτιον (βελτιον-) better

ἐκεῖσε (to) there

ἐν τούτῳ meanwhile

ἐπὶ τῇ χειρί on his/your hand

ἡγεμών (ἡγεμον-), ὁ leader (3a)

ἡγέ-ομαι lead

κόραξ (κορακ-), ὁ crow (3a)

λέγ-οιμι ἄν I will tell (you)

λέγ-οιτε ἄν won't you (pl.) please tell me?

μετ' ἐκείν-ου τοῦ κόρακ-ος with that crow

μῶν surely not?

οἰκίζ-ω found (a city) (fut. οἰκιέ-ω)

Πεισ-έταιρ-ος, ὁ Peisetairos (2a) ('Persuasive-friend')

πολίτ-ης, ὁ citizen (1d)

προσ-ιών approaching (nom. s. m.) (part. of προσ-έρχ-ομαι/ πρόσ-ειμι)

τῆς of the (s.)

τῆς βο-ῆς the shout (*after* αἴτιος)

τῆς πατρίδ-ος our fatherland

τόπ-ος, ὁ place (2a)

τοῦ of the (s.)

τῶν of the (pl.)

χαῖρ-ε hello! greetings!

Vocabulary to be learnt

ἀγορᾱ́, ἡ *market-place, agora (1b)*

βέλτιστος η ον *best*

βελτῑ́ων βέλτῑον (βελτῑον-) *better*

ἐκεῖσε (to) *there*

ἐν τούτῳ *meanwhile*

ἡγεμών (ἡγεμον-), ὁ *leader (3a)*

ἡγέομαι *lead (+ dat.)*

καθοράω (κατιδ-) *see, look down on*

κόραξ (κορακ-), ὁ *crow (3a)*

πέμπω *send*

πολῑ́της, ὁ *citizen (1d)*

προστρέχω (προσδραμ-) *run towards*

χαῖρε *hello! farewell!*

χείρ (χειρ-), ἡ *hand (3a)*

The city of Athens

Even at the end of the fourth century, the size of the city was extremely small by modern standards, one area being within easy walking distance of another. Although large and expensively equipped private houses were not unknown in Athens, most were still basically simple, consisting of a series of small rooms arranged round an inner court. By contrast, private and public money had for generations been spent on public buildings, whether for heated political discussion, athletic or theatrical competitions, legal wrangling or religious celebrations. It was there that the real life of the *polis* had always been lived, and in the fourth century Athenian politicians, in their efforts to castigate their opponents' indulgence in private comfort and display, nostalgically simplified the more public-spirited attitudes of the fifth-century leaders, as in the following speech ascribed to Demosthenes:

'The buildings which they left to adorn our city—the temples and harbours and all that goes with them—are on a scale which their successors cannot hope to surpass; look at the Propylaia, the docks, the colonnades and all the other adornments of the city which they have bequeathed to us. And the private houses of those in power were so modest and in keeping with the title of our constitution that, as those of you who have seen them know, the houses of Themistokles, Kimon and Aristides, the famous men of those days, were no grander than those of their neighbours. But today, my friends, … some of the private individuals who hold any public office have built private houses which are grander not only than those of the ordinary run of citizens but even than our public buildings, and others have bought and cultivate estates on a scale undreamed of before.' ([Demosthenes], *On Organisation* 13.28–9) (*World of Athens*, 2.38)

B

In *World of Athens*: *dikasteria* 6.39; litigiousness 6.54; 'new politicians' 1.58, 6.17.

ΔΙΚ. μείζονα οὖν τινα πόλιν ἢ τὰς Ἀθήνας ζητεῖς;

ΕΥ. οὐ μὰ Δία οὐκ ἐκεῖνο διανοοῦμαι. οὐκ ἔστι μείζων ταύτης⁀τῆς⁀πόλεως πόλις. μέγισται γὰρ νὴ Δία αἱ Ἀθῆναι φαίνονται οὖσαι.

ΡΑΨ. ἔπειτα εὐδαιμονεστέραν ταύτης⁀τῆς⁀πόλεως ζητεῖς πόλιν;

ΕΥ. οὐκ ἔστιν εὐδαιμονεστέρα ἢ αὕτη ἡ πόλις. εὐδαιμονέσταται γὰρ αἱ Ἀθῆναι.

ΔΙΚ. τί οὖν δή; τί ἐν νῷ ἔχετε; μῶν μισεῖτε τὴν πόλιν;

ΠΕΙΣ. ἀλλ' οὐ μὰ Δία οὐκ αὐτὴν μισοῦμεν τὴν πόλιν.

ΔΙΚ. λέγετε οὖν, ὦ φίλοι, τί παθόντες ἢ τί βουλόμενοι ἐκ τῆς⁀πόλεως ἀπέρχεσθε;

ΕΥ. δεινὰ δὴ παθόντες καὶ ἐγὼ καὶ ὁ Πεισέταιρος οὑτοσί, ὦ Δικαιόπολι, ἀπιέναι βουλόμεθα. βαρέως⌜ γὰρ ⌝φέρομεν τὰ τῆς⁀πόλεως πράγματα, μάλιστα δὲ τὰ δικαστήρια. τοιοῦτον γὰρ τὸ πάθος ἐπάθομεν εἰς τὸ δικαστήριον εἰσελθόντες.

ΡΑΨ. ποῖον τὸ πάθος; τί ποιήσαντες ἢ τί ἀδικήσαντες τὸ πάθος ἐπάθετε;

ΕΥ. οὐδὲν οὔτ' ἐποιήσαμεν οὔτ' ἠδικήσαμεν, ἀλλ' οἱ δικασταὶ κατεψηφίσαντο ἡμῶν⁀ἀναιτίων⁀ὄντων διὰ τὴν τῶν μαρτύρων ψευδομαρτυρίαν.

ΔΙΚ. ἀλλ' οὐ θαυμάζω εἰ ἄλλην τινὰ πόλιν ζητοῦντες ἀνίστασθε, ἐπεὶ δίκαια λέγετε περὶ⁀τοῦ⌜ τε ⌝δικαστηρίου⁀καὶ⁀τῶν⁀δικαστῶν. οἱ μὲν γὰρ τέττιγες ὀλίγον χρόνον ἐπὶ⁀τῶν⁀κραδῶν ᾄδουσιν, οἱ δὲ Ἀθηναῖοι ἐπὶ⁀τῶν δικῶν ᾄδουσιν ἀεί. ταῦτ' οὖν εἰκότως ὑμεῖς ποιεῖτε. ἐγὼ δὲ εἰκότως ταῦτα οὐ ποιήσω. φιλόπολις γάρ εἰμι, ὥσπερ οἱ ῥήτορες, οὐδὲ παύσομαι οὐδέποτε φιλόπολις ὤν.

ΠΕΙΣ. ὦ Δικαιόπολι, τί φής; μῶν φιλοπόλιδας ἡγῇ τοὺς ῥήτορας;

ΔΙΚ. ἔγωγε. τί⁀μήν;

ΠΕΙΣ. ἀλλὰ πῶς φιλοῦσι τὸν δῆμον οἱ ῥήτορες; σκόπει γάρ. ὁ μὲν πόλεμος ἕρπει, πανταχοῦ δὲ κλαυθμοὶ καὶ πυραὶ διὰ τὴν νόσον, πανταχοῦ δὲ νεκροί, πολλὴ δ' ἡ ἀνομία. ἆρ' οἰκτίρουσιν οἱ ῥήτορες τὸν δῆμον; οἰκτίρουσιν ἢ οὔ; λέγε. τί σιωπᾷς; οὐκ ἐρεῖς; οὐκ οἰκτίρουσιν, ἀλλ' ἀπολοῦσι τὴν πόλιν, εὖ οἶσθ' ὅτι. ἐγὼ γὰρ ὑπὲρ⁀σοῦ ἀποκρινοῦμαι. καί πλέα μὲν ἡ γῆ τῆς⁀τόλμης αὐτῶν, πλέα δ' ἡ ἐκκλησία, πλέα δὲ τὰ δικαστήρια, ὁ δὲ δῆμος πλέως τῆς⁀ἀπορίας.

Vocabulary for Section Eight B

ἀδικέ-ω do wrong
ἄδ-ω sing
ἀν-ίστα-μαι get up and go, emigrate
ἀπ-ολ-οῦσι they will destroy
βαρέ-ως φέρ-ω find hard to bear, take badly
δῆμ-ος, ὁ the people (2a)
δικαστήρι-ον, τό law-court (2b)
δικαστ-ής, ὁ juror, dikast (1d)
εἰκότ-ως reasonably
ἐκκλησί-α, ἡ assembly, *ekklesia* (1b)
ἐπεί since
ἐπὶ τῶν δικ-ῶν on their lawsuits
ἐπὶ τῶν κραδ-ῶν on their branches
ἐρ-εῖς you (s.) will say (ἐρέ-ω, fut. of λέγ-ω)
ἕρπ-ω go along, take its course
εὐ-δαιμον-έστατ-ος -η -ον wealthiest, most blessed by the gods (εὐ-δαίμων)
εὐ-δαιμον-έστερ-ος -α –ον more wealthy, more blessed (εὐ-δαίμων)
ἡγέ-ομαι consider (x to be y)
ἡμ-ῶν ἀν-αιτί-ων ὄντ-ων us, although we were innocent (*after* καταψηφίσαντο)
κατα-ψηφίζ-ομαι condemn
κλαυθμ-ός, ὁ lamentation (2a)

μάρτυς (μαρτυρ-), ὁ witness (3a)
μέγιστ-ος -η -ον greatest (μέγας)
μείζων μεῖζον (μειζον-) greater (μέγας)
μῶν surely not?
οἰκτίρ-ω pity
πάθ-ος, τό experience (3c)
πανταχοῦ everywhere
περὶ τοῦ δικαστηρί-ου καὶ τῶν δικαστ-ῶν about the law-courts and the dikasts
πλέ-ως -α -ων full of
ποῖ-ος -α -ον; what? what sort of?
ῥήτωρ (ῥητορ-), ὁ politician, speaker (3a)
ταύτ-ης τῆς πόλ- εως than this city (*after* μείζων)
τέττιξ (τεττιγ-), ὁ cicada, grasshopper (3a)
τῆς ἀπορί-ας perplexity (*after* πλέως)
τῆς πόλ-εως the city (*after* ἐκ); of the city
τῆς τόλμ-ης the brazenness (*after* πλέα)
τί μήν; of course
τοι-οῦτ-ος τοι-αύτ-η τοι-οῦτ-ο(ν) like this, of this kind
ὑπὲρ σοῦ for you (s.)
φιλό-πολ-ις (φιλο-πολιδ-), ὁ, ἡ patriotic

χρόν-ος, ὁ time (2a)
ψευδο-μαρτυρί-α, ἡ false-witness, perjury (1b)

Vocabulary to be learnt
ἀδικέω *be unjust, commit a crime, do wrong*
ἄδω/ἀείδω *sing*
ἀνίσταμαι (ἀναστα-) *get up, emigrate*
δῆμος, ὁ *people; deme (2a)*
δικαστήριον, τό *law-court (2b)*
δικαστής, ὁ *juror, dikast (1d)*
ἐκκλησίᾱ, ἡ *assembly, ekklesia (1b)*
εὐδαίμων εὔδαιμον (εὐδαιμον-) *happy, rich, blessed by the gods (comp. εὐδαιμονέστερος ᾱ ον; sup. εὐδαιμονέστατος η ον)*
μέγιστος η ον *greatest (sup. of μέγας)*
μείζων μεῖζον (μειζον-) *greater (comp. of μέγας)*
μῶν; *surely not?*
οἰκτίρω (οἰκτιρα-) *pity*
πάθος, τό *experience, suffering (3C)*
πανταχοῦ *everywhere*
ῥήτωρ (ῥητορ-) ὁ *orator, politician (3a)*
χρόνος, ὁ *time (2a)*

After Pericles

In 430 BC, a virulent plague, the medical identity of which has been long debated, broke out in Athens, and spread rapidly through the population. Thucydides himself caught the plague, but survived to give a vivid account of the suffering. Very large numbers of Athenians died, and the imminence of death led to something close to a collapse of law and order. The disaster almost broke the Athenian spirit. There was a reaction against Pericles, who was tried and fined. An attempt was made to open peace negotiations with Sparta, but nothing came of it. In 429 Pericles died, himself a victim of the plague. The passing of the man who had been a major force in democratic politics for thirty years was bound to have a profound effect on Athens. Contemporary sources present Pericles' death as marking a sea change, after which things could never be the same, only worse. (*World of Athens*, 1.57)

C

In *World of Athens*: benefits of empire 6.74, 81–2; Pericles tried 6.26–7; peace 7.4; festivals 3.40ff.

ΔΙΚ. ἀληθῆ γε δοκεῖς λέγειν, ὦ Πεισέταιρε. ἀλλὰ τίς σώσει τὴν πόλιν, ἐπεὶ
οὐδενὸς ἄξιοι φαίνονται ὄντες οἵ γε ῥήτορες; ἴσως αὐτὸς ὁ δῆμος –
ΕΥ. ὦ Ἡράκλεις, μὴ λέγε τοῦτό γε. ὁ γὰρ δῆμος οἴκοι μέν ἐστι δεξιώτατος, ἐν
δὲ τῇ ἐκκλησίᾳ μωρότατος.
ΡΑΨ. ἀλλ' εἰ Περικλῆς –   5
ΔΙΚ. τὸν Περικλέα μὴ λέγε.
ΡΑΨ. πῶς φῄς, ὦ τᾶν; πάντων ἄριστός γε ἐδόκει ὁ Περικλῆς, ὡς φασίν.
ΠΕΙΣ. ἀλλ' ὁ ἀγαθὸς πολίτης βελτίονας ποιεῖ τοὺς πολίτας ἀντὶ χειρόνων.
τοῦτ' ἐποίει Περικλῆς, ἢ οὔ;
ΡΑΨ. ἐποίει νὴ Δία.   10
ΠΕΙΣ. οὐκοῦν, ὅτε Περικλῆς ἤρχετο λέγειν ἐν τῷ δήμῳ, χείρονες ἦσαν οἱ
Ἀθηναῖοι, ὅτε δὲ ἀπέθανε, βελτίονες;
ΡΑΨ. εἰκός. ὁ γὰρ ἀγαθὸς πολίτης βελτίους ποιεῖ τοὺς ἄλλους.
ΠΕΙΣ. ἀλλ' ἴσμεν σαφῶς καὶ ἐγὼ καὶ σύ, ὅτι πρῶτον μὲν εὐδόκιμος ἦν
Περικλῆς ὅτε χείρους, ὡς σὺ φῄς, ἦσαν οἱ Ἀθηναῖοι, ἐπειδὴ δὲ ἐγένοντο   15
βελτίους διὰ αὐτόν, κλοπὴν κατεψηφίσαντο αὐτοῦ⌐, δῆλον ὅτι
⌐πονηροῦ ὄντος.
ΔΙΚ. ἀληθῆ λέγεις, εὖ οἶδ' ὅτι. τίς οὖν σώσει τὴν πόλιν; ἀνὴρ γὰρ φιλόπολις
σώσει τὴν πόλιν, ἀλλ' οὐκ ἀπολεῖ. τί δεῖ ποιεῖν;
ΡΑΨ. δεῖ σε, ὦ Δικαιόπολι, ζητεῖν τὸ τῆς πόλεως ἀγαθόν.   20
ΔΙΚ. τί τὸ ἀγαθόν, ὦ ῥαψῳδέ; οὐ γὰρ αὐτό, ὅ τι ποτ' ἐστὶ τὸ ἀγαθόν, τυγχάνω εἰδώς.
ΡΑΨ. σὺ δ' οὐκ οἶσθα τί τὸ ἀγαθόν; ἐν δὲ τῇ νηὶ ἔδοξάς γε φιλόσοφός τις εἶναι,
γνοὺς τὰ τῶν φιλοσόφων.
ΔΙΚ. μὴ παῖζε πρὸς ἐμέ, ὦ ῥαψῳδέ. οἱ γὰρ φιλόσοφοι ζητοῦσιν, ὡς ἀκούω,
τί ἐστιν ἀγαθόν, εὑρίσκειν δ' οὐδεὶς δύναται. οἱ μὲν γὰρ ἀρετήν,   25
οἱ δὲ δικαιοσύνην ἡγοῦνται τὸ ἀγαθόν. ἀλλ' οὐδὲν ἴσασιν ἐκεῖνοι. οἱ
δὲ γεωργοὶ τὸ ἀγαθὸν ἴσασι, τί ἐστιν. ἐν ἀγρῷ γὰρ ἔτυχον εὑρόντες
αὐτό. ἔστι δ' εἰρήνη. ὁ μὲν γὰρ πόλεμος πλέως πραγμάτων, ἀπορίας,
νόσου, παρασκευῆς νεῶν, ἡ δ' εἰρήνη πλέα γάμων, ἑορτῶν, συγγενῶν,
παίδων, φίλων, πλούτου, ὑγιείας, σίτου, οἴνου, ἡδονῆς. εἰ δ' ἄλλος τις   30
βούλεται σπονδὰς ποιεῖσθαι καὶ εἰρήνην ἄγειν, οὐκ οἶδα. ἀλλ' ἐγὼ αὐτὸς
ἂν βουλοίμην. ἀλλὰ πῶς μόνος ὢν τὸν δῆμον ἀναπείσω; τί λέγων, ἢ τί
βοῶν, ἢ τί κελεύων, σπονδὰς ποιήσομαι; ἀλλ' οὖν εἶμι, ἕτοιμος ὢν βοᾶν
καὶ κακὰ λέγειν τὸν⌐ ἄλλο τι πλὴν περὶ εἰρήνης ⌐λέγοντα. φέρε νυν, εἰς
τὴν ἐκκλησίαν, Δικαιόπολι.   40
ΕΥ. καὶ ΠΕΙΣ. καίτοι ἡμεῖς γ' ἀνιστάμεθα εἰς τὸν τόπον τὸν ἀπράγμονα. χαίρετε.
ΡΑΨ. μώρους δὴ ἡγοῦμαι τούτους τοὺς ἀνθρώπους. ἐγὼ γὰρ οὐκ ἂν ποιοίην
ταῦτα. οὔτε γὰρ εἰς ἐκκλησίαν σπεύδοιμι ἄν, οὔτε ἂν⌐ ἐκ τῆς πατρίδος

φεύγειν ᵀβουλοίμην. ἆρ' οὐκ ἴσασιν ὅτι ἀληθῆ ἐποίησεν ὁ ποιητὴς ὁ
ποιήσας·   45
'ἀλλ' ἦˉτοι μὲν ταῦτα θεῶν ἐν γούνασι κεῖται·'
δεῖ γὰρ ἡμᾶς τὰ τῶν θεῶν δῶρα καρτερεῖν, καὶ χαλεπὰ καὶ τὰˉβελτίω.
'ἀλλὰ θεῶν μὲν δῶρα, καὶᵀ ἀχνύμενοί ᵀπερ, ἀνάγκη
τέτλαμεν ἄνθρωποι. ἐπὶᵀ γὰρ ζυγὸς ᵀαὐχένι κεῖται.'

Vocabulary for Section Eight C

ἀγρῷ the country
ἄγ-ω live in, be at
ἀλλ' οὖν however that may be
ἀνάγκη of necessity
ἂν βουλ-οίμην (I) would like to
ἀνα-πείθ-ω bring over to one's
    side
ἂν ποι-οίην (I) would do
ἀντὶ χειρόν-ων instead of worse
ἄξι-ος -α -ον worth
ἀπ-ολ-εῖ (he) will destroy
ἀπορί-ας lack of provision;
    perplexity (after πλέα)
ἀ-πράγμων ἄ-πραγμον
    (ἀπραγμον-) free from trouble
ἄρχ-ομαι begin (+ inf.)
αὐτ-οῦ... πονηρ-οῦ ὄντ-ος
    him ... being wicked (after
    κατεψηφίσαντο)
ἀχν-ύμεν-ος -η -ον grieving
βελτί-ους better (nom./acc.)
γν-ούς knowing (nom. s. m.)
    (γιγνώσκ-ω)
γούνασι lap (lit. 'knees')
δεξι-ός -ά -όν clever, handy
δικαιοσύν-η, ἡ justice, being
    just (1a)
δῶρ-ον, τό gift (2b)
εἰκός it is likely
εἰρήν-η, ἡ peace (1a)
ἑορτ-ή, -ή festival (1a)

ἐπεί since
ἐπὶ αὐχένι upon our neck
ἑτοῖμ-ος -η -ον ready (to)
    (+inf.)
εὐ-δόκιμ-ος -ον well thought of
ζυγ-ός, ὁ yoke (2a)
ἦτοι indeed
ἡγέ-ομαι consider (x to be ʏ)
ἡδον-ῆς pleasure (after πλέα)
Ἡράκλεις Herakles! (voc.)
καὶ... περ despite, although
καίτοι nonetheless
κακὰ λέγ-ω speak ill of
καρτερέ-ω endure, put up with
κατα-ψηφίζ-ομαι condemn (x on
    charge of ʏ)
κεῖται (they=ταῦτα) lie;
    (it=ζυγός) lies
κλοπ-ή, ἡ theft (1a)
μόν-ος -η -ον alone
νε-ῶν of ships
νόσ-ον disease (after πλέως)
νυν then
οἴν-ου wine (after πλέα)
οἱ δὲ others
οἱ μὲν some
ὁ Περικλῆς Pericles
ὅ τι what
ὅτι because of
οὐδενὸς nothing (after ἄξιοι)
πάντ-ων of all

παρασκευ-ῆς equipping (after
    πλέως)
περὶ εἰρήν-ης about peace
Περικλῆς Pericles (nom.)
πλέ-ως -α -ων full of
ποιέ-ομαι make
πλήν except
πλούτ-ου riches, wealth (after
    πλέα)
σίτ-ου food (after πλέα)
σπεύδ-οιμι ἄν I would hurry
σπονδ-αί, αἱ truce, treaty (1a)
συγγεν-ής, ὁ relation (3d)
τὰ βελτί-ω the better things (acc.)
τᾶν my dear chap
    (condescendingly)
τέτλαμεν we endure
τῇ ἐκκλησίᾳ the assembly
τῇ νηὶ the ship
τῆς πατρίδ-ος my fatherland
τῆς πόλ-εως of the city
τὸν Περικλέ-α Pericles
τόπ-ος, ὁ place (2a)
τῷ δήμ-ῳ the people
ὑγιεί-ας health (after πλέα)
φέρε come! (s.)
φιλό-πολις patriotic (nom.)
φιλό-σοφ-ος, ὁ philosopher (2a)
χαλεπ-ός -ή -όν difficult, hard
χείρ-ους worse (nom.)
χείρων χεῖρον (χειρον-) worse

Vocabulary to be learnt

ἄγω (ἀγαγ-) *live in, be at; lead, bring*

ἄξιος ᾱ ον *worth, worthy of (+gen.)*

ἀπολέω *I shall kill, destroy*

δεξιός ά όν *clever; right-hand*

διά (+gen.) *through*

ἐγγύς (+gen.) *near*

εἰρήνη, ἡ *peace (1a)*

εἰρήνην ἄγω *live in/be at peace*

ἐναντίον (+gen.) *opposite, in front of*

ἐπεί *since*

ἐπί (+dat., gen.) *on*

ἑτοῖμος η ον *ready (to) (+inf.)*

ἡγέομαι *think, consider; lead (+ dat.)*

ἡδονή, ἡ *pleasure (1a)*

Ἡρακλῆς, ὁ *Herakles (3d uncontr.)*

λαμβάνομαι *take hold of (+gen.)*

μετά (+ gen.) *with*

μόνος η ον *alone*

νυν *then (cf. νῦν now)*

ὁ μέν . . . ὁ δέ *one . . . another*

περί (+gen.) *about*

πλέως α ων *full of (+ gen.) (as if α-ος α-α α-ον contr.)*

ποιέομαι *make*

σῖτος, ὁ *food (2a) (pl. σῖτα, τά 2b)*

σπονδαί, αἱ *treaty, truce (1a)*

συγγενής, ὁ *relation (3d)*

τᾶν *my dear chap (voc.) (condescendingly)*

ὑπέρ (+gen.) *for, on behalf of*

ὑπό (+gen.) *by, at the hands of*

φιλόσοφος, ὁ *philosopher (2a)*

χαλεπός ή όν *difficult, hard*

χείρων χεῖρον (χειρον-) *worse*

Section Nine A–J: Aristophanes' *Wasps*

Introduction

The reason that Euelpides gave for leaving Athens was that he and Peisetairos had been unjustly found guilty in a law-suit. Whatever the actual rights and wrongs of the matter, the Athenians' reputation for litigiousness was notorious throughout the Mediterranean. Pericles (Περικλῆς) had introduced pay for dikasts (δικασταί, jurors) in c. 461 BC, so that even the poorest might be encouraged to take part in the democratic process of judging their fellow-man, and it would appear that some men were happy to scrape a living out of serving as dikasts. The courts handled not only judicial business, but political cases as well: their power was, potentially, enormous, and could be wielded to deadly effect. There was little 'procedure' in the courts; certainly no judge to guide dikasts and clarify the law; no question of the dikasts (usually 501 Athenian males) retiring to discuss what they had heard; few rules of evidence; and no cross-questioning of witnesses. The dikasts listened to both sides, and voted on the issue at once. In such an atmosphere, the law could easily be abused.

In *Wasps*, Aristophanes presents his vision of the 'typical' Athenian dikast, and leaves us to ponder its implications for the administration of justice in Athens.

In *World of Athens*: the law-courts 6.39ff.

Law-court mania in Athens

It has been estimated that, when allowance is made for festivals, ἐκκλησίαι and so on, juries might sit on between 150 and 200 days in the year … If we are to believe Aristophanes' *Wasps* of 422, some elderly Athenians had a passion to serve. Here a slave describes his master's mania:

'He loves it, this juror business; and he groans if he can't sit on the front bench. He doesn't get even a wink of sleep at night, but if in fact he does doze off just for a moment, his mind still flies through the night to the water-clock… And by god, if he saw any graffito by the doorway saying "Demos, son of Pyrilampes, is beautiful", he would go and write beside it, "κημός (the ballot-box) is beautiful"… [see Text 9C l.7]. Straight after supper he shouts for his shoes, and then off he goes to the court in the early hours and sleeps there, clinging to the court-pillar like a limpet. And through bad temper he awards the long line to all the defendants, and then comes home like a bee…with wax plastered under his finger-nails [because, when the jurors had to decide between penalties, they were given a wax tablet on which to mark a longer or shorter line, the former indicating the heavier penalty]. And because he's afraid that some day he may run short of voting-pebbles, he keeps a whole beach in his house. That's how mad he is…' (Aristophanes, *Wasps* 87–112) (*World of Athens*, 6.41)

A

The stage-set represents a house with a door and a window at a higher level. There is a bar across the door and a net draped over the window. In front of the house are standing two slaves, Sosias and Xanthias. They are supposed to be on guard duty, but Xanthias keeps falling asleep.

(ἔμπροσθεν τῆς οἰκίας εἰσὶ δοῦλοι δύο. διαλέγονται πρῶτον μὲν ἀλλήλοις, ἔπειτα τοῖς θεαταῖς.)

ΣΩΣΙΑΣ	οὗτος, τί πάσχεις;
	(again, louder)
	οὗτος, τί πάσχεις; 5
	(louder still)
	σοὶ λέγω, ὦ Ξανθία.
ΞΑΝΘΙΑΣ	*(wakes up with a start)* τίς ἡ βοή;
	(sees Sosias)
	τίνι λέγεις, Σωσία; τί βουλόμενος οὕτω βοᾷς; ἀπολεῖς με βοῶν. 10
Σ.	σοὶ λέγω, ὦ κακόδαιμον Ξανθία, καὶ σοῦ ἕνεκα βοῇ χρῶμαι. ἀλλὰ τί πάσχεις;
Ξ.	καθεύδω ἡδέως.
Σ.	καθεύδεις; ἀλλὰ λέγοιμ' ἄν τί σοι, κακοδαίμονι ἀνθρώπῳ ὄντι, καὶ δυστυχεῖ. 15
Ξ.	τί μοι λέγοις ἄν;
Σ.	λέγοιμ' ἄν σοι ὅτι μέγα κακόν σοι ἐμπεσεῖται. ἀπολεῖ γάρ σε ὁ δεσπότης. μὴ οὖν κάθευδε. ἆρ' οὐ τυγχάνεις εἰδὼς οἷον θηρίον φυλάττομεν;
Ξ.	δοκῶ γ' εἰδέναι.
Σ.	ἀλλ' οὑτοιὶ οὐκ ἴσασιν οἱ θεαταί. κάτειπε οὖν τὸν τοῦ δράματος λόγον τοῖς θεαταῖς, πολλοῖς δὴ οὖσιν. 20
Ξ.	καὶ δὴ καταλέξω τῷ τῶν θεατῶν πλήθει τὸν τοῦ ἡμετέρου δράματος λόγον.

Vocabulary for Section Nine A

> Grammar for 9A–E
> - The dat. case and its uses
> - Time phrases
> - More optatives: δυναίμην, ἀνισταίμην
> - Principal parts: ἐρωτάω, λέγω, λανθάνω

ἀλλήλ-οις to each other
βο-ῇ a shout (*after* χρῶμαι)
δρᾶμα (δραματ-),τό drama, play (3b)
δυσ-τυχεῖ unlucky (*goes with* κακοδαίμονι ἀνθρώπῳ ὄντι)

ἐμ-πεσ-εῖται it will befall (fut. of ἐμ-πίπτ-ω)
ἐμπρόσθεν (+ gen.) in front of, before
θεατ-ής, ὁ spectator, member of the audience (1d)

θηρί-ον,τό beast (2b)
καὶ δή well, all right; look
κακο-δαίμον-ι ἀνθρώπ-ῳ ὄντ-ι unlucky/ill-favoured man that you are
κατα-λέγ-ω (κατ-ειπ-) recount, tell

μοι to me
Ξανθί-ας, ὁ Xanthias (1d)
οἷ-ος -α -ον what sort of
πολλ-οῖς οὖσιν being many
   (*goes with* τοῖς θεατ-αῖς)
σοι to you (s.); you (*after*
   ἐμ-πεσ-εῖται)
σοῦ ἕνεκα for your sake

Σωσί-ας, ὁ Sosias(1d)
τίν-ι to whom? (s.)
τοῖς to/with/by the
τοῖς θεατ-αῖς to the audience
τῷ to/with/by the
τῷ πλήθ-ει to the crowd
χρά-ομαι use, employ

δρᾶμα (δρᾱματ-), τό *play, drama*
   (3b)
θεᾱτ-ής, ὁ *spectator, member of*
   audience (1d)

B

In *World of Athens*: homosexuality 5.32–5.

Ξ.   ἔστιν γὰρ ἡμῖν δεσπότης ἐκεινοσί, ὁ ἄνω ἥσυχος καθεύδων. ἆρ' οὐχ ὁρᾶτε
      αὐτὸν καθεύδοντα;
      (*points up to the roof*)
      ἔστι μὲν οὖν ἡμῖν δεσπότης οὗτος. τῷ δὲ δεσπότῃ πατήρ ἐστι πάνυ γέρων.
      ὁ δὲ δεσπότης ἡμᾶς ἐκέλευε φυλάττειν τὸν πατέρα, κελεύοντι δὲ ἐπιθόμεθα.
      ἐν γὰρ ἀπορίᾳ ἐνέπεσεν ὁ δεσπότης περὶ τοῦ πατρός, ἐπειδὴ ἔγνω αὐτὸν
      πονηρότερον ὄντα τῶν ἄλλων ἐν τῇ πόλει, καὶ αἴτιον κακῶν πολλῶν. ἔστι
      γὰρ τῷ πατρὶ τῷ τοῦ δεσπότου νόσος τις. ἐρωτῶ οὖν ὑμᾶς, ὦ θεαταί, τί
      τυγχάνει ὂν τὸ ὄνομα ταύτῃ τῇ νόσῳ; ὑμεῖς δ' ἀποκρίνεσθε ἡμῖν ἐρωτῶσιν.
      (*appeals to the audience for suggestions*)
      φέρε νυν· τί φησιν οὗτος;
Σ.   οὑτοσὶ μὲν ἡμῖν ἀποκρινόμενος 'φιλόκυβον' ἡγεῖται τὸν γέροντα. ἀλλὰ λέγω
      τῷ ἀνδρὶ ὅτι δῆλός ἐστιν οὐδὲν λέγων, τοιαῦτα ἀποκρινόμενος. οὐ μὴν ἀλλὰ
      'φιλο' μέν ἐστιν ἡ ἀρχὴ τοῦ κακοῦ.
Ξ.   φιλεῖ γάρ τι ὁ γέρων. ἀλλὰ τί φησιν οὗτος;
Σ.   οὗτος δέ μοι ἐρομένῳ ἀποκρίνεται ὅτι 'φιλοθύτην' ἢ 'φιλόξενον' νομίζει τὸν
      πατέρα εἶναι.
Ξ.   μὰ τὸν κύνα, ὦ τᾶν, οὐ φιλόξενος, ἐπεὶ καταπύγων ἐστὶν ὅ γε Φιλόξενος.

Vocabulary for Section Nine B

ἄνω above, up there
ἀπορί-ᾳ perplexity
ἀρχ-ή, ἡ beginning (1a)
ἔ-γνω he realised (γιγνώσκ-
   ω/ἔ-γνω-ν)
ἡμ-ῖν to us
ἡμ-ῖν ἐρωτ-ῶσιν to us asking
ἥσυχ-ος -ον quiet(ly)
κατα-πύγων κατά-πυγον
   (καταπυγον-) homosexual, gay
κελεύ-οντ-ι him ordering (*after*
   ἐπιθόμεθα)

κύων (κυν-), ὁ dog (3a)
μοι ἐρ-ομέν-ῳ to me asking
ὄνομα (ὀνοματ-), τό name (3b)
οὐ μὴν ἀλλὰ nonetheless
πονηρ-ός -ά -όν wicked, bad
ταύτ-ῃ τῇ νόσ-ῳ to this disease
τῇ in/with/by the
τῇ πόλ-ει the city
τοι-οῦτος τοι-αύτη τοι-οῦτ-
   ο(ν) of such a kind, like this
τῷ ἀνδρ-ὶ to the man
τῷ δεσπότ-ῃ to the master

τῷ πατρ-ὶ to the father
φέρε come!
φιλο- lover of
φιλο-θύτ-ης, ὁ lover of sacrifices
   (1d)
φιλό-κυβ-ος -ον lover of dice,
   gambler
φιλό-ξεν-ος -ον loving
   strangers, hospitable
Φιλόξεν-ος, ὁ Philoxenos (2a) (a
   noted homosexual)

Vocabulary to be learnt	ὄνομα (ὀνοματ-), τό *name (3b)*	τοιοῦτος τοιαύτη τοιοῦτο(ν) *of*
ἄνω *up, above*	πονηρός ᾱ́ όν *wicked,*	*this kind, of such a kind*
ἥσυχος ον *quiet, peaceful*	*wretched*	φέρε *come!*

C

In *World of Athens*: the *Eliaia* 6.39; part-source 6.41.

Ξ.   οὐδέποτ' ἐξευρήσετε, ὦ θεαταί. εἰ δὴ βούλεσθε εἰδέναι τίς ἡ νόσος ἡ τῷ πατρὶ
ἐμπεσοῦσα, σιωπᾶτε νῦν. λέξω γὰρ ὑμῖν⌐ ἐν ἀπορίᾳ δὴ ⌐οὖσι τὴν τοῦ γέροντος
νόσον. φιληλιαστής ἐστιν ὥσπερ οὐδεὶς ἀνήρ. δίκας γὰρ ἀεὶ δικάζει καὶ
τὸ δικαστήριον φιλεῖ, τῆς⌐ μὲν ⌐ἡμέρας καθιζόμενος ἐν τῷ⌐ δικαστηρίῳ,
τῆς⌐ δὲ ⌐νυκτὸς ὀνειροπολῶν δίκας. καίτοι οἱ μὲν ἐρασταὶ γράφουσιν ἐν   5
θύρᾳ⌐ τινί 'Δῆμος καλός', οὗτος δὲ ἰδὼν καὶ προσιὼν παραγράφει πλησίον
'Κημὸς καλός'. τοῦτον οὖν φυλάττομεν τούτοις⌐ τοῖς⌐ μοχλοῖς ἐγκλείσαντες,
πολλοῖς⌐ τε οὖσι⌐ καὶ⌐ μεγάλοις. ὁ γὰρ υἱὸς αὐτοῦ, ἐπεὶ τὸν πατέρα ἔμαθεν
φιληλιαστὴν ὄντα, τὴν νόσον βαρέως⌐ φέρων, πρῶτον μὲν ἐπειρᾶτο
ἀναπείθειν αὐτὸν μὴ ἐξιέναι θύραζε, τοιάδε λέγων·   10

    'διὰ τί', ἦ δ' ὅς, 'ἀεὶ δίκας δικάζεις, ὦ πάτερ, ἐν τῷ⌐ δικαστηρίῳ; ἆρ' οὐ
παύσῃ ἡλιαστὴς ὤν; ἆρα τῷ⌐ σῷ⌐ υἱῷ οὐ πείσῃ;'

    ὁ δὲ πατὴρ αὐτῷ⌐ μὴ ἐξιέναι ⌐ἀναπείθοντι οὐκ ἐπείθετο. εἶτα
ὁ υἱὸς τὸν πατέρα ἐκορυβάντιζεν. ὁ δὲ πατήρ, εἰς τὸ δικαστήριον
ἐμπεσών, αὐτῷ⌐ τῷ⌐ τυμπάνῳ ἐδίκαζεν. ἐντεῦθεν ἔνδον ἐγκλείσαντες   15

αὐτῷ τῷ τυμπάνῳ

αὐτὸν ἐφυλάττομεν τούτοις ͡ τοῖς ͡ δικτύοις. ἔστι δ' ὄνομα τῷˈ μὲν ˈγέροντι
Φιλοκλέων, τῷˈ δ' ˈυἱῷˈ γε ˈτούτῳ Βδελυκλέων.

Vocabulary for Section Nine C

ἀνα-πείθ-ω persuade, convince
ἀπορί-ᾳ perplexity
αὐλ-ή, ἡ courtyard (1a)
αὐτ-ῷ ... ἀνα-πείθ-οντ-ι him ...
  trying to persuade (him) (*after*
  ἐπείθετο)
αὐτῷ τῷ τυμπάν-ῳ drum and all
βαρέ-ως φέρ-ω take hard, find
  hard to bear
Βδελυ-κλέων (Βδελυκλεων-), ὁ
  Bdelykleon (3a) ('Loather of
  Kleon')
γράφ-ω write
Δῆμ-ος, ὁ Demos (2a) (*a notably*
  handsome young man)
δικάζ-ω be a juror, decide a case
ἐγ-κλεί-ω shut in
ἐξ-έρχ-ομαι go out
ἐπεὶ when
ἐραστ-ής, ὁ lover (1d)
ἡλιάστ-ης, ὁ juror in the Eliaia
  court (1d)
θύρ-ᾳ τιν-ὶ a door
θυράζε out of doors
καθ-ίζ-ομαι sit down
καίτοι furthermore

κημ-ὸς, ὁ funnel (2a) (*through*
  which the voting pebble goes
  into the voting urn)
κορυβαντίζ-ω introduce into the
  Korybantic rites (*a mystery*
  religion involving wildness of
  all kinds, and the beating of
  drums)
ὀνειρο-πολέ-ω dream
παρα-γράφ-ω write
  alongside
πλησίον nearby
πολλ-οῖς τε οὖσι καὶ
  μεγάλ-οις being many and
  large (*goes with* τούτ-οις τοῖς
  μόχλ-οις)
τῆς ἡμέρ-ας during the day
τῆς νυκτ-ὸς during the night
τοιόσδε τοιάδε τοιόνδε like this,
  as follows
τούτ-οις τοῖς δικτύ-οις with
  these nets
τούτ-οις τοῖς μόχλ-οις with
  these bars
τῷ γέροντ-ι to the old man
τῷ δικαστηρί-ῳ the law-court

τῷ πατρ-ὶ his father (*after*
  ἐμ-πεσ-οῦσ-α)
τῷ σῷ υἱ-ῷ your son (*after*
  πείσ-ῃ)
τῷ υἱ-ῷ τούτ-ῳ to this son here
ὑμ-ῖν ... οὖσι to you (pl.) being
φιλ-ηλιαστ-ής, ὁ lover of being
  a juror in the court of the
  Eliaia (1d)
Φιλο-κλέων (Φιλοκλεων-), ὁ
  Philokleon (3a) ('Lover of
  Kleon')

Vocabulary to be learnt

ἀναπείθω *persuade over to one's*
  side
βαρέως φέρω *take badly, find*
  hard to bear
δικάζω *be a juror; make a*
  judgment
ἐξέρχομαι (ἐξελθ-) *go out; come*
  out
ἐπεί *when; since*
καθίζομαι *sit down*
καθίζω *sit down*
πλησίον *nearby, (+gen.) near*

ΗΟ ΠΑΙΣ ΚΑΛΟΣ

D

In *World of Athens*: Kleon 1.58–9, 63, 67, 6.17, 6.41.

ΒΔΕΛΥΚΛΕΩΝ (βοᾷ τοῖς δούλοις ἀπὸ τοῦ τέγους)
     ὦ Ξανθία καὶ Σωσία, καθεύδετε;
Ξ.   οἴμοι, τάλας.
Σ.   τί ἐστιν;
Ξ.   ὁ δεσπότης οὐκέτι καθεύδει ἀλλ' ἀνίσταται ἤδη καὶ βοῇ χρῆται.   5
Σ.   ἀλλὰ τίσι λέγει ὁ ἀνήρ;
Ξ.   λέγει τι ἡμῖν ὁ Βδελυκλέων, ὡς ἐμοὶ δοκεῖ. καὶ ἡμῖν καθεύδουσιν
    ἐντυχὼν ἀπολεῖ ὁ δεσπότης.
Σ.   κἀμοὶ δοκεῖ λέγειν τι, Ξανθία. ἀλλὰ τί βουλόμενος ἀνίστασαι, ὦ δέσποτα;
ΒΔΕΛ.   (*pointing inside the house*)   10
    ὅ τι; λόγῳ μὲν ὁ πατὴρ ἡσυχάζει, Σωσία, ἔργῳ δὲ βούλεται ἐξιέναι. καὶ
    ἀεὶ τόλμῃ χρῆται ὁ πατὴρ ἐξιέναι βουλόμενος. νῦν δέ, ὡς ἔμοιγε δοκεῖ,
    ὁ πατὴρ εἰς τὸν ἰπνὸν εἰσελθὼν ὀπήν τινα ζητεῖ πολλῇ σπουδῇ.
    (*looking at the chimney*)
    ἄναξ Πόσειδον, τί ποτ' ἄρ' ἡ κάπνη ψοφεῖ;   15
(ἐκ τῆς κάπνης ἐξέρχεται ὁ Φιλοκλέων)
    οὗτος τίς εἶ σύ;
ΦΙΛΟΚΛΕΩΝ (*emerging from the chimney*)
    καπνὸς ἔγωγε ἐξέρχομαι.
ΒΔΕΛ.   καπνός; ἀλλὰ καπνῷ μὲν ἐξιόντι οὐχ ὅμοιος εἶ, ὡς ἔμοιγε δοκεῖ,   20
    Φιλοκλέωνι δ' ὁμοιότερος. τί δέ σοι δοκεῖ, Ξανθία;
Ξ.   οὐδενὶ ὁμοιότερος εἶναί μοι δοκεῖ ἢ τῷ Φιλοκλέωνι, ὦ δέσποτα.
ΒΔΕΛ.   (*puts the cover back on the chimney*)
    ἐνταῦθά νυν ζήτει τιν' ἄλλην μηχανήν.

Vocabulary for Section Nine D

ἄναξ (ἀνακτ-), ὁ lord (3a)
βο-ῆ a shout (*after* χρῆται)
ἐμ-οὶ to me
ἔμ-οιγε to me at least
ἐνταῦθα (from) here
ἐν-τυγχάν-ω (ἐν-τυχ-) meet,
    chance upon
ἔργ-ῳ in fact, indeed (i.e. actually)
ἡμ-ῖν to us
ἡμ-ῖν καθεύδ-ουσιν us sleeping
    (*after* ἐντυχὼν)
ἰπν-ός, ὁ oven (2a)
κάπν-η, ἡ chimney (1a)
καπν-ῷ . . . ἐξ-ιόντ-ι smoke
    coming out (*after* ὅμοι-ος)

καπν-ός, ὁ smoke (2a)
λόγ-ῳ in word (i.e.
    supposedly)
μηχαν-ή, ἡ device, scheme (1a)
μοι to me
ὅμοι-ος -α -ον like
ὀπ-ή, ἡ hole (1a)
ὅ τι; what?
οὐδεν-ὶ no one (*after*
    ὁμοιότερος)
πολλ-ῇ σπουδ-ῇ with much
    urgency (i.e. very urgently)
σοί to you (s.)
τάλας wretched (me)
τέγ-ος, τό roof (3c)

τίσι; to whom? (pl.)
τοῖς δούλ-οις to the slaves
τόλμ-η brazenness (*after*
    χρῆται)
τῷ Φιλο-κλέων-ι Philokleon
    (*after* ὁμοιότερος)
Φιλο-κλέων-ι Philokleon (*after*
    ὅμοιος)
χρά-ομαι use, employ (3rd s.
    χρῆται)
ψοφέ-ω make a noise

Vocabulary to be learnt
ἄναξ (ἀνακτ-), ὁ *prince, lord,*
    king (3a)

ἐνταῦθα (*t*)*here, at this that point*   μέλᾱς μέλαινα μέλαν (μελαν-) *black*   τάλᾱς τάλαινα τάλαν (ταλαν-) *wretched, unhappy*

E

ΦΙΛ.   (*commandingly*)
       ἀλλ' ἄνοιγε τὴν θύραν.

ΒΔΕΛ.   (*resolutely*)
       μὰ τὸν Ποσειδῶ, πάτερ, οὐδέποτέ γε.

ΦΙΛ.   (*a pause, then craftily*)   5
       ἀλλ' ἔστι νουμηνία τήμερον.

ΒΔΕΛ.   ὁ ἄνθρωπος οὗτος μέγα τι κακὸν παρασκευάζεται, ὡς ἔμοιγε δοκεῖ. τί σοι
       δοκεῖ, Ξανθία;

Ξ.   καὶ ἔμοιγε δοκεῖ.

ΦΙΛ.   (*overhears*)   10
       μὰ τὸν Δία οὐ δῆτα, ἀλλ' ἔξειμι, ἐπεὶ τὸν ἡμίονον ἐν τῇ ἀγορᾷ πωλεῖν
       βούλομαι αὐτοῖς τοῖς κανθηλίοις.

ΒΔΕΛ.   πωλεῖν βούλῃ τὸν ἡμίονον αὐτοῖς τοῖς κανθηλίοις; ἀλλ' ἐγὼ τοῦτο ἂν
       δρᾶν δυναίμην.

ΦΙΛ.   ἐγὼ δὲ τοῦτο ἂν δυναίμην ἄμεινον ἢ σύ.   15

ΒΔΕΛ.   οὐ μὰ τὸν Δία, ἀλλ' ἐγὼ σοῦ ἄμεινον.

ΦΙΛ.   ἀλλὰ εἰσιὼν τὸν ἡμίονον ἔξαγε.

The mule is led out of the courtyard.

ΒΔΕΛ.   ἀλλὰ τί παθὼν στένεις, ἡμίονε; ἆρα ὅτι τήμερον πωλήσομέν σε; ἀλλὰ
       μὴ στένε μηκέτι, ἡμίονε. τί δὲ τουτὶ τὸ πρᾶγμα; τί στένεις, εἰ μὴ φέρεις   20
       Ὀδυσσέα τινά;

Vocabulary for Section Nine E

ἄμεινον better
ἄνοιγε open!
αὐτ-οῖς τοῖς κανθηλί-οις pack-
   saddle and all
ἔμοι-γε to me

ἐξ-άγ-ω bring out, lead out
μηκέτι no longer
νου-μηνί-α, ἡ first of the month
   (1b) (*market-day*)
Ὀδυσσ-εύς, ὁ Odysseus (3g)

παρα-σκευάζ-ομαι devise,
   prepare
πωλέ-ω sell
στέν-ω groan
τῇ ἀγορ-ᾷ the market-place

ὁ ἡμίονος . . .

. . . φέρει Ὀδυσσέα τινά

Σ.   (*looks under the mule*)
        ἀλλὰ ναὶ μὰ Δία φέρει κάτω γε τουτονί τινα.
ΒΔΕΛ.   τίνα φέρει ὁ ἡμίονος; τίς εἶ ποτ', ὦ 'νθρωπε;
ΦΙΛ.   Οὖτις νὴ Δία.   25
ΒΔΕΛ.   Οὖτις σύ; ποδαπὸς εἶ;
ΦΙΛ.   Ἰθακήσιος, ὁ τοῦ Ἀποδρασιππίδου.
ΒΔΕΛ.   (*to Sosias*)
        ὕφελκε αὐτόν.
        (*looks at Philokleon with disgust*)   30
        ὦ μιαρώτατος. γιγνώσκω γάρ σε πάντων πονηρότατον ὄντα. τῷ⌐ γὰρ⌐
        Ὀδυσσεῖ δὴ ὁμοιότατός ἐστιν ὁ πατήρ, ὡς ἔμοιγε δοκεῖ. ἀλλ' ὦ πάτερ,
        σπουδῇ⌐ πάσῃ ὤθει τὸν ἡμίονον καὶ σεαυτὸν εἰς τὴν οἰκίαν.
        (*points to a pile of stones*)
        σὺ δέ, Σωσία, ὤθει ταῖς⌐ χερσὶ πολλοὺς τῶν λίθων πρὸς τὴν θύραν. 35
Σ.   (*busies himself with the task. Suddenly . . .*)
        οἴμοι τάλας. τί τοῦτο; πόθεν ποτ' ἐνέπεσέ μοι τὸ βῶλιον;
Ξ.   (*points to the roof*)
        ἰδού, ὦ δέσποτα. ὁ ἀνὴρ στρουθὸς γίγνεται.
ΒΔΕΛ.   οἴμοι κακοδαίμων. οὐ γάρ με λανθάνει ὁ πατὴρ στρουθὸς γιγνόμενος. 40
        ἀλλὰ φθήσεται ἡμᾶς ἐκφυγών. ποῦ ποῦ ἐστί μοι τὸ δίκτυον; σοῦ σοῦ,
        πάλιν σοῦ.
(τῷ⌐ δικτύῳ διώκει τὸν πατέρα)
Σ.   (*with relief, determined that the old man will give no more trouble*)
        ἄγε νυν. ἐπειδὴ τουτονὶ μὲν ἐνεκλείσαμεν, ἐγκλείσασι⌐ δ' ⌐ἡμῖν καὶ   45
        φύλαξιν⌐ οὖσι πράγματα⌐ οὐκ αὖθις ⌐παρέξει ὁ γέρων οὐδὲ λήσει ἡμᾶς
        ἀποδραμών, τί οὐ καθεύδομεν ὀλίγον χρόνον;

ἀπο-δραμ-ών *see* ἀπο-τρέχ-ω
ἀπο-τρέχ-ω (ἀπο-δραμ-) run away
Ἀπο-δρασ-ιππ-ίδης, ὁ the son of
    Runawayhorse (1d) (*comic
    name*)
βώλι-ον, τό clod of earth (2b)
δίκτυ-ον, τό net (2b)
δυν-αίμην ἀν I would be able
    (opt. of δύν-αμαι)
ἐγ-κλείσ-ασι . . . ἡμ-ῖν to us
    shutting (him) in
ἐγ-κλεί-ω shut in
ἐκ-φεύγ-ω (ἐκ-φυγ-) escape
ἡμίον-ος, ὁ mule (2a)
Ἰθακήσι-ος, ὁ (an) Ithakan (2a)
κάτω below, underneath
λήσ-ει he will escape notice (fut.
    of λανθάν-ω)

λίθ-ος, ὁ stone (2a)
μιαρ-ός -ά -όν foul
μοι me (*after* ἐνέπεσε); *my* (*after*
    ἐστί)
ὅμοι-ος -α -ον like
ὅτι because
Οὖ-τις No-man
πάντ-ων of all
ποδαπός from which country?
πράγματα παρ-έχ-ω cause
    problems (fut. παρ-έξ-ω)
σοί to you (s.)
σοῦ (ll.46–7) shoo!
σπουδ-ῇ πάσ-ῃ with all urgency
    (i.e. most urgently)
στρουθ-ός, ὁ sparrow (2a)
ταῖς χερσὶ with your
    hands

τῷ δικτύ-ῳ with the net
τῷ Ὀδυσσ-εῖ Odysseus (*after*
    ὁμοιότατος)
ὑφ-έλκ-ω drag from beneath
φθήσ-εται he will anticipate (fut.
    of φθάν-ω)
φύλαξιν οὖσι (to us) being
    guards (*goes with* ἐγκλείσασι
    . . . ἡμῖν)
ὠθέ-ω push

Vocabulary to be learnt
ἀμείνων ἄμεινον (ἀμεινον-)
    better
ἀποτρέχω (ἀποδραμ-) *run away*
ἐγκλείω *shut in, lock in*
ἐκφεύγω (ἐκφυγ-) *escape*
ἐξάγω (ἐξαγαγ-) *lead/bring out*

ἡμίονος, ὁ *mule (2a)*
μηκέτι *no longer*
μιαρός ᾱ́ όν *foul, polluted*

ὅμοιος ᾱ ον *like, similar to (+dat.)*
παρέχω (παρασχ-) *give to, provide*
πρᾱ́γματα παρέχω *cause trouble*

πωλέω *sell*
στένω *groan*
χράομαι *use, employ (+ dat.)*

Bdelykleon now persuades Philokleon that he should not go out to the court, but stay at home and judge offences committed by members of his own household. The old man agrees, and they begin to set up the courtroom.

In *World of Athens*: pay for jurors 6.41.

(Βδελυκλέων τῷ πατρὶ λέγει)

ΒΔΕΛ.   ἄκουε, ὦ πάτερ, οὐκέτι σε ἐάσω εἰς τὸ δικαστήριον ἀπιέναι, οὐδ' ἐμὲ
λήσεις πειρώμενος ἐξιέναι.

ΦΙΛ.   *(dismayed)*
τί τοῦτο; ἀλλ' ἀπολεῖς με, οὐκ ἐάσας ἐξιέναι.   5

ΒΔΕΛ.   *(firmly)*
ἐνθάδε μένειν σε χρή, πάτερ, καὶ ἐμοὶ πιθέσθαι.

ΦΙΛ.   ἀλλ' ὅμως ἐγὼ δικάζειν βούλομαι.
(falls to the floor in a rage)

ΒΔΕΛ.   ἀνίστασο, ὦ πάτερ, ἐπεὶ τήμερον δικάσαι δυνήσῃ.   10

ΦΙΛ.   ἀλλὰ πῶς δικάζειν μοι ἐξέσται, ἐνθάδε μένοντι;

Vocabulary for Section Nine F

> **Grammar for 9F–G**
> - Aorist infinitives, first and second, active and middle
> - Aspect in the infinitive
> - Aorist imperatives, first and second, active and middle
> - Present imperatives: εἰμί, εἶμι, οἶδα, δύναμαι, ἀνίσταμαι
> - ἔξεστι, δεινός
> - Vocatives
> - Adjectives: πᾶς

ἀν-ίστασο *get up! (s.)*
   (ἀν-ίστα-μαι)
δυνήσ-ῃ *you (s.) will be able*
   (fut. of δύν-αμαι)

ἐά-ω (ἐασ-) *allow*
ἐνθάδε *here*
ἔξ-εστι *it is possible (for x (dat.)*
   to -)

ὅμως *nevertheless, however*
πιθ-έσθαι *to obey (πείθ-ομαι/ἐ-*
   πιθ-όμην)
χρή *it is necessary (for x [acc.] to-)*

ΒΔΕΛ.   ἐν τῇ σαυτοῦ οἰκίᾳ ἔσται σοι δικαστήριον καὶ τοῖς οἰκέταις δικάσαι
        ἐξέσται.

ΦΙΛ.   τί φῄς; ἀλλὰ τίνι τρόπῳ καὶ περὶ τίνος;

ΒΔΕΛ.   περὶ πολλῶν. φέρε γάρ. εἰσὶ γάρ σοι πολλοὶ οἰκέται, ἀλλὰ εὖ οἶσθ' ὅτι   15
        οἱ οἰκέται οὐ βούλονται παύσασθαι ἀδικοῦντες, ἀλλ' αἴτιοί εἰσι πολλῶν
        κακῶν. χρὴ οὖν σε κατάσκοπον γενέσθαι τῶν πραγμάτων τῶν ἐν τῇ
        οἰκίᾳ γιγνομένων. καὶ ταῦτα τὰ κακὰ ἐξέσται σοι σκοπουμένῳ τήμερον
        ἐξευρεῖν, ἐξευρόντι δὲ δίκην λαβεῖν. οὔκουν ἂν βούλοιο τοῦτο δρᾶν, καὶ
        ἀναγκάζειν τοὺς οἰκέτας τῶν κακῶν παύσασθαι καὶ βελτίους γενέσθαι;   20

ΦΙΛ.   (eagerly)
        καὶ πάνυ βουλοίμην ἄν. ἀναπείθεις γάρ με τοῖς λόγοις. ἀλλ' ἐκεῖνο οὔπω
        λέγεις, τὸν μισθὸν ὁπόθεν λαβεῖν δυνήσομαι. οὔκουν βούλοιο ἂν τὸ
        πρᾶγμα δηλοῦν;

ΒΔΕΛ.   λήψῃ παρ' ἐμοῦ.   25

ΦΙΛ.   (satisfied)
        καλῶς λέγεις.

ΒΔΕΛ.   καὶ ποιῆσαι τοῦτο ἐθέλοις ἄν;

ΦΙΛ.   τοῦτο ἂν ποιοίην.

ΒΔΕΛ.   ἀνάμενέ νυν. ἐγὼ γὰρ ταχέως ἥξω φέρων τὰ τοῦ δικαστηρίου ταῖς χερσί.   30
        νὴ Δία, ἐξοίσω πάντα.

(ἀναμένει μὲν ὁ γέρων, ὁ δ' υἱὸς εἰς τὴν οἰκίαν εἰσέρχεται. δι' ὀλίγου Βδελυκλέων
ἐξελθὼν τὰ τοῦ δικαστηρίου ταῖς χερσὶ μόγις ἐκφέρει.)

ΒΔΕΛ.   (panting, and finally depositing the equipment)
        ἰδού. τέλος γὰρ ἐξήνεγκον τὰ τοῦ δικαστηρίου ἐγώ.   40

ΦΙΛ.   (looking at what Bdelykleon brought in)
        ἐξήνεγκας δὴ σὺ πάντα;

ΒΔΕΛ.   νὴ Δία, δοκῶ γ' ἐνεγκεῖν πάντα.
        (points to a brazier)
        καὶ πῦρ γε τουτὶ ἐξήνεγκον. ἰδού, ἐγγὺς τοῦ πυρὸς φακῆ τίς σοί ἐστιν.   45

ΦΙΛ.   (joyfully)
        ἰοὺ ἰού. ἔξεσται γάρ μοι δικάζοντι τὴν φακῆν ἐσθίειν. καὶ νὴ τὸν Δία
        αὐτὴν ἔδομαι, ὡς ἔμοιγε δοκεῖ, πάσῃ προθυμίᾳ, δεινὸς δὴ ὢν φαγεῖν.
        (pointing at a cockerel)
        ἀτὰρ τί βουλόμενος τὸν ἀλεκτρυόνα ἐξήνεγκας;   50

ΒΔΕΛ.   ὅ τι; ὁ ἀλεκτρυών σ' ἐγείρειν οἷός τ' ἔσται τῇ φωνῇ. μακροὶ μὲν γὰρ
        εἰσιν οἱ τῶν κατηγόρων λόγοι, σὺ δὲ δεινὸς καθεύδειν, καίπερ ἐν τῷ
        δικαστηρίῳ καθιζόμενος.

ἀλεκτρυών (ἀλεκτρυον-), ὁ
    cockerel (3a)
ἀναγκάζ-ω force, compel
ἀνα-μέν-ω hold on, wait
    around
ἀτὰρ but

γεν-έσθαι to become
    (γίγν-ομαι/ἐ-γεν-όμην)
δειν-ὸς καθεύδειν clever at
    sleeping
δειν-ὸς φαγ-εῖν clever at
    eating

δι' ὀλίγου after a short while
δικάσ-αι to give a judgment
    (δικάζ-ω)
δυνήσ-ομαι I will be able (fut. of
    δύν-αμαι)
ἐγείρ-ω wake up

ἔδ-ομαι I shall eat (fut. of
  ἐσθί-ω)
ἐθέλ-ω wish, want (to)
ἐκ-φέρ-ω (ἐξ-ενεγκ–) carry out
ἐνεγκ-εῖν to bring (φέρ-ω/
  ἤνεγκ-ον)
ἐξ-ευρ-εῖν to discover (ἐξ-
  ευρίσκ-ω/ἐξ-ηῦρ-ον)
ἐξ-ήνεγκ-ας you (s.) brought out
  (aor. ἐκ-φέρ-ω)
ἐξ-οίσ-ω I shall bring out (fut. of
  ἐκ-φέρ-ω)
ἐσθί-ω (φαγ-) eat
ἥκ-ω come
ἰού hurrah!
κατά-σκοπ-ος, ὁ scout, spy,
  inspector (2a)
κατήγορος, ὁ prosecutor (2a)
λαβ-εῖν to exact (λαμβάν-ω/
  ἔ-λαβ-ον)

μακρ-ός -ά -όν long
μισθ-ός, ὁ pay (2a)
μόγις with difficulty
οἷ-ός τ᾽ εἰμί be able (to)
  (+ inf.)
ὁπόθεν from where
ὅ τι; what?
οὔπω=οὐδέπω not yet
παρά (+ gen.) from
πάντ-α everything (acc.)
πάσ-ῃ προθυμί-ᾳ with all
  eagerness (i.e. most eagerly)
παύσ-ασθαι to stop; to cease
  from (+ gen.) (παύ-ομαι)
ποιῆσ-αι to act on (ποιέ-ω)
πῦρ (πυρ-), τό fire, brazier (3b)
σκοπέομαι investigate, examine
τίν-ι τρόπ-ῳ how? in what way?
  (τρόπ-ος, ὁ way [[2a]])
φακ-ῆ, ἡ lentil-soup (1a)

Vocabulary to be learnt
ἀναμένω (ἀναμεινα-) *wait, hold*
  on
ἀτάρ *but*
δεινός ἡ όν *clever at (+inf.);*
  dire, terrible
ἐάω (ἐᾱσα-, aor. εἴᾱσα) *allow*
ἐκφέρω (ἐξενεγκ-) *carry out;*
  (often: carry out for
  burial)
ἐνθάδε *here*
ἔξεστι *it is possible (for X [dat.]*
  to – [inf.])
ἐσθίω (φαγ -) *eat (fut. ἔδομαι)*
ὅμως *nevertheless, however*
ὅ τι; *what? (in reply to τί;)*
χρή *it is necessary (for X (acc.)*
  to – [inf.])

Law-court procedure

Because the court is one set up at home, Philokleon can enjoy all the home com-
forts he presumably would not have had in a real court – hot soup, for example,
(ll. 45–7). But there are two specific items mentioned in 9G. The *kados* (of which
there were two) was the urn in which one placed one's vote. Each juror had two
'pebbles' for voting. One was 'live'. One placed one's 'live' one in either the
innocent or guilty *kados*, and dropped the other pebble in the other. The *klepsudra* illustrated on p. 110 – the only one found in the Athenian *agora* – controlled the length of the speeches: it was filled with water, and the plug was removed
when the speech began (one juror was appointed to be in charge of it). The
speech had to end when the water had emptied. Both sides were thereby allotted the same time for their speeches. The illustrated *klepsudra* holds two χόες of
water (note the two capital χs on the side), and runs out in six minutes. But we
learn from Aristotle's *Constitution of Athens* that different sorts of cases were
granted speeches of different lengths, measured in numbers of χόες – anything
from three to forty-four. But we do not know whether the plugs were of the same
size as the example we possess; further, that *klepsudra* belonged to the Antiokhis
tribe (as the inscription indicates: ΑΝΤΙΟΧΙΔΟΣ, 'of Antiokhis'), not the courts.

G

In *World of Athens*: water-clock 6.46.

ΒΔΕΛ.	ἆρα πάντ' ἀρέσκει σοι, πάτερ; εἰπέ μοι.
ΦΙΛ.	πάντα δή μοι ἀρέσκει, εὖ ἴσθ' ὅτι.
ΒΔΕΛ.	οὐκοῦν κάθιζε, πάτερ. ἰδού· τὴν γὰρ πρώτην δίκην καλῶ.
ΦΙΛ.	μὴ κάλει τὴν δίκην, ὦ παῖ, ἀλλ' ἄκουσον.
ΒΔΕΛ.	καὶ δὴ ἀκούω. τί λέγεις; ἴθι, ὦ πάτερ, λέξον.

5

ΦΙΛ.	ποῦ εἰσιν οἱ κάδοι; οὐ γὰρ δύναμαι τὴν ψῆφον θέσθαι ἄνευ τῶν κάδων,
	εὖ ἴσθ' ὅτι.

(ἐκτρέχων ἄρχεται ὁ γέρων)

ΒΔΕΛ.	(shouting after him)
	οὗτος, σὺ ποῖ σπεύδεις;

10

ΦΙΛ.	κάδων ἕνεκα ἐκτρέχω.
ΒΔΕΛ.	μὴ ἄπιθι μηδαμῶς, ἀλλ' ἐμοὶ πιθοῦ καὶ ἄκουσον, ὦ πάτερ.
ΦΙΛ.	(looking back over his shoulder)
	ἀλλ' ὦ παῖ, δεῖ με τοὺς κάδους ζητήσαντα τὴν ψῆφον θέσθαι. ἀλλ' ἔασον.

(αὖθις ἄρχεται ἐκτρέχων)

15

ΒΔΕΛ.	(points to some cups)
	παῦσαι ἐκτρέχων, πάτερ, ἐπειδὴ τυγχάνω ἔχων ταῦτα τὰ κυμβία. μὴ οὖν
	ἄπιθι.
ΦΙΛ.	(satisfied)
	καλῶς γε. πάντα γὰρ τὰ τοῦ δικαστηρίου πάρεστι –
	(has a sudden thought)
	πλήν –

20

ΒΔΕΛ.	λέξον· τὸ τί;

αἱ κλεψύδραι

ἡ ἄμις κλεψύδρα ἀρίστη

ΦΙΛ.   πλὴν τῆς κλεψύδρας. ποῦ ἐστιν ἡ κλεψύδρα; ἔνεγκέ μοι.

ΒΔΕΛ.   ἰδού.   25

(τὴν τοῦ πατρὸς ἀμίδα δηλοῖ)

          εἰπέ, αὕτη δὴ τίς ἐστιν; οὐχὶ κλεψύδραν ἀρίστην ἡγῇ τὴν ἀμίδα ταύτην;

          πάντα νῦν πάρεστιν.

Sosias enters, leading two dogs. It seems that one, Labes (Λάβης 'Grabber'), has

wolfed a whole cheese. It is decided that the other dog should charge him with theft.   30

Bdelykleon orders the slaves to clear the 'courtroom' and asks for ritual prayers.

ΒΔΕΛ.   κάθιζε οὖν, πάτερ, καὶ παῦσαι φροντίζων. ἀκούσατε, παῖδες, καὶ ἐμοὶ

          πίθεσθε, καὶ ἐξενέγκατε τὸ πῦρ. ὑμεῖς δὲ εὔξασθε πᾶσι τοῖς θεοῖς,

          εὐξάμενοι δὲ κατηγορεῖτε.

(ἐξενεγκόντες τὸ πῦρ ἀπέρχονται πάντες οἱ δοῦλοι, εὔχονται δὲ τοῖς θεοῖς οἱ   35

παρόντες)

κάδον φέρει   'ΚΑΔΟΣ ΕΙΜΙ'

Vocabulary for Section Nine G

ἀκούσ-ατε listen! pay attention! (pl.) (ἀκού-ω)

ἄκουσ-ον listen! pay attention! (s.) (ἀκού-ω)

ἀμίς (ἀμιδ-), ἡ chamber-pot (3a)

ἄνευ + gen.) without

ἄπ-ιθι go away! (s.) (ἀπ-έρχ-ομαι/ἄπ-ειμι)

ἀρέσκ-ει it pleases (+dat.)

ἄρχ-ομαι begin (+ part.)

ἔασ-ον (lit. 'allow!') leave off! (s.) (ἐά-ω)

ἐκ-τρέχ-ω run out

ἔνεγκ-έ fetch! (φέρ-ω/ἤνεγκ-ον)

ἐξ-ενέγκ-ατε fetch out! (pl.) (ἐκ-φέρ-ω/ἐξ-ήνεγκ-α)

εὔξ-ασθε pray! (pl.) (εὔχ-ομαι)

θέ-σθαι to cast (τίθεμαι/ἐ-θέ-μην)

ἴθι come! (s.) (ἔρχ-ομαι/εἶμι)

ἴσθι know! (s.) (οἶδα)

κάδ-ος, ὁ voting-urn (2a)

κάδ-ων ἕνεκα because of the urns

καὶ δὴ well, all right (you have my attention)

καλῶς γε fine!

κατηγορέ-ω accuse, prosecute

κλεψύδρ-α, ἡ water-clock (1b)

κυμβί-ον, τό cup (2b)

λέξ-ον (lit. 'speak!') out with it! (λέγ-ω)

μηδαμ-ῶς in no way

πάντ-α everything; all (nom.)

πάντ-ες all (nom. pl. m.)

πᾶσι to all (dat. pl. m.)

παῦσ-αι stop! (s.) (παύ-ομαι)

πίθ-εσθε obey! (pl.) (πείθ-ομαι/ἐ-πιθ-όμην)

πιθ-οῦ obey! (s.) (πείθ-ομαι/ἐ-πιθ-όμην)

πλὴν (+ gen.) except

πῦρ (πυρ-),τό fire (3b)

ψῆφ-ος, ἡ vote (2a) (lit. pebble)

Vocabulary to be learnt

ἄρχομαι *begin (+inf. or part.)*

ἐκτρέχω (ἐκδραμ-) *run out*

ἕνεκα (+gen.) *because, for the sake of* (usually placed after the noun)

πᾶς πᾶσα πᾶν (παντ-) *all*

ὁ πᾶς *the whole of*

πλήν (+gen.) *except*

πῦρ (πυρ-), τό *fire (3b)*

H

*After the prayers, Bdelykleon acts as herald and opens the proceedings.
Philokleon eats happily as he listens to the case, which is α γραφή for theft
brought by Dog against Labes.*

In *World of Athens*: coming to trial 6.49–50.

ΒΔΕΛ.	εἴ τις ἡλιαστὴς ἔξω ὢν τυγχάνει, εἰσίτω καὶ σπευδέτω.
ΦΙΛ.	*(looks about expectantly)*
	τίς ἐσθ' ὁ φεύγων; προσίτω.

(προσέρχεται ὁ φεύγων, κύων ὤν)

ΒΔΕΛ.	ἀκούσατ' ἤδη τῆς γραφῆς.	5
	(he reads out the charge)	
	ἐγράψατο Κύων Κυδαθηναιεὺς κύνα Λάβητ' Αἰξωνέα κλοπῆς. ἠδίκησε	
	γὰρ ὁ φεύγων, μόνος τὸν τυρὸν καταφαγών. καὶ μὴν ὁ φεύγων οὑτοσὶ	
	Λάβης πάρεστιν.	
ΦΙΛ.	*(regarding the dog balefully)*	10
	προσίτω. ὦ μιαρὸς οὗτος, γιγνώσκω σε κλέπτην ὄντα. ἀλλ' ἐξαπατήσειν	
	μ' ἐλπίζεις, εὖ οἶδα. ποῦ δ' ἐσθ' ὁ διώκων, ὁ Κυδαθηναιεὺς κύων; ἴθι,	
	κύον.	
ΚΥΩΝ	αὖ͡ αὖ.	
ΒΔΕΛ.	πάρεστιν οὗτος.	15
ΞΑΝΘΙΑΣ	ἕτερος οὗτος αὖ Λάβης εἶναί μοι δοκεῖ, λόγῳ μὲν ἀναίτιος ὤν, ἔργῳ δὲ	
	κλέπτης καὶ αὐτός, καὶ ἀγαθός γε καταφαγεῖν πάντα τὸν τυρόν.	

The trial of Labes from Aristophanes' *Wasps*

Vocabulary for Section Nine H

> **Grammar for 9H–J**
> - Third person imperatives, present and aorist, active and middle, incl. εἰμί, εἶμι, οἶδα
> - Future infinitive and its uses
> - Root aorists: ἔβην, ἔγνων
> - ἐπίσταμαι 'I know'
> - Principal parts: αἱρέω, αἱρέομαι, πάσχω, φέρω, πείθω, πείθομαι

ἀγαθ-ός -ή -όν good (at)
(+ inf.)
Αἰξων-εύς, ὁ man from the deme
Aixone (3g)
ἀν-αίτι-ος -ον innocent
αὖ αὖ woof! woof!
γράφ-ομαι indict x (acc.) for
γ (gen.)
διώκ-ω prosecute

ἐλπίζ-ω hope, expect (to)
ἐξ-απατήσ-ειν to deceive
(ἐξ-απατά-ω)
ἔξω outside
ἡλιάστ-ης, ὁ juror in the Eliaia
court (1d)
καὶ μήν and look . . .
κλέπτ-ης, ὁ thief (1d)
κλοπ-ή, ἡ theft (1a)

Κυδαθηναι-εύς, ὁ man from the
deme Kydathene (3g)
Λάβης (Λαβητ-), ὁ Labes (3a)
('Grabber')
προσ-ίτω let him come forward
(προσ-έρχ-ομαι/πρός-ειμι)
σπευδ-έτω let him hurry!
(σπεύδ-ω)
φεύγ-ω be a defendant

Kleon and Lakhes

The trial between the two dogs is an extended satire on two contemporary politicians, Kleon and Lakhes. The dog from Kudathenaion represents Kleon, Labes from Aixone represents Lakhes. Kleon is already at the heart of *Wasps* because it was he who had raised jury pay: hence Philokleon 'Love-Kleon', and Bdelukleon 'Loathe-Kleon'. Here Aristophanes sees a further chance to mock Kleon by turning him into a dog and having him prosecute Labes/Lakhes for 'eating up all the Sicilian cheese'. Lakhes had been involved with an expedition round Sicily in 427–4, and it seems he had been accused of helping himself to the money that Athens' allies in Sicily had been providing for the upkeep of the fleet. Whether Kleon had actually prosecuted Lakhes on these grounds is not known; but since Kleon was renowned for putting himself forward as a 'champion of the people' by prosecuting officials whose financial conduct was dodgy, and had recently been making comments about Lakhes' behaviour, Aristophanes saw a chance to have a bit of fun at his expense. It is notable that, throughout the trial, the dog Kleon is presented as every bit as bad as Labes/Lakhes (see e.g. *Text* 9H l.16, 9I ll.23–4). Aristophanes always had it in for Kleon. The point is that the majority of leaders of the people before Pericles had been from traditional families whose wealth was in land; but after the death of Pericles, the new breed of politicians came from un-landed, *nouveau-riche* families, whom Aristophanes despised.

ΒΔΕΛ.   σῖγα, κάθιζε. σὺ δέ, ὦ κύον, ἀναβὰς κατηγόρει.
(ὁ δὲ κύων, ἀναβῆναι οὐκ ἐθέλων, ἀποτρέχει)
The dog runs off round the courtroom. At last he is caught and put on the rostrum.   20

ΦΙΛ.   εὖ γε. τέλος γὰρ ἀνέβη ὁ κύων. ἐγὼ δέ, ἅμα δικάζων, πᾶσαν τὴν φακῆν
ἔδομαι, τῆς δὲ κατηγορίας ἀκούσομαι ἐσθίων.

ΚΥΩΝ   τῆς μὲν γραφῆς ἠκούσατ', ὦ ἄνδρες δικασταί. οὗτος γὰρ ὁ ἀδικήσας με
ἔλαθε ἀπιὼν μόνος, καὶ πάντα τὸν τυρὸν καταφαγών. καὶ ὅτε μέρος
ᾔτησα ἐγώ, οὐ παρεῖχέ μοι αἰτοῦντι. παύσομαι κατηγορῶν· δίκασον.   25

ΦΙΛ.   ἀλλ' ὦ 'γαθέ, τὸ πρᾶγμα φανερόν ἐστιν. αὐτὸ γὰρ βοᾷ. τὴν ψῆφον οὖν
θέσθαι με δεῖ, καὶ ἑλεῖν αὐτόν.

ΒΔΕΛ.   *(appeals to Philokleon)*
ἴθι, πάτερ, πρὸς τῶν θεῶν, ἐμοὶ πιθοῦ καὶ μὴ προκαταγίγνωσκε. δεῖ γάρ
σε ἀμφοτέρων ἀκοῦσαι, ἀκούσαντα δὲ οὕτω τὴν ψῆφον θέσθαι.   30

ΚΥΩΝ   κολάσατε αὐτόν, ὡς ὄντα αὖ πολὺ κυνῶν ἁπάντων ἄνδρα
μονοφαγίστατον, καὶ ἕλετε τοῦτον.

ΒΔΕΛ.   νῦν δὲ τοὺς μάρτυρας εἰσκαλῶ ἔγωγε.
(calls out a summons)
προσιόντων πάντες οἱ Λάβητος μάρτυρες, κυμβίον, τυρόκνηστις, χύτρα,   35
καὶ τὰ ἄλλα σκεύη πάντα. ἴθι, ὦ κύον, ἀνάβαινε, ἀπολογοῦ.
(there is a long silence from Labes)
τί παθὼν σιωπᾷς; λέγοις ἄν. ἔξεστι γάρ· καὶ δὴ δεῖ σε ἀπολογεῖσθαι.

ΦΙΛ.   ἀλλὰ οὐ δύναται οὗτός γ', ὡς ἔμοιγε δοκεῖ. οὐ γὰρ ἐπίσταται λέγειν.

ΒΔΕΛ.   κατάβηθι, ὦ κύον. ἐγὼ γὰρ μέλλω ἀπολογήσεσθαι, εὖ εἰδὼς περὶ τὰ   40
δικανικά.

χύτρα καὶ τὰ ἄλλα σκεύη

αἱρέ-ω (ἑλ-) convict

αἰτέ-ω ask (for)

ἀκού-ω listen (to) (+gen.)

ἀμφότερ-οι –αι -α both

ἀνα-βάς going up
   (ἀνα-βαίν-ω/ἀν-έ-βην)

ἀνα-βῆν-αι to go up
   (ἀνα-βαίν-ω/ἀν-έ-βην)

ἀν-έ-βη (he) went up
   (ἀνα-βαίν-ω/ἀν-έ-βην)

ἅπας ἅπασ-α ἅπαν (ἁπαντ-) all

ἀπο-λογέ-ομαι make speech for
   the defence

ἀπο-λογήσ-εσθαι to make the
   defence speech

αὖ again, moreover

γραφ-ή, ἡ indictment, charge
   (1a)

δικανικ-ά, τά court affairs, legal
   matters (2b)

ἐθέλ-ω wish, want (to)

εἰσ-ίτω let him come in!
   (εἰσ-έρχ-ομαι/εἴσ-ειμι)

εἰσ-καλέ-ω call in,
   summon

ἑλ-εῖν see αἱρέ-ω

ἕλ-ετε see αἱρέ-ω

ἐπ-ίστα-μαι know how (to)
   (+ inf.)

εὖγε well done! hurrah!

θέ-σθαι to cast (τίθε-μαι/
   ἐ-θέ-μην)

καὶ δή and indeed

κατά-βηθι get down! (s.)
   (κατα-βαίν-ω/κατ-έ-βην)

κατ-εσθί-ω (κατα-φαγ-) eat up

κατηγορέ-ω prosecute, make a
   prosecution speech

κατηγορί-α, ἡ prosecution (1b)

κηρύττ-ω announce

κυμβί-ον, τό cup (2b)

κύων (κυν-), ὁ dog (3a)

μάρτυς (μαρτυρ-), ὁ witness (3a)

μέλλ-ω be about (to)

μέρ-ος, τό share (3c)

μονο-φαγ-ίστατ-ος most selfish
   (lit. 'alone') eater

πολὺ much

προ-κατα-γιγνώσκ-ω
   prejudge

πρός (+ gen.) in the name of

προσ-ιόντων let them come
   forward! (προσ-έρχ-ομαι/
   πρόσ-ειμι)

σιγά-ω be quiet

τυρό-κνηστις (τυροκνηστιδ-), ἡ
   cheese-grater (3a)

τυρ-ός, ὁ cheese (2a)

φακ-ῆ, ἡ lentil-soup (1a)

φανερ-ός -ά -όν clear,
   obvious

χυτρ-ά, ἡ cooking-pot

ψῆφ-ος, ἡ vote (2a) (lit.
   'pebble')

Vocabulary to be learnt

ἀκούω *hear, listen to (+ gen. of*
   person/thing)

ἀπολογέομαι *defend oneself,*
   make a speech in one's own
   defence

γραφή, ἡ *indictment, charge,*
   case (1a)

γράφομαι *indict, charge*

γραφὴν γράφομαι *indict*
   X (acc.) on charge of Y
   (gen.)

διώκω *prosecute, pursue*

ἐθέλω *wish, want (to)*

κατηγορέω *prosecute*
   X (gen.) on a charge of
   Y (acc.)

κατηγορίᾱ, ἡ *speech for the*
   prosecution (1b)

κύων (κυν-), ὁ *dog (3a)*

μάρτυς (μαρτυρ-), ὁ *witness*
   (3a)

μέρος, τό *share, part (3c)*

πολύ *(adv.) much*

πρός *(+gen.) in the name of,*
   under the protection of

φεύγω (φυγ-) *be a defendant, be*
   on trial; flee

ψῆφος, ἡ *vote, voting-pebble*
   (2a)

In *World of Athens*: witnesses and evidence 6.46; cheese 2.16.

(ὁ Βδελυκλέων, τῆς ἀπολογίας ἀρχόμενος, λέγει)

ΒΔΕΛ.	χαλεπὸν μέν, ὦνδρες, ἐστὶν ὑπὲρ κυνὸς τοσαύτης διαβολῆς
	τυχόντος ἀποκρίνασθαι, λέξω δ' ὅμως. γιγνώσκω γὰρ αὐτὸν ἀγαθὸν ὄντα
	καὶ διώκοντα τοὺς λύκους.
ΦΙΛ.	*(dissenting)* 5
	κλέπτης μὲν‿οὖν οὗτός γ' εἶναί μοι δοκεῖ καὶ ἄξιος θανάτου. δεῖ οὖν με
	ἑλεῖν αὐτὸν κλέψαντα, ἑλόντα δ' ἑτέραν αὖ δίκην δικάζειν.
ΒΔΕΛ.	μὰ Δί', ἀλλ' ἄριστός ἐστι πάντων τῶν νυνὶ κυνῶν, ἐπειδὴ οἷός‿τ'‿ἐστὶ
	πολλὰ πρόβατα φυλάττειν.
ΦΙΛ.	τί οὖν ὄφελος, εἰ τὸν τυρὸν ὑφαιρεῖται, ὑφελόμενος δὲ κατεσθίει; 10
ΒΔΕΛ.	ὅ τι; φυλάττει γὰρ καὶ τὴν θύραν. εἰ δ' ὑφείλετο τὸν τυρόν,
	συγγνώμην‿ἔχετε. κιθαρίζειν γὰρ οὐκ ἐπίσταται. ἄκουσον, ὦ δαιμόνιε,
	τῶν μαρτύρων. ἀνάβηθι, τυρόκνηστι, καὶ λέξον μέγα. σὺ γὰρ τὸν τυρὸν
	φυλάττουσα ἔτυχες.

(ἀνίσταται ἡ τυρόκνηστις)   15

	ἀπόκριναι σαφῶς· ἆρα κατέκνησας τὸν τυρὸν ἀμφοτέροις τοῖς κυσίν;
	(bends his head towards the grater and pretends to listen)
	λέγει ὅτι πάντα κατέκνησεν ἀμφοτέροις.
ΦΙΛ.	νὴ Δία, ἀλλὰ γιγνώσκω αὐτὴν ψευδομένην.
ΒΔΕΛ.	*(pleading)* 20
	ἀλλ' ὦ δαιμόνιε, οἴκτιρε τοὺς κακὰ πάσχοντας. οὗτος γὰρ ὁ Λάβης
	οὐδέποτε ἐν τῇ οἰκίᾳ μένει, ἀλλὰ τὰ σιτία ζητῶν ἐκ τῆς οἰκίας ἐξέρχεται.
	ὁ δ' ἕτερος κύων τὴν οἰκίαν φυλάττει μόνον. ἐνθάδε γὰρ μένων ἐλπίζει
	τὰ σιτία ὑφαιρήσεσθαι παρὰ τῶν ἄλλων. καὶ ὑφελόμενος μηδέν, δάκνει.
ΦΙΛ.	*(feels his resolve breaking)* 25
	αἰβοῖ. τί κακόν πότ' ἐστι τόδε; κακόν τι περιβαίνει με, καὶ ὁ λέγων με
	πείθει τοῖς λόγοις.
ΒΔΕΛ.	*(still pleading)*
	ἴθ' ἀντιβολῶ σε, οἰκτίρατε αὐτόν, ὦ πάτερ, κακὰ παθόντα, καὶ
	ἀπολύσατε. ποῦ τὰ παιδία; ἀναβαίνετε, ὦ πονηρά, αἰτεῖτε καὶ ἀντιβολεῖτε 30
	δακρύοντα.
ΦΙΛ.	*(exasperated)*
	κατάβηθι, κατάβηθι, κατάβηθι, κατάβηθι.
ΒΔΕΛ.	καταβήσομαι. καίτοι τὸ 'κατάβηθι' τοῦτο πολλοὺς δὴ πάνυ ἐξαπατᾷ. οἱ
	γὰρ δικασταὶ τὸν φεύγοντα καταβῆναι κελεύουσιν, εἶτα καταβάντος 35
	αὐτοῦ καταδικάζουσιν. ἀτὰρ ὅμως καταβήσομαι.

γυνή τις τυροκνήστιδι χρωμένη

Vocabulary for Section Nine I

αἰβοῖ yuk! arghh!
αἱρέ-ω (ἑλ-) convict
αἰτέ-ω ask
ἀμφότερ-οι -αι -α both
ἀνά-βηθι go up! (s.)
  (ἀνα-βαίν-ω/ἀν-έ-βην)
ἀντι-βολέ-ω beg, plead (with)
ἀπο-λογί-α, ἡ defence speech (1b)
ἀπο-λύ-ω acquit
ἀπο-λύσ-ατε pl., as if to a whole
  jury
ἄρχ-ομαι begin (+gen.)
αὖ again, further
δαιμόνι-ε my good fellow
δακρύ-ω weep
ἐλ-εῖν
ἐλ-όντ-α } see αἱρέ-ω
ἐλπίζ-ω hope, expect
ἐξ-απατά-ω deceive
ἐπ-ίστα-μαι know (how to)
  (+ inf.)
θάνατ-ος, ὁ death (2a)
καίτοι and yet
κατα-βάντ-ος getting down (gen.
  s. m.) (κατα-βαίν-ω/
  κατ-έ-βην)
κατά-βηθι get down! (s.)
  (κατα-βαίν-ω/κατ-έ-βην)
κατα-βῆναι to get down
  (κατα-βαίν-ω/κατ-έ-βην)
κατα-βής-ομαι I shall get down
  (κατα-βαίν-ω/κατ-έ-βην)

κατα-δικάζ-ω convict, find guilty
  (+gen.)
κατα-κνά-ω grate
κατ-εσθί-ω eat up
κιθαρίζ-ω play the kithara (i.e.
  be educated)
κλέπτ-ης, ὁ thief (1d)
λύκ-ος, ὁ wolf (2a)
μέγα loudly
μὲν οὖν no, rather
μηδείς μηδεμί-α μηδέν (μηδεν-)
  no
νυνὶ=νῦν
ὅδε ἥδε τόδε this (here)
οἰκτίρ-ατε pl., as if to a whole
  jury
οἷ-ός τ' εἰμί be able (to)
ὄφελ-ος, τό use (3c)
παιδί-ον, τό puppy (2b)
παρά (+gen.) from
περι-βαίν-ω surround
πονηρ-ός –ά -όν poor,
  wretched
πρόβατ-α, τά sheep (2b)
σιτί-α, τά provisions, food (2b)
συγγνώμ-ην ἔχ-ω forgive
τόδε see ὅδε
τοσ-οῦτ-ος, τοσ-αύτ-η
  τοσ-οῦτ-ο(ν) so great
τυγχάν-ω (τυχ-) chance on,
  happen upon, hit upon
  (+ gen.)

τυρό-κνηστις (τυροκνηστιδ-), ἡ
  cheese-grater (3a)
ὑφ-αιρέ-ομαι (ὑφ-ελ-) steal, take
  by stealth for oneself
ὑφ-αιρήσ-εσθαι to steal
  (ὑφ-αιρέ-ομαι)
ψεύδ-ομαι lie

Vocabulary to be learnt

αἱρέω (ἑλ-) take, capture,
  convict
αἰτέω ask (for)
ἀμφότεροι αι α both
ἀπολογίᾱ, ἡ speech in one's own
  defence (1b)
ἄρχομαι begin (+gen.); begin to
  (+part. or inf.)
αὖ again, moreover
ἐλπίζω hope, expect (+fut. inf.)
θάνατος, ὁ death (2a)
καταδικάζω condemn, convict
  (X [gen.] on charge of
  Y [acc.])
κλέπτης, ὁ thief (1d)
παιδίον, τό child; slave (2b)
παρά (+gen.) from
τυγχάνω (τυχ-) hit, chance
  on, happen on, be subject
  to (+gen.); happen (to), be
  actually (+part.)
ὑφαιρέομαι (ὑφελ-) steal, take
  for oneself by stealth

J

In *World of Athens*: voting 6.51.

ΦΙΛ.   (*weeping*)
          εἰς κόρακας. ὡς οὐκ ἀγαθὴν νομίζω τὴν φακῆν. ἐγὼ γὰρ ἀπεδάκρυσα,
          τὴν φακῆν ταύτην κατεσθίων.
ΒΔΕΛ.   οὔκουν ἀποφεύγει δῆτα ὁ κύων;
ΦΙΛ.   χαλεπόν μοί ἐστιν εἰδέναι.   5
ΒΔΕΛ.   (*pleads again*)
          ἴθ', ὦ πατρίδιον, ἐπὶ τὰ βελτίω τρέπου.
          (*hands him a voting-pebble*)
          τήνδε λαβὼν τὴν ψῆφον τῇ χειρί, θὲς ἐν τῷ ὑστέρῳ κάδῳ, καὶ
          ἀπόλυσον, ὦ πάτερ.   10
ΦΙΛ.   (*his resolve returns*)
          οὐ δῆτα. κιθαρίζειν γὰρ οὐκ ἐπίσταμαι.
ΒΔΕΛ.   φέρε⌜ νύν σε τῇδε ⌝περιάγω.
(περιάγων οὖν περίπατον πολύν, ἐπὶ τὸν ὕστερον κάδον πρῶτον βαδίζει)
ΦΙΛ.   ὅδε ἐσθ' ὁ πρότερος;   15
ΒΔΕΛ.   οὗτος. θὲς τὴν ψῆφον.
ΦΙΛ.   αὕτη ἡ ψῆφος ἐνταῦθ' ἔνεστιν.
          (*puts pebble into the acquittal urn*)
ΒΔΕΛ.   (πρὸς ἑαυτὸν λέγει)
          εὖ⌢ γε. ἐξηπάτησα αὐτόν. ἀπέλυσε γὰρ Φιλοκλέων τὸν κύνα   20
          οὐχ ἑκών, τὴν ψῆφον θεὶς ἐν τῷ ὑστέρῳ κάδῳ.
ΦΙΛ.   πῶς ἄρ' ἠγωνισάμεθα;
ΒΔΕΛ.   δηλώσειν μέλλω.
          (*looks in the urn, counts, and then declares*)
          ἀπέφυγες, ὦ Λάβης.   25
          (*Philokleon faints*)
          πάτερ, πάτερ. τί πάσχεις; οἴμοι ποῦ ἐσθ' ὕδωρ; ἔπαιρε σεαυτόν, ἀνίστασο.
ΦΙΛ.   (*still not believing what has happened*)
          εἰπέ νυν ἐκεῖνό μοι, ὄντως ἀπέφυγεν; ἀπολεῖς με τῷ λόγῳ.
ΒΔΕΛ.   νὴ Δία.   30
ΦΙΛ.   οὐδέν εἰμ' ἄρα.
ΒΔΕΛ.   μὴ φρόντιζε, ὦ δαιμόνιε, ἀλλ' ἀνίστασο.
ΦΙΛ.   ἀλλ' ἐγὼ φεύγοντα ἀπέλυσα ἄνδρα τῇ ψήφῳ; τί πάσχω; τί ποτε πείσομαι;
          ἀλλ' ὦ πολυτίμητοι θεοί, συγγνώμην⌜ μοι ⌝ἔχετε, ὅτι ἄκων αὐτὸ ἔδρασα,
          τὴν ψῆφον θεὶς καὶ οὐχ ἑλών.   35

Vocabulary for Section Nine J

ἀγωνίζ-ομαι contest
ἄκων ἄκουσ-α ἆκον (ἀκοντ-)
    unwilling(ly)
ἀπο-δακρύ-ω burst into tears
ἀπο-λύ-ω acquit
ἀπο-φεύγ-ω (ἀποφυγ-) be
    acquitted
βαδίζ-ω walk
δαιμόνι-ε my dear fellow
δηλώσ-ειν to reveal (δηλό-ω)
ἑκών ἑκοῦσ-α ἑκόν (ἑκοντ-)
    willing(ly)
ἐξ-απατά-ω deceive
ἐπ-αίρ-ω raise up, lift
ἐπ-ίστα-μαι know (how to)
    (+ inf.)
εὖγε hurrah!
θὲ-ς put! (s.) (τίθη-μι/-θε-)
θε-ὶς putting (nom. s. m.)
    (τίθη-μι/-θε-)
κάδ-ος, ὁ voting-urn (2a)

κατ-εσθί-ω eat up
κιθαρίζ-ω play the kithara (i.e.
    be educated)
μέλλ-ω be about to
ὅδε ἥδε τόδε this (here)
ὄντ-ως really
ὅτι because
πατρίδιον daddy dear (2b)
πείσ-ομαι I shall suffer (fut. of
    πάσχ-ω)
περι-άγ-ω lead round
περί-πατ-ος, ὁ walkabout (2a)
πολυ-τίμητ-ος –ον much-
    honoured
πρότερ-ος –α -ον first (of two),
    former
συγγνώμ-ην ἔχ-ω forgive
    (+dat.)
τῇδε this way
τήνδε *see* ὅδε
ὕδωρ (ὑδατ-), τό water (3b)

ὕστερ-ος –α -ον last (of two),
    further
φακ-ῆ, ἡ lentil-soup (1a)
φέρε . . . περιάγω come . . .
    let me take you round

Vocabulary to be learnt
ἀπολύ́ω *acquit, release*
ἐξαπατάω *deceive, trick*
ἐπίσταμαι *know how to (+inf.);*
    understand
μέλλω *be about to (+fut. inf.);*
    intend; hesitate (+pres. inf.)
ὅδε ἥδε τόδε *this here*
ὅτι *because*
συγγνώμην ἔχω *forgive, pardon*
    (+dat.)
ὕστερος ᾱ ον *later, last*
    (of two)
ὕστερον *later, further*

Section Ten A–E: Aristophanes' *Lysistrata*

Introduction

Peisetairos and Euelpides decided that the only solution to the troubles of Athens was to escape to Cloudcuckooland. In *Lysistrata*, Aristophanes envisages the women of Athens finding a different solution.

   An Athenian woman had no political rights at all, but that did not mean that she had no influence, and Aristophanes could make good comedy from the idea of women taking command of their men and of public affairs, as he often did.

In *World of Athens*: women 5.23ff; in myth 3.11–12; Athens vs. Sparta 1.75ff.

A

Lysistrata has gathered together a group of women from all over Greece to talk of ways to end the war. Lampito is a Spartan.

ΛΥΣΙΣΤΡΑΤΗ (Λυσιστράτη, ἣ Ἀθηναία ἐστὶ γυνή, παρελθοῦσα λέγει)
    ἆρα ἐλπίζετε, ὦ γυναῖκες, μετ' ἐμοῦ καταλύσειν τὸν πόλεμον; εὖ γὰρ ἴστε ὅτι,
    τὸν πόλεμον καταλύσασαι, τὴν εἰρήνην αὖθις ὀψόμεθα.
ΜΥΡΡΙΝΗ (Μυρρίνη, ἣ φίλη ἐστὶ Λυσιστράτῃ, ὁμολογεῖ)
    νὴ τοὺς θεοὺς ἡδέως ἂν ἴδοιμι ἔγωγε τὴν εἰρήνην, τὸν πόλεμον καταλύσασα.   5
ΚΛΕΟΝΙΚΗ (καὶ Κλεονίκη, ἣ ἑτέρα φίλη τυγχάνει οὖσα, ὁμολογεῖ)
    κἀμοὶ δοκεῖ τὸν πόλεμον καταλῦσαι. ἀλλὰ πῶς ἔξεστιν ἡμῖν, γυναιξὶν
    οὔσαις; ἆρα μηχανήν τιν' ἔχεις; δεῖ γὰρ τοὺς ἄνδρας, οἳ τὰς μάχας μάχονται,
    καταλύσαντας τὸν πόλεμον σπονδὰς ποιεῖσθαι.
ΛΥ.   λέγοιμ' ἄν. οὐ γὰρ δεῖ σιωπᾶν. ἀλλ', ὦ γυναῖκες, εἴπερ μέλλομεν   10
    ἀναγκάσειν τοὺς ἄνδρας εἰρήνην ἄγειν, ἡμᾶς χρὴ ἀπέχεσθαι –
ΜΥ.   τίνος; τίς ἡ μηχανή; λέξον ἐκεῖνο ὃ ἐν νῷ ἔχεις.
ΛΥ.   ποιήσετ' οὖν ὃ κελεύω;
ΜΥ.   ποιήσομεν πάνθ' ἃ κελεύεις.
ΛΥ.   δεῖ τοίνυν ἡμᾶς ἀπέχεσθαι τῶν ἀφροδισίων.   15
(αἱ γυναῖκες πᾶσαι, ἀκούσασαι τοὺς λόγους, οὓς λέγει Λυσιστράτη, ἀπιέναι ἄρχονται)
ΛΥ.   ποῖ βαδίζετε; τί δακρύετε; ποιήσετ' ἢ οὐ ποιήσετε ἃ κελεύω; ἢ τί μέλλετε;
ΜΥ.   *(resolutely)*
    οὐκ ἂν ποιήσαιμι τοῦθ' ὃ λέγεις, ὦ Λυσιστράτη, ἀλλ' ὁ πόλεμος ἑρπέτω.
ΚΛ.   μὰ Δί' οὐδ' ἐγὼ γάρ, ἀλλ' ὁ πόλεμος ἑρπέτω. κέλευσόν με διὰ τοῦ πυρὸς   20
    βαδίζειν. τοῦτο μᾶλλον⌐ ἐθελήσαιμι⌐ ἂν ποιεῖν ⌐ἢ τῶν ἀφροδισίων
    ἀπέχεσθαι. οὐδὲν γὰρ τοῖς ἀφροδισίοις ὅμοιον, ὦ φίλη Λυσιστράτη. οὐκ
    ἂν ποιήσαιμι οὐδαμῶς.
ΛΥ.   *(turns back to Myrrhine)*
    τί δαὶ σύ; ποιήσειας ἂν ἃ κελεύω;   25

MY.   κἀγὼ ἐθελήσαιμ'‿ἂν διὰ τοῦ πυρός. οὐ μὰ Δία, οὐκ ἂν ποιήσαιμι ἐγώ.

ΛΥ.   ὦ παγκατάπυγον τὸ ἡμέτερον ἅπαν γένος. ἆρ' οὐδεμία ποιήσειε‿ἂν, ὃ κελεύω;
      (*addresses the Spartan, Lampito*)
      ἀλλ' ὦ φίλη Λάκαινα, ἆρα συμψηφίσαιο‿ἂν μοι; οὕτω γὰρ τὸ πρᾶγμα
      σώσαιμεν‿ἂν ἔτι.   30

ΛΑΜΠΙΤΩ   χαλεπὸν μὲν ναὶ‿τὼ‿σιὼ ἐστιν ἡμῖν ἄνευ τῶν ἀφροδισίων
      καθεύδειν. ἀλλὰ δεῖ ἡμᾶς, τὸν πόλεμον καταλυσάσας, εἰρήνην ἄγειν.
      συμψηφισαίμην‿ἂν σοι.

ΛΥ.   (*joyfully*)
      ὦ φιλτάτη σὺ καὶ μόνη τούτων γυνή.   35

MY.   (*reluctantly*)
      εἴ τοι δοκεῖ ὑμῖν ταῦτα, καὶ ἡμῖν συνδοκεῖ.

Vocabulary for Section Ten A

> **Grammar for 10A–E**
> - Aorist optative, active and middle
> - Verbs: δίδωμι, γιγνώσκω
> - Adjectives: ἀμελής, γλυκύς
> - Relatives: 'who/which/what/that'

ἅ what, which (acc. pl. n.)
ἀναγκάζ-ω compel
ἄνευ (+gen.) without
ἂν ἴδ-οιμι I would (like to) see
  (ὁρά-ω/εἶδ-ον)
ἂν ποιήσ-αιμι I will do (ποιέ-ω)
ἅπας ἅπασ-α ἅπαν (ἅπαντ-) all,
  the whole
ἀπ-έχ-ομαι refrain from (+gen.)
ἀφροδίσι-α, τά sex (2b)
βαδίζ-ω walk
γέν-ος, τό race, kind (3c)
δαί then
δακρύ-ω weep
δοκ-εῖ it seems a good idea (to x
  (dat.) to Y [inf.])
ἐθελήσ-αιμι ἂν I would (like to)
  (ἐθέλ-ω)
εἴπερ if indeed, if really (-περ
  *strengthens the word to which
  it is attached*)
ἕρπ-ω go along, take its course
ἥ who (nom. s. f.)
κατα-λύ-ω bring to an end
Κλεονίκ-η, ἡ Kleonike (1a)
Λάκαιν-α, ἡ Spartan woman (1c)

Λυσι-στράτ-η, ἡ Lysistrata (1a)
  ('Destroyer of the army')
μᾶλλον . . . ἤ rather than
μέλλ-ω intend
μηχαν-ή, ἡ plan, scheme (1a)
Μυρρίν-η, ἡ Myrrhine (1a)
ναὶ τὼ σιὼ (*Spartan dialect*) by
  the Two Gods! (Castor and
  Pollux)
ὃ what, which (acc. s. n.)
οἵ who (nom. pl. m.)
οὐδαμ-ῶς not at all, in no
  way
οὓς which, who (acc. pl. m.)
ὀψ-όμεθα we shall see (fut. of
  ὁρά-ω)
παγ-κατάπυγον totally
  lascivious
παρ-έρχ-ομαι (παρ-ελθ-) come
  forward
ποιήσ-ειας ἂν will you (s.) do
  (ποιέ-ω)
ποιήσ-ειε ἂν will (he) do
  (ποιέ-ω)
συμ-ψηφισ-αίμην ἂν I will vote
  with (+dat.) (συμ-ψηφίζ-ομαι)

συμ-ψηφίσ-αιο ἂν will you (s.)
  vote with (συμ-ψηφίζ-ομαι)
  (+dat.)
συν-δοκ-εῖ it seems a good idea
  to x (dat.) also
σώσ-αιμεν ἂν we might save
  (σῴζ-ω)
τοι then
τοίνυν so, then
φίλτατ-ος –η -ον most dear
  (φίλ-ος)
χἠμῖν=καὶ ἡμῖν

Vocabulary to be learnt
ἅπας ἅπασα ἅπαν (ἅπαντ-) *all,
  the whole*
ἀπέχομαι *refrain, keep away
  (from) (+gen.)*
βαδίζω *walk, go (fut.
  βαδιέομαι)*
δοκεῖ *it seems a good idea to X
  (dat.) to do Y (inf.); X (dat.)
  decides to do Y (inf.)*
καταλύω *bring to an end; finish*
μηχανή, ἡ *device, plan (1a)*
οὐδαμῶς *in no way, not at all*

B

In *World of Athens*: treasury 8.95; economics of empire 6.75ff.

ΛΑΜ.   ἡμεῖς οὖν, τοὺς ἡμετέρους ἄνδρας πείσασαι, ἀναγκάσομεν εἰρήνην ἄγειν.
         τίνι ⌐τρόπῳ τοὺς ὑμετέρους δυνήσεσθε πεῖσαι, οἳ τὰς τριήρεις γ' ἔχουσι
         καὶ τἀργύριον; ἢ χρήμασιν ἢ δώροις ἢ τί ποιοῦσαι;
ΛΥ.   ἀλλὰ καὶ τοῦτ' εὖ παρεσκευασάμεθα, ὅτι καταληψόμεθα τήμερον τὴν
         ἀκρόπολιν, θύειν δοκοῦσαι. καταλαβοῦσαι δέ, φυλάξομεν αὐτὴν αὐτῷ   5
         τῷ ἀργυρίῳ.
(βοήν τινα ἐξαίφνης ἀκούει ἡ Λαμπιτώ, ἀκούσασα δὲ τὴν Λυσιστράτην προσαγορεύει)
ΛΑΜ.   τίς ἐβόησε; τίς αἴτιος τῆς βοῆς;
ΛΥ.   τοῦτ' ἐκεῖνο ὃ ἔλεγον. αἱ γὰρ γρᾶες, ἃς ἔδει τὴν ἀκρόπολιν τῆς θεοῦ
         καταλαβεῖν, νῦν ἔχουσιν. ἀλλ' ὦ Λαμπιτοῖ, σὺ μὲν, οἴκαδε ἐλθοῦσα, τὰ   10
         παρ' ὑμῖν εὖ θές, ἡμεῖς δ' εἰσελθοῦσαι τὴν ἀκρόπολιν, ἣν ἄρτι κατέλαβον
         αἱ γρᾶες, φυλάξομεν.
(ἡ μὲν Λαμπιτώ ἀπιοῦσα βαδίζει τὴν ὁδόν, ἣ εἰς Λακεδαίμονα φέρει, αἱ δ' ἄλλαι
εἰσελθοῦσαι τὴν ἀκρόπολιν φυλάττουσιν. ἐξαίφνης δὲ βοᾷ ἡ Λυσιστράτη, ἰδοῦσα
ἄνδρα τινά, ὃς τυγχάνει προσιών.)   15
ΛΥ.   ἰοὺ ἰοὺ γυναῖκες, ἴτε δεῦρο ὡς ἐμὲ ταχέως.
ΚΛ.   τί δ' ἐστίν; εἰπέ μοι, τίς ἡ βοή;
ΛΥ.   ἄνδρα ἄνδρα ὁρῶ προσιόντα. ὁρᾶτε. γιγνώσκει τις ὑμῶν τὸν ἄνδρα ὃς
         προσέρχεται;
ΜΥ.   οἴμοι.   20
ΚΛ.   ἀλλὰ δῆλον, Λυσιστράτη, ὅτι ἡ Μυρρίνη αὐτὸν ἔγνω. ἰδοῦσα γὰρ καὶ
         γνοῦσα ᾤμωξε.
ΛΥ.   λέγε, ὦ Μυρρίνη. ἆρ' ἡ Κλεονίκη ἀληθῆ λέγει; τὸν ἄνδρα ἔγνως σύ; κἀμοὶ
         γὰρ δοκεῖς τὸν ἄνδρα γνῶναι.
ΜΥ.   νὴ Δία ἔγνων ἔγωγε. ἔστι γὰρ Κινησίας, οὗ γυνή εἰμι ἐγώ.   25
ΛΥ.   (reveals her plan)
         σὸν ἔργον ἤδη τοῦτον, ᾧ συνοικεῖς, ἐξαπατᾶν καὶ φιλεῖν καὶ μὴ φιλεῖν.
ΜΥ.   ποιήσω ταῦτ' ἐγώ.
ΛΥ.   καὶ ⌐μὴν ἐγὼ συνεξαπατήσαιμ'⌐ ἂν σοι παραμένουσα ἐνθάδε,
         ἀποπέμψασα τὰς γραῦς, ὧν ἔργον ἐστὶ τὴν ἀκρόπολιν φυλάττειν.   30

Vocabulary for Section Ten B

ἀκρόπολ-ις, ἡ acropolis (3e)	ἄρτι just now, recently	δῶρ-ον, τό gift, bribe (2b)
ἀναγκάζ-ω compel	ἃς [for] whom (acc. pl. f.) (after	ἔ-γνω-ν (I) recognised
ἀπο-πέμπ-ω send away, dismiss	ἔδει)	(γιγνώσκ-ω/ἔ-γνω-ν)
ἀργύρι-ον, τό silver (2b)	γν-οῦσ-α recognising (nom. s. f.)	ἔ-γνω-ς you (s.) recognised
(deposited in the Parthenon;	(γιγνώσκ-ω/ἔ-γνω-ν)	(γιγνώσκ-ω/ἔ-γνω-ν)
these were reserves built	γνῶ-ναι to recognise (γιγνώσκ-	ἔ-γνω (she) recognised
up from the silver mines at	ω/ἔ-γνω-ν)	(γιγνώσκ-ω/ἔ-γνω-ν)
Laurion)	γραῦς (γρα-), ἡ old woman (3a)	ἐξαίφνης suddenly

ἥ which (nom. s. f.)

ἥν which (acc. s. f.)

ἰού oh!

καὶ μὴν look!

Κινησί-ας, ὁ Kinesias (1d)
 (comic name implying sexual prowess)

Λακεδαίμων (Λακεδαιμον-), ἡ Sparta (3a)

Λαμπιτώ, ἡ Lampito (voc. Λαμπιτοῖ)

ὅ which (acc. s. n.)

ὁδ-ός, ἡ road (2a)

οἵ who (nom. pl. m.)

οἰμώζ-ω cry οἴμοι

ὅς who (nom. s. m.)

οὗ whose (gen. s. m.)

παρά (+dat.) with, at, beside

παρα-μέν-ω remain beside

παρα-σκευάζ-ομαι prepare

προσ-αγορεύ-ω address

συν-εξ-απατήσ-αιμ' ἂν I will join with x (dat.) in deceiving (συν-εξ-απατά-ω)

συν-οικέ-ω live (with) (+dat.)

τριήρ-ης, ἡ trireme (3d)

τίν-ι τρόπ-ῳ how? in what way?

φέρ-ω lead

ᾧ with whom (dat. s. m.)

ὧν whose (gen. pl. f.)

ὡς (+acc.) to

Vocabulary to be learnt

ἀναγκάζω force, compel

ἄρτι *just now, recently*

γραῦς (γρα-), ἡ *old woman (3 irr.) (acc. s. γραῦν; acc. pl. γραῦς)*

δῶρον, τό *gift, bribe (2b)*

ἐξαίφνης *suddenly*

παρά (+dat.) *with, beside, in the presence of*

συνοικέω *live with, live together*

Athenian finances

Lysistrata is known as the play about a sex-strike. But that was only one side of Lysistrata's plan. She knew that while the men controlled the finances, they could keep the war going, sex-strike or not. So her second plan was to capture the Parthenon, where the money was kept. Only then could she be certain of forcing the men to give in to her. The passage from *World of Athens* below describes the state of Athenian finances in the years preceding *Wasps*. The tribute referred to came from Athens' allies in the Delian league, an alliance of states of which Athens was the predominant member, formed after the Persian Wars to guarantee Greek security against further Persian invasion. Members paid Athens in money or ships:

'Thucydides made Pericles declare in 431 that Athens' reserve fund stood at the gigantic figure of 6,000 talents – and this despite the expenditure on the Acropolis building programme and the heavy cost of putting down the revolt of Samos in 440/39; further, that the annual external income from tribute, fines and other sources, amounted to 600 talents. With reason did Pericles stress Athens' financial preparedness for the coming war. Five years later, however, the demands of the war were proving unmanageable, and in these circumstances the Athenian attitude to their allies seems to have changed markedly. First of all they tightened up on tribute collection. From 430 onwards we hear of the Athenians sending out ships to collect the tribute, and in 426 the Athenians passed a decree making it a treasonable offence to impede the collection of tribute. Second, they put up the amounts of tribute they demanded. Tribute levels seem to have been steady over the previous three decades, adjusted only in the light of local circumstances, but in 425 the amount of tribute demanded from cities was increased by anything up to a factor of five, bringing the total demanded to perhaps as much as 1,460 talents per annum.' (*World of Athens*, 6.80)

C

(αἱ μὲν οὖν γρᾶες ἀπέρχονται, ὁ δὲ Κινησίας ἀφικνεῖται, προσιὼν δ' ὀλοφύρεται)

KINHΣIAΣ   οἴμοι κακοδαίμων, οἷος ὁ σπασμός μ' ἔχει.

ΛΥ.   (ἀπὸ τοῦ τείχους λέγουσα)
           τίς οὗτος ὃς διὰ τῶν φυλάκων λαθὼν ἐβιάσατο;

KIN.   ἐγώ.   5

ΛΥ.   ἀνὴρ εἶ;

KIN.   ἀνὴρ δῆτα.

ΛΥ.   οὐκ ἄπει δῆτ' ἐκποδών;

KIN.   σὺ δ' εἶ τίς, ἢ ἐκβάλλεις με;

ΛΥ.   φύλαξ.   10

KIN.   οἴμοι.

(πρὸς ἑαυτὸν λέγων)
           δῆλον ὅτι δεῖ με - δυστυχῆ - ὄντα εὔξασθαι τοῖς θεοῖς ἅπασιν. ἴσως δὲ οἱ
           θεοί, οἷς εὔχομαι, δώσουσί μοι τὴν γυναῖκα ἰδεῖν.
           (εὔχεται ὁ ἀνήρ)   15
           ἀλλ' ὦ πάντες θεοί, δότε μοι τὴν γυναῖκα ἰδεῖν.
           (αὖθις τὴν Λυσιστράτην προσαγορεύει)
           πρὸς τῶν θεῶν νῦν ἐκκάλεσόν μοι Μυρρίνην.

ΛΥ.   (appearing to soften)
           σὺ δὲ τίς εἶ;   20

KIN.   ἀνὴρ ἐκείνης, Κινησίας Παιονίδης, ᾧ συνοικεῖ.

(πρὸς ἑαυτὸν λέγων)
           εὖ‿γε, ὡς εὐξαμένῳ ἔδοσάν μοι οἱ θεοὶ τὴν Μυρρίνην ἰδεῖν.

ΛΥ.   (very friendly)
           ὦ χαῖρε, φίλτατε Κινησία. εὖ ἴσμεν γὰρ τὸ σὸν ὄνομα καὶ ἡμεῖς. ἀεὶ γὰρ   25
           ἡ γυνή σ' ἔχει διὰ‿στόμα. καὶ‿μὴν λαβοῦσα μῆλον 'ὡς ἡδέως', φησί,
           'Κινησίᾳ τοῦτ' ἂν‿διδοίην.'

KIN.   (his passion increasing)
           ὦ πρὸς τῶν θεῶν· ἐγὼ ὁ ἀνὴρ ᾧ Μυρρίνη βούλεται μῆλα διδόναι;

ΛΥ.   νὴ τὴν Ἀφροδίτην. καὶ δὴ καὶ χθές, ὅτε περὶ ἀνδρῶν ἐνέπεσε λόγος τις, ἡ σὴ   30
           γυνή 'πάντων', ἔφη, 'ἄριστον νομίζω τὸν Κινησίαν.'

KIN.   (desperately)
           ἴθι νυν κάλεσον αὐτήν.

ΛΥ.   (stretching out her hand)
           τί οὖν; δώσεις τί μοι;   35

KIN.   νὴ τὸν Δία ἔγωγέ σοί τι δώσω. ἔχω δὲ τοῦτο· ὅπερ οὖν ἔχω δίδωμί σοι. σὺ
           οὖν, ᾗ δίδωμι τόδε, κάλεσον αὐτήν.

(ὃ ἔχει ἐν τῇ χειρὶ δίδωσι τῇ Λυσιστράτῃ)

ΛΥ.   εἶεν· καταβᾶσα καλῶ σοι αὐτήν.

(καταβαίνει ἀπὸ τοῦ τείχους)   40

KIN.   ταχέως.

MY.   (ἔνδον οὖσα)

σὺ δ' ἐμὲ τούτῳ μὴ κάλει, Λυσιστράτη. οὐ γὰρ βούλομαι καταβῆναι.

KIN.   ὦ Μυρρινίδιον, τί ταῦτα δρᾷς; καταβᾶσα πάσῃ σπουδῇ δεῦρ' ἐλθέ.

MY.   μὰ Δί' ἐγὼ μὲν οὔ. ἀλλ' ἄπειμι.   45

KIN.   μὴ δῆτ' ἄπιθι, ἀλλὰ τῷ γοῦν παιδίῳ ὑπάκουσον.

(τῷ παιδίῳ λέγει, ὃ θεράπων τις φέρει)

         οὗτος, οὐ καλεῖς τὴν μαμμίαν;

ΠΑΙΣ   μαμμία μαμμία μαμμία.

KIN.   αὕτη, τί πάσχεις; ἆρ' οὐκ οἰκτίρεις τὸ παιδίον, ὃ ἄλουτον ὂν τυγχάνει;   50

MY.   ἔγωγε οἰκτίρω δῆτα.

KIN.   κατάβηθι οὖν, ὦ δαιμονία, τοῦ παιδίου ἕνεκα.

MY.   *(sighing)*

         οἷον τὸ⁀τεκεῖν. χρὴ καταβῆναι.

Vocabulary for Section Ten C

ἄ-λουτ-ος -ον unwashed
ἂν διδ-οίην I would like to give (δίδω-μι/δο-)
γοῦν at any rate
δαιμονί-α my dear lady
διὰ στόμα on her lips
διδό-ναι to give (δίδω-μι/δο-)
δίδω-μι I give, offer
δώσ-ω I shall give (δίδω-μι/δο-)
δώσ-εις you (s.) will give (δίδω-μι/δο-)
δώσ-ουσι they will grant (δίδω-μι/δο-)
ἔ-δο-σαν they granted (δίδω-μι/δο-)
δό-τε grant! (pl.) (δίδω-μι/δο-)
δυσ-τυχ-ῆ unlucky (acc. s. m.)
εἶεν very well
ἐκ-καλέ-ω call out
ἐκποδών out of the way
εὖ γε hurrah! good!

ἥ who (nom. s. f.)
θεράπων (θεραποντ-), ὁ slave, servant (3a)
καὶ μὴν look!
καλ-ῶ I shall call (fut. of καλέ-ω; ἐ-ω contr.)
μαμμί-α, ἡ mummy (1b)
μῆλ-ον, τό apple (2b)
Μυρρινίδιον Myrrhine baby
ὃ which (acc. s. n.); which (nom. s. n.)
οἷ-ος-α-ον what sort of a!
οἷς to whom (dat. pl. m.)
ὅπερ what indeed, the very thing which (acc. s. n.)
ὅς who (nom. s. m.)
Παιονίδ-ης, ὁ of the deme Paionis (1d) *(comic name implying sexual prowess)*
προσ-αγορεύ-ω address
σπασμ-ός, ὁ agony (2a)

σπουδ-ή, ἡ haste (1a)
τεῖχ-ος, τό wall (of a city) (3c)
τὸ τεκ-εῖν to be a mother, motherhood (τίκτ-ω/ ἔ-τεκ-ον)
ὑπ-ακού-ω obey, listen to (+dat.)
φίλτατ-ος -η -ον dearest (φίλ-ος)
φύλαξ (φυλακ-), ὁ, ἡ guard (3a)
ᾧ with/to whom (dat. s. m.)
ὡς since, because

Vocabulary to be learnt

οἷος ᾱ ον *what a! what sort of a!*
προσαγορεύω *address, speak to*
σπουδή, ἡ *haste, zeal, seriousness (1a)*
τεῖχος, τό *wall (of a city) (3c)*
φίλτατος η ον *most dear (φίλος)*
φύλαξ (φυλακ-), ὁ, ἡ *guard (3a)*

D

In *World of Athens*: purification 3.33; slaves 5.63.

(καταβᾶσα δὲ καὶ ἀφικομένη ἡ Μυρρίνη εἰς τὴν πύλην, τὸ παιδίον προσαγορεύει)

MY.   (*cuddling the child*)
           ὦ τέκνον, ὡς γλυκὺς εἶ σύ. φέρε⌐ σε ⌐φιλήσω. γλυκὺ γὰρ τὸ τῆς μητρὸς
           φίλημα. γλυκεῖα δὲ καὶ ἡ μήτηρ· ἀλλ' οὐ γλυκὺν ἔχεις τὸν πατέρα,
           ἀλλ' ἀμελῆ. ἐγὼ δὲ μέμφομαι τῷ σῷ πατρὶ ἀμελεῖ ὄντι. ὦ τέκνον, ὡς   5
           δυστυχὴς φαίνῃ ὢν διὰ τὸν πατέρα.

KIN.   (*angrily*)
           ἀλλὰ σὺ τὸν ἄνδρα ἀμελῆ καλεῖς; οὐδεμία μὲν γάρ ἐστι σοῦ ἀμελεστέρα,
           οὐδεὶς δὲ δυστυχέστερος ἐμοῦ.

(προσάγων τῇ γυναικὶ τὴν χεῖρα, λέγει)   10
           τί βουλομένη, ὦ πονηρά, ταῦτα ποιεῖς, γυναιξὶ πιθομένη τοιαύταις;

MY.   (*brushing aside his advances*)
           παῦσαι, κάκιστε, καὶ μὴ πρόσαγε τὴν χεῖρά μοι.

KIN.   (*pleading*)
           οἴκαδε δ' οὐ βαδιῇ πάλιν;   15

MY.   (*firmly*)
           μὰ Δί' οὐκ ἔγωγε οἴκαδε βαδιοῦμαι. ἀλλὰ πρότερον τοὺς ἄνδρας δεῖ, τοῦ
           πολέμου παυσαμένους, σπονδὰς ποιεῖσθαι. ποιήσετε ταῦτα;

KIN.   σὺ δὲ τί οὐ κατακλίνῃ μετ' ἐμοῦ ὀλίγον χρόνον;

MY.   οὐ δῆτα· καίτοι σ' οὐκ ἐρῶ γ' ὡς οὐ φιλῶ.   20

KIN.   φιλεῖς; τί οὖν οὐ κατακλίνῃ;

MY.   ὦ καταγέλαστε, ἐναντίον τοῦ παιδίου;

KIN.   (*turning to the slave*)
           μὰ Δί', ἀλλὰ τοῦτό γ' οἴκαδε, ὦ Μανῆ, φέρε.

(ὁ θεράπων, ὃς τὸ παιδίον φέρει, οἴκαδε ἀπέρχεται)   25
           ἰδού, τὸ μέν σοι παιδίον καὶ⌐δὴ ἐκποδών, σὺ δ' οὐ κατακλίνῃ;

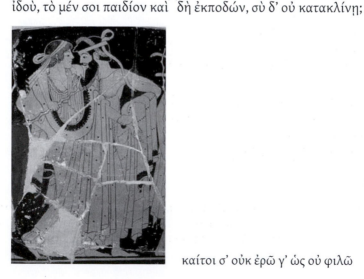

καίτοι σ' οὐκ ἐρῶ γ' ὡς οὐ φιλῶ

MY.   ἀλλὰ ποῦ γὰρ ἄν⌐ τις ⌐δράσειε τοῦτο; πρῶτον γὰρ δεῖ μ' ἐνεγκεῖν κλινίδιον.
KIN.   μηδαμῶς, ἐπειδὴ ἔξεστιν ἡμῖν χαμαὶ κατακλίνεσθαι.
MY.   *(firmly)*
      μὰ τὸν Ἀπόλλω, οὐκ ἐάσω σ' ἐγώ, καίπερ τοιοῦτον ὄντα, κατακλίνεσθαι χαμαί.   30
      (ἐξέρχεται)
KIN.   *(joyfully)*
      ὦ τῆς εὐτυχίας· ἤ τοι γυνὴ φιλοῦσά με δήλη ἐστίν.

Vocabulary for Section Ten D

ἀ-μελ-εῖ uncaring (dat. s. m.)
ἀ-μελέστερ-ος –α -ον more
   uncaring (ἀ-μελ-ής)
ἀ-μελ-ῆ uncaring (acc. s. m.)
ἂν δράσ-ειε (he) might do (δρά-ω)
βαδι-οῦμαι I shall walk (fut. of
   βαδίζ-ω; έ-ω contr.)
βαδι-ῇ you (s.) will walk (fut. of
   βαδίζ-ω; έ-ω contr.)
γλυκ-εῖ-α sweet (nom. s. f.)
γλυκ-ὺ sweet (nom. s. n.)
γλυκ-ὺν sweet (acc. s. m.)
γλυκ-ύς sweet (nom. s. m.)
δυσ-τυχέστερ-ος –α -ον more
   unlucky (δυσ-τυχ-ής)
ἐκποδών out of the way
εὐ-τυχί-α, ἡ good luck (1b)

θεράπων (θεραποντ-), ὁ servant,
   slave (3a)
καὶ δὴ there!
καίτοι and yet
κατα-γέλαστ-ος -ον laughable,
   silly
κατα-κλίν-ομαι lie down
κλινίδι-ον, τό little couch (2b)
Μαν-ῆς, ὁ Manes (voc. Μαν-ῆ)
   (1d)
μέμφ-ομαι criticise (+dat.)
μηδαμ-ῶς not at all
μήτηρ (μητ(ε)ρ-), ἡ mother (3a)
ὅς who (nom. s. m.)
παύ-ομαι cease from (+gen.)
προσ-άγ-ω bring (to) (+dat.)
πρότερον before, first

πύλ-η, ἡ gate (1a)
τέκν-ον, τό child (2b)
τοι then
φέρε . . . φιλήσω come . . . let
   me kiss
φίλημα (φιληματ-), τό kiss (3b)
χαμαὶ on the ground

Vocabulary to be learnt
καίτοι *and yet*
κατακλῑ́νομαι *lie down*
μέμφομαι *blame, criticise, find
   fault with (+acc. or dat.)*
μηδαμῶς *not at all, in no way*
μήτηρ (μητ(ε)ρ-), ἡ *mother (3a)*
παύομαι *cease from (+gen.)*
τοι *then (inference)*

E

(ἐπανέρχεται ἡ Μυρρίνη κλινίδιον φέρουσα)
MY.   ἰδοὺ ἐγὼ ἐκδύομαι.
      (has a sudden thought)
      καίτοι ψίαθον χρή μ' ἐνεγκεῖν.
KIN.   *(surprised)*   5
      ποία ψίαθος; μὴ μοί γε. ἀλλὰ δός μοί νυν κύσαι.
MY.   ἰδού.
(κύσασα τὸν ἄνδρα, αὖθις ἐξέρχεται. φέρουσα δὲ ψίαθον, πάνυ ταχέως ἐπανέρχεται.)
      ἰδού, ψίαθος. ἀλλὰ τί οὐ κατακλίνη; καὶ⌐δὴ ἐκδύομαι.
      (another sudden thought)   10
      καίτοι προσκεφάλαιον οὐκ ἔχεις.

Vocabulary for Section Ten E

δός grant! (s.) (δίδω-μι/δο-)
ἐκ-δύ-ομαι undress
καί δὴ there!

κλινίδι-ον, τό small couch (2b)
κυνέ-ω (κυσ-) kiss
ποῖ-ος –α -ον; what sort of?

προσ-κεφάλαι-ον, τό pillow (2b)
ψίαθ-ος, ἡ mattress (2a)

KIN.   *(belligerently)*
          ἀλλ' οὐ δέομαι οὐδὲν ἔγωγε.
MY.   *(firmly)*
          νὴ Δί', ἀλλ' ἐγὼ δέομαι.   15
(αὖθις ἐξέρχεται. ἐπανέρχεται δὲ προσκεφάλαιον φέρουσα.)
MY.   ἀνίστασο, ἀναπήδησον.
KIN.   *(shaking his head)*
          ἤδη πάντ' ἔχω, ὅσων δέομαι.
MY.   ἄπαντα δῆτα;   20
KIN.   δεῦρό νυν, ὦ Μυρρινίδιον.
MY.   *(teasing, then seriously)*
          τὸ στρόφιον ἤδη λύομαι. ἀλλὰ φύλαξαι⁀μή μ' ἐξαπατᾶν περὶ τῶν
          σπονδῶν, περὶ ὧν ἄρτι λόγους ἐποιούμεθα.
KIN.   *(absently)*   25
          νὴ Δί', ἀπολοίμην ἄρα.
MY.   (ἐξαίφνης παύεται ἐκδυομένη)

τὸ στρόφιον ἤδη λύομαι   νῦν σε φιλήσω

          σισύραν οὐκ ἔχεις.
KIN.   *(shouting out in frustration)*
          μὰ Δί', οὐδὲ δέομαί γε, ἀλλὰ βινεῖν βούλομαι.   30
MY.   *(teasing again)*
          ἀμέλει ποιήσεις τοῦτο. ταχὺ γὰρ ἔρχομαι.
          (ἐξέρχεται)
KIN.   *(sighing wearily)*
          ἡ ἄνθρωπος διαφθερεῖ με ταῖς σισύραις.   35
(ἐπανέρχεται ἡ Μυρρίνη σισύραν φέρουσα)
          (firmly)
          νῦν σε φιλήσω. ἰδού.
MY.   *(holds him off)*

		40

ἀνάμενε. ἆρα μυριῶ σε;   40

KIN. μὰ τὸν Ἀπόλλω, μὴ ἐμέ γε.

MY. *(firmly, picking up a flask of ointment)*

νὴ τὴν Ἀφροδίτην, ποιήσω τοῦτο. πρότεινε δὴ τὴν χεῖρα καὶ ἀλείφου

λαβών, ὅ σοι δώσω.

KIN. *(suspiciously)*   45

οὐχ ἡδὺ τὸ μύρον ὅ μοι ἔδωκας. διατριβῆς γὰρ ὄζει, ἀλλ' οὐκ ὄζει γάμων.

MY. *(looking in mock anger at the flask)*

τάλαιν' ἐγώ, τὸ Ῥόδιον ἤνεγκον μύρον.

KIN. *(impatiently)*

ἀγαθόν. ἔα αὐτό, ὦ δαιμονία. κάκιστ' ἀπόλοιτο, ὅστις πρῶτος ἐποίησε   50

μύρον. ἀλλὰ κατακλίνηθι καὶ μή μοι φέρε μηδέν.

MY. ποιήσω ταῦτα, νὴ τὴν Ἄρτεμιν. ὑπολύομαι γοῦν. ἀλλ', ὦ φίλτατε,

σπονδὰς ποιεῖσθαι ψηφιεῖ;

KIN. *(absently)*

ψηφιοῦμαι.   55

(ἡ Μυρρίνη ἀποτρέχει)

τί δὲ τουτὶ τὸ πρᾶγμα; ἡ γυνὴ ἀπελθοῦσά μ' ἔλιπεν. οἴμοι, τί πάσχω; τί

πείσομαι; οἴμοι, ἀπολεῖ με ἡ γυνή. τίνα νῦν βινήσω; οἴμοι. δυστυχέστατος

ἐγώ.

ἀλείφ-ομαι anoint (oneself)

ἀμέλει of course

ἀνα-πηδά-ω jump up

ἀπ-ολ-οίμην may I die
    (ἀπ-όλλ-υμαι/ἀπ-ολ-)

ἀπ-όλ-οιτο may he die
    (ἀπ-όλλ-υμαι/ἀπ-ολ-)

Ἄρτεμις, ἡ Artemis (3a) (acc.
    Ἄρτεμιν) (goddess of hunting
    and chastity)

βινέ-ω screw (colloquial)

γοῦν at any rate

δαιμονί-α my dear lady

δέ-ομαι need, ask for (+gen.)

δια-τριβ-ή, ἡ delay (1a)

δυσ-τυχέστατ-ος -η -ον most
    unlucky (δυσ-τυχ-ής)

δώσ-ω I shall give (δίδω-μι/
    δο-)

ἔ-δωκ-ας you (s.) gave
    (δίδω-μι/δο-)

ἔ-λιπ-ον see λείπ-ω

ἡδ-ύ sweet, pleasant (nom. s. n.)

κάκιστα most badly (tr. 'an
    awful death')

κατα-κλίν-ηθι lie down! (s.)

λείπ-ω (λιπ-) leave

λύ-ομαι undo (one's own)

μηδείς μηδεμί-α μηδέν (μηδεν-)
    no one, nothing

μυρίζ-ω anoint with myrrh (fut.
    μυριέ-ω)

μύρ-ον, τό myrrh (2b)

Μυρρινίδιον Myrrhine, darling

ὅ what, which (acc. s. n.)

ὄζ-ω smell of (+gen.)

ὅσ-ων of all the things which
    (gen. pl. n.) (lit. 'as many as')

ὅσ-τις he who (nom. s. m.)

προ-τείν-ω stretch forth

Ῥόδι-ος -α -ον from Rhodes

σισύρ-α, ἡ blanket (1b)

στρόφι-ον, τό sash (2b)

ταχὺ quickly

ὑπο-λύ-ομαι undo one's shoes

φιλέ-ω kiss

φυλάττ-ομαι μὴ take care not
    (to)

ψηφίζ-ομαι vote (fut.
    ψηφιέ-ομαι)

ὧν which (gen. pl. f.)

Vocabulary to be learnt

ἀμελής ές uncaring

γλυκύς εῖα ύ sweet

γοῦν at any rate

δέομαι need, ask, beg (+gen.)

δίδωμι (δο-) give, grant

ἐκδύομαι undress

μηδείς μηδεμία μηδέν (μηδεν-)
    no, no one

ὅς ἥ ὅ who, what, which

ὅσπερ ἥπερ ὅπερ who/which
    indeed

ὅστις ἥτις ὅ τι who(ever),
    what(ever)

ποῖος ᾱ ον; what sort of?

ψηφίζομαι vote (fut.
    ψηφιέομαι)

Section Eleven A–C: Aristophanes' *Akharnians*

Introduction

We return for the last time to Dikaiopolis, who ceases to be a mere observer of the troubles which seem to him to infect Athens, and which he attributes chiefly to the war and the Athenians' obstinate refusal to end it. Dikaiopolis is the hero of Aristophanes' comedy *Akharnians*.

In *World of Athens*: democracy in Athens 6.1ff.; comic technique 8.77; the rope 6.10; prutaneis 6.9; herald 6.33–4; Scythian archer 5.63, 6.31; embassies 6.35–7.

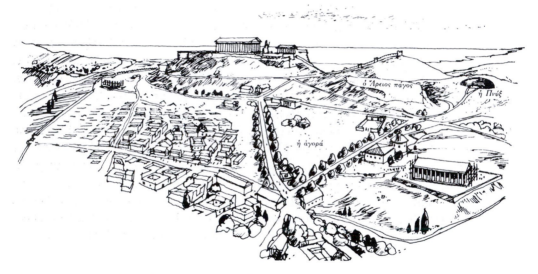

View across the agora from the north west (c. 425)

Comic plots

Aristophanes' plots usually follow this sort of pattern: (1) a great and fantastic idea is put forward (the more outrageous the better), frequently involving salvation for oneself, one's family or the whole of Greece. The originator of this idea becomes the hero(ine). (2) The idea is advanced and after a series of minor setbacks, the main struggle takes place, after which the 'great idea' is realised. (3) The consequences of the success of the 'great idea' are worked out.

So in the following extract from *Akharnians*. The great idea is to end the war with Sparta. That being impossible, Dikaiopolis decides to make his own personal treaty with the Spartans. Many people resist this idea, including the warlike people of Akharnes who live nearby. But Dikaiopolis triumphs over them all, and the play ends with Dikaiopolis celebrating the rural festival of Dionysus with a drunken, sexual orgy.

Aristophanes generally pulled no punches and took no hostages. It is true he never called for a change in the radical democratic constitution of fifth-century Athens, nor did he (in his surviving work) seriously attack public figures such as Nikias or Alcibiades. But apart from these, all was grist to his mill: the audience, the gods, politicians, intellectuals, homosexuals, jurors, bureaucrats, students, the military. In all this, his purpose was to win first prize; but the appeal to his audience, which included farmers, city men, the poor, sailors, soldiers, the successful and the disillusioned, the educated and the illiterate, surely resided in the *hope* he gave them. Aristophanes' heroes like Dikaiopolis were all little people of no importance, but still individuals who felt passionately about something probably close to the heart of the audience and who made heroic efforts to achieve their ends – usually successfully. In the strongly competitive world of Athenian society, this reassertion of the little man's will to win and to overcome his superiors must have been as reassuring as the discomfiture of the high and mighty. (*World of Athens*, 8.73, 78)

A

*Dikaiopolis has made his way to the Assembly on the Pnyx, and is determined
to take action to find peace for himself. He looks around in surprise at the empty
Assembly.*

ΔΙΚΑΙΟΠΟΛΙΣ ἀλλὰ τί τοῦτο; οἶδα γὰρ ὅτι κυρία ἐκκλησία γενήσεσθαι μέλλει
τήμερον. ἀλλ' ἔρημος ἡ Πνὺξ αὑτή.
(looks down into the agora)
οἱ δὲ ἐν τῇ ἀγορᾷ, πρὸς ἀλλήλους διαλεγόμενοι, ἄνω καὶ κάτω τὸ
σχοινίον φεύγουσιν. ὀψὲ δὲ οἱ πρυτάνεις ἥξουσιν, εὖ οἶδα. ἀλλ' ὅπως   5
εἰρήνη ἔσται, φροντίζει οὐδείς, ἐγὼ δ' ἀεὶ πρῶτος εἰς τὴν ἐκκλησίαν
εἰσιὼν καθίζω, καὶ μόνος ὤν, ἀποβλέπω εἰς τὸν ἀγρόν, εἰρήνην φιλῶν,
μισῶν μὲν ἄστυ, τὸν δ' ἐμὸν δῆμον ποθῶν.
(pauses; looks at the entrance)
ἀλλ' οἱ πρυτάνεις γὰρ οὑτοιὶ ὀψὲ ἥκουσι. τοῦτ' ἐκεῖνο ὃ ἐγὼ ἔλεγον.   10
Proceedings begin: the herald invites speakers.
ΚΗΡΥΞ   (κηρύττει)
πάριτ' εἰς τὸ πρόσθεν. πάριτ' ἐντὸς τοῦ καθάρματος.
(παρέρχονται εἰς τὸ πρόσθεν πάντες οἱ παρόντες. παρελθόντων δὲ πάντων, ἐξαίφνης
τὸν κήρυκα προσαγορεύει τις, Ἀμφίθεος ὀνόματι.)   15
ΑΜΦΙΘΕΟΣ *(anxiously)*
ἤδη τις εἶπε;
(ὁ μὲν Ἀμφίθεος μένει, ὁ δὲ κῆρυξ οὐκ ἀποκρίνεται. μένοντος δ' Ἀμφιθέου, κηρύττει ἔτι.)
ΚΗΡΥΞ   τίς ἀγορεύειν βούλεται;
ΑΜΦΙ.   (αὖθις τὸν κήρυκα προσαγορεύει)   20
ἐγώ.
ΚΗΡΥΞ   τίς ὤν;
ΑΜΦΙ.   Ἀμφίθεος.
ΚΗΡΥΞ   οὐκ ἄνθρωπος;
ΑΜΦΙ.   οὔκ, ἀλλὰ ἀθάνατος, ὃν ἐκέλευσαν οἱ θεοὶ σπονδὰς ποιῆσαι πρὸς   25
Λακεδαιμονίους. ἀλλ' ἀθανάτῳ ὄντι, ὦνδρες, ἐφόδια οὐκ ἔστι μοι ἃ δεῖ.
οὐ γὰρ διδόασιν οἱ πρυτάνεις. ἐλπίζω οὖν δέξεσθαι τὰ ἐφόδια –
ΡΗΤΩΡ ΤΙΣ   εὖ ἴστε, ὦ ἄνδρες Ἀθηναῖοι, ὅτι εὔνους εἰμὶ τῷ πλήθει. μὴ οὖν ἀκούετε
τούτου, εἰ μὴ περὶ πολέμου λέγοντος.
(ἐπαινοῦσι καὶ θορυβοῦσιν οἱ Ἀθηναῖοι)   30
ΚΗΡΥΞ   οἱ τοξόται.
(εἰσελθόντες οἱ τοξόται τὸν Ἀμφίθεον ἀπάγουσιν. ἀπαγόντων δὲ αὐτῶν, ὀργίζεται
Δικαιόπολις.)
ΔΙΚ.   ὦνδρες πρυτάνεις, ἀδικεῖτε τὴν ἐκκλησίαν, τὸν ἄνδρα ἀπάγοντες ὅστις
ἡμῖν ἔμελλε σπονδὰς ποιήσειν.   35
ΚΗΡΥΞ   κάθιζε, σίγα
ΔΙΚ.   μὰ τὸν Ἀπόλλω, ἐγὼ μὲν οὔ, ἀλλὰ περὶ εἰρήνης χρηματίσατε.
ΚΗΡΥΞ   οἱ πρέσβεις οἱ παρὰ βασιλέως.

Vocabulary for Section Eleven A

> **Grammar for 11A–C**
> - Present and imperfect passive
> - Genitive absolute
> - Comparative adverbs and two-termination adjectives
> - Optative of φημί 'I say'

ἀγορεύ-ω speak
ἀγρ-ός, ὁ country (2a)
ἀ-θάνατ-ος -ον immortal
Ἀμφί-θε-ος, ὁ Amphitheos (2a)
    (*comic name;* 'god on both
    sides')
ἀπαγόντων . . . αὐτῶν them
    leading (him) off
ἀπο-βλέπ-ω look out
ἐντός (+gen.) inside
ἐρήμ-ος -ον empty, deserted
εὔ-νους -ουν well-disposed
ἐφ-όδι-α, τά
travelling-expenses,
journey-money (2b)
ἥκ-ω come
θορυβέ-ω clamour, raise a clamour
κάθαρμα (καθαρματ-), τό
    purified place (3b)
κάτω down
κηρύττ-ω proclaim, herald,
    announce
κύρι-ος –α -ον sovereign, with
    power

μένοντος Ἀμφιθέου
Amphitheos remaining
ὅπως how, that
ὀργίζ-ομαι become/be made angry
ὄψε late
παρελθόντων πάντων all
    coming forward
παρ-έρχ-ομαι/πάρ-ειμι
    (παρελθ-) come forward
Πνύξ (Πυκν-), ἡ Pnyx(3a)
    (*meeting-place of the ekklesia*)
ποθέ-ω desire
πρόσθεν in front
πρύταν-ις, ὁ prytanis (3e)
    (*current administrative officer
    of the* βουλή)
σιγά-ω be quiet
σχοινί-ον, τό rope (2b) (*this
    was stained with red dye, and
    swept up and down the agora
    by slaves to drive the citizens
    into the ekklesia*)
τοξότ-ης, ὁ archer (1d) (*Scythian
    archers in Athens were public*

*slaves used for a variety of
    policing duties*)
χρηματίζ-ω do business

Vocabulary to be learnt

ἀγορεύω *speak (in assembly),
    proclaim*
ἀγρός, ὁ *field, country(side) (2a)*
ἀθάνατος ον *immortal*
ἀποβλέπω *look steadfastly at (and
    away from everything else)*
ἥκω *come, have come*
θορυβέω *make a disturbance, din*
κάτω *below*
κηρΰττω *announce, proclaim*
ὅπως *how? (answer to* πῶς;*),
    how (indir. q.)*
παρέρχομαι (παρελθ-) *come
    forward, pass by, go by*
πρύτανις, ὁ *prytanis (3e)*
    (member of the βουλή
    committee currently in charge
    of public affairs)
σῑγάω *be quiet*

τοξότης τις

B

In *World of Athens*: debate and democracy 6.16; citizen power 6.9; trade and manufacture 1.100, 5.55–7.

ΔΙΚ.   ὄλοιντο πάντες Ἀθηναῖοι ὅσοι ἐπαινοῦσί τε καὶ πείθονται οἷς λέγουσιν
        οἱ πρυτάνεις, κάκιστα δ' ἀπόλοιντο οἱ ῥήτορες οἳ τὸν δῆμον θωπεύουσι
        καὶ ἐξαπατῶσιν ἀεί. τί γὰρ οὐ πάσχομεν ἡμεῖς οἱ γεωργοὶ ὑπ' αὐτῶν;
        ἀεὶ γὰρ ὑπ' αὐτῶν ἐξαπατώμεθα καὶ ἀδικούμεθα καὶ ἀπολλύμεθα. ἀλλὰ
        τί ἔξεστιν ἡμῖν ποιεῖν, οὕτως ἀεὶ ὑπ' αὐτῶν ἀδικούμενοις; ὁ γὰρ δῆμος   5
        δοκεῖ γ' ἥδεσθαι πειθόμενος ὑπὸ τῶν ῥητόρων, καὶ τοῖς λόγοις αὐτῶν
        θωπευόμενος καὶ ἐξαπατώμενος καὶ διαφθειρόμενος. ἀεὶ γὰρ τιμᾶται
        ὑπὸ τοῦ δήμου ὁ λέγων ὅτι 'εὔνους εἰμὶ τῷ πλήθει', οὐδέποτε τιμᾶται ὁ
        χρηστὸς ὁ τὰ χρηστὰ συμβουλεύων.
             ἴσως δὲ ἂν φαίη τις 'τί οὖν; ἐλεύθερός γ' ὁ δῆμος καὶ αὐτὸς ἄρχει, καὶ   10
        ὑπ' οὐδενὸς ἄλλου ἄρχεται. εἰ δὲ τυγχάνει βουλόμενος ὑπὸ τῶν ῥητόρων
        ἐξαπατᾶσθαι καὶ πείθεσθαι καὶ θωπεύεσθαι, ἔστω.'
             ἐγὼ δ' ἀποκρίνομαι, 'καίτοι οἱ μὲν ναῦται κρατοῦσιν ἐν τῇ ἐκκλησίᾳ,
        οἱ δὲ γεωργοὶ ἄκοντες ἀναγκάζονται οἰκεῖν ἐν τῷ ἄστει, ἀπολλύμενοι τῇ
        οἰκήσει καὶ τῇ ἀπορίᾳ καὶ τῇ νόσῳ.'   15
             ἴσως δὲ ἀποκρίναιτ' ἂν οὗτος 'σὺ δὲ ἐλεύθερος ὢν οὐ τυγχάνεις;
        μὴ οὖν φρόντιζε μηδέν, μήτε τοῦ δήμου μήτε τῶν ῥητόρων μήτε τοῦ
        πολέμου μήτε τῶν νόμων ἢ γεγραμμένων ἢ ἀγράφων. ἐν γὰρ ταύτῃ
        τῇ πόλει οὐδεὶς ὑπ' οὐδενὸς οὐδέποτε ἀναγκάζεται ποιεῖν ἃ μὴ ἐθέλει.
        ἀτεχνῶς δὲ ἐλευθέρους ἡγοῦμαι τούς τε ἵππους καὶ τοὺς ἡμιόνους τοὺς   20
        ἐν τῇ πόλει, οἳ κατὰ τὰς ὁδοὺς πορευόμενοι ἐμβάλλειν φιλοῦσι τοῖς
        ὁδοιπόροις τοῖς μὴ ἐξισταμένοις.'
             εἶεν. γνοὺς οὖν ἐμαυτὸν ἐλεύθερόν γ' ὄντα καὶ οὐκ ἀναγκαζόμενον
        ὑπ' οὐδενὸς ποιεῖν ἃ μὴ ἐθέλω, τῶν ἄλλων πολεμούντων, ἐγὼ αὐτὸς οὐ
        πολεμήσω, ἀλλ' εἰρήνην ἄξω. Ἀμφίθεε, δεῦρ' ἐλθέ· ἀλλ' Ἀμφίθεός μοι   25
        ποῦ ἐστιν;
ΑΜΦΙ.   πάρειμι.
ΔΙΚ.   (δοὺς τῷ Ἀμφιθέῳ ὀκτὼ δραχμάς)
        σύ, ταυτασὶ λαβὼν ὀκτὼ δραχμάς, σπονδὰς ποίησαι πρὸς Λακεδαιμονίους
        ἐμοὶ μόνῳ καὶ τοῖς παιδίοις.   30
(τοῦ Δικαιοπόλεως δόντος τὰ ἐφόδια, ἀπέρχεται ὁ Ἀμφίθεος)
        (turns to the Prytanes)
        ὑμεῖς δὲ πρεσβεύεσθε, ἔπειτα δὲ ἐκδικάζετε, ἔπειτα χρηματίζετε περὶ
        τοῦ πολέμου καὶ περὶ πόρου χρημάτων καὶ περὶ νόμων θέσεως καὶ περὶ
        συμμάχων καὶ περὶ τριήρων καὶ περὶ νεωρίων καὶ περὶ ἱερῶν. ἀλλ' οὔτε   35
        τριήρων οὔτε νεωρίων δεῖται ἡ πόλις, εἰ μέλλει εὐδαιμονήσειν, οὔτε
        πλήθους οὔτε μεγέθους, ἄνευ εἰρήνης.

Vocabulary for Section Eleven B

ἄ-γραφ-ος -ον unwritten
ἀδικ-ούμεθα we are being
  wronged (ἀδικέ-ω)
ἀδικ-ουμέν-οις being wronged
  (ἀδικέ-ω)
ἄκων ἄκουσ-α ἆκον (ἀκοντ-)
  unwilling(ly)
ἀναγκάζ-εται he is forced
  (ἀναγκάζ-ω)
ἀναγκαζ-όμεν-ον being forced
  (ἀναγκάζ-ω)
ἀναγκάζ-ονται they are (being)
  forced (ἀναγκάζ-ω)
ἄνευ (+gen.) without
ἀπ-ολλύ-μεθα we are being
  ruined (ἀπ-όλλυ-μι/ἀπολ-)
ἀπ-ολλύ-μεν-οι being ruined
  (ἀπ-όλλυ-μι)
ἀπ-όλ-οιντο may they perish!
  (ἀπ-όλλυ-μαι/ἀπολ-)
ἄρχ-εται (it) is ruled (ἄρχ-ω)
ἄρχ-ω rule
ἀτεχν-ῶς really, utterly
γεγραμμέν-ος -η -ον written
δια-φθειρ-όμεν-ος being
  corrupted (δια-φθείρ-ω)
δραχμ-ή, ἡ drachma (1a)
εἶεν all right then
ἐκ-δικάζ-ω make judgment
ἐμ-βάλλ-ω bump into
  (+dat.)
ἐξ-απατ-ᾶσθαι to be deceived
  (ἐξ-απατά-ω)
ἐξ-απατ-ώμεθα we are (being)
  deceived (ἐξ-απατά-ω)
ἐξ-απατ-ώμεν-ος being deceived
  (ἐξ-απατά-ω)

ἐξ-ίστα-μαι get out of the way
ἔστω let it be; so be it
εὐ-δαιμονέ-ω be happy
εὔ-νους -ουν well-disposed
ἐφ-όδι-α, τά travelling expenses
  (2b)
θέσ-ις, ἡ making (3e)
θωπευ-όμεν-ος being flattered
  (θωπεύ-ω)
θωπεύ-εσθαι to be flattered
  (θωπεύ-ω)
θωπεύ-ω flatter
ἱερ-ά, τά sacrifices (2b)
κάκιστα most horribly
μέγεθ-ος, τό great size (3c)
μήτε . . . μήτε neither . . . nor
νεώρι-ον, τό dockyard (2b)
ὁδοι-πόρ-ος, ὁ traveller (2a)
ὁδ-ός, ἡ road (2a)
οἷς what (after πείθ-ομαι)
ὅσ-οι -αι- α as many as
ὀκτώ eight
ὄλ-οιντο may they die
  (ὄλλυ-μαι/ὀλ-)
πείθ-εσθαι to be persuaded
  (πείθ-ω)
πειθ-όμεν-ος being persuaded
  (πείθ-ω)
πείθ-ονται they are (being)
  persuaded (πείθ-ω)
πολεμέ-ω make war
πόρ-ος, ὁ ways of raising,
  provision (2a)
πρεσβεύ-ομαι deal with
  ambassadors
συμ-βουλεύ-ω give advice
σύμ-μαχ-ος, ὁ ally (2a)

τιμ-ᾶται (he) is (being) honoured
  (τιμά-ω)
τριήρ-ης, ἡ trireme (3d)
τοῦ Δικαιοπόλεως δόντος
  Dikaiopolis giving
τῶν ἄλλων πολεμούντων the
  others making war
χρηματίζ-ω do business
φαίη he might say (with ἄν)
  (opt. of φημί)
φιλέ-ω be accustomed, used to

Vocabulary to be learnt
ἄκων ἄκουσα ἆκον (ἀκοντ-)
  unwilling(ly)
ἄνευ *(+gen.) without*
ἀπόλλῡμι (ἀπολεσα-, ἀπολ-)
  kill, ruin, destroy; (in pass.)
  be killed etc. (aor. ἀπωλόμην)
δραχμή, ἡ *drachma (1a) (coin;*
  pay for two days' attendance
  at the ekklesia)
εἶεν *very well then!*
εὔνους ουν *well-disposed*
μήτε . . . μήτε *neither. . . nor*
ὁδοιπόρος, ὁ *traveller (2a)*
ὁδός, ἡ *road, way (2a)*
ὄλλῡμι (ὀλεσα-, ὀλ-) *destroy,*
  kill; (in pass.) be killed, die,
  perish (aor. ὠλόμην)
ὅσ-ος η ον *as much as (pl. as*
  many as)
πολεμέω *make war*
τριήρης, ἡ *trireme (3d)*
φιλέω *be used to; love; kiss*
χρηματίζω *do business*

Critics of Athenian democracy

Dikaiopolis' rant at ll.1–22 is taken from those critics of democracy who felt
that the δῆμος, male citizens over 18 who in the ἐκκλησία made all the decisions
that politicians make for us today, was basically irresponsible. In his *Republic*
(563), Plato argues that excess of freedom ultimately leads to excess of slavery
and points out that in democracy, pets have more freedom than anywhere else:
'horses and donkeys learn to strut about with absolute freedom, bumping into
anyone they happen to meet who doesn't get out of the way'!

C

In *World of Athens*: Akharnai and Akharnians 2.22; Marathon-fighters 1.30; peace 7.4; festivals 8.45–7; city Dionysia 2.21, 2.29, 3.43–4.

ΔΙΚ.   ἀλλ᾽ ἐκ Λακεδαίμονος γὰρ Ἀμφίθεος ὁδί. χαῖρ᾽, Ἀμφίθεε.
(Δικαιοπόλεως δὲ ταῦτα εἰπόντος, ὁ Ἀμφίθεος τρέχει ἔτι)
ΑΜΦΙ.   μήπω γε, Δικαιόπολι. δεῖ γάρ με φεύγοντ᾽ ἐκφυγεῖν Ἀχαρνέας.
ΔΙΚ.   τί δ᾽ ἐστίν;
ΑΜΦΙ.   *(looks around anxiously)*   5
         ἐγὼ μὲν δεῦρό σοι σπονδὰς φέρων ἔσπευδον. ἀλλ᾽ οὐκ ἔλαθον τοὺς
         Ἀχαρνέας. οἱ δὲ γέροντες ἐκεῖνοι, Μαραθωνομάχαι ὄντες, εὐθὺς αἰσθόμενοί
         με σπονδὰς φέροντα, ἐβόησαν πάντες, ʻὦ μιαρώτατε, σπονδὰς φέρεις,
         Λακεδαιμονίων τὴν ἡμετέραν γῆν ὀλεσάντων;ʼ καὶ λίθους ἔλαβον. λίθους
         δὲ λαβόντων αὐτῶν, ἐγὼ ἔφευγον. οἱ˘δ᾽ ἐδίωκον καὶ ἐβόων.   10
ΔΙΚ.   οἱ˘δ᾽ οὖν βοώντων. ἀλλὰ τὰς σπονδὰς φέρεις;
ΑΜΦΙ.   ἔγωγέ φημι.
         (produces some sample bottles from his pouch)
         τρία γε ταυτὶ γεύματα..
(δίδωσιν αὐτῷ γεῦμά τι)   15
         αὗται μέν εἰσι πεντέτεις. γεῦσαι λαβών.
ΔΙΚ.   (δόντος Ἀμφιθέου, γεύεται Δικαιόπολις)
         αἰβοῖ.
ΑΜΦΙ.   τί ἐστιν;
ΔΙΚ.   οὐκ ἀρέσκουσί μοι ὅτι ὄζουσι παρασκευῆς νεῶν.   20
ΑΜΦΙ.   (δοὺς ἄλλο τι γεῦμα)
         σὺ δ᾽ ἀλλά, τασδὶ τὰς δεκέτεις, γεῦσαι λαβών.
ΔΙΚ.   ὄζουσι χαῦται πρεσβέων εἰς τὰς πόλεις ὀξύτατα.

δίδωσιν αὐτῷ γεῦμά τι

ΑΜΦΙ.   ἀλλ' αὗταί εἰσι σπονδαὶ τριακοντούτεις κατὰ γῆν τε καὶ θάλατταν.
ΔΙΚ.   (*joyfully*)   25
        ὦ Διονύσια, αὗται μὲν ὄζουσ' ἀμβροσίας καὶ νέκταρος. ταύτας ἥδιστ' ἂν
        αἱροίμην, χαίρειν πολλὰ κελεύων τοὺς Ἀχαρνέας. ἐγὼ δέ, πολέμου καὶ
        κακῶν παυσάμενος, ἄξειν μέλλω εἰσιὼν τὰ κατ' ἀγροὺς Διονύσια.
ΑΜΦΙ.   (κατιδὼν προσιόντας τοὺς Ἀχαρνέας)
        ἐγὼ δὲ φεύξομαί γε τοὺς Ἀχαρνέας.   30

Vocabulary for Section Eleven C

αἰβοῖ yuk!
αἱρέ-ομαι choose
αἰσθάν-ομαι (αἰσθ-) perceive,
    notice
ἀμβροσί-α, ἡ ambrosia (1b)
ἀρέσκ-ω please (+dat.)
Ἀχαρν-εύς, ὁ member of the
    deme Akharnai (3g) (*in
    central Attica, in the path of
    Spartan attacks*)
γεῦμα (γευματ-), τό taste,
    sample (3b)
γεύ-ομαι taste
δεκέτ-ης -ες for ten years
Δικαιοπόλεως … εἰπόντος
    Dikaiopolis saying
Διονύσι-α, τά festival of
    Dionysos (2b)
δόντος Ἀμφιθέου Amphitheos
    giving
ἥδιστα most pleasurably (ἡδ-ύς)

λαβόντων αὐτῶν them taking
Λακεδαιμονίων … ὀλεσάντων
    the Spartans destroying
Λακεδαίμων (Λακεδαιμον-), ἡ
    Sparta (3a)
λίθ-ος, ὁ stone (2a)
Μαραθωνο-μάχ-ης, ὁ fighter at
    the battle of Marathon (*which
    took place in 490*) (1d)
μήπω not yet
νέκταρ (νεκταρ-), τό nectar (3b)
ὄζ-ω smell of (+gen.)
ὀξ-ύτατ-α most sharply (ὀξ-ύς)
παρα-σκευ-ή, ἡ preparation,
    equipping (1a)
πεντέτ-ης -ες for five years
τρία three (n. of τρεῖς)
τριακοντούτ-ης -ες for thirty
    years
χαίρειν πολλὰ κελεύων bidding
    a long farewell to

Vocabulary to be learnt
αἱρέομαι (ἑλ-) *choose*
αἰσθάνομαι (αἰσθ-) *perceive,
    notice*
ἀρέσκω *please (+dat.)*
ἄρχομαι *be ruled*
ἄρχω *rule (+gen.)*
γεῦμα (γευματ-), τό *taste,
    sample (3b)*
γεύομαι *taste*
ἥδιστος η ον *most pleasant (sup.
    of ἡδύς)*
λίθος, ὁ *stone (2a)*
ὅδέ *and/but he*
οἵδέ *and/but they*
ὀξύς εῖα ύ *sharp; bitter; shrill*
παρασκευή, ἡ *preparation,
    equipping; force (1a)*
τρεῖς τρία *three*

Part Four Women in Athenian society

Introduction

Institutionally, Athenian society was male-dominated; and nearly all Greek literature was written by men. How then can we assess the impact and importance of women in Athenian society, especially when we cannot help but see them through twentieth-century eyes? A straight, short and true answer is 'With much difficulty'. But the question is an important one for many reasons, particularly because women play such a dominant role in much Greek literature (e.g. Homer, tragedy and, as we have seen, comedy).

One of the best sources we have for the attitudes and prejudices of the ordinary people in Athenian society is the speeches from the law courts, and much information about women's lives emerges almost incidentally from these to balance the silence of some literary sources and the 'tragic' stature of the great dramatic heroines.

In the *Prosecution of Neaira* the prosecutor, Apollodoros, charges the woman Neaira with being an alien (i.e. non-Athenian) and living with an Athenian Stephanos as if she were his wife, so falsely claiming the privileges of Athenian citizenship. Apollodoros describes her early life in Corinth as a slave and prostitute, and how her subsequent career took her all over Greece and brought her into contact with men in the first rank of Athenian society, before she eventually settled down with Stephanos. Apollodoros' condemnation of her behaviour, which he denounces as a threat and affront to the status and security of native Athenian women, indicates by contrast his attitude to citizen women.

An Athenian wedding

It is important to remember that Apollodoros' aim is to win his case. We can therefore assume that everything he says is, in his opinion, calculated to persuade the hearts and minds of the jury, 501 Athenian males over the age of 30. You must continually ask yourself the question 'What do Apollodoros' words tell us about the average Athenian male's attitude to the subject under discussion?'

Counterpointing the speech are discussions of some of the prosecutor's points by three listening dikasts, Komias, Euergides and Strymodoros. Their reactions serve to bring out some of the attitudes and prejudices which the prosecutor was trying to arouse. The dikast dialogue is invented, but most of it is based closely on arguments in the speech.

The picture of the status of women in Athens given in Apollodoros' prosecution of Neaira is balanced by the figure of a mythical heroine. Alkestis was traditionally the supreme example of a woman's devotion. Euripides enables us to see the mythical heroine very much in terms of a fifth-century Athenian woman in her concern for her husband and children.

In *World of Athens*: law-courts 6.38ff.; Apollodoros 5.70, 6.45–6.

Sources

Demosthenes 59, *The Prosecution of Neaira (pass.)*
Euripides, *Alkestis* 150–207

(For the dikast dialogue) Extracts from Plato, Aristophanes, Solon, Theokritos, Demosthenes, Lysias

The best edition of the whole of the prosecution of Neaira, with text, facing-page translation and commentary on the translation, is by Christopher Carey, *Apollodoros* Against Neaira *[Demosthenes] 59* (Greek Orators vol. VI, Aris and Phillips 1992). Debra Hamel, *Trying Neaira* (Yale 2003) tells the 'true story' of Neaira's life.

Time to be taken

Seven weeks

Sections Twelve to Fourteen: The prosecution of Neaira

Introduction

These selections are adapted from the speech Κατὰ Νεαίρας, *The Prosecution of Neaira* (attributed to Demosthenes), given by Apollodoros in the Athenian courts about 340. Neaira is accused of being non-Athenian and of claiming marriage to the Athenian Stephanos, and so usurping the privileges of citizenship. Citizenship at Athens was restricted to the children of two Athenian citizen parents, legally married, and it was a jealously guarded privilege. Apollodoros was therefore able to bring the charge as a matter of public interest, in a γραφή. He sketches Neaira's past to prove that she is an alien, but also makes great play of the fact that she was a slave and prostitute as well, thus making her 'pretence' to Athenian citizenship all the more shocking; and goes on to show that Stephanos and Neaira were treating Neaira's alien children as if they were entitled to Athenian citizenship. This evidence gives Apollodoros the occasion to claim that Neaira and Stephanos are undermining the whole fabric of society.

Apollodoros had a personal interest in the matter as well, for he had a long-standing feud with Stephanos, as the start of the speech makes clear. If Apollodoros secured Neaira's conviction, she would be sold into slavery: Stephanos' 'family' would be broken up (and Neaira and Stephanos, formally married or not, had been living together for probably thirty years by the time of this case) and Stephanos himself would be liable to a heavy fine; if he could not pay it, he would lose his rights of citizenship (ἀτιμία). It is revenge on Stephanos that Apollodoros is really after, which is why Stephanos is so heavily implicated in the incidents cited. Neaira just happens to be the weak point through which Apollodoros can hit at Stephanos.

The speech draws attention to a number of important points about the Athenian world, among which we draw especial attention to:

(i) Personal security for oneself, one's property and one's family depended first and foremost on being a full citizen of the πόλις. In return for this personal security, the citizen was expected to do his duty by the community of which he was a member. This bond of obligation between citizen and πόλις, expressed most powerfully in the laws of the community, was shaken if outsiders forced their way in, and consequently the πόλις was at risk if those who had no duty to it inveigled their way in. The close link which the native inhabitants felt with their local patron god, on whose protection they had a strong claim, could also be weakened by the intrusion of outsiders.

(ii) Athenians were extremely sensitive about their status in other people's eyes. In the face of a personal affront (however justified), an Athenian would be applauded for taking swift and decisive steps to gain revenge (remember that Christianity was some 500 years away from fifth-century Athens). Any citizen whose rights to citizenship had been put at risk (as Apollodoros' had been by Stephanos) would be quick to seek retribution, on whatever grounds he could find, and he would not be afraid to explain that personal revenge was the motive for the attack (imagine the consequences of saying that to a jury today).

(iii) While it is dangerous to generalise about the status of women in the ancient world, Apollodoros in this speech says what he thinks he *ought* to say about Neaira in particular and women in general in order to win over a jury of 501 males over the age of 30. He paints an unpleasant and quite unsympathetic picture of Neaira because he hopes the jury will respond favourably to that; and while we may feel moved to sympathy by Neaira's experience as a slave and prostitute (over which she almost certainly had no choice) and by her efforts to gain security for her children by marriage with Stephanos, Apollodoros clearly presumed that his audience's response would be very different.

Again, Apollodoros' picture of citizen women as either highly virtuous or rather weak-headed was not drawn because he necessarily believed it or because it was the case. It was supposed to strike a chord in the hearts of his listeners – nothing more or less. The speech thus gives us an invaluable glimpse into what an average Athenian male might be presumed to think about the opposite sex, both citizen and alien. With such evidence of attitudes and prejudices before us, it should be easier for us to assess, for example, the emotional impact that a figure such as Antigone or Medea might have had upon an Athenian audience.

(iv) In a world where the spoken word is the main means of communication and persuasion, and the mass meeting the main context, the orator's art is of the highest importance. It was a skill much cultivated and admired by Athenian writers, and much suspected by thinkers like Plato (himself, of course, a master of the art). However unsympathetic the twenty-first century may be to the orator's art (though it is simply one variant of a number of means of persuading people, with which we are far more conversant than the Greeks who did not have radio, T.V., newspapers or the Internet), it is important to understand it and the impact it had on the Greek world.

The speech

The speech is set in the context of a meeting between three of the dikasts who will be judging the case – the experienced Komias and Euergides, and the inexperienced Strymodoros. They appear at the beginning and end of the speech, but hardly interrupt the flow of evidence at all.

The speech is divided up as follows:

Section Twelve: Neaira as slave

A–B: The dikasts enter the court.

C. Apollodoros outlines in general his motives for bringing the action and the dikasts urge Strymodoros not to believe everything that he hears.

D: Apollodoros reviews his grudge against Stephanos and details the charge against Neaira.

E: The dikasts argue about the validity of Apollodoros' motives.

F: Apollodoros sketches Neaira's past as a slave in Corinth.

G: Strymodoros' memory lets him down.

H: Neaira runs away from Phrynion and meets Stephanos.

I: Neaira sets up home with Stephanos in Athens.

Section Thirteen: Neaira as married woman

A: Stephanos marries off Neaira's daughter Phano to the Athenian Phrastor, briefly.

B: Phrastor falls ill and re-adopts Phano's son.

C: Phrastor recovers and marries someone else.

D: The incident between Phano and Phrastor is reviewed.

E: Stephanos marries Phano off to Theogenes.

F: The Areopagos find out and call Theogenes to account.

G: Komias suggests arguments Stephanos will use to clear his name.

I: Apollodoros implicates Stephanos along with Neaira in the charges.

Section Fourteen: guarding a woman's purity

A–B: How could anyone not condemn a woman like Neaira?

C–D: Komias argues that the acquittal of Neaira would be intolerable.

E: Apollodoros' final appeal to the dikasts.

F. The dikasts await the speech for the defence – and their pay.

The characters

The main characters involved are:

Komias, Euergidcs, Strymodoros: three listening dikasts.

Apollodoros: the prosecutor, making the speech, a man with a reputation for litigiousness.

Neaira: the defendant, a woman now living in Athens with Stephanos. It is her past that Apollodoros uncovers in an attempt to prove that she is non-Athenian and pretending to be married to Stephanos.

Stephanos: a personal enemy of Apollodoros and an old adversary in several legal and political battles in the past. He brought Neaira back to Athens from Megara, and is claimed by Apollodoros to be living with Neaira as if they were husband and wife.

Nikarete: Neaira's owner and 'madam' in Corinth in her youth.

Phrynion: one of Neaira's lovers, a wealthy and well-connected figure in Athenian society. She went to live with him after buying her freedom from her two previous lovers Timanoridas and Eukrates (largely because he gave her most of the money for her freedom). She ran away from him to Megara; on her return to Athens with Stephanos, Phrynion and Stephanos clashed over who rightfully owned her.

Phano: Neaira's daughter, and therefore non-Athenian. But Stephanos tried to palm her off as *his* own Athenian daughter to a number of Athenian men. These included:

Phrastor: a self-made man who had quarrelled with his family, and Theogenes: a poor man who had been chosen by lot as *archon basileus,* the position of greatest importance in conducting the religious rites of the Athenian state.

Section Twelve A–I: Neaira as slave

A

κελεύοντος τοῦ κήρυκος, ἥκουσιν οἱ δικασταὶ εἰς τὸ δικαστήριον. καὶ ἄλλος ἄλλον
ὡς ὁρῶσιν ἥκοντα, εὐθὺς ἀσπάζονται, λαβόμενοι τῆς χειρός. ἐπεὶ δὲ ἥκουσιν ὁ
Κωμίας καὶ Εὐεργίδης εἰς τὸ δικαστήριον – οὗ μέλλουσι δικάσειν γραφήν τινα περὶ
Νεαίρας – ἀσπάζεται ὁ ἕτερος τὸν ἕτερον.

5

ΕΥΕΡΓΙΔΗΣ	χαῖρε, ὦ Κωμία.
ΚΩΜΙΑΣ	νὴ⌢καὶ⌢σύ⌢γε, ὦ Εὐεργίδη. ὅσος ὁ ὄχλος. ἀλλὰ τίς ἐστι οὑτοσί; οὐ δήπου
	Στρυμόδωρος ὁ γείτων; ναὶ μὰ τὸν Δία, αὐτὸς δῆτ᾽ ἐκεῖνος. ὦ τῆς τύχης.
	ἀλλ᾽ οὐκ ἤλπιζον Στρυμοδώρῳ ἐντεύξεσθαι ἐν δικαστηρίῳ διατρίβοντι,
	νέῳ δὴ ὄντι καὶ ἀπείρῳ τῶν δικανικῶν. 10
ΕΥ.	τί οὐ καλεῖς αὐτὸν δεῦρο; ἐξέσται γὰρ αὐτῷ μεθ᾽ ἡμῶν καθίζειν.
ΚΩ.	ἀλλὰ καλῶς λέγεις καὶ καλοῦμεν αὐτόν. ὦ Στρυμόδωρε, Στρυμόδωρε.
ΣΤΡΥΜΟΔΩΡΟΣ	χαίρετε, ὦ γείτονες. ὅσον τὸ χρῆμα τοῦ ὄχλου.
(ὠθεῖται ὑπὸ δικαστοῦ τινος, ὃς τοῦ ἱματίου λαμβάνεται)	
	οὗτος, τί βουλόμενος ἐλάβου τοῦ ἐμοῦ ἱματίου; ὄλοιο. 15
ΕΥ.	εὖ γε. κάθιζε.

The agora area of Athens, where the law-courts were.

Vocabulary for Section Twelve A

Note: from now on, prefixes in compounds will not be hyphenated, and new
forms will be glossed as a whole, without hyphens.

> **Grammar for 12A–D**
> - Aorist passive
> - Verbs: ἵστημι, καθίστημι

ἄλλος . . . ἄλλον one . . . another
ἄπειρ-ος -ον inexperienced in
   (+gen.)
Ἀπολλόδωρ-ος, ὁ Apollodoros
   (2a) (*prosecuting in the case*)
ἀσπάζ-ομαι greet, welcome
διατρίβ-ω pass time, be
δικανικ-ός -ή -όν judicial
ἐντεύξεσθαι fut. inf. of
ἐντυγχάνω
ἐντυγχάν-ω meet (+dat.)
ἕτερος . . . ἕτερον one . . .
   another (of two)
Εὐεργίδ-ης, ὁ Euergides (1d)
   (*a dikast*)
ἱμάτι-ον, τό cloak (2b)

Κωμί-ας, ὁ Komias (1d) (*a
   dikast*)
λαμπρ-ός -ά -όν famous,
   notorious
μηδέ . . . μηδέ neither . . . nor
Νέαιρ-α, ἡ Neaira (1b)
   (*defendant in the case*)
νὴ καὶ σύ γε and you, too
οὗ where (at)
ὄχλ-ος, ὁ crowd (2a)
Στρυμόδωρ-ος, ὁ Strymodoros
   (2a) (*a young dikast*)
τύχ-η, ἡ fortune, piece of luck
   (1a)
χρῆμα (χρηματ-), τό astonishing
   size, amount (3b)

ὠθέ-ω push, shove

Vocabulary to be learnt
ἄλλος . . . ἄλλον *one . . .
   another*
ἀσπάζομαι *greet, welcome*
δικανικός ή όν *judicial*
ἐντυγχάνω (ἐντυχ-) *meet with,
   come upon (dat.)*
ἕτερος . . . ἕτερον *one . . .
   another (of two)*
ἱμάτιον, τό *cloak (2b)*
μηδέ . . . μηδέ *neither . . . nor*
τύχη, ἡ *chance, fortune (good or
   bad) (1a)*
ὠθέω *push, shove*

B

In *World of Athens*: meddling 6.54; persuasion 8.20–1.

(εἰσέρχεται Ἀπολλόδωρος ὁ κατήγορος)

ΣΤΡ.   ἀλλὰ τίς ἐστιν ἐκεῖνος, ὃς πρὸς τὸ βῆμα προσέρχεται ταχέως βαδίζων;

ΚΩ.   τυγχάνει κατηγορῶν ἐν τῇ δίκῃ οὗτος, ᾧ ὄνομά ἐστιν Ἀπολλόδωρος,
       φύσις δὲ αὐτοῦ πολυπράγμων.

ΕΥ.   ἀλλ᾽ οὐδὲν διαφέρει εἴτε πολυπράγμων ἡ φύσις αὐτοῦ ἢ οὔ. δεῖ γὰρ ἡμᾶς   5
       κοινὴν τὴν εὔνοιαν τοῖς ἀγωνιζομένοις παρέχειν, καὶ ὁμοίως ἀκοῦσαι
       τοὺς λόγους οἷς χρῆται ἑκάτερος, κατὰ τὸν ὅρκον ὃν ἀπέδομεν.
       καὶ μὴν ὁ Ἀπολλόδωρος ἑαυτῷ καὶ ἄλλοις πολλοῖς δοκεῖ εὐεργετεῖν τὴν
       πόλιν καὶ κυρίους ποιεῖν τοὺς νόμους, τὴν Νέαιραν γραψάμενος γραφὴν
       ξενίας.   10

Vocabulary for Section Twelve B

ἀγωνίζ-ομαι go to law
ἀποδίδω-μι (ἀποδο-) pledge,
   give back
βῆμα (βηματ-), τό stand, podium
   (3b)
διαφέρ-ω make a difference
εἴτε . . . εἴτε whether . . . or

εὐεργετέ-ω benefit
εὔνοι-α, ἡ good will (1b)
κατά (+acc.) in accordance with
κατήγορ-ος, ὁ prosecutor,
   accuser (2a)
κοιν-ός –ή -όν common,
   undivided

κύρι-ος -α -ον valid
ξενί-α, ἡ alien status (1b)
ὄρκ-ος, ὁ oath (2a)
πολυπράγμων πολύπραγμον
   meddling
φύσ-ις, ἡ nature (3e)

ΚΩ.   ἴσως δὴ φιλόπολις ἔφυ ὁ Ἀπολλόδωρος. ἀλλὰ γιγνώσκω σέ, ὦ Εὐεργίδη,
        κατήγορον ὄντα πάνυ δεινὸν λέγειν. ἀεὶ γὰρ ὑπὸ τῶν διωκόντων λέγεται
        τὰ τοιαῦτα. καὶ Ἀπολλόδωρος, εὖ οἶδ᾽ ὅτι, τὰ αὐτὰ ἐρεῖ· ᾽οὐχ ὑπῆρξα τῆς
        ἔχθρας᾽, φήσει, καὶ ᾽ὁ φεύγων ἡμᾶς ἠδίκησε μάλιστα᾽, καὶ ᾽βούλομαι
        τιμωρεῖσθαι αὐτόν.᾽ ἐγὼ δὲ οὐκ ἀεὶ ὑπὸ τῶν τοιούτων πείθομαι.   15
ΕΥ.   εἰκός. νῦν δὲ οὐκ ἂν σιγῴης καὶ προσέχοις⌒τὸν⌒νοῦν; χρέμπτεται
        γὰρ ἤδη ὁ Ἀπολλόδωρος, ὅπερ ποιοῦσιν οἱ ἀρχόμενοι λέγοντες, καὶ
        ἀνίσταται.
ΚΩ.   σιγήσομαι, ὦ Εὐεργίδη. ἀλλ᾽ ὅπως σιωπήσεις καὶ σύ, ὦ Στρυμόδωρε, καὶ
        προσέξεις⌒τὸν⌒νοῦν.   20

εἰκός rightly, reasonably
ἑκάτερ-ος -α -ον each (of two)
ἔφυ-ν be, be naturally (from
    φύ-ομαι)
ἔχθρ-α, ἡ hostility, enmity
    (1b)
καὶ μήν what's more
ὅπως see to it that (+ fut. ind.)
προκαταγιγνώσκ-ω
    (προκαταγνο-) pre-judge
προσέχ-ω τὸν νοῦν pay attention

τιμωρέ-ομαι revenge oneself on
ὑπάρχ-ω begin, start (+gen.)
φιλόπολις patriotic, loyal
φύ-ομαι grow (see ἔφυν)
χρέμπτ-ομαι clear one's
    throat

Vocabulary to be learnt
διαφέρ-ω make a difference;
    differ from (+gen.); be
    superior to (+gen.)

εἴτε . . . εἴτε whether . . . or
ἑκάτερος ᾶ ον both (of two)
εὔνοια, ἡ good will (1b)
καὶ μήν what's more; look!
κατά (+ acc.) according to; down;
    throughout; in relation to
κατήγορος, ὁ prosecutor
    (2a)
ὅρκος, ὁ oath (2a)
προσέχω τὸν νοῦν pay attention
    to (+ dat.)

C

Apollodoros outlines in general his motives for bringing the action, and the
dikasts urge Strymodoros not to believe everything that he hears.

In *World of Athens*: revenge 4.8ff.; friends and enemies 4.2, 14–16; poverty 4.21; *atimia*
4.12, 6.55–8.

πολλῶν ἕνεκα, ὦ ἄνδρες Ἀθηναῖοι, ἐβουλόμην γράψασθαι Νέαιραν τὴν γραφήν, ἣν
νυνὶ διώκω, καὶ εἰσελθεῖν εἰς ὑμᾶς. καὶ γὰρ ἠδικήθην μεγάλα ὑπὸ Στεφάνου, οὗ γυνή
ἐστιν ἡ Νέαιρα αὕτη. καὶ ἀδικηθεὶς ὑπ᾽ αὐτοῦ εἰς κινδύνους τοὺς ἐσχάτους κατέστην, καὶ
οὐ⌒μόνον⌐ἐγὼ⌐ἀλλὰ⌐καὶ αἱ θυγατέρες καὶ ἡ γυνὴ ἡ ἐμή. τιμωρίας οὖν ἕνεκα ἀγωνίζομαι
τὸν ἀγῶνα τουτονί, καταστὰς εἰς τοιοῦτον κίνδυνον. οὐ γὰρ ὑπῆρξα τῆς ἔχθρας ἐγώ,   5
ἀλλὰ Στέφανος, οὐδὲν ὑφ᾽ ἡμῶν πώποτε οὔτε λόγῳ οὔτε ἔργῳ ἀδικηθείς. βούλομαι δ᾽
ὑμῖν προδιηγήσασθαι πάνθ᾽ ἃ ἐπάθομεν καὶ ὡς ἀδικηθέντες ὑπ᾽ αὐτοῦ εἰς τοὺς ἐσχάτους
κινδύνους κατέστημεν περί τε τῆς πενίας καὶ περὶ ἀτιμίας.

ΣΤΡ.   δεινὸς δὴ λέγειν, ὡς ἔοικεν, Ἀπολλόδωρος, ὃς ὑπὸ Στεφάνου ἠδικήθη.   10
        εὔνοιαν δ᾽ ἔχω εἰς αὐτὸν ὅτι ὑπῆρξε τῆς ἔχθρας Στέφανος. τίς γὰρ οὐκ ἂν
        βούλοιτο τιμωρεῖσθαι τὸν ἐχθρόν; πάντες γὰρ ἐθέλουσι τοὺς μὲν φίλους
        εὖ⌒ποιεῖν, τοὺς δ᾽ ἐχθροὺς κακῶς.

ΚΩ.   ὅπως μὴ ῥᾳδίως τοῖς ἀντιδίκοις πιστεύσεις, ὦ Στρυμόδωρε. ἀναστάντες
        γὰρ ἐν τῷ δικαστηρίῳ οἱ ἀντίδικοι τοὺς δικαστὰς, πάσαις χρώμενοι   15
        τέχναις, εἰς εὔνοιαν καθίστασιν.
ΣΤΡ.   ἀλλ' ἡδέως ἄν τι μάθοιμι. ὁ γὰρ Ἀπολλόδωρος λέγει ὅτι ἀδικηθεὶς ὑπὸ
        τοῦ Στεφάνου εἰς κίνδυνον κατέστη περὶ τῆς πενίας. τί ποιῶν ὁ Στέφανος
        κατέστησε τὸν Ἀπολλόδωρον εἰς τοῦτον τὸν κίνδυνον;
ΕΥ.   ἀλλ' ἄκουε. περὶ γὰρ τῆς τοῦ ἀγῶνος ἀρχῆς διατελεῖ λέγων ὁ   20
        Ἀπολλόδωρος.

Vocabulary for Section Twelve C

ἀγών (ἀγων-), ὁ trial, contest (3a)
ἀγωνίζ-ομαι go to law, fight
ἀδικηθείς harmed, wronged (nom. s. m.) (ἀδικέ-ω)
ἀδικηθέντες harmed, wronged (nom. pl. m.) (ἀδικέ-ω)
ἀναστάντες standing up (nom. pl. m.) (ἀνίσταμαι/ἀναστα-)
ἀντίδικ-ος, ὁ contestant (2a)
ἀρχ-ή, ἡ start (1a)
διατελέ-ω continue
ἔοικε it seems
ἔσχατ-ος -η -ον furthest, worst
εὖ ποιέ-ω do good to, treat well
ἔχθρ-α, ἡ hostility (1b)
ἐχθρ-ός, ὁ an enemy (2a)
ἠδικήθη (he) was harmed, wronged (ἀδικέ-ω)
ἠδικήθην I was harmed, wronged (ἀδικέ-ω)
θυγάτηρ (θυγατ(ε)ρ-), ἡ daughter (3a)
καθίστη-μι (καταστησ-) set up, put, place (x in y position)
καὶ γάρ in fact

καταστάς being put, made (nom. s. m.) (καθίσταμαι/καταστα-)
κατέστην I was placed, found myself in (καθίσταμαι/καταστα-)
κατέστη he was placed, found himself in (καθίσταμαι/καταστα-)
κατέστημεν we were placed, found ourselves in (καθίσταμαι/ καταστα-)
κατέστησε (he) placed (καθίστημι/καταστησ-)
μεγάλα very much, greatly
ὅπως see to it that (+fut. ind.)
οὐ μόνον . . . ἀλλὰ καί not only . . . but also
πενί-α, ἡ poverty (1b)
πιστεύ-ω trust (+dat.)
προδιηγέ-ομαι give a preliminary outline of
πώποτε ever, yet
Στέφαν-ος, ὁ Stephanos (2a) *(who lived with Neaira in Athens)*
τιμωρέ-ομαι take revenge on

τιμωρί-α, ἡ revenge (1b)
ὑπάρχ-ω begin (+gen.)

Vocabulary to be learnt
ἀγών (ἀγων-), ὁ *contest, trial (3a)*
ἀγωνίζομαι *contest, go to law*
ἀντίδικος, ὁ *contestant in lawsuit (2a)*
ἀρχή, ἡ *beginning, start (1a)*
εὖ ποιέω *treat well, do good to*
ἔχθρᾱ, ἡ *enmity, hostility (1b)*
ἐχθρός, ὁ *enemy (2a)*
ἐχθρός ᾱ́ όν *hostile, enemy*
θωπεύω *flatter*
καὶ γάρ *in fact; yes, certainly*
οὐ μόνον . . . ἀλλὰ καί *not only . . . but also*
πιστεύω *trust (+dat.)*
τῑμωρέομαι *take revenge on*
τῑμωρίᾱ, ἡ *revenge, vengeance (1b)*
ὑπάρχω *begin (+gen.)*

D

Apollodoros reviews his grudge against Stephanos—that some time ago Stephanos had successfully brought a charge (γραφὴ παρανόμων) against him for proposing an illegal change in the law, and this had almost reduced him to poverty. He details the charge against Neaira.

In *World of Athens*: *psephisma* 6.9; *proix* 5.19, 6.45, 9.3; family; marriage and property 5.17–18; state and religion 3.56–7.

ἐγὼ μὲν γὰρ βουλευτής ποτε καταστὰς ἔγραψα ψήφισμά τι ὃ ἐξήνεγκα εἰς τὸν δῆμον. ὁ δὲ Στέφανος οὑτοσί, γραψάμενος παρανόμων τὸ ἐμὸν ψήφισμα, τῆς ἔχθρας ὑπῆρξεν. ἑλὼν γὰρ τὸ ψήφισμα, ψευδεῖς μάρτυρας παρασχόμενος, ᾔτησε τίμημα μέγα, ὃ οὐχ οἷός τ᾽ ἦ ἐκτεῖσαι. ἐζήτει γάρ, εἰς τὴν ἐσχάτην ἀπορίαν καταστήσας ἐμέ, ἄτιμον ποιεῖσθαι, ὀφείλοντα τὰ χρήματα τῇ πόλει καὶ οὐ δυνάμενον ἐκτεῖσαι.   5

ἐμέλλομεν οὖν ἡμεῖς ἅπαντες εἰς ἔνδειαν καταστήσεσθαι. μεγάλη δ᾽ ἔμελλεν ἔσεσθαι ἡ συμφορά, καὶ μεγάλη ἡ αἰσχύνη μοι, ὑπέρ τε τῆς γυναικὸς καὶ τῶν θυγατέρων, εἰς πενίαν καταστάντι καὶ προῖκα οὐ δυναμένῳ παρασχεῖν καὶ τὸ τίμημα τῇ πόλει ὀφείλοντι. πολλὴν οὖν χάριν οἶδα τοῖς δικασταῖς, οἳ οὐκ ἐπείσθησαν ὑπὸ Στεφάνου, ἀλλ᾽ ἐλάττονά μοι ἐτίμησαν δίκην.   10

οὐκοῦν τοσούτων κακῶν αἴτιος ἡμῖν πᾶσιν ἐγίγνετο Στέφανος, οὐδέποτε ὑφ᾽ ἡμῶν ἀδικηθείς. νῦν δέ, πάντων τῶν φίλων παρακαλούντων με καὶ κελευόντων τιμωρεῖσθαι Στέφανον, ὑφ᾽ οὗ τοιαῦτα ἠδικήθην, εἰσάγω εἰς ὑμᾶς ταύτην τὴν δίκην.

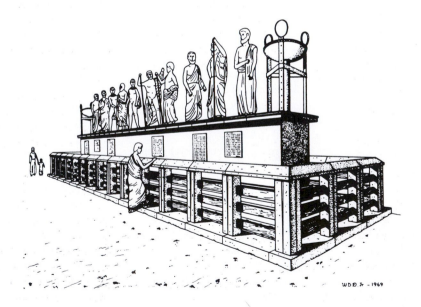

Proposals for new laws were displayed in front of the monument of the Eponymous Heroes in the agora

ὀνειδίζουσι γάρ μοι οἱ φίλοι, ἀνανδρότατον ἀνθρώπων καλοῦντες, εἰ μὴ λήψομαι
δίκην ὑπέρ τε τῶν θυγατέρων καὶ τῆς γυναικὸς τῆς ἐμῆς.   15

εἰσάγω οὖν εἰς ὑμᾶς καὶ ἐξελέγχω τὴν Νέαιραν ταυτηνί, ἣ εἰς τοὺς θεοὺς ἀσεβεῖ,
καὶ εἰς τὴν πόλιν ὑβρίζει, καὶ τῶν νόμων τῶν ὑμετέρων καταφρονεῖ. Στέφανος
γὰρ ἐπειρᾶτό με ἀφαιρεῖσθαι τοὺς οἰκείους παρὰ τοὺς νόμους. οὕτω καὶ ἐγὼ ἥκω
εἰς ὑμᾶς καὶ φάσκω Στέφανον τοῦτον συνοικεῖν μὲν ξένῃ γυναικὶ παρὰ τὸν νόμον,
εἰσαγαγεῖν δὲ ἀλλοτρίους παῖδας εἴς τε τοὺς φράτερας καὶ εἰς τοὺς δημότας, ἐγγυᾶν   20
δὲ τὰς τῶν ἑταιρῶν θυγατέρας ὥσπερ αὑτοῦ οὔσας, ἀσεβεῖν δὲ εἰς τοὺς θεούς.

ὅτι μὲν οὖν ὑπὸ τοῦ Στεφάνου πρότερον ἠδικήθην, εὖ ἴστε. ὅτι δὲ Νέαιρά ἐστι ξένη
καὶ συνοικεῖ Στεφάνῳ παρὰ τοὺς νόμους, ταῦθ' ὑμῖν βούλομαι σαφῶς ἐπιδεῖξαι.

Vocabulary for Section Twelve D

ἀδικηθείς wronged, harmed
(nom. s. m.) (ἀδικέω)
αἰσχύν-η, ἡ sense of shame,
humiliation (1a)
ἀλλότρι-ος -α -ον alien
ἄνανδρ-ος -ον cowardly, feeble
ἀσεβέ-ω εἰς commit sacrilege upon
ἄτιμ-ος -ον deprived of all rights
ἀφαιρέ-ομαι take X (acc.) from
Y (acc.), claim
βουλευτ-ής, ὁ member of βουλή
(1d)
γράφ-ω propose
δημότ-ης, ὁ member of deme,
demesman (1d)
ἐγγυά-ω give in marriage
εἰσάγ-ω (εἰσαγαγ-) introduce
ἐκτίν-ω (ἐκτεισ-) pay (a fine)
ἐλάττων (ἐλαττον-) less, smaller
(comp. of ὀλίγος)
ἔνδει-α, ἡ poverty (1b)
ἐξελέγχ-ω convict, expose
ἐπείσθησαν (they) were
persuaded (πείθω)
ἐπιδείκνυ-μι (ἐπιδειξ-)
demonstrate, prove
ἔσχατ-ος -η -ον worst, most severe
ἑταίρ-α, ἡ whore, prostitute (1b)
ἠδικήθην I was wronged,
harmed (ἀδικέω)
θυγάτηρ (θυγατ(ε)ρ-), ἡ
daughter (3a)
καταστάς (κατασταντ-) placed,
put, made (καθίσταμαι/
καταστα-)

κατάστησας (καταστησαντ-)
placing, putting, making
(καθίστημι/καταστησ-)
καταστήσεσθαι to be put
(καθίσταμαι/καταστα-)
καταφρονέ-ω despise, hold in
contempt (+gen.)
οἰκεῖ-ος ὁ relative (2a)
οἷός τ' εἰμί be able to (+inf.)
ὀνειδίζ-ω rebuke, reproach
(+ dat.)
παρά (+acc.) against
παρακαλέ-ω encourage, urge
παρανόμων as illegal
πενί-α, ἡ poverty (1b)
προίξ (προικ-), ἡ dowry (3a)
πρότερον previously, first
συμφορ-ά, ἡ chance, misfortune,
disaster (1b)
τιμά-ω fine (+dat.)
τίμημα (τιμημat-), τό a fine (3b)
τοσ-οῦτος -αύτη -οῦτο(ν) so
great
ὑβρίζ-ω εἰς act violently against
φάσκ-ω allege
φράτηρ (φρατερ-), ὁ member of
a phratry (3a) (a phratry is a
group of families: as such it
fulfilled various religious and
social functions)
ψευδ-ής -ές false, lying
ψήφισμα (ψηφισμat-), τό decree
(3b)
χάριν οἶδα be grateful to (+dat.)

Vocabulary to be learnt

ἀλλότριος ᾱ ον someone else's,
alien
ἀσεβέω εἰς commit sacrilege
upon
ἄτῑμος ον deprived of citizen
rights
ἀφαιρέομαι (ἀφελ-) take X
(acc.) from Y (acc.), claim
εἰσάγω (εἰσαγαγ-) introduce
ἔσχατος η ον worst, furthest, last
θυγάτηρ (θυγατ(ε)ρ-), ἡ
daughter (3a)
καθίστημι (καταστησα-) set up,
make, place, put X (acc.) in
(εἰς) Y
καθίσταμαι (καταστα-) be
placed, find oneself in, be
made
ξένη, ἡ foreign/alien woman (1a)
οἷός τ' εἰμί be able to (+inf.)
παρά (+acc.) against; to;
compared with; except; along,
beside
πενίᾱ, ἡ poverty (1b)
πρότερος ᾱ ον first (of two),
previous
πρότερον (adv.) previously
τῑμάω fine (+dat.)
τίμημα (τῑμημat-),τό a fine (3b)
τοσοῦτος αύτη οὗτο(ν) so great
ψευδής ές false, lying
ψήφισμα (ψηφισμat-), τό decree
(3b)

E

The dikasts argue about the validity of Apollodoros' motives.

ΚΩ.   οὐχ ὁρᾷς; τοῦτ' ἐκεῖνο ὃ ἔλεγον. τοιαῦτα δὴ ἀεὶ λέγουσιν οἱ ἀντίδικοι,
        ἀλλ' οὐ πείθομαι ὑπ' αὐτῶν ἔγωγε.

ΣΤΡ.   εἰκός γε· φησὶ γὰρ ὁ Ἀπολλόδωρος τὸν Στέφανον ἄρξαι τῆς ἔχθρας, καὶ
        αὐτὸς τιμωρίας ἕνεκα ἀγωνίζεσθαι ἀδικηθεὶς ὑπ' αὐτοῦ. ἃ πάντα ἔλεγες
        σύ, ὦ Κωμία.   5

ΕΥ.   ταῦτα δὴ ἐλέχθη ὑπὸ Ἀπολλοδώρου, ἀλλ' ἡγοῦμαι τὸν Ἀπολλόδωρον
        ἴσως γέ τι σπουδαῖον λέγειν. πρῶτον μὲν γὰρ ἔφη Ἀπολλόδωρος εἰς
        κίνδυνον καταστῆναι περὶ πενίας καὶ ἀτιμίας, καὶ οὐ δυνήσεσθαι τὰς
        θυγατέρας ἐκδοῦναι· ἔπειτα δὲ Στέφανον καὶ Νέαιραν τῶν νόμων
        καταφρονεῖν καὶ εἰς τοὺς θεοὺς ἀσεβεῖν. τίς οὐκ ἂν σπουδάζοι περὶ ταῦτα; 10

ΣΤΡ.   οὐδείς, μὰ Δία. πῶς γὰρ οὐκ ἂν αἰσχύνοιτο ὁ Ἀπολλόδωρος, τὰς
        θυγατέρας ἀνεκδότους ἔχων; καὶ τίς ἂν γαμοίη γυναῖκα προῖκα οὐκ
        ἔχουσαν παρὰ τοιούτου πατρός;

ΕΥ.   ἀλλ' ἴσως ὁ Κωμίας οὐκ ἂν ὁμολογοίη;

ΚΩ.   περὶ τῆς πενίας ὁμολογοίην ἄν. πῶς γὰρ οὔ; περὶ δὲ τῶν νόμων καὶ τῶν   15
        θεῶν, οὐ σαφῶς οἶδα. τεκμηρίων δὲ βεβαίων ὑπὸ τοῦ Ἀπολλοδώρου
        παρεχομένων, ἀκριβῶς μαθησόμεθα.

Vocabulary for Section Twelve E

┌───┐
│ Grammmar for 12E   │
│ • Infinitives in reported speech   │
└───┘

αἰσχύν-ομαι feel shame, be
  ashamed
ἀνέκδοτ-ος -ον unmarried
ἄρχ-ω begin (+gen.)
ἀτιμί-α, ἡ loss of rights (1b)
γαμέ-ω marry
εἰκός right(ly)
ἐκδίδω-μι (ἐκδο-) give in
  marriage
καταφρονέ-ω despise (+gen.)
πᾶς τις everyone

προίξ (προικ-), ἡ dowry (3a)
σπουδάζ-ω be concerned
σπουδαῖ-ος -α -ον important,
  serious
τεκμήρι-ον, τό evidence (2b)

Vocabulary to be learnt
αἰσχύνομαι be ashamed, feel
  shame
ἄρχω begin (+gen.); rule
  (+gen.)

ἀτῑμίᾱ, ἡ *loss of citizen rights
  (1b)*
εἰκός *likely, probable,
  reasonable, fair*
καταφρονέω *despise, look down
  on (+gen.)*
σπουδάζω *be concerned,
  serious; do seriously*
σπουδαῖος ᾱ ον *important,
  serious*

F

Introduction

Apollodoros has introduced the case by indicating his personal and political motives for bringing it, and has outlined the charges he is making against Neaira. The law he is invoking runs as follows:

'If a ξένος lives with (συνοικεῖν) an ἀστή in any way at all, any qualified Athenian who wishes to may bring a case against him before the Thesmothetai. If he is convicted, both the man and his property shall be sold and a third of the proceeds shall go to the man who secured the conviction. The same shall apply if a ξένη lives with an ἀστός. In this case, the man living with the convicted ξένη shall be fined 1,000 drachmas in addition.'

ξένος   a non-Athenian male, without Athenian citizen rights; an alien.
ξένη   a non-Athenian female, without Athenian citizen rights; an alien.
ἀστός   a male Athenian citizen.
ἀστή   a female Athenian citizen.

Apollodoros has then to establish two charges. First, that Neaira is an alien; second, that Stephanos is living with her as if she were his wife. The proof of the first charge will occupy the rest of Section Twelve; the proof of the second charge will occupy Section Thirteen.

In *World of Athens*: *sunoikein* 5.19; Lysias 1.82, 2.24, 3.45, 5.69; the Mysteries 2.22, 3.50–2; witnesses and evidence 6.47.

Apollodoros sketches Neaira's past as a slave in Corinth, under the 'care' of Nikarete.

τοῦ νόμου τοίνυν ἠκούσατε, ὦ ἄνδρες δικασταί, ὃς οὐκ ἐᾷ τὴν ξένην τῷ ἀστῷ συνοικεῖν, οὐδὲ τὴν ἀστὴν τῷ ξένῳ, οὐδὲ παιδοποιεῖσθαι. ὅτι οὖν ἐστιν οὐ μόνον ξένη Νέαιρα ἀλλὰ καὶ δούλη καὶ ἑταίρα, τοῦθ' ὑμῖν βούλομαι ἐξ ἀρχῆς ἀκριβῶς ἐπιδεῖξαι.

Vocabulary for Section Twelve F

> **Grammar for 12F**
> - τίθημι 'I place, put' δείκνῡμι 'I show, reveal'

ἀστ-ή, ἡ female citizen (1a)
ἀστ-ός, ὁ male citizen (2a)

ἐπιδείκνῡ-μι (ἐπιδειξ-) show, prove

ἑταίρ-α, ἡ whore, prostitute (1b)
παιδοποιέ-ομαι have children

ἡ γὰρ Νέαιρα πρῶτον μὲν δούλη ἐν Κορίνθῳ ἦν Νικαρέτης, ὑφ' ἧς ἐτρέφετο παῖς   5
μικρὰ οὖσα. καὶ τόδε φανερὸν καὶ βέβαιον τεκμήριόν ἐστι τούτου· ἦν γὰρ δὴ ἑτέρα
δούλη Νικαρέτης, Μετάνειρα ὀνόματι, ἧς ἐραστὴς ὢν Λυσίας ὁ σοφιστὴς πολλὰς
δραχμὰς ἔθηκεν ὑπὲρ αὐτῆς. ἀλλ' ἐπειδὴ ὑπὸ Νικαρέτης ἐλήφθησαν πᾶσαι αἱ
δραχμαὶ ἃς ἔθηκεν, ἔδοξεν αὐτῷ μυῆσαι αὐτὴν καὶ πολλὰ χρήματα καταθεῖναι εἴς τε
τὴν ἑορτὴν καὶ τὰ μυστήρια, βουλομένῳ ὑπὲρ Μετανείρας καὶ οὐχ ὑπὲρ Νικαρέτης   10
τιθέναι τὰ χρήματα. καὶ ἐπείσθη Νικαρέτη ἐλθεῖν εἰς τὰ μυστήρια, ἄγουσα τὴν
Μετάνειραν. ἀφικομένας δὲ αὐτὰς ὁ Λυσίας εἰς μὲν τὴν αὐτοῦ οἰκίαν οὐκ εἰσάγει
(ᾐσχύνετο γὰρ τὴν γυναῖκα ἣν εἶχε καὶ τὴν μητέρα τὴν αὐτοῦ, ἣ γραῦς οὖσα ἐν τῇ
οἰκίᾳ συνῴκει). καθίστησι δ' αὐτὰς ὁ Λυσίας ὡς Φιλόστρατον, ἠίθεον ἔτι ὄντα καὶ
φίλον αὐτῷ. μεθ' ὧν συνῆλθεν Ἀθήναζε Νέαιρα, δούλη Νικαρέτης οὖσα καὶ αὐτή,   15
ἐργαζομένη μὲν ἤδη τῷ σώματι, νεωτέρα δὲ οὖσα. ὡς οὖν ἀληθῆ λέγω, ὅτι Νέαιρα
Νικαρέτης ἦν καὶ συνῆλθε μετ' αὐτῆς, τούτων ὑμῖν αὐτὸν τὸν Φιλόστρατον μάρτυρα
καλῶ.

The courtesan Niinnion set up this plaque to commemorate her initiation into the Mysteries
at Eleusis

Evidence

(The heading EVIDENCE means that the passage quoted was read out in court. It was *not* spoken by the witness, nor was it cross-examined.)

'Philostratos, son of Dionysios, from Kolonos, gives evidence that he knows that Neaira was Nikarete's property, as was Metaneira too; that they were residents of Corinth; and that they lodged at his house when they came to Athens for the Mysteries; and that Lysias, a close friend of his, brought them to his house.'

Ἀθήναζε to Athens
ἔθηκεν he put down (τίθημι/θε-)
ἐλήφθησαν aor. pass. of
   λαμβάνω
ἑορτ-ή, ἡ festival (1a)
ἐραστ-ής, ὁ lover (1d)
ἐργάζ-ομαι work, earn a living
ἤθε-ος, ὁ bachelor (2a)
καταθεῖναι to put down
   (κατατίθημι/καταθε-)
Κόρινθ-ος, ἡ Corinth (2a)
Λυσί-ας, ὁ Lysias (1d) *(lover of*
   Metaneira)
Μετάνειρ-α, ἡ Metaneira (1a)
   (slave of Nikarete)
μικρ-ός -ά -όν small

μυέ-ω initiate
μυστήρι-α, τά the Mysteries (2b)
Νικαρέτ-η, ἡ Nikarete (1a)
   (slave-owner)
συνέρχ-ομαι (συνελθ-) come
   together
σῶμα (σωματ-), τό body (3b)
τεκμήρι-ον, τό evidence, proof (2b)
τιθέναι to be putting down
   (τίθημι)
τοίνυν well now *(resuming a*
   narrative)
τρέφ-ω rear, raise
φανερ-ός -ά -όν clear, obvious
Φιλόστρατ-ος, ὁ Philostratos
   (2a) *(Lysias' friend)*

ὡς (+ acc.) to (the house of), with

Vocabulary to be learnt
Ἀθήναζε *to Athens*
ἀστή, ἡ *female citizen (1a)*
ἀστός, ὁ *male citizen (2a)*
ἑταίρᾱ, ἡ *whore, prostitute (1b)*
ἑταῖρος, ὁ *(male) companion (2a)*
(σ)μῑκρός ᾱ́ όν *small, short, little*
παιδοποιέομαι *have children*
συνέρχομαι (συνελθ-) *come*
   together
τεκμήριον, τό *evidence, proof (2b)*
τίθημι (θε-) *put, place, make*
φανερός ᾱ́ όν *clear, obvious*
ὡς (+ acc.) *towards, to the house*
   of

The Eleusinian mysteries

The Eleusinian Mysteries were open to anyone, slave or free, who was a Greek speaker and had been initiated. The emphasis was not upon the community but firmly upon personal revelation and salvation. A character in Sophocles is recorded as saying 'Thrice blessed are those among men who, after beholding these rites, go down to Hades. Only for them is there life' (Plutarch, *Moralia* 21f.). Initiation was in two stages. At the 'Lesser Mysteries', the initiates (*mustai*) wore wreaths and carried in procession branches of myrtle. A woman bore on her head the sacred vessel (*kernos*) which held a variety of seeds and grains to symbolise Demeter's gifts, as Demeter was goddess of the crops. For the 'Greater Mysteries', a truce of fifty-five days was declared so that people could travel safely from all over Greece to the festival. Little is known of the central ritual, except that it was divided into 'things said', 'things done' and 'things revealed'. Initiates who were allowed to see the last stage were known as *epoptai* ('viewers'). The Mysteries provided an intense personal involvement and an emotional experience of the highest order. Initiation, as the quotation from Sophocles shows, was regarded with reverence. The rites were said to 'inspire those who take part in them with sweeter hopes regarding both the end of life and all eternity'. (*World of Athens*, 3.50–2)

G

[The incident with Lysias and Metaneira is not the only one that Apollodoros quotes. He goes on to Neaira's later career, which takes her all over Greece, but always in the company of men of wealth and high social position. They include Simos, a Thessalian, who brought her to Athens for the great Panathenaia, Xenokleides the poet and Hipparchos the actor; then Timanoridas from Corinth and Eukrates from Leukadia eventually decide to buy Neaira outright from Nikarete, and do so for 30 mnas. She lives a long time with them. No wonder that Strymodoros struggles to keep up…]

In *World of Athens*: Solon 1.20; Hippias 5.48; sophists 5.44–9, 8.22ff.

Strymodoros' memory lets him down.

ΣΤΡ.   ἀπολοίμην, εἰ μνημονεύω –

ΚΩ.   δοκεῖς μοι, ὦ Στρυμόδωρε, εἰς ἀπορίαν τινὰ καταστῆναι. μὴ οὖν
       ἐπικάλυπτε τὴν ἀπορίαν, αἰσχυνόμενος τὸν Εὐεργίδην, ἀλλὰ λέγε μοι ὃ
       ἀπορεῖς.

ΣΤΡ.   ἐγώ σοι ἐρῶ, ὦ Κωμία, ὃ ἀπορῶ. διὰ τί μνείαν ἐποιήσατο ὁ Ἀπολλόδωρος   5
       τοῦ Λυσίου καὶ τῆς Μετανείρας; οὐ γὰρ μνημονεύω ἔγωγε. βουλοίμην
       μεντἂν νὴ Δία μνημονεύειν ἃ λέγει ὁ ἀντίδικος. εἴθε μνημονεύοιμι πάνθ'
       ἃ λέγει, καὶ ἀπολοίμην, εἰ μνημονεύω. πῶς γὰρ ἂν δικαίως τιθεῖτό τις
       τὴν ψῆφον, μὴ μνημονεύσας τοὺς λόγους;

ΚΩ.   χαλεπὸν δή ἐστι τῷ δικαστῇ διακρίνειν τὴν δίκην, μὴ μνημονεύοντι   10
       πάνθ' ἃ λέγει ὁ κατήγορος. εἰ μέντοι σοφιστὴς γένοιο σύ, ῥᾳδίως ἂν
       μνημονεύσαις πάντας τοὺς λόγους, ὦ Στρυμόδωρε, ὡς ἔοικε, καὶ οὐκ ἂν
       ἐπιλάθοιο τῶν λεχθέντων. ἀλλ' ὥσπερ Ἱππίας τις, ἅπαξ ἀκούσας, πάντα
       μνημονεύσαις ἄν.

ΣΤΡ.   ὥσπερ Ἱππίας; εἴθε Ἱππίας γενοίμην ἐγώ.   15

ΚΩ.   εἰ νῦν Ἱππίας ἦσθα, οἷός τ' ἂν ἦσθα καταλέγειν πάντας τοὺς ἀπὸ
       Σόλωνος ἄρχοντας. ὁ γὰρ Ἱππίας, ἅπαξ ἀκούσας, ἐμνημόνευε πεντήκοντα
       ὀνόματα.

ΣΤΡ.   ὦ τῆς τέχνης. εἴθε τοσαῦτα μνημονεύσαιμι. ἀλλ' ἐγὼ φύσει σοφὸς οὐκ εἰμί.
       εἰ πάντες οἱ σοφισταί με διδάσκοιεν, οὐκ ἂν οἷοί τ' εἶεν σοφιστήν με ποιεῖν.   20
       ἀλλ' εἰ Ἱππίας ἡμῖν νῦν συνεγίγνετο, πῶς ἂν ἐδίδασκέ με, καὶ τί ἂν ἔλεγεν;
       καὶ πῶς ἂν ἐμάνθανον ἐγώ;

ΚΩ.   εἴθε ταῦτα εἰδείην, ὦ Στρυμόδωρε. εἰ γὰρ ταῦτα ἤδη ἐγώ, πλούσιος ἂν ἦ
       τὸ νῦν, καὶ οὐ πένης οὐδὲ δικαστής.

ΣΤΡ.   οἴμοι. ἐγὼ γάρ, ὥσπερ γέρων τις, ἐπιλανθάνομαι πάνθ' ἃ ἀκούω, τῶν τε   25
       νόμων καὶ τῶν λόγων καὶ τῶν μαρτυριῶν. εἰ δέ τις τοσαῦτα ἐπιλάθοιτο,
       πῶς ἂν δικάσειε τὴν δίκην καὶ τὴν ψῆφον θεῖτο ἄν;

ΚΩ.   οὐκ οἶδ' ἔγωγε, ὦ Στρυμόδωρε. οὐ γὰρ ἂν γένοιτό ποτε ἀγαθὸς
       δικαστής, εἰ μὴ μνημονεύσειε τὰ ὑπὸ τοῦ κατηγόρου λεχθέντα. ἀλλ'

ΨΗΦΟΙ ΔΗΜΟΣΙΑΙ

ὅπως προθύμως προσέξεις τὸν νοῦν τοῖς λόγοις καὶ τοῖς νόμοις καὶ   30
ταῖς μαρτυρίαις. τοῦτο γὰρ ποιοῦντες, ῥᾳδίως τὴν ψῆφον τίθενται οἱ
δικασταί.

ΣΤΡ.   ἀπόλοιντο οἵτινες, δικασταὶ ὄντες, ἐπιλανθάνονται ἃ λέγουσιν οἱ
ἀντίδικοι.

Vocabulary for Section Twelve G

Grammar for 12G
- 'Would-should' conditions: future 'remote' and present 'contrary to fact'
- Wishes: 'Would that/O that …'
- ὅπως + future indicative 'see to it that'
- Optative forms of εἰμί 'I am', εἶμι 'I (shall) go', οἶδα 'I know'

ἄν (+ opt.) 'would'
ἄν (+ impf.) 'would'
ἅπαξ once
ἄρχων (ἀρχοντ-), ὁ archon (3a)
διακρίν-ω determine, judge
εἰ (+ opt.) 'if. . . were to'
εἰ (+ impf.) 'if. . . were –ing'
εἰδείην optative of οἶδα
εἴθε (+opt.) I wish that! would
   that!
ἔοικε it seems (reasonable)
ἐπικαλύπτ-ω conceal, hide
ἐπιλανθάν-ομαι (ἐπιλαθ-) forget
   (+ gen.)
Ἱππί-ας, ὁ Hippias (1d) (a sophist)
καταλέγ-ω recite, list
μαρτυρί-α, ἡ evidence, witness (1b)

μέντἄν=μέντοι ἄν
μνεί-α, ἡ mention (1b)
μνημονεύ-ω remember
ὅπως (+ fut. ind.) see to it that
πένης (πενητ-), ὁ poor man
   (3a)
πεντήκοντα fifty
πλούσι-ος -α -ον rich, wealthy
Σόλων (Σολων-), ὁ Solon (3a)
   (famous statesman)
συγγίγν-ομαι (συγγεν-) be with
   (+ dat.)
φύσ-ις, ἡ nature (3e)

Vocabulary to be learnt
ἄν (use of, in conditionals, see
   Grammar **151–2**)

εἴθε (+ opt.) I wish that! would
   that!
ἐπιλανθάνομαι (ἐπιλαθ-) forget
   (+gen.)
καταλέγω (κατειπ-) recite, list
μαρτυρίᾱ, ἡ evidence, witness
   (1b)
μνείᾱ, ἡ mention (1b)
μνημονεύω remember
ὅπως (+fut. ind.) see to it that
πένης (πενητ-), ὁ poor man (3a)
   (or adj., poor)
πλούσιος ᾱ ον rich, wealthy
συγγίγνομαι (συγγεν-) be with,
   have intercourse with
   (+ dat.)

H

[Eventually, Timanoridas and Eukrates both decide to get married. They give Neaira the chance to buy her freedom for 20 mnas (as against the 30 they gave for her). She collects donations from old admirers, of which the handsomest sum comes from an Athenian acquaintance, Phrynion. In gratitude to Phrynion, Neaira goes to live with him in Athens, where she mixes with the highest and wealthiest levels of Athenian male society.]

In *World of Athens*: metics and *xenoi* 5.4, 5.67ff.; symposia 5.25, 5.30, 8.90.

Neaira runs away from Phrynion and meets Stephanos.

ὁ τοίνυν Φρυνίων, καταθεὶς τὸ ἀργύριον ὑπὲρ Νεαίρας ἐπ' ἐλευθερίᾳ, ᾤχετο
Ἀθήναζε ἀπάγων αὐτήν, ἀλλ' ἀφικόμενος Ἀθήναζε ἀσελγῶς ἐχρῆτο αὐτῇ καὶ ἐπὶ
τὰ δεῖπνα ἔχων αὐτὴν πανταχοῖ ἐπορεύετο, ἐκώμαζέ τ' ἀεὶ μετ' αὐτῆς. Νέαιρα δέ,
ἐπειδὴ ἀσελγῶς προὐπηλακίζετο ὑπὸ τοῦ Φρυνίωνος καὶ οὐχ, ὡς ᾤετο, ἠγαπᾶτο,   5
συνεσκευάσατο πάντα τὰ Φρυνίωνος ἐκ τῆς οἰκίας καὶ τὰ ἱμάτια καὶ τὰ χρυσία, ἃ
Φρυνίων αὐτῇ ἔδωκεν. ἔχουσα δὲ ταῦτα πάντα, καὶ θεραπαίνας δύο, Θρᾷτταν καὶ
Κοκκαλίνην, ἀποδιδράσκει εἰς Μέγαρα. διέτριψε δὲ Νέαιρα ἐν τοῖς Μεγάροις δύο
ἔτη, ἀλλ' οὐκ ἐδύνατο ἱκανὴν εὐπορίαν παρέχειν εἰς τὴν τῆς οἰκίας διοίκησιν. τότε
δ' ἐπιδημήσας ὁ Στέφανος οὑτοσὶ εἰς τὰ Μέγαρα, κατήγετο ὡς αὐτήν, ἑταίραν οὖσαν.   10
ἡ δὲ Νέαιρα, διηγησαμένη πάντα τὰ πράγματα καὶ τὴν ὕβριν τοῦ Φρυνίωνος, ἔδωκε
Στεφάνῳ πάνθ' ἃ ἔχουσα ἐξῆλθεν ἐκ τῶν Ἀθηνῶν, ἐπιθυμοῦσα μὲν τῆς ἐνθάδε
οἰκήσεως, φοβουμένη δὲ τὸν Φρυνίωνα. ᾔδει γὰρ ἀδικηθέντα μὲν τὸν Φρυνίωνα
ὑφ' αὑτῆς καὶ ὀργιζόμενον αὐτῇ, σοβαρὸν δὲ καὶ ὀλίγωρον αὐτοῦ τὸν τρόπον ὄντα.
δοῦσα οὖν Νέαιρα πάντα τὰ αὑτῆς τῷ Στεφάνῳ, προΐσταται ἐκεῖνον αὑτῆς.   15

ἐκώμαζέ τ' ἀεὶ μετ' αὐτῆς

Vocabulary for Section Twelve H

> **Grammar for 12H–I**
> - Participial constructions in reported speech
> - The future passive

ἀγαπά-ω love
ἀπο-διδράσκ-ω run off
ἀργύρι-ον, τό silver, money (2b)
ἀσελγῶς disgracefully
δεῖπν-ον, τό dinner-party (2b)
διατρίβ-ω spend time
διηγέ-ομαι reveal, describe,
   explain
διοίκησ-ις, ἡ management (3e)
ἐπί (+ dat.) for the purpose of
ἐπιδημέ-ω come into town, live
ἐπιθυμέ-ω desire (+ gen.)
ἔτ-ος, τό year (3c)
εὐπορί-α, ἡ resources (1b)
θεράπαιν-α, ἡ slave girl (1c)
Θρᾶττ-α, ἡ Thratta (1c) (one of
   Neaira's slaves)
ἱκαν-ός -ή -όν sufficient

κατάγ-ομαι lodge
κατατίθη-μι (καταθε-) pay
Κοκκαλίν-η, ἡ Kokkaline (1a)
   (slave of Neaira)
κωμάζ-ω revel
Μέγαρ-α, τά Megara (2b) (a
   town on the isthmus)
οἴχ-ομαι go
ὀλίγωρ-ος -ον contemptuous
ὀργίζ-ομαι grow angry with
   (+ dat.)
πανταχοῖ everywhere
προΐστα-μαι make x (acc.)
   sponsor of y (gen.)
προπηλακίζ-ω treat like dirt,
   insult
σοβαρ-ός -ά -όν pompous
συσκευάζ-ομαι gather up, collect

τοίνυν well then (resuming
   argument)
τρόπ-ος, ὁ manner, way (2a)
Φρυνίων (Φρυνιων-), ὁ
   Phrynion (3a) (owner of
   Neaira)
χρυσί-ον, τό gold (trinkets or
   money) (2b)

Vocabulary to be learnt
ἀργύριον, τό *silver, money (2b)*
διατρίβω *pass time, waste time*
ὀργίζομαι *grow angry with
   (+ dat.)*
τοίνυν *well then (resuming and
   pushing argument on
   further)*
τρόπος, ὁ *way, manner (2a)*

Men's other women

Concubines (*pallakai*), courtesans (*hetairai*, literally 'companions') and prostitutes (*pornai*) would normally not be of Athenian birth. Alcibiades was notorious for not merely having numerous mistresses but also keeping concubines, slave and free, in addition to his aristocratic wife ... Concubines had some legal status and offering one's services as a prostitute was legal, and indeed taxed (the *pornikon telos*). Prostitutes seem to have been readily available ... They ranged in class and expensiveness from the brothel-girls of the Peiraieus; through the rather more sophisticated *aulos*-girls an Athenian might hire to enliven a male drinking-party (*sumposion*); to the educated courtesans euphemistically known as *hetairai*. The ways in which some *hetairai* verged on respectability is well brought out in Xenophon's *Memoirs of Socrates*, in the story of Socrates' conversation with a woman named Theodote. In an artful display of studied innocence Socrates, noting Theodote's wealth, gradually teases out of her its true source – her rich lovers. The passage incidentally lists the chief sources of wealth in Athens, in order of their importance: 'Socrates asked "Have you an estate, Theodote?" "No." "Then perhaps you get your income from house-property". "No." "Well, does it come from some manufacturing business?" "No." "Then what *do* you live on?" "The contributions of kind friends ..."' (*World of Athens*, 5.30–1)

I

Neaira sets up home with Stephanos in Athens. Phrynion hears of it and demands Neaira's return and compensation from Stephanos.

In *World of Athens*: phratries 3.53–4; sycophants 6.54; polemarch 1.17; arbitration 6.49.

ὁ δὲ Στέφανος οὑτοσὶ εἰς μεγίστην ἐλπίδα κατέστησε Νέαιραν ἐν τοῖς Μεγάροις τῷ λόγῳ. ἐκόμπαζε γὰρ τὸν μὲν Φρυνίωνα οὐχ ἅψεσθαι αὐτῆς οὐδέποτε, αὐτὸς δὲ γυναῖκα αὐτὴν ἕξειν. ἔφη δὲ καὶ τοὺς παῖδας αὐτῆς εἰσαχθήσεσθαι εἰς τοὺς φράτερας ὡς αὐτοῦ ὄντας, καὶ πολίτας γενήσεσθαι, ἀδικηθήσεσθαι δ' αὐτὴν ὑπ' οὐδενὸς ἀνθρώπων. ταῦτα δ' εἰπών, ἀφικνεῖται αὐτὴν ἔχων δεῦρο ἐκ τῶν Μεγάρων, καὶ παιδία μετ' αὐτῆς τρία, Πρόξενον καὶ Ἀρίστωνα καὶ παῖδα κόρην, ἣ νυνὶ Φανὼ καλεῖται.　　　　　　　5
　　καὶ εἰσάγει αὐτὴν καὶ τὰ παιδία εἰς τὸ οἰκίδιον ὃ ἦν αὐτῷ Ἀθήνησι παρὰ τὸν ψιθυριστὴν Ἑρμῆν, μεταξὺ τῆς Δωροθέου τοῦ Ἐλευσινίου οἰκίας καὶ τῆς Κλεινομάχου. δυοῖν δὲ ἕνεκα ἦλθεν ἔχων αὐτήν, ὡς⌐ ἐξ ἀτελείας ⌐ἕξων καλὴν ἑταίραν καὶ ὡς ἐργασομένην‿ αὐτὴν‿ καὶ‿ θρέψουσαν τὴν οἰκίαν. εὖ γὰρ ᾔδει Στέφανος ἄλλην πρόσοδον οὐκ ἔχων οὐδὲ βίον, εἰ μή τι λαβὼν διὰ τὴν　　　10
συκοφαντίαν. ὁ δὲ Φρυνίων, πυθόμενος Νέαιραν ἐπιδημοῦσαν καὶ οὖσαν παρὰ Στεφάνῳ, παραλαβὼν νεανίσκους μεθ' αὑτοῦ, ἦλθεν ἐπὶ τὴν οἰκίαν τὴν τοῦ Στεφάνου, ὡς‿ ἄξων αὐτήν. ἀφαιρουμένου δὲ αὐτὴν τοῦ Στεφάνου κατὰ τὸν νόμον εἰς ἐλευθερίαν, κατηγγύησεν αὐτὴν ὁ Φρυνίων πρὸς τῷ πολεμάρχῳ, ἡγούμενος αὐτὴν δούλην εἶναι αὐτῷ, τὰ χρήματα ὑπὲρ αὐτῆς καταθέντι.　　　　　　　15

Vocabulary for Section Twelve I

ἀδικηθήσεσθαι 'would be harmed' *(ἀδικέω)*
Ἀθήνησι at Athens
ἅπτ-ομαι touch (+ gen.)
Ἀρίστων (Ἀριστων-), ὁ Ariston (3a) *(Neaira's son)*
ἀτέλει-α, ἡ exemption, immunity (ἐξ ἀτελείας=free) (1b)
ἅψεσθαι fut. inf. of ἅπτομαι
δυοῖν two (sc. 'reasons')
Δωρόθε-ος, ὁ Dorotheos (2a) *(Athenian householder)*
εἰσαχθήσεσθαι 'would be introduced' *(εἰσάγω)*
Ἐλευσίνι-ος -α -ον of Eleusis
ἐλπ-ίς (ἐλπιδ-), ἡ hope (3a)
ἐξ- =fut. stem ἔχω
ἐπιδημέ-ω be in town
ἐργάζ-ομαι work
Ἑρμ-ῆς, ὁ Hermes (1d)

θρεψ- = fut./aor. stem of τρέφω
κατατίθη-μι (καταθε -) pay
κατεγγυά-ω compel x (acc.) to give securities
Κλεινόμαχ-ος, ὁ Kleinomakhos (2a) *(Athenian householder)*
κομπάζ-ω boast
κόρ-η, ἡ girl, maiden (1a)
Μέγαρ-α, τά Megara (2b)
μεταξύ (+ gen.) between
οἰκίδι-ον, τό house, small house (2b)
παραλαμβάν-ω (παραλαβ-) take
πολέμαρχ-ος, ὁ Polemarch (2a) *(state official)*
Πρόξεν-ος, ὁ Proxenos (2a) *(son of Neaira)*
πρός (+ dat.) before
πρόσοδ-ος, ἡ income (2a)

πυνθάν-ομαι (πυθ-) learn, hear, discover
συκοφαντί-α, ἡ informing (1b)
τρέφ-ω (θρεψ-) maintain, keep
Φανώ, ἡ Phano *(Neaira's daughter)*
φράτηρ (φρατερ-), ὁ member of phratry (3a) *(a group of families, with certain religious and social functions)*
ψιθυριστ-ής ὁ whisperer (1d)
ὡς (+ fut. part.) in order to
ὡς ἄξων in order to take
ὡς ἕξων in order to have
ὡς ἐργασομένην αὐτὴν καὶ θρέψουσαν in order for her to work and maintain

Vocabulary to be learnt
Ἀθήνησι(ν) *at Athens*

ἐλπίς (ἐλπιδ-), ἡ *hope,*
expectation (3a)
ἐπιδημέω *come to town, be in*
town

ἐργάζομαι *work, perform*
κατατίθημι (καταθε-) *put down,*
pay, perform
οἰκίδιον, τό *small house (2b)*

παραλαμβάνω (παραλαβ-) *take,*
receive from

The settlement

One way of avoiding a court-case was to appoint three arbitrators to reach a decision. Both parties would appoint their own representative, and would agree on a third 'neutral'. The decision of these three was final and binding. Here is the translation of the passage in which Apollodoros explains what happened, giving the details of the arbitration and the evidence for it:

'The case Phrynion brought against Stephanos rested on two points: first, that Stephanos had taken Neaira from him and had asserted that she was free, and second, that Stephanos had taken possession of all the goods that Neaira had brought with her from Phrynion's house. But their friends brought them together and persuaded them to submit their quarrel to arbitration (δίαιτα). Satyros, from Alopeke, the brother of Lakedaimonios, acted as arbitrator on Phrynion's behalf, while Saurias from Lamptrai acted for Stephanos here. Both sides also agreed to make Diogeiton from Akharnai the third member of the panel. These men met in the sacred place and heard the facts from both sides and from Neaira herself. They then gave their decision, which met with agreement from both sides. It was:

(a) that the woman should be free and her own mistress (αὐτῆς κυρία);
(b) that she should return to Phrynion everything she had taken with her from his house, apart from the clothes and gold jewellery and the female servants (since these had been bought for her own personal use);
(c) that she should live with each man on alternate days, although if the men reached any other mutually satisfactory arrangement, it should be binding;
(d) that maintenance for the woman should be provided by whichever of them had her in his keeping at the time;
(e) that from now on the two men should be on friendly terms and should harbour no further resentment against each other.

Such were the terms of the reconciliation between Phrynion and Stephanos which the arbitrators brought about in regard to this woman Neaira.

To prove that these statements of mine are true, the clerk shall read you the depositions regarding these matters.

Evidence

'Satyros from Alopeke, Saurias from Lamptrai and Diogeiton from Akharnai depose that, having been appointed arbitrators in the matter of Neaira, they brought about a reconciliation between Stephanos and Phrynion, and that the terms on which the reconciliation was brought about were such as Apollodoros produces.'

Section Thirteen A–I: Neaira as married woman

Introduction

Apollodoros has now established that Neaira is non-Athenian. He has sketched her past as a slave and prostitute in Corinth, detailed a number of her lovers, and shown how she came to live with Stephanos in Athens. Now that it has been proved that Neaira is non-Athenian, Apollodoros has to prove that she is living with Stephanos *as his wife*. A formal betrothal was normally validated by witnesses and the marriage itself confirmed by cohabitation to produce legitimate heirs. Apollodoros, however, produces no evidence of the birth of children to Neaira and Stephanos. In the absence of evidence from such children, Apollodoros concentrates on establishing the marriage of Stephanos and Neaira in other ways. The most important evidence is that Stephanos attempted to pass off Neaira's children *as if they were his own children* (as he indeed boasted that he would do at 12. I.).

In *World of Athens*: divorce and dowry 5.11, 16, 19.

Proving identity

Athenians had no birth certificates and no state registry of births. Nor were scientific methods of proof available to decide paternity. Instead, legitimacy and citizenship were most easily demonstrated to the satisfaction of a large citizen jury by producing witnesses who would testify to a child's introduction as an infant into a phratry at the *Apatouria* festival and into the deme at the age of majority. One of the best examples of what could be involved is provided by a speech ([Demosthenes], *Against Euboulides* 57) written for a man who had been voted off the register of his deme in 346/5 … The speaker needed to show not that he had been registered in the deme, for that was not in question – he had even served as its chief official (δήμαρχος) – but that he had been *legitimately* so registered. To do so he first cites as witnesses of his father's legitimacy five of his father's male kinsmen by birth and several of his male kinsmen by marriage (his father's female cousins' husbands); then his father's φράτερες (fellow phratry members), those with whom he shares his Ἀπόλλων Πατρῷος and Ζεὺς Ἑρκεῖος and the same family tombs, and his father's fellow deme members. With women, on the other hand, it was much harder to establish legitimacy, since they were not registered in a deme. So to prove his mother's Athenian descent, the speaker cites, apart from a similar range of male kinsmen, only the φράτερες and fellow deme members of his mother's male kinsmen. As for his own life history, he first calls witnesses to his mother's (second) marriage and then presents evidence of his induction into phratry and, most important, deme. (*World of Athens*, 5.12–14)

A

Stephanos marries off Neaira's daughter Phano to the Athenian Phrastor,
pretending that Phano was a true-born Athenian girl. Phrastor discovers the
truth, and wants a divorce.

ὅτι μὲν τοίνυν ἐξ ἀρχῆς δούλη ἦν Νέαιρα καὶ ἑταίρα, καὶ ἀπέδρα ἀπὸ τοῦ Φρυνίωνος
εἰς Μέγαρα, καὶ ὁ Φρυνίων ἐπανελθοῦσαν Ἀθήναζε αὐτὴν κατηγγύησε πρὸς τῷ
πολεμάρχῳ ὡς ξένην οὖσαν, δῆλά ἐστι τὰ τεκμήρια.

νῦν δὲ βούλομαι ὑμῖν ἐπιδεῖξαι ὅτι Στέφανος αὐτὸς καταμαρτυρεῖ Νεαίρας ὡς,
ξένη οὖσα, συνοικεῖ αὐτῷ ὡς γυνή.   5

ἦν γὰρ τῇ Νεαίρᾳ θυγάτηρ, ἣν ἦλθεν ἔχουσα εἰς τὴν τοῦ Στεφάνου οἰκίαν. καὶ
Ἀθήναζε ἐλθόντες, τὴν κόρην ἐκάλουν Φανώ. πρότερον γὰρ Στρυβήλη ἐκαλεῖτο,
πρὶν Ἀθήναζε ἐλθεῖν. αὕτη δὲ ἡ κόρη ἐξεδόθη ὑπὸ τοῦ Στεφάνου τουτουί, ὥσπερ
αὐτοῦ θυγάτηρ οὖσα καὶ ἐξ ἀστῆς γυναικός, ἀνδρὶ Ἀθηναίῳ, Φράστορι Αἰγιλεῖ. καὶ
προῖκα ἔδωκεν ὁ Στέφανος τριάκοντα μνᾶς. καὶ δὴ ἴστε τὴν Φανώ, πρὶν συνοικεῖν   10
τῷ Φράστορι, τὴν τῆς μητρὸς φύσιν καὶ ἀκολασίαν μαθοῦσαν. ἐπειδὴ οὖν ἦλθεν ὡς
τὸν Φράστορα, ὃς ἀνὴρ ἐργάτης ἦν καὶ ἀκριβῶς τὸν βίον συνελέγετο, οὐκ ἠπίστατο
τοῖς τοῦ Φράστορος τρόποις ἀρέσκειν.

ὁρῶν δὲ ὁ Φράστωρ αὐτὴν οὔτε κοσμίαν οὖσαν οὔτ' ἐθέλουσαν πείθεσθαι αὐτῷ,
ἅμα δὲ πυθόμενος σαφῶς τὴν Φανὼ οὐ Στεφάνου ἀλλὰ Νεαίρας θυγατέρα οὖσαν,   15
ὠργίσθη μάλιστα, ἡγούμενος ὑπὸ Στεφάνου ὑβρισθῆναι καὶ ἐξαπατηθῆναι. ἔγημε
γὰρ τὴν Φανὼ πρὶν εἰδέναι αὐτὴν Νεαίρας οὖσαν θυγατέρα. ἐκβάλλει οὖν τὴν Φανώ,
ἐνιαυτὸν συνοικήσας αὐτῇ, κυοῦσαν, καὶ τὴν προῖκα οὐκ ἀποδίδωσιν. ἀλλ' εἰ ὑπὸ
Στεφάνου μὴ ἐξηπατήθη ὁ Φράστωρ καὶ Φανὼ γνησία ἦν, ἢ οὐκ ἂν ἐξέβαλεν αὐτὴν
ὁ Φράστωρ, ἢ ἀπέδωκεν ἂν τὴν προῖκα.   20

ἐκπεσούσης δὲ Φανοῦς, ἔλαχε Στέφανος δίκην τῷ Φράστορι, κατὰ τὸν νόμον ὃς
κελεύει τὸν ἄνδρα τὸν ἀποπέμποντα τὴν γυναῖκα ἀποδιδόναι τὴν προῖκα. λαχόντος
δὲ Στεφάνου τὴν δίκην ταύτην, γράφεται Φράστωρ Στέφανον τουτονὶ γραφὴν
κατὰ τὸν νόμον ὃς οὐκ ἐᾷ τινα ἐγγυῆσαι τὴν ξένης θυγατέρα ἀνδρὶ Ἀθηναίῳ.
γνοὺς δὲ Στέφανος ὅτι ἐξελεγχθήσεται ἀδικῶν καὶ ὅτι, ἐξελεγχθείς, κινδυνεύσει   25

Women working in the home weaving and spinning

ταῖς ἐσχάταις ζημίαις περιπεσεῖν (ξένης γὰρ θυγάτηρ ἦν ἡ Φανώ), διαλλάττεται πρὸς τὸν Φράστορα καὶ ἀφίσταται τῆς προικὸς καὶ ἀνείλετο τὴν δίκην. καὶ πρὶν εἰς δικαστήριον εἰσελθεῖν, καὶ ὁ Φράστωρ ἀνείλετο τὴν γραφήν. ἀλλ' εἰ ἀστῆς θυγάτηρ ἦν Φανώ, οὐκ ἂν διηλλάχθη Στέφανος.

Vocabulary for Section Thirteen A

> **Grammar for 13A–B**
> - Aorist infinitive passive
> - Future participles active, middle and passive
> - ὡς + future participle
> - πρίν + infinitive

Αἰγιλ-εύς, ὁ of the deme Aigileia (3g)

ἀκολασί-α, ἡ extravagance (1b)

ἄν (+ aor. indic.) 'would have . . .'

ἀναιρέ-ομαι (ἀνελ-) take away

ἀπέδρα 3rd s. aor. of ἀποδιδράσκω

ἀποδιδράσκ-ω (ἀποδρα-) run off

ἀποδίδω-μι (ἀποδο-) return, give back

ἀποπέμπ-ω send away, divorce

ἀφίστα-μαι give up any claim to (+gen.)

γαμέ-ω (γημ-) marry

γνήσι-ος –α -ον legitimate

διαλλάττ-ομαι πρός be reconciled with

ἐγγυά-ω engage, promise

εἰ (+ aor. ind.) 'if. . . had–ed . . .'

ἐκβάλλ-ω (ἐκβαλ-) divorce

ἐκδίδω-μι (ἐκδο-) give in marriage

ἐκπίπτ-ω (ἐκπεσ-) be divorced

ἐνιαυτ-ός, ὁ year (2a)

ἐξαπατηθῆναι 'had been deceived' (ἐξαπατάω)

ἐξεδόθη aor. pass. of ἐκδίδωμι

ἐξελέγχ-ω convict

ἐπιδείκνυ-μι (ἐπιδειξ-) show, demonstrate

ἐργάτ-ης, ὁ working man (1d)

ζημί-α, ἡ penalty (1b)

ἠπίστατο impf. of ἐπίσταμαι know how to (+ inf.)

καὶ δή and really, and as a matter of fact

καταμαρτυρέ-ω give evidence against (+ gen.)

κατεγγυά-ω demand securities from

κινδυνεύ-ω run a risk of (+ inf.)

κόρ-η, ἡ maiden, girl (1a)

κόσμι-ος -α -ον well-behaved

κυέ-ω be pregnant

λαγχάν-ω (λαχ-) bring (a suit) against (+ dat.)

Μέγαρα, τά Megara (2b)

μν-ᾶ, ἡ mina (=60 drachmas) (1b)

περιπίπτ-ω (περιπεσ-) meet with (+ dat.)

πολέμαρχ-ος, ὁ the Polemarch (2a) (magistrate dealing with lawsuits involving aliens)

πρίν before (+ inf.)

προίξ (προικ-), ἡ dowry (3a)

πρός (+ dat.) before

πυνθάν-ομαι (πυθ-) learn, hear

Στρυβήλ-η, ἡ Strybele (1a) (Phano's former name)

συλλέγ-ομαι make, collect

τριάκοντα thirty (indecl.)

ὑβρίζ-ω treat disgracefully

ὑβρισθῆναι 'had been treated disgracefully' (aor. pass. inf. of ὑβρίζω)

Φανοῦς Phano (gen. s.) (see List of Proper Names for full declension)

Φανώ Phano (acc. s.) (see List of Proper Names for full declension)

Φράστωρ (Φραστορ-), ὁ Phrastor (3a) (Phano's husband)

φύσ-ις, ἡ nature, temperament (3e)

Vocabulary to be learnt

ἀποδίδωμι (ἀποδο-) *give back, return*

ἀποπέμπω *send away, divorce*

ἀφίσταμαι (ἀποστα-) *relinquish claim to; revolt from*

ἐγγυάω *engage, promise*

ἐκβάλλω (ἐκβαλ-) *throw out; divorce*

ἐκδίδωμι (ἐκδο-) *give in marriage*

ἐκπίπτω (ἐκπεσ-) *be thrown out, divorced*

ἐξελέγχω *convict, refute, expose*

ζημία, ἡ *fine (1b)*

ἠπιστάμην *impf. of ἐπίσταμαι know how to (+inf)*

καὶ δή *and really; as a matter of fact; let us suppose; there! look!*

κατεγγυάω *demand securities from (+acc.)*

κόρη, ἡ *maiden, girl (1a)*

μνᾶ, ἡ *mina (100 drachmas) (1b)*

προίξ (προικ-), ἡ *dowry (3a)*

ὑβρίζω *treat violently, disgracefully*

φύσις, ἡ *nature, temperament, character (3e)*

B

Phrastor then falls ill but, not wishing to die childless, decides to take back Phano and her son.

In *World of Athens*: women in the family 5.17ff.

βούλομαι δ' ὑμῖν παρέχειν ἑτέραν μαρτυρίαν τοῦ τε Φράστορος καὶ τῶν φρατέρων
αὐτοῦ καὶ τῶν γεννητῶν, ὡς ἔστι ξένη Νέαιρα αὑτηί. οὐ πολλῷ χρόνῳ γὰρ ὕστερον
ἢ ἐξεπέμφθη ἡ τῆς Νεαίρας θυγάτηρ, ἠσθένησεν ὁ Φράστωρ καὶ πάνυ πονηρῶς
διετέθη καὶ εἰς πᾶσαν ἀπορίαν κατέστη. καί, πρὶν αὐτὸν ἀσθενεῖν, πρὸς τοὺς
οἰκείους αὐτοῦ διαφορὰ ἦν παλαιὰ καὶ ὀργὴ καὶ μῖσος. καὶ ἄπαις ἦν Φράστωρ.   5
ἀλλ' εἰς ἀπορίαν καταστάς, ὑπό τε τῆς Νεαίρας καὶ τῆς Φανοῦς ἐψυχαγωγεῖτο.
ἐβάδιζον γὰρ πρὸς αὐτόν, ὡς ⌐θεραπεύσουσαι⌐ καὶ⌐ προθύμως ⌐ἐπιμελησόμεναι
(ἔρημος δὲ τῶν ⌐θεραπευσόντων ἦν Φράστωρ), καὶ ἔφερον τὰ πρόσφορα τῇ νόσῳ καὶ
ἐπεσκοποῦντο. ἴστε δήπου καὶ ὑμεῖς αὐτοί, ὦ ἄνδρες δικασταί, ὡς ἀξία πολλοῦ ἐστὶ
γυνὴ ἐν ταῖς νόσοις, παροῦσα κάμνοντι ἀνθρώπῳ.   10
   τοῦτο οὖν ποιουσῶν αὐτῶν, ἐπείσθη Φράστωρ, πρὶν ὑγιαίνειν, πάλιν λαβεῖν τὸ
τῆς Φανοῦς παιδίον καὶ ποιήσασθαι υἱὸν αὐτοῦ. τοῦτο δὲ τὸ παιδίον ἔτεκε Φανὼ
ὅτε ἐξεπέμφθη ὑπὸ τοῦ Φράστορος κυοῦσα. καὶ πρὶν ὑγιαίνειν, ὑπέσχετο δὴ τοῦτο
ποιήσειν ὁ Φράστωρ, λογισμὸν ἀνθρώπινον καὶ ἐοικότα λογιζόμενος, ὅτι πονηρῶς
μὲν ἔχει καὶ οὐκ ἐλπίζει περιγενήσεσθαι, ἐβούλετο δὲ ἀναλαβεῖν τὸ τῆς Φανοῦς   15
παιδίον πρὶν ἀποθανεῖν (καίπερ εἰδὼς αὐτὸν οὐ γνήσιον ὄντα), οὐκ ἐθέλων τοὺς
οἰκείους λαβεῖν τὰ αὑτοῦ, οὐδ' ἄπαις ἀποθανεῖν. εἰ γὰρ ἄπαις ἀπέθανε Φράστωρ, οἱ
οἰκεῖοι ἔλαβον ἂν τὰ αὑτοῦ.

Vocabulary for Section Thirteen B

ἄν (+ aor. ind.) 'would have . . .'
ἀναλαμβάν-ω take back
ἀνθρώπιν-ος -η -ον human,
   mortal
ἄπαις (ἀπαιδ-) childless
ἀπέθανεν aor. of ἀποθνήσκω
   (ἀποθαν-) die
ἀσθενέ-ω fall ill
γεννήτ-ης, ὁ member of *genos*
   (a smaller grouping of
   families within the phratry)
   (1d)
γνήσι-ος -α -ον legitimate
διατίθε-μαι be put in x *(adv.)*
   state
διαφορ-ά, ἡ disagreement,
   differences (1b)
εἰ (+aor. ind.) 'if. . . had–ed'
ἐκπέμπ-ω divorce

ἐοικ-ώς (ἐοικοτ-)
   reasonable
ἐπιμελέ-ομαι take care of
   (+ gen.)
ἐπισκοπέ-ομαι visit
ἔρημος -ον lacking in (+ gen.)
ἔτεκε *see* τίκτω
ἔχ-ω (+adv.) be (in x
   condition)
θεραπεύ-ω look after
κάμν-ω be ill
κυέ-ω be pregnant
λογισμ-ός, ὁ calculation (2a)
μῖσ-ος, τό hatred (3c)
οἰκεῖ-ος, ὁ relative (2a)
ὀργ-ή, ἡ anger (1a)
παλαι-ός -ά -όν of old
παροῦσα being with (+ dat.)
   (part. of πάρειμι)

περιγίγν-ομαι survive
πονηρῶς poorly
πρίν before (+ inf.)
προθύμως readily, actively
πρόσφορ-ος -ον useful for
   (+ dat.)
τίκτ-ω (τεκ-) bear
τῶν θεραπευσόντων 'of those
   who would look after him'
ὑγιαίν-ω be healthy, well
ὑπισχνέ-ομαι (ὑποσχ-) promise
   (to) (+ fut. inf.)
φράτηρ (φρατερ-), ὁ member of
   phratry *(family group)* (3a)
ψυχαγωγέ-ω win over
ὡς (+ fut. part.) in order to
ὡς θεραπεύσουσαι καὶ. . .
   ἐπιμελησόμεναι 'to look after
   and take care of' (nom. pl. f.)

Vocabulary to be learnt

ἀναλαμβάνω (ἀναλαβ-) *take back, take up*

ἄπαις (ἀπαιδ-) *childless*

ἐκπέμπω *send out, divorce*

ἐπιμελέομαι *care for (+ gen.)*

ἐρῆμος ον *empty, deserted; devoid of (+ gen.)*

ἔχω *(+ adv.) be (in X condition)*

λογισμός, ὁ *calculation (2a)*

μῖσος, τό *hatred (3c)*

οἰκεῖος, ὁ *relative (2a)*

οἰκεῖος ᾱ ον *related, domestic, family*

ὀργή, ἡ *anger (1a)*

παλαιός ᾱ όν *ancient, old, of old*

πρίν *(+ inf.) before*

πρόθῡμος -ον *ready, eager, willing, active*

φρᾱ́τηρ (φρᾱτερ-), ὁ *member of a phratry (a group of families with certain religious and social functions) (3a)*

ὡς *(+fut. part.) in order to*

Phrastor recovers and at once marries someone else. The status of Phano's son in the eyes of the Athenian γένος is made quite clear.

In *World of Athens*: citizenship 5.1ff., 13–14; legitimacy 5.12; oaths 3.27.

νῦν δὲ μεγάλῳ τεκμηρίῳ καὶ περιφανεῖ ἐγὼ ὑμῖν ἐπιδείξω ὅτι οὐκ ἄν ποτε ἔπραξε τοῦτο ὁ Φράστωρ, εἰ μὴ ἠσθένησε. ὡς⌐ γὰρ ἀνέστη ⌐τάχιστα ἐξ ἐκείνης τῆς ἀσθενείας ὁ Φράστωρ, λαμβάνει γυναῖκα ἀστὴν κατὰ τοὺς νόμους, Σατύρου μὲν τοῦ Μελιτέως θυγατέρα γνησίαν, Διφίλου δὲ ἀδελφήν· ὃ ὑμῖν ἐστι τεκμήριον, ὅτι οὐχ ἑκὼν ἀνέλαβε τὸ παιδίον, ἀλλὰ βιασθεὶς διὰ τὸ⌐ νοσεῖν καὶ τὸ⌐ ἄπαις⌐ εἶναι καὶ τὸ⌐ θεραπεύειν αὐτὰς αὐτὸν καὶ τὸ⌐ τοὺς οἰκείους ⌐μισεῖν. εἰ γὰρ μὴ ἠσθένησε Φράστωρ, οὐκ ἂν ἀνέλαβε τὸ παιδίον.   5

Vocabulary for Section Thirteen C

Grammar for 13C
- Conditional clauses: past 'unfulfilled'; 'mixed'; and 'open/simple' (no ἄν)

ἀδελφ-ή, ἡ *sister (1a)*

ἀσθένει-α, ἡ *illness (1b)*

ἀσθενέ-ω *be ill*

γνήσι-ος -α -ον *legitimate*

Δίφιλ-ος, ὁ *Diphilos (2a) (the brother of Phrastor's new wife)*

ἐκ-ών -οῦσα -όν *willing(ly)*

ἐπιδείκνυ-μι (ἐπιδειξ-) *show, prove*

Μελιτ-εύς, ὁ *of the deme Melite (3g)*

περιφαν-ής -ές *very evident*

Σάτυρ-ος, ὁ *Satyros (2a) (father of Phrastor's new wife)*

τό + inf.=noun

τὸ ἄπαις εἶναι *childlessness*

τὸ θεραπεύειν *care, looking after*

τὸ μισεῖν *hating, hatred*

τὸ νοσεῖν *being sick, illness*

ὡς τάχιστα *as soon as*

καὶ δὴ καὶ ἄλλο τεκμήριον βούλομαι ὑμῖν ἐπιδεῖξαι ὅτι ξένη ἐστὶ Νέαιρα αὐτή. ὁ γὰρ
Φράστωρ, ἐν τῇ ἀσθενείᾳ ὤν, εἰσήγαγε τὸν Φανοῦς παῖδα εἰς τοὺς φράτερας καὶ τοὺς
Βρυτίδας, ὧν Φράστωρ ἐστί γεννήτης. ἀλλὰ οἱ γεννῆται, εἰδότες τὴν γυναῖκα θυγατέρα   10
Νεαίρας οὖσαν, καὶ ἀκούσαντες Φράστορα αὐτὴν ἀποπέμψαντα, ἔπειτα διὰ τὸ‾ἀσθενεῖν
ἀναλαβεῖν τὸ παιδίον, ἀποψηφίζονται τοῦ παιδὸς καὶ οὐκ ἐνέγραφον αὐτὸν εἰς
τὸ γένος. ἀλλ᾽ εἰ ἀστῆς θυγάτηρ ἦν Φανώ, οὐκ ἂν ἀπεψηφίσαντο τοῦ παιδὸς οἱ
γεννῆται, ἀλλ᾽ ἐνέγραψαν ἂν εἰς τὸ γένος. λαχόντος οὖν τοῦ Φράστορος αὐτοῖς δίκην,
προκαλοῦνται αὐτὸν οἱ γεννῆται ὀμόσαι καθ᾽ ἱερῶν τελείων ἦ‾μὴν νομίζειν τὸν παῖδα   15
εἶναι αὐτοῦ υἱὸν ἐξ ἀστῆς γυναικὸς καὶ ἐγγυητῆς κατὰ τὸν νόμον. προκαλουμένων δ᾽
αὐτὸν τῶν γεννητῶν, ἔλιπεν ὁ Φράστωρ τὸν ὅρκον καὶ ἀπῆλθε πρὶν ὀμόσαι τὸν παῖδα
γνήσιον εἶναι. ἀλλ᾽ εἰ ὁ παῖς γνήσιος ἦν καὶ ἐξ ἀστῆς γυναικός, ὤμοσεν ἄν.

ἄν (+aor. ind.) 'would have'
ἀποψηφίζ-ομαι vote against,
  reject (+gen.)
ἀσθένει-α, ἡ illness (1b)
Βρυτίδ-αι, οἱ the Brytidai (3a)
  (name of genos to which
  Phrastor belonged)
γεννήτ-ης, ὁ member of genos
  (1d)
γέν-ος, τό genos (a smaller
  group of families within the
  phratry) (3c)
γνήσι-ος -α -ον legitimate
ἐγγράφ-ω enlist, register
ἐγγυητ-ός -ή- όν legally married
εἰ (+aor. ind.) 'if . . . had–ed'
ἐπιδείκνυ-μι (ἐπιδειξ-) show,
  prove

ἦ μήν indeed, truly
θεραπεύ-ω tend, look after
ἱερ-ά, τά sacrifices (2b)
κατά (+gen.) by, in name of
λαγχάν-ω (λαχ-) bring (a suit)
  against (+dat.)
λείπ-ω (λιπ-) leave, abandon
νοσέ-ω be sick
ὄμνυ-μι (ὀμοσ-) swear
πράττ-ω (πραξ-) do
προκαλέ-ομαι challenge
τέλει-ος -α -ον perfect,
  unblemished
τὸ ἀσθενεῖν illness

Vocabulary to be learnt
ἀσθένεια, ἡ illness, weakness (1b)
ἀσθενέω be ill, fall ill

γεννήτης, ὁ member of genos
  (1d)
γένος, τό genos (smaller
  groupings of families within
  the phratry) (3c)
γνήσιος ᾱ ον legitimate,
  genuine
ἐγγράφω enrol, enlist, register
ἑκών οὖσα ὄν willing(ly)
ἐπιδείκνῡμι (ἐπιδειξα-) prove,
  show, demonstrate
θεραπεύω look after, tend
λαγχάνω (δίκην) (λαχ-) bring
  (suit) against, obtain by lot,
  run as candidate for office
λείπω (λιπ-) leave, abandon
νοσέω be sick
ὄμνῡμι (ὀμοσα-) swear

D

The incident between Phrastor and Phano is reviewed by Apollodoros.

οὐκοῦν περιφανῶς ἐπιδεικνύω ὑμῖν καὶ αὐτοὺς τοὺς οἰκείους Νεαίρας ταυτησὶ
καταμαρτυρήσαντας αὐτὴν ξένην εἶναι, Στέφανόν τε τουτονὶ τὸν ἔχοντα ταύτην νυνὶ
καὶ συνοικοῦντ' αὐτῇ καὶ Φράστορα τὸν λαβόντα τὴν θυγατέρα. ὁ μὲν γὰρ Στέφανος
καταμαρτυρεῖ Νεαίρας διὰ τὸ ⌐μὴ⌐ ἐθελῆσαι ἀγωνίσασθαι ὑπὲρ τῆς θυγατρὸς περὶ τῆς
προικός, Φράστωρ δὲ μαρτυρεῖ ἐκβαλεῖν τε τὴν θυγατέρα τὴν Νεαίρας ταυτησὶ καὶ   5
οὐκ ἀποδοῦναι τὴν προῖκα, ἔπειτα δὲ αὐτὸς ὑπὸ Νεαίρας καὶ Φανοῦς πεισθῆναι, διὰ
τὴν ἀσθένειαν καὶ τὸ ⌐ἄπαις⌐ εἶναι καὶ τὴν ἔχθραν τὴν πρὸς τοὺς οἰκείους, ἀναλαβεῖν
τὸ παιδίον καὶ υἱὸν ποιήσασθαι, αὐτὸς δὲ εἰσαγαγεῖν τὸν παῖδα εἰς τοὺς γεννήτας,
ἀλλ' οὐκ ὀμόσαι τὸν υἱὸν ἐξ ἀστῆς γυναικὸς εἶναι· ὕστερον δὲ γῆμαι γυναῖκα
ἀστὴν κατὰ τὸν νόμον. αὗται δὲ αἱ πράξεις, περιφανεῖς οὖσαι, μεγάλας μαρτυρίας   10
διδόασιν, ὅτι ᾔδεσαν ξένην οὖσαν τὴν Νέαιραν ταυτηνί. εἰ γὰρ ἀστὴ ἦν Νέαιρα,
οὐκ ἂν ἐξεπέμφθη ἡ Φανώ. Φανὼ γὰρ ἀστὴ ἂν ἦν. καὶ δὴ καί, εἰ Φανὼ ἀστὴ ἦν, οἱ
γεννῆται οὐκ ἂν ἀπεψηφίσαντο τοῦ παιδὸς αὐτῆς. διὰ οὖν τὸ ⌐μὴ⌐ ἐθέλειν ὀμόσαι τὸν
Φράστορα καὶ τὸ⌐ τοὺς γεννήτας τοῦ παιδὸς ⌐ἀποψηφίσασθαι, Στέφανος δῆλός ἐστιν
ἀδικῶν καὶ ἀσεβῶν εἴς τε τὴν πόλιν καὶ τοὺς θεούς.   15

Vocabulary for Section Thirteen D

> **Grammar for 13D**
> - Gerunds (verbs used as nouns): τό + infinitive

ἀποψηφίζ-ομαι reject, vote
   against (+gen.)
γαμέ-ω (γημ-) marry
ἐπιδεικνύ-ω=ἐπιδείκνυ-μι
καταμαρτυρέ-ω give evidence
   against (+gen.)
μαρτυρέ-ω give evidence, bear
   witness
περιφαν-ής -ές very clear

πρᾶξ-ις, ἡ deed, action, fact (3e)
τό + inf.=noun
τὸ ἄπαις εἶναι childlessness
τὸ ἀποψηφίζεσθαι rejection
τὸ μὴ ἐθέλειν/ἐθελῆσαι not
   wanting, refusal

Vocabulary to be learnt
ἀποψηφίζομαι *reject (+gen.)*

γαμέω (γημα-) *marry*
καταμαρτυρέω *give evidence
   against (+gen.)*
μαρτυρέω *give evidence, bear
   witness*
περιφανής ές *very clear*

The marriage dowry

The new wife brought a 'dowry' with her to a marriage, given her by her father,
usually a sum of money … It was her husband who controlled how it was spent,
under two constraints: first, he was (essentially) looking after it to hand it on to
the male children of the marriage; second, in the event of divorce, the husband
had to see that the dowry was repaid to the wife's father. Divorce proceedings could be initiated by either party. It was easier for the husband to obtain a
divorce, and he was obliged to divorce if he found out his wife had been unfaith-
ful. (*World of Athens*, 5.19)

E

Introduction

The incident between Phrastor and Phano is the first major piece of evidence that Apollodoros brings to bear on his contention that Stephanos and Neaira are living together as man and wife.

The second incident would have appeared yet more heinous to the dikasts – for Stephanos tried to marry Phano off to a man who was standing for the office of ἄρχων βασιλεύς, an office which entailed performing, with one's wife, some of Athens' most sacred rites on behalf of the state.

In *World of Athens*: king *arkhon* 2.33, 3.47, 6.30; offices of state 6.23ff.; purity of family 5.20; piety and the city 3.57; marriage to Dionysos 3.47; defiance of the gods 3.56.

Stephanos takes advantage of Theogenes' poverty to win political power for himself and a marriage for Phano.

διὰ οὖν ταῦτα, πάντες ἔγνωσαν τὴν Φανὼ περιφανῶς ξένην οὖσαν καὶ οὐκ ἀστήν. σκοπεῖτε τοίνυν ὁποία ἦν ἡ ἀναίδεια ἡ τοῦ Στεφάνου καὶ Νεαίρας, καὶ ὅπως τὴν πόλιν ἠδίκησαν. ἐμφανῶς γὰρ ἐτόλμησαν φάσκειν τὴν θυγατέρα τὴν Νεαίρας ἀστὴν εἶναι. ἦν γάρ ποτε Θεογένης τις, ὃς ἔλαχε βασιλεύς, εὐγενὴς μὲν ὤν, πένης δὲ καὶ ἄπειρος τῶν πραγμάτων. καὶ πρὶν εἰσελθεῖν τὸν Θεογένη εἰς τὴν ἀρχήν,   5
χρήματα παρεῖχεν ὁ Στέφανος, ὡς πάρεδρος γενησόμενος καὶ τῆς ἀρχῆς μεθέξων. ὅτε δὲ Θεογένης εἰσῄει εἰς τὴν ἀρχήν, Στέφανος οὑτοσί, πάρεδρος γενόμενος διὰ τὸ Θεογένει χρήματα παρασχεῖν, δίδωσι τὴν Νεαίρας θυγατέρα γυναῖκα Θεογένει καὶ ἐγγυᾷ αὐτὴν ὡς αὐτοῦ θυγατέρα οὖσαν. οὐ γὰρ ᾔδει ὁ Θεογένης ὅτου θυγάτηρ ἐστί, οὐδὲ ὁποῖά ἐστιν αὐτῆς τὰ ἔθη. οὕτω πολὺ τῶν νόμων καὶ ὑμῶν κατεφρόνησεν   10
οὗτος. καὶ αὕτη ἡ γυνὴ ὑμῖν ἔθυε τὰ ἄρρητα ἱερὰ ὑπὲρ τῆς πόλεως, καὶ εἶδεν ἃ οὐ προσῆκεν αὐτῇ ὁρᾶν, ξένη οὖσα. καὶ εἰσῆλθεν οἷ οὐδεὶς ἄλλος Ἀθηναίων εἰσέρχεται ἀλλ' ἢ ἡ τοῦ βασιλέως γυνή, ἐξεδόθη δὲ τῷ Διονύσῳ γυνή, ἔπραξε δ' ὑπὲρ τῆς πόλεως τὰ πάτρια τὰ πρὸς τοὺς θεούς, πολλὰ καὶ ἅγια καὶ ἀπόρρητα.

βούλομαι δ' ὑμῖν ἀκριβέστερον περὶ τούτων διηγήσασθαι. οὐ μόνον γὰρ ὑπὲρ   15
ὑμῶν αὐτῶν καὶ τῶν νόμων τὴν ψῆφον θήσεσθε, ἀλλὰ καὶ ὑπὲρ τῆς πρὸς θεοὺς εὐλαβείας. δεδήλωκα τοίνυν ὑμῖν ὅτι Στέφανος ἀσεβέστατα πεποίηκε. τοὺς γὰρ νόμους ἀκύρους πεποίηκε καὶ τῶν θεῶν καταπεφρόνηκε, τὴν Νεαίρας θυγατέρα γυναῖκα Θεογένει βασιλεύοντι ἐκδούς. καὶ μὴν αὕτη πεποίηκε τὰ ἱερά, καὶ τὰς θυσίας ὑπὲρ τῆς πόλεως τέθυκεν. ὅτι δ' ἀληθῆ λέγω, αὗται αἱ πράξεις δηλώσουσιν.   20

Vocabulary for Section Thirteen E

> Grammar for 13E
> - The perfect indicative active, 'have –ed'

ἅγι-ος -α -ον holy
ἄκυρ-ος -ον invalid
ἀναίδει-α, ἡ shamelessness (1b)
ἄπειρ-ος -ον inexperienced in
 (+ gen.)
ἀπόρρητ-ος -ον forbidden
ἄρρητ-ος -ον secret, mysterious
ἀρχ-ή, ἡ office, position (1a)
ἀσεβ-ής -ές unholy, impious
βασιλ-εύς, ὁ *basileus archon*
 (3g) *(state officer, in charge*
 of certain important religious
 rites)
βασιλεύ-ω be *basileus*
δεδήλωκ-α I have shown
 (δηλό-ω)
διηγέ-ομαι explain
Διόνυσ-ος, ὁ Dionysos (2a) *(god*
 of nature, especially of wine)
ἔθ-ος, τό manner, habits (3c)
ἐμφαν-ής -ές open
εὐγεν-ής -ές well-born,
 aristocratic

εὐλάβει-α, ἡ respect (1b)
Θεογέν-ης, ὁ Theogenes (3d)
 (Phano's husband for a short
 while)
ἱερ-ά, τά rites, sacrifice (2b)
καταπεφρόνηκ-ε(ν) he has
 despised (καταφρονέω)
λαγχάν-ω (λαχ-) run as
 (candidate for office)
μετέχ-ω take part in (+ gen.)
οἷ (to) where
ὁποῖ-ος -α -ον of what sort
ὅτου=οὗτινος (ὅστις)
πάρεδρ-ος, ὁ assistant (2a)
πάτρι-α, τά ancestral rites (2b)
πεποίηκ-ε(ν) (she) has done
 (ποιέω)
πρᾶξ-ις, ἡ fact, action (3e)
πράττ-ω (πραξ-) do, act
προσήκ-ει it is fitting, right (for,
 +dat.)
τέθυκ-ε(ν) (she) has sacrificed
 (θύω)

φάσκ-ω allege, claim

Vocabulary to be learnt
ἄπειρος ον *inexperienced in*
 (+gen.)
ἀρχή, ἡ *position, office; start;*
 rule (1a)
ἀσεβής ές *unholy*
βασιλεύς, ὁ *king, king archon*
 (3g)
βασιλεύω *be king, be king*
 archon
ἔθος, τό *manner, habit (3c)*
ἐμφανής ές *open, obvious*
ἱερά, τά *rites, sacrifices (2b)*
οἷ *(to) where*
ὁποῖος ᾱ ον *of what kind*
πρᾶξις, ἡ *fact, action (3e)*
πράττω (πραξ-) *do, perform,*
 fare

The festival of *Anthesteria*

This festival in honour of Dionysos gave its name to the month in which it took place (Ἀνθεστηρίων, January-February). Its name derives from the Greek for 'flowers', and the festival took place at a time when the first signs of life in nature, blossom, began to show. The main concern of the festival was with the new wine (i.e. the reappearance of Dionysos) and the spirits of ill omen. The festival lasted three days. On day 1 (πιθοίγια, 'jar opening'), the new wine was opened and tested; on day 2 (χόες, 'wine-jugs'), there was a procession in which Dionysos rode in a ship-chariot and the wife of the king ἄρχων (ἄρχων βασιλεύς) was 'married' to him in a 'holy marriage'. In the evening, drinking-parties were the order of the day, but each guest brought his own wine and drank it in silence, the very antithesis of community fellowship. The Greek explanation lay in myth. Orestes, infected with blood-pollution for killing his mother, arrived in Athens on χόες. In order that he should not be excluded from the celebrations and that the people should not be polluted, the king ordered that all drink their own wine from their own cups. We may prefer to explain the ritual rather as an attempt to put a boundary around the potentially destructive effects of too much alcohol. The third day was χύτραι, 'pots', and of a completely different character. Vegetables were boiled in these pots not for the living but for the spirits of the dead. It was a day of ill omen, when these spirits were said to roam abroad. When the day was over, the householders shouted 'Get out, κῆρες ['evil demons'], the Ἀνθεστήρια are over!' (*World of Athens*, 3.47)

The Areopagos Council finds out about Phano's true status, and calls Theogenes to account.

In *World of Athens*: Areopagus 6.38; priestly authority 3.5.

Στέφανος μὲν τοίνυν τὴν θυγατέρα γυναῖκα Θεογένει βασιλεύοντι ἠγγύησεν,
αὕτη δὲ ἐποίει τὰ ἱερὰ ταῦτα. γενομένων δὲ τούτων τῶν ἱερῶν, καὶ ἀναβάντων
εἰς Ἄρειον πάγον τῶν ἐννέα ἀρχόντων, ἤρετο ἡ βουλὴ ἡ ἐν Ἀρείῳ πάγῳ
περὶ τῶν ἱερῶν, τίς αὐτὰ ποιήσειε καὶ πῶς πράξειαν οἱ ἄρχοντες. καὶ εὐθὺς
ἐζήτει ἡ βουλὴ τὴν γυναῖκα ταύτην τὴν Θεογένους, ἥτις εἴη. καὶ πυθομένη   5
ἥστινος θυγατέρα γυναῖκα ἔχοι Θεογένης, καὶ ὁποῖα ποιήσειεν αὐτή, περὶ τῶν
ἱερῶν πρόνοιαν ἐποιεῖτο καὶ ἐζημίου τὸν Θεογένη. γενομένων δὲ λόγων, καὶ
χαλεπῶς φερούσης τῆς ἐν Ἀρείῳ πάγῳ βουλῆς, καὶ ζημιούσης τὸν Θεογένη, ὅτι
τοιαύτην λάβοι γυναῖκα καὶ ταύτην ἐάσειε ποιῆσαι τὰ ἱερὰ τὰ ἄρρητα ὑπὲρ τῆς
πόλεως, ἐδεῖτο ὁ Θεογένης, ἱκετεύων καὶ ἀντιβολῶν. ἔλεγεν γὰρ ὅτι οὐκ εἰδείη   10
Νεαίρας αὐτὴν οὖσαν θυγατέρα, ἀλλ᾽ ἐξαπατηθείη ὑπὸ Στεφάνου, καὶ αὐτὸς λάβοι
Φανὼ ὡς θυγατέρα αὐτοῦ οὖσαν γνησίαν κατὰ τὸν νόμον· διὰ δὲ τὸ ἄπειρος εἶναι
τῶν πραγμάτων, καὶ τὴν ἀκακίαν τὴν αὐτοῦ, ποιήσασθαι πάρεδρον τὸν Στέφανον,
ὡς διοικήσοντα τὴν ἀρχήν· εὔνουν γὰρ φαίνεσθαι εἶναι τὸν Στέφανον· διὰ δὲ τοῦτο,
κηδεῦσαι αὐτῷ πρὶν μαθεῖν σαφῶς ὁποῖος εἴη. 'ὅτι δέ', ἔφη, 'οὐ ψεύδομαι, μεγάλῳ   15
τεκμηρίῳ ἐπιδείξω ὑμῖν. τὴν γὰρ ἄνθρωπον ἀποπέμψω ἐκ τῆς οἰκίας, ἐπειδὴ οὐκ ἔστι
Στεφάνου θυγάτηρ ἀλλὰ Νεαίρας.' ὑποσχομένου δὲ ταῦτα ποιήσειν Θεογένους καὶ
δεομένου, ἡ ἐν Ἀρείῳ πάγῳ βουλή, ἅμα μὲν ἐλεήσασα αὐτὸν διὰ τὸ ἄκακον εἶναι,
ἅμα δὲ ἡγουμένη ὑπὸ τοῦ Στεφάνου ἀληθῶς ἐξαπατηθῆναι, ἐπέσχεν. ὡς δὲ κατέβη
ἐξ Ἀρείου πάγου ὁ Θεογένης, εὐθὺς τήν τε ἄνθρωπον, τὴν τῆς Νεαίρας θυγατέρα,   20
ἐκβάλλει ἐκ τῆς οἰκίας, τόν τε Στέφανον, τὸν ἐξαπατήσαντα αὐτόν, ἀπελαύνει ἀπὸ
τοῦ συνεδρίου. καὶ ἐκπεσούσης τῆς Φανοῦς, ἐπαύσαντο οἱ Ἀρεοπαγῖται κρίνοντες
τὸν Θεογένη καὶ ὀργιζόμενοι αὐτῷ, καὶ συγγνώμην εἶχον ἐξαπατηθέντι.

Evidence

'Theogenes from Erkhia deposes that when he was βασιλεὺς ἄρχων he married
Phano, believing her to be the daughter of Stephanos and that, when he found he
had been deceived, he divorced the woman and ceased to live with her, and that
he expelled Stephanos from his post of Assistant, and no longer allowed him to
serve in that capacity.'

Vocabulary for Section Thirteen F

> **Grammar for 13F**
> - the aorist optative passive
> - the use of the optative in indirect speech
> - sequence of tenses
> - the future optative

ἀκακί-α, ἡ innocence (1b)
ἄκακ-ος -ον innocent
ἄνθρωπ-ος, ἡ woman (2a)
ἀντιβολέ-ω entreat
ἀπελαύν-ω exclude, reject
Ἀρεοπαγίτ-ης, ὁ member of the
  Areopagos council (1d)
Ἄρε-ος πάγ-ος, ὁ Areopagos hill
  (2a) *(where the council met)*
ἄρρητ-ος -ον secret, mysterious
ἄρχων (ἀρχοντ-), ὁ archon (3a)
βουλ-ή, ἡ council (1a)
διοικέ-ω administer
ἐλεέ-ω pity
ἐννέα nine (indecl.)
ἐξαπατηθείη he was deceived
  (ἐξαπατάω)
ἐπέχ-ω (ἐπισχ-) hold off

ζημιό-ω fine
ἱκετεύ-ω beg
κηδεύ-ω ally oneself by
  marriage to (+dat.)
κρίν-ω judge, accuse
πάρεδρ-ος, ὁ assistant (2a)
πρόνοιαν ποιέ-ομαι show
  concern
πυνθάν-ομαι (πυθ-) learn, hear,
  discover
συνέδρι-ον, τό council board
  (2b)
ὑπισχνέ-ομαι (ὑποσχ-) promise
φαίν-ομαι (+inf.) seem to – (but
  not in fact to –)
χαλεπῶς φέρ-ω be angry,
  displeased
ψεύδ-ομαι lie

Vocabulary to be learnt
ἄνθρωπος, ἡ *woman (2a)*
ἄρχων (ἀρχοντ-), ὁ *archon*
  (3a)
βουλή, ἡ *council (1a)*
διοικέω *administer, run*
ἱκετεύω *beg, supplicate*
κρίνω (κρῖνα-) *judge, decide*
πυνθάνομαι (πυθ-) *learn, hear*
  by inquiry
φαίνομαι (+inf.) *seem to – (but*
  not in fact to –)
χαλεπῶς φέρω *be angry at,*
  displeased with
ψεύδομαι *lie, tell lies*

G

Komias suggests arguments that Stephanos will use to clear his name.

ΣΤΡ.   ὦ τῆς ἀνομίας. πολλὰ γὰρ αἰσχρῶς διεπράξατο Στέφανος.
ΕΥ.   εἰ ἀληθῆ γε λέγει Ἀπολλόδωρος, ἀσεβέστατα δὴ πεποιήκασι Στέφανος

Vocabulary for Section Thirteen G

> **Grammar for 13G–I**
> - More forms of the perfect:
>   - perfect indicative middle and passive
>   - perfect infinitive
>   - perfect participle
> - Some irregular perfects

αἰσχρ-ός -ά -όν base, shameful   διαπράττ-ομαι do

καὶ Νέαιρα. τῶν γὰρ νόμων τῶν ὑπὲρ τῆς πολιτείας καὶ τῶν θεῶν
καταπεφρονήκασιν.

ΣΤΡ.   εἰκός γε. πολλοὶ γὰρ μεμαρτυρήκασιν αὐτοὺς καταπεφρονηκέναι τῆς τε   5
πόλεως καὶ τῶν θεῶν. θαυμάζω δὲ τί ποτ' ἐρεῖ Στέφανος ἐν τῇ ἀπολογίᾳ.

ΚΩ.   τοιαῦτα ἐρεῖ Στέφανος οἷα πάντες οἱ φεύγοντες ἐν τῷ ἀπολογεῖσθαι
λέγουσιν, ὡς 'εὖ πεπολίτευμαι' καὶ 'αἴτιος γεγένημαι οὐδεμιᾶς συμφορᾶς
ἐν τῇ πόλει.' εὖ γὰρ οἶσθ' ὅτι πάντες οἱ φεύγοντες φάσκουσι φιλοτίμως
τὰς λειτουργίας λελειτουργηκέναι, καὶ νίκας πολλὰς καὶ καλὰς ἐν τοῖς   10
ἀγῶσι νενικηκέναι, καὶ πολλὰ κἀγαθὰ διαπεπρᾶχθαι τῇ πόλει.

ΕΥ.   εἰκότως. πολλάκις γὰρ ἀπολελύκασιν οἱ δικασταὶ τοὺς ἀδικοῦντας οἳ ἂν
ἀποφαίνωσι τὰς τῶν προγόνων ἀρετὰς καὶ τὰς σφετέρας εὐεργεσίας. ἀλλ'
εὖ ἴσμεν τὸν Στέφανον οὔτε πλούσιον ὄντα, οὔτε τετριηραρχηκότα, οὔτε
χορηγὸν καθεστῶτα, οὔτε εὖ πεπολιτευμένον, οὔτε ἀγαθὸν οὐδὲν τῇ   15
πόλει διαπεπραγμένον.

ἀποφαίνωσι (they) display
  (ἀποφαίνω)
γεγένημαι I have become, been
  (γίγνομαι)
διαπεπραγμένον having done
  (διαπράττομαι)
διαπεπρᾶχθαι to have done
  (διαπράττομαι)
εἰκότως reasonably
εὐεργεσί-α, ἡ good service,
  public service (1b)
καθεστῶτα having been made
  (καθίσταμαι)
καταπεφρονηκέναι to have
  despised (καταφρονέω)
λειτουργέ-ω perform (a state duty)
λειτουργί-α, ἡ a state duty (1b)

λελειτουργηκέναι to have
  performed (λειτουργέω)
νενικηκέναι to have won
  (νικάω)
οἳ ἄν who (ever)
πολιτεί-α, ἡ state, constitution (1b)
πεπολίτευμαι I have governed
  (πολιτεύομαι)
πολιτεύ-ομαι govern
πρόγον-ος, ὁ forebear, ancestor
  (2a)
συμφορ-ά, ἡ disaster (1b)
σφέτερ-ος -α -ον their own
τετριηραρχηκότα having served
  as trierarch (τριηραρχέω)
τριηραρχέ-ω serve as trierarch
φάσκ-ω allege

φιλότιμ-ος -ον ambitious
χορηγ-ός, ὁ chorus-financier
  (2a) *(a duty which the state
  imposed on the rich)*

Vocabulary to be learnt
αἰσχρός ᾱ όν *base, shameful;
  ugly (of people) (comp.
  αἰσχῑων; sup.* αἴσχιστος)
διαπράττομαι (διαπρᾱξ-) *do, act,
  perform*
εἰκότως *reasonably, rightly*
πολῑτείᾱ, ἡ *state, constitution (1b)*
πολῑτεύομαι *be a citizen*
πρόγονος, ὁ *forebear, ancestor
  (2a)*
φάσκω *allege, claim, assert*

H

The dikasts have found Apollodoros very persuasive.

ΣΤΡ.   τί δέ; τί ποτ' ἐρεῖ Στέφανος ἐν τῷ ἀπολογεῖσθαι; ἆρα ὅτι ἀστὴ ἔφυ ἡ
Νέαιρα καὶ κατὰ τοὺς νόμους συνοικεῖ αὐτῷ;

ΚΩ.   ἀλλὰ τεκμηρίοις ἰσχυροτάτοις κέχρηται Ἀπολλόδωρος, φαίνων Νέαιραν
ἑταίραν οὖσαν καὶ δούλην Νικαρέτης γεγενημένην, ἀλλ' οὐκ ἀστὴν
πεφυκυῖαν. ὥστε δῆλον ὅτι ἐξελεγχθήσεται ὁ Στέφανος ψευδόμενος,   5
φάσκων τοιαῦτα.

ΣΤΡ.   τί δέ; ὅτι οὐκ εἴληφε τὴν Νέαιραν ὡς γυναῖκα, ἀλλ' ὡς παλλακὴν ἔνδον;

ΕΥ.   ἀλλὰ καταμεμαρτύρηται Στέφανος αὐτὸς ὑφ' αὑτοῦ. οἱ γὰρ παῖδες,
           Νεαίρας ὄντες καὶ εἰσηγμένοι εἰς τοὺς φρατέρας ὑπὸ Στεφάνου, καὶ ἡ
           θυγάτηρ, ἀνδρὶ Ἀθηναίῳ ἐκδοθεῖσα, περιφανῶς Νέαιραν ἀποφαίνουσι   10
           συνοικοῦσαν τῷ Στεφάνῳ ὡς γυναῖκα.
ΣΤΡ.   καὶ γὰρ δῆλον ὅτι τὰ ἀληθῆ εἴρηται ὑπὸ Ἀπολλοδώρου. ἐν τοῖς
           δεινοτάτοις οὖν κινδύνοις καθέστηκε Νέαιρα δι' ἃ πέπρακται ὑπὸ
           Στεφάνου.
ΕΥ.   ἀλλ' ἀπόλωλε καὶ ὁ Στέφανος, ὡς ἐμοὶ δοκεῖ· πεφύκασί τοι πάντες   15
           ἁμαρτάνειν.

Vocabulary for Section Thirteen H

ἁμαρτάν-ω make a mistake
ἀπόλωλεν he is done for
   (ἀπόλλυμι)
γεγενημένην having been
   (γίγνομαι)
εἴληφε he has taken (λαμβάνω)
εἴρηται (it) has been spoken
   (λέγω)
εἰσηγμένος having been
   introduced (εἰσάγω)
ἰσχυρ-ός -ά -όν strong, powerful
καταμεμαρτύρηται he has had
   evidence brought against him
   (καταμαρτυρέω)
κεχρῆται he has used
   (χράομαι)

παλλακ-ή, ἡ kept slave,
   concubine (1a)
πέπρακται (it) has been done
   (πράττω)
πεφύκασιν (they) are born to
   (φύομαι) (+inf.)
πεφυκυῖαν born (acc. s. f.)
   (φύομαι)
φαίν-ω reveal, declare
φύ-ω bear; mid., grow (ἔφυν=I
   am naturally)
ὥστε so that; and so

Vocabulary to be learnt
ἁμαρτάνω (ἁμαρτ-) *err; do
   wrong, make a mistake*

ἀπόλωλα (*perf. of ἀπόλλῡμαι*)
   I am lost
γεγένημαι (*perf. of γίγνομαι*) I
   have been
εἴληφα (*perf. of λαμβάνω*) *I
   have taken*
εἴρημαι (*perf. of λέγω*) *I have
   been said*
ἰσχυρός ᾱ́ όν *strong, powerful*
καθέστηκα (*perf. pass. of
   καθίσταμαι*) *I have been
   made, put*
φαίνω *reveal, declare, indict*
φῡ́ω *bear; mid., grow; aor.
   mid. ἔφῡν, perf. πέφῡκα be
   naturally*

Apollodoros implicates Stephanos along with Neaira in the charges he is bringing.

τὰς μαρτυρίας οὖν ἀκηκόατε, ὦ ἄνδρες δικασταί, καὶ ἀκριβῶς μεμαθήκατε, Νέαιραν
μὲν ξένην οὖσαν καὶ εἰς τοὺς θεοὺς ἠσεβηκυῖαν, αὐτοὶ δὲ μεγάλα ἠδικημένοι καὶ
ὑβρισμένοι. καὶ πρὶν δικάζειν, ἴστε ὅτι οὗτος ὁ Στέφανος ἄξιός ἐστιν οὐκ

Vocabulary for Section Thirteen I

ἀκηκόατε you have heard
   (ἀκούω)
ἠδικημένοι having been injured
   (nom. pl. m.) (ἀδικέω)

ἠσεβηκυῖαν having been
   impious (acc. s. f.)
   (ἀσεβέω)

ὑβρισμένοι having been
   violently treated (nom. pl. m.)
   (ὑβρίζω)

ἐλάττω δοῦναι⌐δίκην ἢ καὶ Νέαιρα αὐτή, ἀλλὰ καὶ πολλῷ μείζω, δι' ἃ εἴργασται.
δεδήλωκα γὰρ αὐτόν, Ἀθηναῖον φάσκοντα εἶναι, οὕτω πολὺ τῶν νόμων καὶ ὑμῶν   5
καταπεφρονηκέναι καὶ εἰς τοὺς θεοὺς ἠσεβηκέναι. τιμωρίαν⌐ οὖν ⌐ποιεῖσθε τῶν
εἰς τοὺς θεοὺς ἠσεβηκότων, καὶ κολάζετε τοὺς τὴν πόλιν ἠδικηκότας, καὶ πρὸς τὸ
ἀσεβεῖν μᾶλλον ἢ πρὸς τὸ εὐσεβεῖν πεφυκότας.

δίκην δίδωμι (δο-) pay penalty,
　be punished
εἴργασται he has done
　(ἐργάζομαι)
ἐλάττων (ἐλαττον-) smaller
εὐσεβέ-ω act righteously
ἠδικηκότας having committed
　crimes against (acc. pl. m.)
ἠσεβηκέναι to have been
　impious (ἀσεβέω)

ἠσεβηκότων having been
　impious (gen. pl. m.) (ἀσεβέω)
καταπεφρονηκέναι to have
　despised (καταφρονέω)
μᾶλλον ἤ rather than, more than
πεφυκότας inclined by nature
　(acc. pl. m.) (φύομαι)
τιμωρίαν ποιέ-ομαι take revenge
　on (+gen.)

Vocabulary to be learnt
ἀκήκοα (*perf. of* ἀκούω) *I have
　heard*
δίκην δίδωμι (δο-) *be punished,
　pay penalty*
ἐλάττων (ἐλαττον-) *smaller,
　less, fewer*
εὐσεβέω *act righteously*
μᾶλλον ἤ *rather than; more
　than*

Section Fourteen A-F: Guarding a woman's purity

Introduction

The evidence is over. Apollodoros has shown to his own satisfaction that Neaira is an alien and is living with Stephanos as his wife. But the matter cannot simply rest there, on the 'facts'. An appeal to the heart may carry far more weight than one to the intellect; and in an Athenian court, where there was no judge to warn the dikasts against such appeals or to guide them in what the issue at hand really was, pleas directed at the dikasts' emotions were common. Apollodoros thus makes a final emotional appeal to the dikasts and sketches an imagined picture of the likely reaction of their own womenfolk to Neaira, especially were she to be acquitted. Clearly, Apollodoros felt that the male dikasts would respond readily to such a picture.

In *World of Athens*: creating citizens 5.3–4; citizen solidarity 2.1, 5.83.

ἡ πολῖτις καὶ ἡ πόρνη

A

How could any Athenian not condemn a woman like Neaira? The slur upon Athenian womanhood would be intolerable.

ἆρ' οὖν ἐάσετε, ὦ ἄνδρες δικασταί, τὴν Νέαιραν ταύτην αἰσχρῶς καὶ ὀλιγώρως
ὑβρίζειν εἰς τὴν πόλιν, ἣν οὔτε οἱ πρόγονοι ἀστὴν κατέλιπον, οὔθ' ὁ δῆμος πολῖτιν
ἐποιήσατο; ἆρ' ἐάσετε αὐτὴν ἀσεβεῖν εἰς τοὺς θεοὺς ἀτιμώρητον, ἢ περιφανῶς ἐν
πάσῃ τῇ Ἑλλάδι πεπόρνευται; ποῦ γὰρ αὕτη οὐκ εἴργασται τῷ σώματι; ἢ ποῖ οὐκ
ἐλήλυθεν ἐπὶ τῷ καθ' ἡμέρας μισθῷ; ἆρα τὴν Νέαιραν περιφανῶς ἐγνωσμένην   5
ὑπὸ πάντων τοιαύτην οὖσαν ψηφιεῖσθε ἀστὴν εἶναι; καὶ τί καλὸν φήσετε πρὸς τοὺς
ἐρωτῶντας διαπεπρᾶχθαι, οὕτω ψηφισάμενοι;
   πρότερον γὰρ τὰ μὲν ἀδικήματα ταύτης ἦν, ἡ δ' ἀμέλεια τῆς πόλεως, πρὶν
γραφῆναι ὑπ' ἐμοῦ ταύτην καὶ εἰς ἀγῶνα καταστῆναι καὶ πυθέσθαι πάντας ὑμᾶς
ἥτις ἦν καὶ οἷα ἠσέβηκεν. ἐπειδὴ δὲ πέπυσθε καὶ ἴστε ὑμεῖς πάντες, καὶ κύριοί ἐστε   10
κολάσαι, ἀσεβήσετε καὶ ὑμεῖς αὐτοὶ πρὸς τοὺς θεούς, ἐὰν μὴ ταύτην κολάσητε.

Vocabulary for Section Fourteen A

> **Grammar for 14A–F**
> * The subjunctive mood: present, aorist and perfect
> * Indefinite constructions with ἄν

ἀδίκημα (ἀδικημat-), τό crime (3b)
ἀμέλει-α, ἡ indifference (1b)
ἀτιμώρητ-ος -ον unavenged
γραφῆναι aor. inf. pass. of γράφω
ἐάν if
ἐγνωσμένην known (γιγνώσκω)
εἴργασται she has worked
   (ἐργάζομαι)
ἐλήλυθεν she has gone
   (ἔρχομαι)
Ἑλλάς (Ἑλλάδ-), ἡ Greece (3a)
ἐπί (+dat.) for the purpose of
καθ' ἡμέρας daily, day by day
καταλείπ-ω (καταλιπ-)
   bequeath, leave by right

κολάσητε you punish (κολάζω)
κύρι-ος -α -ον able, empowered
μισθ-ός, ὁ pay (2a)
ὀλίγωρ-ος -ον contemptuous
πέπυσθε you have learnt
   (πυνθάνομαι)
πολῖτις (πολιτιδ-), ἡ female
   citizen (3a: but acc. s. πολῖτιν)
πορνεύ-ομαι prostitute oneself
σῶμα (σωματ-), τό body, person
   (3b)

Vocabulary to be learnt
ἀδίκημα (ἀδικημat-), τό *crime*
   (3b)

ἐλήλυθα *perf. of* ἔρχομαι *I have
   come*
Ἑλλάς (Ἑλλάδ-), ἡ *Greece (3a)*
ἐπί (+dat.) for the purpose of,
   at, near
ἡμέρᾱ, ἡ *day (1b)*
καταλείπω (καταλιπ-) *leave
   behind, bequeath*
κύριος ᾱ ον *able, with power, by
   right, sovereign*
μισθός, ὁ *pay (2a)*
σῶμα (σωματ-), τό *body, person
   (3b)*

B

In *World of Athens*: protection of women 5.16–18; their dangerous habits 5.24; impiety and the state 3.57; family breakdown 8.54.

τί δὲ καὶ φήσειεν ἂν ὑμῶν ἕκαστος, εἰσιὼν πρὸς τὴν αὑτοῦ γυναῖκα ἢ παῖδα κόρην ἢ
μητέρα, ἀποψηφισάμενος Νεαίρας; ἐπειδὰν γάρ τις ἔρηται ὑμᾶς 'ποῦ ἦτε;' καὶ εἴπητε
ὅτι 'ἐδικάζομεν', ἐρήσεταί τις εὐθὺς 'τίνι ἐδικάζετε;' ὑμεῖς δὲ φήσετε 'Νεαίρᾳ' (οὐ
γάρ;) 'ὅτι ξένη οὖσα ἀστῷ συνοικεῖ παρὰ τὸν νόμον, καὶ ὅτι τὴν θυγατέρα ἐξέδωκε
Θεογένει τῷ βασιλεύσαντι, καὶ αὕτη ἔθυε τὰ ἱερὰ τὰ ἄρρητα ὑπὲρ τῆς πόλεως,   5
καὶ τῷ Διονύσῳ γυνὴ ἐδόθη.' (καὶ τὰ ἄλλα περὶ τῆς κατηγορίας διηγήσεσθε, ὡς
εὖ καὶ ἐπιμελῶς καὶ μνημονικῶς περὶ ἑκάστου κατηγορήθη.) αἱ δέ, ἀκούσασαι,
ἐρήσονται 'τί οὖν ἐποιήσατε;' ὑμεῖς δὲ φήσετε 'ἀπεψηφισάμεθα'. οὔκουν ἤδη αἱ
σωφρονέσταται τῶν γυναικῶν, ἐπειδὰν πύθωνται, ὀργισθήσονται ὑμῖν διότι, ὁμοίως
αὐταῖς, κατηξιοῦτε Νέαιραν μετέχειν τῶν τῆς πόλεως καὶ τῶν ἱερῶν; καὶ δὴ καὶ   10
ταῖς ἀνοήτοις γυναιξὶ δόξετε ἄδειαν διδόναι ποιεῖν ὅ τι ἂν βούλωνται. δόξετε γὰρ
ὀλίγωροι εἶναι καὶ αὐτοὶ ὁμογνώμονες τοῖς Νεαίρας τρόποις.

Vocabulary for Section Fourteen B

ἄδει-α, ἡ freedom, *carte-blanche*
  (1b)
ἀνόητ-ος -ον foolish,
  thoughtless
ἀποψηφίζ-ομαι acquit (+gen.)
ἄρρητ-ος -ον secret, mysterious
βούλωνται they wish (βούλομαι)
διηγέ-ομαι explain, go through
Διόνυσ-ος, ὁ Dionysos (2a) *(god
  of nature, transformation and
  especially wine)*
ἕκαστ-ος -η -ον each
εἴπητε you say (εἶπον)

ἐπειδὰν when (ever)
ἐπιμελ-ής -ές careful
ἔρηται she asks (ἠρόμην)
καταξιό-ω think it right
μετέχ-ω share in (+gen.)
μνημονικῶς indelibly,
  unforgetably
ὀλίγωρ-ος -ον contemptuous
ὁμογνώμων (ὁμογνωμον-) in
  agreement with, content with,
  acquiescent in (+dat.)
ὁμοίως equally with (+dat.)
πύθωνται they learn (ἐπυθόμην)

σώφρων (σωφρον-) sensible,
  law-abiding
ὅ τι ἂν whatever

Vocabulary to be learnt
ἀποψηφίζομαι *acquit (+gen.);
  reject (+gen.)*
διηγέομαι *explain, relate, go
  through*
ἕκαστος η ον *each*
ἐπιμελής ές *careful*
μετέχω *share in (+gen.)*
ὀλίγωρος ον *contemptuous*

The exclusivity of citizenship

The Athenians took practical steps to see that they remained a restricted descent group; a citizenship law introduced by Pericles in 451 insisted that only men who had an Athenian mother as well as an Athenian father should qualify as citizens … Among the free population of Athens, all women, whatever their status, and all males lacking the correct parentage, were by definition excluded from full citizenship (though a woman with an Athenian mother and father counted as a 'citizen' for the purpose of producing legitimate Athenian children). It was very exceptional indeed for a resident alien (μέτοικος, hence 'metic') or non-resident foreigner (ξένος) to be voted citizenship; it would be a reward for some extraordinary service to the democracy. In short, only a fraction of the total population of the Athenian state enjoyed political rights under the democracy. (World of Athens, 5.3–4)

C

Komias argues that the acquittal of a woman like Neaira would pose an intolerable threat to Athenian public and private life.

ΣΤΡ.   σὺ δὲ δὴ τί σιγᾷς, ὦ Εὐεργίδη, καὶ οὔτε συνεπαινεῖς τοὺς λόγους οὔτε
ἐλέγχεις; ἥδομαι γὰρ ἔγωγε μάλιστα ἀκούσας τὸν λόγον ὃν διέρχεται
Ἀπολλόδωρος. τί οὖν λέγεις περὶ ὧν διῆλθεν; ἆρ' ἤδει καὶ σύ γε τοῖς
λόγοις;

ΕΥ.   μάλιστά γε⌢δήπου, ὦ Στρυμόδωρε, τοῖς λόγοις ἥδομαι οἷς διελήλυθεν   5
Ἀπολλόδωρος. ἐπειδὰν γάρ τις καλῶς λέγῃ καὶ ἀληθῆ, τίς οὐχ ἥδεται
ἀκούσας;

ΣΤΡ.   τί δέ; ἆρα δεῖ ἡμᾶς καταδικάσαι τῆς Νεαίρας;

ΕΥ.   πῶς γὰρ οὔ; ἐὰν γὰρ ἀποψηφισώμεθα Νεαίρας, ἐξέσται ταῖς πόρναις
συνοικεῖν οἷς⌢ἂν βούλωνται, καὶ φάσκειν τοὺς παῖδας εἶναι οὗ⌢ἂν   10
τύχωσιν.

ΣΤΡ.   οὐ μόνον γε, ὦ Εὐεργίδη, ἀλλὰ καὶ οἱ μὲν καθεστῶτες νόμοι ἄκυροι
ἔσονται, αἱ δὲ ἑταῖραι κύριαι διαπράττεσθαι ὅ τι⌢ἂν βούλωνται. τί φῄς, ὦ
Κωμία; ἆρ' οἴει τοὺς νόμους ἀκύρους ἔσεσθαι;

ΚΩ.   ὑμῖν μὲν μέλει τῶν τε ἑταιρῶν καὶ τῶν νόμων, ἐμοὶ δὲ οὐδὲν τούτων   15
μέλει. τῶν γὰρ πολιτίδων μοι μέλει.

ΣΤΡ.   σοὶ τῶν πολιτίδων μέλει; πῶς φῄς; ἴσως μέν τι λέγεις, ἐγὼ δ' οὐ
μανθάνω.

ΚΩ.   εἰ σὺ γυνὴ ἦσθα, ὦ Στρυμόδωρε, ἐμάνθανες ἄν, καί σοι ἂν ἔμελε τῶν
πολιτίδων. σκόπει δή, ὦ Στρυμόδωρε.   20

Vocabulary for Section Fourteen C

ἄκυρ-ος -ον invalid
ἀποψηφισώμεθα we acquit
   (ἀποψηφίζομαι)
βούλωνται they wish (βούλομαι)
γε δήπου of course
ἐὰν if
ἐλέγχ-ω refute, argue against
ἐπειδὰν when (ever)
λέγῃ (he) speaks (λέγω)
μέλει x (dat.) is concerned about
   Y (gen.)

οἷς ἂν with whomever
ὅ τι ἂν whatever
οὗ ἂν of whomever
πολῖτ-ις (πολιτιδ-), ἡ female
   citizen (3a)
πόρν-η, ἡ prostitute (1a)
συνεπαινέ-ω join in
   praising
τύχωσιν they happen upon
   (ἔτυχον)

Vocabulary to be learnt
ἄκῡρος ον *invalid*
ἐάν *if (ever)*
ἐλέγχω *refute, argue against*
ἐπειδάν *when(ever)*
μέλει *[impersonal] X (dat.) is
   concerned about Y (gen.)*
πολῖτις (πολῑτιδ-), ἡ *female
   citizen (3a: but acc. s.*
   πολῖτιν)

D

In *World of Athens*: importance of the   5.9–10; jealousy of citizenship 5.4.

ΚΩ.   νῦν μὲν γάρ, καὶ ἐὰν ἀπορηθῇ γυνή τις καὶ ὁ πατὴρ εἰς πενίαν καθεστήκῃ
       καὶ μὴ δύνηται προῖκα δοῦναι τῇ θυγατρί, ἱκανὴν τὴν προῖκα παρέχει ὁ
       νόμος.

ΣΤΡ.   πῶς λέγεις;

ΚΩ.   ἐάν τις βούληται παῖδας ἀστοὺς τρέφειν, δεῖ αὐτὸν ἀστοῦ θυγατέρα γαμεῖν,   5
       εἰ καὶ πένητος ὄντος. οὕτως οἱ νομοθέται σκοποῦσιν ὅπως αἱ τῶν πολιτῶν
       θυγατέρες μὴ ἀνέκδοτοι γενήσονται –

ΣΤΡ.   ἐὰν ἡ φύσις μετρίαν ὄψιν τῇ κόρῃ ἀποδῷ.

ΕΥ.   τί οὖν δή;

ΚΩ.   ἐὰν δὲ ἀπολυθῇ Νέαιρα, ἐξέσται τοῖς Ἀθηναίοις συνοικεῖν ταῖς   10
       ἑταίραις καὶ παιδοποιεῖσθαι ὡς ἂν βούλωνται. ἀλλ' ἐὰν οἱ Ἀθηναῖοι
       παιδοποιῶνται ὡς ἂν βούλωνται, πῶς ἐξέσται ἡμῖν διακρίνειν τόν τε
       ἀστὸν καὶ τὸν ξένον; ἐὰν δὲ μὴ δυνώμεθα διακρίνειν τόν τε ἀστὸν καὶ
       τὸν ξένον, οὐ δεήσει τοὺς Ἀθηναίους γαμεῖν τὰς ἀστάς, ἀλλ' ἥντινα ἂν
       βούλωνται. ἐὰν οὖν οἱ Ἀθηναῖοι γαμῶσιν ἥντινα ἂν βούλωνται, τίς γαμεῖ   15
       τὰς τῶν πενήτων θυγατέρας, τὰς προῖκας μὴ ἐχούσας; παντελῶς οὖν ἡ μὲν
       τῶν πορνῶν ἐργασία ἥξει εἰς τὰς τῶν πολιτῶν θυγατέρας διὰ τὸ προῖκα
       μηδεμίαν ἔχειν, τὸ δὲ τῶν ἐλευθέρων γυναικῶν ἀξίωμα εἰς τὰς ἑταίρας.
       ἐξέσται γὰρ ταῖς ἑταίραις παιδοποιεῖσθαι ὡς ἂν βούλωνται καὶ τελετῶν
       καὶ ἱερῶν καὶ τιμῶν μετέχειν ἐν τῇ πόλει. οὕτως μοι μέλει τῶν πολιτίδων.   20

ΕΥ.   καλῶς μὲν διελήλυθε τὸν λόγον Ἀπολλόδωρος, κάλλιον δὲ καὶ
       ἀληθέστερον δὴ τὸ πρᾶγμα ὑπὸ Κωμίου εἴρηται. ἀλλὰ σιγᾶτε, ὦ φίλοι.
       παύεται γὰρ λέγων Ἀπολλόδωρος.

Vocabulary for Section Fourteen D

ἀνέκδοτ-ος -ον unmarried
ἀξίωμα (ἀξιωματ-), τό
   reputation (3b)
ἀποδιδῷ (it) gives (ἀποδίδωμι)
ἀπολυθῇ (she) is acquitted
   (ἀπολύω)
ἀπορηθῇ (she) is in dire straits
   (ἀπορέω)
βούληται (he) wishes
   (βούλομαι)
βούλωνται they wish (βούλομαι)
γαμῶσίν (they) marry (γαμέω)
διακρίν-ω differentiate between
δύνηται he is able (δύναμαι)
δυνώμεθα we are able (δύναμαι)

ἐργασί-α, ἡ function, work (1b)
ἥντινα ἂν whomever
ἱκαν-ός -ή -όν adequate,
   sufficient
καθεστήκῃ he is placed, finds
   himself in (καθέστηκα)
κάλλιον better
μέτρι-ος -α -ον reasonable,
   acceptable
νομοθέτ-ης, ὁ lawgiver (1d)
ὄψ-ις, ἡ face, looks (3e)
παιδοποιῶνται (they) have
   children (παιδοποιέομαι)
παντελῶς completely, outright
πόρν-η, ἡ prostitute (1a)

σκοπέω ὅπως see to it that (+fut.
   ind.)
τελετ-ή, ἡ rite (1a)
τιμ-ή, ἡ privilege, honour (1a)
τρέφ-ω rear, raise
ὡς ἂν in whatever way

Vocabulary to be learnt
διακρῑ́νω *decide, judge between*
ἱκανός ή όν *sufficient, able*
παντελῶς *completely, outright*
πόρνη, ἡ *prostitute (1a)*
τῑμή, ἡ *honour, privilege, right (1a)*
τρέφω (θρεψα-) *rear, raise, feed,
   nourish*

E

Apollodoros appeals to the dikasts to vote in the interests of their families and of the state and its laws.

In *World of Athens*: female sexuality 4.23, 9.3; being *sophron* 4.19.

βούλομαι οὖν ἕνα ἕκαστον ὑμῶν εἰδέναι ὅτι τίθεσαι τὴν ψῆφον ὁ μὲν ὑπὲρ γυναικός,
ὁ δὲ ὑπὲρ θυγατρός, ὁ δὲ ὑπὲρ μητρός, ὁ δὲ ὑπὲρ τῆς πόλεως καὶ τῶν νόμων καὶ
τῶν ἱερῶν. μὴ οὖν τιμᾶτε αὐτὰς ὁμοίως Νεαίρᾳ τῇ πόρνῃ. τρέφετε γάρ, ὦ ἄνδρες
δικασταί, τρέφετε αὐτὰς μετὰ πολλῆς καὶ καλῆς σωφροσύνης καὶ ἐπιμελείας, καὶ
ἐκδίδοτε κατὰ τοὺς νόμους. Νέαιρα δέ, μετὰ πολλῶν καὶ ἀσελγῶν τρόπων, πολλοῖς   5
πολλάκις ἑκάστης ἡμέρας συγγεγένηται. καὶ ὅταν μὲν ἐπὶ τοῦ κατηγορεῖν γένησθε,
τῶν νόμων αὐτῶν ἀκούετε, δι᾽ ὧν οἰκοῦμεν τὴν πόλιν, καὶ καθ᾽ οὓς ὀμωμόκατε
δικάσειν. ὅταν δὲ ἐπὶ τοῦ ἀπολογεῖσθαι ἦτε, μνημονεύετε τὴν τῶν νόμων
κατηγορίαν καὶ τὸν τῶν εἰρημένων ἔλεγχον ὃν ἀκηκόατε. καὶ ὅταν εἰς τὴν Νεαίρας
ὄψιν ἀποβλέπητε, ἐνθυμεῖσθε τοῦτο μόνον, εἰ Νέαιρα οὖσα ταῦτα διαπέπρακται.   10

Vocabulary for Section Fourteen E

ἀποβλέπητε you gaze at
    (ἀποβλέπω)
ἀσελγ-ής -ές disgusting
γένησθε you are (ἐγενόμην)
ἔλεγχ-ος, ὁ examination,
    refutation (2a)
ἐπί (+gen.) on, concerned with
ἐπιμέλει-α, ἡ care, concern (1b)
ἦτε you are (εἰμί)

ὀμωμόκατε you have sworn
    (ὄμνυμι)
ὅταν when (ever)
συγγίγν-ομαι (συγγεν-) have
    intercourse with (+dat.)
σωφροσύν-η, ἡ discipline,
    sense of right and wrong
    (1a)

Vocabulary to be learnt
ἔλεγχος, ὁ *examination,
    refutation (2a)*
ἐπιμέλεια, ἡ *care, concern (1b)*
ὅταν *whenever*

F

The dikasts await the speech for the defence – and their pay.

In *World of Athens*: state pay 6.13, 59.

ΕΥ.   εἶεν. τοσαύτη ἥ γε κατηγορία ἣν διελήλυθεν Ἀπολλόδωρος. τὴν δὲ
        ἀπολογίαν τὴν τοῦ Στεφάνου νῦν δεῖ ἡμᾶς ἀκούειν, ἀκούσαντας δὲ τὴν
        ψῆφον θέσθαι.
ΣΤΡ.   ἀλλὰ τί ἐρῶ, ὅταν οἱ παῖδες οἱ ἐμοὶ καὶ ἡ γυνὴ ἔρωνται πότερον
        κατεδίκασα ἢ ἀπεψηφισάμην;   5
ΕΥ.   ἐὰν μὲν καταδικασθῇ Νέαιρα, ὦ Στρυμόδωρε, ἐρεῖς ὅτι κατεδίκασας, ἐὰν
        δὲ ἀπολυθῇ, ὅτι ἀπεψηφίσω.
ΣΤΡ.   πῶς γὰρ οὔ; ἀλλὰ καίπερ προθυμούμενος οὐχ οἷός τ᾽ εἰμὶ μνημονεύειν τὴν
        κατηγορίαν· περιέλκει γάρ με κύκλῳ ὁ κατήγορος, ὥσπερ σοφιστής τις, καὶ εἰς
        πολλὴν ἀπορίαν με καθίστησιν.   10

ΚΩ.	καὶ περιέλξει σε κύκλῳ ὁ ἀπολογούμενος, ὡς ἔοικεν, ὦ Στρυμόδωρε.
ΣΤΡ.	πῶς οὖν μοι ἐξέσται διακρίνειν τὴν δίκην;
ΕΥ.	πρῶτον μὲν ἄκουσον, ἔπειτα δὲ διάκρινον.
ΣΤΡ.	εἶεν. ὅταν δὲ τὴν ψῆφον θώμεθα, τί;
ΚΩ.	ὅ τι; ἐκ τῆς ἕδρας ἀνεστῶτες καὶ τὴν ψῆφον θέμενοι, τὸ τριώβολον 5
	ληψόμεθα, ὦ Στρυμόδωρε. ἥδιστον δή ἐστι τοῦτο, ὅταν οἴκαδ' ἴω, τὸ
	τριώβολον ἔχων ἐν τῷ στόματι, καὶ πάντες οἱ οἰκεῖοι ἀσπάζωνταί με διὰ
	τὸ τριώβολον.
ΕΥ.	εἰκότως. ἀλλὰ παῦε φλυαρῶν, ὦ Κωμία. ἀνέστηκε γὰρ ἤδη Στέφανος
	ὡς ἀπολογησόμενος. σιγῴης ἄν, καὶ τὸν νοῦν προσέχοις ἄν. καὶ σύ γε, 10
	ὦ Στρυμόδωρε, ὅπως μνημονεύσεις τὰ εἰρημένα ὑπὸ Ἀπολλοδώρου καὶ
	προσέξεις τὸν νοῦν πρὸς πάνθ' ἃ ἂν λέγῃ Στέφανος.

Vocabulary for Section Fourteen F

ἀπολυθῇ (she) is acquitted
 (ἀπολύω)
ἀσπάζωνται (they) greet
 (ἀσπάζομαι)
ἕδρ-α, ἡ seat (1b)
ἔοικε it seems, it is reasonable
ἔρωνται (they) ask (ἠρόμην/
 ἐρωτάω)
θώμεθα we cast (τίθημι/θε-)

ἴω I go (subj. of εἶμι)
καταδικασθῇ (she) is condemned
 (καταδικάζω)
κύκλ-ος, ὁ circle (2a)
λέγῃ (he) says (λέγω)
περιέλκ-ω drag round
προθυμέ-ομαι be eager, willing
στόμα (στοματ-), τό mouth
 (3b)

τριώβολ-ον, τό three obols
 (dikast's pay) (2b)
φλυαρέ-ω talk nonsense

Vocabulary to be learnt
ἔοικε *it seems, it is*
 reasonable, it resembles
 (+ dat.)

So ends the speech for the prosecution of Neaira. To the questions 'What did Stephanos reply? Who won?' we have no answer. But however damning Apollodoros' case may seem, it has a number of weaknesses that Stephanos would have exploited. Firstly, he could claim that Neaira was no wife of his, but simply a 'kept woman' (ἑταίρα), a normal practice in ancient Athens. Secondly, he could claim that Phano was not Neaira's child, but his own by a previous citizen woman, and therefore fully entitled to Athenian citizenship (and one may imagine how emotionally he would have described to the jury how his own dear child had had her reputation slurred simply because of his perfectly normal extra-marital relationship with Neaira). If you have read Apollodoros' evidence on one side of the case, there is absolutely no doubt at all that Stephanos would have produced plenty of quite contrary evidence on the other side. Apollodoros' case rested on his claim that by passing off Phano as free-born, Stephanos and Neaira have asserted the validity of their marriage and that this is an act of criminal collusion in which they are both implicated. His pleas for the preservation of public morality against the threat of people like Neaira must have added considerable emotional weight to his argument. If the birth of citizen children from marriage was the *sole* criterion for judging whether two people were married or not, Apollodoros had not a leg to stand on. The fact that he still brought the case illustrates that there were many other considerations which could sway the jury.

Whatever your feelings about the people involved (and remember you have heard only one side of the argument), bear in mind, as you leave Neaira to whatever fate she met, that at the time of the trial she was probably between fifty and sixty, and that a great number of the incidents referred to must have happened anything up to fifty years previously; and that she had been living with Stephanos in Athens for up to thirty years before this case. Apollodoros' desire for revenge was strong, and he left few stones unturned in his quest for it, however deeply time had buried them. One is left reflecting on what Neaira herself must have been thinking as her past was so ruthlessly dug up in the cause of Apollodoros' revenge on her man.

Section Fifteen A–C: Alkestis in Euripides' play

Introduction

The extracts from *The Prosecution of Neaira* may have given you one impression of the responsibilities, dignity and status of Athenian women, and of other women, seen through the eyes of one man. In the following brief extract, taken from Greek drama – the circumstances and conventions of which place it on a far different level from a speech in a courtroom (though both are written to win – the one a case, the other a dramatic prize) – you may receive a quite different impression, and one no less important than that given by *Neaira.*

The god Apollo, sentenced by Zeus to live a life of serfdom to a mortal (because he had killed Zeus' firemakers, the Cyclopes), serves his time under the human Admetos and, finding Admetos a pious man, tricks the Fates into offering him a reprieve from imminent death – on the condition that another will die in his place. Only Admetos' wife, Alkestis, can be found to take his place. The day has now come on which Death is to take Alkestis away.

In *World of Athens*: Greek tragedy 8.49ff.; women, marrriage and the home 5.9ff.; death and burial 5.78ff.

Note

For verse metre, see *Grammar,* **179, 228.** The text is unadapted.

Wedding preparations

A

A Chorus (χορός) of townsmen has come to Admetos' palace to find out whether Alkestis is already dead. A maidservant (θεράπαινα) comes weeping from Alkestis' rooms; she heartily agrees with the Chorus' praise of Alkestis' noble death, and describes Alkestis' last actions and her prayer for her husband and children.

ΧΟΡΟΣ	ἴστω νυν εὐκλεής γε κατθανουμένη	
	γυνή τ' ἀρίστη τῶν ὑφ' ἡλίῳ μακρῷ.	
ΘΕΡΑΠΑΙΝΑ	πῶς δ' οὐκ ἀρίστη; τίς δ' ἐναντιώσεται;	
	τί χρὴ λέγεσθαι τήνδ' ὑπερβεβλημένην	
	γυναῖκα; πῶς δ' ἂν μᾶλλον ἐνδείξαιτό τις	5
	πόσιν προτιμῶσ' ἢ θέλουσ' ὑπερθανεῖν;	
	καὶ ταῦτα μὲν δὴ πᾶσ' ἐπίσταται πόλις·	
	ἃ δ' ἐν δόμοις ἔδρασε θαυμάσῃ κλύων.	
	ἐπεὶ γὰρ ᾔσθεθ' ἡμέραν τὴν κυρίαν	
	ἥκουσαν, ὕδασι ποταμίοις λευκὸν χρόα	10
	ἐλούσατ', ἐκ⌈ δ' ⌉ἑλοῦσα κεδρίνων δόμων	
	ἐσθῆτα κόσμον τ' εὐπρεπῶς ἠσκήσατο,	
	καὶ στᾶσα πρόσθεν Ἑστίας κατηύξατο·	
	'δέσποιν', ἐγὼ γὰρ ἔρχομαι κατὰ χθονός,	
	πανύστατόν σε προσπίτνουσ' αἰτήσομαι,	15
	τέκν' ὀρφανεῦσαι τἀμά· καὶ τῷ μὲν φίλην	
	σύζευξον ἄλοχον, τῇ δὲ γενναῖον πόσιν.	
	μηδ' (ὥσπερ αὐτῶν ἡ τεκοῦσ' ἀπόλλυμαι)	
	θανεῖν ἀώρους παῖδας, ἀλλ' εὐδαίμονας	
	ἐν γῇ πατρῴᾳ τερπνὸν ἐκπλῆσαι βίον.'	20

Notes

1. κατθανουμένη: nom. fut. part. after ἴστω (see vocab: οἶδα) 'that she will die'

1–2. εὐκλεής … γυνή τ' : 'glorious … and the [best] woman'; τῶν 'of those…'

4. τί χρὴ λέγεσθαι: 'what should [τήνδ' ὑπ. γυν.] be called?' i.e. 'how can one describe…?'

5–6. μᾶλλον … ἢ θέλουσ': 'more, than by being willing'

8. ἃ: ' the things which', object of κλύων. Begin with θαυμάσῃ (fut., 2s.)

11. κεδρίνων δόμων: 'from the …'

16–17. τῷ μέν … τῇ δέ: 'for the one [boy], the other [girl]'. σύζευξον is aor. imperat.

19. θανεῖν: see vocabulary, and understand 'grant that they [+ infin.] (i) μὴ θανεῖν (ii) ἐκπλῆσαι'

Vocabulary for Section Fifteen A

> **Grammar for 15A–C**
> - The future perfect
> - Tragic usages
> - Scanning Greek verse
> - Iambic trimeters

αἰτέ-ομαι beg, ask
ἄλοχ-ος, ἡ wife (2a)
ἀσκέ-ομαι adorn oneself
ἄωρ-ος -ον untimely, before time
γενναῖ-ος -α -ον noble, fine
δέσποιν-α, ἡ mistress (1c)
δόμ-οι, οἱ house, home; (with κέδριν-ος) chest, box (2a)
ἐκ ... ἑλοῦσα taking out from
ἐκπίμπλη-μι (ἐκπλησ-) complete
ἐναντιό-ομαι deny, disagree
ἐνδείκνυ-μαι (ἐνδειξ-) declare oneself as (+ part.)
ἔσθης (ἐσθητ-), ἡ clothes (3a)
Ἑστί-α, ἡ household hearth (1b)
εὐκλε-ής -ές glorious, of good reputation
εὐπρεπ-ής -ές becoming, proper
ᾔσθεθ'=ᾔσθετο (aor. of αἰσθάνομαι)
θανεῖν ... παῖδας 'that my children (do not) die'
θέλουσα=ἐθέλουσα
θεράπαιν-α, ἡ female servant (of Alkestis) (1c)
θνήσκ-ω (θαν-) die
ἵστα-μαι (στα-) stand
ἴστω γυνή 'let the woman know (that she)'
κατά (+ gen.) beneath
καταθνήσκ-ω die away (fut. κατθανοῦμαι)

κατεύχ-ομαι pray earnestly
κατθανουμένη see καταθνήσκω
κέδριν-ος -η -ον of cedar
κλύ-ω hear
κόσμ-ος, ὁ decoration (2a)
λευκ-ός -ή -όν white
λού-ω wash
μακρῷ by far
ὀρφανεύ-ω look after as orphans
πανύστατ-ος -η -ον for the very last time
πατρῷ-ος -α -ον father's, ancestral
πόσ-ις, ὁ husband (3e)
ποτάμι-ος -α -ον from a river
πρόσθεν (+ gen.) in front of
προσπίτν-ω=προσπίπτ-ω fall upon, embrace
προτιμά-ω hold in honour
συζεύγνυ-μι (συζευξ-) join in marriage
τέκν-ον, τό child (2b)
τεκοῦσα, ἡ mother (τίκτω [τεκ-] bear)
τερπν-ός -ή -όν joyful, pleasant
ὕδωρ (ὑδατ-), τό water (3b)
ὑπερβεβλημένην 'who surpasses' (sc. Alkestis) (ὑπερβάλλομαι)
ὑπερθνήσκ-ω (ὑπερθαν-) die for another
ὑπό (+dat.) under
χθών (χθον-), ἡ earth (3a)

χορ-ός, ὁ chorus (of townsmen) (2a)
χρώς (χρωτ-), ὁ skin, flesh (3a) (acc. χρόα)

Vocabulary to be learnt

γενναῖος ᾱ ον *noble, fine*
δέσποινα, ἡ *mistress (1c)*
δόμοι, οἱ *house, home (2a)*
εὐπρεπής ές *seemly, proper, becoming*
θνήσκω (θαν-) *die*
ἵστημι/ἵσταμαι *set up, stand, raise*
κατά (+gen.) *below*
καταθνήσκω (καταθαν-) *die away*
κλύω *hear*
κόσμος, ὁ *decoration, ornament; order; universe (2a)*
μακρός ᾱ όν *large, big, long*
πανύστατος η ον *for the very last time*
πατρῷος ᾱ ον *of one's father, ancestral*
πόσις, ὁ *husband, spouse (3e)*
προσπίτνω *fall upon, embrace*
τέκνον, τό *child (2b)*
τίκτω (τεκ-) *bear, give birth to*
ὕδωρ (ὑδατ-), τό *water (3b)*
ὑπό (+dat.) *under, beneath*
χρώς (χρωτ-), ὁ *flesh, skin (acc. χρόα) (3a)*

B

The servant describes Alkestis' calm, and then her breakdown as she approaches her marriage bed.

πάντας δὲ βωμούς, οἳ κατ' Ἀδμήτου δόμους,
προσῆλθε κἀξέστεψε καὶ προσηύξατο,
ἄκλαυτος ἀστένακτος, οὐδὲ τοὐπιὸν
κακὸν μεθίστη χρωτὸς εὐειδῆ φύσιν.
κἄπειτα θάλαμον ἐσπεσοῦσα καὶ λέχος,   5
ἐνταῦθα δὴ 'δάκρυσε καὶ λέγει τάδε·
'ὦ λέκτρον, ἔνθα παρθένει' ἔλυσ' ἐγὼ
κορεύματ' ἐκ τοῦδ' ἀνδρός, οὗ θνήσκω πέρι,
χαῖρ'· οὐ γὰρ ἐχθαίρω σ'· ἀπώλεσας δ' ἐμὲ
μόνην· προδοῦναι γάρ σ' ὀκνοῦσα καὶ πόσιν   10
θνήσκω. σὲ δ' ἄλλη τις γυνὴ κεκτήσεται,
σώφρων μὲν οὐκ ἂν μᾶλλον, εὐτυχὴς δ' ἴσως.'

Vocabulary for Section Fifteen B

Ἄδμητ-ος, ὁ Admetos (2a)
ἄκλαυτ-ος -ον unweeping
ἀστένακτ-ος -ον without
   lamentation
δακρύ-ω weep
ἐσπίπτ-ω (ἐσπεσ-) fall into, on
ἐκστέφ-ω garland, crown
ἔνθα there
εὐειδ-ής -ές graceful, pleasant
εὐτυχ-ής -ές fortunate
ἐχθαίρ-ω hate
θάλαμ-ος, ὁ bedroom (2a)
κἀξέστεψε=καὶ ἐξέστεψε
κἄπειτα=καὶ ἔπειτα
κατά (+acc.) throughout

κορεύματ-α, τά maidenhood (3b)
κεκτήσεται (she) will have
   gained (κτάομαι)
λέκτρ-ον, τό bed (2b)
λέχ-ος, τό bed (3c)
μεθίστη-μι change, alter
ὀκνέ-ω shrink from (+ inf.)
παρθένει-ος -α -ον maiden,
   virgin
προδίδω-μι (προδο-) betray
προσεύχ-ομαι address in prayer
σώφρων (σώφρον-) modest,
   chaste
τοὐπιόν=τὸ ἐπιόν (pres. part. n.
   of ἐπέρχομαι)

Vocabulary to be learnt
δακρύω *weep*
εἰσπίπτω (εἰσπεσ-) *fall into,*
   on
ἔνθα *there*
εὐτυχής ἐς *fortunate, lucky*
θάλαμος, ὁ *bedchamber (2a)*
κτάομαι *acquire, get, gain*
προδίδωμι (προδο-) *betray*
σώφρων (σωφρον-) *modest,*
   chaste, discreet, sensible,
   law-abiding, prudent,
   disciplined, temperate

Notes

B8.   οὗ: take with πέρι
C4.   ἐκπεσοῦσα: 'stumbling from the δεμνίων'
  5.   πολλά: 'often'; θαλάμων: 'from the…' (controlled by ἐξιοῦσ')

C

The reaction of her children and servants is described – and finally, Admetos' tearful lament.

κυνεῖ δὲ προσπίτνουσα, πᾶν δὲ δέμνιον
ὀφθαλμοτέγκτῳ δεύεται πλημμυρίδι.
ἐπεὶ δὲ πολλῶν δακρύων εἶχεν κόρον,
στείχει. προνωπὴς ἐκπεσοῦσα δεμνίων,
καὶ πολλὰ θαλάμων ἐξιοῦσ' ἐπεστράφη   5
κἄρριψεν αὑτὴν αὖθις ἐς κοίτην πάλιν.
    παῖδες δὲ πέπλων μητρὸς ἐξηρτημένοι
ἔκλαιον· ἡ δὲ λαμβάνουσ' ἐς ἀγκάλας
ἠσπάζετ' ἄλλοτ' ἄλλον, ὡς θανουμένη.
πάντες δ' ἔκλαιον οἰκέται κατὰ στέγας   10
δέσποιναν οἰκτίροντες. ἡ δὲ δεξιὰν
προὔτειν' ἑκάστῳ, κοὔτις ἦν οὕτω κακὸς
ὃν οὐ προσεῖπε καὶ προσερρήθη πάλιν.

παῖδες δὲ πέπλων μητρὸς ἐξηρτημένοι ἔκλαιον

Vocabulary for Section Fifteen C

ἀγκάλ-η, ἡ arm (1a)
ἄλλοτ' ἄλλον now one, now the
    other
δάκρυ-ον, τό tear (2b)
δέμνι-ον, τό bed, bedding (usu.
    pl.) (2b)
δεύ-ω wet, bedew, besprinkle
ἐξηρτημέν-ος clinging to (+gen.)
ἐπεστράφη she turned back
    (ἐπιστρέφω)

κἄρριψεν=καὶ ἔρριψεν
κλαί-ω weep
κοίτ-η, ἡ bed (1a)
κόρ-ος, ὁ sufficiency, enough,
    fill (2a)
κυνέ-ω kiss
οὔτις (οὔτιν-) no one
ὀφθαλμότεγκτ-ος -ον welling
    from the eyes
πέπλ-ος, ὁ robe (2a)

πλημμυρίς (πλημμυριδ-), ἡ flood
    (3a)
προνωπ-ής -ές forward,
    headlong
προσλέγ-ω (προσειπ-) address
    (aor. pass. προσερρήθην)
προτείν-ω stretch out
σμικρ-ός -ά -όν=μικρός
στέγ-αι, αἱ house (1c)
στείχ-ω go

τοιαῦτ' ἐν οἴκοις ἐστὶν Ἀδμήτου κακά.
καὶ κατθανὼν τἂν ὤλετ', ἐκφυγὼν δ' ἔχει   15
τοσοῦτον ἄλγος, οὗ ποτ' – οὐ λελήσεται.

ΧΟΡΟΣ   ἦ που στενάζει τοισίδ' Ἄδμητος κακοῖς,
ἐσθλῆς γυναικὸς εἰ στερηθῆναί σφε χρή;

ΘΕΡ.   κλαίει γ' ἄκοιτιν ἐν χεροῖν φίλην ἔχων,
καὶ μὴ προδοῦναι λίσσεται, τἀμήχανα   20
ζητῶν· φθίνει γὰρ καὶ μαραίνεται νόσῳ.
παρειμένη δέ, χειρὸς ἄθλιον βάρος,
ὅμως δὲ (καίπερ σμικρὸν) ἐμπνέουσ' ἔτι
βλέψαι πρὸς αὐγὰς βούλεται τὰς ἡλίου
ὡς οὔποτ' αὖθις, ἀλλὰ νῦν πανύστατον.   25

ἄθλι-ος -α -ον pathetic, miserable
ἄκοιτ-ις, ἡ wife (3e)
ἄλγ-ος, τό pain, agony (3c)
ἀμήχαν-ος -ον hopeless, impossible
αὐγ-ή, ἡ ray (1a)
βάρ-ος, τό weight, burden (3c)
ἐμπνέ-ω breathe
ἐσθλ-ός -ή -όν noble, fine
ἦ που no doubt
κλαί-ω weep
λελήσεται he will have forgotten (λανθάνομαι)
λίσσ-ομαι beg

μαραίν-ομαι die away (pass.)
οἶκ-ος, ὁ household (often pl.) (2a)
οὔποτε never
παρειμέν-ος -η -ον exhausted
στενάζ-ω weep, lament
στερέ-ω deprive of (+ gen.)
σφέ he (= Admetos)
τἀμήχανα=τὰ ἀμήχανα
τἄν=τοι ἄν 'truly, he would have ...'
τοισίδ'=τοῖσδε
φθίν-ω die, waste away
χειρός i.e. on Admetos' hand

χεροῖν 'in both hands' (dual form)

Vocabulary to be learnt
ἄθλιος ᾱ ον *pathetic, miserable, wretched*
βάρος, τό *weight, burden (3c)*
δάκρυον, τό *tear (2b)*
ἐσθλός ή όν *noble, fine, good*
κλαίω *weep*
οἶκος, ὁ *household, house (2a)*
οὔποτε *never*
οὔτις *no one*
προσλέγω *address*
στείχω *go, come*

Notes

15.   κατθανών: Admetos is the subject
21.   φθίνει: Alkestis is the subject
22.   χειρός: see vocabulary

A fight

Part Five Athenian views of justice

Introduction

A number of Greek writers and thinkers were greatly concerned with the question of the nature of justice – what is it? What should it be? What is the relationship between justice and law? Why should one be so concerned about it? What are the origins of law and justice in our society?

The extracts from *Neaira* have already shown you something of legal process. Part Five concentrates on the actual workings of justice in the Athenian world, and shows the problems of enforcing it and making it work (Sections 16–17). It ends with a μῦθος, ascribed by Plato to the Greek sophist Protagoras (Πρωταγόρας), which explains the origins of human civilisation and shows how δίκη became an essential ingredient of it (Section 18).

Sources

Demosthenes 47, *Against Mnesiboulos and Euergos (passim.).*

Plato, *Phaidros (passim.),* and other dialogues.
Plato, *Protagoras 321d–323a*

NRE Fisher, *Social Values in Classical Athens* (Dent 1976) has excellent part-translations and discussions of both *Neaira* and *Against Mnesiboulos and Euergos.*

Time to be taken

Five weeks

Sections Sixteen to Seventeen: Official and private justice

Aristarkhos had been appointed in succession to Theophemos as a trierarch, whose duty it was to equip and man, at his own expense, a trireme of the Athenian navy. It was Theophemos' duty to hand over the state-provided ship's gear to his successor, but this he refused to do. In his attempts to recover the gear Aristarkhos got into a fight with Theophemos: Theophemos then brought a charge of assault and battery which he won, thanks to false evidence and the suppression of the testimony of a slave woman. Aristarkhos sought an extension of time in which to pay the fine, but at this Theophemos and a bunch of friends descended on Aristarkhos' farm, grabbing all they could lay their hands on and mauling an old servant so badly that she subsequently died.

Aristarkhos is uncertain what action he can take against Theophemos, and consults the *Exegetai,* state officials who advised on what to do in cases of murder. He is returning home when he meets Apollodoros, and tells him the whole story.

The speech is datable to the time of the Social War in 357.

Note

Aristarkhos' monologue is almost entirely unadapted.

In *World of Athens*: liturgies 6.62; trierachies 7.43–6; *exegetai* 3.33; blood-guilt 3.26; revenge 4.8ff.; Social War 1.100.

Section Sixteen A–H: Official justice: ships, state and individuals

A

Aristarkhos is on his way home from the agora *where he has been taking the advice of the* Exegetai *about the death of a faithful servant. By the city gate he meets Apollodoros, who is taking a walk outside the walls. Aristarkhos agrees to tell Apollodoros the whole story.*

πορεύεται ὁ Ἀπολλόδωρος εὐθὺς Ἰλισοῦ, τὴν ἔξω τείχους ὁδὸν βαδίζων ὑπ᾽ αὐτὸ
τὸ τεῖχος. ἐπειδὴ δὲ γίγνεται κατὰ τὴν πύλην, ἐνταῦθα συντυγχάνει Ἀριστάρχῳ τῷ
Ἀριστῶνος πάνυ ἀθύμως ᾽ἔχοντι. καὶ Ἀρίσταρχον προσιόντα ὁ Ἀπολλόδωρος ἰδὼν
προσαγορεύει.

5

ΑΠΟΛΛΟΔΩΡΟΣ ποῖ δὴ πορεύει καὶ πόθεν, ὦ Ἀρίσταρχε;
ΑΡΙΣΤΑΡΧΟΣ ἐξ ἀγορᾶς, ὦ Ἀπολλόδωρε, πορεύομαι οἴκαδε.
ΑΠ.   ἀλλά, ὦ βέλτιστε, δοκεῖς μοι ἀθύμως ᾽ἔχειν. ἔοικας γὰρ βαρέως φέρειν τι.
        εἰπὲ οὖν, τί βουλόμενος ἐν ἀγορᾷ διέτριβες;
ΑΡ.   ἦλθον, ὦ Ἀπολλόδωρε, πρὸς τοὺς ἐξηγητάς.   10
ΑΠ.   τί φῄς; περὶ καθάρσεως, ὡς ἔοικεν, ἢ περὶ ταφῆς πρὸς αὐτοὺς ἦλθες;
ΑΡ.   μάλιστά γε, ὦ φίλε. ὀργιζόμενος γὰρ ἀνθρώπῳ τινὶ ὑβριστῇ, Θεοφήμῳ
        ὀνόματι, δι᾽ ἃ ἐπεποιήκει, οὕτως ἦλθον. οὗτος γὰρ ἠδικήκει με μάλιστα,
        εἰσελθὼν εἰς τὸ χωρίον καὶ ὑβρίζων εἰς τοὺς οἰκείους καὶ δὴ καὶ
        φονεύσας γραῦν τινα, ἀπελευθέραν οὖσαν. ταύτην οὖν τὴν συμφορὰν   15
        ἐνθυμούμενος καὶ τιμωρεῖσθαι βουλόμενος τοῦτον, ὡς τοὺς ἐξηγητὰς
        ἦλθον, διεξελθόντι δέ μοι ἃ ἐπεπόνθη ἐγὼ καὶ Θεόφημος διεπέπρακτο,
        οὐκ ἔφασαν ἐξεῖναι τιμωρεῖσθαι τρόπῳ ᾧ ἐν νῷ εἶχον.

Vocabulary for Section Sixteen A

> **Grammar for 16A–B**
> * The pluperfect 'I had -ed'
> * Imperatives using μή + the aorist subjunctive
> * Verbs of 'fearing': φοβοῦμαι μή + subjunctive
> * Verb-forms in –τέος, expressing necessity

ἀθύμως ἔχ-ω be gloomy,
  disheartened
ἀπελευθέρ-α, ἡ freedwoman
  (1b)
Ἀπολλόδωρ-ος, ὁ Apollodoros
  (2a) *(friend of Aristarkhos)*

Ἀρίσταρχ-ος, ὁ Aristarkhos (2a)
  (whose story is told)
Ἀρίστων, ὁ Ariston (3a) *(father
  of Aristarkhos)*
διεξέρχ-ομαι *(διεξελθ-)* tell, go
  through in detail

διεπέπρακτο (he) had done
  (διαπράττομαι)
ἐνθυμέ-ομαι take to heart
ἐξηγητ-ής, ὁ Adviser (1d)
ἔξω (+gen.) outside
ἔοικ-α seem

ἐπεποιήκει he had done (ποιέω)
ἐπεπόνθη I had suffered (πάσχω)
εὐθύς (+gen.) straight towards
ἠδικήκει (he) had wronged
(ἀδικέω)
Θεόφημ-ος, ὁ Theophemos (2a)
(enemy of Aristarkhos and responsible for the death of a freedwoman)
Ἰλισ-ός, ὁ River Ilisos (2a)
κάθαρσ-ις, ἡ purification (3e)
πύλ-η, ἡ gate (1a)
συμφορ-ά, ἡ disaster, occurrence
(1b)
συντυγχάν-ω (συντυχ-) meet
with (+dat.)

ταφ-ή, ἡ burial (1a)
ὑβριστ-ής, ὁ violent, criminal
character (1d)
ὑπό (+acc.) up under, along
under
φονεύ-ω kill, murder
χωρί-ον, τό farm (2b)

Vocabulary to be learnt
ἀπελεύθερος, ὁ *freedman*
(2a)
ἀπελευθέρᾱ, ἡ *freedwoman*
(1b)
διεξέρχομαι (διεξελθ-) *go
through, relate*
ἔξω (+gen.) *outside*

ἔοικα *seem, resemble*
εὐθύς (+gen.) *straight
towards*
πύλη, ἡ *gate* (1a)
συμφορᾱ̃, ἡ *disaster, mishap,
occurrence (1b)*
συντυγχάνω (συντυχ-) *meet
with (+dat.)*
ὑβριστής, ὁ *violent, criminal
person (1d)*
ὑπό *(+ acc.) under, along under,
up under*
χωρίον, τό *farm; place, space,
region (2b)*

Ritual purification

Faced with the vagaries of climate, disease, etc., Greeks chose to assume that the decisions and actions of divine powers accounted for things beyond human control. So anything abnormal could indicate the intervention of a divinity and might therefore need careful handling. Ritual purification was the key here. It was required for approaches to a deity, especially sacrifice, and a sacrifice could itself purify. So before every meeting of the Athenian ἐκκλησία, a pig was sacrificed and its blood sprinkled to render the place ritually pure. Before a sacrifice, a ceremonial washing of hands was usually all that was needed, together with purification of the place of sacrifice, thenceforth called the κάθαρμα, 'the purified place'. More elaborate ritual purification was needed in certain cases, particularly for murderers who were excluded from sacred ground, and for those who came into contact with murder or with the dead. It might be required after sexual intercourse and childbirth. Some cities set up lists of situations that brought impurity and what actions were required to restore purity, and one particularly full list survives from fourth-century Kyrene. There were also official bodies of people in Athens to whom one could apply for advice. One such body was the ἐξηγηταί in Athens, who were official ministers of Apollo. Some of them were named by the oracle at Delphi for this task, others were elected by the Athenian people from one or two noble families with hereditary authority in such matters (one such family was the Eumolpidai). They advised on such matters as temples, cult procedure, sacrifices, and particularly purification following homicide. See *Text* 17D, l.17, where the ἐξηγηταί recommend purification rather than any further legal action. (*World of Athens*, 3.7, 33)

B

In *World of Athens*: climate 2.5–6.

ΑΠ.   μὴ ἀπορήσῃς, ὦ Ἀρίσταρχε, μηδὲ ἀθυμήσῃς ἔτι. καὶ γὰρ οὐ δεῖ βαρέως
        φέρειν τὰ γεγενημένα οὐδὲ ἀθυμεῖν. οὐ γὰρ ἀθυμητέον ἀλλὰ προθυμητέον.
        ἐξ ἀρχῆς ἄρα σκεπτέον ἡμῖν περὶ τοῦ πράγματος. μὴ οὖν μ᾽ ἀτιμάσῃς, ἀλλὰ
        παντὶ τρόπῳ προσέχων τὸν νοῦν προθυμοῦ τοῦτο, ὅπως σαφέστατά μοι τὸ
        πρᾶγμα διέξει. εἰπὲ οὖν, ὦ βέλτιστε, καὶ μὴ ἀποκρύψῃς μηδέν.   5
ΑΡ.   ἀλλὰ φοβοῦμαι⌐μή σ᾽ ἀπολέσω λέγων. οὐ γὰρ βραχὺς ὁ λόγος.
ΑΠ.   μὴ φοβοῦ⌐μὴ τοῦτο γένηται. σχολὴ γάρ μοί ἐστιν. εἰπὲ οὖν καὶ μὴ
        ἐπίσχῃς.
ΑΡ.   διηγητέον ἄρα μοι πάντα ἐξ ἀρχῆς, ὡς ἔοικε. καὶ δή, ὦ Ἀπολλόδωρε,
        προσήκουσά γέ σοι ἡ ἀκοή. σὺ γὰρ κατήγορος δεινὸς εἶ καὶ ἐπιεικῶς   10
        ἔμπειρος περὶ τὰ δικανικά. τί δέ; ἆρα περίπατον ποιούμενος βούλη
        ἀκούειν, ἢ καθήμενος; πάντως δὲ ἡ ὁδὸς ἡ παρὰ τὸν Ἰλισὸν ἐπιτηδεία
        πορευομένοις καὶ λέγειν καὶ ἀκούειν.
ΑΠ.   πῶς δ᾽ οὔ; οὔπω γὰρ πνῖγός ἐστι τὸ νῦν. ἐγὼ γὰρ μάλιστα ἐπιθυμῶ
        ἀκοῦσαι, ἵνα σοι βοηθήσω ἐν ἀπορίᾳ ὄντι καὶ ἀθυμοῦντι. ὥστε, ἐὰν   15
        βαδίζων ποιῇ τὸν περίπατον καὶ Μέγαράδε, οὐ παύσομαι ἑπόμενός
        σοι, ἵνα τὰ γεγενημένα μάθω. σὺ δὲ λέγε, ἵνα ἀκούσας μετὰ σοῦ
        συμβουλεύσωμαι.
ΑΡ.   πάνυ⌐μὲν⌐οὖν. χάριν⌐γὰρ⌐εἴσομαί σοι, ἐὰν ἀκούῃς.
ΑΠ.   καὶ μὴν κἀγώ σοι, ἐὰν λέγῃς.   20
ΑΡ.   διπλῆ ἂν εἴη ἡ χάρις. ἀλλ᾽ οὖν ἄκουε.

Vocabulary for Section Sixteen B

ἀθυμέ-ω be gloomy,
    disheartened, downhearted
ἀθυμητέον (you) should be
    gloomy
ἀκο-ή, ἡ hearing (1a)
ἀλλ᾽ οὖν well, anyway; however
    that might be
ἀποκρύπτ-ω conceal, hide
βραχ-ύς -εῖα -ύ brief, short
γεγενημένα, τά events
διηγητέον I (dat.) must tell/relate
διπλ-οῦς -ῆ -οῦν double
εἴσομαι fut. of οἶδα
ἐπέχ-ω (ἐπισχ-) hold on, hold
    back
ἐπιεικῶς pretty, fairly
ἐπιθυμέ-ω desire
ἐπιτήδει-ος -α -ον suitable

ἵνα (+subj.) in order that
κάθη-μαι be seated
Μέγαράδε to Megara
μή (+aor. subj.) don't
πάντως in every way, wholly
πάνυ μὲν οὖν certainly
περίπατ-ος, ὁ walk, stroll
    (2a)
πνῖγ-ος, τό midday heat, stifling
    heat (3c)
προθυμέ-ομαι be eager, ready
προθυμητέον (you) should be
    ready (for action)
προσήκ-ων -ουσα -ον fitting for
    (+ dat.)
σκέπτ-ομαι consider
σκεπτέον we (dat.) must
    consider

συμβουλεύ-ομαι debate with,
    take counsel with
σχολ-ή, ἡ leisure (1a)
φοβέ-ομαι μή I am afraid that/
    lest (+ subj.)
χάρις (χαριτ-), ἡ thanks (3a)
χάριν οἶδα feel grateful to
    (+dat.)
ὥστε so that, and so

Vocabulary to be learnt
ἀθῡμέω *be downhearted, gloomy*
ἀκοή, ἡ *hearing (1a)*
ἀλλ᾽ οὖν *well anyway; however
    that may be*
βραχύς εῖα ύ *short, brief*
γεγενημένα, τά *events,
    occurrences (2b)*

ἐπέχω (ἐπισχ-) *hold on, restrain, check*

ἐπιθῡμέω *desire, yearn for (+gen.)*

ἐπιτήδειος ᾱ ον *suitable, useful for*

κάθημαι *be seated*

μή *(+aor. subj.) don't*

πάνυ μὲν οὖν *certainly, of course*

προθῡμέομαι *be ready, eager*

σκέπτομαι *examine, look carefully at*

σχολή, ἡ *leisure (1a)*

φοβέομαι μή *fear that/lest (+ subj.)*

χάριν οἶδα *be grateful to (+ dat.)*

χάρις (χαριτ-), ἡ *thanks, grace (3a)*

Athens: climate and character

Apart from some mountainous areas of the central Peloponnese and Crete, southern Greece enjoys the type of climate called 'Mediterranean': winter rains and summer droughts. In the winter, rainfall is heavy but intermittent, and there are many days when the sky is clear, the sun warm and the breeze cool. In summer there is virtually no rain for two to four months, apart from an occasional thunderstorm or brief mist, and the intense heat of noontime can bring activity to a halt. Particularly in south-eastern Greece, where Athens lies, levels of rainfall vary very significantly from year to year, and more than once a decade rainfall is insufficient to sustain cereal crops. Unlike the cold of northern Europe which invites a private, indoor existence, the Mediterranean climate encouraged an outdoor life. Until modern heavy industrialisation, the atmosphere everywhere had a piercing clarity which sharpened the outline of landscape and buildings, so that even distant landmarks could be seen …

Attica, situated in the driest part of Greece, has rather shallow soils on the hills and mountains. Ancient authors could not agree as to whether it was unusually good (so Xenophon) or unusually bad (so Thucydides) for agriculture. Plato, blaming deluges (evidence for deforestation is very meagre), likened Attica to 'the skeleton of a body wasted by disease; the rich soft soil has all run away, leaving the land nothing but skin and bone' (*Kritias* 111b–c). Despite Plato's gloomy picture, Attica still had a variety of trees: planes, cypresses and elms, and in Athens itself these trees were planted in the ἀγορά.

The plain of Athens is the largest in Attica; it is enclosed to the west, north and east by hills (Aigaleos, Parnes, Pentelikon and Hymettos) but is open to the sea on the south … The plain was watered by two seasonal rivers, destructive in winter, much reduced in summer. These flow close to the Acropolis: the Kephisos on the west rising in Mt Parnes and flowing into the bay of Phaleron, and the Ilisos on the east rising in Mt Hymettos and flowing into the Kephisos … A traveller ('Herakleides') who first saw Athens in the early third century sets the scene: 'He then comes to the city of the Athenians; the road is pleasant; the ground is cultivated all the way, and has a kindly look. The city is all dry, not well-watered; the streets are badly laid out because of their antiquity. The houses are mostly mean; few are commodious. Strangers visiting the city might be struck by sudden doubt, whether this is really the renowned city of the Athenians; but after a little while one might well believe it.' (*World of Athens*, 2.5–6, 12, 26)

Aristarkhos tells how his feud with Theophemos arose. In a time of state crisis, Aristarkhos had been appointed a trierarch, but Theophemos had refused to co-operate with him.

In *World of Athens*: personal enmity 4.14–16; trierach 7.43ff.; *stasis* 4.16; ship's gear 7.44.

βούλομαι οὖν σοι διηγήσασθαι ὅθεν ἐγένετο ἡ ἔχθρα πρὸς Θεόφημον, ἵνα μάθῃς τί
ἐγένετο καὶ γιγνώσκῃς ὅτι οὐ μόνον ἐμὲ ἠδίκησεν, ἀλλὰ καὶ τόν τε δῆμον καὶ τὴν
βουλήν. ἔτυχον γὰρ ἐγὼ τριηραρχῶν, καὶ τριηραρχοῦντα ἔδει με τὰ σκεύη καὶ τὴν
τριήρη παρὰ Θεοφήμου παραλαβεῖν· εὖ γὰρ οἶσθα ὅτι δεῖ τὸν τριηραρχήσαντα, ἐξιούσης
τῆς ἀρχῆς, παραδοῦναι τήν τε τριήρη καὶ τὰ σκεύη τῷ μέλλοντι τριηραρχήσειν, ἵνα καὶ   5
αὐτὸς δύνηται παρασκευάζειν τὴν ναῦν. ἀλλὰ καίπερ δέον τὸν Θεόφημον ἀποδοῦναι
τὰ σκεύη, οὐ παρέλαβον ἐγὼ παρὰ τούτου τῶν σκευῶν οὐδέν. καὶ δὴ καί, ἦν τότε, ὅτε
τριηραρχήσειν ἔμελλον, κίνδυνος μέγας τῇ πόλει διὰ τὴν τῶν συμμάχων στάσιν, ὥστε
ἔδει τοὺς τριηράρχους διὰ τάχους τριήρων βοήθειαν ἀποστέλλειν. ἀλλὰ καίπερ δέον
ἡμᾶς ὡς τάχιστα ἀποστέλλειν τὰς ναῦς, σκεύη ἐν τῷ νεωρίῳ οὐχ ὑπῆρχε ταῖς ναυσίν·   10
οὐ γὰρ ἀπέδωκαν τὰ σκεύη οἱ ὀφείλοντες, ἐν οἷς ἦν Θεόφημος.
   πρὸς δὲ τούτοις, οὐδ' ἐν τῷ Πειραιεῖ ἦν ἄφθονα ὀθόνια καὶ στυππεῖον καὶ σχοινία,
ὥστε οὐκ ἐξῆν πρίασθαι. καὶ οὐκ ἐξὸν πρίασθαι, οὐδὲ τῶν ὀφειλόντων ἀποδόντων,
γράφει Χαιρέδημος ψήφισμα ἵνα ἡμεῖς οἱ καθεστῶτες τριήραρχοι προστάττωμεν
καὶ ἀναγκάζωμεν τοὺς τριηραρχήσαντας ἀποδοῦναι τὰ σκεύη, ὃς ἂν μὴ ἀποδιδῷ.   15
καὶ δὴ ἡμᾶς κελεύει τὸ ψήφισμα κομίζεσθαι τὰ σκεύη τρόπῳ ᾧ ἂν δυνώμεθα, ἵνα
ὡς τάχιστα τὰς ναῦς παρασκευάζωμεν καὶ βοήθειαν ἀποστέλλωμεν.
   πολλὴ οὖν ἦν μοι ἀνάγκη κομίζεσθαι τὰ σκεύη ἵνα τὴν ναῦν παρασκευάζοιμι
καὶ παρασκευάσας ἀποστέλλοιμι ὡς τάχιστα. δέον οὖν με ταῦτα ποιεῖν, Θεοφήμῳ
προσῆλθον ἵνα τὰ σκεύη κομισαίμην.   20

Vocabulary for Section Sixteen C

> **Grammar for 16C**
> * The accusative absolute
> * ὡς + the superlative

ἀποστέλλ-ω send out
ἄφθον-ος -ον unlimited
βοήθει-α, ἡ rescue operation
   (1b)
γράφ-ω propose (a decree)
δέον it being necessary (δεῖ)
διὰ τάχους with all speed
ἐξέρχ-ομαι end, finish
ἐξόν it being possible (ἔξεστι)

ἵνα (+ subj./opt.) in order that, to
κομίζ-ομαι collect
νεώρι-ον, τό dockyard (2b)
ὅθεν from where
ὀθόνι-ον, τό sail-cloth (2b)
παραδίδω-μι (παραδο-) hand
   over
παρασκευάζ-ω equip, prepare
Πειραι-εύς, ὁ Piraeus (3g)

πρίασθαι to buy (aor. inf. of
   ὠνέομαι)
πρός (+ dat.) in addition to
προστάττ-ω (προσταξ-) instruct,
   order
σκεύ-η, τά ship's gear (pl.) (3c)
στάσ-ις, ἡ revolution (3e)
στυππεῖ-ον, τό tow, coarse flax
   (2b)

σύμμαχ-ος, ὁ ally (2a)
σχοινί-ον, τό rope (2b)
τριηραρχέ-ω serve as trierarch
ὑπάρχ-ω be in supply
Χαιρέδημ-ος, ὁ Khairedemos
(2a) *(proposer of a decree
about ship's gear in 357)*
ὡς τάχιστα as quickly as
possible
ὥστε consequently, so that, and
so

Vocabulary to be learnt
βοήθεια, ἡ *help, rescue
operation (1b)*
γράφω *propose (a decree);
write*
δέον *it being necessary*
ἐξόν *it being permitted, possible*
ὅθεν *from where*
παραδίδωμι (παραδο-) *hand
over*
παρασκευάζω *prepare, equip*

πρός *(+dat.) in addition to, near*
σκεύη, τά *ship's gear; gear,
furniture (3c)*
σύμμαχος, ὁ *ally (2a)*
τριηραρχέω *serve as trierarch*
ὠνέομαι (πρια-) *buy*
ὡς *(+sup.) as - as possible*
ὥστε *so that, with the result that,
consequently*

Ship's gear

The city kept meticulous lists of the equipment which each trierarch was supposed to have in order to equip his ship. The following is an excerpt from an inscription detailing such equipment.

ὅσοι τῶν τριηράρχων γεγραμμένοι εἰσὶν ἔχοντες εἰς πλοῦν ἐντελῆ σκεύη κρεμαστὰ ἢ ξύλινα, ὅσοι μὲν κρεμαστά, τάδε ἔχουσιν· ὑποζώματα, ἱστίον, τοπεῖα, ὑπόβλημα, κατάβλημα, παραρύματα λευκά, παραρύματα τρίχινα, σχοινία ὀκτωδάκτυλα ||||, ἑξδάκτυλα ||||, ἀγκύρας σιδηρᾶς ||· ὅσοι δὲ ξύλινα, ἔχουσιν ταρρόν, πηδάλια, κλιμακίδας, ἱστόν, κεραίας, κοντούς.

'All the trierarchs who are listed as having gear complete for their voyage, whether hanging or wooden, have the following: those with hanging gear, swifters, sails, sail-tackle, hypoblema, katablema, canvas side-screens, hair side-screens, 4 heavy ropes of eight fingers, 4 heavy ropes of six fingers, 2 iron anchors: those with wooden gear have a set of oars, steering-oars, ladders, a mast, sail-yards, poles.'

swifters	heavy cables passed around the outside of a ship's hull and made tight, to hold the fabric together
hypoblema ⎫ katablema ⎭	unknown
side-screens	for the protection of the rowers during battle

(From: *Inscriptiones Graecae*, 11, 2, 1627)

Since Theophemos is not at home, Aristarkhos approaches Theophemos' brother Euergos for information about their property.

In *World of Athens: boule* 6.6–22; evidence 6.47; *huperetes* 5.63.

ἀλλὰ ἀπόντος Θεοφήμου καὶ οὐκ ἐξόν μοι ἰδεῖν, προσελθὼν τῷ Εὐέργῳ, τῷ τοῦ
Θεοφήμου ἀδελφῷ, ἀπήτησα τὰ σκεύη καὶ ἐκέλευον αὐτὸν φράσαι Θεοφήμῳ.
ἔστι γὰρ τὸ τῆς βουλῆς ψήφισμα κομίζεσθαι τὰ σκεύη, ὁπόταν οἱ ὀφείλοντες μὴ
ἀποδιδῶσι, τρόπῳ ᾧ ἂν δυνώμεθα. ἐκέλευον μὲν οὖν ἐγώ, καὶ διέλιπον ἡμέρας
τινάς, ἵνα Εὔεργος φράσειε Θεοφήμῳ, Εὔεργος δὲ οὐκ ἀπεδίδου τὰ σκεύη, ἀλλὰ   5
κακά⌐ μ' ⌐ἔλεγεν. παραλαβὼν οὖν μάρτυρας ὡς πλείστους, ἠρόμην αὐτὸν πότερον
κοινὴ εἴη ἡ οὐσία ἢ οὔ, ἐρομένῳ δέ μοι ἀπεκρίνατο Εὔεργος ὅτι κοινὴ οὐκ εἴη ἡ
οὐσία, καὶ χωρὶς οἰκοίη ὁ ἀδελφός.
    πυθόμενος οὖν ἄλλοθεν οὗ οἰκεῖ Θεόφημος, καὶ λαβὼν ὑπηρέτην παρὰ τῆς ἀρχῆς,
ἦλθον ἐπὶ τὴν τοῦ Θεοφήμου οἰκίαν ἵνα αὐτὸν ἴδοιμι.   10

Vocabulary for Section Sixteen D

> **Grammar for 16D**
> * ἵνα or ὅπως + subjunctive or optative

ἀδελφ-ός, ὁ brother (2a)
ἄλλοθεν from elsewhere
ἀπαιτέ-ω demand x (acc.) from
   Υ (acc.)
ἄπειμι be absent
ἀρχ-ή, ἡ board of officials (1a)
διαλείπ-ω (διαλιπ-) leave
Εὔεργ-ος, ὁ Euergos (2a)
   (Theophemos' brother)
ἵνα (+ opt.) in order that, to
κακὰ λέγ-ω curse, insult (+ acc.)
κοιν-ός -ή -όν common, shared
κομίζ-ομαι collect

ὁπόταν whenever
οὗ where (at)
οὐσί-α, ἡ property (1b)
πλεῖστ -ος -η -ον very many,
   most (sup. of πολύς)
φράζ-ω mention, talk
χωρίς separately, apart

Vocabulary to be learnt
ἀδελφός, ὁ brother (2a)
ἀπαιτέω demand X (acc.) from
   Υ (acc.)
ἄπειμι be absent

διαλείπω (διαλιπ-) leave
ἵνα (+subj., opt.) in order to, that
κοινός ή όν common, shared
κομίζομαι collect
ὁπόταν whenever
οὗ where (at)
οὐσίᾱ, ἡ property, wealth (1b)
πλεῖστος η ον very much, most
   (sup. of πολύς)
φράζω utter, mention, talk
χωρίς apart; separately; (prep.)
   apart/ separately from (+gen.)

Witnesses (i)

The orator Isaios emphasises that you must have friends on your side in court: 'You all
know that when we are acting without concealment and need witnesses, we normally
make use of our close relatives and intimate friends as witnesses of such actions; but
for the unforeseen and unexpected, we call on anyone who happens to be present.'
That was why Aristarkhos brought witnesses when he asked whether Euergos shared
the property with Theophemos. Had Euergos done so, Aristarkhos could have tried to
seize some of it against the missing ship's gear. (*World of Athens*, 6.47)

E

Aristarkhos demands the gear from Theophemos.

In *World of Athens*: self-help in law 6.42.

κόψας δὲ τὴν θύραν, ἠρόμην ὅπου εἴη, ἀποκρίνεται δὲ ἡ ἄνθρωπος ὅτι 'οὐκ ἔνδον,
ὅπου ἂν νῦν γε τυγχάνῃ ὤν.' καταλαβὼν οὖν αὐτὸν ἔνδον οὐκ ὄντα, ἐκέλευον τὴν
ἄνθρωπον τὴν ὑπακούσασαν μετελθεῖν αὐτὸν ὅπου ὢν τυγχάνοι. ὡς δ' ἀφικνεῖται
Θεόφημος, μετελθούσης αὐτὸν τῆς ἀνθρώπου, ἀπήτουν αὐτὸν τὸ διάγραμμα τῶν
σκευῶν καὶ ἐδείκνυον τὸ ψήφισμα τῆς βουλῆς, ὃ ἐκέλευέ με κομίζεσθαι τὰ σκεύη   5
τρόπῳ ᾧ δυναίμην. καὶ γὰρ οὐκ ἐγὼ μόνος οὕτως ἔπραξα, ἀλλὰ καὶ ἄλλοι τῶν
τριηράρχων, ὁπότε τις τὰ σκεύη μὴ ἀποδιδοίη.

  ἀλλ' ἐπειδὴ ἐδείχθη τὸ ψήφισμα ἐκείνῳ καὶ ἀπητήθη τὸ διάγραμμα, ὁ Θεόφημος
οὐκ ἀπεδίδου. πρὶν οὖν ἄλλο τι ποιῆσαι, ἐκέλευον τὸν παῖδα καλέσαι τοὺς ἐκ τῆς
ὁδοῦ πολίτας, εἴ τινας ἴδοι, ἵνα μάρτυρές μοι εἶεν τῶν λεχθέντων. καλέσαντος δὲ   10
τοῦ παιδός, καὶ παρόντων μαρτύρων τῶν ὑπ' αὐτοῦ κληθέντων, ἐκέλευον πάλιν ἐγὼ
τὸν Θεόφημον ἢ αὐτὸν ἀκολουθεῖν πρὸς τὴν βουλήν, εἰ μή φησιν ὀφείλειν τὰ σκεύη,
ἢ ἀποδιδόναι τὰ σκεύη. εἰ δὲ μή, ἔλεγον ὅτι ληψοίμην ἐνέχυρα κατά τε τοὺς νόμους
καὶ τὰ ψηφίσματα.

Vocabulary for Section Sixteen E

> **Grammar for 16E**
> - Indefinite clauses in secondary sequence

ἀκολουθέ-ω follow, accompany
δείκνυ-μι (δειξ-) show
διάγραμμα (διαγραμματ-), τό,
  register (3b)
ἐνέχυρ-ον, τό security, pledge
  (2b)

μετέρχ-ομαι (μετελθ-) send for
ὁπότε when (+opt.= whenever)
ὑπακού-ω reply, answer

Vocabulary to be learnt
δείκνῡμι (δειξα-) *show*

ὁπότε *when (+opt.= whenever)*
ὑπακούω *reply, answer; obey*
  (+dat.)

Witnesses (ii)

Aristarkhos took only a slave official with him (16D l.9: presumably one from
the dockyards' board – the 'boy' of 16E l.9) to Theophemos' house. When
Theophemos still refused to deliver the ship's gear, Aristarkhos needed *someone*
to witness his efforts to seize Theophemos' property in reparation (16F). This
was not ideal, as Isaios hints (see 'Witnesses' at 16D), but vital. As Isaios went
on 'When evidence is needed in court, we have to bring as witnesses persons who
were actually present, whoever they are.' Note that Aristarkhos will ascertain that
Theophemos had no wife (16F, l.5): it was not 'done' for non-family males to
intrude uninvited (contrast Theophemos' behaviour at 17A).

Theophemos refuses to comply, and a fight at the house ensues. Worsted, Aristarkhos takes his grievance to the βουλή, who encourage him to bring a (successful) case against Theophemos.

In *World of Athens*: protection of women in law 5.27.

ἐθέλοντος δὲ αὐτοῦ οὐδὲν τούτων ποιεῖν, καίπερ κελευσθέντος ὑπ' ἐμοῦ, ἦγον τὴν ἄνθρωπον ἑστηκυῖαν ἐπὶ τῇ θύρᾳ, τὴν μετελθοῦσαν αὐτόν, ἵνα μάρτυρα ἔχοιμι. καὶ ὁ Θεόφημός με ἀφηρεῖτο αὐτήν, καὶ ἐγὼ τὴν μὲν ἄνθρωπον ἀφῆκα, εἰς δὲ τὴν οἰκίαν εἰσῇα ἵνα ἐνέχυρόν τι λάβοιμι τῶν σκευῶν. ἔτυχε γὰρ ἡ θύρα ἀνεῳγμένη. καὶ πρὶν εἰσιέναι, ἐπεπύσμην ὅτι οὐ γεγαμηκὼς‿εἴη. εἰσιόντος δέ μου, παίει πὺξ τὸ στόμα ὁ   5
Θεόφημος, καὶ ἐγώ, ἐπιμαρτυράμενος τοὺς παρόντας, ἠμυνάμην.

ἐπειδὴ οὖν τὰ ἐνέχυρα ἐλήφθη ὑπὸ Θεοφήμου, καὶ συνεκόπην ἐγώ, ἦλθον εἰς τὴν βουλὴν ἵνα δείξαιμι τὰς πληγὰς καὶ εἴποιμι πάνθ' ἃ πεπονθὼς‿ἦ, κομιζόμενος τὰ σκεύη τῇ πόλει. ἡ δὲ βουλή, ἀγανακτήσασα ἐφ' οἷς ἐπεπόνθη, καὶ ἰδοῦσα ὡς διεκείμην ὑπὸ Θεοφήμου, ἐβούλετο αὐτὸν ἁλῶναι καὶ ζημιωθῆναι. ἐκελεύσθην οὖν   10
ὑπὸ τῆς βουλῆς εἰσαγγέλλειν αὐτὸν ὡς ἀδικοῦντα καὶ διακωλύοντα τὸν ἀπόστολον. ἡγήσατο γὰρ ἡ βουλὴ ὑβρισθῆναι οὐκ ἐμὲ ἀλλ' ἑαυτὴν καὶ τὸν δῆμον καὶ τὸν νόμον. καὶ γὰρ εὖ ᾔδει ἡ βουλὴ ὅτι εἰσαγγελθεὶς ὁ Θεόφημος ἁλώσεται καὶ ζημιωθήσεται. γενομένης τοίνυν τῆς κρίσεως ἐν τῇ βουλῇ, καὶ πυθομένων τῶν βουλευτῶν τὴν πόλιν ὑβρισθεῖσαν καὶ ἀδικηθέντα ἐμέ, ἑάλω ὁ Θεόφημος καὶ ἐζημιώθη. καὶ ἐξὸν   15
ταῖς πεντακοσίαις δραχμαῖς ζημιῶσαι αὐτόν, ἐγώ, καίπερ ἀδικηθείς, μέτριος καὶ ἐπιεικὴς ἐγενόμην καὶ συνεχώρησα πέντε καὶ εἴκοσι δραχμαῖς.

Vocabulary for Section Sixteen F

> **Grammar for 16F**
> - **The perfect optative**
> - ἀλίσκομαι 'I am captured'

ἀγανακτέ-ω be angry
ἀλίσκ-ομαι ([ἑ]αλ-) be convicted, caught (aor. ἑάλων)
ἁλῶναι to be convicted (ἀλίσκομαι)
ἁλώσεται he will be convicted (ἀλίσκομαι)
ἀμύν-ομαι defend oneself
ἀνεῳγμένη open (perf. part. pass. of ἀνοίγνυμι)
ἀπόστολ-ος, ὁ sailing, mission (2a)
ἀφῆ-κα I released (ἀφίημι)

βουλευτ-ής, ὁ member of council (1d)
γεγαμηκὼς εἴη he was married (perf. opt. of γαμέω)
διάκει-μαι be in x (adv.) state
διακωλύ-ω prevent
ἑάλω see ἀλίσκομαι
εἴκοσι twenty (indecl.)
εἰσαγγέλλ-ω (εἰσαγγειλ-) impeach
ἐνέχυρ-ον, τό security, pledge (2b)
ἐπεπόνθη I had suffered (πάσχω)

ἐπεπύσμην I had ascertained (πυνθάνομαι)
ἐπί (+ dat.) at, on
ἐπιεικ-ής -ές fair, moderate
ἐπιμαρτύρ-ομαι call as witnesses
ζημιό-ω fine, punish
κρίσ-ις, ἡ judgment (3e)
μετέρχ-ομαι (μετελθ-) send for
μέτρι-ος -α -ον reasonable, fair
παί-ω strike
πεντακόσι-οι -αι -α five hundred
πέντε five

πεπονθὼς ἦ 'I had suffered'
  (πάσχω)
πληγ-ή, ἡ blow (1a)
πύξ with the fist
στόμα (στοματ-), τό mouth (3b)
συγκόπτ-ω hit, strike (aor. pass.
  συνεκόπ-ην)
συγχωρέ-ω agree with, to (+ dat.)

Vocabulary to be learnt
ἁλίσκομαι (ἁλ-) be caught,
  convicted (aor. ἑάλων)

βουλευτής, ὁ member of council
  (1d)
διακωλῦω prevent
εἴκοσι twenty
εἰσαγγέλλω (εἰσαγγειλα-)
  impeach
ἐνέχυρον, τό security, pledge
  (2b)
ἐπί (+ dat.) at, on; for the
  purpose of
ζημιόω fine, penalise, punish

κρίσις, ἡ judgment, dispute, trial,
  decision (3e)
μετέρχομαι (μετελθ-) send for,
  chase after
μέτριος ᾱ ον fair, moderate
  reasonable
στόμα (στοματ-), τό mouth (3b)
συγχωρέω agree with, to
  (+ dat.); yield to

G

The heat of the day is too much for Apollodoros, who asks for a rest in the shade by the river. Aristarkhos now explains how the tables were turned on him by Theophemos.

ΑΠ.   ἐπιεικὴς δὴ καὶ μέτριος ἐγένου περὶ ὧν ἐπεποιήκει ὁ Θεόφημος, ὦ
       Ἀρίσταρχε. ἀλλὰ τί οὐ παυόμεθα περιπατοῦντες; πνῖγος γὰρ γίγνεται
       νῦν, καὶ ἐὰν πλέον περιπατήσω, εἰς πολλὴν ἀπορίαν καταστήσομαι.
       παυώμεθα οὖν, ἕως ἂν ἐκ τῆς ἀσθενείας συλλέγω ἐμαυτόν.
ΑΡ.   οὕτως οὖν ποιητέον, εἴ σοι δοκεῖ. παυώμεθα οὖν καὶ ἐν ἡσυχίᾳ καθιζώμεθα   5
       παρὰ τὸν Ἰλισόν, ἕως ἂν ἠπιώτερον γένηται τὸ πνῖγος.
ΑΠ.   πρόαγε δή, καὶ σκοπῶμεν ἅμα ὅπου καθιζησόμεθα.
ΑΡ.   ὁρᾷς οὖν ἐκείνην τὴν ὑψηλοτάτην πλάτανον;
ΑΠ.   τί μήν;

Vocabulary for Section Sixteen G

> **Grammar for 16G**
> - 'Jussive' subjunctive
> - ἕως ἄν 'until'

ἐπιεικ-ής -ές fair, moderate
ἤπι-ος -α -ον mild
καθιζώμεθα let us sit

παυώμεθα let us stop
περιπατέ-ω walk, stroll
πλάταν-ος, ἡ plane-tree (2a)

πνῖγ-ος, τό stifling heat (3c)
σκοπῶμεν let us survey, consider
ὑψηλ-ός -ή -όν high, tall

AP.	ἐκεῖ σκιά τ' ἐστὶ καὶ πνεῦμα μέτριον καὶ πόα καθίζεσθαι, ἐὰν βουλώμεθα. 10
	ἐκεῖσε οὖν ἴωμεν, ἵνα καθιζώμεθα ἀναπαυόμενοι.
ΑΠ.	προάγοις ἄν. νὴ τὴν Ἥραν, καλή γε ἡ καταγωγή. νῦν οὖν δεῦρο ἀφικόμενοι
	μένωμεν ἕως ἂν ἐκ τῆς ἀσθενείας συλλέγω ἐμαυτόν.
	ἀλλὰ σύ, ὦ Ἀρίσταρχε, ὡς ἔφης, ἐνίκησας τὴν εἰσαγγελίαν. τί
	οὖν τὰ μετὰ ταῦτα; πῶς πρὸς σὲ διέκειτο ὁ Θεόφημος; κακῶς, ἔμοιγε 15
	δοκεῖ τεκμαιρομένῳ τῇ σῇ ἀθυμίᾳ. τί οὖν οὐ διατελεῖς τὸν λόγον
	διηγούμενος, εἰ μή τί σε κωλύει; ὥς μοι δοκῶ καθέξειν σε ἐνθάδε ἕως ἂν
	εἴπῃς ἅπαντα.
AP.	ἀλλὰ μὴν⌐ οὐδέν ⌐γε κωλύει με διατελεῖν διεξιόντα τὸν λόγον, ἕως ἂν
	λεχθῇ ἅπαντα. ἄκουε οὖν, ἵνα σαφέστερον μάθῃς. 20

ἀθυμί-α, ἡ lack of spirit,
  depression (1b)
ἀλλὰ μήν . . . γε but naturally
ἀναπαύ-ομαι rest, take a
  breather
διάκει-μαι be in x (adv.)
  condition
διατελέ-ω finish, complete
εἰσαγγελί-α, ἡ impeachment
  (1b)
ἐκεῖ there
ἕως ἄν (+subj.) until
Ἥρ-α, ἡ Hera *(1b) (wife of Zeus)*
ἴωμεν let us go
καταγωγ-ή, ἡ place, spot (1a)

κατέχ-ω restrain, hold
μένωμεν let us stay
πλέον (any) more
πνεῦμα (πνευματ-), τό breeze (3a)
πό-α, ἡ grass (1c)
προάγ-ω lead on
σκι-ά, ἡ shade (1b)
συλλέγ-ω gather, collect
τεκμαίρ-ομαι conclude, infer
τί μήν; of course, so what
  follows?

Vocabulary to be learnt
ἀθῡμίᾱ, ἡ *lack of spirit,*
  depression (1b)

διάκειμαι *be in X (adv.) state,*
  mood
εἰσαγγελίᾱ, ἡ *impeachment*
  (1b)
ἐκεῖ *there*
ἐπιεικής ἐς *fair, reasonable,*
  moderate
ἕως ἄν (+ subj.) until
πλέον *more (adv.)*
προάγω *lead on*
συλλέγω *collect, gather*
τεκμαίρομαι *conclude, infer*

H

In *World of Athens*: slave-evidence 6.48; banking 2.23, 5.60, 63.

ἐνενικήκη τοίνυν ἐγὼ τὴν εἰσαγγελίαν, ἀλλὰ τοῦτο, φασίν, ἡ ἀρχὴ τοῦ κακοῦ. ὁ
μὲν γὰρ Θεόφημος, αὐτίκα μάλα ἐνθυμούμενος τὴν καταδίκην καὶ τιμωρεῖσθαι
βουλόμενος, ἔλαχέ μοι δίκην αἰκείας, φάσκων ἐμὲ ἄρξαι τῶν πληγῶν τῶν ἐπὶ
τῇ θύρᾳ. ἐγὼ δ' ἡσύχαζον, οὐ φοβούμενος μὴ καταδικάσειαν ἐμοῦ οἱ δικασταί.
ἥκιστα γὰρ ἡγούμην ἐξελεγχθήσεσθαι, ἀναίτιος ὤν. ὁ δὲ Θεόφημος, ψευδεῖς   5
παρασχόμενος μάρτυρας, Εὔεργον τόν τε ἀδελφὸν καὶ Μνησίβουλον τὸν κηδεστήν,
καὶ ὑποσχόμενος παραδώσειν τὸ σῶμα τῆς ἀνθρώπου τῆς ἐπὶ τῇ θύρᾳ ἑστηκυίας
(ὃ οὐ πεποίηκε), ἐξηπάτησε τοὺς δικαστάς, οἳ ὑπὲρ Θεοφήμου ἐπείσθησαν τὴν
ψῆφον θέσθαι. ἐγὼ οὖν οὕτω ζημιωθείς, οὐ πολλαῖς ἡμέραις ὕστερον προσελθὼν
Θεοφήμῳ ἐκέλευον ἐπὶ τὴν τράπεζαν ἀκολουθοῦντα κομίζεσθαι τὴν καταδίκην. ὁ δὲ   10
Θεόφημος, ἀντὶ τοῦ καταδίκην ἀπολαβεῖν, ἦλθεν ἐπὶ τὸ χωρίον μου.

Vocabulary for Section Sixteen H

> **Grammar for 16H**
> - φοβοῦμαι μή + optative

αἰκεί-α, ἡ assault (1b)
ἀκολουθέ-ω follow
ἀναίτι-ος –ον
innocent
ἀντί (+ gen.) instead of
ἀπολαμβάν-ω (ἀπολαβ-) take
αὐτίκα at once, directly
ἐνθυμέ-ομαι take to heart
ἥκιστα least of all, not
καταδίκ-η, ἡ fine (1a)
κηδεστ-ής, ὁ cousin (1d)
μάλα virtually, quite, very

Μνησίβουλ-ος, ὁ Mnesiboulos
(2a) (*Theophemos' cousin*)
τράπεζ-α, ἡ bank (1c)
ὑπισχνέ-ομαι (ὑποσχ-) promise
(to) (+ fut. inf.)
φοβέ-ομαι μή fear that/lest
(+ opt.)

Vocabulary to be learnt
ἀναίτιος ον *innocent*
ἀντί *(+gen.) instead of, for*
ἀπολαμβάνω (ἀπολαβ-) *take*

ἐνθῡμέομαι *take to heart, be
angry at*
ἥκιστα *least of all, no, not*
καταδίκη, ἡ *fine (1a)*
μάλα *very, quite, virtually
(cf. μᾶλλον, μάλιστα)*
ὑπισχνέομαι (ὑποσχ-) *promise
(to) (+fut. inf.)*
φοβέομαι μή *fear that/lest
(+ opt.)*

Section Seventeen A–E: Private justice: trouble down at the farm

Introduction

Aristarkhos has thus had the tables turned on him by Theophemos. Thanks to false evidence, Theophemos managed to convince the dikasts that Aristarkhos had been responsible for the fight at the house, and has landed him with a substantial fine to pay. Aristarkhos needed time, but set a date for payment. Theophemos refused to wait, but took his own measures to collect the fine.

In *World of Athens*: houses 5.28–9; farming 2.13–17, 5.51–2; sheep 2.16; slavery 5.61ff.; female seclusion 5.25ff.

ἡ αὐλή

ὁ πύργος

ὁ κῆπος

Reconstruction of a country house in Attica

A

Theophemos and his cronies swoop on Aristarkhos' farm.

ὁ οὖν Θεόφημος οὐκ εἴασέ με ἐκτεῖσαι τὰ χρήματα. οὐ γὰρ ἔμεινε ἕως τὰ
χρήματα παρέχοιμι, ἀλλ' ἐλθών μου τὰ πρόβατα λαμβάνει, πεντήκοντα μαλακά,
ποιμαινόμενα ὑπὸ τοῦ ποιμένος. πρὶν οὖν με εἰδέναι τὰ γεγενημένα, λαμβάνεται
ὑπὸ Θεοφήμου οὐ μόνον τὰ πρόβατα ἀλλὰ καὶ πάντα τὰ ἀκόλουθα τῇ ποίμνῃ καὶ ὁ
ποιμὴν μετ' αὐτῶν, ἔπειτα καὶ παῖς διάκονος, ἀποφέρων ὑδρίαν χαλκῆν, παρὰ φίλου   5
τινὸς ᾐτημένην, πολλοῦ ἀξίαν. τούτων δὲ πάντων ληφθέντων, ἐπεισελθόντες

ὑδρία χαλκῆ

Vocabulary for Section Seventeen A

> **Grammar for 17A**
> * ἕως + optative 'until such time as'
> * (ἀφ)ἵημι

ἀκόλουθ-ος -ον accompanying (+dat.)
ἀποφέρ-ω carry back, return
διάκον-ος, ὁ servant (2a)
ἐκτίν-ω (ἐκτεισ-) pay

ἐπεισέρχ-ομαι (ἐπεισελθ-) invade
ἕως (+opt.) until
μαλακ-ός -ή -όν soft-fleeced
πεντήκοντα fifty
ποιμαίν-ω tend

ποιμήν (ποιμεν-), ὁ shepherd (3a)
ποίμν-η, ἡ flock of sheep (1a)
πρόβατ-ον, τό sheep (2b)
ὑδρί-α, ἡ hydria, large vessel (1b)
χαλκ-οῦς -ῆ -οῦν bronze

ὁ Θεόφημος καὶ Εὔεργος εἰς τὸ χωρίον (γεωργῶ δὲ πρὸς τῷ ἱπποδρόμῳ, καὶ οἰκῶ
ἐνταῦθα ἐκ μειρακίου), πρῶτον μὲν ἐπὶ τοὺς οἰκέτας ᾖξαν. ἐπεὶ δὲ οἱ οἰκέται οὐκ
ἔμειναν ἕως ἅλοιεν ἀλλ᾿ ἔφθασαν διαφυγόντες, ἐλθόντες πρὸς τὴν οἰκίαν ἐξέβαλον
τὴν θύραν τὴν εἰς τὸν κῆπον φέρουσαν. ἐκβληθείσης δὲ τῆς θύρας, εἰσελθόντες ἐπὶ   10
τὴν γυναῖκά μου καὶ τὰ παιδία, ἐξεφόρησαν πάντα τὰ σκεύη, ὅσα ἔτι ὑπόλοιπά μοι
ἦν ἐν τῇ οἰκίᾳ, καὶ ᾤχοντο λαβόντες ἃ βούλοιντο.
    πρὸς δὲ τούτοις, πρὶν αὐτοὺς εἰσελθεῖν εἰς τὴν οἰκίαν, ἔτυχεν ἡ γυνή μου
μετὰ τῶν παιδίων ἀριστῶσα ἐν τῇ αὐλῇ, καὶ μετ᾿ αὐτῆς τίτθη τις ἐμὴ γενομένη
πρεσβυτέρα, ἄνθρωπος εὔνους καὶ πιστὴ καὶ ἐλευθέρα ἀφειμένη (ἀφῆκε γὰρ αὐτὴν   15
ὁ πατὴρ ὁ ἐμός. ἐπειδὴ δὲ ἀφείθη ἐλευθέρα ὑπὸ τοῦ πατρὸς τοῦ ἐμοῦ, συνῴκησεν
ἀνδρί. ἀποθανόντος δὲ τοῦ ἀνδρός, ὡς αὐτὴ γραῦς ἦν καὶ οὐδεὶς ἔτρεφεν αὐτήν,
ἐπανῆλθεν ὡς ἐμέ. ἀναγκαῖον οὖν ἦν μοι τρέφειν αὐτήν, τίτθην γενομένην.)
ἀριστώντων δ᾿ αὐτῶν ἐν τῇ αὐλῇ, ὁρμῶνται οὗτοι καὶ καταλαμβάνουσιν αὐτὰς καὶ
ἥρπαζον τὰ σκεύη. τῶν δὲ σκευῶν ὑπ᾿ αὐτῶν ἁρπαζομένων, αἱ ἄλλαι θεράπαιναι (ἐν   20
γὰρ τῷ πύργῳ ἦσαν, οὗπερ διαιτῶνται), ὡς ἤκουσαν κραυγῆς καὶ βοῆς, οὐκ ἐπέσχον
ἕως εἰσέλθοιεν ἐκεῖνοι ἀλλὰ κλείουσι τὸν πύργον πρὶν αὐτοὺς ὁρμᾶσθαι.

ἀναγκαῖ-ος -α -ον necessary
ἀριστά-ω have breakfast
ἁρπάζ-ω seize, plunder
ᾄσσ-ω dart, dash
αὐλ-ή, ἡ courtyard (1a)
ἀφείθη she was let go (aor. pass. of ἀφίημι)
ἀφειμένη let go, released (perf. pass. of ἀφιήμι)
ἀφῆκε (he) let go (aor. of ἀφίημι)
γεωργέ-ω farm
διαιτά-ομαι live
διαφεύγ-ω (διαφυγ-) get away from
ἐκβάλλ-ω (ἐκβαλ-) break open
ἐκφορέ-ω carry off
ᾖξαν see ᾄσσω
θεράπαιν-α, ἡ servant (1c)
ἱππόδρομ-ος, ὁ race-course, downs (2a)
κῆπ-ος, ὁ garden (2a)
κλεί-ω close

κραυγ-ή, ἡ shouting, tumult (1a)
μειράκι-ον, τό youth (2b)
    ἐκ μειρακίου from a young boy
οἴχ-ομαι be off, be gone
ὁρμά-ομαι charge
οὗπερ where
πιστ-ός -ή -όν trustworthy, reliable
πρεσβύτερ-ος -α -ον older, rather old
πρός (+dat.) near; in addition to
πύργ-ος, ὁ tower (2a)
τίτθ-η, ἡ nurse (1a)
ὑπόλοιπ-ος -ον remaining, left over
φέρ-ω lead

Vocabulary to be learnt

ἀναγκαῖος ᾱ ον *necessary*
ἀποφέρω (ἀπενεγκ-) *carry back*
αὐλή, ἡ *courtyard (1a)*
ἀφῑημι (ἀφε-) *release, let go*

διαφεύγω (διαφυγ-) *get away, flee*
ἐκβάλλω (ἐκβαλ-) *break open; throw out*
ἐπεισέρχομαι (ἐπεισελθ-) *attack*
ἕως *(+opt.) until*
θεράπαινα, ἡ *maidservant (1c)*
κλείω *close, shut*
ὁρμάομαι *charge, set off, make a move*
οὗπερ *where*
πιστός ή όν *faithful, trustworthy, reliable*
ποιμήν (ποιμεν-), ὁ *shepherd (3a)*
πρεσβύτερος ᾱ ον *older, rather old*
πρός *(+dat.) near; in addition to*
φέρω (ἐνεγκ-) *lead*
χαλκοῦς ῆ οῦν *bronze (χάλκε-ος)*

B

Despite the intervention of Aristarkhos' wife, the plundering continues, and the old maidservant is badly beaten up. Aristarkhos' neighbours witness the scene.

In *World of Athens*: female rights in the home 5.23–4; the *kurios* 5.11.

ἐνταῦθα μὲν οὖν οὐκ εἰσῆλθον ἐκεῖνοι, τὰ δ' ἐκ τῆς ἄλλης οἰκίας σκεύη ἐξέφερον.
ἀπεῖπε δ' ἡ γυνή, λέγουσα ὅτι αὐτῆς εἴη τὰ σκεύη, ἐν τῇ προικὶ τετιμημένα, καὶ
ὅτι 'ἔχετε τὰ πρόβατα πεντήκοντα καὶ τὸν παῖδα καὶ τὸν ποιμένα, ἃ ἄξιά ἐστι τῆς
καταδίκης. (ἀπήγγειλε γάρ τις τῶν γειτόνων, κόψας τὴν θύραν.) καὶ δὴ καὶ τὸ ἀργύριον
ὑμῖν κεῖται ἐπὶ τῇ τραπέζῃ. (ἠκηκόει γὰρ ἐμοῦ.) μὴ οὖν λάβητε τὰ λοιπὰ σκεύη, πρὶν   5
ἐπανελθεῖν τὸν ἄνδρα τὸ τίμημα ἔχοντα, ἄλλως τε καὶ ἔχοντες ἄξια τῆς καταδίκης.'

ἐκφορεῖ τὰ σκεύη

Vocabulary for Section Seventeen B

> **Grammar for 17B**
> - ἕως + indicative 'while, until'
> - πρὶν ἄν + subjunctive and πρίν + optative 'until'
> - διατίθημι, διάκειμαι

ἄλλως τε καί especially
ἀπαγγέλλ-ω announce, report
ἀπαγορεύ-ω (ἀπειπ-) forbid
ἀπεῖπε *see* ἀπαγορεύ-ω

ἠκηκόει plup. of ἀκούω (3rd s.)
κεῖ-μαι lie
λοιπ-ός -ή -όν left,
    remaining

πεντήκοντα fifty
τιμά-ω value, reckon
τράπεζ-α, ἡ bank (1c)

ἀλλὰ καίπερ ταῦτα λεγούσης τῆς γυναικός, οὐ παύονται πρὶν ἂν λάβωσι
πάνυ πολλά. ἡ δὲ τίτθη, ἐπειδὴ εἶδεν αὐτοὺς ἔνδον ὄντας, λαβοῦσα τὸ κυμβίον
παρακείμενον αὐτῇ, ἐξ οὗ ἔπινεν, ἐνετίθετο εἰς τὸν κόλπον, ἵνα μὴ οὗτοι λάβοιεν.
Θεόφημος δὲ καὶ Εὔεργος, ὁ ἀδελφὸς αὐτοῦ, κατιδόντες αὐτήν, ἀφείλοντο καὶ οὕτω   10
διέθεσαν τὴν γραῦν ὥστε ὕφαιμοι μὲν ἐγένοντο οἱ βραχίονες καὶ οἱ καρποὶ τῶν
χειρῶν αὐτῆς, ἀποστρεφομένης ὑπ' αὐτῶν καὶ ἑλκομένης. καὶ δὴ ἀμυχὰς εἶχεν ἐν
τῷ τραχήλῳ, ἀγχομένη ὑπὸ τούτων, πελιὸν δὲ ἐγένετο τὸ στῆθος. οὕτω δὲ πονηροὶ
ἦσαν ὥστε οὐκ ἐπαύσαντο ἄγχοντες καὶ τύπτοντες τὴν γραῦν, πρὶν πέσοι μὲν αὐτὴ
πρὸς τὴν γῆν, ἐκεῖνοι δὲ ἀφέλοιντο τὸ κυμβίον ἐκ τοῦ κόλπου αὐτῆς.   15

ἀκούοντες δ' οἱ τῶν γειτόνων θεράποντες τῆς τε κραυγῆς καὶ βοῆς, εἶδον τὴν
οἰκίαν τὴν ἐμὴν ὑπ' αὐτῶν πορθουμένην. οἱ μὲν οὖν ἀπὸ τῶν τεγῶν τῶν ἑαυτῶν
ἐκάλουν τοὺς παριόντας, οἱ δέ, εἰς τὴν ἑτέραν ὁδὸν ἐλθόντες καὶ ἰδόντες τὸν
Ἁγνόφιλον παριόντα, ἐκέλευον αὐτὸν παραγενέσθαι. προσελθὼν δ' ὁ Ἁγνόφιλος,
προσκληθεὶς ὑπὸ τοῦ Ἀνθεμίωνος, ὅς ἐστί μοι γείτων, εἰς μὲν τὴν οἰκίαν οὐκ   20
εἰσῆλθεν (οὐ γὰρ παρῆν ὁ τῆς οἰκίας κύριος· παρόντος δὲ τοῦ κυρίου, εἰσῆλθεν
ἄν), ἐν δὲ τῷ χωρίῳ ὢν τῷ τοῦ Ἀνθεμίωνος, ἑώρα τά τε σκεύη ἐκφερόμενα καὶ
Εὔεργον καὶ Θεόφημον ἐξιόντας ἐκ τῆς ἐμῆς οἰκίας. οὐ μόνον τοίνυν λαβόντες μου
τὰ σκεύη ᾤχοντο, ἀλλὰ καὶ τὸν υἱὸν ἦγον ὡς οἰκέτην ὄντα, ἕως Ἑρμογένης, τῶν
γειτόνων τις, ἀπαντήσας αὐτοῖς, εἶπεν ὅτι υἱός μου εἴη.   25

Ἁγνόφιλ-ος, ὁ Hagnophilos (2a)
(*a friend of Aristarkhos*)
ἄγχ-ω throttle, strangle
ἀμυχ-ή, ἡ scratching, tearing
(1a)
Ἀνθεμίων (Ἀνθεμιων-), ὁ
Anthemion (*3a*) (*a neighbour
of Aristarkhos*)
ἀπαντά-ω meet (+dat.)
ἀποστρέφ-ω twist back
βραχίων (βραχιον-), ὁ arm
(3a)
διατίθη-μι (διαθε-) dispose
ἕλκ-ω drag
ἐντίθη-μι (ἐνθε-) insert, put in
Ἑρμογέν-ης, ὁ Hermogenes (3d)
ἑώρα impf. of ὁράω (3rd s.)
ἕως (+ind.) until
θεράπων (θεραποντ-), ὁ servant
(3a)
καρπ-ός, ὁ wrist (2a)
κόλπ-ος, ὁ bosom, lap (2a)
κραυγ-ή, ἡ shout, cry (1a)
κυμβί-ον, τό cup (2b)

οἴχ-ομαι go, depart
παραγίγν-ομαι (παραγεν-) be
present, turn up
παράκει-μαι lie beside (+dat.)
παριόντας part. of παρέρχομαι,
pass by
πελι-ός -ά -όν bruised
πίν-ω (πι-) drink
πορθέ-ω ransack
πρὶν ἄν (+subj.) until
πρίν (+opt.) until
πρόβατ-ον, τό sheep (2b)
προσκαλέ-ω summon (aor. part.
pass. προσκληθείς)
στῆθ-ος, τό chest (3c)
τέγ-ος, τό roof (3c)
τίτθ-η, ἡ nurse (1a)
τράχηλ-ος, ὁ throat (2a)
ὕφαιμ-ος -ον bloody

Vocabulary to be learnt
ἀπαγγέλλω (ἀπαγγειλα-)
announce, report
ἀπαγορεύω (ἀπειπ-) *forbid*

διατίθημι (διαθε-) *dispose, put X
in Y (adv.) state*
ἐντίθημι (ἐνθε-) *place in,
put in*
θεράπων (θεραποντ-), ὁ *servant
(3a)*
κεῖμαι *lie, be placed, be
made*
λοιπός ή όν *left, remaining*
οἴχομαι *be off, depart*
παραγίγνομαι (παραγεν-) *be
present, turn up at (+dat.)*
παράκειμαι *lie beside, be placed
beside (+dat.)*
πεντήκοντα *fifty*
πίνω (πι-) *drink*
πρὶν ἄν (+subj.) *until*
πρίν (+opt.) *until*
πρόβατον, τό *sheep (2b)*
προσκαλέω *summon, call (aor.
part. pass. προσκληθείς)*
τῑμάω *value, reckon; honour*
τίτθη, ἡ *nurse (1a)*
τράπεζα, ἡ *bank; table (1c)*

C

Aristarkhos is informed of what has happened, and orders Theophemos to appear at the bank next day, to receive payment of the fine. Euergos makes a second swoop on the farm.

In *World of Athens*: doctors 5.72–7, 8.12.

ἐπειδὴ τοίνυν μοι ἀπηγγέλθη εἰς Πειραιᾶ τὰ γεγενημένα ὑπὸ τῶν γειτόνων,
ἐλθὼν εἰς ἀγρόν, τούτους μὲν οὐκέτι καταλαβεῖν ἐδυνήθην (οὐ γὰρ ἀφικόμην
πρὶν ἀπῆλθον), ἰδὼν δὲ πάντα τὰ ἐκ τῆς οἰκίας ἐκπεφορημένα καὶ τὴν γραῦν
οὕτω διακειμένην ὥστε περὶ τῆς ψυχῆς κινδυνεύειν, καὶ ἀκούων τῆς γυναικὸς τὰ   5
γενόμενα, σφόδρα ὠργίσθην καὶ προσῆλθον τῷ Θεοφήμῳ τῇ ὑστεραίᾳ ἕωθεν ἐν τῇ
πόλει, μάρτυρας ἔχων. ἐκέλευον δ᾽ αὐτὸν πρῶτον μὲν τὴν καταδίκην ἀπολαμβάνειν
καὶ ἀκολουθεῖν ἐπὶ τὴν τράπεζαν, ἔπειτα τὴν γραῦν θεραπεύειν ἣν συνέκοψαν καὶ
ἰατρὸν εἰσάγειν ὃν βούλοιντο. ταῦτα δέ μου λέγοντος καὶ διαμαρτυρομένου, ὠργίσθη
καὶ κακά ⌜με⌝ πολλὰ ⌢εἶπεν ὁ Θεόφημος. ἔπειτα δ᾽ ὁ μὲν Θεόφημος ἠκολούθει μόλις,   10

τὰ σκεύη

διατριβὰς ἐμποιῶν καὶ φάσκων βούλεσθαι καὶ αὐτὸς παραλαβεῖν μάρτυρας. ὁ δ᾽

Vocabulary for Section Seventeen C

> **Grammar for 17C**
> - ὥστε clauses 'so as to, so that' + indicative and infinitive
> - Numerals

ἀκολουθέ-ω follow,
  accompany
διαμαρτύρ-ομαι beg earnestly
διατριβ-ή, ἡ delay (1a)
ἐδυνήθην aor. of δύναμαι
ἐμποιέ-ω engender, cause
ἔωθεν at dawn

ἰατρ-ός, ὁ doctor (2a)
κακά . . . πολλὰ λέγω curse
  vehemently
κινδυνεύ-ω be in danger, run a
  risk
μόλις scarcely, reluctantly
Πειραι-εύς, ὁ Piraeus (3g)

συγκόπτ-ω beat up (aor. pass.
  συνεκόπην)
σφόδρα very much,
  exceedingly
ὑστεραῖ-ος -α -ον next, of next
  day
ψυχ-ή, ἡ life, soul (1a)

Εὔεργος οὑτοσὶ εὐθὺς ἐκ τῆς πόλεως μεθ' ἑτέρων ὁμοίων αὐτῷ ἦλθεν εἰς ἀγρὸν τὸν
ἐμόν. τὰ δ' ὑπόλοιπα σκεύη, εἴ τινα τῇ προτεραίᾳ ἐν τῷ πύργῳ ἦν καὶ οὐκ ἔτυχεν ἔξω
ὄντα, κατηνέχθη ὑπ' ἐμοῦ διὰ τὴν χρείαν. ἐκβαλὼν δὲ τὴν θύραν ὁ Εὔεργος (ἥνπερ
καὶ τῇ προτεραίᾳ ἐξέβαλον), ᾤχετό μου λαβὼν τὰ σκεύη.

ἐν δὲ τούτῳ, ἐκτίνοντός μου τὸ ἀργύριον τῷ Θεοφήμῳ, χιλίας τριακοσίας δέκα   15
τρεῖς δραχμὰς δύ' ὀβολούς, πολλῶν παρόντων μαρτύρων, καὶ ἀπαιτοῦντος τά τε
πρόβατα καὶ τὰ ἀνδράποδα καὶ τὰ σκεύη τὰ ἡρπασμένα ὑπ' αὐτοῦ, Θεόφημος οὐκ
ἔφη ἀποδώσειν μοι. ταῦτα δ' ἀποκρινομένου αὐτοῦ, μάρτυρας μὲν ἐποιησάμην
τῆς ἀποκρίσεως τοὺς παρόντας, τὴν δὲ δίκην ἐξέτεισα. οὐ γὰρ ἤδη Εὔεργον
εἰσεληλυθότα μου εἰς τὴν οἰκίαν ταύτῃ τῇ ἡμέρᾳ, ἀλλ' αὐτίκα τὴν δίκην ἐξέτεισα.   20
ἀλλ' οὕτως ἐπλεονέκτει ὁ Θεόφημος ὥστε λαβεῖν τὴν δίκην καὶ ἔχειν τὰ πρόβατα καὶ
τὰ ἀνδράποδα καὶ τὰ σκεύη, καὶ αὐτίκα ἐκτετεισμένης τῆς δίκης ἄγγελος ἦλθέ μοι,
λιθοκόπος τις, τὸ πλησίον μνῆμα ἐργαζόμενος, λέγων ὅτι πάλιν οἴχοιτο Εὔεργος, τὰ
ὑπόλοιπα σκεύη ἐκφορήσας ἐκ τῆς οἰκίας.

ἄγγελ-ος, ὁ messenger (2a)
ἀνδράποδ-ον, τό slave (2b)
ἀπόκρισ-ις, ἡ reply (3e)
ἁρπάζ-ω seize, plunder
αὐτίκα at once
δέκα ten
δίκ-η, ἡ fine (1a)
ἐκτίν-ω (ἐκτεισ-) pay
ἐκφορέ-ω carry off
καταφέρ-ω carry down
κατηνέχθη aor. pass. of
　καταφέρω
λιθοκόπ-ος, ὁ stone-mason (2a)
μνῆμα (μνηματ-), τό memorial,
　monument (3b)
ὀβολ-ός, ὁ obol (2a) (one-sixth
　of a drachma)
πλεονεκτέ-ω be greedy
πλησί-ος -α -ον nearby

προτεραῖ-ος -α -ον previous, of
　previous day
τῇ προτεραίᾳ on the previous
　day
πύργ-ος, ὁ tower (2a)
τριακόσι-οι -αι -α three hundred
ὑπόλοιπ-ος -ον remaining, left
τῇ ὑστεραίᾳ on the next day
χίλι-οι -αι -α thousand
χρεί-α, ἡ need, necessity (2b)

Vocabulary to be learnt
ἄγγελος, ὁ messenger (2a)
ἀκολουθέω follow, accompany
ἀπόκρισις, ἡ reply, answer (3e)
ἁρπάζω seize, plunder, snatch
δέκα ten
διατριβή, ἡ delay; pastime;
　discussion; way of life (1a)

δίκη, ἡ fine; case; justice (1a)
ἐκτίνω (ἐκτεισ-) pay
ἐκφορέω carry off
καταφέρω (κατενεγκ-) carry
　down
κινδῡνεύω be in danger, run
　risk, be likely to
πλησίος ᾱ ον nearby
προτεραῖος ᾱ ον previous, of
　previous day
πύργος, ὁ tower (2a)
συγκόπτω beat up, strike (aor.
　pass., συνεκόπην)
σφόδρα very much,
　exceedingly
ὑπόλοιπος ον remaining
ὑστεραῖος ᾱ ον next day
χῑλιοι αι α thousand
ψῡχή, ἡ soul, life (1a)

Grave monuments

Grave reliefs were made in their thousands for the great cemeteries of Athens itself,
the Peiraieus, and the demes of Attica. Imposing funerary enclosures dominated
several of the roads into Athens, the road from the sanctuary to the settlement and
fort at Rhamnous, and no doubt elsewhere. Although many reliefs are conservative
in their iconography, there is a tendency over time for the more elaborate monuments to show ever higher relief and larger groups of figures … high relief was connected with grand monuments, and the greater Athenian tolerance of individual display can be measured both in the way in which some *stelai* 'heroise' the individual
dead person and in the sheer scale of some monuments. (*World of Athens*, 8.102)

D

Despite medical treatmen, the old servant dies. Aristarkhos goes to the Exegetai
to see what action he can take in revenge, but meets with an unsatisfactory
response.

In *World of Athens: exegetai* 3.33; purification 3.33; family and murder 6.42.

τί οὖν ἔδει με ποιεῖν, ὦ Ἀπολλόδωρε, καὶ ποῖ τρέπεσθαι, ἐκπεφορημένων μὲν τῶν
σκευῶν, τῆς δὲ γραὸς περὶ ψυχῆς κινδυνευούσης, ἐκτετεισμένης δὲ τῆς καταδίκης;
ἀλλ' οὖν, εἰ μή τι ἄλλο, ἐπήγγειλα τὸν Θεόφημον θεραπεύειν τὴν ἄνθρωπον ἢ
συνεκόπη καὶ ἰατρὸν εἰσάγειν ὃν βούλοιτο. ἐπειδὴ οὐκ ἐβουλήθη Θεόφημος οὐδ'
ἐδυνήθην ἐγὼ πεῖσαι αὐτόν, εἰσήγαγον ἰατρὸν ᾧ πολλὰ ἔτη ἐχρώμην. χθὲς δέ,   5
ἕκτῃ οὔσῃ ἡμέρᾳ ὕστερον ἢ οὗτοι ὡρμήθησαν εἰς τὴν οἰκίαν, ἐτελεύτησεν ἡ τίτθη.
ἐγὼ οὖν αὐτίκα μὲν ὠργίσθην, πρῷ δ' ἦλθον (ὡς εἴρηκα) ὡς τοὺς ἐξηγητάς, ἵνα
εἰδείην ὅ τι ποιητέον περὶ τούτων, καὶ διηγησάμην αὐτοῖς ἅπαντα τὰ γενόμενα,
τό τε ὁρμηθῆναι αὐτοὺς εἰς τὸ χωρίον καὶ εἰς τοῦτο ἀσελγείας ἐλθεῖν, ὥστε μὴ
αἰσχυνθῆναι ἐπὶ τὴν γυναῖκα καὶ τὰ παιδία εἰσελθεῖν, καὶ τὴν γραῦν συγκόψαι,   10
κυμβίου ἕνεκα, καὶ τὰ σκεύη ἐκφορῆσαι. πρὸς δὲ τούτοις, ἐμνήσθην τὴν εὔνοιαν τῆς
ἀνθρώπου καὶ ὡς διὰ τὸ μὴ ἀφεῖναι τὸ κυμβίον τελευτήσειεν.
   ἀκούσαντες δέ μου οἱ ἐξηγηταὶ ταῦτα, τάδε παρήνεσαν· 'ἐπειδὴ αὐτὸς μὲν
οὐ παρεγένου, ἡ δὲ γυνὴ καὶ τὰ παιδία, ἄλλοι δέ σοι μάρτυρες οὐκ ἐφάνησαν,
εὐλαβήθητι μὴ προαγορεύῃς μηδενὶ ὀνομαστί, μηδὲ πρὸς τὸν βασιλέα δίκην φόνου   15
λάχῃς. οὐ γάρ ἐστιν ἐν γένει σοι ἡ ἄνθρωπος, οὐδὲ θεράπαινα, ἐξ ὧν σὺ λέγεις. ἀλλ'
ὑπὲρ σεαυτοῦ καὶ τῆς οἰκίας ἀφοσιωσάμενος, ὡς ῥᾷστα τὴν συμφορὰν φέρε, ἄλλῃ
δέ, εἴ πῃ βούλει, τιμωροῦ.'

Vocabulary for Section Seventeen D

> Grammar for 17D
> - Aorist passive imperatives
> - Root aorist imperatives
> - Middle verbs which take passive forms in the aorist

αἰσχυνθῆναι aor. inf. of
   αἰσχύνομαι
ἄλλῃ in some other way
ἀσέλγει-α, ἡ disreputable
   behaviour (1b)
αὐτίκα at once
ἀφοσιό-ομαι purify oneself
ἐβουλήθη aor. of βούλομαι
ἐδυνήθην aor. of δύναμαι
εἰ μή τι ἄλλο if nothing else

εἰς τοῦτο (X, gen.) ἔρχομαι
   reach such a pitch of . . .
ἐμνήσθην aor. of μιμνήσκομαι
ἐν γένει σοι related to you
ἐξηγητ-ής, ὁ Adviser (1d)
ἕκτ-ος -η -ον sixth
ἐπαγγέλλ-ω (ἐπαγγειλ-) order
ἔτ-ος, τό year (3c)
εὐλαβέ-ομαι μή take care not to
   (+subj.)

εὐλαβήθητι aor. imper. s. of
   εὐλαβέομαι
ἐφάνησαν aor. of φαίνομαι
ἰατρ-ός, ὁ doctor (2a)
κυμβί-ον, τό cup (2b)
μιμνήσκ-ομαι remember
ὀνομαστί by name
ὁρμηθῆναι aor. of ὁρμάομαι
παραινέ-ω advise
πῃ in any way

προαγορεύ-ω make a public
  denunciation against (+dat.)
πρῷ early
ῥᾷστα most easily (sup. adv. of
  ῥᾴδιος)
τελευτά-ω die
φέρ-ω (ἐνεγκ-) bear, endure
φόν-ος, ὁ murder (2a)
χθές yesterday

ὡρμήθησαν aor. of
  ὁρμάομαι

Vocabulary to be learnt
αὐτίκα at once
ἐπαγγέλλω (ἐπαγγειλα-)
  order
ἔτος, τό year (3c)
ἰᾱτρός, ὁ doctor (2a)

μιμνῄσκομαι (μνησθ-)
  remember, mention
ῥᾷστος η ον *very easy*
τελευτάω *die, end, finish*
φέρω (ἐνεγκ-) *carry; bear,*
  endure; lead
φόνος, ὁ *murder (2a)*
χθές *yesterday*

E

Apollodoros agrees to help Aristarkhos in any way he can.

In *World of Athens*: friends and enemies 4.2–4, 14–16; climate 2.5–6.

ΑΡ.	εἶεν. ἔχεις τὸ πρᾶγμα. τί⌐ οὖν ⌐ποιήσω; ποῖ⌐ τράπωμαι; τί⌐ γένωμαι; οὐ
	γὰρ οἶδα ὅ τι⌐ χρῶμαι⌐ ἐμαυτῷ. οὐ γὰρ δήπου οὕτως ἀνόητός γ' ἂν εἴην
	ὥστε τολμῆσαι ψεύσασθαι πρὸς τοὺς δικαστάς, οὐδ' ἂν εἰ εὖ εἰδείην ὅτι
	αἱρήσοιμι τοὺς ἐχθροὺς ἀδικήσαντας. οὐ γὰρ οὕτω τούτους μισῶ ὡς
	ἐμαυτὸν φιλῶ. ὅρα οὖν τί⌐ δρῶμεν. 5
ΑΠ.	σκοπῶμεν κοινῇ, ὦ 'γαθέ, καὶ μὴ φοβηθῇς μὴ οὐ συμπροθυμῶμαί σοι. καὶ
	γὰρ δεινὸν ἂν εἴη ἀνδρὶ φίλῳ τοῦτό γε, τὸ μὴ ἐθέλειν συμπροθυμεῖσθαι
	τοῖς φίλοις ὅπως τιμωρήσονται τοὺς ἐχθρούς. ὥστε δεῖ με μάλιστα
	πάντων βοηθῆσαί σοι ἐν ἀπορίᾳ ὄντι.
ΑΡ.	καὶ χάριν εἴσομαί σοι, ὦ βέλτιστε, συμπροθυμηθέντι. 10
ΑΠ.	ἀλλὰ ὕστερον ποιώμεθα ταῦτα καὶ ἀναλάβωμεν τὸν λόγον. ὕει γάρ, καὶ
	οὐ κυνὶ μὰ τοὺς θεοὺς νυνὶ πλανητέον. σὺ δέ μοι οὑτωσὶ ποίησον. αὔριον
	ἕωθεν ἀφικοῦ οἴκαδε καὶ μὴ ἄλλως ποιήσῃς, ἵνα βουλευσώμεθα περὶ
	αὐτῶν τούτων.
ΑΡ.	ἐμοὶ ἀρέσκει ἃ σὺ λέγεις, ὦ Ἀπολλόδωρε, καὶ ὁμολογῶ ὡς οὐ ποιητέον 15
	οὐδὲν πρὶν ἂν μετὰ σοῦ συμβουλεύωμαι. ἥξω οὖν παρὰ σὲ αὔριον, ἐὰν
	θεὸς ἐθέλῃ.
ΑΠ.	πράττωμεν ταῦτα. ἴωμεν οὖν.

Vocabulary for Section Seventeen E

Grammar for 17E
- Deliberative subjunctives
- χράομαι
- Correlatives

ἄλλως otherwise
ἀνόητ-ος -ον foolish
βουλεύ-ομαι discuss
ἕωθεν daybreak
κοινῇ together, in common
ὅτι χρῶμαι ἐμαυτῷ; what I am
  to do with myself?
πλανά-ομαι wander, roam about
ποῖ τράπωμαι; where am I to
  turn?

συμβουλεύ-ομαι discuss with
  (+dat.)
συμπροθυμέ -ομαι share
  enthusiasm of (+dat.)
τί γένωμαι; what will become
  of me?
τί δρῶμεν; what are we to do?
τί ποιήσω; what am I to do?
ὕει it is raining

Vocabulary to be learnt
ἄλλως *otherwise; in vain*
ἀνόητος ον *foolish*
βουλεύομαι *discuss, take
  advice*
συμβουλεύομαι *discuss with
  (+dat.)*
συμπροθῡμέομαι *share
  enthusiasm of (+dat.)*

Section Eighteen A–E: How Zeus gave justice to men

Introduction

Whether Aristarkhos was telling the truth or not (and it was probably six of one and half a dozen of the other), the fact was that the actual working of justice could be a slow, messy and unsatisfactory business – slow because of the variety of claims and counter-claims that could be lodged, messy because it was always up to individuals to bring cases, gather evidence, present the case and enforce the verdict, and unsatisfactory because the scanty rules of legal process made dikasts liable to be swayed by purely emotional or personal appeals. Nevertheless, there is no denying that the law was an intensely *personal* concern for a Greek (far more, perhaps, than it is for us with our batteries of solicitors, policemen, barristers and judges) and that the Greeks regarded the laws, by means of which justice was upheld, as the absolute heart and soul of the πόλις. Indeed, Greek citizens actually *made* the laws by their vote in the ἐκκλησία; and, as we have seen, thousands of citizens could be daily involved in the process of law as dikasts. The word νόμος also had much deeper associations for a Greek than 'law' does for us, because it meant much more than statutory law: it meant also 'custom', 'convention', the collected wisdom of the past, the 'accepted inheritance which formed the permanent background of [a Greek's] life' (Dodds).

The following passage is taken from Plato's dialogue *Protagoras*. Socrates has asked Protagoras, the great sophist and thinker, whether it is possible to teach people to be good citizens, a skill that Protagoras himself claimed to teach. Socrates suggests that it is not, for experts are called to advise on subjects that can be taught, like carpentry and ship-building, but on questions of e.g. state policy everyone in the ἐκκλησία has a say – as if expertise on that topic did not exist. Protagoras, with the agreement of his listeners, elects to answer with a μῦθος (myth? story? parable?), which describes the creation of the world and

ὁ Προμηθεύς

the implantation in man of δίκη and αἰδώς (i.e. a sense of right and a moral awareness of others and of their response to one's actions.).

In *World of Athens: nomos-physis* 8.32, 9.7; sophists and civilisation 8.29; myth 3.7–12; speculation 8.7–8.

Note

This text (Plato, *Protagoras* 320D-323A) is unadapted.

There is a very good translation with notes by CCW Taylor, *Plato Protagoras* (Clarendon Plato Series, Oxford 1976).

A

The Creation story, and how Epimetheus, Prometheus' brother, distributed various characteristics and capacities amongst the animals.

ἦν γάρ ποτε χρόνος ὅτε θεοὶ μὲν ἦσαν, θνητὰ δὲ γένη οὐκ ἦν. ἐπειδὴ δὲ καὶ τούτοις χρόνος ἦλθεν εἱμαρμένος γενέσεως, τυποῦσιν αὐτὰ θεοὶ γῆς ἔνδον, ἐκ γῆς καὶ πυρὸς μείξαντες καὶ τῶν ὅσα πυρὶ καὶ γῇ κεράννυται. ἐπειδὴ δ' ἄγειν αὐτὰ πρὸς φῶς ἔμελλον, προσέταξαν Προμηθεῖ καὶ Ἐπιμηθεῖ κοσμῆσαί τε καὶ νεῖμαι δυνάμεις ἑκάστοις, ὡς πρέπει. Προμηθέα δὲ παραιτεῖται Ἐπιμηθεὺς αὐτὸς νεῖμαι, 'νείμαντος   5
δέ μου', ἔφη, 'ἐπίσκεψαι'. καὶ οὕτω πείσας νέμει, νέμων δὲ τοῖς μὲν ἰσχὺν ἄνευ τάχους προσῆπτε, τοὺς δ' ἀσθενεστέρους τάχει ἐκόσμει· τοὺς δ' ὥπλιζε, τοῖς δ' ἄοπλον διδοὺς φύσιν ἄλλην τιν' αὐτοῖς ἐμηχανᾶτο δύναμιν εἰς σωτηρίαν. ἃ μὲν γὰρ αὐτῶν σμικρότητι ἤμπισχε, πτηνὸν φυγὴν ἢ κατάγειον οἴκησιν ἔνεμεν· ἃ δὲ ηὖξε μεγέθει, τῷδε αὐτῷ αὐτὰ ἔσῳζε· καὶ τἆλλα οὕτως ἐπανισῶν ἔνεμε. ταῦτα δὲ ἐμηχανᾶτο,   10
εὐλάβειαν ἔχων μή τι γένος ἀϊστωθείη.

Vocabulary and notes for Section Eighteen A

> **In Grammar for 18A–E**
> - Deliberatives in secondary sequence
> - ἄτε + participle 'as one who'
> - Duals

Notes

1. χρόνος: to be taken with γενέσεως.
2. γῆς ἔνδον: take together. The idea that humans were originally born from the earth was common.
2. ἐκ: to be taken with γῆς καὶ πυρὸς ... καὶ τῶν ('those things'). There was a commonly-held Greek theory that everything was made up of four elements – earth, air, fire and water. Protagoras must have thought that air and water were produced by a mixture of earth and fire.
4. Προμηθεῖ καὶ Ἐπιμηθεῖ: Pro-metheus means 'Fore-sight', Epi-metheus 'After-sight'. As will become apparent, Epimetheus forgets all about man.
5. αὐτός: i.e. by himself.
8. ἄλλην τιν': take with δύναμιν.
8. ἃ ... αὐτῶν: 'which of them', 'those of them which' (obj. of ἤμπισχε); in the main clause, understand 'to them he...'. ἃ δὲ ηὖξε (9–10) works in the same way, and is picked up by αὐτὰ (10).

ἀϊστό-ω destroy
ἀμπίσχ-ω surround, clothe
ἄοπλ-ος -ον unarmed
ἀσθεν-ής -ές weak
αὐξάν-ω (αὐξ-) make grow,
  increase
γένεσ-ις, ἡ birth (3e)
δύναμ-ις, ἡ power, faculty (3e)
εἱμαρμέν-ος -η -ον allotted
ἔνδον (+gen.; take with
  preceding γῆς) inside, within
ἐπανισό-ω put on a par, make
  equal
Ἐπιμηθ-εύς, ὁ Epimetheus (3g)
  ('Aftersight')
ἐπισκοπέ-ομαι (ἐπισκεψ-)
  review
εὐλάβει-α, ἡ care (1b)
ἰσχ-ύς, ἡ strength (3h)
κατάγει-ος -ον under the earth

κεράννυ-μι mix with, compound
  of (+dat.)
κοσμέ-ω equip
μέγεθ-ος, τό size (3c)
μηχανά-ομαι contrive, devise
μίγνυ-μι (μιξ-) mix
νέμ-ω (νειμ-) allot, distribute,
  assign
ὁπλίζ-ω arm
παραιτέ-ομαι beg
πρέπει it is fitting, suitable
Προμηθ-εύς, ὁ Prometheus (3g)
  ('Foresight')
προσάπτ-ω attach, give
προστάττ-ω (προσταξ-) order
  (+dat.)
πτην-ός -ή -όν winged
σμικρότης (σμικροτητ-), ἡ
  smallness (3a)
τάχ-ος, τό speed (3c)

τυπέ-ω fashion, shape
φυγ-ή, ἡ flight (1a)
φῶς (φωτ-), τό light (3b)

Vocabulary to be learnt
ἀσθενής ές weak, ill
γένεσις, ἡ birth (3e)
δύναμις, ἡ power, ability, faculty
  (3e)
ἐπισκοπέομαι (ἐπισκεψα-)
  review
μηχανάομαι devise, contrive
νέμω (νειμα-) distribute, allot,
  assign
παραιτέομαι beg
προστάττω (προσταξα-) order
  (+dat.)
τάχος, τό speed (3c)
φυγή, ἡ flight (1a)

The evolution of man

Considerable interest was taken in the origins of human society. A sort of evolutionary theory was developed: early man, Plato makes Protagoras suggest in this section, found survival difficult because of wild animals, illness, and lack of food, and so on pragmatic grounds was spurred to invent τέχναι ('skills, the results of applied intelligence') like hunting, medicine and agriculture in order to survive. But men were still at risk from other men. So social compacts were formed, giving rise to φιλία ('making common cause with another', cf. φίλος), for example, and πειθώ ('getting someone to acquiesce peacefully'). These utilitarian practices became enshrined in time into a moral code, giving rise to constraints such as αἰδώς ('conscience', 'sense of shame', 'respect for others') and δίκη ('justice, rule of law'). From these beginnings fully civilised societies, characterised by laws, religious observances and democratic practices, were able to develop. The basis of this view of man's development was ultimately utilitarian, and this fact reflects the enlightened self-interest and ethically relativistic view of many sophists, against which Plato and Socrates reacted strongly. (*World of Athens*, 8.29)

Protagoras explained his view of the development of civilization in a μῦθος that he had invented for the purpose. But as the tragedians' highly flexible treatment of the subject-matter of myth makes clear, μῦθος did not mean anything like 'revealed scripture' or 'truth about the gods'. It ranged in meaning over 'myth', 'fiction', 'story', 'parable'. Its antithesis was λόγος, 'rational account'. Observe that, while Protagoras made the gods the 'first cause' of the αἰδώς and δίκη implanted in men, it was up to humans to work out what those imperatives actually meant in practice. Greek gods were not generally felt to impose commandments or moral guidelines on men.

B

Further attributes are distributed.

ἐπειδὴ δὲ αὐτοῖς ἀλληλοφθοριῶν διαφυγὰς ἐπήρκεσε, πρὸς τὰς ἐκ Διὸς ὥρας
εὐμάρειαν ἐμηχανᾶτο ἀμφιεννὺς αὐτὰ πυκναῖς τε θριξὶ καὶ στερεοῖς δέρμασιν,
ἱκανοῖς μὲν ἀμῦναι χειμῶνα, δυνατοῖς δὲ καὶ καύματα, καὶ εἰς εὐνὰς ἰοῦσιν ὅπως
ὑπάρχοι τὰ αὐτὰ ταῦτα στρωμνὴ οἰκεία τε καὶ αὐτοφυὴς ἑκάστῳ· καὶ ὑποδῶν τὰ
μὲν ὁπλαῖς, τὰ δὲ δέρμασι στερεοῖς καὶ ἀναίμοις, τοὐντεῦθεν τροφὰς ἄλλοις ἄλλας   5
ἐξεπόριζε, τοῖς μὲν ἐκ γῆς βοτάνην, ἄλλοις δὲ δένδρων καρπούς, τοῖς δὲ ῥίζας· ἔστι⌐
δ' ⌐οἷς ἔδωκεν εἶναι τροφὴν ζώων ἄλλων βοράν· καὶ τοῖς μὲν ὀλιγογονίαν προσῆψε,
τοῖς δ' ἀναλισκομένοις ὑπὸ τούτων πολυγονίαν, σωτηρίαν τῷ γένει πορίζων.

Vocabulary for Section Eighteen B

Notes

3.   δυνατοῖς: supply ἀμῦναι.
3.   ἰοῦσιν: dat. pl., 'for them [=the beasts] going'.
3–4. καὶ ... ὅπως ὑπάρχοι: and [he contrived] so that there should be'.
4.   τὰ μὲν: referring to animals; take as object of 'he clothed' (understood).
6–7. ἔστι . . . οἷς: 'to some'
7.   εἶναι τροφὴν: 'to be as food' (in apposition to βοράν)

ἀλληλοφθορί-α, ἡ mutual
  destruction (1b)
ἀμύν-ω keep off, withstand
ἀμφιέννυ-μι dress, clothe
ἀναλίσκ-ω kill, consume
ἄναιμ-ος -ον bloodless
αὐτοφυ-ής -ές natural
βορ-ά, ἡ meat (1b)
βοτάν-η, ἡ grass (1a)
δένδρ-ον, τό tree (2b)
δέρμα (δερματ-), τό skin (3b)
διαφυγ-ή, ἡ means of escape
  from (1a)
δυνατ-ός -ή -όν able
ἐκπορίζ-ω supply
ἐπαρκέ-ω provide enough (of)
εὐμάρει-α, ἡ comfort (1b)
εὐν-ή, ἡ bed (1a)
ζῷ-ον, τό animal (2b)
θρίξ (τριχ-), ἡ hair (3a) (dat. pl.
  θριξί)
ἱκαν-ός -ή -όν sufficient (+inf. 'to')
καρπ-ός, ὁ fruit (2a)

καῦμα (καυματ-), τό heat (3b)
οἰκεῖ-ος -α -ον personal
ὀλιγογονί-α, ἡ production of few
  young (1b)
ὁπλ-ή, ἡ hoof (1a)
ὅπως (+opt.)=ἵνα (+opt.)
πολυγονί-α, ἡ fertility (1b)
πορίζ-ω provide, offer
προσάπτ-ω give, attach to (+dat.)
πυκν-ός -ή -όν thick
ῥίζ-α, ἡ root (1c)
στερε-ός -ά -όν hard
στρωμν-ή, ἡ bedding (1a)
τοὐντεῦθεν=τὸ ἐντεῦθεν next
τροφ-ή, ἡ food (1a)
ὑπάρχ-ω serve as, be
ὑποδέ-ω shoe
χειμών (χειμων-), ὁ winter,
  storm (3a)
ὥρα, ἡ season (1b)

Vocabulary to be learnt
ἀμῡ́νω *keep off, withstand*

ἀναλίσκω (ἀνάλωσα-) *spend;*
  use; kill
δένδρον, τό *tree (2b)*
δέρμα (δερματ-), τό *skin (3b)*
διαφυγή, ἡ *flight, means of*
  escape (1a)
δυνατός ή όν *able, possible*
ἐκπορίζω *supply, provide*
ζῷον, τό *animal, creature, living*
  thing (2b)
ἱκανός ή όν *sufficient, capable,*
  able (+inf.)
ὅπως=ἵνα (+subj./opt.) in order
  to
πορίζω *provide, offer*
προσάπτω *give, attach to*
  (+dat.)
στρωμνή, ἡ *bedding (1a)*
τροφή, ἡ *food, nourishment (1a)*
χειμών (χειμων-), ὁ *winter,*
  storm (3a)

C

But when it comes to man, Epimetheus has run out of characteristics to distribute. Prometheus takes a hand.

ἅτε δὴ⌢ οὖν οὐ πάνυ τι σοφὸς ὤν, ὁ Ἐπιμηθεὺς ἔλαθεν αὐτὸν καταναλώσας τὰς δυνάμεις εἰς τὰ ἄλογα· λοιπὸν δὴ ἀκόσμητον ἔτι αὐτῷ ἦν τὸ ἀνθρώπων γένος, καὶ ἠπόρει ὅ τι⌢ χρήσαιτο. ἀποροῦντι δὲ αὐτῷ, ἔρχεται Προμηθεὺς ἐπισκεψόμενος τὴν νομήν, καὶ ὁρᾷ τὰ μὲν ἄλλα ζῷα ἐμμελῶς⌐ πάντων ⌐ἔχοντα, τὸν δὲ ἄνθρωπον γυμνόν τε καὶ ἀνυπόδητον καὶ ἄστρωτον καὶ ἄοπλον· ἤδη δὲ καὶ ἡ εἱμαρμένη   5 ἡμέρα παρῆν, ἐν ᾗ ἔδει καὶ ἄνθρωπον ἐξιέναι ἐκ γῆς εἰς φῶς. ἀπορίᾳ οὖν σχόμενος ὁ Προμηθεὺς ἥντινα σωτηρίαν τῷ ἀνθρώπῳ εὕροι, κλέπτει Ἡφαίστου καὶ Ἀθηνᾶς τὴν ἔντεχνον σοφίαν σὺν πυρί – ἀμήχανον γὰρ ἦν ἄνευ πυρὸς αὐτὴν κτητήν τῳ ἢ χρησίμην γενέσθαι – καὶ οὕτω δὴ δωρεῖται ἀνθρώπῳ. τὴν μὲν οὖν περὶ τὸν βίον σοφίαν ἄνθρωπος ταύτῃ ἔσχεν, τὴν δὲ πολιτικὴν οὐκ εἶχεν· ἦν γὰρ παρὰ τῷ Διί. τῷ   10

Vocabulary for Section Eighteen C

Notes

1. τι: at all (lit. 'in any respect').
2. αὐτῷ: 'by him' - dat. of agent; so too τῳ (8).
8. αὐτὴν κτητήν: f., picking up σοφίαν.
10. πολιτικήν: i.e. σοφίαν.

ἀκόσμητ-ος -ον unprovided for
ἄλογ-ος -ον speechless
ἀμήχανον ἦν it was impossible to (inf.)
ἀνυπόδητ-ος -ον unshod
ἄοπλ-ος -ον unarmed
ἄστρωτ-ος -ον without a bed
γυμν-ός -ή -όν naked
δὴ οὖν but

δωρέ-ω bestow, give as a gift
εἱμαρμέν-ος -η -ον allotted, appointed
ἐμμελῶς ἔχ-ω be well off for (+gen.)
ἔντεχν-ος -ον artistic
καταναλίσκ-ω
κτητ-ός -ή -όν possessed
νομ-ή, ἡ distribution (1a)

ὅ τι χρήσαιτο what he should make of it
πολιτικ-ός -ή -όν political
σύν (+dat.) with, with the help of
ταύτῃ in this way
τῳ=τινι
φῶς (φωτ-), τό light (3b)

An alternative Prometheus story

Protagoras describes how Prometheus brought the blessings of fire to men and was later punished for it by Zeus (p. 220, ll. 15–16). But according to the early poet Hesiod (c. 680 BC), Zeus also punished *men* – by giving them woman. 'And when he had made this lovely, evil thing as the price of fire, he led her to a place where gods and men were gathered, and she showed her delight at the finery which Athene had given her. And immortal gods and mortal men were amazed when they saw how deep was the trap from which there was no escape for men. For from her the whole female sex is descended, a great curse to mortal men with whom they live, no help in accursed poverty but ready enough to share wealth'. Being irrelevant to Protagoras, this feature of the myth was omitted. (Cf. *World of Athens*, 3.11)

δὲ Προμηθεῖ εἰς μὲν τὴν ἀκρόπολιν τὴν τοῦ Διὸς οἴκησιν οὐκέτι ἐνεχώρει εἰσελθεῖν
– πρὸς δὲ καὶ αἱ Διὸς φυλακαὶ φοβεραὶ ἦσαν – εἰς δὲ τὸ τῆς Ἀθηνᾶς καὶ Ἡφαίστου
οἴκημα τὸ κοινόν, ἐν ᾧ ἐφιλοτεχνείτην, λαθὼν εἰσέρχεται, καὶ κλέψας τήν τε
ἔμπυρον τέχνην τὴν τοῦ Ἡφαίστου καὶ τὴν ἄλλην τὴν τῆς Ἀθηνᾶς δίδωσιν
ἀνθρώπῳ, καὶ ἐκ τούτου εὐπορία μὲν ἀνθρώπῳ τοῦ βίου γίγνεται, Προμηθέα δὲ δι'   15
Ἐπιμηθέα ὕστερον, ᾗπερ λέγεται, κλοπῆς δίκη⁀ μετῆλθεν.

10–12.   ἦν … ἦσαν: this explains where 'political wisdom' (i.e. wisdom to do with the formation of a πόλις) resided and why Prometheus could not get it. At εἰς δέ (12) Plato returns to the topic to elaborate on how Prometheus obtained skills/technology and fire for men.

14.   τὴν ἄλλην … Ἀθηνᾶς: presumably spinning, weaving, olive-cultivation and pottery, all closely associated with Athene.

16.   κλοπῆς: presumably this refers to the punishment that was visited by Zeus on Prometheus for helping man: he was nailed to a cliff and a vulture daily pecked out his liver, which re-grew overnight.

Ἀθην-ᾶ, ἡ Athene (1b)
ἀκρόπολ-ις, ἡ acropolis (3e)
τὰ ἄλογα brute beasts
ἀμήχαν-ος -ον impracticable,
    impossible
ἅτε in that, since, seeing that
    (+part.)
δίκη μετέρχεται a charge of x
    (gen.) is brought against y (acc.)
ἐγχωρεῖ it is permitted for x
    (dat.)
ἔμπυρ-ος -ον of fire
εὐπορί-α, ἡ abundance, means
    (1b)
ἐφιλοτεχνείτην the two of them
    practised their skills
ᾗπερ as
Ἥφαιστ-ος, ὁ Hephaistos (2a)
    (god of fire)

(καταναλωσ-) spend lavishly
κλοπ-ή, ἡ theft (1a)
οἴκημα (οἰκηματ-), τό dwelling
    (3b)
πρός (adv.) in addition
σχόμεν-ος -η -ον being in (+dat.)
    (aor. mid. of ἔχω)
φοβερ-ός -ά -όν terrible,
    awe-inspiring
φυλακ-ή, ἡ sentinel, guard (1a)

Vocabulary to be learnt
ἀκόσμητος ον unprovided for
ἀκρόπολις, ἡ acropolis, citadel
    (3e)
ἄλογος ον speechless, without
    reason
ἀμήχανος ον impossible,
    impracticable

ἄοπλος ον unarmed
δωρέω bestow, give as a gift
εἱμαρμένος η ον allotted,
    appointed
εὐπορίᾱ, ἡ abundance, means
    (1b)
κλοπή, ἡ theft (1a)
νόμη, ἡ distribution (1a)
οἴκημα (οἰκηματ-), τό dwelling
    (3b)
πολῑτικός ή όν political
πρός (adv.) in addition
σύν with, together with
    (+dat.)
φοβερός ᾶ όν terrible,
    frightening
φυλακή, ἡ sentinel, guard
    (1a)
φῶς (φωτ-), τό light (3b)

D

Men form communities for protection, but this is not enough.

ἐπειδὴ δὲ ὁ ἄνθρωπος θείας μετέσχε μοίρας, πρῶτον μὲν διὰ τὴν τοῦ θεοῦ
συγγένειαν ζῴων μόνον θεοὺς ἐνόμισε, καὶ ἐπεχείρει βωμούς τε ἱδρύεσθαι καὶ
ἀγάλματα θεῶν· ἔπειτα φωνὴν καὶ ὀνόματα ταχὺ διηρθρώσατο τῇ τέχνῃ, καὶ
οἰκήσεις καὶ ἐσθῆτας καὶ ὑποδέσεις καὶ στρωμνὰς καὶ τὰς ἐκ γῆς τροφὰς ηὕρετο.
οὕτω δὴ παρεσκευασμένοι κατ᾽ ἀρχὰς ἄνθρωποι ᾤκουν σποράδην, πόλεις δὲ   5
οὐκ ἦσαν· ἀπώλλυντο οὖν ὑπὸ τῶν θηρίων διὰ τὸ πανταχῇ αὐτῶν ἀσθενέστεροι
εἶναι, καὶ ἡ δημιουργικὴ τέχνη αὐτοῖς πρὸς μὲν τροφὴν ἱκανὴ βοηθὸς ἦν, πρὸς
δὲ τὸν τῶν θηρίων πόλεμον ἐνδεής – πολιτικὴν γὰρ τέχνην οὔπω εἶχον, ἧς
μέρος πολεμική – ἐζήτουν δὴ ἀθροίζεσθαι καὶ σῴζεσθαι κτίζοντες πόλεις· ὅτ᾽ οὖν
ἀθροισθεῖεν, ἠδίκουν ἀλλήλους ἅτε οὐκ ἔχοντες τὴν πολιτικὴν τέχνην, ὥστε πάλιν   10
σκεδαννύμενοι διεφθείροντο.

Vocabulary for Section Eighteen D

Notes

1. θείας … μοίρας: i.e. the share in/gift of technical skill, till then the preserve
solely of the gods.

2. συγγένειαν: i.e. the relationship with the gods forged by the 'divine' skills
man now possessed.

3. τέχνῃ: it was because of his skills that man was able to invent speech and
words.

9. ἧς μέρος [ἐστί]: one element/aspect of communal life in the πόλις was the
ability to fight a successful war.

10. ἀθροισθεῖεν: note the optative (**300**).

ἄγαλμα (ἀγαλματ-), τό image,
   statue (3b)
ἀθροίζ-ω gather, collect
ἅτε since, seeing that (+part.)
βοηθ-ός, ὁ helper, assistant (2a)
δημιουργικ-ός -ή -όν technical
διαρθρό-ομαι articulate (i.e.
   invent)
ἐνδε-ής -ές insufficient, lacking
ἐπιχειρέ-ω undertake, set to
   work
ἐσθής (ἐσθητ-), ἡ clothes (3a)
θεῖ-ος -α -ον divine
θηρί-ον, τό beast (2b)

ἱδρύ-ομαι erect
κτίζ-ω found
μοῖρ-α, ἡ portion (1b)
μόνον alone among (+gen.)
πανταχῇ in every respect
παρασκευασμένος perf. part.
   pass. of παρασκευάζω
   prepare, equip
πολεμικ-ός -ή -όν military,
   martial
σκεδάννυ-μι scatter
σποράδην scattered, in groups
συγγένει-α, ἡ kinship (1b)
ὑπόδεσ-ις, ἡ shoe (3e)

Vocabulary to be learnt
ἄγαλμα (ἀγαλματ-), τό *image,*
   statue (3b)
ἀθροίζω *gather, collect*
ἅτε *since, seeing that (+part.)*
ἐπιχειρέω *undertake, set to work*
   (+inf.)
ἐσθής (ἐσθητ-), ἡ *clothing*
   (3a)
θεῖος ᾱ ον *divine*
θηρίον, τό *beast (2b)*
πολεμικός ή όν *military, of war,*
   martial
συγγένεια, ἡ *kinship (1b)*

Zeus sends Hermes to ensure that men are all given a share of those moral qualities which are essential for their survival.

Ζεὺς οὖν, δείσας περὶ τῷ γένει ἡμῶν μὴ ἀπόλοιτο πᾶν, Ἑρμῆν πέμπει ἄγοντα
εἰς ἀνθρώπους αἰδῶ τε καὶ δίκην, ἵν' εἶεν πόλεων κόσμοι τε καὶ δεσμοὶ φιλίας
συναγωγοί. ἐρωτᾷ οὖν Ἑρμῆς Δία τίνα οὖν τρόπον δοίη δίκην καὶ αἰδῶ ἀνθρώποις·
'πότερον ὡς αἱ τέχναι νενέμηνται, οὕτω καὶ ταύτας νείμω; νενέμηνται δὲ ὧδε· εἷς
ἔχων ἰατρικὴν πολλοῖς ἱκανὸς ἰδιώταις, καὶ οἱ ἄλλοι δημιουργοί· καὶ δίκην δὴ καὶ   5
αἰδῶ οὕτω θῶ ἐν τοῖς ἀνθρώποις, ἢ ἐπὶ πάντας νείμω;' 'ἐπὶ πάντας', ἔφη ὁ Ζεύς, 'καὶ
πάντες μετεχόντων· οὐ γὰρ ἂν γένοιντο πόλεις, εἰ ὀλίγοι αὐτῶν μετέχοιεν ὥσπερ
ἄλλων τεχνῶν· καὶ νόμον γε θὲς παρ' ἐμοῦ τὸν μὴ δυνάμενον αἰδοῦς καὶ δίκης
μετέχειν κτείνειν ὡς νόσον πόλεως.' οὕτω δή, ὦ Σώκρατες, καὶ διὰ ταῦτα οἵ τε ἄλλοι
καὶ Ἀθηναῖοι, ὅταν μὲν περὶ ἀρετῆς τεκτονικῆς ἢ λόγος ἢ ἄλλης τινὸς δημιουργικῆς,   10
ὀλίγοις οἴονται μετεῖναι συμβουλῆς, καὶ ἐάν τις ἐκτὸς ὢν τῶν ὀλίγων συμβουλεύῃ,
οὐκ ἀνέχονται, ὡς σὺ φής – εἰκότως, ὡς ἐγώ φημι – ὅταν δὲ εἰς συμβουλὴν
πολιτικῆς ἀρετῆς ἴωσιν, ἣν δεῖ διὰ δικαιοσύνης πᾶσαν ἰέναι καὶ σωφροσύνης,
εἰκότως ἅπαντος ἀνδρὸς ἀνέχονται, ὡς παντὶ προσῆκον ταύτης γε μετέχειν τῆς
ἀρετῆς ἢ μὴ εἶναι πόλεις. αὕτη, ὦ Σώκρατες, τούτου αἰτία.   15

Ζεὺς Ἑρμῆν πέμπει

Vocabulary for Section Eighteen E

Notes

Remember that 4thC Athens was a genuine democracy, in which the citizen body meeting in Assembly (ἐκκλησία) every eight days took all the decisions. Protagoras is thinking of the way in which the Assembly made a distinction between the discussion of technical and political (i.e. communal) issues.

4, 6.   νείμω: aorist subj., 'am I to…?' (deliberative: 325); so too θῶ (6).

4–5.   εἷς … δημιουργοί: i.e. expertise was given not to all, but to selected individuals (e.g. doctors) who could use it for the benefit of all.

9–10.   οἵ τε ἄλλοι καί: 'everyone else, including …'.

10.   περί: take after λόγος with ἀρετῆς… and [ἀρετῆς] ἄλλης… .

12.   ὅταν δέ: 'but when'.

13.   ἰέναι: see vocabulary: the subject is ἥν (=συμβουλήν).

14.   προσῆκον: acc. absolute (296).

αἰδ-ώς (-ῶ -οῦς -οῖ), ἡ respect for others
ἀνέχ-ομαι put up with (+gen.)
δείδ-ω (δεισ-) fear
δεσμ-ός, ὁ bond (2a)
δημιουργικ-ός -ή -όν technical
δημιουργ-ός, ὁ expert (2a)
δικαιοσύν-η, ἡ justice (1a)
εἷς μία ἕν (ἑν-) one
ἐκτός (+gen.) outside
ἰατρικ-ός -ή -όν medical
ἰδιώτ-ης, ὁ layman, private citizen (1d)
ἰέναι (to) be conducted, (to) go along
κτείν-ω kill
μέτεστι x (dat.) has a share in y (gen.)
περί (+dat.) about

προσήκει it is fitting for (+dat.)
συμβουλ-ή, ἡ discussion, advice (1a)
συναγωγ-ός -όν uniting, unifying
σωφροσύν-η, ἡ moderation, good sense (1a)
τεκτονικ-ός -ή –όν architectural
φιλία, ἡ friendship (1b)
ὧδε thus, so

Vocabulary to be learnt

αἰδώς, ἡ respect for others (acc. αἰδῶ; gen. αἰδοῦς; dat. αἰδοῖ)
ἀνέχομαι put up with (+gen.)
δεσμός, ὁ bond (2a)
δημιουργικός ή όν technical, of a workman

δημιουργός, ὁ craftsman, workman, expert (2a)
δικαιοσύνη, ἡ justice (1a)
εἷς μία ἕν (ἑν-) one
ἰατρικός ή όν medical, of healing
ἰδιώτης, ὁ layman, private citizen (1d)
κτείνω (κτεινα-) kill
περί (+dat.) about
προσήκει it is fitting (for) (+dat.)
συμβουλή, ἡ discussion, recommendation (1a)
σωφροσύνη, ἡ moderation, good sense (1a)
φιλίᾱ, ἡ friendship (1b)
ὧδε thus, as follows

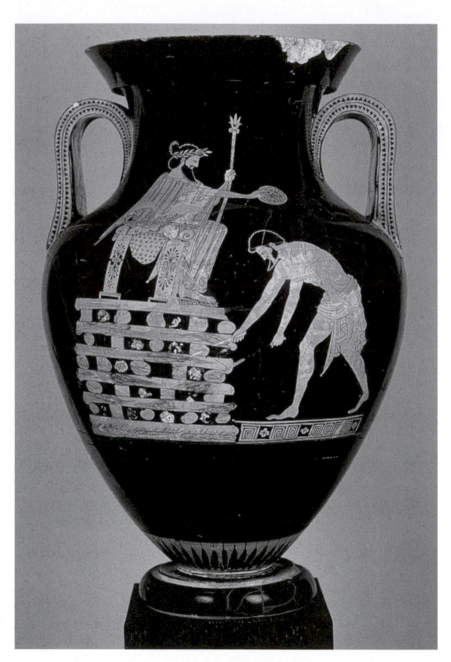

ὁ Κροῖσος ἐπὶ τῆς πυρᾶς

Part Six   Gods, fate and man

Introduction

Section Nine, the story of Adrastos, is taken from Herodotus. All places referred to will be found on the map. Croesus is king of Lydia, whose capital city was Sardis. The story takes place *c*. 590. For the previous 150 years, Asia Minor had seen many different peoples come and go. The Lydians and Phrygians between them now controlled most of the mainland, but the Greeks, through assiduous colonisation, had established a firm foothold on the coastal regions and were (generally) welcomed by the locals. It was through this crucial contact with Near East culture that Greek art, literature and philosophy developed as they did. Croesus was especially well-disposed to the Greeks and had adopted a number of their customs.

Croesus' wealth was legendary (cf. 'as rich as Croesus'). The tale you are about to read, one of the most powerful and tragic in the whole of Herodotus, is just one incident in the saga of Croesus' life which Herodotus uses at the very start of his *Histories* to tell us about the way in which gods deal with men. The 'reason' that Herodotus propounds for Croesus' tragedy will be found in the translation of the episode immediately prior to the Adrastos story (given below) – the visit of the great Athenian politician and law-giver Solon to Croesus' court.

The story of Croesus ends in 546 with the capture of Sardis by the Persians, who swiftly emerged as a major power. Within sixty years (550–490) they had absorbed the empire of the Medes, Babylonia, Egypt, the whole of Asia Minor, and were threatening mainland Greece.

Greek dialect

Greece is a mountainous country, and communication between one πόλις and another could be a difficult business. This geographical fragmentation of the country is reflected not only in the number of small, self-governing πόλεις it contained (e.g. Athens, Sparta, Corinth) but also in the number of dialects spoken. Since the Greeks colonised heavily overseas as well, Greek dialects emerged in places other than the Greek mainland. One such area of heavy colonisation was the Ionian coast (see map) and perhaps the most important literary dialect after Attic – the dialect of Athens and Attica which you have been learning so far – is Ionic, the dialect used for his *Histories* by Herodotus (who came from Halikarnassos) and an important element in the dialect of the Ionian

Homer, though Homer's language is a mixture of a great number of dialects, of all eras and provenances. In the course of reading the story of Adrastos, you will meet the most important features of Ionic dialect which, because Attic and Ionic are quite similar, are mercifully fairly few and easy to recognise. You will find the major features of Ionic dialect summarised for you in the accompanying grammar section.

Note

This text is unadapted, as the rest of the reading in this Course will be from now on. The linking device is now used to indicate word-groups which might be difficult to spot. These are no longer necessarily glossed under the first word of the group in the vocabulary.

Source

Herodotus *Histories* 1.34–45

A good modern edition of Herodotus 1 in English is awaited. GA Sheets, *Herodotus Book 1* (Bryn Mawr 1981) – text and mainly grammatical commentary – is useful.

Time to be taken

Three weeks.

Section Nineteen A–F: The story of Adrastos

Introduction

Solon's visit to Croesus (translated from Herodotus Histories *1.29–33)*

When Sardis was at its most prosperous, all the teachers (σοφισταί) of the Greek world paid a visit, including Solon the Athenian … On arrival, he was entertained by Croesus in the palace, and after three or four days slaves at Croesus' command showed him around the treasury in all its greatness and magnificence. When he had dutifully examined and admired everything as best he could, Croesus asked him, 'Guest from Athens, we have frequently been told of your wisdom and of the sight-seeing journeys you have undertaken all over the world to foster it. Now then, I find myself quite unable to resist asking you if you have ever seen anyone who is the happiest (ὄλβιος) man in the world.' He asked this hoping that he himself was the happiest. Solon did not flatter him, but spoke the plain truth. 'Yes, O King, Tellos the Athenian.' Croesus, astonished at this reply, acidly asked the reason for his judgment. Solon replied, 'First, Tellos' city was prosperous, and he had fine sons, and he saw children born to them all, and all of them survived; second, he was as well off as a man can expect, and his death was glorious. For in a battle between the Athenians and their neighbours in Eleusis, it was he who rescued the situation, routed the enemy and died gloriously. And the Athenians demonstrated the high honour in which they held him by giving him a public funeral on the spot where he fell.'

This tale of Tellos' many blessings (πολλά τε καὶ ὄλβια) aroused Croesus' curiosity, and he asked who was the next happiest man Solon had seen, certain that he was bound to take at least second prize. 'Cleobis and Biton', said Solon, 'two young Argives. They

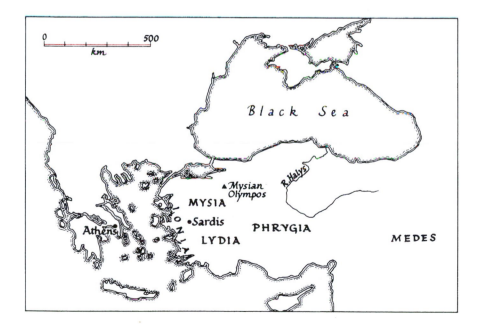

Map of Greece and Asia Minor

had sufficient to live on, and were also endowed with great physical strength. While both carried off prizes in athletics, there is this story in particular which is told of them. It was the Argive festival of Hera, and the young men's mother had to drive an ox-cart to the temple. But the oxen were late in arriving from the fields. So the young men, left no option because of the lack of time, harnessed themselves to the cart and dragged it off, with their mother sitting on it. They pulled it the six miles to the temple and were witnessed by the whole assembly. And then they met a magnificent end (clear proof from the gods how much better it is to die than to live). While men and women crowded round, congratulating the boys on their strength and the mother on her children, their mother, overcome with joy at what they had done and what everyone was saying about them, stood before the statue of Hera and prayed that the goddess would give her sons, Cleobis and Biton, the finest gift (ἄριστον) that man could hope for, in return for the signal honour they had done her. After this prayer the young men sacrificed, feasted and fell asleep in the temple itself – never to wake again. That, then, was how they died, and the Argives made statues of them which they set up in Delphi to mark the recognition of their outstanding excellence (ἀρίστων γενομένων).'

So Solon gave the second prize to these two, but Croesus heatedly said, 'Guest from Athens, does my own happiness (εὐδαιμονίη) count for so little that you cannot rank me even with ordinary mortals?' Solon said, 'My experience is that divinity is characterised by envy at man's prosperity (φθονερός) and by love of upheaval (ταραχώδης) – and do you ask *me* about the lot of man? In the fullness of time, a man must see and experience much which he would rather not. I put it to you that the span of a man's life is 70 years or (counting intercalary months), 26,250 days. Of all those days, none brings the same as the next. Man, then, is entirely a creature of chance (συμφορή). As for you, you seem to me to be very rich and king over many people. But the question you ask me I will not answer yet – that is, until I hear that you have ended your life well (τελευτᾶν καλῶς τὸν αἰῶνα). For the multi-millionaire is no happier than the man who lives from hand to mouth, unless fortune grants that he should end his life well (εὖ), in full possession of every good thing (πάντα καλά). I do not need to tell you that many very rich men are unhappy (ἀνόλβιος), while many of moderate means are blessed with good fortune (εὐτυχής). The rich, but unhappy, man has two advantages over the man who is poor but blessed with good fortune: first, he is more able to fulfil his earthly desires, and second, he is in a better position to ride disaster. But the poor man, who is blessed with good fortune, has the advantage in many more ways. If he is not so able to deal with either material desires or disaster, yet good fortune protects him from these anyway, and he is granted a sound body, excellent health, freedom from trouble, a fine family and good looks. If, on top of all this, he also ends his life well, this will be precisely the man you are looking for, and he really will deserve to be called happy. But until he is dead, hold back: call him "lucky", but not yet "happy".

'No mortal can, of course, have all these things, just as no country will be entirely self-sufficient in what it produces. Different countries specialise in different things, and the best is the one which has most. So with mankind. We are self-sufficient in some things, but not in others; but the man who has the most advantages and holds on to them and dies at peace (εὐχαρίστως), that man, O King, in my view deserves the accolade. It is to the end of all things that mankind must look, to see how they will eventually turn out. God holds out the prospect of happiness to many men, and then utterly uproots them.'

It was out of the question that these sentiments could bring any pleasure to Croesus, so he dismissed Solon as a man of no account, firmly convinced that only a fool could disregard present prosperity and suggest one should look to the end of all things.

(The Greek text takes the story on from here)

A

Croesus has a dream, in which he is told that his son will be killed by a metal spear. He takes measures accordingly.

In *World of Athens: hubris* 4.17; dreams 3.14–16.

μετὰ δὲ Σόλωνα οἰχόμενον, ἔλαβε ἐκ θεοῦ νέμεσις μεγάλη Κροῖσον, ὡς ̄ εἰκάσαι, ὅτι
ἐνόμισε ἑωυτὸν εἶναι ἀνθρώπων ἁπάντων ὀλβιώτατον. αὐτίκα δέ οἱ εὕδοντι ἐπέστη
ὄνειρος, ὅς οἱ τὴν ἀληθείην ἔφαινε τῶν μελλόντων γενέσθαι κακῶν κατὰ τὸν παῖδα.
ἦσαν δὲ τῷ Κροίσῳ δύο παῖδες, τῶν οὕτερος μὲν διέφθαρτο, (ἦν γὰρ δὴ κωφός,) ὁ δὲ
ἕτερος τῶν ἡλίκων μακρῷ τὰ ̄ πάντα πρῶτος· οὔνομα δέ οἱ ἦν Ἄτυς. τοῦτον δὲ ὦν   5
τὸν Ἄτυν σημαίνει τῷ Κροίσῳ ὁ ὄνειρος, ὡς ἀπολέει μιν αἰχμῇ σιδηρέῃ βληθέντα. ὁ
δὲ ἐπείτε ἐξηγέρθη καὶ ἑωυτῷ λόγον ̄ ἔδωκε, καταρρωδήσας τὸν ὄνειρον, ἄγεται μὲν
τῷ παιδὶ γυναῖκα, ἐωθότα δὲ στρατηγέειν μιν τῶν Λυδῶν, οὐδαμῇ ἔτι ἐπὶ τοιοῦτο
πρῆγμα ἐξέπεμπε, ἀκόντια δὲ καὶ δοράτια καὶ τὰ τοιαῦτα πάντα, τοῖσι χρέωνται ἐς
πόλεμον ἄνθρωποι, ἐκ τῶν ἀνδρεώνων ἐκκομίσας, ἐς τοὺς θαλάμους συνένησε, μή   10
τί οἱ κρεμάμενον τῷ παιδὶ ἐμπέσῃ.

Vocabulary for Section Nineteen A

> Grammar for 19A–F
> * Herodotus' dialect
> * Accusative of respect
> * οὐ φημί 'I say that ... not', 'I deny'

Notes

2, 3, 5, 11.	οἱ: see vocabulary. οἱ in this usage is an enclitic. Note its effect on the accent of the preceding words.
5.	μακρῷ: by far.
5.	Ἄτυς: the name recalls ἄτη, 'delusion, punishment, woe'.
5.	ὦν: see vocabulary. Distinguish from ὤν.
6.	ἀπολέει: Croesus is the subject; remember that ἀπόλλυμι can mean 'lose' and 'destroy'.
8.	ἐωθότα ... μιν (=Atys) is the object of ἐξέπεμπε.
9.	τοῖσι: see vocabulary.

ἄγ-ομαι bring in marriage
αἰχμ-ή, ἡ point of a spear (1a)
ἀκόντι-ον, τό javelin (2b)
ἀληθείη=ἀλήθεια
ἀνδρεών (ἀνδρεων-), ὁ men's apartment (3a)
ἀπολέει=ἀπολεῖ (fut. of ἀπόλλυμι)
Ἄτ-υς, ὁ Atys (3e) *(Croesus' healthy son)*
βάλλ-ω (βαλ-) hit, strike (aor. pass. ἐβλήθην)
βληθέντα aor. part. pass. of βάλλω
διέφθαρτο he was disabled (plup. pass. of διαφθείρω)
δοράτι-ον, τό spear (2b)
ἐκκομίζ-ω carry out
ἐξεγείρ-ομαι wake up (aor. ἐξηγέρθην)
ἐπείτε when
εὕδ-ω sleep
ἐφίστα-μαι (ἐπιστα-) stand near (+dat.)
ἐωθώς (ἐωθοτ-) accustomed to (+ inf.)

ἑωυτόν=ἑαυτόν
ἑωυτῷ=ἑαυτῷ
ἧλιξ (ἡλικ-), ὁ comrade, companion (3a)
κατά (+acc.) in relation to, concerning
καταρρωδέ-ω fear
κρέμα-μαι hang over (+dat.)
Κροῖσ-ος, ὁ Croesus (2a) *(king of Lydia)*
κωφός -ή -όν deaf and dumb
λόγον δίδω-μι take counsel with (+dat.)
Λυδ-οί, οἱ the Lydians (2a) *(Croesus' people)*
μιν him, her (acc.) *(goes with* (i) βληθέντα 1.3; (ii) ἐωθότα 1.5)
νέμεσ-ις, ἡ retribution (3e)
οἱ to him, her (dat.) *(goes with* εὕδοντι)
ὄλβι-ος -α -ον happy, blest
ὄνειρ-ος, ὁ dream (2a)
οὐδαμῇ (to) nowhere
οὔνομα=ὄνομα
οὔτερος=ὁ ἕτερος

πρῆγμα=πρᾶγμα
σημαίν-ω tell, announce, point out
σιδηρέ-ος -η -ον iron, metal
Σόλων (Σολων-), ὁ Solon (3a) *(Athenian lawgiver)*
στρατηγέ-ω lead (as commander) (+ gen.)
συννέ-ω pile up
τὰ πάντα in all respects
τοῖσι=οἷς which (relative)
τῶν=ὧν of whom (relative)
χρέωνται=χρῶνται
ὦν=οὖν
ὡς εἰκάσαι to make a reasonable guess

Vocabulary to be learnt
διεφθάρ-μην *I was disabled, ruined (plup. pass. of* διαφθείρω)
μιν *him, her (acc.) (enclitic)*
οἱ *to him, her (dat.) (enclitic)*
ὄνειρος, ὁ *dream (2a)*

Tragic vision

This magnificent story could well have been used by Aristotle in his *Poetics* to define 'tragedy' (instead he used Sophocles' *Oedipus Tyrannus*). Aristotle says that 'plot' is at the heart of tragedy – by which he means, the structure or design of the pattern of events that shape it. It must contain a change of circumstances, from good fortune to bad. The sequence of events must be 'probable or necessary' and the events must arise naturally one from the other; and it must exemplify something universal about human experience. Further, it must evoke 'wonder' and feelings of 'pity and fear'. There will be a change 'from ignorance to knowledge' (ἀναγνώρισις), and a 'reversal' (περιπάτεια), i.e. things will not turn out as expected (so ἀναγνώρισις and περιπάτεια are connected). These will be brought about by the ἁμαρτία of the main character, i.e. an unintentional 'mistake' of some sort – arising out of ignorance or misjudgement – which hardly deserves the dreadful consequences, most dreadful when visited on a φίλος. A strong sense of irony will underlie the whole story. [On all this, see M. Heath, *Aristotle: Poetics*, Penguin 1996]. In *Poetics*, Aristotle was doing with tragedy what he did with the natural world: seeing what was there and trying to draw universal conclusions about it. The story of Croesus fits perfectly into the pattern Aristotle elucidates.

B

Adrastos, a Phrygian of the royal household, arrives at Croesus' palace and begs for purification for having accidentally killed his brother. Croesus welcomes him in.

In *World of Athens*: purification 3.33; *nomos* 8.32; *atimia* 4.12.

ἔχοντος δέ οἱ ἐν χερσὶ τοῦ παιδὸς τὸν γάμον, ἀπικνέεται ἐς τὰς Σάρδις ἀνὴρ συμφορῇ
ἐχόμενος καὶ οὐ καθαρὸς χεῖρας, ἐὼν Φρὺξ μὲν γενεῇ, γένεος δὲ τοῦ βασιληίου.
παρελθὼν δὲ οὗτος ἐς τὰ Κροίσου οἰκία, κατὰ νόμους τοὺς ἐπιχωρίους καθαρσίου
ἐδέετο ἐπικυρῆσαι, Κροῖσος δέ μιν ἐκάθηρε. ἔστι δὲ παραπλησίη ἡ κάθαρσις τοῖσι
Λυδοῖσι καὶ τοῖσι Ἕλλησιν. ἐπείτε δὲ τὰ νομιζόμενα ἐποίησε ὁ Κροῖσος, ἐπυνθάνετο   5
ὁκόθεν τε καὶ τίς εἴη, λέγων τάδε. 'ὦ 'νθρωπε, τίς τε ἐὼν καὶ κόθεν τῆς Φρυγίης
ἥκων, ἐπίστιός μοι ἐγένεο; τίνα τε ἀνδρῶν ἢ γυναικῶν ἐφόνευσας;' ὁ δὲ ἀμείβετο·
'ὦ βασιλεῦ, Γορδίεω μὲν τοῦ Μίδεω εἰμι παῖς, ὀνομάζομαι δὲ Ἄδρηστος, φονεύσας
δὲ ἀδελφεὸν ἐμεωυτοῦ ἀέκων πάρειμι, ἐξεληλαμένος τε ὑπὸ τοῦ πατρὸς καὶ
ἐστερημένος πάντων.' Κροῖσος δέ μιν ἀμείβετο τοισίδε· 'ἀνδρῶν τε φίλων τυγχάνεις   10
ἔκγονος ἐών, καὶ ἐλήλυθας ἐς φίλους, ἔνθα ἀμηχανήσεις χρήματος οὐδενός, μένων
ἐν ‾ἡμετέρου. συμφορὴν δὲ ταύτην ὡς κουφότατα φέρων κερδανέεις πλεῖστον.'

Vocabulary for Section Nineteen B

Notes

1. ἔχοντος … τοῦ παιδός: genitive absolute.
2. γένεος: genitive of description or source.
6. κόθεν τῆς Φρυγίης: 'from where in Phrygia'.
8. Ἄδρηστος: the name hints at ἀ + δράω, 'unable to run/escape'.

ἀδελφεόν = ἀδελφόν
Ἄδρηστ-ος, ὁ Adrastos (2a)
   ('Unable to escape')
ἀέκων = ἄκων
ἀμείβ-ομαι answer, reply
ἀμηχανέ-ω be in need of
   (+ gen.)
ἀπικνέεται = ἀφικνεῖται
βασιλήϊ-ος -η -ον of the king,
   royal
γενε-ή, ἡ birth (1a)
γένεος = γένους (gen. s. of
   γέν-ος, τό family [3c])
Γορδί-ας, ὁ Gordias (gen. s.
   Γορδίεω) (1d)
ἐγένεο = ἐγένου
ἐδέετο = ἐδεῖτο
ἔκγον-ος, ὁ son (2a)

ἐμεωυτοῦ = ἐμαυτοῦ
ἐν ἡμετέρου in our
   house
ἔνθα where (relative)
ἐξελαύν-ω drive out (perf. part.
   pass. ἐξεληλαμέν-ος -η -ον)
ἐπείτε when
ἐπικυρέ-ω receive, partake of
   (+ gen.)
ἐπίστι-ος -ον suppliant
ἐπιχώρι-ος -η -ον of the land,
   native
ἐών = ὤν
καθαίρ-ω (καθηρ-) cleanse,
   purify
καθαρ-ός -ή -όν pure, clean
καθάρσι-ον, τό purification (2b)
κάθαρσ-ις, ἡ purification (3e)

κερδαίν-ω profit (fut. κερδανέω)
κόθεν = πόθεν
κουφ-ός -ή -όν light
Λυδοῖσι = Λυδοῖς
Μίδ-ας, ὁ Midas (gen. s. Μιδέω)
   (1d)
νομίζ-ομαι be accustomed τὰ
   νομιζόμενα the customary
   things (2b)
οἰκί-α, τά palace (2b)
ὀκόθεν = ὁπόθεν from where
ὀνομάζ-ω name, call
παραπλήσι-ος -η -ον similar
Σάρδι-ες, αἱ Sardis (*Croesus'
   capital*)
στερέ-ω deprive of (+ gen.)
   (perf. part. pass. ἐστερημέν-ος
   -η -ον)

συμφορῇ = συμφορᾷ
συμφορήν = συμφοράν
τοῖσι = τοῖς
φονεύ-ω kill, murder
Φρυγι-ή, ἡ Phrygia (1a)
Φρύξ (Φρυγ-), ὁ Phrygian (3a)
χεῖρας in respect of his hands
χρῆμα (χρηματ-), τό thing
   (3b)

Vocabulary to be learnt
ἀέκων = ἄκων
ἐμεωυτόν = ἐμαυτόν
ἐν (+gen.) in the house of
ἐών = ὤν
ἑωυτόν = ἑαυτόν
ἐπείτε when, since
Dropping of aspirates in
   some verb compounds, e.g.
   ἀφικνέομαι = ἀπικνέομαι

νομίζομαι be accustomed
ὁπόθεν (ὁκόθεν) from where
οὔνομα = ὄνομα
στερέω deprive of (+gen.) (perf.
   part. pass. ἐστερημένος)
τοῖσι = τοῖς
χρῆμα (χρηματ-), τό thing (3b)

*News is brought of a wild boar which is causing havoc in Mysia. The Mysians
beg Croesus to send an expedition to kill it, and Croesus agrees.*

ὁ μὲν δὴ δίαιταν εἶχε ἐν Κροίσου, ἐν δὲ τῷ αὐτῷ χρόνῳ τούτῳ, ἐν τῷ Μυσίῳ Ὀλύμπῳ,
ὑὸς χρῆμα γίνεται μέγα· ὁρμώμενος δὲ οὗτος ἐκ τοῦ ὄρεος τούτου, τὰ τῶν Μυσῶν
ἔργα διαφθείρεσκε, πολλάκις δὲ οἱ Μυσοὶ ἐπ᾽ αὐτὸν ἐξελθόντες ποιέεσκον μὲν κακὸν
οὐδέν, ἔπασχον δὲ πρὸς αὐτοῦ. τέλος δέ, ἀπικόμενοι παρὰ τὸν Κροῖσον, τῶν Μυσῶν
ἄγγελοι ἔλεγον τάδε. ʼὦ βασιλεῦ, ὑὸς χρῆμα μέγιστον ἀνεφάνη ἡμῖν ἐν τῇ χώρῃ, ὃς   5
τὰ ἔργα διαφθείρει, τοῦτον προθυμεόμενοι ἑλεῖν οὐ δυνάμεθα. νῦν ὦν προσδεόμεθά
σευ τὸν παῖδα καὶ λογάδας νεηνίας καὶ κύνας συμπέμψαι ἡμῖν, ὡς ἄν μιν ἐξέλωμεν ἐκ
τῆς χώρης.ʼ οἱ μὲν δὴ τούτων ἐδέοντο, Κροῖσος δέ, μνημονεύων τοῦ ὀνείρου τὰ ἔπεα,
ἔλεγέ σφι τάδε· ʼπαιδὸς μὲν πέρι τοῦ ἐμοῦ, μὴ μνησθῆτε ἔτι· οὐ γὰρ ἄν ὑμῖν

Vocabulary for Section Nineteen C

Notes

7. συμπέμψαι: infinitive after προσδεόμεθα (6).

ἀναφαίν-ομαι (ἀναφαν-) appear
γίνεται = γίγνεται
δίαιτ-α, ἡ dwelling (1c)
διαφθείρεσκε = διέφθειρε
   (the -εσκ- suffix implies
   continuation, repetition)
ἐξαιρέ-ω (ἐξελ-) remove
ἔπ-ος, τό word (3c) (uncontr. pl.
   ἔπεα)
ἔργ-ον, τό result of work (i.e.
   tilled field) (2b)

Μύσι-ος -η -ον in Mysia
Μυσ-ός, ὁ a Mysian (2a)
Ὄλυμπ-ος, ὁ Mt Olympos
   (2a)
ὄρεος= ὄρους (gen. s. of ὄρος, τό
   mountain [3c])
ποιέεσκον = ἐποίουν (the
   -εσκ- suffix implies continuation,
   repetition)
προθυμεόμενοι =
πρός (+ gen.) at the hands of

προσδέ-ομαι beg x (gen.) for Y
   (acc.)
σευ = σου
συμπέμπ-ω send with (+ dat.)
σφι to them (dat.)
ὑὸς χρῆμα μέγα/μέγιστον huge
   monster of a boar
ὦν = οὖν
ὡς ἄν (+ subj.) so that, in order
   that

συμπέμψαιμι· νεόγαμός τε γάρ ἐστι καὶ ταῦτά οἱ νῦν μέλει. Λυδῶν μέντοι λογάδας καὶ   10
τὸ κυνηγέσιον πᾶν συμπέμψω, καὶ διακελεύσομαι τοῖσι ἰοῦσι εἶναι ὡς προθυμοτάτοισι
συνεξελεῖν ὑμῖν τὸ θηρίον ἐκ τῆς χώρης.' ταῦτα ἀμείψατο.

ἀμείβ-ομαι reply
διακελεύ-ομαι exhort, direct
    (+ dat.)
ἰοῦσι dat. pl. m. of ἰών (part. of
    ἔρχομαι)
κυνηγέσι-ον, τό dog-pack (2b)
λογάς (λογαδ-), ὁ picked, chosen
    (man) (3a)
νεηνί-ης, ὁ = νεανίας
νεόγαμ-ος -ον newly married

προθυμούμενοι
συνεξαιρέ-ω (συνεξελ-) join x
    (dat.) in destroying
ὗς, ὁ boar (3h)
χώρ-η, ἡ country (1a)

Vocabulary to be learnt
γίνομαι=γίγνομαι
ἔπος, τό word (3c) (uncontr. pl.
    ἔπεα)

νεηνίης = νεᾱνίᾱς
συμπέμπω send with (+dat.)
χώρη, ἡ land (1a)
ὦν= οὖν so, therefore
Note uncontracted -ε- in ὄρεος
    (= ὄρους), προθῡμεόμενοι
    (προθῡμούμενοι) etc.
Note η for ᾱ in e.g., χώρη
    (= χώρᾱ), συμφορή (συμφορᾷ)
    etc.

D

Croesus' son begs to be allowed to join the expedition.

In *World of Athens*: public eye 4.5–7; envy 4.9–11; persuasion and psychology 8.56ff.

ἀποχρεωμένων δὲ τούτοισι τῶν Μυσῶν, ἐπεσέρχεται ὁ τοῦ Κροίσου παῖς, ἀκηκοὼς
τῶν ἐδέοντο οἱ Μυσοί. οὐ φαμένου δὲ τοῦ Κροίσου τόν γε παῖδά σφι συμπέμψειν,
λέγει πρὸς αὐτὸν ὁ νεηνίης τάδε· 'ὦ πάτερ, τὰ κάλλιστα πρότερόν κοτε καὶ
γενναιότατα ἡμῖν ἦν ἔς τε πολέμους καὶ ἐς ἄγρας φοιτέοντας εὐδοκιμέειν. νῦν
δὲ ἀμφοτέρων με τούτων ἀποκληίσας ἔχεις, οὔτε τινὰ δειλίην μοι παριδὼν οὔτε   5
ἀθυμίην. νῦν τε τέοισί με χρὴ ὄμμασι ἔς τε ἀγορὴν καὶ ἐξ ἀγορῆς φοιτέοντα
φαίνεσθαι; κοῖος μέν τις τοῖσι πολιήτῃσι δόξω εἶναι, κοῖος δέ τις τῇ νεογάμῳ
γυναικί; κοίῳ δὲ ἐκείνη δόξει ἀνδρὶ συνοικέειν; ἐμὲ ὦν σὺ ἢ μέθες ἰέναι ἐπὶ τὴν
θήρην, ἢ λόγῳ ἀνάπεισον ὅκως μοι ἀμείνω ἐστὶ ταῦτα οὕτω ποιεόμενα.' ἀμείβεται
Κροῖσος τοισίδε· 'ὦ παῖ, οὔτε δειλίην οὔτε ἄλλο οὐδὲν ἄχαρι παριδών τοι ποιέω   10
ταῦτα, ἀλλά μοι ὄψις ὀνείρου, ἐν τῷ ὕπνῳ ἐπιστᾶσα, ἔφη σε ὀλιγοχρόνιον ἔσεσθαι·
ὑπὸ γὰρ αἰχμῆς σιδηρέης ἀπολέεσθαι. πρὸς ὦν τὴν ὄψιν ταύτην, τόν τε γάμον τοι
τοῦτον ἔσπευσα, καὶ ἐπὶ τὰ παραλαμβανόμενα οὐκ ἀποπέμπω, φυλακὴν ἔχων, εἴ
κως δυναίμην ἐπὶ τῆς ἐμῆς σε ζόης διακλέψαι. εἷς γάρ μοι μοῦνος τυγχάνεις ἐὼν
παῖς· τὸν γὰρ δὴ ἕτερον διεφθαρμένον τὴν ἀκοὴν οὐκ εἶναί μοι λογίζομαι.' ἀμείβεται   15
ὁ νεηνίης τοισίδε· 'συγγνώμη μέν, ὦ πάτερ, τοι, ἰδόντι γε ὄψιν τοιαύτην, περὶ ἐμὲ
φυλακὴν ἔχειν· τὸ δὲ οὐ μανθάνεις, ἀλλὰ λέληθέ σε τὸ ὄνειρον, ἐμέ τοι δίκαιόν ἐστι
φράζειν. φῂς τοι τὸ ὄνειρον ὑπὸ αἰχμῆς σιδηρέης φάναι ἐμὲ τελευτήσειν·

Vocabulary for Section Nineteen D

Notes

2.   τῶν: see vocabulary.

2.   οὐ … συμπέμψειν: '[with] Croesus saying that he would not send …'.

3–4. τὰ κάλλιστα … καὶ γενναιότατα ἡμῖν ἦν: 'It was the best and noblest [thing] for us that …' + acc. and inf.

5.   ἀποκληίσας ἔχεις: take together as a perfect.

6.   φαίνεσθαι: 'to be seen/looked at' after με χρή. Atys is worried about how people will look at him.

8.   κοίῳ: with ἀνδρί, after συνοικέειν.

9.   ἀμείνω: complement to ταῦτα οὕτω ποιεόμενα (subject).

12.   ἀπολέεσθαι: '[it said that you] would be killed'.

13.   τὰ παραλαμβόμενα: take as a noun, 'the matter in hand'.

14.   ἐπί: see vocabulary. With τῆς ἐμῆς ζόης it = 'while I am still alive'.

15.   τὴν ἀκοήν: acc. of respect.

16.   τοι: see vocabulary, and take with ἰδόντι. Understand ἐστί with συγγνώμη.

17.   τό: see vocabulary.

17–18. δίκαιόν ἐστι: 'it is right for (acc.)'.

ἄγρ-η, ἡ hunt (1a)
αἰχμ-ή, ἡ spear-point (1a)
ἀμείβ-ομαι reply, answer
ἀποκληΐ-ω shut x (acc.) off from Υ (gen.)
ἀποχρέ-ομαι be content with (+ dat.)
ἄχαρις ἄχαρι (ἀχαριτ-) disagreeable
δειλί-η, ἡ cowardice
διακλέπτ-ω steal (i.e. snatch from the jaws of death)
ἐπί (+ gen.) in the time of
εὐδοκιμέ-ω win a glorious reputation

ἐφίστα-μαι (ἐπιστα-) stand by (+dat.)
ζό-η, ἡ life (1a)
θήρ-η, ἡ hunt (1a)
κοῖος=ποῖος
κως=πως
μεθ-/μετ-ίημι allow; let go
μοῦνος=μόνος
νεόγαμ-ος -ον newly wed
ὅκως=ὅπως
ὀλιγοχρόνι-ος -ον short-lived
ὄμμα (ὀμματ-), τό eye (3b)
ὄνειρ-ον, τό dream (2b)
ὄψ-ις, ἡ sight, vision (3e)
παραλαμβάν-ω undertake

παρορά-ω (παριδ-) notice x (acc.) in Υ (dat.)
πολιήτησι=πολίταις
σιδηρέ-ος -η -ον metal, iron
σφι to them (dat.)
τέοισι=τίσι with what (goes with ὄμμασι)
το (l. 17) this
τοι=σοι
τῶν=ὧν what (relative)
φοιτέ-ω go
φοιτέοντας (understand e.g. ἄνδρας, i.e. 'that men should go …')
φυλακὴν ἔχω take care

ὑὸς δὲ κοῖαι μέν εἰσι χεῖρες, κοίη δὲ αἰχμὴ σιδηρέη, τὴν σὺ φοβέαι; εἰ μὲν γὰρ ὑπὸ
ὀδόντος τοι εἶπε τελευτήσειν με, ἢ ἄλλου τευ ὅ τι τούτῳ οἶκε, χρῆν δή σε ποιέειν τὰ   20
ποιέεις· νῦν δὲ ὑπὸ αἰχμῆς. ἐπείτε ὦν οὐ πρὸς ἄνδρας ἡμῖν γίνεται ἡ μάχη, μέθες με.'
ἀμείβεται Κροῖσος· 'ὦ παῖ, ἔστι τῇ με νικᾷς, γνώμην ἀποφαίνων περὶ τοῦ ἐνυπνίου·
ὡς ὦν νενικημένος ὑπὸ σέο, μεταγινώσκω, μετίημί τέ σε ἰέναι ἐπὶ τὴν ἄγρην.'

---

19.   τήν: see vocabulary.
20.   τά: see vocabulary.

ἄγρ-η, ἡ hunt (1a)
αἰχμ-ή, ἡ spear-point (1a)
ἀμείβ-ομαι reply, answer
ἐνύπνι-ον, τό dream (2b)
ἔστι τῇ it is the case that
κοῖος=ποῖος
κοτε=ποτε
μεθ-/μετ-ίημι allow; let go
μεταγινώσκ-ω change one's
   mind
ὀδούς (ὀδοντ-), ὁ tusk (3a)
οἶκε=ἔοικε resemble, be like
   (+ dat.)
πρός (+ acc.) with a mind
   to
σέο/σευ=σοῦ
σιδηρέ-ος -η -ον metal, iron
τά=ἅ what (relative)

τευ=τινος
τήν=ἥν which (relative)
τοι=σοι
ὕπν-ος, ὁ sleep (2a)
ὗς, ὁ boar (3h)
φοβέαι=φοβῇ
χρῆν past of χρή

Vocabulary to be learnt
αἰχμή, ἡ *spear-point (1a)*
ἀμείβομαι *answer, reply to
   (+ acc.)*
ἐπί (+gen.) *in the time of*
μετ-/μεθίημι (μεθε-) *allow; let
   go*
οἶκε=ἔοικε *resemble, be like
   (+dat.)*
ὄψις, ἡ *vision, sight (3e)*

παραλαμβάνω (παραλαβ-)
   undertake; take from
παροράω (παριδ-) *notice*
σέο/σευ=σοῦ
σιδηρέος η ον *iron, metal*
σφι *to them (dat.)*
τευ=τίνος
τοι=σοι
ὕπνος, ὁ *sleep (2a)*
ὗς, ὁ *boar (3h)*
Note κ *for* π *in e.g.* κοτε (ποτε),
   κοῖος (ποῖος), κως (πως),
   ὁκόθεν (ὁπόθεν) *etc.*
Note the declension of σφεῖς
   'they':
Attic: σφεῖς σφᾶς σφῶν σφίσι(ν)
Ionic: σφεῖς σφέας σφέων σφί(ν)
   (σφέα *n.*)

E

Adrastos is placed in charge of Croesus' son and promises to bring him safely back.

In *World of Athens*: reciprocity in human relations 3.4, 4.5.

εἴπας δὲ ταῦτα, ὁ Κροῖσος μεταπέμπεται τὸν Φρύγα Ἄδρηστον, ἀπικομένῳ δέ οἱ
λέγει τάδε· ' Ἄδρηστε, ἐγώ σε, συμφορῇ πεπληγμένον ἀχάριτι (τήν τοι οὐκ ὀνειδίζω),
ἐκάθηρα καὶ οἰκίοισι ὑποδεξάμενος ἔχω, παρέχων πᾶσαν δαπάνην· νῦν ὦν, ὀφείλεις
γάρ, ἐμεῦ προποιήσαντος χρηστὰ ἐς σέ, χρηστοῖσί με ἀμείβεσθαι, φύλακα παιδός
σε τοῦ ἐμοῦ χρηίζω γενέσθαι ἐς ἄγρην ὁρμωμένου, μή τινες κατ' ὁδὸν κλῶπες   5
κακοῦργοι ἐπὶ δηλήσι φανέωσι ὑμῖν. πρὸς δὲ τούτῳ, καὶ σέ τοι χρεόν ἐστι ἰέναι ἔνθα
ἀπολαμπρυνέαι τοῖσι ἔργοισι· πατρώιόν τε γάρ τοί ἐστι καὶ προσέτι ῥώμη ὑπάρχει.'
ἀμείβεται ὁ Ἄδρηστος· 'ὦ βασιλεῦ, ἄλλως μὲν ἔγωγε ἂν οὐκ ἤια ἐς ἄεθλον τοιόνδε·

Vocabulary for Section Nineteen E

Notes

   2. τήν: relative, picking up συμφορῇ.

   3. ὑποδεξάμενος ἔχω: treat as a perfect (cf. 19D l.5).

   4. ἀμείβεσθαι: infinitive after ὀφείλεις.

   5. φύλακα … σε … γενέσθαι: object after χρηίζω.

   5. ὁρμωμένου: with παιδός.

   6. ἐπὶ [+ dat., 'for the purpose of'] ; δηλήσι is the dat. s. of δήλησις 'harm,
      injury'.

ἄγρ-η, ἡ hunt (1a)
ἄεθλ-ον, τό contest (2b)
ἄλλως in other circumstances
ἀπολαμπρύν-ομαι distinguish
   oneself in (-έαι = -ει/ῃ 2nd s.
   pres. [possibly fut. here])
ἄχαρις ἄχαρι (ἀχαριτ-)
   unpleasant
δαπάν-η, ἡ expense, money (1a)
δήλησ-ις, ἡ harm (3e)
εἴπας=εἴπων (first aorist is εἴπα
   'I said')

ἔνθα where (relative)
καθαίρ-ω cleanse, purify
κακοῦργ-ος -ον evil
κλώψ (κλωπ-), ὁ thief (3a)
μεταπέμπ-ομαι send for
οἰκί-α, τά palace (2b)
ὀνειδίζ-ω blame x (acc.) on y
   (dat.)
πλήσσ-ω strike (perf. part. pass.
   πεπληγμένος)
προποιέ-ω do first, do
   before

προσέτι besides
ῥώμ-η, ἡ strength (1a)
ὑπάρχ-ω be, be sufficient
ὑποδέκ-ομαι welcome, entertain
   (=ὑποδέχ-ομαι)
φανέωσι=φανῶσι (3rd pl. aor.
   subj. of φαίνομαι)
Φρύξ (Φρυγ-), ὁ Phrygian (3a)
χρεόν ἐστι=χρή
χρηίζ-ω desire

οὔτε γὰρ συμφορῇ τοιῇδε κεχρημένον οἰκός ἐστι ἐς ὁμήλικας εὖ πρήσσοντας ἰέναι,
οὔτε τὸ βούλεσθαι πάρα, πολλαχῇ τε ἂν ἴσχον ἐμεωυτόν. νῦν δέ, ἐπείτε σὺ σπεύδεις   10
καὶ δεῖ τοι χαρίζεσθαι (ὀφείλω γάρ σε ἀμείβεσθαι χρηστοῖσι), ποιέειν εἰμὶ ἕτοιμος
ταῦτα, παῖδά τε σόν, τὸν διακελεύεαι φυλάσσειν, ἀπήμονα, τοῦ φυλάσσοντος
εἵνεκεν, προσδόκα τοι ἀπονοστήσειν.'

9. οἰκός: see vocabulary. Understand 'for one who κεχρημένον … ἰέναι'.
10. τὸ βούλεσθαι: verb-noun/gerund (257), subject of πάρα.
12. παῖδα σόν … ἀπήμονα: object of προσδόκα (imperative), 1.13.

ἀπήμων ἄπημον (ἀπημον-)
  unharmed
ἀπονοστέ-ω return
διακελεύ-ομαι exhort, direct
  (-έαι = -ει/ῃ, 2nd s. pres.)
εἵνεκεν=ἕνεκα
ἐμεῦ=ἐμοῦ
ἐπὶ δήλησι bent on mischief
εὖ πρήσσω=εὖ πράττω
ἤια=ᾖα (past of ἔρχομαι/εἶμι)
ἴσχ-ω hold back, restrain
κεχρημένον 'for one who has met'
οἰκός=εἰκός likely
ὁμήλιξ (ὁμηλικ-), ὁ companion
  (3a)

πάρα=πάρεστι it is in one's
  power, possible
πολλαχῇ for many reasons
προσδοκά-ω expect
τοιόσδε τοιήδε τοιόνδε like this
χαρίζ-ομαι oblige (+ dat.)

Vocabulary to be learnt
ἄγρη, ἡ *hunt (1a)*
εὖ πράττω *fare well, be*
  prosperous
πάρα, πάρεστι *it is possible for*
  X (dat.)
τοιόσδε τοιήδε τοιόνδε *of this*
  kind

ὑπάρχω *be, be sufficient; begin*
  (+gen.)
ὑποδέχομαι *welcome, entertain*
χαρίζομαι *oblige; please; be*
  dear to (+ dat.)
Note that -έαι *is used for* -ει *or*
  -ῃ *in the 2nd s. middle, mostly*
  of ε *contr. verbs only, but*
  occasionally of other verbs
  as well, e.g. διακελεύεαι,
  ἀπολαμπρῡνέαι *(where the* ε
  may indicate the future*)*

περιστάντες αὐτὸ κύκλῳ, ἐσηκόντιζον

F

ἐκ θεοῦ νέμεσις μεγάλη

In *World of Athens*: Zeus 3.3; *xenia* 4.2; divine injustice 3.7; human responsibility 4.25–7; Herodotus and history 8.41.

τοιούτοισι ἐπείτε οὗτος ἀμείψατο Κροῖσον, ἤισαν μετὰ ταῦτα, ἐξηρτυμένοι λογάσι τε νεηνίῃσι καὶ κυσί. ἀπικόμενοι δὲ ἐς τὸν Ὄλυμπον τὸ ὄρος, ἐζήτεον τὸ θηρίον, εὑρόντες δὲ καὶ περιστάντες αὐτὸ κύκλῳ, ἐσηκόντιζον. ἔνθα δὴ ὁ ξεῖνος, οὗτος δὴ ὁ καθαρθεὶς τὸν φόνον, καλεόμενος δὲ Ἄδρηστος, ἀκοντίζων τὸν ὗν, τοῦ μὲν ἁμαρτάνει, τυγχάνει δὲ τοῦ Κροίσου παιδός. ὁ μὲν δή, βληθεὶς τῇ αἰχμῇ, ἐξέπλησε   5 τοῦ ὀνείρου τὴν φήμην, ἔθεε δέ τις ἀγγελέων τῷ Κροίσῳ τὸ γεγονός, ἀπικόμενος δὲ ἐς τὰς Σάρδις τήν τε μάχην καὶ τὸν τοῦ παιδὸς μόρον ἐσήμηνέ οἱ. ὁ δὲ Κροῖσος, τῷ θανάτῳ τοῦ παιδὸς συντεταραγμένος, μᾶλλόν τι ἐδεινολογέετο ὅτι μιν ἀπέκτεινε τὸν αὐτὸς φόνου ἐκάθηρε. περιημεκτέων δὲ τῇ συμφορῇ, δεινῶς ἐκάλεε μὲν Δία καθάρσιον, μαρτυρόμενος τὰ ὑπὸ τοῦ ξείνου πεπονθὼς εἴη, ἐκάλεε δὲ ἐπίστιόν τε   10 καὶ ἑταιρήιον, τὸν αὐτὸν τοῦτον ὀνομάζων θεόν, τὸν ͡ μὲν ἐπίστιον καλέων, διότι δὴ οἰκίοισι ὑποδεξάμενος τὸν ξεῖνον φονέα τοῦ παιδὸς ἐλάνθανε βόσκων, τὸν ͡ δὲ ἑταιρήιον, ὡς φύλακα συμπέμψας αὐτὸν εὑρήκοι πολεμιώτατον. παρῆσαν δὲ μετὰ τοῦτο οἱ Λυδοὶ φέροντες τὸν νεκρόν, ὄπισθε δὲ εἵπετό οἱ ὁ φονεύς. στὰς δὲ οὗτος

Vocabulary for Section Nineteen F

Notes

8.   ἀπέκτεινε: the subject is Adrastus, picked up by τόν 'whom'.

9.   αὐτός: '[Croesus] himself'.

9–11. Δία καθάρσιον … ἐπίστιον … ἑταιρήιον: 'Zeus [as god] of purification … and [as god] of the hearth and [god] of friendship'.

10.   τά: 'the things that/what' (relative).

13.   φύλακα: 'as a guard'.

ἀγγέλλ-ω announce, report (fut. ἀγγελέω)
ἁμαρτάν-ω miss (+gen.)
βάλλ-ω (βαλ-) hit (aor.pass. ἐβλήθην)
βόσκ-ω nurture, feed
γέγονα irr. perf. of γίγνομαι (part. γεγονώς or γεγώς)
δεινολογέ-ομαι grieve
ἐκπίμπλη-μι (ἐκπλησ-) fulfil
ἐξαρτύ-ω equip
ἐπίστι-ος -ον (sc. 'Zeus, god') of the hearth
ἐσακοντίζ-ω hurl a javelin at
ἑταιρήϊ-ος (sc. 'Zeus, god') of friendship

ἤισαν = ᾖσαν (past of ἔρχομαι/ εἶμι)
θέ-ω run
καθαίρ-ω purify, cleanse
καθάρσι-ος -ον (sc. 'Zeus, god') of purification
κύκλ-ος, ὁ circle (2a)
λογάς (λογαδ-), ὁ selected
μαρτύρ-ομαι invoke
μόρ-ος, ὁ fate (2a)
οἰκί-α, τά palace (2b)
Ὄλυμπ-ος, ὁ Olympos (2a)
ὀνομάζ-ω name
ὄπισθε behind
πεπονθώς perf. part. of πάσχω

περιημεκτέ-ω be grieved at (+ dat.)
περιίστα-μαι (περιστα-) stand round
πρό (+ gen.) in front of
Σάρδι-ες, αἱ Sardis (*Croesus' capital*)
σημαίν-ω tell
συνταράσσ-ω overwhelm
τὸν δὲ 'and on Zeus as ἑταιρήϊος, because . . .'
τὸν μὲν 'and on Zeus as ἐπίστιος, because . . .'
φήμ-η, ἡ prophecy (1a)
φον-εύς, ὁ murderer (3g)

πρὸ τοῦ νεκροῦ, παρεδίδου ἑωυτὸν Κροίσῳ, προτείνων τὰς χεῖρας, ἐπικατασφάξαι   15
μιν κελεύων τῷ νεκρῷ, λέγων τήν τε προτέρην ἑωυτοῦ συμφορήν, καὶ ὡς ἐπ' ἐκείνῃ
τὸν καθήραντα ἀπολωλεκὼς εἴη, οὐδέ οἱ εἴη βιώσιμον. Κροῖσος δέ, τούτων ἀκούσας,
τόν τε Ἄδρηστον κατοικτίρει, καίπερ ἐὼν ἐν κακῷ οἰκηίῳ τοσούτῳ, καὶ λέγει πρὸς
αὐτόν· 'ἔχω, ὦ ξεῖνε, παρὰ σεῦ πᾶσαν τὴν δίκην, ἐπειδὴ σεωυτοῦ καταδικάζεις
θάνατον. εἰς δὲ οὐ σύ μοι τοῦδε τοῦ κακοῦ αἴτιος, εἰ μὴ ὅσον ἀέκων ἐξεργάσαο,   20
ἀλλὰ θεῶν κού τις, ὅς μοι καὶ πάλαι προεσήμαινε τὰ μέλλοντα ἔσεσθαι.' Κροῖσος
μέν νυν ἔθαψε, ὡς οἰκὸς ἦν, τὸν ἑωυτοῦ παῖδα· Ἄδρηστος δέ, ὁ Γορδίεω τοῦ Μίδεω,
οὗτος δὴ ὁ φονεὺς μὲν τοῦ ἑωυτοῦ ἀδελφεοῦ γενόμενος, φονεὺς δὲ τοῦ καθήραντος,
ἐπείτε ἡσυχίη τῶν ἀνθρώπων ἐγένετο περὶ τὸ σῆμα, συγγινωσκόμενος ἀνθρώπων
εἶναι, τῶν αὐτὸς ᾔδεε, βαρυσυμφορώτατος, ἐπικατασφάζει τῷ τύμβῳ ἑωυτόν.   25

---

16.   κελεύων: supply 'Croesus' as object.
16.   προτέρην: i.e. Adrastus' unintentional slaughter of his brother (19B, 8-9).
16.   ἐπὶ ἐκείνῃ: see vocabulary.
25.   εἶναι ... βαρυσυμφορώτατος: 'that he was the most [lit.] heavy-fated'.
25.   τῶν: attracted into the gen. by its antecedent ἀνθρώπων (**218b**).

ἀκοντίζ-ω throw javelin at
ἀπολωλεκώς perf. part. of
    ἀπόλλυμι
βαρυσύμφορ-ος –ον accursed
βιώσιμ-ος -ον worth living
Γορδί-ας, ὁ Gordias (1d) (gen.
    Γορδιέ-ω)
εἰ μὴ ὅσον except in as far as
εἶς = εἶ you are
ἔνθα where (tr. 'at this point')
ἐξεργάζ-ομαι do a deed
    (ἐξεργάσαο = ἐξηργάσω, 2nd
    s. aor.)
ἐπὶ ἐκείνῃ 'in addition to that
    (previous tragedy)'
ἐπικατασφάζ-ω slay x (acc.)
    over y (dat.)
ᾔδεε = ᾔδει (past of οἶδα)
θάπτ-ω bury
καθαίρ-ω purify, cleanse
κατοικτίρ-ω pity

κου = που
Μίδ-ας, ὁ Midas (1d) (gen.
    Μιδέ -ω)
οἰκήϊ-ος -η -ον personal
οἰκός = εἰκός
ὄρ-ος, τό mountain (3c)
πάλαι long ago
προσημαίν-ω prophesy
προτείν-ω stretch out
σῆμα (σηματ-), τό mound (3b)
    (marking a grave)
συγγιγνώσκ-ομαι
    acknowledge
τύμβ-ος, ὁ grave (2a)
φον-εύς, ὁ murderer (3g)

Vocabulary to be learnt
ἀγγέλλω (ἀγγειλα-; fut.
    ἀγγελέω) report, announce
ἁμαρτάν-ω (ἁμαρτ-) miss; make
    a mistake

βάλλω (βαλ-) hit (aor. pass.
    ἐβλήθην)
γέγον-α irr. perf. of γίγνομαι
    (part. γεγον-ώς or
    γεγ-ώς)
ἔνθα where, there
θέω run
καθαίρω (καθηρα-) purify,
    cleanse
μαρτύρομαι invoke, call to
    witness
οἰκία, τά palace (2b)
οἰκός = εἰκός
ὄρ-ος, τό mountain (3c)
πάλαι long ago
κου = που
πρό (+gen.) before, in
    front of
προτείνω stretch out
σημαίνω tell, signal

So ends the story of Adrastos. Croesus continued to be hounded, yet loved, by
the gods, as you can now read in the following account, by Herodotus, of his end
as king of Lydia. As you have read on p. 225, the Persians were already pushing
against Croesus' frontiers and eventually Sardis fell. Cyrus is the Persian king.
He has placed Croesus on a pyre:

And as Croesus stood on the pyre, he remembered the words of Solon and realised how divinely inspired they had been, that no man was happy while he still lived. As this memory came back to him, he broke his silence and groaning deeply called aloud three times 'Solon'.

When Cyrus heard this, he instructed his interpreters to ask Croesus who it was on whom he was calling. Croesus at first maintained silence in the face of their questions, but eventually, under compulsion, said, 'He was a man whom I would have given much money to see in conversation with every ruler in the world.' The interpreters could not understand this and asked again what he meant. Under the pressure of their insistent questioning, Croesus explained how the Athenian Solon had come to visit him in Sardis, had seen all the magnificence he had to offer, and had dismissed it in so many words; and how everything Solon had said had turned out to be the case, although his words had not been directed so much at Croesus as at all mankind, especially at those who considered themselves happy.

While Croesus spoke, the fire had been lit and the edges of the pyre were already burning. But when Cyrus heard what the interpreters said, he had a change of heart, moved by the consideration that he, a mortal, was burning alive another whose happiness had been no less than his own; besides, he feared retribution (for it occurred to him that instability was the hallmark of all human life). So he ordered his men to put the fire out as quickly as possible and to bring Croesus and those with him down from the pyre. But try as they might, the fire was too strong for them.

Then, as the Lydians relate, Croesus, who had learnt of Cyrus' change of heart and saw the men's vain efforts to douse the fire, called in supplication upon Apollo to come down and save him from his plight, if ever he had offered pleasing gifts to him. So in tears he called upon the god; and suddenly, from out of a clear and windless sky, storm clouds gathered and burst in a torrential downpour, extinguishing the fire. So Cyrus, realising that Croesus was a good man and loved by the gods, brought him down from the pyre and questioned him as follows: 'Who was it, Croesus, who persuaded you to march against my country and make yourself my enemy rather than my friend?' And Croesus replied, 'O king, it was I who *did* it – to your great advantage, though to my own great misfortune. But responsibility for what has happened rests with the god of the Greeks, who encouraged me to fight. No one is so foolish that he prefers war to peace. For in the one, sons bury their fathers, in the other fathers bury their sons. But I must suppose it was the gods' will that these things should happen.'

When Croesus said this, Cyrus had him released and brought him to sit near himself and treated him with much consideration; and it was with the greatest respect that both he and all those with him looked upon Croesus.

Odysseus, Athene and Nausikaa

Part Seven   Homeric hero and heroine

Introduction

Section Twenty, the final section of the first half of the Course, introduces Homer through the story of Odysseus and Nausikaa. The shift of emphasis apparent in Section Nineteen, which took you away from the secular society of Neaira and Aristarkhos to an interpretation of history which depended on the intervention of the gods in man's affairs, is continued here. Homer's world is one in which the gods move easily amongst the (mortal) heroes of the Greeks (whom the gods are made, in many ways, to resemble), and heroes are quite often, as a result, called 'godlike'. Yet there is a deeper sense of the value of mere humanity in Homer than perhaps in any other Greek writer.

Homer and his poems

The *Iliad* and *Odyssey* are the very first works of literature of Western civilisation, and some would say they are rivalled only by Shakespeare. In reading them, you will be placing yourself in a mainstream of human experience which stretches back for some 2,700 years, and will stretch forward for as long as books are read. No other works have made, directly or indirectly, such a profound impact upon Western literature, or exercised such a compelling grip upon the human imagination over so long a period.

The two poems had probably reached the form in which we now have them by about 700. Tradition tells us that their composer was Homer and that he was blind. Both poems deal with events surrounding the Trojan War which, if it did take place (and it may have), occurred about 1200. What is certain is that the poems are the result of hundreds of years of oral (not written) story-telling, passed on down through generations of singers who altered, adapted and modified the traditional tales to suit their own vision, ability and audience. Homer is the culmination of that tradition.

The *Iliad* describes an incident that occurred during the Greek siege of Troy, triggered off by an ugly clash between Agamemnon, the Greek commander-in-chief, and Akhilleus, mainstay of the Greek army. The *Odyssey* describes the home-coming of the Greek hero Odysseus from Troy after the war is over, and Odysseus' re-establishment as lord of his homeland, Ithaka, in the face of the opposition of 108 suitors who have spent the years of his absence courting

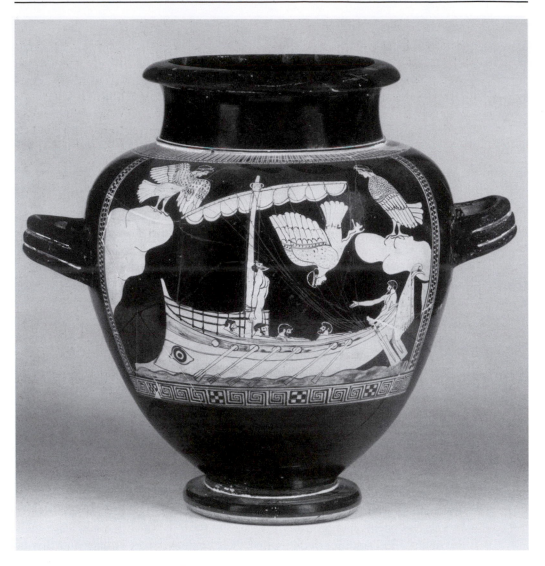

Odysseus, on his way home from Troy, hears the song of the Sirens unscathed. One of the Sirens, doomed to die in this event, falls to her death.

his wife Penelope. The incident you are about to read is taken from Odysseus' adventures on his way home from Troy to Ithaka.

The most striking feature of Homer's work is its repetition of words, phrases and clauses. This is the direct consequence of the oral style of composition in which Homer worked. But, as you will quickly find out, far from acting as a constraint upon the poetry, this repetition actually enhances it.

Homeric dialect

Homeric dialect consists of a mixture of Aeolic and Ionic forms, with a scattering of Attic, Arcado-Cypriot and others. Forms you will not know are noted in the vocabulary, and a summary of the main differences between Homeric and Attic Greek is contained in the accompanying section of the grammar. If you have a good grasp of Ionic, you will not find Homeric dialect difficult, and sentences tend to be straightforward grammatically. It is the very large Homeric vocabulary which always presents problems, although the repetition helps considerably.

For a brief description of the hexameter, the metre in which all Greek epics are composed, see the *Grammar*, **226**.

Source

Homer, *Odyssey* 6

Time to be taken

Three weeks

Section Twenty A–G: Odysseus and Nausikaa

Introduction

Odysseus has left Troy for home with his contingent of ships, but is swept off course and, in a series of adventures with such mythical creatures as the Cyclopes, the Lotus Eaters, Kirke, the Sirens and Skylla and Kharybdis, loses all his ships and men. He himself is washed up on the island of the demi-goddess Kalypso, where he is kept against his will for a number of years. Eventually, the gods order his release and Odysseus builds himself a boat and sets sail for his home, Ithaka. But Poseidon the sea-god, still enraged at Odysseus for blinding his son the Cyclops, wrecks the boat. Odysseus swims to land and arrives at Scheria, where he hauls himself ashore and collapses joyfully under a bush to sleep. Meanwhile his patron goddess, Athene, is working on his behalf to arrange a welcome for him amongst the Phaiakians, who inhabit the island.

The interleaved translation is by Richmond Lattimore.

In *World of Athens*: Homer 1.10–11, 17, 8.1; dreams 3.8, 12, 14–16; display and reputation 4.5–8.

There is a good edition by Janet Watson, *Homer: Odyssey VI and VII* (Bristol 2005); and for more advanced students by AF Garvie, *Homer: Odyssey VI–VIII* (Cambridge 1994).

While Odysseus sleeps, Athene visits Nausikaa, the daughter of Alkinoös (king of the Phaiakians), in a dream and suggests that she should go to the river next day to wash the royal linen. Her part played, Athene returns to Mount Olympos.

ὣς ὁ μὲν ἔνθα καθεῦδε πολύτλας δῖος Ὀδυσσεὺς
ὕπνῳ καὶ καμάτῳ ἀρημένος· αὐτὰρ Ἀθήνη
βῆ ῥ' ἐς Φαιήκων ἀνδρῶν δῆμόν τε πόλιν τε,
men, who formerly lived in the spacious land, Hypereia,
next to the Cyclopes, who were men too overbearing,   5
and who had kept harrying them, being greater in strength. From here
godlike Nausithoös had removed and led a migration,
and settled in Scheria, far away from men who eat bread,
and driven a wall about the city, and built the houses,
and made the temples of the gods, and allotted the holdings.   10
But now he had submitted to his fate, and gone to Hades,
and Alkinoös, learned in designs from the gods, now ruled there.
It was to his house that the gray-eyed goddess Athene
went, devising the homecoming of great-hearted Odysseus,

and she went into the ornate chamber, in which a girl   15
was sleeping, like the immortal goddesses for stature and beauty,
Nausikaa, the daughter of great-hearted Alkinoös,
and beside her two handmaidens with beauty given from the Graces
slept on either side of the post with the shining doors closed.

ἡ δ', ἀνέμου ὡς πνοιή, ἐπέσσυτο δέμνια κούρης,   20
στῆ δ' ἄρ' ὑπὲρ κεφαλῆς, καί μιν πρὸς μῦθον ἔειπεν,
εἰδομένη κούρῃ ναυσικλειτοῖο Δύμαντος,
ἥ οἱ ὁμηλικίη μὲν ἔην, κεχάριστο δὲ θυμῷ.

Vocabulary for Section Twenty A

Grammar for 20A–G
- Homeric dialect
- Homeric hexameters

Notes

1.   ὁ μέν: 'he', shortly to be qualified as πολύτλας δῖος Ὀδυσσεύς, and con-
     trasted with Athene (l.2).
20. ἡ δέ: 'and she' (Athene).
20. ἐπέσσυτο: the 2nd aorist of ἐπισεύομαι (ἐπεσσύμην). Note the doubled σσ.
21. μιν πρὸς μῦθον ἔειπεν: πρός here is strictly an adverb ('directionally')
     with a double acc., [spoke] a μῦθον [to] μιν. Note the doubled augment
     of ἔειπεν.
23. οἱ: i.e. as Nausikaa.

Ἀθήν-η, ἡ Athene (1a)
ἄνεμ-ος, ὁ wind (2a)
ἄρα straightaway, then
ἀρημέν-ος -η -ον overcome
αὐτάρ but
βῆ=ἔβη
δέμνι-α, τά bed (2b)
δῖ-ος -α -ον godlike
Δύμας (Δυμαντ-), ὁ Dymas (3a)
ἔην=ἦν

εἰδόμεν-ος -η -ον making
   oneself like (+dat.)
ἐπισεύ-ομαι hurry to (+acc.)
ἐς=εἰς
θυμ-ός, ὁ heart, soul (2a)
καθεῦδε=ἐκάθευδε
κάματ-ος, ὁ weariness (2a)
κεχάριστο 3rd s. perf. of
   χαρίζομαι
κούρ-η, ἡ maiden (1a)

μῦθ-ος, ὁ word (2a)
ναυσικλειτ-ός -ή -όν famous for
   ships
Ὀδυσσ-εύς, ὁ Odysseus (3g)
ὁμηλικί-η of same age as (+dat.)
πνοι-ή, ἡ breath (1a)
πολύτλας long-suffering
στῆ=ἔστη
Φαίηκες, οἱ Phaiakians (3a)
ὥς thus, so

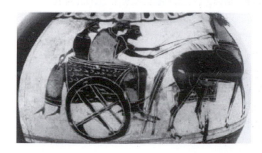

ἡμιόνους καὶ ἄμαξαν

τῇ μιν ἐεισαμένη προσέφη γλαυκῶπις Ἀθήνη·
'Ναυσικάα, τί νύ σ' ὧδε μεθήμονα γείνατο μήτηρ; 25
εἵματα μέν τοι κεῖται ἀκηδέα σιγαλόεντα,
σοὶ δὲ γάμος σχεδόν ἐστιν, ἵνα χρὴ καλὰ μὲν αὐτὴν
ἕννυσθαι, τὰ δὲ τοῖσιˈ παρασχεῖν ˈοἵ κέ σ' ἄγωνται.
ἐκ γάρ τοι τούτων φάτις ἀνθρώπους ἀναβαίνει
ἐσθλή, χαίρουσιν δὲ πατὴρ καὶ πότνια μήτηρ. 30
ἀλλ' ἴομεν πλυνέουσαι ἅμ' ἠοῖ φαινομένηφι·
καί τοι ἐγὼ συνέριθος ἅμ' ἕψομαι, ὄφρα τάχιστα
ἐντύνεαι, ἐπεὶ οὔ τοι ἔτι δὴν παρθένος ἔσσεαι·
ἤδη γάρ σε μνῶνται ἀριστῆες κατὰ δῆμον
πάντων Φαιήκων, ὅθι τοι γένος ἐστὶ καὶ αὐτῇ. 35
ἀλλ' ἄγ' ἐπότρυνον πατέρα κλυτὸν ἠῶθιˉ πρὸ
ἡμιόνους καὶ ἄμαξαν ἐφοπλίσαι, ἥ κεν ἄγῃσι
ζῶστρά τε καὶ πέπλους καὶ ῥήγεα σιγαλόεντα.
καὶ δὲ σοὶ ὧδ' αὐτῇ πολὺ κάλλιον ἠὲ πόδεσσιν
ἔρχεσθαι· πολλὸν γὰρ ἀπὸˈ πλυνοί ˈεἰσι πόληος.' 40
ἡ μὲν ἄρ' ὣς εἰποῦσ' ἀπέβη γλαυκῶπις Ἀθήνη
Οὔλυμπόνδ', ὅθι φασὶ θεῶν ἕδος ἀσφαλὲς αἰεὶ
ἔμμεναι· οὔτ' ἀνέμοισι τινάσσεται οὔτε ποτ' ὄμβρῳ
δεύεται οὔτε χιὼν ἐπιπίλναται, ἀλλὰ μάλ' αἴθρη
πέπταται ἀνέφελος, λευκὴ δ' ἐπιδέδρομεν αἴγλη· 45
τῷ ἔνι τέρπονται μάκαρες θεοὶ ἤματα πάντα.
ἔνθ' ἀπέβη γλαυκῶπις, ἐπεὶ διεπέφραδε κούρῃ.

---

24.   τῇ μιν ἐεισαμένη: 'likening herself [μιν] to her [=the daughter of Dymas]'. This repeats l.22. It is a very common device in Homer, known as 'ring-composition'. The poet uses it to deal with digressions, bringing his audience back to the point where the digression started. Compare l.3 with ll.13-14 above.

26.   τοι: the equivalent of 'your' [the clothes for you] or perhaps 'by you', after ἀκηδέα.

27.   ἵνα: see vocabulary: here it takes the indicative.

27.   καλά: i.e. εἵματα, object of ἕννυσθαι.

27.   αὐτήν: '[you] yourself', subject of χρή.

28.   παρασχεῖν: a second inf. after χρή, with τά ('them' =εἵματα) as its object.

29–30. φάτις ἐσθλή: subject.

31.   ἴομεν: (see vocabulary); a subjunctive often shows a short vowel in Homer.

31.   φαινομένηφι: (see vocabulary); the –φι ending is often used as a dative.

35.   τοι: take with αὐτῇ.

39.   κάλλιον: supply ἐστί.
46.   τῷ ἔνι: = ἐν τῷ, i.e. 'there'.
47.   ἀπέβη … διεπέφραδε: ring composition with 41 εἰποῦσ' ἀπέβη.

ἄγῃσι=ἄγῃ (3rd s. pres. subj.)
ἄγ-ομαι lead in marriage
Ἀθήν-η, ἡ Athene (1a)
αἴγλ-η, ἡ light, radiance (1a)
αἰεί=ἀεί
αἴθρ-η, ἡ clear sky (1a)
ἀκηδ-ής -ές uncared for
ἅμα (+dat.) at the same time as
ἅμαξ-α, ἡ wagon (1c)
ἀνέφελ-ος -ον unclouded
ἀπό . . . εἰμί be distant from
   (+gen.)
ἀριστ-εύς, ὁ nobleman (3g)
ἀσφαλ-ής -ές safe, secure
γείνατο=ἐγείνατο
γείν-ομαι (γειν-) bear
γλαυκῶπις (γλαυκωπιδ-), ἡ
   grey-eyed
δεύ-ω besprinkle, bedew
δήν for a long time
διεπέφραδε aor. of διαφράζω
   speak to
ἕδ-ος, τό seat (3c)
ἐεισάμεν-ος -η -ον likening x
   (acc.) to y (dat.)
εἵματα, τά clothes (3b)
ἔμμεναι=εἶναι
ἐνί=ἐν
ἔννυ-μαι put on
ἐντύν-ομαι get oneself ready
   (ἐντυνέαι=2nd s. subj.)
ἐπιδέδρομεν (it) is spread over
   (perf. of ἐπιτρέχω)
ἐπιπίλνα-μαι come near
ἐποτρύν-ω urge, persuade
ἔσσεαι=ἔσει (2nd s. fut. of εἰμί)

ἐφοπλίζ-ω get ready
ζῶστρ-ον, τό belt, girdle (2b)
ἠέ=ἤ
ἦμαρ (ἠματ-), τό day (3b)
ἠῶθι πρό before dawn
ἠώς, ἡ dawn (dat. ἠοῖ)
ἵνα (+ind.) where, when
ἴομεν=ἴωμεν
κάλλιον (understand ἐστί) it is
   better
κε=ἄν
κλυτ-ός -ή -όν famous
κούρ-η, ἡ maiden (1a)
λευκ-ός -ή -όν white
μάκαρ (μακαρ-), ὁ blessed
μεθήμων μέθημον (μεθημον-)
   lax, careless
μνά-ομαι woo, court
Ναυσικά-α, ἡ Nausikaa (1b)
   (daughter of Alkinoos, king of
   the Phaiakians)
νυ=νυν
ὅθι where; in which place
ὄμβρ-ος, ὁ shower, rain (2a)
Οὔλυμπόνδε to Olympos
ὄφρα =ἵνα (+subj.) in order to
παρθέν-ος, ἡ maiden, unwedded
   girl (2a)
πέπλ-ος, ὁ robe, mantle (2a)
πετάννυ-μι spread out (perf.
   pass. πέπταμαι)
πλυν-ός, ὁ washing place (2a)
πλύν-ω wash (fut. πλυνέω)
ποδέσσι(ν)=ποσί (ν) on foot
   (πούς)
πόληος=πόλεως

πολλόν far, a long way
πότνια lady (nom. s. f.)
πρός . . . εἶπεν addressed x (acc.)
   to y (acc.)
πρόσφημι speak to
ῥῆγ-ος, τό rug, blanket (3c)
σιγαλό-εις -εσσα -εν
   (σιγαλοεντ-) shining
συνέριθ-ος, ἡ fellow-worker,
   companion (2a)
τά (1.28) =αὐτά 'things'
τέρπ-ομαι enjoy oneself
τῇ (1.24) =αὐτῇ (i.e. Dymas'
   daughter)
τινάσσ-ω shake
τοι 'let me tell you/look
   here'
τοῖσι . . . οἳ (1.29) =αὐτοῖς. . . οἳ
   'for those . . . who'
τῷ (1.46) =αὐτῷ
ὑπέρ (+ gen.) above
φαινομένηφι =φαινομένη
φάτ-ις, ἡ reputation (3e)
χαίρ-ω rejoice
χιών (χιον-), ἡ snow (3a)

Vocabulary to be learnt
αἰεί=ἀεί
ἄρα straightaway
ἀσφαλής ές safe, secure
δέμνια, τά bed, bedding (2b)
κε (κεν) (enclitic)=ἄν
κούρη=κόρη, ἡ daughter, girl
   (1a)
χαίρω rejoice
ὥς thus, so

B

Prompted by the dream, Nausikaa approaches her father and, with the innocent guile of a favourite daughter, suggests that he should grant her permission to do the washing for the family at the river next day.

αὐτίκα δ' Ἠὼς ἦλθεν ἐΰθρονος, ἥ μιν ἔγειρε
Ναυσικάαν εὔπεπλον· ἄφαρ δ' ἀπεθαύμασ' ὄνειρον,
βῆ δ' ἴμεναι διὰ δώμαθ', ἵν' ἀγγείλειε τοκεῦσι,   50
πατρὶ φίλῳ καὶ μητρί· κιχήσατο δ' ἔνδον ἐόντας·
ἡ ͜ μὲν ἐπ' ἐσχάρῃ ἧστο, σὺν ἀμφιπόλοισι γυναιξίν,
ἠλάκατα στρωφῶσ' ἁλιπόρφυρα· τῷ δὲ θύραζε
ἐρχομένῳ ξύμβλητο μετὰ κλειτοὺς βασιλῆας
ἐς βουλήν, ἵνα μιν κάλεον Φαίηκες ἀγαυοί.   55
ἡ δέ, μάλ' ἄγχι στᾶσα, φίλον πατέρα προσέειπε·
'πάππα φίλ', οὐκ ἂν δή μοι ἐφοπλίσσειας ἀπήνην
ὑψηλὴν εὔκυκλον, ἵνα κλυτὰ εἵματ' ἄγωμαι
ἐς ποταμὸν πλυνέουσα, τά μοι ῥερυπωμένα κεῖται;
καὶ δὲ σοὶ αὐτῷ ἔοικε μετὰ πρώτοισιν ἐόντα   60
βουλὰς βουλεύειν καθαρὰ χροῒ εἵματ' ἔχοντα.
πέντε δέ τοι φίλοι υἷες ἐνὶ μεγάροις γεγάασιν,
οἱ δύ' ὀπυίοντες, τρεῖς δ' ἠΐθεοι θαλέθοντες·
οἱ δ' αἰεὶ ἐθέλουσι, νεόπλυτα εἵματ' ἔχοντες,
ἐς χορὸν ἔρχεσθαι· τὰ δ' ἐμῇ φρενὶ πάντα μέμηλεν.'   65
ὣς ἔφατ'· αἴδετο γὰρ θαλερὸν γάμον ἐξονομῆναι
πατρὶ φίλῳ· ὁ δὲ πάντα νόει καὶ ἀμείβετο μύθῳ·
'οὔτε τοι ἡμιόνων φθονέω, τέκος, οὔτε τευ ἄλλου.
ἔρχευ· ἀτάρ τοι δμῶες ἐφοπλίσσουσιν ἀπήνην
ὑψηλὴν εὔκυκλον, ὑπερτερίῃ ἀραρυῖαν.'   70
ὣς εἰπών, δμώεσσιν ἐκέκλετο, τοὶ δ' ἐπίθοντο.

Vocabulary for Section Twenty B

Notes

48.   μιν: 'her', to be shortly explained as Ναυσικάαν εὔπεπλον.
50.   βῆ δ' ἰμέναι: 'and she went to go…'
51.   ἐόντας: see vocabulary.
53.   τῷ: see vocabulary; take with ἐρχομένῳ after ξύμβλητο.
55.   ἵνα: here with the indicative; contrast l.11.
60–1.   ἐόντα … ἔχοντα: see vocabulary.
67.   πάντα: 'everything'.
71.   τοί: the accent indicates that this = οἱ, 'they'.

ἀγαυ-ός -ή -όν noble
ἄγ-ομαι bring for oneself
ἄγχι close
αἴδ-ομαι feel reticence about
   (+ inf.)
ἀλιπόρφυρ-ος -ον purple
Ἀλκίνο-ος, ὁ Alkinoos (2a) *(king
   of the Phaiakians, Nausikaa's
   father)*
ἀμφίπολ-ος, ἡ servant,
   handmaiden (2a)
ἀπήν-η, ἡ wagon (1a)
ἀποθαυμάζ-ω wonder at
ἀραρυῖαν fitted (acc. s. f. perf.
   part. of ἀραρίσκω)
ἄφαρ at once
γεγάασιν 3rd pl. perf. of
   γίγνομαι
διά (+acc.) through
δμῶς (δμω-), ὁ slave (3a) (dat.
   pl. δμώεσσιν)
δώματ-α, τά house, palace (3b)
ἐγείρ-ω rouse
ἔγειρε=ἤγειρε
εἴματ-α, τά clothes (3b)
ἐνί=ἐν
ἐξονομαίν-ω (ἐξονομην-)
   mention
ἔοικε it is right for (+dat.)
ἐόντα l.60 take with σοι l.60
ἐόντας l. 22 understand 'parents'
ἔρχευ=ἔρχου
ἐς=εἰς
ἐσχάρ-η, ἡ hearth (1a)
εὔθρον-ος -ον lovely,
   fair-throned

εὔκυκλ-ος -ον with fine wheels
εὔπεπλ-ος -ον fair-robed
ἐφοπλίζ-ω get ready (fut.
   ἐφοπλίσσω)
ἔχοντα l.61 take with σοι l.60
ἤϊθε-ος, ὁ bachelor (2a)
ἠλάκατ-α, τά wool (on the
   distaff) (2b)
ἧμαι be seated (ἧστο 3rd s. past)
ἡ μέν i.e. her mother
ἠώς, ἡ dawn
θαλέθ-ω thrive
θαλερ-ός -ή -όν fruitful
θύραζε to the outside, out
ἴμεναι=ἰέναι
ἵνα (+ind.) where
καθαρ-ός -ή -όν clean
κάλεον=ἐκάλουν
κέλ-ομαι command (+dat.)
   (ἐκέκλετο 3rd s. aor.)
κιγχάν-ω (κιχησ-) meet
κλειτ-ός -ή -όν famous
κλυτ-ός -ή -όν splendid, lovely
μέγαρ-α, τά house, palace (2b)
μέμηλεν perf. of μέλει
μετά (+acc.) among; (+dat.)
   among, in company with
μῦθ-ος, ὁ word (2a)
νεόπλυτ-ος -ον newly washed
ξύμβλητο=ξυνέβλητο (3rd s. aor.
   mid. of ξυμβάλλομαι meet
   [+dat.])
ὀπυί-ω be married
πάππας, ὁ father (voc. πάππα)
πέντε five
πλύν-ω wash (fut. πλυνέω)

προσέειπε=προσεῖπε spoke to
ῥερυπωμέν-ος -η -ον dirty
στρωφά-ω twist, spin
τέκ-ος, τό child (3c
   uncontr.)
τοκ-εύς, ὁ parent (3g)
τῷ (1.6)=αὐτῷ (i.e. father)
ὑπερτερί-η, ἡ covering, canopy
   (1a)
ὑψηλ-ός -ή -όν high
φθον-έω begrudge (+gen.)
φρήν (φρεν-), ἡ heart, mind (3a)
χορός, ὁ dance (2a)
χρώς, ὁ body, flesh (dat. χροί)

Vocabulary to be learnt
ἄγομαι (ἀγαγ-) *bring (for
   oneself), lead, marry*
εἵματα, τά *clothes (3b)*
ἔοικε *it is right for (+dat.)*
ἐνί=ἐν
ἐς=εἰς
ἐφοπλίζω *equip, get ready (fut.
   ἐφοπλίσσω)*
ἠώς, ἡ *dawn (=Attic ἕως) (acc.
   ἠῶ; gen. ἠοῦς; dat. ἠοῖ)*
μετά *(+dat.) among, in company
   with*
μῦθος, ὁ *word, story (2a)*
πλύνω *wash (fut. πλυνέω)*
προσεῖπον (προσέειπον) *spoke
   X (acc.) to Y (acc.)*
*Lack of augment on past
   tenses e.g. στῆ=ἔστη,
   κάλεον=ἐκάλουν etc.*

and brought the mule wagon with good wheels outside and put it
together, and led the mules under the yoke and harnessed them,
and the girl brought the bright clothing out from the inner chamber
and laid it in the well-polished wagon. Meanwhile her mother   75
put in a box all manner of food, which would preserve strength,
and put many good things to eat with it, and poured out
wine in a goatskin bottle, and her daughter put that in the wagon.
She gave her limpid olive oil in a golden oil flask
for her and her attendant women to use for anointing.   80
Nausikaa took up the whip and the shining reins, then

whipped them into a start and the mules went noisily forward
and pulled without stint, carrying the girl and the clothing.
She was not alone. The rest, her handmaidens, walked on beside her.
Now when they had come to the delightful stream of the river,   85
where there was always a washing place, and plenty of glorious
water that ran through to wash what was ever so dirty,
there they unyoked the mules and set them free from the wagon,
and chased them out along the bank of the swirling river
to graze on the sweet river grass, while they from the wagon   90
lifted the wash in their hands and carried it to the black water,
and stamped on it in the basins, making a race and game of it
until they had washed and rinsed all dirt away, then spread it
out in line along the beach of the sea, where the water
of the sea had washed the most big pebbles up on the dry shore.   95
Then they themselves after bathing and anointing themselves with olive oil,
ate their dinner all along by the banks of the river
and waited for the laundry to dry out in the sunshine.
But when she and her maids had taken their pleasure in eating,
they all threw off their veils for a game of ball, and among them   100
it was Nausikaa of the white arms who led in the dancing;
and as Artemis, who showers arrows, moves on the mountains
either along Taÿgetos or on high-towering
Erymanthos, delighting in boars and deer in their running,
and along with her the nymphs, daughters of Zeus of the aegis,   105
range in the wilds and play, and the heart of Leto is gladdened,
for the head and the brows of Artemis are above all the others,
and she is easily marked among them, though all are lovely,
so this one shone among her handmaidens, a virgin unwedded.

C

*As the girls play ball by the beach, Athene engineers an encounter with
Odysseus.*

ἀλλ' ὅτε δὴ ἄρ' ἔμελλε πάλιν οἶκόνδε νέεσθαι,   110
ζεύξασ' ἡμιόνους, πτύξασά τε εἵματα καλά,
ἔνθ' αὖτ' ἄλλ' ἐνόησε θεὰ γλαυκῶπις Ἀθήνη,
ὡς Ὀδυσεὺς ἔγροιτο, ἴδοι τ' εὐώπιδα κούρην,
ἥ οἱ Φαιήκων ἀνδρῶν πόλιν ἡγήσαιτο.
σφαῖραν ἔπειτ' ἔρριψε μετ' ἀμφίπολον βασίλεια·   115
ἀμφιπόλου μὲν ἅμαρτε, βαθείῃ δ' ἔμβαλε δίνῃ,
αἱ δ' ἐπὶ μακρὸν ἄϋσαν. ὁ δ' ἔγρετο δῖος Ὀδυσσεύς,
ἑζόμενος δ' ὅρμαινε κατὰ φρένα καὶ κατὰ θυμόν·

ὤ ͜ μοι ἐγώ, τέων αὖτε βροτῶν ἐς γαῖαν ἱκάνω;
ἦ ῥ’ οἵ γ’ ὑβρισταί τε καὶ ἄγριοι οὐδὲ δίκαιοι,   120
ἦε φιλόξεινοι, καί σφιν νόος ἐστί θεουδής;
ὥς τέ με κουράων ἀμφήλυθε θῆλυς ἀϋτή,
νυμφάων, αἳ ἔχουσ’ ὀρέων αἰπεινὰ κάρηνα
καὶ πηγὰς ποταμῶν καὶ πίσεα ποιήεντα.
ἦ νύ που ἀνθρώπων εἰμὶ σχεδὸν αὐδηέντων;   125
ἀλλ’ ἄγ’, ἐγὼν αὐτὸς πειρήσομαι ἠδὲ ἴδωμαι.’

Vocabulary for Section Twenty C

Notes

112. ἄλλ’ = ἄλλα ‘other [things], something else’; do not confuse with ἀλλά ‘but’.
113. ὥς: indicating purpose.
119. ὤ μοι: = οἴμοι.
122. ὥς: how!
126. πειρήσομαι: i.e. carry out a test by using my eyes (ἴδωμαι).

ἄγρι-ος -η -ον wild
αἰπειν-ός -ή -όν steep
ἀμφέρχ-ομαι (aor. ἀμφήλυθ-ον) surround (+acc.)
ἀμφίπολ-ος, ἡ handmaiden (2a)
αὐδή-εις -εσσα -εν (αὐδηεντ-) speaking with human voices
αὖτε again, on the contrary, this time
ἀϋτ-ή, ἡ cry, shriek (1a)
ἀΰ-ω scream
βασίλει-α, ἡ princess (1b)
βροτ-ός, ὁ mortal (2a)
γαῖ-α, ἡ (1c)=γῆ
γλαυκῶπις (γλαυκωπιδ-), ἡ grey-eyed
δίν-η, ἡ eddy (1a)
δῖ-ος -α -ον god-like
ἐγείρ-ομαι (aor. ἐγρό-μην) wake up
ἐγών =ἐγώ
ἕζ-ομαι sit
ἐμβάλλ-ω (ἐμβαλ-) throw in (+ dat.)
εὐῶπις (εὐωπιδ-), ἡ beautiful
ζεύγνυ-μι (ζευξ-) yoke

ἦ = ? (dir. or indir.)
ἦ . . . ἦε double question
ἠδέ and
θεουδ-ής -ές god-fearing
θῆλ-υς -εια -υ female
θυμ-ός, ὁ heart (2a)
ἱκάν-ω come
κάρην-ον, τό peak (2b)
μετά (+acc.) to
νέ-ομαι return
νοέ-ω plan
νό-ος, ὁ =νοῦς, ὁ
νυ=νυν
νύμφ-η, ἡ nymph (1a)
οἴκόνδε home, homewards
ὁρμαίν-ω debate, consider
πειρήσομαι let me try (aor. subj. of πειράομαι)
πηγ-ή, ἡ source (1a)
πίσε-α, τά meadows (3c uncontr.)
ποιή-εις -εσσα -εν (ποιηεντ-) grassy
που somewhere, anywhere (enclitic)
πτύσσ-ω (πτυξ-) fold

ῥα=ἄρα
σφαῖρ-α, ἡ ball (1b)
σχεδόν (+ gen.) near
τέων= τίνων
φιλόξειν-ος -ον loving strangers, hospitable
φρήν (φρεν-), ἡ mind (3a)
ὥς =ἵνα (+ subj./opt.) in order that

Vocabulary to be learnt
ἀμφέρχομαι surround (+acc.) (aor. ἀμφήλυθον)
ἀμφίπολος, ἡ handmaiden (2a)
γλαυκῶπις (γλαυκωπιδ-), ἡ grey-eyed (used of Athene)
δῖος ᾱ ον godlike
θῡμός, ὁ heart, anger (2a)
νοέω plan, devise; notice
νυ=νυν (enclitic)
φρήν (φρεν-), ἡ heart, mind (3a)
ὥς (+subj./opt.)=ἵνα in order to/that

D

*Naked, but discreetly clutching a leafy branch, Odysseus emerges. The girls flee
– all except Nausikaa. Odysseus considers how he may best address her.*

In *World of Athens*: supplication 3.35–6.

> ὡς εἰπών, θάμνων ὑπεδύσετο δῖος Ὀδυσσεύς,
> ἐκ πυκινῆς δ' ὕλης πτόρθον κλάσε χειρὶ παχείῃ
> φύλλων, ὡς ῥύσαιτο περὶ χροῒ μήδεα φωτός.
> βῆ δ' ἴμεν ὥς τε λέων ὀρεσίτροφος, ἀλκὶ πεποιθώς,   130
> ὅς τ' εἶσ' ὑόμενος καὶ ἀήμενος, ἐν δέ οἱ ὄσσε
> δαίεται· αὐτὰρ ὁ βουσὶ μετέρχεται ἢ ὀίεσσιν
> ἠὲ μετ' ἀγροτέρας ἐλάφους· κέλεται δέ ἑ γαστήρ,
> μήλων πειρήσοντα, καὶ ἐς πυκινὸν δόμον ἐλθεῖν·
> ὡς Ὀδυσεὺς κούρῃσιν ἐϋπλοκάμοισιν ἔμελλε   135
> μίξεσθαι, γυμνός περ ἐών· χρειὼ γὰρ ἵκανε.
> σμερδαλέος δ' αὐτῇσι φάνη κεκακωμένος ἅλμῃ,
> τρέσσαν δ' ἄλλυδις ἄλλη ἐπ' ἠϊόνας προὐχούσας·
> οἴη δ' Ἀλκινόου θυγάτηρ μένε· τῇ γὰρ Ἀθήνη
> θάρσος ἐνὶ φρεσὶ θῆκε, καὶ ἐκˤ δέος ⌉εἵλετο γυίων.   140
> στῆ δ' ἄντα σχομένη· ὁ δὲ μερμήριξεν Ὀδυσσεύς,
> ἢ γούνων λίσσοιτο λαβὼν εὐώπιδα κούρην,
> ἦ αὔτως ἐπέεσσιν ἀποσταδὰ μειλιχίοισι
> λίσσοιτ', εἰ δείξειε πόλιν καὶ εἵματα δοίη.
> ὡς ἄρα οἱ φρονέοντι δοάσσατο κέρδιον εἶναι,   145
> λίσσεσθαι ἐπέεσσιν ἀποσταδὰ μειλιχίοισι,
> μή οἱ γοῦνα λαβόντι χολώσαιτο φρένα κούρη.
> αὐτίκα μειλίχιον καὶ κερδαλέον φάτο μῦθον·

Vocabulary for Section Twenty D

Notes

127. ὥς: 'so, in this way', like 135 and 145; cf. ὡς 129 expressing purpose; ὥς
   130 'like'.
129. ῥύσαιτο: the subject is πτόρθος.
131. εἶσ(ι): εἶμι 'go'.
134. ἐλθεῖν: after κέλεται; πειρήσοντα (agreeing with ἑ) is future, expressing
   purpose.
134. δόμον: here 'sheepfold'.
141. σχομένη: aor. middle participle of ἔχω.
144. εἰ: 'in the hope that she would' (implied purpose).
147. μή: 'lest'; φρένα 'in her mind'.

ἀγρότερ-ος -η -ον wild
ἄη-μι blow upon (of wind)
ἀλκί strength, prowess (dat.)
ἄλλυδις (ἄλλη) in different directions
ἅλμ-η, ἡ brine (1a)
ἄντα face to face
ἀποσταδά at a distance
αὐτάρ but, now
αὔτως simply
γαστήρ (γαστερ-), ἡ stomach, hunger (3a)
γοῦν-α, τά knees (2b) (take γούνων [l.142] after λαβών 'taking hold of')
γυῖ-α, τά limbs (2b)
γυμν-ός -ή -όν naked
δαί-ομαι blaze
δέ-ος, τό fear (3c)
δοάσσατο it seemed to x (dat.)
ἑ (l.133) =αὐτόν
ἐκ . . . εἵλετο (aor. of ἐξαιρέομαι) remove from (+ gen.)
ἔλαφ-ος, ἡ hind (2a)
εὐπλόκαμ-ος -ον with pretty hair
εὐῶπις (εὐωπιδ-), ἡ beautiful
ἔχ-ομαι (σχ-) hold one's ground
ἤ . . . ἠέ either ... or
ἤ ...ἤ whether ... or
ἠιών (ἠιον-), ἡ shore, strand (3a)

θάμν-ος, ὁ bush (2a)
θάρσ-ος, τό courage, boldness (3c)
ἱκάν-ω come to, come upon
ἴμεν=ἰέναι
κακό-ω disfigure
κέλ-ομαι order
κερδαλέ-ος -η -ον cunning
κέρδιον more profitable
κλάζ-ω break
λίσσ-ομαι beseech
μειλίχι-ος -η -ον winning, soothing
μερμηρίζ-ω consider, debate
μετέρχ-ομαι attack (+dat., or μετά+acc.)
μήδε-α, τά genitals (3c uncontr.)
μῆλ-ον, τό sheep (2b)
μίγνυ-μαι meet with (+dat.) (fut μίξομαι)
ὀΐεσσιν dat. pl. of ὄϊς
οἶ-ος -η -ον alone
ὄϊς, ὁ, ἡ sheep
ὀρεσίτροφ-ος -ον mountain-bred
ὄσσε both eyes (nom.)
παχ-ύς -εῖα -ύ thick, clenched
πειρά-ω test (+gen.)
πεποιθώς trusting in (+dat.) (perf. part. of πείθ-ω)
περ=καίπερ
περί (+dat.) around, about

προέχ-ω jut out
πτόρθ-ος, ὁ branch (2a)
πυκιν-ός -ή -όν dense, thick-foliaged
ῥύ-ομαι protect, hide
σμερδαλέ-ος -η -ον frightful, terrible
τῇ (l.139) =αὐτῇ
τρέ-ω tremble, flee
ὕλ-η, ἡ bush, tree (1a)
ὑποδύ-ομαι emerge from (+gen.)
ὕ-ω rain (upon)
φρονέ-ω consider
φύλλ-ον, τό leaf (2b)
φώς (φωτ-), ὁ mortal (3a)
χολό-ομαι be angry with (+dat.)
χρείω, ἡ need
χρώς, ὁ flesh, body (dat. χροΐ)

Vocabulary to be learnt
γοῦνα, τά *knees (2b) (sometimes* γούνατα *[3b])*
ἱκάνω *come, come to/upon (+acc.)*
ἴμεν =ἰέναι
λίσσομαι *beseech*
ὁ ἡ τό *he, she, it*
φρονέω *think, consider*
χρώς, ὁ *flesh (Attic* χρωτ- *3a) (Ionic/Epic acc.* χρόα; *gen.* χροός; *dat.* χροΐ)

τρέσσαν δ' ἄλλυδις ἄλλη

E

Odysseus' speech. He indicates his awe of Nausikaa, relates his past sufferings (hinting at his own importance in passing), and closes with a plea for help.

'γουνοῦμαί σε, ἄνασσα· θεός νύ τις ἦ βροτός ἐσσι;
εἰ μέν τις θεός ἐσσι, τοὶ οὐρανὸν εὐρὺν ἔχουσιν,   150
Ἀρτέμιδί σε ἐγώ γε, Διὸς κούρη μεγάλοιο,
εἶδός τε μέγεθός τε φυήν τ' ἄγχιστα ἐΐσκω·
εἰ δέ τίς ἐσσι βροτῶν, τοὶ ἐπὶ χθονὶ ναιετάουσι,
τρισμάκαρες μέν σοί γε πατὴρ καὶ πότνια μήτηρ,
τρισμάκαρες δὲ κασίγνητοι· μάλα πού σφισι θυμὸς   155
αἰὲν ἐϋφροσύνῃσιν ἰαίνεται εἵνεκα σεῖο,
λευσσόντων τοιόνδε θάλος χορὸν εἰσοιχνεῦσαν.
κεῖνος δ' αὖ περὶ κῆρι μακάρτατος ἔξοχον ἄλλων,
ὅς κέ σ', ἐέδνοισι βρίσας, οἶκόνδ' ἀγάγηται.
οὐ γάρ πω τοιοῦτον ἐγὼ ἴδον ὀφθαλμοῖσιν,   160
οὔτ' ἄνδρ' οὔτε γυναῖκα· σέβας μ' ἔχει εἰσορόωντα.
Δήλῳ δή ποτε τοῖον, Ἀπόλλωνος παρὰ βωμῷ,
φοίνικος νέον ἔρνος ἀνερχόμενον ἐνόησα·
ἦλθον γὰρ καὶ κεῖσε, πολὺς δέ μοι ἕσπετο λαός
τὴν ὁδὸν ᾗ δὴ μέλλεν ἐμοὶ κακὰ κήδε' ἔσεσθαι.   165
ὣς ͡δ' ͡αὔτως, καὶ κεῖνο ἰδών, ἐτεθήπεα θυμῷ
δήν, ἐπεὶ οὔ πω τοῖον ἀνήλυθεν ἐκ δόρυ γαίης,
ὣς σέ, γύναι, ἄγαμαί τε τέθηπά τε δείδιά τ' αἰνῶς
γούνων ἅψασθαι· χαλεπὸν δέ με πένθος ἱκάνει.

Vocabulary for Section Twenty E

Notes

151–2. take in order ἐΐσκω σε Ἀρτέμιδι, κούρη Διὸς μεγάλοιο, in respect of
        your (acc.) εἶδος etc.
157.   λευσσόντων: lit. 'of them [= σφισί 155, i.e. parents and siblings]
        seeing…'.
157.   τοιόνδε θάλος: i.e. such a budding branch as you (hence εἰσοιχνεῦσαν,
        f. acc.).
162.   τοῖον … νέον ἔρνος ἀνερχόμενον: object of ἐνόησα.
165.   τὴν ὁδὸν ᾗ: 'on the journey by which…'.
167.   ἐκ: see vocabulary.

ἄγα-μαι admire, look at in awe
ἄγχιστα most closely
αἰέν=ἀεί
αἰνῶς terribly
ἄνασσ-α, ἡ princess (1c)
ἀνέρχ-ομαι (ἀνηλυθ-) come up
Ἄρτεμις (Ἀρτεμιδ-), ἡ Artemis
    (3a) (goddess of hunting and
    chastity)
βρίθ-ω load down
βροτ-ός, ὁ mortal (2a)
γουνό-ομαι beseech
δείδια I fear
Δῆλ-ος, ἡ Delos (2a) (island
    birthplace and sanctuary of
    Apollo)
δήν for a long time
δόρυ (δορατ-), τό piece of wood,
    shaft (3b)
ἕεδν-α, τά bridal gifts (2b)
εἶδ-ος, τό looks, appearance (3c)
εἵνεκα =ἕνεκα
ἐΐσκ-ω liken x (acc.) to y (dat.)
    in z (acc.)

εἰσοιχνέ-ω enter
εἰσορά-ω behold, look upon
ἐκ l.167 goes with γαίης
ἔξοχον (+gen.) above, more
    than
ἔρν-ος, τό young stem (3c)
ἐσσι=εἶ you (s.) are
εὐρ-ύς -εῖα -ύ broad, wide
εὐφροσύν-η, ἡ pleasure (1a)
θάλ-ος, τό budding branch (3c)
ἰαίν-ω warm
κασίγνητ-ος, ὁ brother (2a)
κεῖν-ος=ἐκεῖν-ος
κεῖσε=ἐκεῖσε
κήδε-α, τά troubles (3c uncontr.)
κῆρ (κηρ-), τό heart (3a)
λα-ός, ὁ people (2a)
λεύσσ-ω see (take λευσσόντων
    with σφισι)
μάκαρ (μακαρ-) blessed
    (μακάρτατ-ος -η -ον is the
    sup.)
μέγεθ-ος, τό size (3c)
ναιετά-ω dwell

οἰκόνδε home, homewards
ὀφθαλμ-ός, ὁ eye (2a)
πένθ-ος, τό grief (3c)
περί (+dat.) in
πότνι-α lady (nom. s. f.)
που somewhere, anywhere; I
    suppose (enclitic)
πω yet (enclitic)
σέβας, τό respect (3c)
σεῖο=σοῦ
σφισι=σφι
τέθηπα be astonished (perf.)
    (past ἐτεθήπεα)
τοι=οἵ
τοῖ-ος=τοιοῦτος
τρισμάκαρ (τρισμακαρ-)
    thrice-blessed
φοίνιξ (φοινικ-), ὁ, ἡ
    date-palm
φυ-ή, ἡ stature (1a)
χθών (χθον-), ἡ earth (3a)
χορ-ός, ὁ dance (2a)
ὡς δ' αὔτως in the same way

Ἄρτεμις   Ἀπόλλων

χθιζὸς ἐεικοστῷ φύγον ἤματι οἴνοπα πόντον·   170
τόφρα δέ μ' αἰεὶ κῦμ' ἐφόρει κραιπναί τε θύελλαι
νήσου ἀπ' Ὠγυγίης· νῦν δ' ἐνθάδε κάββαλε δαίμων,
ὄφρα τί που καὶ τῇδε πάθω κακόν· οὐ γὰρ ὀΐω
παύσεσθ', ἀλλ' ἔτι πολλὰ θεοὶ τελέουσι πάροιθεν.
ἀλλά, ἄνασσ', ἐλέαιρε· σὲ γὰρ κακὰ πολλὰ μογήσας   175
ἐς πρώτην ἱκόμην, τῶν δ' ἄλλων οὔ τινα οἶδα
ἀνθρώπων, οἳ τήνδε πόλιν καὶ γαῖαν ἔχουσιν.
ἄστυ δέ μοι δεῖξον, δὸς δὲ ῥάκος ἀμφιβαλέσθαι,
εἴ τί που εἴλυμα σπείρων ἔχες ἐνθάδ' ἰοῦσα.
σοὶ δὲ θεοὶ τόσα δοῖεν ὅσα φρεσὶ σῇσι μενοινᾷς,   180
ἄνδρα τε καὶ οἶκον καὶ ὁμοφροσύνην ὀπάσειαν
ἐσθλήν· οὐ μὲν γὰρ τοῦ γε κρεῖσσον καὶ ἄρειον,
ἢ ὅθ' ὁμοφρονέοντε νοήμασιν οἶκον ἔχητον
ἀνὴρ ἠδὲ γυνή· πόλλ' ἄλγεα δυσμενέεσσι,
χάρματα δ' εὐμενέτῃσι· μάλιστα δέ τ' ἔκλυον αὐτοί.'   185

---

174.   παύσεσθαι: understand κακόν as subject.
175.   σε: with ἐς πρώτην.
180.   δοῖεν: note optative, expressing a wish, like ὀπάσειαν (181).
182.   τοῦ: see vocabulary.
184.   πολλ' … εὐμενέτῃσι: see vocabulary under ἄλγος.

ἄλγ-ος, τό source of grief
  (3c uncontr.) (*understand*
  'these things are . . .')
ἀμφιβάλλ-ομαι (ἀμφιβαλ-) put on
ἅπτ-ομαι touch (+gen.)
ἄρειον better
γαῖ-α, ἡ (1c)=γῆ
δυσμεν-ής, ὁ enemy
ἐεικοστ-ός -ή -όν twentieth
εἴλυμα, τό wrapping (3b)
ἐλεαίρ-ω show mercy
εὐμενέτ-ης, ὁ friend (1d)
ἔχες=εἶχες
ἔχητον 'the two of them keep'
  (3rd dual)
ἢ or
ἠδέ and
ἦμαρ (ἠματ-), τό day (3b)
θύελλ-α, ἡ storm (1c)
ἱκνέ-ομαι (ἱκ-) come to
κάββαλε=κατέβαλε
καταβάλλ-ω (καταβαλ-) cast
  down

κλύ-ω be respected
κραιπν-ός -ή -όν swift
κῦμα (κυματ-), τό wave (3b)
μενοινά-ω desire
μογέ-ω suffer
νόημα (νοηματ-), τό thought
  (3b)
οἶνοψ (οἰνοπ-) wine-faced
  (wine-dark)
οἴ-ω think
ὁμοφρονέ-ω be in agreement,
  compatible
ὁμοφρονέοντε nom. part. dual
ὁμοφροσύν-η, ἡ compatibility
  (1a)
ὀπάζ-ω grant
ὄφρα=ἵνα (+subj.) in order that
πάροιθεν before then
πόντ-ος, ὁ sea (2a)
που somewhere, anywhere; I
  suppose (enclitic)
ῥάκ-ος, τό tattered garment (3c)
σπεῖρ-ον, τό garment (2b)

τελέ-ω complete, bring to pass
  (fut. τελέ-ω)
τῇδε here
τόσ-ος -η -ον as many (*take with*
  ὅσος 'as many as')
τοῦ=τούτου (gen. of
  comparison)
τόφρα for so long
φορέ-ω carry
χάρμα (χαρματ-), τό source of
  joy (3b)
χθιζ-ός -ή -όν yesterday's
  (tr. 'yesterday')
Ὠγυγί-η, ἡ Ogygia (1a) (*island
  of Kalypso*)

Vocabulary to be learnt
ἄνασσα, ἡ *princess, queen (1c)*
ἅπτομαι *touch (+gen.)*
βροτός, ὁ *mortal (2a)*
γαῖα, ἡ=γῆ
εἰσοράω (εἰσιδ-) *behold, look at*
ἔσσι=εἶ *you (s.) are*

ἦ *or*
ἦμαρ (ἤματ-), τό *day (3b)*
ἱκνέομαι (ἱκ-) *come to, arrive at*
κεῖνος=ἐκεῖνος
μέγεθος, τό *size (3c)*

οἴκόνδε *home, homewards*
ὀφθαλμός, ὁ *eye (2a)*
περί *(+dat.) in, on*
που *somewhere, anywhere (enclitic)*

πω *yet (enclitic)*
τοί=οἵ *(relative)*
χορός, ὁ *dance; chorus (2a)*

Enjoying Homer

One important feature of Homer's practice is his tendency to restrict the third-person narrative to reporting of facts, without any obvious authorial evaluation or interpretation added. To put it simply, Homer says 'X happened and Y happened and Z happened' without saying anything more about the significance of the events. He puts evaluation, judgement and moral perspective in the mouths of his characters – again, as if merely reporting what they say. The result is that Homer's work has an air of 'objectivity' too it, as if the poet is entirely divorced from the proceedings – he is merely the mouthpiece – and we have to make what sense of it we can. Look, for example, at 20B ll.56–71. Homer does not say 'Look how Nausikaa winds her father round her little finger!' He just lets her talk, and her father answer. Nevertheless, is there a gentle narratorial steer at ll. 66–7?

Odysseus' speech in 20E is a masterpiece. It starts with a lightly humorous touch (a good beginning for a man in desperate need of help but not exactly dressed to kill). Odysseus has decided not to supplicate Nausikaa in the usual way (i.e. seize her knees) for the reason he gives. But his first words are 'I seize your knees'! He compliments her on her beauty by likening her to Artemis (151), goddess of – ? Virginity. In other words, Odysseus flatters her beauty (152), but does not threaten (she would have run a mile had he likened her to, for example, Aphrodite, goddess of sex). He blesses her parents and siblings, but most of all, the one who marries her. Here is a man who respects the family and marriage – an unlikely sentiment for someone who had evil designs on her. He summarises his reaction to her by one word – σέβας (161) – which he proceeds to explain with a story that hints at an interesting past (162–5), ending with a more detailed account of his feelings towards her (166-8). Now is the time to wring her heart with a brief hint at the sufferings that have brought him here (170–4), and to throw himself on her mercy (175–9). He ends by wishing her everything a young and attractive woman of that world would long for – a marriage in which both parties see eye–to–eye (the marriage theme returns). The wily, intelligent, delicately tactful Odysseus sees perfectly into her heart. What a masterful speech, from a master poet. But that is Homer for you – speaking to us with such sensitive human understanding over nearly 3000 years.

Nausikaa, with halting formality, promises help, introduces herself and recalls her terrified servants.

τὸν δ' αὖ Ναυσικάα λευκώλενος ἀντίον ηὔδα·
'ξεῖν', ἐπεὶ οὔτε κακῷ οὔτ' ἄφρονι φωτὶ ἔοικας,
Ζεὺς δ' αὐτὸς νέμει ὄλβον Ὀλύμπιος ἀνθρώποισιν,
ἐσθλοῖς ἠδὲ κακοῖσιν, ὅπως ἐθέλησιν, ἑκάστῳ·
καί που σοὶ τάδ' ἔδωκε, σὲ δὲ χρὴ τετλάμεν ἔμπης.   190
νῦν δ', ἐπεὶ ἡμετέρην τε πόλιν καὶ γαῖαν ἱκάνεις,
οὔτ' οὖν ἐσθῆτος δευήσεαι οὔτε τευ ἄλλου,
ὧν ἐπέοιχ' ἱκέτην ταλαπείριον ἀντιάσαντα.
ἄστυ δέ τοι δείξω, ἐρέω δέ τοι οὔνομα λαῶν.
Φαίηκες μὲν τήνδε πόλιν καὶ γαῖαν ἔχουσιν,   195
εἰμὶ δ' ἐγὼ θυγάτηρ μεγαλήτορος Ἀλκινόοιο,
τοῦ δ' ἐκ Φαιήκων ἔχεται κάρτος τε βίη τε.'
ἦ ῥα, καὶ ἀμφιπόλοισιν ἐϋπλοκάμοισι κέλευσε·
'στῆτέ μοι, ἀμφίπολοι· πόσε φεύγετε, φῶτα ἰδοῦσαι;
ἦ μή πού τινα δυσμενέων φάσθ' ἔμμεναι ἀνδρῶν;   200
οὐκ ἔσθ' οὗτος ἀνὴρ διερὸς βροτὸς οὐδὲ γένηται,
ὅς κεν Φαιήκων ἀνδρῶν ἐς γαῖαν ἵκηται
δηϊοτῆτα φέρων· μάλα γὰρ φίλοι ἀθανάτοισιν.
οἰκέομεν δ' ἀπάνευθε, πολυκλύστῳ ἐνὶ πόντῳ,
ἔσχατοι, οὐδέ τις ἄμμι βροτῶν ἐπιμίσγεται ἄλλος.   205
ἀλλ' ὅδε τις δύστηνος ἀλώμενος ἐνθάδ' ἱκάνει,
τὸν νῦν χρὴ κομέειν· πρὸς γὰρ Διός εἰσιν ἅπαντες
ξεῖνοί τε πτωχοί τε, δόσις δ' ὀλίγη τε φίλη τε.
ἀλλὰ δότ', ἀμφίπολοι, ξείνῳ βρῶσίν τε πόσιν τε,
λούσατέ τ' ἐν ποταμῷ, ὅθ' ἐπὶ⌐ σκέπας ⌐ἔστ' ἀνέμοιο.'   210

Vocabulary for Section Twenty F

Notes

193. ὧν: gen., as if the sentence continued 'ὧν it is right for a ἱκέτης not to lack'.
197. ἐκ, ἔχεται: see vocabulary.
200. φάσθ(ε): φημί in Homer often means 'think', as here: 'surely you do not think [him] to be τινα…' etc.
203. φίλοι: understand 'we are'.
207. πρός: see vocabulary.
208. ὀλίγη τε φίλη τε: = 'doesn't cost us much but will mean a lot to the beggar'.

ἀλά-ομαι wander
Ἀλκινόοιο=Ἀλκινόου
ἄμμι=ἡμῖν
ἀνέμοιο=ἀνέμου
ἄνεμος, ὁ wind (2a)
ἀντιά-ω meet, encounter
ἀντίον in reply
ἀπάνευθε far away
αὐδά-ω speak, say
ἄφρων ἄφρον (ἀφρον-) stupid,
   thoughtless
βί-η, ἡ dominion (1a)
βρῶσ-ις, ἡ meat, food (3e)
γένηται (1.201) '(he) will
   ever be' (*subj. in general
   statement*)
δεύ-ομαι lack (+gen.) (fut.
   δευήσομαι)
δηϊοτής (δηϊοτητ-), ἡ slaughter
   (3a)
διερ-ός -ά -όν living
δόσ-ις, ἡ gift, giving (3e)
δυσμεν-ής -ές hostile
δύστην-ος -ον wretched

ἐθέλησιν=ἐθέλη (3rd s. pres.
   subj.)
ἐκ (l. 25) governs τοῦ
ἔμμεναι=εἶναι
ἔμπης doubtless, at any rate
ἐπέοικε it befits, it is right for
   (+dat.)
ἐπί . . . ἔστ' is, is found
ἐπιμίσγ-ομαι have to do with
   (+dat.)
εὐπλόκαμ-ος -ον with pretty hair
ἔχ-ομαι (ἐκ) depend (on)
ἦ (1.198) she spoke
ἦ μή surely you don't
ἠδέ and
κάρτ-ος, τό power (3c)
κομέ-ω look after, care for
λα-ός, ὁ people, inhabitant (2a)
λευκώλεν-ος -ον white-armed
λού-ω wash
μεγαλήτωρ (μεγαλητορ-)
   great-hearted
ὄλβ-ος, ὁ happiness, wealth
   (2a)

πολύκλυστ-ος -ον loud-roaring
πόντ-ος, ὁ sea (2a)
πόσε; (to) where?
πόσ-ις, ἡ drink (3e)
πρός (+gen.) under the
   protection of
πτωχ-ός, ὁ beggar (2a)
σκέπας, τό cover, shelter (sc.
   'from')
ταλαπείρι-ος -ον weary
τετλάμεν to endure (perf. inf. of
   τλάω)
φώς (φωτ-), ὁ mortal, man (3a)

Vocabulary to be learnt
ἄνεμος, ὁ *wind (2a)*
ἔμμεναι=εἶναι
εὐπλόκαμος ον *with pretty hair*
ἠδέ *and*
λᾱός, ὁ *people, inhabitant (2a)*
λούω *wash (mid. wash oneself)*
πόντος, ὁ *sea (2a)*
φώς (φωτ-), ὁ *man, mortal (3a)*

G

As Odysseus bathes, Athene increases his attractiveness. Nausikaa describes to her servants the effect upon her of his transformation.

ὣς ἔφαθ', αἱ δ' ἔσταν τε καὶ ἀλλήλῃσι κέλευσαν,
κὰδ⌐ δ' ἄρ' Ὀδυσσῆ' ⌐εἷσαν ἐπὶ σκέπας, ὡς ἐκέλευσε
Ναυσικάα, θυγάτηρ μεγαλήτορος Ἀλκινόοιο·
πὰρ δ' ἄρα οἱ φαρός τε χιτῶνά τε εἵματ' ἔθηκαν,
δῶκαν δὲ χρυσέῃ ἐν ληκύθῳ ὑγρὸν ἔλαιον,   215
ἤνωγον δ' ἄρα μιν λοῦσθαι ποταμοῖο ῥοῇσι.

Vocabulary for Section Twenty G

ἔλαι-ον, τό olive oil (2b)
ἤνωγον they ordered
κάδ (= κατά) . . . ἕζ-ω to seat
   (aor. εἷσα)
λήκυθ-ος, ἡ oil-jar (2a)

μεγαλήτωρ (μεγαλητορ-)
   great-hearted
ῥο-ή, ἡ stream, current (1a)
σκέπας, τό cover, shelter
ὑγρ-ός -ή -όν moist

φᾶρ-ος, τό cloak (3c)
χιτών (χιτων-), ὁ tunic (3a)
χρύσε-ος -η -ον golden

δή ῥα τότ' ἀμφιπόλοισι μετηύδα δῖος Ὀδυσσεύς·
'ἀμφίπολοι, στῆθ' οὕτω ἀπόπροθεν, ὄφρ' ἐγὼ αὐτὸς
ἅλμην ὤμοιϊν ἀπολούσομαι, ἀμφὶ δ' ἐλαίῳ
χρίσομαι· ἦ γὰρ δηρὸν ἀπὸ⌐ χροός ⌐ἐστιν ἀλοιφή.   220
ἄντην δ' οὐκ ἂν ἐγώ γε λοέσσομαι· αἰδέομαι γὰρ
γυμνοῦσθαι κούρῃσιν ἐϋπλοκάμοισι μετελθών.'
ὣς ἔφαθ', αἱ δ' ἀπάνευθεν ἴσαν, εἶπον δ' ἄρα κούρῃ.
αὐτὰρ ὁ ἐκ ποταμοῦ χρόα νίζετο δῖος Ὀδυσσεὺς
ἅλμην, ἥ οἱ νῶτα καὶ εὐρέας ἄμπεχεν ὤμους·   225
ἐκ κεφαλῆς δ' ἔσμηχεν ἁλὸς χνόον ἀτρυγέτοιο.
αὐτὰρ ἐπεὶ δὴ πάντα λοέσσατο καὶ λίπ' ἄλειψεν,
ἀμφὶ⌐ δὲ εἵματα ⌐ἕσσαθ' ἅ οἱ πόρε παρθένος ἀδμής,
τὸν μὲν Ἀθηναίη θῆκεν, Διὸς ἐκγεγαυῖα,
μείζονά τ' εἰσιδέειν καὶ πάσσονα, κὰδ δὲ κάρητος   230
οὔλας ἧκε κόμας, ὑακινθίνῳ ἄνθει ὁμοίας.
ὡς δ' ὅτε τις χρυσὸν περιχεύεται ἀργύρῳ ἀνήρ,
ἴδρις, ὃν Ἥφαιστος δέδαεν καὶ Παλλὰς Ἀθήνη
τέχνην παντοίην, χαρίεντα δὲ ἔργα τελείει,
ὣς ἄρα τῷ κατέχευε χάριν κεφαλῇ τε καὶ ὤμοις.   235
ἕζετ' ἔπειτ' ἀπάνευθε, κιὼν ἐπὶ θῖνα θαλάσσης,
κάλλεϊ καὶ χάρισι στίλβων· θηεῖτο δὲ κούρη.
δή ῥα τότ' ἀμφιπόλοισιν ἐϋπλοκάμοισι μετηύδα·
'κλῦτέ μευ, ἀμφίπολοι λευκώλενοι, ὄφρα τι εἴπω.
οὐ πάντων ἀέκητι θεῶν, οἳ Ὄλυμπον ἔχουσι,   240
Φαιήκεσσ' ὅδ' ἀνὴρ ἐπιμίσγεται ἀντιθέοισι·
πρόσθεν μὲν γὰρ δή μοι ἀεικέλιος δέατ' εἶναι,
νῦν δὲ θεοῖσιν ἔοικε, τοὶ οὐρανὸν εὐρὺν ἔχουσιν.
αἲ γὰρ ἐμοὶ τοιόσδε πόσις κεκλημένος εἴη
ἐνθάδε ναιετάων, καί οἱ ἅδοι αὐτόθι μίμνειν.   245
ἀλλὰ δότ', ἀμφίπολοι, ξείνῳ βρῶσίν τε πόσιν τε.'
ὣς ἔφαθ', αἱ δ' ἄρα τῆς μάλα μὲν κλύον ἠδ' ἐπίθοντο,
πὰρ δ' ἄρ' Ὀδυσσῆϊ ἔθεσαν βρῶσίν τε πόσιν τε.
ἦ τοι ὁ πῖνε καὶ ἦσθε πολύτλας δῖος Ὀδυσσεὺς
ἁρπαλέως· δηρὸν γὰρ ἐδητύος ἦεν ἄπαστος.   250

Notes

224. ὁ: 'he', soon to be qualified '[that is] δῖος Ὀδυσσεύς'.
229. τὸν μέν: = Odysseus, object of Ἀθηναίη [another form of 'Athene'] θῆκεν,
     agreeing with μείζονα … καὶ πάσσονα (230).
231. ἧκε: 'she let fall'.
232. ὡς δ' ὅτε: 'as when …', the start of a simile, to be picked up at 235 ὣς ἄρα
     τῷ 'so then on him…'.
244. κεκλημένος: from καλέω.
245. ἅδοι: see vocabulary ἀνδάνω.

ἀδμής (ἀδμητ-), ἡ unwed
ἀεικέλι-ος -η -ον wretched
ἀέκητι against the will of (+gen.)
αἲ γάρ = εἰ γάρ
αἰδέ-ομαι feel shame at (+inf.)
ἀλείφ-ω anoint
ἅλμ-η, ἡ brine (1a)
ἀλοιφ-ή, ἡ ointment (1a)
ἅλς (ἁλ-), ὁ sea (3a)
ἀμπέχ-ω cover, lie thick upon
ἀμφί round about (adv.)
ἀμφί . . . ἔννυμαι put on (aor.
    ἑσσάμην)
ἀνδάν-ω (ἁδ-) please (+dat.)
ἄνθ-ος, τό flower (3c)
ἄντην face to face, in front of
    (sc. 'you')
ἀντίθε-ος -η -ον god-like
ἀπάνευθεν afar off
ἄπαστ-ος -ον not having tasted
    (+gen.)
ἀπό . . . ἐστίν has been absent
    (from +gen.)
ἀπολούσομαι 1st s. aor. subj. of
    ἀπολού-ομαι wash off oneself
ἀπόπροθεν far off
ἄργυρ-ος, ὁ silver (2a)
ἁρπαλέως greedily
ἀτρυγέτοιο=ἀτρυγέτου
ἀτρύγετ-ος -ον unharvested
αὐτάρ then, but
αὐτόθι here
βρῶσ-ις, ἡ meat, food (3e)
γυμνό-ομαι strip
δέατο he seemed
δέδαεν 3rd s. perf. of
    δι-δά-σκω
δηρόν for a long time
ἐδητύς, ἡ food (3h)
ἕζ-ομαι sit
ἐκγεγαυῖα born of (+gen.) (nom.
    s. f.)
ἐπιμίσγ-ομαι meet with (+dat.)

εὐρ-ύς -εῖα -ύ broad
ἦ indeed
ἦεν=ἦν
ἦσθε =ἤσθιε (he) ate
ἦ τοι then indeed
θηέ-ομαι look at admiringly
θίς (θιν-), ὁ shore (3a)
ἴδρις skilful, cunning (nom.)
ἴσαν =ᾖσαν they went
κάδ=κατά
κάλλ-ος, τό beauty (3c)
κάρη (καρητ-), τό head (3b)
καταχεύ-ω pour down x (acc.)
    on γ (dat.) over z (acc.)
κί-ω go
κόμ-η, ἡ hair (1a)
λευκώλεν-ος -ον white-armed
λίπα richly
λοέσσατο 3rd s. aor. mid. of
    λούω
λοέσσομαι fut. mid. of λούω
μεταυδά-ω say (to)
μετέρχ-ομαι (μετελθ-) go among
    (+dat.)
μίμν-ω=μένω
ναιετά-ω dwell, live
νίζ-ομαι wash x (acc.) from γ
    (acc.)
νῶτ-ον, τό back (2b)
Ὄλυμπ-ος, ὁ Olympus (2a)
οὖλ-ος -η -ον thick, bushy
ὄφρα =ἵνα (+subj.) in order that
Πάλλας (Παλλαδ-), ἡ Pallas (3a)
παντοῖ-ος -η -ον of all
    kinds
πάρ = παρά beside (adv.)
παρθέν-ος, ἡ maiden (2a)
πάσσων -ον (πασσον-) broader
περιχεύ-ομαι inlay, gild x (acc.)
    on γ (dat.)
πολύτλας ὁ long-enduring
πόρε (she) provided, gave (3rd s.
    of ἔπορον)

πόσ-ις, ἡ drink (3e)
πρόσθεν previously
σμήχ-ω wipe
στίλβ-ω shine
τελεί-ω complete
ὑακίνθιν-ος -η -ον of a wild
    hyacinth
χαρί-εις -εσσα -εν (χαριεντ-)
    graceful
χνό-ος, ὁ scum, scurf (2a)
χρί-ομαι anoint oneself
χρῦσ-ός -ό gold (2a)
ὤμοϊιν 'from my two shoulders'
    (gen. dual of ὦμος)
ὦμ-ος, ὁ shoulder (2a)

Vocabulary to be learnt

ἀπάνευθεν *afar off*
αὐδάω *speak, say*
αὐτάρ *then, but*
εὐρύς εῖα ύ *broad,*
    wide
κάδ=κατά
κατά *(+gen.) down from,*
    against; below
κάρη (καρητ-), τό=κάρα
    (κρατ- *(3b); Attic) head*
μεταυδάω *speak to*
μετέρχομαι (μετελθ-) *go among*
    (+dat.); attack (+dat. or
    μετά); send for
ὄφρα=ἵνα+*subj./ opt. in order*
    to/that
πάρ=παρά
παρθένος, ἡ *maiden (2a)*
πρόσθεν *(+gen.) previously,*
    before
χρύσεος η ον *golden (Attic*
    χρυσοῦς ῆ οῦν)
ὦμος, ὁ *shoulder (2a)*
Genitive s. of Type 2 nouns
    (-οιο for -ου)

Then Nausikaa of the white arms thought what to do next.
She folded the laundry and put it away in the fine mule wagon,
and yoked the mules with powerful hooves, and herself mounted,
and urged Odysseus and spoke a word and named him by title:
'Rise up now, stranger, to go to the city, so I can see you   255
to the house of my own prudent father, where I am confident
you will be made known to all the highest Phaiakians.
Or rather, do it this way; you seem to me not to be thoughtless.
While we are still among the fields and the lands that the people
work, for that time follow the mules and the wagon, walking   260
lightly along with the maids, and I will point the way to you.
But when we come to the city, and around this is a towering
wall, and a handsome harbor either side of the city,
and a narrow causeway, and along the road there are oarswept
ships drawn up, for they all have slips, one for each vessel;   265
and there is the place of assembly, put together with quarried
stone, and built around a fine precinct of Poseidon,
and there they tend to all that gear that goes with the black ships,
the hawsers and the sails, and there they fine down their
     oarblades;   270
for the Phaiakians have no concern with the bow or the quiver,
but it is all masts and the oars of ships and the balanced vessels
themselves, in which they delight in crossing over the gray sea;
and it is their graceless speech I shrink from, for fear one may mock us
hereafter, since there are insolent men in our community,   275
and see how one of the worse sort might say when he met us,
'Who is this large and handsome stranger whom Nausikaa
has with her, and where did she find him? Surely, he is
to be her husband, but is he a stray from some ship of alien
men she found for herself, since there are no such hereabouts?   280
Or did some god after much entreaty come down in answer
to her prayers, out of the sky, and all his days will he have her?
Better so, if she goes out herself and finds her a husband
from elsewhere, since she pays no heed to her own Phaiakian
neighbors, although many of these and the best ones court her.'   285
So they will speak, and that would be a scandal against me,
and I myself would disapprove of a girl who acted
so, that is, without the good will of her dear father
and mother making friends with a man, before being formally
married. Then, stranger, understand what I say, in order   290
soon to win escort and a voyage home from my father.
You will find a glorious grove of poplars sacred to Athene
near the road, and a spring runs there, and there is a meadow
about it, and there is my father's estate and his flowering orchard,

as far from the city as the shout of a man will carry.   295
Sit down there and wait for time enough for the rest of us
to reach the town and make our way to my father's palace.
But when you estimate that we shall have reached the palace,
then go to the city of the Phaiakians and inquire for
the palace of my father, great-hearted Alkinoös. This is   300
easily distinguished, so an innocent child could guide you
there, for there are no other houses built for the other
Phaiakians anything like the house of the hero Alkinoös.
But when you have disappeared inside the house and the
     courtyard,   305
then go on quickly across the hall until you come to
my mother, and she will be sitting beside the hearth, in the firelight,
turning sea-purple yarn on a distaff, a wonder to look at,
and leaning against the pillar, and her maids are sitting behind her;
and there is my father's chair of state, drawn close beside her,   310
on which he sits when he drinks his wine like any immortal.
Go on past him and then with your arms embrace our mother's
knees; do this, so as to behold your day of homecoming
with happiness and speed, even if you live very far off.
For if she has thoughts in her mind that are friendly to you,   315
then there is hope that you can see your own people, and come back
to your strong-founded house, and to the land of your fathers.'
So Nausikaa spoke and with the shining lash whipped up
her mules, and swiftly they left the running river behind them,
and the mules, neatly twinkling their feet, ran very strongly,   320
but she drove them with care, so that those on foot, Odysseus
and the serving maids, could keep up, and used the whip with
     discretion.
And the sun went down and they came to the famous grove, sacred
to Athene; and there the great Odysseus sat down   325
and immediately thereafter prayed to the daughter of great Zeus:
'Hear me, Atrytone child of Zeus of the aegis,
and listen to me now, since before you did not listen
to my stricken voice as the famous shaker of the earth battered me.
Grant that I come, as one loved and pitied, among the Phaiakians.'   330
So he spoke in prayer, and Pallas Athene heard him,
but she did not yet show herself before him, for she respected
her father's brother, Poseidon, who still nursed a sore anger
at godlike Odysseus until his arrival in his own country.

A total Greek–English vocabulary of all words to be learnt*

Finding the lexicon form of a verb

The essence is to isolate the present stem, since it is most often this form which will be shown in the lexicon.

(i) Look at the front of the word, and remove any augment, or reduplication.

η could be the augmented form of α, ε, η

ῃ	„	„	αι, ει
ηυ	„	„	αυ, ευ
ω	„	„	ο
ῳ	„	„	οι
ῑ, ῡ	„	„	ι, υ
ει	„	„	ε, ει

Bear in mind that the augment might be hidden by a prefix such as κατά, ἐκ, πρό, εἰς, ἐν, so check the prefix as well.

προὔβαλον = προ-έ-βαλον
ἐξέβαλον = ἐκ-έ-βαλον
ἐνέβαλον from ἐμβάλλω

Here is a list of common prepositions and prefixes, with their various forms:

ἀνά ἀν’	ἐν ἐμ- ἐγ-	παρά παρ’
ἀπό ἀπ’ ἀφ’	ἐπί ἐπ’ ἐφ’	πρό προε- πρου-
διά δι’	κατά κατ’ καθ’	σύν συμ- συγ-
ἐκ ἐξ	μετά μετ’ μεθ’	ὑπό ὑπ’ ὑφ’

(ii) Having made an adjustment for augment/reduplication and prefix, examine the stem and the ending. Remove any personal endings.

(iii) If the remaining stem ends in σ, ξ, ψ, especially if an α follows, it is probably an aorist. Try dropping the σα (e.g. ἔ-λυ-σα = λύω) or converting σ to ζ (ἐ-νόμισ-α = νομίζω). Try restoring a terminal ξ→κ or →ττ (ἔ-πραξ-α = πράττω), and a terminal ψ to π (ἔ-πεμψ-α = πέμπω).

If the stem ends in some form of θη, remember that χ may hide ττ or κ (ἐπράχθην = πράττω), φ may hide π or β (ἐπέμφθην = πέμπω). See **359(x)**.

(iv) If there is no augment, check the endings for some sign of σ (ξ, ψ) or ε-contract in the stem, when it may be future. Check also endings for signs of

*This vocabulary also includes difficult parts of verbs, assigned to the grammatical section where they were met, with or without prefix.

participle, infinitive, etc. and remember that the stem you so isolate may be present or aorist or perfect or future.

Convention

Bold square brackets (e.g. **[3A]**) refer to the chapter where the word or root was learned, or to the grammatical section (e.g. **[223]**) where the form was met. Other difficult forms met in the *Text* are also included.

† = Principle parts at **389** in the *Grammar* volume (remove any prefixes).

A

ἀγαγ- aor. stem of ἄγω **[7H]**

ἀγαθός ἡ όν good; noble; courageous **[2B]**

ἄγαλμα (ἀγαλματ-), τό image, statue (3b) **[18D]**

†ἀγγέλλω (ἀγγειλα-) report, announce **[19F]**

ἄγγελος, ὁ messenger (2a) **[17C]**

ἄγε come! (s.) **[3A]**

ἄγομαι bring for oneself, lead; marry **[20B]**

ἀγορᾷ, ἡ gathering (-place); market-place; agora (1b) **[8A]**

ἀγορεύω speak (in assembly); proclaim **[11A]**

ἄγρη, ἡ hunt (1a) **[19E]**

ἄγροικος ον from the country; boorish **[6A]**

ἀγρός, ὁ field; country (side)(2a) **[11A]**

†ἄγω (ἀγαγ-) lead, bring **[7H]**; live in, be at **[8C]**
    εἰρήνην ἄγω live in/be at peace **[8C]**

ἀγών (ἀγων-), ὁ contest; trial (3a) **[12C]**

ἀγωνίζομαι contest, go to law **[12C]**

ἀδελφός, ὁ brother (2a) **[16D]**

ἀδικέω be unjust; commit a crime; wrong **[8B]**

ἀδίκημα (ἀδικηματ-), τό crime, wrong (3b) **[14A]**

ἄδικος ον unjust **[5D]**

ἀδύνατος ον impossible **[6B]**

†ᾄδω = ἀείδω **[8B]**

ἀεί always **[1J]**

†ἀείδω sing **[8B]**

ἀέκων= ἄκων **[19B]**

ἀθάνατος ον immortal **[11A]**

’Αθήνᾱζε to Athens **[12F]**

’Αθῆναι, αἱ Athens (1a) **[6B]**

’Αθηναῖος, ὁ Athenian (2a) **[2B]**

’Αθήνησι at Athens **[12I]**

ἄθλιος ᾱ ον pathetic, miserable, wretched **[15C]**

ἀθροίζω gather, collect **[18D]**

ἀθῡμέω be downhearted, gloomy, disheartened **[16B]**

ἀθῡμίᾱ, ἡ lack of spirit, depression (1b) **[16G]**

αἰδώς, ἡ respect for others, shame (acc. αἰδῶ; gen. αἰδοῦς; dat. αἰδοῖ) **[18E]**

αἰεί = ἀεί **[20A]**

αἱρέομαι (ἑλ-) choose **[11C]**

†αἱρέω (ἑλ-) take, capture; convict **[9I]**

†αἰσθάνομαι (αἰσθ-) perceive, notice (+ acc. or gen.) **[11C]**

αἰσχρός ᾱ́ όν ugly (of people); base, shameful (comp. αἰσχῑ́ων; sup. αἴσχιστος) **[13G]**

†αἰσχῡ́νομαι be ashamed, feel shame (before) **[12E]**

αἰτέω ask (for) **[9I]**

αἰτίᾱ, ἡ reason, cause; responsibility (1b) **[5C]**

αἴτιος ᾱ ον responsible (for), guilty (of) (+gen.) **[5A]**

αἰχμή, ἡ spear-point (1a) **[19D]**

ἀκήκοα perf. ind. of ἀκούω **[13I]**

ἀκηκοώς υἶα ός (-οτ-) perf. part. of ἀκούω

ἀκοή, ἡ hearing (1a) **[16B]**

ἀκολουθέω follow, accompany (+ dat.) **[17C]**

ἀκόσμητος ον unprovided for **[18C]**

†ἀκούω hear **[1C-D]**; listen (to) (+gen. of person, gen. or acc. of thing) (fut. ἀκούσομαι) **[9H]**

ἀκρῑβῶς accurately, closely **[1E-F]**

ἀκρόπολις, ἡ Acropolis, citadel (3e) **[1A-B]**; **[18C]**

ἄκῡρος ον invalid **[14C]**

ἄκων ἄκουσα ἄκον (ἀκοντ-) unwilling(ly) **[11B]**

ἀλ- aor. stem of ἀλίσκομαι **[16F]**

ἀλήθεια, ἡ truth (1b) **[7A]**

ἀληθῆ, τά the truth **[1D]**

†ἀλίσκομαι (ἀλ-) be convicted; be caught **[16F]**

ἀλλά but [1C]

ἀλλήλους each other, one another (2a) [3C]

ἄλλος η ο other, the rest of [3C]

ἄλλος . . . ἄλλον one . . . another [12A]

ἀλλότριος ᾱ ον someone else's; alien [12D]

ἀλλ' οὖν well anyway; however that may be [16B]

ἄλλως otherwise; in vain [17E]

ἄλογος ον speechless; without reason [18C]

ἅμα at the same time [2C]

ἀμαθής ές ignorant [6D]

†ἁμαρτάνω (ἁμαρτ-) err; do wrong; make a mistake [13H]; miss (+ gen.) [19F]

ἅμαρτε 3rd s. (2nd) aor. of ἁμαρτάνω *(no augment)*

ἀμείβομαι answer, reply to (+acc.) [19D]

ἀμείνων ἄμεινον (ἀμεινον-) better [9E]

ἀμελής ές uncaring [10E]

ἀμήχανος ον impossible, impracticable [18C]

†ἀμύνω keep off, withstand [18B]

ἀμφέρχομαι (ἀμφηλυθ-) surround (+ acc.) [20C]

ἀμφίπολος, ἡ handmaiden (2a) [20C]

ἀμφότερος ᾱ ον both [9I]

*ἄν (+ind.) *conditional* (+opt.) [12G]; *potential* [8A-C]; (+subj.) *indefinite* [14]

ἀναβαίνω (ἀναβα-) go up, come up [1G]

ἀναβάς (ἀναβαντ-) aor. part of ἀναβαίνω [209]

ἀναγκάζω force, compel [10B]

ἀναγκαῖος ᾱ ον necessary [17A]

ἀνάγκη, ἡ necessity (1a) [7B]

ἀνάγκη ἐστί it is obligatory (for x [acc. or dat.] to – [inf.]) [7B]

ἀναιρέω (ἀνελ-) pick up [7G]

ἀναίτιος ον innocent [16H]

ἀναλαμβάνω (ἀναλαβ-) take back, up [13B]

†ἀνᾱλίσκω (ἀνᾱλωσα-) spend, use, kill [18B]

ἀναμένω (ἀναμείνα-) wait, hold on [9F]

ἄναξ (ἀνακτ-), ὁ lord, prince, king (3a) [9D]

ἀναπείθω persuade over to one's side [9C]

ἄνασσα, ἡ princess (1c) [20E]

ἀναχωρέω retreat [2D]

ἀνδρεῖος ᾱ ον brave, manly [7D]

ἄνεμος, ὁ wind (2a) [20F]

ἀνέστην I stood up (aor. of ἀνίσταμαι) [231-3]

ἀνέστηκα I am standing (perf. of ἀνίσταμαι) [231-3]

ἀνεστώς ῶσα ός (ἀνεστωτ-) standing (perf. part, of ἀνίσταμαι) [231-3]

ἄνευ (+ gen.) without [11B]

†ἀνέχομαι put up with (+ gen.) [18E]

ἀνήρ (ἀνδρ-), ὁ man (3a) [3A-B]

ἄνθρωπος, ὁ man, fellow (2a) [1G]; ἡ, woman [13F]

ἀνίσταμαι (ἀναστα-) get up, stand up, emigrate [8B]

ἀνόητος ον foolish [17E]

ἀνομίᾱ, ἡ lawlessness (1b) [4C]

ἀντί (+gen.) instead of, for [16H]

ἀντίδικος, ὁ contestant in lawsuit (2a) [12C]

ἄνω above [9B]

ἄξιος ᾱ ον worth, worthy of (+gen.) [8C]

ἄοπλος ον unarmed [18C]

ἀπαγγέλλω (ἀπαγγειλα-) announce, report [17B]

ἀπαγορεύω (ἀπειπ-) forbid [17A]

ἀπάγω (ἀπαγαγ-) lead, take away [4C]

ἄπαις (ἀπαιδ-) childless [13B]

ἀπαιτέω demand (X [acc.] from Y [acc.]) [16D]

ἀπάνευθε(ν) afar off [20G]

ἅπᾶς ἅπᾶσα ἅπᾶν (ἁπαντ-) all, the whole of [10A]

ἀπέβην aor. of ἀποβαίνω

ἀπέδωκα aor. of ἀποδίδωμι [214]

ἀπέθανον aor. of ἀποθνήσκω

ἄπειμι be absent [16D]

ἄπειρος ον inexperienced in (+ gen.) [13E]

ἀπελεύθερ-ος, -ᾱ, ὁ, ἡ freedman, freedwoman (2a) [16A]

ἀπελθ- aor. stem of ἀπέρχομαι [6C]

ἀπέρχομαι (ἀπελθ-) go away, depart [6C]

ἀπέχομαι (ἀποσχ-) refrain, keep away from (+ gen.) [10A]

ἀπῆλθον aor. of ἀπέρχομαι [146]

ἀπιέναι inf. of ἀπέρχομαι/ἄπειμι [152]

ἄπιθι imper. of ἀπέρχομαι/ἄπειμι [201]

ἀπικνέομαι = ἀφικνέομαι

ἀπιών οὖσα όν part. of ἀπέρχομαι/ἄπειμι [123]

ἀπό (+ gen.) from, away from [1G]

ἀποβαίνω (ἀποβα-) leave, depart [7G]

ἀποβλέπω look steadfastly at (and away from everything else) [11A]

ἀποδίδωμι (ἀποδο-) give back, return [13A]

ἀποδο- aor. stem of ἀποδίδωμι [13A]

ἀποδραμ- aor. stem of ἀποτρέχω

ἀποδώσειν fut. inf. of ἀποδίδωμι **[214]**
ἀποθαν- aor. stem of ἀποθνήσκω
†ἀποθνήσκω (ἀποθαν-) die **[1G]**
ἀποκρίνομαι (ἀποκρīνα-) answer **[7D]**
ἀπόκρισις, ἡ reply, answer (3e) **[17C]**
ἀποκτείνω (ἀποκτεινα-) kill **[4D]**
ἀπολαβα- aor. stem of ἀπολαμβάνω **[16H]**
ἀπολαμβάνω take **[16H]**
ἀπολεσα- aor. stem of ἀπόλλῡμι **[11B]**
ἀπολέ-ω I shall kill, ruin, destroy **[8C]**
†ἀπόλλῡμι (ἀπολεσα-) kill, ruin, destroy;
    mid./pass. be killed (aor. ἀπωλόμην) **[11B]**;
    perf. mid. I have been killed, I am done for
    (ἀπόλωλα)
ἀπολογέομαι make a speech in defence, defend
    oneself **[9H]**
ἀπολογίā, ἡ speech in one's defence (1b) **[9I]**
ἀπολ- aor. stem of ἀπόλλυμαι
ἀπολύω acquit, release **[9J]**
ἀπόλωλα perf. of ἀπόλλῡμαι I am lost **[13H]**
ἀποπέμπω send away, divorce **[13A]**
ἀπορέω have no resources, be at a loss **[2B]**
ἀπορίā, ἡ lack of provisions, perplexity (1b) **[2]**
ἀποτρέχω (ἀποδραμ-) run away, run off **[9E]**
ἀποφαίνω reveal, show **[7B]**
ἀποφέρω (ἀπενεγκ-) carry back **[17A]**
ἀποφεύγω (ἀποφυγ-) escape, run off **[4C]**
ἀποχωρέω go away, depart **[1G]**
ἀποψηφίζομαι vote against; reject **[13D]**; acquit
    (+ gen.) **[14B]**
ἅπτομαι touch (+ gen.) **[20E]**
†ἅπτω light, fasten, fix **[5B]**
ἀπώλεσα aor. of ἀπόλλῡμι
*ἄρα then, consequently (*marking an inference*)
    [6D]; straightaway **[20A]**
*ἆρα ? (direct q.) **[1B]**
ἀργύριον, τό silver, money (2b) **[12H]**
†ἀρέσκω please (+ dat.) **[11C]**
ἀρετή, ἡ courage, excellence, quality (1a) **[7D]**
ἄριστος η ον best, very good **[1J]**
†ἁρπάζω seize, plunder, snatch **[17C]**
ἄρτι just now, recently **[10B]**
ἀρχή, ἡ beginning, start **[12C]**; rule, office,
    position **[13E]**; board of magistrates (1a)
ἄρχομαι (mid.) begin (+ gen.) **[9G]**; (+ inf./part.)
    [9I]; (pass.) be ruled over **[11C]**
†ἄρχω rule (+ gen.) **[11C]**; begin (+gen.) **[12E]**

ἄρχων (ἀρχοντ-), ὁ archon (3a) **[13F]**
ἀσέβεια, ἡ irreverence to the gods (1b) **[4D]**
ἀσεβέω (εἰς) commit sacrilege upon **[12D]**
ἀσεβής ἐς impious, unholy **[13E]**
ἀσθένεια, ἡ illness, weakness (1b) **[13C]**
ἀσθενέω be ill, fall ill **[13C]**
ἀσθενής ἐς weak, ill **[18A]**
ἀσπάζομαι greet, welcome **[12A]**
ἀστή, ἡ female citizen (1a) **[12F]**
ἀστός, ὁ male citizen (2a) **[12F]**
ἄστυ, τό city (3f) **[4A-B]**
ἀσφαλής ἐς safe, secure **[20A]**
ἀτάρ but **[9F]**
ἅτε since, seeing that (+ part.) **[18D]**
ἀτῑμάζω hold in dishonour, dishonour **[4B]**
ἀτῑμίā, ἡ loss of citizen rights (1b) **[12E]**
ἄτῑμος ον deprived of citizen rights **[12D]**
αὖ again, moreover **[9I]**
αὐδάω speak, say **[20G]**
αὖθις again **[2C]**
αὐλή, ἡ courtyard (1a) **[17A]**
αὔριον tomorrow **[5D]**
αὐτάρ but, then **[20G]**
αὐτίκα at once **[17D]**
αὐτόν ήν ό him, her, it, them **[4D]**
αὐτός ή ό self **[7H]**
    ὁ αὐτός the same **[7H]**
ἀφαιρέομαι (ἀφελ-) take x (acc.) from y (acc.)
    [12D]; claim
ἀφειλόμην aor. of ἀφαιρέομαι **[211]**
ἀφεῖναι aor. inf. of ἀφῑημι **[318]**
†ἀφέλκω (ἀφελκυσα-) drag off **[4D]**
ἀφελ- aor. stem of ἀφαιρέομαι **[12D]**
†ἀφῑημι (ἀφε-) release, let go **[17A]**
†ἀφικνέομαι (ἀφῑκ-) arrive, come **[3A]**
ἀφῑκόμην aor. of ἀφικνέομαι
ἀφίσταμαι relinquish claim to (+ gen.), revolt
    from (+ gen.) **[13A]**

B

βαδίζω walk, go (fut. βαδιοῦμαι) **[10A]**
βαθέως deeply **[1E-F]**
βαθύς εῖα ύ deep **[5A]**
†βαίνω (βα-) go, come, walk **[1A-B]**
†βάλλω (βαλ-) hit, throw **[19F]**; βάλλ' εἰς
    κόρακας go to hell! **[6A]**

βάρβαρος, ὁ barbarian, foreigner (2a) **[2C]**
βάρος, τό weight, burden (3c) **[15C]**
βαρύς εῖα ύ heavy, weighty **[5A]**; βαρέως φέρω
    take badly, find hard to bear **[9C]**
βασιλεύς, ὁ king **[4D]**; king archon (3g) **[13E]**
βασιλεύω be king, be king archon; be queen
    [13E]
βέβαιος (ᾱ) ον secure **[2B]**
βέλτιστος η ον best **[8A]**
βελτῑ́ων βέλτῑον (βελτῑον-) better **[8A]**
βιάζομαι use force **[6C]**
βίος, ὁ life; means, livelihood (2a) **[5A]**
βλέπω look (at) **[1C-D]**
βληθείς εῖσα έν (βληθεντ-) aor. part. pass. of
    βάλλω
βοάω shout (for) **[3D]**
βοή, ἡ shout (1a) **[2]**
βοήθεια, ἡ help, rescue operation (1b) **[16C]**
βοηθέω run to help (+ dat.) **[1E-F]**
βουλεύομαι discuss, take advice **[17E]**
βουλευτής, ὁ member of council (1d) **[16F]**
βουλή, ἡ council (1a) **[13F]**
†βούλομαι wish, want **[7A]**
βραδέως slowly **[2B]**
βραχύς εῖα ύ short, brief **[16B]**
βροτός, ὁ mortal, man (2a) **[20E]**
βωμός, ὁ altar (2a) **[4D]**

Γ

ʼγαθέ = ἀγαθέ
γαῖα (1c)=γῆ, ἡ (1a) **[20E]**
†γαμέω (γημα-) marry **[13D]**
γάμος, ὁ marriage (2a) **[5A]**
*γάρ for **[1C]**; γάρ δή really, I assure you **[7B]**
*γε at least (*denotes some sort of reservation*)
    [1G, 5D]
γεγένημαι perf. of γίγνομαι **[13H]**
γεγενημένα, τά events, occurrences (2b) (perf.
    part. of γίγνομαι) **[16B]**
γέγονα perf. of γίγνομαι (part. γεγονώς or
    γεγώς) **[19F]**
γείτων (γειτον-), ὁ neighbour (3a) **[3A-B]**
†γελάω (γελασα-) laugh **[7F]**
γεν- aor. stem of γίγνομαι **[2]**
γένεσις, ἡ birth (3e) **[18A]**
γενναῖος ᾱ ον noble, fine **[15A]**

γεννήτης, ὁ member of a *genos* (1d) **[13C]**
γένος, τό *genos* **[13C]**; race, kind (3c)
γέρων (γεροντ-), ὁ old man (3a) **[6D]**
γεῦμα (γευματ-), τό taste, sample (3b) **[11C]**
γεύομαι taste **[11C]**
γεωργός, ὁ farmer (2a) **[4A]**
γῆ, ἡ land, earth (1a) **[1A-B]**
γημα- aor. stem of γαμέω
†γίγνομαι (γεν-) become, be born, happen, arise
    [2]
†γιγνώσκω (γνο-) know, think, resolve **[1I]**
γίνομαι = γίγνομαι **[19C]**
γλαυκῶπις (γλαυκωπιδ-), ἡ grey-eyed **[20C]**
γλυκύς εῖα ύ sweet **[10E]**
γνήσιος ᾱ ον legitimate, genuine **[13C]**
γνούς γνοῦσα γνόν (γνοντ-) aor. part. of
    γιγνώσκω **[209]**
γνώμη, ἡ judgment, mind, purpose, plan (1a)
    [6D]
*γοῦν at any rate **[10E]**
γοῦνα, τά knees (2b) (sometimes γούνατα [3b])
    [20D]
γραῦς (γρα-), ἡ old woman (3a; but acc. s. γραῦν;
    acc. pl. γραῦς) **[10B]**
γραφή, ἡ indictment, charge, case (1a) **[9H]**
    γραφὴν γράφομαι indict x (acc.) on charge of
    γ (gen.) **[9H]**
γράφομαι indict, charge **[9H]**
†γράφ-ω propose (a decree); write **[16C]**
γυνή (γυναικ-), ἡ woman, wife (3a) **[4A]**

Δ

δαίμων (δαιμον-), ὁ god, demon (3a) **[4A]**
†δάκνω (δακ-) bite, worry **[6A]**
δάκρυον, τό tear (2b) **[15C]**
δακρῡ́ω weep **[15B]**
*δέ and, but **[1A]**
δεήσει fut. of δεῖ
†δεῖ it is necessary for x (acc.) to – (inf.) **[7B]**
†δείκνῡμι (δειξα-) show **[16E]**
δεινός ή όν terrible, dire, astonishing, clever
    [3B]; clever at (+ inf.) **[9F]**
δέκα ten **[17C]**
δέμνια, τά bed, bedding (2b) **[20A]**
δένδρον, τό tree (2b) **[18B]**
δεξιᾱ́, ἡ right hand (1b) **[6D]**

δεξιός ά όν right [6D]; clever [8C]

†δέομαι need, ask, beg (+ gen.) [10E]

δέον it being necessary [16C]

δέρμα (δερματ-), τό skin (3b) [18B]

δεσμός, ὁ bond (2a) [18E]

δέσποινα, ἡ mistress (1c) [15A]

δεσπότης, ὁ master (1d) [4B]

δεῦρο here, over here [1B]

†δέχομαι receive [5D]

*δή then, indeed (adds stress) [3E]

δῆλος η ον clear, obvious [1H]

δηλόω show, reveal [1E-F]

δημιουργικός ή όν technical, of a workman [18E]

δημιουργός, ὁ craftsman, workman, expert, (2a) [18E]

δῆμος, ὁ people [6B]; deme [8B] (2a)

δήπου of course, surely [7D]

*δῆτα then [6D]

*διά (+ acc.) because of [2D]; (+ gen.) through [8C]; διὰ τί; why? [1G]

διαβαίνω (διαβα-) cross [7H]

διαβάλλω (διαβαλ-) slander [7A]

διαβολή, ἡ slander (1a) [7C]

διάκειμαι be in x (adv.) state, mood [16G]

διακρίνω (διακρῑνα-) judge between, decide [14D]

διακωλύω prevent [16F]

διαλέγομαι converse [5A]

διαλείπω (διαλιπ-) leave [16D]

διανοέομαι intend, plan [5C]

διάνοια, ἡ intention, plan (1b) [5C]

διαπράττομαι (διαπραξα-) do, perform, act [13G]

διατίθημι (διαθε-) dispose, put x (acc.) in y (adv.) state [17B]

διατριβή, ἡ delay, pastime, discussion, way of life (1a) [17C]

διατρίβω pass time, waste time [12H]

διαφέρω differ from (gen.); make a difference; be superior to (gen.) [12B]

διαφεύγω (διαφυγ-) get away, flee [17A]

†διαφθείρω (διαφθειρα-) destroy; kill [4B]; corrupt [7C]

διαφυγή, ἡ means of escape, flight (1a) [18B]

διδάσκαλος, ὁ teacher (2a) [7E]

†διδάσκω teach [5D]

†δίδωμι (δο-) give, grant [10E]

δίκην δίδωμι be punished, pay the penalty [13I]

διεξέρχομαι (διεξελθ-) go through, relate (fut. διέξειμι) [16A]

διέρχομαι (διελθ-) go through, relate [2]

διεφθάρμην plup. pass. of διαφθείρω [19A]

διηγέομαι explain, relate, go through [14B]

δικάζω be a juror; make a judgment [9C]

δίκαιος ᾱ ον just [5D]

δικαιοσύνη, ἡ justice (1a) [18E]

δικανικός ή όν judicial [12A]

δικαστήριον, τό law-court (2b) [8B]

δικαστής, ὁ juror, dikast (1d) [8B]

δίκη, ἡ lawsuit; justice; penalty (1a) [5A]; fine, case [17C]

δίκην δίδωμι be punished, pay the penalty [13I]

δίκην λαμβάνω punish, exact one's due from (παρά + gen.) [5A]

διοικέω administer, run [13F]

δῖος ᾱ ον godlike [20C]

διότι because [5A]

διώκω pursue [1C-D]; prosecute [9H]

δο- aor. stem of δίδωμι [10E]

δοκεῖ it seems a good idea to x (dat.) to do y (inf.); x (dat.) decides to – (inf.) [9A-E, 10A]

δοκέω seem, consider (self) to be [7C]

δόμοι, οἱ house, home (2a) [15A]

δόξα, ἡ reputation, opinion (1c) [7A]

δοῦλος, ὁ slave (2a) [4C]

δουλόομαι enslave (for oneself) [2A-D]

δούς δοῦσα δόν (δοντ-) aor. part. of δίδωμι [214]

δρᾶμα (δρᾱματ-), τό play, drama (3b) [9A]

δραχμή, ἡ drachma (coin) (pay for two days' attendance at ekklesia) (1a) [11B]

†δράω (δρᾱσα-) do, act [6D]

†δύναμαι be able [7H]

δύναμις, ἡ power, ability, faculty (3e) [18A]

δυνατός ή όν able, possible [18B]

δύο two [7H]

δύω sink [1G]

δυστυχής ές unlucky [5A]

δῶκαν 3rd pl. aor. of δίδωμι

δωρέω bestow, give as a gift [18C]

δῶρον, τό gift, bribe (2b) [10B]

ἐ- augment (remove this and try again under stem of verb)

*ἐάν (+ subj.) if (ever) [14C]

ἑαυτόν ἥν ὁ himself/herself/itself [7A]

†ἐάω allow [9F]

ἐγγράφω enrol, enlist, register [13C]

ἐγγυάω engage, promise [13A]

ἐγγύς nearby [3C]; near + gen. [8C]

ἐγκλείω shut in, lock in [9E]

ἔγνων aor. of γιγνώσκω [209]

ἐγώ I [1B]

ἔγωγε I at least, for my part [1D]

ἐδόθην aor. pass. of δίδωμι [228(i)]

ἔδομαι fut. of ἐσθίω [9F]

ἔδωκα aor. of δίδωμι [214]

ἐθέλω (ἐθελησ-) wish, want [9H]

ἔθεσαν 3rd pl. aor. of τίθημι [237]

ἔθηκα aor. of τίθημι [237]

ἔθος, τό manner, habit (3c) [13E]

*εἰ if [6D]

εἶ 2nd s. of εἰμί or εἶμι [44, 123]

εἴασα aor. ἐάω [9F]

εἰδείην opt. of οἶδα

εἰδέναι inf. of οἶδα [152]

εἶδον aor. of ὁράω [146]

εἰδώς εἰδυῖα εἰδός (εἰδοτ-) knowing (part. of
    οἶδα) [7C]

εἶεν very well, then! [11B]

*εἴθε (+opt.) I wish that! would that! if only!
    [12G]

εἰκός probable, reasonable, fair [12E]

εἴκοσι(ν) twenty [16F]

εἰκότως reasonably, rightly [13G]

εἴληφα perf. of λαμβάνω [13H]

εἱλόμην aor. of αἱρέομαι [211]

εἱμαρμένος η ον allotted, appointed
    [18C]

εἵματα, τά clothes (3b) [20B]

†εἰμί be [1J]

†εἶμι I shall go (inf. ἰέναι; impf. ᾖα I went) [7C]

εἶναι to be (inf. of εἰμί) [152]

εἰπ- aor. stem of λέγω [146]

εἰπέ speak! tell me! [3C]

εἶπον aor. of λέγω [146]

εἴρηκα I have said (perf. act. of λέγω)

εἴρημαι I have been said (perf. pass. of λέγω)
    [13H]

εἰρήνη, ἡ peace (1a) [8C]

    εἰρήνην ἄγω live in, be at peace [8C]

*εἰς (+ acc.) to, into, onto [1G]

εἷς μία ἕν (ἑν-) one [18E]

εἰσαγγελίᾱ, ἡ impeachment (1b) [16G]

εἰσαγγέλλω (εἰσαγγειλα-) impeach [16F]

εἰσάγω (εἰσαγαγ-) introduce [12D]

εἰσβαίνω I go onto, on board [1C-D]

εἰσεληλυθώς υῖα ός (-οτ-) perf. part. of
    εἰσέρχομαι

εἰσελθ- aor. stem of εἰσέρχομαι [5D]

εἰσέρχομαι (εἰσελθ-) enter [5D]

εἰσήγαγον aor. of εἰσάγω

εἰσῄα impf. of εἰσέρχομαι/εἴσειμι [161]

εἰσῆλθον aor. of εἰσέρχομαι [146]

εἰσιδ- aor. stem of εἰσοράω [1E-F]

εἰσιέναι inf. of εἰσέρχομαι/εἴσειμι [152]

εἰσιών οὖσα όν (-οντ-) part. of εἰσέρχομαι/εἴσειμι
    [123]

εἴσομαι fut. of οἶδα

εἰσοράω (εἰσιδ-) behold, look at [20E]

εἰσπεσ- aor. stem of εἰσπίπτω [15B]

εἰσπίπτω (εἰσπεσ-) fall into, on [15B]

εἰσφέρω (εἰσενεγκ-) bring, carry in [5A]

εἶτα then, next [6C]

εἴτε . . . εἴτε whether ... or [12B]

εἶχον impf. of ἔχω

ἐκ/ἐξ (+ gen.) out of [1G]

ἕκαστος η ον each [14B]

ἑκάτερος ᾱ ον each /both (of two)

ἐκβαλ- aor. stem of ἐκβάλλω [6A]

ἐκβάλλω (ἐκβαλ-) throw out [6A]; divorce
    [13A]; break down, break open [17A]

ἐκβληθείς εἶσα έν (-εντ-) aor. part. pass. of
    ἐκβάλλω

ἐκδέχομαι receive in turn [7F]

ἐκδίδωμι (ἐκδο-) give in marriage [13A]

ἐκδο- aor. stem of ἐκδίδωμι [13A]

ἐκδύομαι undress [10E]

ἐκεῖ there [16G]

ἐκεῖνος η ο that, (s)he [3C-E]

ἐκεινοσί that there (pointing) [72]

ἐκεῖσε there, (to) there [8A]

ἐκκλησίᾱ, ἡ assembly, ekklesia (1b) [8B]

ἐκπέμπω send out, divorce [13B]

ἔκπεσ – aor. stem of ἐκπίπτω [13A]

ἐκπίπτω (ἔκπεσ-) be thrown out, divorced [13A]

ἐκπορίζω supply, provide [18B]

†ἐκτίνω (ἐκτεισ-) pay [17C]

ἐκτρέχω (ἐκδραμ-) run out [9G]

ἐκφέρω (ἐξενεγκ-) carry out; (often: carry out for burial) [9F]

ἐκφεύγω (ἐκφυγ-) escape [9E]

ἐκφορέω carry off [17C]

ἐκφυγ- aor. stem of ἐκφεύγω [92]

ἑκών οὖσα όν (ἑκοντ-) willing(ly) [13C]

ἔλαβον aor. of λαμβάνω [146]

ἔλαθον aor. of λανθάνω [146]

ἐλάττων ἔλᾱττον (ἐλᾱττον-) smaller; fewer; less [13I]

ἔλαχον aor. of λαγχάνω

ἔλεγχος, ὁ examination, refutation (2a) [14E]

ἐλέγχω refute, argue against [14C]

ἐλ- aor. stem of αἱρέω/ομαι [11C]

ἐλευθερίᾱ, ἡ freedom (1b) [2]

ἐλεύθερος ᾱ ον free [2D]

ἐλευθερόω set free [2]

ἐλήλυθα perf. of ἔρχομαι [14A]

ἐλήφθην aor. pass. of λαμβάνω

ἐλθέ come! (s.) [1G]

ἐλθ- aor. stem of ἔρχομαι [2]

ἔλιπον aor. of λείπω

Ἕλλας (Ἑλλαδ-), ἡ Greece (3a) [14A]

Ἕλλην (Ἑλλην-), ὁ Greek (3a) [1J]

†ἐλπίζω hope, expect (+ fut. inf.) [9I]

ἐλπίς (ἐλπιδ-), ἡ hope, expectation (3a) [12I]

ἔμαθον aor. of μανθάνω [146]

ἐμαυτόν ήν myself [6D]

ἐμβαίνω (ἐμβα-) embark [3E]

ἔμεινα aor. of μένω [135]

ἐμεωυτόν = ἐμαυτόν [19B]

ἔμμεναι = εἶναι [20F]

ἐμός ή όν my, mine [2C]

ἔμπειρος ον skilled, experienced [1I]

ἐμπεσ- aor. stem of ἐμπίπτω [7F]

ἐμπίπτω (ἐμπεσ-) (ἐν) (εἰς) fall into, on, upon [7F]

ἐμπόριον, τό market-place (2b) [1G]

ἐμφανής ές open, obvious [13E]

*ἐν (+dat.) in, on, among [1G]; (+ gen.) in the house of [19B]

ἐν τούτῳ meanwhile [8A]

ἐν- stem of εἷς one

ἐναντίον (+gen.) opposite, in front of [8C]

ἔνδον inside [5D]

ἐνεγκ- aor. stem of φέρω [4B]

ἔνειμι be in [5B]

ἕνεκα (+gen.) because, for the sake of (usually follows its noun) [9G]

ἐνέπεσον aor. of ἐμπίπτω

ἐνέχυρον, τό security, pledge (2b) [16F]

ἔνθα there [15B]; where [19F]

ἐνθάδε here [9F]

ἐνθῡμέομαι take to heart, be angry at [16H]

ἐνί = ἐν [20B]

ἐνταῦθα (t)here, at this/that point [9D]

ἐντεῦθεν from then, from there [7B]

ἐντίθημι (ἐνθε-) place in, put in [17B]

ἐντυγχάνω (ἐντυχ-) meet with, come upon (+dat.) [9A-E] [12A]

ἐξ = ἐκ

ἐξάγω (ἐξαγαγ-) lead, bring out [9E]

ἐξαίφνης suddenly [10B]

ἐξαπατάω deceive, trick [9J]

ἐξέβαλον aor. ἐκβάλλω

ἐξεδόθην aor. pass. of ἐκδίδωμι [228(i)]

ἐξέδωκα aor. act. of ἐκδίδωμι [214]

ἐξελέγχω convict, refute, expose [13A]

ἐξελθ- aor. stem of ἐξέρχομαι [9C]

ἐξέρχομαι (ἐξελθ-) go out, come out [9C]

ἔξεστι it is possible for x (dat.) to – (inf.) [9F]

ἐξετάζω question closely [7C]

ἐξευρ- aor. stem of ἐξευρίσκω [6C]

ἐξευρίσκω (ἐξευρ-) find out [6C]

ἐξῆλθον aor. of ἐξέρχομαι [146]

ἐξήνεγκα 1st aor. of ἐκφέρω [211]

ἐξιέναι inf. of ἐξέρχομαι/ἔξειμι [152]

ἐξόν it being permitted, possible [16C]

ἔξω (+gen.) outside [16A]

ἔοικα seem; resemble (+dat.) [19D]

ἔοικε it seems, is reasonable [16A]; it is right for (+ dat.) [14F]; [20B]

ἐπαγγέλλω (ἐπαγγειλα-) order [17D]

ἔπαθον aor. of πάσχω [211]

†ἐπαινέω (ἐπαινεσα-) praise, agree [7F]

ἐπανελθ- aor. stem of ἐπανέρχομαι [7H]

ἐπανέρχομαι (ἐπανελθ-) return [7H]

ἐπανῆλθον aor. of ἐπανέρχομαι [146]

ἐπεί since [8C]; when [9C]

*ἐπειδάν (+ subj.) when(ever) [14C]

ἐπειδή when [2D]; since, because [3C]

ἐπεισέρχομαι (ἐπεισελθ-) attack [17A]

ἔπειτα then, next [1A]

ἐπείτε when, since [19B]
ἐπέρχομαι (ἐπελθ-) go against, attack [2]
ἐπέσχον aor. of ἐπέχω
ἐπέχω (ἐπισχ-) hold on, restrain, check [16B]
*ἐπί (+acc.) against, at, to, to get [2D]; (+ gen.) on [8C]; in the time of [19D]; (+ dat.) at, near, on [16F]; for the purpose of [14A]
ἐπιδείκνῡμι (ἐπιδειξα-) prove, show, demonstrate [13C]
ἐπιδημέω come to town, be in town [12I]
ἐπιεικής ές reasonable, moderate, fair [16G]
ἐπιθόμην aor. of πείθομαι
ἐπιθῡμέω desire, yearn for (+ gen.) [16B]
ἐπικαλέομαι call upon (to witness) [4D]
ἐπιλανθάνομαι (ἐπιλαθ-) forget (+gen.) [12G]
ἐπιμέλεια, ἡ concern, care (1b) [14E]
ἐπιμελέομαι care for (+ gen.) [13B]
ἐπιμελής ές careful [14B]
ἐπισκοπέομαι (ἐπισκεψα-) review [18A]
†ἐπίσταμαι know how to (+ inf.); understand [9J]
ἐπισχ- aor. stem ἐπέχω [16B]
ἐπιτήδειος ᾱ ον suitable, useful for [16B]
ἐπιχειρέω undertake, set to work [18D]
†ἕπομαι (σπ-) follow (+dat.) [7G]
ἔπος, τό word (3c) (uncontr. pl. ἔπεα) [19C]
ἐρ- see ἐρωτάω or ἐρέω [3A]
†ἐργάζομαι work, perform [12I]
ἔργον, τό task, job (2b) [1G]
ἐρέω fut. of λέγω [9A-E]
ἐρῆμος ον empty, deserted, devoid of [13B]
†ἔρχομαι (ἐλθ-) go, come [2]
†ἐρωτάω (ἐρ-) ask [3A]
ἐς = εἰς [20B]
ἐσθής (ἐσθητ-), ἡ clothing (3a) [18D]
†ἐσθίω (φαγ-) eat [9F]
ἐσθλός ή όν fine, noble, good [15C]
ἔσομαι fut. of εἰμί (be) (3rd s. ἔσται) [122]
ἐσπόμην aor. of ἕπομαι [7G]
ἔσσι = εἶ you (s.) are [20E]
ἔσται 3rd s. fut. of εἰμί (be) [122]
ἔσταν they stopped (3rd pl. aor. of ἵσταμαι)
ἐστερημένος η ον perf. part. pass. of στερέω [19B]
ἑστηκώς υῖα ός (-οτ-) standing (perf. part. of ἵσταμαι)
ἔσχατος η ον worst, furthest, last [12D]
ἔσχον aor. of ἔχω [146]
ἑταίρᾱ, ἡ prostitute, courtesan (1b) [12F]

ἑταῖρος, ὁ male companion (2a) [12F]
ἕτερος ᾱ ον one (or the other) of two [6D]
ἕτερος ... ἕτερον one ... another [12A]
ἔτι still, yet [3D]
ἔτι καὶ νῦν even now, still now [4A]
ἕτοῖμος η ον ready (to) (+ inf.) [8C]
ἔτος, τό year (3c) [17D]
ἐτραπόμην aor. of τρέπομαι
ἔτυχον aor. of τυγχάνω [146]
εὖ well [3B]
    εὖ ποιέω treat well, do good to [12C]
    εὖ πράττω fare well, be prosperous [19E]
εὐδαίμων εὔδαιμον (εὐδαιμον-) happy, rich, blessed by the gods [8B]
εὐθύς at once, straightaway [7F]; straight towards (+ gen.) [16A]
εὔνοια, ἡ good will (1b) [12B]
εὔνους ουν well-disposed [11B]
ἐϋπλόκαμος ον with pretty hair [20F]
εὐπορίᾱ, ἡ abundance, means (1b) [18C]
εὐπρεπής ές seemly, proper, becoming [15A]
εὑρ- aor. stem of εὑρίσκω [7C]
εὕρηκα perf. of εὑρίσκω
†εὑρίσκω (εὑρ-) find, come upon [7C]
εὐρύς εῖα ύ broad, wide [20G]
εὐσεβέω act righteously [13I]
εὐτυχής ές fortunate, lucky [15B]
εὔφρων εὔφρον well-disposed [4A-B]
εὐχή, ἡ prayer (1a) [3E]
εὔχομαι pray [3E]
ἐφ'=ἐπί
ἐφάνην aor. of φαίνομαι
ἔφην impf. of φημί [168]
ἐφοπλίζω equip, get ready [20B]
ἔφῡν be naturally (aor. of φύομαι) [13H]
ἔχθρᾱ, ἡ enmity, hostility (1b) [12C]
ἐχθρός, ὁ enemy (2a) [12C]
ἐχθρός ᾱ όν hostile, enemy [12C]
†ἔχω (σχ-) have, hold [1G]; (+adv.) be in x [adv.] condition [13B]
ἐν νῷ ἔχω have in mind, intend [6A]
ἐών=ὤν being [19B]
ἑώρᾱ 3rd s. impf. of ὁράω
ἕως, ἡ dawn [20B]
*ἕως (+ ἄν + subj.) until [16G]; until, while (+ ind.); (+ opt.) until [17A]
ἑωυτόν=ἑαυτόν [19B]

Z

Ζεύς (Δι-), ὁ Zeus (3a) **[3C-E]**
ζημίᾱ, ἡ fine(1b) **[13A]**
ζημιόω fine, penalise, punish **[16F]**
ζητέω look for, seek **[3D]**
ζῷον, τό animal, creature, living thing (2b) **[18B]**

H

ἠ – augment (if not under ἠ – look under ἀ – or
   ἐ -)
ἤ or **[1J]**; than **[7A]**
ἦ 1st s. impf. of εἰμί (be) **[110]**
ἦ or **[20E]**
ἦ δ’ ὅς he said **[7D]**
ᾖα impf. of ἔρχομαι/εῖμι **[161]**
ἡγεμών (ἡγεμον-), ὁ leader (3a) **[8A]**
ἡγέομαι lead (+dat.) **[8C]**; think, consider **[8A]**
ἠδέ and **[20F]**
ᾔδει 3rd s. past of οἶδα **[167]**
ᾔδεσαν 3rd pl. past οἶδα **[167]**
ἡδέως with pleasure, happily **[2A]**
ἤδη by now, now, already **[2A]**
ἤδη past of οἶδα **[167]**
ἥδιστος most pleasant (sup. of ἡδύς) **[11C]**
†ἥδομαι enjoy, be pleased with (+dat.) **[7D]**
ἡδονή, ἡ pleasure (1a) **[8C]**
ἡδύς εῖα ύ agreable, pleasant (sup. ἥδιστος) **[5A]**
ἥκιστα least of all, no, not **[16H]**
ἥκω have come, come **[11A]**
ἦλθον aor. of ἔρχομαι/εῖμι **[146]**
ἥλιος, ὁ sun (2a) **[6C]**
ἦμαρ (ἡματ-), τό day (3b) **[20E]**
ἡμεῖς we **[1C]**
ἦμεν 1st pl. impf. of εἰμί **[110]**
ἡμέρᾱ, ἡ day (1b) **[9A-E]**
ἡμέτερος ᾱ ον our **[1G]**
ἡμίονος, ὁ mule (2a) **[9E]**
ἦν 3rd s. impf. of εἰμί **[110]**
ἦν δ’ ἐγώ I said **[7D]**
ἤνεγκον aor. of φέρω **[211]**
ἠπιστάμην impf. of ἐπίσταμαι **[13A]**
Ἡρακλῆς, ὁ Herakles (3d uncontr.) **[8C]**
ἠρόμην aor. of ἐρωτάω **[194]**
ἦσαν 3rd pl. impf. of εἰμί **[110]**
ἦσθα 2nd s. impf. of εἰμί **[110]**
ἠσθόμην aor. of αἰσθάνομαι

ἡσυχάζω be quiet, keep quiet **[2C]**
ἡσυχίᾱ, ἡ quiet, peace (1b) **[2]**
ἥσυχος η ον quiet, peaceful **[9B]**
ἦτε 2nd pl. impf. of εἰμί or 2nd pl. subj. of εἰμί
ἥττων ἧττον (ἡττον-) lesser, weaker **[6D]**
ηὗρον aor. of εὑρίσκω **[146]**
ἠώς, ἡ (=ἕως, ἡ) dawn (acc. ἠῶ; gen. ἠοῦς; dat.
   ἠοῖ) **[20B]**

Θ

θάλαμος, ὁ bedchamber (2a) **[15B]**
θάλαττα, ἡ sea (1c) **[1G]**
θαν- aor. stem of θνήσκω **[15A]**
θάνατος, ὁ death (2a) **[9I]**
θαυμάζω wonder at **[6B]**
θε- aor. stem of τίθημι **[6C]**
θεᾱ́, ἡ goddess (1b) **[2]**
θεάομαι watch, gaze at **[3B]**
θεᾱτής, ὁ spectator, (pl.) audience (1d) **[9A]**
θεῖος ᾱ ον divine **[18D]**
θεῖτο 3rd s. aor. opt. of τίθεμαι **[237]**
θέμενος η ον aor. part of τίθεμαι **[237]**
θεός, ὁ ἡ god (2a) **[4B]**
θεράπαινα, ἡ maidservant (1c) **[17A]**
θεραπεύω look after, tend **[13C]**
θεράπων (θεραποντ-), ὁ servant (3a) **[17B]**
θές place! set! put! (aor. imper. [s.] of τίθημι)
   [237]
θέσθαι aor. inf. of τίθεμαι **[237]**
θέω run **[19F]**
θῆκε(ν) 3rd s. aor. of τίθημι (no augment)
θηρίον, τό beast (2b) **[18D]**
θήσεσθε 2nd pl. fut. of τίθεμαι **[237]**
†θνήσκω (θαν-) die **[15A]**
θνητός ή όν mortal **[4B]**
θορυβέω make a disturbance, din **[11A]**
θόρυβος, ὁ noise, din, clamour, hustle and bustle
   (2a) **[3B]**
θυγάτηρ (θυγατ(ε)ρ-), ἡ daughter (3a) **[12D]**
θῡμός, ὁ heart; anger (2a) **[20C]**
θύρᾱ, ἡ door (1b) **[3D]**
θυσίᾱ, ἡ sacrifice (1b) **[3E]**
θύω sacrifice **[3E]**
θώμεθα 1st pl. aor. subj. of τίθεμαι
θωπεύω flatter **[12C]**

I

ἰᾱτρικός ή όν medical, of healing **[18E]**

ἰᾱτρός, ὁ doctor (2a) **[17D]**

ἰδ- aor. stem of ὁράω **[1E-F]**

ἰδιώτης, ὁ layman, private citizen (1d) **[18E]**

ἴδον 1st s. aor. of ὁράω (*no augment*)

ἰδού look! here! hey! **[3A]**

ἰέναι inf. of ἔρχομαι/εἶμι **[152]**

ἱερά, τά rites, sacrifices (2b) **[13E]**

ἱερόν, τό sanctuary (2b) **[4C]**

ἴθι imper. s. of ἔρχομαι/εἶμι **[201]**

ἱκανός ή όν sufficient; able to (+ inf.) **[18B]**; capable of (+ inf.) **[14D]**

ἱκάνω come, come to/upon (+ acc.) **[20D]**

ἱκετεύω beg, supplicate **[13F]**

ἱκέτης, ὁ suppliant (1d) **[4C]**

†ἱκνέομαι (ἱκ-) come to, arrive at **[20E]**

ἱκόμην aor. of ἱκνέομαι

ἱμάτιον, τό cloak (2b) **[12A]**

ἴμεν = ἰέναι **[20D]**

*ἵνα (+subj./opt.) in order to/that **[16D]**; (+indic.) where

ἵππος, ὁ horse (2a) **[5A]**

ἴσᾱσι(ν) 3rd pl. of οἶδα **[44]**

ἴσμεν 1st pl. of οἶδα **[44]**

ἴστε 2nd pl. imperative of οἶδα **[44, 201]**

†ἵστημι (στησ-) set up, raise

ἵσταμαι (στα-) stand **[15A]**

ἰσχυρός ά όν strong, powerful **[13H]**

ἴσως perhaps **[7A]**

ἴω subj. of ἔρχομαι/εἶμι **[279]**

ἰών ἰοῦσα ἰόν (ἰοντ-) part. of ἔρχομαι/εἶμι **[123]**

K

κάδ = κατά **[20G]**

καθαίρω (καθηρα-) cleanse, purify **[19F]**

καθέστηκα I have been put (perf. of καθίσταμαι) **[13H]**

καθεστώς ῶσα ός (καθεστωτ-) having been made (perf. part. of καθίσταμαι)

καθεύδω sleep **[3D]**

†κάθημαι be seated **[16B]**

καθίζομαι sit down **[9C]**

καθίζω sit down **[9C]**

καθίσταμαι (καταστα-) be placed, put, made **[12D]**

καθίστημι (καταστησα-) set up, make, place, put x (acc.) in (εἰς) γ **[12D]**

καθοράω (κατιδ-) see, look down on **[8A]**

*καί and **[1A]**; also **[1B]**, even

*τε . . . καί both A and B

*καὶ γάρ in fact; yes, certainly **[12C]**

*καὶ δή and really; as a matter of fact; look! let us suppose **[13A]**

*καὶ δὴ καί moreover **[5D]**

*καὶ μήν what's more; look! **[12B]**; yes, and; and anyway

καίπερ although (+part.) **[6A]**

*καίτοι and yet **[10D]**

κακοδαίμων κακόδαιμον (κακοδαιμον-) unlucky, dogged by an evil daimon **[4A-B]**

κακός ή όν bad, evil, cowardly, mean, lowly **[1G]**

κακά (κακῶς) ποιέω treat badly, do harm to **[5B]**

κακῶς badly, evilly **[1E-F]**

καλεσα- aor. stem of καλέω

†καλέω (καλεσα-) call, summon **[3D]**

κάλλιστος η ον most (very) fine, good, beautiful **[2C]**

καλός ή όν beautiful, good **[1A-B]**

καλῶς well, finely, beautifully **[1E-F]**

κάρη (καρητ-), τό head (Attic κάρα [κρατ-], τό **[3b]**) **[20G]**

*κατά (+acc.) in, on, by, according to **[3C]**; down, throughout, in relation to **[12B]**; (+ gen.) below **[15A]**; down from, against **[20G]**

καταβαίνω (καταβα-) go down, come down **[1C-D]**

καταδικάζω condemn; convict x (gen.) of γ (acc.) **[9I]**

καταδίκη, ἡ fine (1a) **[16H]**

καταθε- aor. stem of κατατίθημι **[12I]**

καταθνῄσκω (καταθαν-) die away **[15A]**

κατακλίνομαι lie down **[10D]**

καταλαβ- aor. stem of καταλαμβάνω **[7H]**

καταλαμβάνω (καταλαβ-) overtake, come across, seize **[7H]**

καταλέγω (κατειπ-) recite, list **[12G]**

καταλείπω (καταλιπ-) leave behind, bequeath **[14A]**

καταλήψομαι fut. of καταλαμβάνω

καταλύω bring to an end, finish **[10A]**

καταμαρτυρέω give evidence against (gen.) [13D]

καταστάς ᾶσα άν (κατασταντ-) being placed, put (aor. part. of καθίσταμαι) [231]

καταστῆναι to be put (aor. inf. of καθίσταμαι) [232]

καταστήσομαι fut. of καθίσταμαι [232]

κατατίθημι (καταθε-) put down, pay, perform [12I]

καταφέρω (κατενεγκ-) carry down [17C]

καταφρονέω despise, look down on (+ gen.) [12E]

κατεγγυάω demand securities from (+ acc.) [13A]

κατέλαβον aor. of καταλαμβάνω [146]

κατέλιπον aor. of καταλείπω

κατέστην I was put (aor. of καθίσταμαι)

κατέστησα I put (aor. of καθίστημι)

κατηγορέω prosecute x (gen.) on charge of y (acc.) [9H]

κατηγορίᾱ, ἡ speech for the prosecution (1b) [9H]

κατήγορος, ὁ prosecutor (2a) [12B]

κατθανών aor. part. of καταθνῄσκω

κατιδ- aor. stem of καθοράω [8A]

κάτω below [11A]

κε (κεν) = ἄν (enclitic) [20A]

†κεῖμαι lie, be placed, be made [17B]

κεῖνος η ο = ἐκεῖνος [20E]

κέλευσαν 3rd pl. aor. of κελεύω (no augment)

κέλευσε 3rd s. aor. of κελεύω (no augment)

κελευστής, ὁ boatswain (1d) [3D]

κελεύω order [3E]

κεν = κε [20A]

κεφαλή, ἡ head (1a) [6A]

κῆρυξ (κηρῡκ-), ὁ herald (3a) [4D]

κηρῡ́ττω announce, proclaim [11A]

κινδῡνεύω be in danger, run a risk; be likely to (+ inf.) [17C]

κίνδῡνος, ὁ danger (2a) [3A]

κλαίω (κλαυσ-) weep [15C]

κλείω close, shut [17A]

κλέπτης, ὁ thief (1d) [9I]

†κλέπτω steal [6D]

κληθείς εῖσα έν (κληθεντ-) aor. part. pass. of καλέω

κλοπή, ἡ theft (1a) [18C]

κλύον 3rd pl. aor. of κλύω (no augment)

κλῦτε 2nd pl. imper. of κλύω

κλύω hear [15A]

κοινός ή όν common, shared [16D]

κοῖος = ποῖος

κολάζω punish [5B]

κομίζομαι collect [16D]

†κόπτω knock (on); cut [5D]

κόραξ (κορακ-), ὁ crow (3a) [8A]
 βάλλ' εἰς κόρακας go to hell! [6A]

κόρη, ἡ maiden, girl, daughter (1a) [13A]

κόσμος, ὁ decoration, ornament; order; universe (2a) [15A]

κοτε = ποτε

κου = που [19F]

κούρη, ἡ = κόρη, ἡ girl, daughter (1a) [20A]

κρατέω hold sway, power over (+ gen.) [4A]

κρείττων κρεῖττον (κρειττον-) stronger, greater [6D]

†κρῑ́νω (κρῑνα-) judge, decide [13F]

κρίσις, ἡ judgment, decision; dispute; trial (3e) [16F]

†κτάομαι acquire, get, gain [15B]

†κτείνω (κτεινα-) kill [18E]

κτῆμα (κτηματ-), τό possession (3b) [7H]

κυβερνήτης, ὁ captain, helmsman (1d) [1G]

κῡ́ριος ᾱ ον able, with power, sovereign, by right [14A]

κύων (κυν-), ὁ dog (3a) [9H]

κωλῡ́ω prevent, stop [4B]

κως = πως

Λ

λαβ- aor. stem of λαμβάνω [3C]

†λαγχάνω (λαχ-) obtain by lot; run as a candidate for office [13C]

δίκην λαγχάνω bring suit against

λαθ- aor. stem of λανθάνω [4D], [9A-E]

Λακεδαιμόνιος, ὁ Spartan (2a) [3C]

λαμβάνομαι (λαβ-) take hold of (+ gen.) [8C]

†λαμβάνω (λαβ-) take, capture [3C]
 δίκην λαμβάνω punish, exact one's due from (παρά + gen.)

λαμπάς (λαμπαδ-), ἡ torch (3a) [3A-B]

†λανθάνω (λαθ-) escape notice of x (acc.) –ing (nom. part.) [4D]

λᾱός, ὁ people, inhabitant (2a) [20F]

λαχ- aor. stem of λαγχάνω [13C]

†λέγω (εἰπ-) speak, say, tell, mean [1G]

†λείπω (λιπ-) leave, abandon [13C]

λέληθε 3rd s. perf. of λανθάνω

λέμβος, ὁ boat, life-boat (2a) [1G]

ληφθ- aor. pass. stem of λαμβάνω

λήψομαι fut. of λαμβάνω

λίθος, ὁ stone (2a) [11C]

λιμήν (λιμεν-), ὁ harbour (3a) [3A-B]

λιπ- aor. stem of λείπω

λίσσομαι beseech [20D]

λογίζομαι calculate, reckon, consider [7B]

λογισμός, ὁ calculation (2a) [13B]

λόγος, ὁ story, tale [2C]; speech, word [3C]; reason, argument [5D] (2a)

λοιπός ή όν left, remaining [17B]

λούω wash (mid. wash oneself) [20F]

λύω release [6A]

M

μά by! (+ acc.) [4C]

μαθ- aor. stem of μανθάνω [3C]

μαθήσομαι fut. of μανθάνω

μαθητής, ὁ student (1d) [5D]

μακρός ᾱ όν large, big, long [15A]

μάλα very, quite, virtually [16H]

μάλιστα (μάλα) especially, particularly; yes [4B]

μᾶλλον (μάλα) . . . ἤ more, rather than [13I]

μανθάνω (μαθ-) learn, understand [3C]

μαρτυρέω give evidence, bear witness [13D]

μαρτυρίᾱ, ἡ evidence, testimony (1b) [12G]

μαρτύρομαι invoke, call to witness [19F]

μάρτυς (μαρτυρ-), ὁ witness (3a) [9H]

μάχη, ἡ fight, battle (1a) [7G]

†μάχομαι (μαχεσ-) fight [2]

μεγάλοιο gen. s. m. of μέγας

μέγας μεγάλη μέγα (μεγαλ-) great, big [3C-E]

μέγεθος, τό size (3c) [20E]

μέγιστος η ον greatest (sup. of μέγας) [8B]

μέθες 2nd s. aor. imper. of μεθίημι [318]

μεθίημι (μεθε-) allow, let go [19D]

μείζων μεῖζον (μειζον-) greater (comp. of μέγας) [8B]

μέλᾱς αινα αν (μελαν-) black [9D]

†μέλει x (dat.) is concerned about (+ gen.) [14C]

†μέλλω be about to (+ fut. inf.); hesitate; intend (+ pres. inf.) [9J]

μέμφομαι blame, criticise, find fault with (+ acc. or dat.) [10D]

*μέν ... δέ on one hand ... on the other [1E]

*μέντοι however, but [7G]

†μένω (μεινα-) remain, wait for [1C-D]

μέρος, τό share, part (3c) [9H]

*μετά (+ acc.) after [7H]; (+ gen.) with [8C]; (+ dat.) among, in company with [20B]

μεταυδάω speak to [20G]

μετελθ- aor. stem of μετέρχομαι [16F]

μετέρχομαι (μετελθ-) send for, chase after [16F]; go among (+ dat.); attack (+ dat. or μετά + acc.) [20G]

μετέχω share in (+gen.) [14B]

μετίημι = μεθίημι [19D]

μέτριος ᾱ ον moderate, reasonable, fair [16F]

*μή (+imper.) don't! [1C]; not [7C]; (+aor. subj.) don't! [16B]

μηδαμῶς not at all, in no way [10D]

*μηδέ . . . μηδέ neither . . . nor [12A]

μηδείς μηδεμία μηδέν (μηδεν-) no, no one [10E]

μηκέτι no longer [9E]

*μήτε . . . μήτε neither . . . nor [11B]

μήτηρ (μητ(ε)ρ-), ἡ mother (3a) [10D]

μηχανάομαι devise, contrive [18A]

μηχανή, ἡ device, plan (1a) [10A]

μιαρός ᾱ όν foul, polluted [9E]

μῑκρός ᾱ όν small, short, little [12F]

†μιμνήσκομαι (μνησθ-) remember, mention [17D]

μιν him, her (acc.) (enclitic) [19A]

μῑσέω hate [4D]

μισθός, ὁ pay (2a) [14A]

μῖσος, τό hatred (3c) [13B]

μνᾶ, ἡ mina (100 drachmas) (1b) [13A]

μνείᾱ, ἡ mention (1b) [12G]

μνημονεύω remember [12G]

μνησθ- aor. stem of μιμνήσκομαι [17D]

μόνος η ον alone [8C]

μόνον only, merely [8C]
    οὐ μόνον . . . ἀλλὰ καί not only . . . but also [12C]

μῦθος, ὁ word, story (2a) [20B]

μῶν surely not? [8B]

μῶρος ᾱ ον stupid, foolish [1I]

N

ναί yes [1I]

ναυμαχίᾱ, ἡ naval battle (1b) [2]

ναῦς, ἡ ship (3 irr.) [1J]; [3C-E]

ναύτης, ὁ sailor (1d) [1A-B]

ναυτικός ή όν naval [3C]

νεᾱνίᾱς, ὁ young man (1d) [5B]

νεᾱνίσκος, ὁ young man (2a) [7D]

νεηνίης, ὁ = νεᾱνίᾱς, ὁ [19C]

νειμα- aor. stem of νέμω [18A]

νεκρός, ὁ corpse (2a) [4B]

†νέμω (νειμα-) distribute, allot, assign [18A]

νέος ᾱ ον young [5B]

νεώριον, τό dockyard [1A-B]

νή by! (+acc.) [4A]

νῆσος, ἡ island (2a) [3A]

'νθρωπε = ἄνθρωτε

νῑκάω win, defeat [2B]

νῑκη, ἡ victory, conquest (1a) [2]

νοέω plan, devise [20C]; think, mean, intend, notice [7B]

νομή, ἡ distribution (1a) [18C]

νομίζομαι be accustomed [19B]

†νομίζω acknowledge, think x (acc.) to be y (acc. or acc. + inf.) [7G]

νόμος, ὁ law, convention (2a) [4B]

νοσέω be sick [13C]

νόσος, ἡ illness, plague, disease (2a) [4B]

νοῦς, ὁ (νόος, contr.) mind, sense (2a) [5C]

ἐν νῷ ἔχω have in mind, intend [6A]

νυ = νυν [20C]

νυν now, then (enclitic) [8C]

νῦν now [1G]

νύξ (νυκτ-), ἡ night (3a) [3A-B]

Ξ

ξεῖνος = ξένος

ξένη, ἡ foreign woman (1a) [12D]

ξένος, ὁ foreigner, guest, host (2a) [4C]

O

ὁ ἡ τό the [1A-B]; in Ionic = he, she, it [20D]

ὁ αὐτός the same [176]

ὁ δέ and/but he [11C]

ὁ μέν... ὁ δέ one... another [8C]

ὅ τι; what? (sometimes in reply to τί;) [9F]

ὅδε ἥδε τόδε this here [9J]

ὁδί this here (pointing)

ὁδοιπόρος, ὁ traveller (2a) [11B]

ὁδός, ἡ road, way (2a) [11B]

ὅθεν from where [5C-D]; [16C]

οἱ = αὐτῷ to him, her (dat.) (Ionic) [19A]

οἷ (to) where [5C-D] [13E]

†οἶδα know [1J]

χάριν οἶδα be grateful to (+ dat.) [16B]

οἴκαδε homewards [3B]

οἶκε = ἔοικε resemble, be like (+ dat.) [19D]

οἰκεῖος, ὁ relative (2a) [13B]

οἰκεῖος ᾱ ον related, domestic, family [13B]

οἰκέτης, ὁ house-slave (1d) [5B]

οἰκέω dwell (in), live [7H]

οἴκημα (οἰκηματ-), τό dwelling (3b) [18C]

οἴκησις, ἡ dwelling (3e) [4A-B]

οἰκίᾱ, ἡ house (1b) [3B]

οἰκία, τά palace (2b) [19F]

οἰκίδιον, τό small house (2b) [12I]

οἴκοι at home [3D]

οἰκόνδε home, homewards [20E]

οἶκος, ὁ household, house (2a) [15C]

οἰκός = εἰκός reasonable [19F]

οἰκτῑρω (οἰκτῑρα-) pity [8B]

†οἶμαι think [7C]

οἴμοι alas! oh dear! [1F]

οἷος ᾱ ον what a! what sort of a! [10C]

οἷός τ' εἰμί be able to (+inf.) [12D]

οἴχομαι be off, depart [17B]

ὁκόθεν = ὁπόθεν [19B]

ὀλ- aor. stem ὄλλῡμαι [11B]

ὀλεσα- aor. stem of ὄλλῡμι [11B]

ὀλίγος η ον small, few [4A]

ὀλίγωρος ον contemptuous [14B]

ὄλλῡμαι (aor. ὠλόμην) be killed, die, perish [11B]

†ὄλλῡμι (ὀλεσα-) destroy, kill [11B]

ὅλος η ον whole of [5A]

ὀλοφῡρομαι lament [4D]

†ὄμνῡμι (ὀμοσ-) swear [13C]

ὅμοιος α ον like, similar to (+dat.) [9E]

ὁμολογέω agree [7E]

ὁμόνοια, ἡ agreement, harmony (1b) [2]

ὅμως nevertheless, however [9F]

ὄνειρος, ὁ dream (2a) [19A]
ὄνομα (ὀνοματ-), τό name (3b) [9B]
ὀξύς εῖα ύ sharp, bitter, shrill [11C]
ὅπλα, τά weapons, arms (2b) [3B]
ὁπόθεν from where [5C-D]; [19B]
ὅποι to where [5C-D]
ὁποῖος ᾱ ον of what kind [13E]
ὁπόσος η ον how many, how great [6C]
*ὁπόταν whenever (+ subj.) [16D]
*ὁπότε when [5C-D]; whenever (+opt.) [16E]
ὅπου where [5C-D, 6B]
*ὅπως how (answer to πῶς;) [11A]; how (indir.
    q.) [5C-D]
    (+ fut. ind.) see to it that [12G]
    (+subj. or opt.)= ἵνα in order to/that [18B]
†ὁράω (ἰδ -) see [1E-F]
ὀργή, ἡ anger (1a) [13B]
ὀργίζομαι grow angry with (+ dat.) [12H]
ὄρεος = ὄρους gen. of ὄρος, τό
ὀρθός ή όν straight, correct, right [4C]
ὅρκος, ὁ oath (2a) [12B]
ὁρμάομαι charge, set off [17A]
ὄρος, τό mountain (3c) [19F]
ὅς ἥ ὅ who, what, which [10E]
ὅσος η ον how great! [2B]; as much/many as
    [11B]
ὅσπερ ἥπερ ὅπερ who/which indeed [10E]
ὅστις ἥτις ὅτι who(ever), which(ever) [10E]
*ὅταν (+ subj.) whenever [14E]
ὅτε when [5C-D, 6A]
ὅτι that [1H]; because [9J]
*οὐ (οὐκ, οὐχ) no, not [1C]
οὐ μόνον . . . ἀλλὰ καί not only … but also [12C]
οὗ where (at) [16D]
οὐδαμῶς in no way, not at all [10A]
οὐδέ and not, not even [3C]
οὐδέν nothing [1D]
οὐδείς οὐδεμία οὐδέν (οὐδεν-) no, no one,
    nothing [4A-B]
οὐδέποτε never [5C]
οὐδέπω not yet [5A]
οὐκ=οὐ no, not [1C]
οὐκέτι no longer [2D]
*οὐκοῦν therefore [7E]
*οὔκουν not. . . therefore [7E]
*οὖν so, then, really, therefore [1D]
οὔνομα = ὄνομα, τό [19B]

οὗπερ where [17A]
οὔποτε never [15C]
οὔπω not yet [5A]
οὐρανός, ὁ sky, heavens (2a) [6B]
οὐσίᾱ, ἡ property, wealth (1b) [16D]
*οὔτε . . . οὔτε neither . . . nor [5D]
οὔτις (οὔτιν-) no one [15C]
οὗτος αὕτη τοῦτο this; (s)he, it [3C-E]
οὗτος hey there! you there! [6D]
οὑτοσί this here (*pointing*) [3A-E]
οὕτως/οὕτω thus, so; in this way [2D]
οὐχ = οὐ [1C]
†ὀφείλω owe [5A]
ὀφθαλμός, ὁ eye (2a) [20E]
ὄφρα (+subj./opt.) = ἵνα (+ind./subj./opt.) [20G];
    while, until
ὀφρῦς, ἡ eyebrow (3h) [6A]
ὄψις, ἡ vision, sight (3e) [19D]

Π

παθ- aor. stem of πάσχω [4D]
πάθος, τό suffering, experience (3c) [8B]
παιδίον, τό child, slave (2b) [9I]
παιδοποιέομαι beget, have children [12F]
παίζω play, joke at (πρός + acc.) [1H]
παῖς (παιδ-),ὁ, ἡ child; slave (3a) [3A-B]
πάλαι long ago [19F]
παλαιός ᾱ όν ancient, of old, old [13B]
πάλιν back, again [7H]
πανταχοῦ everywhere [8B]
παντελῶς completely, outright [14D]
*πάνυ very (much); at all [6D]
*πάνυ μὲν οὖν certainly, of course [16B]
πανύστατος η ον for the very last time [15A]
πάρα = πάρεστι(ν) [19E]
πάρ = παρά [20G]
*παρά (+ acc.) along, beside [2A]; against, to;
    compared with; except [12D]
    (+gen.) from [9I]
    (+dat.) with, beside, in the presence of [10B]
πάρα=πάρεστι it is possible for (+dat.) [19E]
παραγίγνομαι (παραγεν-) be present, turn up at
    (+ dat.) [17B]
παραδίδωμι (παραδο-) hand over [16C]
παραδώσειν fut. inf. of παραδίδωμι [214]
παραιτέομαι beg [18A]

παράκειμαι lie, be placed beside (+ dat.) **[17B]**

παραλαβ- aor. stem of παραλαμβάνω **[12I]**

παραλαμβάνω (παραλαβ-) take, receive from **[12I]**; undertake **[19D]**

παρασκευάζω prepare, equip **[16C]**

παρασκευή, ἡ preparation, equipping; force (1a) **[11C]**

παρασχ- aor. stem of παρέχω **[9E]**

παρεγενόμην aor. of παραγίγνομαι **[17B]**

πάρειμι be at hand, be present (+dat.) **[7B]**

παρέλαβον aor.of παραλαμβάνω **[146]**

παρελθ- aor. stem of παρέρχομαι **[11A]**

παρέρχομαι (παρελθ-) pass. go by, come forward **[11A]**

πάρεστι it is possible for (+ dat.) **[19E]**

παρέχω (παρασχ-) give to, provide **[9E]**

πράγματα παρέχω cause trouble (to) **[9E]**

παρθένος, ἡ maiden (2a) **[20G]**

Παρθενών, ὁ the Parthenon (3a) **[1A-B]**

πάριτε 2nd pl. imper. of παρέρχομαι/πάρειμι **[201]**

παριών οὖσα όν (-οντ-) part. of παρέρχομαι **[123]**

παροράω (παριδ-) notice **[19D]**

παρών οὖσα όν (παρονт-) part. of πάρειμι **[87]**

πᾶς πᾶσα πᾶν (παντ-) all **[9G]**
  ὁ πᾶς the whole of **[9G]**

†πάσχω (παθ-) suffer, experience **[4D]**

πατήρ (πατ(ε)ρ-), ὁ father (3a) **[5A]**

πατρίς (πατριδ-), ἡ fatherland (3a) **[3A-B]**

πατρῷος ᾱ ον ancestral, of one's father **[15A]**

παύομαι stop, cease (+ part.) **[4D]**; cease from (+gen.) **[10D]**

παύω stop x (acc.) from y (ἐκ + gen.); stop x (acc.) doing y (acc. part.) **[5B]**

πείθομαι (πιθ-) trust, obey **[5B]**; believe **[6B]** (+dat.)

πείθω persuade **[5D]**

πειράομαι (πειρᾱσα-) test, try **[7C]**

πείσομαι fut. of πάσχω or πείθομαι **[211]**

†πέμπω send **[8A]**

πένης (πενητ-) poor man (3a); (adj.) poor **[12G]**

πενίᾱ, ἡ poverty (1b) **[12D]**

πεντήκοντα fifty **[17B]**

*περί (+acc.) about, concerning **[1I]**
  (+ gen.) about, around **[8C]**
  (+dat.) in, on **[20E]**; about **[18E]**

περιφανής ές very clear, obvious **[13D]**

πεσ- aor. stem of πίπτω **[2B]**

πέφῡκα tend naturally to (perf. of φύομαι) **[13H]**

πηδάω leap, jump **[6C]**

πιθ- aor. stem of πείθομαι **[5B]**

†πῑνω (πι-) drink **[17B]**

†πῑπτω (πεσ-) fall, die **[2B]**

πιστεύω trust (+dat.) **[12C]**

πιστός ή όν reliable, trustworthy, faithful **[17A]**

πλεῖστος η ον very much, most (sup. of πολύς) **[16D]**

πλέον more (adv.) (comp. of πολύς) **[16G]**

†πλέω (πλευσα-) sail **[1G]**

πλέως α ων full of (+ gen.) **[8C]**

πλῆθος, τό number, crowd; the people (3c) **[4A-B]**

πλήν (+gen.) except **[9G]**

πλησίον nearby, (+ gen.) near **[9C]**

πλησίος ᾱ ον near, close to (+ gen.) **[17C]**

πλοῖον, τό vessel, ship (2b) **[1A-B]**

πλούσιος ᾱ ον rich, wealthy **[12G]**

πλῡνω wash **[20B]**

πόθεν; from where? **[3A, 5C-D]**; ποθεν from somewhere **[5C-D]**

ποῖ; where to? **[1E]** ; ποι to somewhere **[5C-D]**

ποιέομαι make **[8C]**

ποιέω make, do **[1E-F]**
  κακά (κακῶς) ποιέω treat badly, harm **[5B]**

ποιητής, ὁ poet (1d) **[7B]**

ποιμήν (ποιμεν-), ὁ shepherd (3a) **[17A]**

ποῖος ᾱ ον; what sort of? **[10E]**

πολεμέω make war **[11B]**

πολεμικός ή όν of war, military, martial **[18D]**

πολέμιοι, οἱ the enemy (2a) **[2D]**

πολέμιος ᾱ ον hostile, enemy **[2D]**

πόλεμος, ὁ war (2a) **[2D]**

πόλις, ἡ city, city-state (3e) **[4A-B]**

πολῑτείᾱ, ἡ state, constitution (1b) **[13G]**

πολῑτεύομαι be a citizen **[13G]**

πολῑτης, ὁ citizen (1d) **[8A]**

πολῑτικός ή όν political, to do with the πόλις **[18C]**

πολῖτις (πολιτιδ -), ἡ female citizen (3a) **[14C]**

πολλά many things **[1I]**

πολλάκις many times, often **[7C]**

πολύς πολλή πολύ (πολλ-) much, many **[3C-E]**
  πολύ (adv.) much **[9H]**

πονηρός ᾱ́ όν wicked, wretched **[9B]**
πόντος, ὁ sea (2a) **[20F]**
πορεύομαι march, journey, go **[3B]**
πορίζω provide, offer **[18B]**
πόρνη, ἡ prostitute (1a) **[14D]**
πόρρω far, afar off **[6C]**
Ποσειδῶν (Ποσειδων-), ὁ Poseidon, god of sea
    (3a) (voc. Πόσειδον; acc. Ποσειδῶ) **[5C]**
πόσις, ὁ husband, spouse (3e) **[15A]**
ποταμοῖο gen. s. of ποταμός
ποταμός, ὁ river (2a) **[7H]**
ποτε once, ever (*enclitic*) **[5C-D, 7B]**
πότε when? **[5C-D]**
πότερον . . . ἤ whether ... or **[2C]**
πότερος ᾱ ον; which (of two)? **[6D]**
που somewhere, anywhere (*enclitic*) **[5C-D]**;
    [20E]
ποῦ; where? **[1F, 5C-D]**
πούς (ποδ-), ὁ foot (3a) **[6A]**
πρᾶγμα (πράγματ-), τό thing, deed, matter, affair;
    (pl.) troubles (3b) **[4A-B]**
πράγματα παρέχω cause trouble **[9E]**
πρᾶξις, ἡ fact, action (3e) **[13E]**
†πρᾱ́ττω do, perform, fare **[13E]**
    εὖ πρᾱ́ττω fare well, be prosperous **[19E]**
πρέσβεις, οἱ ambassadors (3e) **[4D]**
πρεσβευτής, ὁ ambassador (1d) **[4D]**
πρεσβύτερος ᾱ ον older, rather old **[17A]**
*πρίν (+inf.) before **[13B]**
πρὶν ἄν (+ subj.) until **[17B]**
πρίν (+opt.) until **[17B]**
πρό (+gen.) before, in front of **[19F]**
προάγω lead on **[16G]**
πρόβατον, τό sheep (2b) **[17B]**
πρόγονος, ὁ forebear, ancestor (2a) **[13G]**
προδίδωμι (προδο-) betray **[15B]**
προδο- aor. stem of προδίδωμι **[15B]**
προθῡμέομαι be ready, eager **[16B]**
πρόθῡμος ον ready, eager, willing **[13B]**
προίξ (προικ-), ἡ dowry (3a) **[13A]**
*πρός (+acc.) to, towards **[1G]**
    (+ gen.) in the name/under the protection of
    [9H]
    (+ dat.) in addition to, near **[9A-E]**; **[16C]**;
    [17A]
    (adverbial) in addition **[18C]**
προσαγορεύω address, speak to **[10C]**

προσάπτω give, attach to (+ dat.) **[18B]**
προσδραμ- aor. stem of προστρέχω **[8A]**
προσεῖπον I spoke x (acc.) to y (acc.)
    (προσέειπον Ionic) **[20B]**
προσελθ- aor. stem of προσέρχομαι **[146]**
προσέρχομαι (προσελθ-) go/come towards,
    advance **[2]**
προσέχω bring near, apply to
    προσέχω τὸν νοῦν pay attention to (+dat.)
    [12B]
προσήκει it is fitting for x (dat.) to – (+ inf.)
    [18E]
προσῆλθον aor. of προσέρχομαι **[146]**
πρόσθεν previously; before (+ gen.) **[20G]**
προσιών οὖσα όν (προσιοντ-) part. of
    προσέρχομαι/πρόσειμι **[123]**
προσκαλέω summon, call **[17B]**
προσλέγω (προσειπ-) address **[15C]**
προσπίτνω fall upon, embrace **[15A]**
προστάττω (προσταξα-) order (+dat.) **[18A]**
προστρέχω (προσδραμ-) run towards **[8A]**
προτείνω stretch out **[19F]**
προτεραῖος ᾱ ον of the previous day **[17C]**
πρότερον formerly, previously **[12D]**
πρότερος ᾱ ον first (of two); previous **[12D]**
προτρέπω urge on, impel **[7D]**
πρύτανις, ὁ prytanis (3e) **[11A]**
πρῶτον first, at first **[6C]**
πρῶτος η ον first **[6C]**
πυθ- aor. stem of πυνθάνομαι **[13F]**
πύλη, ἡ gate (1a) **[16A]**
†πυνθάνομαι (πυθ-) learn, hear, get to know
    [13F]
πῦρ (πυρ-), τό fire (3b) **[9G]**
πυρά, τά fire-signal (2b) **[3A]**
πυρά̄, ἡ funeral pyre (1b) **[4B]**
πύργος, ὁ tower (2a) **[17C]**
πω yet (*enclitic*) **[20E]**
†πωλέω sell **[9E]**
πως somehow (*enclitic*) **[5C, C-D]**
πῶς; how? **[5C-D]**
*πῶς γὰρ οὔ; of course **[1J]**

Ρ

ῥᾴδιος ᾱ ον easy **[6A]**
ῥᾳδίως easily **[6A]**

ῥᾷστος η ον very easy [17D]
ῥαψῳδός, ὁ rhapsode (2a) [1A-B]; [1H]
ῥήτωρ (ῥητορ-), ὁ orator, politician (3a) [8B]
†ῥίπτω throw [1G]

Σ

σαφῶς clearly [1E-F]; [1H]
σεαυτόν yourself (s.) [1E]
σελήνη, ἡ moon (1a) [6D]
σέο=σοῦ of you [19D]
σεῦ=σοῦ of you
σημαίνω (σημην-) tell, signal [19F]
σημεῖον, τό sign, signal (2b) [7H]
σῑγάω be quiet [11A]
σιδηρέος η ον of iron, metal [19D]
σῖτος, ὁ food (2a) (pl. σῖτα, τά [2b]) [8C]
σιωπάω be silent [2C]
†σκέπτομαι examine, look carefully at [16B]
σκεύη, τά gear, furniture [4A-B]; ship's gear (3c) [16C]
†σκοπέω consider, examine [2C]
σμῑκρός ᾱ όν small, short, little [12F]
σός σή σόν your (s.) [6D]
σοφίᾱ, ἡ wisdom (1b) [7A]
σοφιστής, ὁ sophist, thinker (1d) [5D]
σοφός ή όν wise, clever [5D]
†σπένδω pour a libation [3E]
σπεύδω hurry [3A]
σπονδαί, αἱ treaty, truce (1a) [8C]
σπονδή, ἡ libation (1a) [3E]
σπουδάζω be concerned; do seriously [12E]
σπουδαῖος ᾱ ον serious, important [12E]
σπουδή, ἡ zeal, haste, seriousness (1a) [10C]
στᾱ́ς στᾶσα στᾱ́ν (σταντ-) standing (aor. part. of ἵσταμαι) [232]
στείχω go, come [15C]
στένω groan [9E]
στερέω deprive of [19B]
στή = ἔστη he/she stood (aor. of ἵσταμαι) (no augment)
στῆθ' = στῆτε [232]
στῆτε stand! (2nd pl. imper. aor. of ἵσταμαι) [232]
στόμα (στοματ-), τό mouth (3b) [16F]
στρατηγός, ὁ general (2a) [1J]
στρατιᾱ́, ἡ army (1b) [2]
στρωμνή, ἡ bed (1a) [18B]

σύ you (s.) [1B]
συγγεγένημαι perf. of συγγίγνομαι [13H]
συγγένεια, ἡ kinship (1b) [18D]
συγγενής, ὁ relation (3d) [8C]
συγγίγνομαι (συγγεν-) be with, have intercourse, dealings with (+ dat.) [12G]
συγγνώμη, ἡ pardon, forgiveness (1a) [9J]
συγγνώμην ἔχω forgive, pardon [9J]
συγκόπτω beat up, strike (aor. pass. συνεκόπην) [17C]
συγχωρέω agree with, to; yield to (+ dat.) [16F]
συλλέγω collect, gather [16G]
συμβουλεύομαι discuss with (+ dat.) [17E]
συμβουλή, ἡ discussion, recommendation (1a) [18E]
συμμαχός, ὁ ally (2a) [16C]
συμπέμπω send with (+ dat.) [19C]
συμπροθῡμέομαι share enthusiasm of (+ dat.) [17E]
συμφορᾱ́, ἡ disaster, mishap, occurrence (1b) [16A]
συμφορή = συμφορᾱ́
*σύν (+dat.) with the help of [9A-E]; together with [18C]
συνέρχομαι (συνελθ-) come together [12F]
συνῆλθον aor. of συνέρχομαι
συνοικέω live with, together (+dat.) [10B]
συντυγχάνω (συντυχ-) meet with (+dat.) [16A]
σφεῖς they (Attic σφᾶς σφῶν σφίσι) (Ionic σφεῖς σφέας σφέων σφι) [19D]
σφι to them (dat. of σφεῖς) [19D]
σφόδρα very much, exceedingly [17C]
σχ- aor. stem of ἔχω/ἔχομαι [1A-E]
σχεδόν near, nearly, almost [5A]
σχολή, ἡ leisure (1a) [16B]
†σῴζω save, keep safe [1G]
Σωκράτης, ὁ Socrates (3d) [6C]
σῶμα (σωματ-), τό body, person (3b) [14A]
σῶος ᾱ ον safe [1G]
σωτήρ (σωτηρ-), ὁ saviour (3a) [3A-B]
σωτηρίᾱ, ἡ safety (1b) [1G]
σωφροσύνη, ἡ good sense, moderation (1a) [18E]
σώφρων (σωφρον-) sensible, temperate, modest, chaste, discreet, prudent, law-abiding, disciplined [15B]

T

τάλᾱς αινα αν wretched, unhappy [9D]

τᾶν my dear chap (condescending) [8C]

τάξις, ἡ order, rank, battle-array (3e) [4A-B]

ταχέως quickly [2D]

τάχος, τό speed (3c) [18A]

τε . . . καί both . . . and [1A]

τεῖχος, τό wall (of a city) (3c) [10C]

τεκμαίρομαι conclude, infer [16G]; assign, ordain

τεκμήριον, τό evidence, proof (2b) [12F]

τέκνον, τό child (2b) [15A]

τελευτάω die, end, finish [17D]

τέλος in the end, finally [2B]

τευ = τινος [19D]

τέχνη, ἡ skill, art, expertise (1a) [3C]

τήμερον today [6D]

τι a, something (enclitic) [2D]

τί; what? [1D] why? [6C]

†τίθημι (θε-) put, place [6C] [12F]

†τίκτω (τεκ-) bear, give birth to [15A]

τῑμάω honour [4B]; value, reckon [17B]; (+dat.) fine [12D]

τῑμή, ἡ privilege, honour (1a) [14D]

τίμημα (τιμημᾱτ-), τό fine (3b) [12D]

τῑμωρέομαι take revenge on [12C]

τῑμωρίᾱ, ἡ revenge, vengeance (1b) [12C]

τις τι (τιν-) a certain, someone (enclitic) [4A-B]

τίς τί (τίν-); who? what? which? [1B]

τίτθη, ἡ nurse (1a) [17B]

*τοι then (inference) [10D]

τοι = σοι [19D]

τοί = οἵ (relative) [20E]

*τοίνυν well then (resuming argument) [12H]

τοιόσδε ἥδε όνδε of this kind [19E]

τοι-οῦτος -αύτη -οῦτο of this kind, of such a kind [9B]

τοῖσι = τοῖς [19B]

τόλμα, ἡ daring (1c) [2]

τολμάω dare, be daring, undertake [2D]

τοσοῦτος αύτη οῦτο so great [12D]

τότε then [5A]

τούτῳ dat. of οὗτος

  ἐν τούτῳ meanwhile, during this [8A]

τράπεζα, ἡ bank (1c) [17B]

τραπ- aor. stem of τρέπομαι

τρεῖς τρία three [11C]

τρέπομαι (τραπ-) turn (self), turn in flight [4D]

†τρέπω cause to turn, put to flight

†τρέφω (θρεψα-) rear, raise, feed, nourish [14D]

†τρέχω (δραμ-) run [3D]

τριηραρχέω serve as a trierarch [16C]

τριήραρχος, ὁ trierarch (2a) [3D]

τριήρης, ἡ trireme (3d) [11B]

τρόπος, ὁ way, manner (2a) [12H]

τροφή, ἡ food, nourishment (1a) [18B]

†τυγχάνω (τυχ-) chance, happen (to be –ing + nom.part.); be actually –ing (+nom. part.) [4D] (+ gen.) hit, chance/happen on, be subject to [9I]

†τύπτω strike, hit [4B]

τυχ- aor. stem of τυγχάνω [4D]

τύχη, ἡ chance, good/bad fortune (1a) [12A]

Y

ὑβρίζω treat violently, disgracefully [13A]; humiliate

ὕβρις, ἡ aggression, violence, insult, humiliation (3e) [4D]

ὑβριστής, ὁ violent, criminal person (1d) [16A]

ὕδωρ (ὑδατ-), τό water (3b) [15A]

υἱός, ὁ son (2a; also, except for acc. s., like m. forms of γλυκύς) [5A]

ὑμεῖς you (pl.) [1D]

ὑμέτερος ᾱ ον your (when 'you' is more than one person) [7H]

ὑπακούω reply, answer; obey (+ dat.) [16E]

ὑπάρχω be, be sufficient [19E]; begin (+ gen.) [12C]

*ὑπέρ (+gen.) for, on behalf of [8C]

ὑπηρέτης, ὁ servant, slave (1d) [4D]

†ὑπισχνέομαι (ὑποσχ-) promise (to) (+ fut. inf.) [16H]

ὕπνος, ὁ sleep (2a) [19D]

*ὑπό (+acc.) under, along under, up under [16A]
  (+gen.) by, at the hand of [8C]
  (+dat.) under, beneath [15A]

ὑποδέχομαι welcome, entertain [19E]

ὑπόλοιπος ον remaining [17C]

ὗς, ὁ boar (3h) [19D]

ὑσταραῖος ᾱ ον of the next day [17C]

ὕστερον later, further [9J]

ὕστερος ᾱ ον later, last (of two) [9J]

ὑφ' = ὑπό

ὑφαιρέομαι (ὑφελ-) steal, take for oneself by stealth [9I]

Φ

φαγ- aor. stem of ἐσθίω [9F]

φαίνομαι (φαν-) appear, seem [3B]; seem (to be) (+nom. part.) [4D]; seem to be but not *really* to be (+inf.) [13F]

†φαίνω (φην-) reveal, declare, indict [13H]

φάμενος η ον aor. part. mid. of φημί (ἐφάμην) [168]

οὐ φάμενος saying . . . not, refusing [336]

φάναι inf. of φημί [168]

φανερός ᾱ́ όν clear, obvious [12F]

φάνη 3rd s. aor. of φαίνομαι (*no augment*)

φάσθ' you say (2nd pl. mid. of φημί) [168]

φάσκω allege, claim, assert [13G]

φάτο he spoke (3rd s. aor. mid. of φημί)

φέρε come! [9B]

†φέρω (ἐνεγκ-) carry [4B]; bear, endure [17D]; lead [17A]

   χαλεπῶς φέρω be angry, displeased at [13F]

†φεύγω (φυγ-) run off, flee [1C-D]; be a defendant, be on trial [9H]

φεύξομαι fut. of φεύγω

†φημί/ἔφην I say/I said [7F]

φής you say [5B]

φήσω fut. of φημί [168]

φήσειεν 3rd s. aor. opt. of φημί

†φθάνω (φθασ-) anticipate x (acc.) by/in –ing (nom. part.) [4D]

φιλέω love, kiss [5C]; be used to (+inf.) [11B]

φιλίᾱ, ἡ friendship (1b) [18E]

φίλος, ὁ friend (2a) [1G]

φίλος η ον dear; one's own [1G]

φιλοσοφίᾱ, ἡ philosophy (1b) [7D]

φιλόσοφος, ὁ philosopher (2a) [8C]

φίλτατος η ον most dear (sup. of φίλος) [10C]

φοβέομαι fear, be afraid of, respect [2]

φοβέομαι μή (+subj.) fear that, lest [16B]; (+ opt.) [16H]

φοβερός ᾱ́ όν terrible, frightening [18C]

φόβος, ὁ fear (2a) [4B]

φόνος, ὁ murder (2a) [17D]

φράζω utter, mention, talk [16D]

φρά́τηρ (φρᾱτερ-), ὁ member of phratry (3a) [13B]

φρήν (φρεν-), ἡ heart, mind (3a) [20C]

φρονέω think, consider [20D]

φροντίζω think, worry [1G]

φροντίς (φροντιδ-), ἡ thought, care, concern (3a) [6A]

φυγή, ἡ flight (1a) [18A]

φύγον 1st s. aor. of φεύγω (no augment)

φυλακή, ἡ guard (1a) [18C]

φύλαξ (φυλακ-), ὁ, ἡ guard (3a) [10C]

φυλάττω guard (Ionic φυλάσσω) [7G]

φύσις, ἡ nature, character, temperament (3e) [13A]

†φύ́ω bear; mid. grow; (aor. mid.) ἔφῡν be naturally; (perf.) πέφῡκα be inclined by nature [13H]

φωνέω speak, utter [7H]

φωνή, ἡ voice, language, speech (1a) [7H]

φῶς (φωτ-), τό light (3b) [18C]

φώς (φωτ-), ὁ man, mortal (3a) [20F]

Χ

χαῖρε greetings! hello! [8A] farewell!

†χαίρω (χαρ-) rejoice [20A]

χαλεπός ή όν difficult, hard [8C]

χαλεπῶς φέρω be angry, displeased at [13F]

χαλκοῦς ῆ οῦν of bronze [17A]

χαρίζομαι oblige, please; be dear to (+dat.) [19E]

χάρις (χαριτ-), ἡ reciprocal action, thanks, grace, (3a) [16B]

χάριν οἶδα be grateful to (+dat.) [16B]

χειμών (χειμων-), ὁ winter, storm (3a) [18B]

χείρ (χειρ-), ἡ hand (3a) [8A]

χείρων χεῖρον (χειρον-) worse (comp. of κακός) [8C]

χθές yesterday [17D]

χί́λιοι αι α thousand [17C]

χορός, ὁ dance; chorus (2a) [20E]

†χράομαι use, employ (+dat.) [9E]

χρέα, τά debts (3c uncontr.) [5B]

†χρή it is necessary for x (acc.) to – (infin.) [9F]

χρῆμα (χρημᾱτ-), τό thing (3b) [19B]

χρήματα, τά money (3b) [5A]

χρηματίζω do business **[11B]**
χρῆσθαι pres. inf. of χράομαι
χρήσιμος η ον profitable, useful **[6D]**
χρηστός ή όν good, fine, serviceable **[5B]**
χρῆται 3rd s. pres. of χράομαι
χρόα acc. of χρώς **[20D]**
χροΐ dat. of χρώς **[20D]**
χρόνος, ὁ time (2a) **[8B]**
χροός gen. of χρώς **[20D]**
χρύσεος η ον golden **[20G]**
χρώς (χρωτ-), ὁ flesh, skin, body (3a) **[15A]**
  (Ionic acc. χρόα; gen. χροός; dat. χροΐ **[20D]**)
χωρέω go, come **[3A]**
χώρη, ἡ land (1a) (*Attic* χώρᾱ, ἡ [1b]) **[19C]**
χωρίον, τό place; space; region **[6C]**; farm (2b)
  [16A]
χωρίς apart, separately (from) (+gen.) **[16D]**

ψευδής ές false, lying **[12D]**
ψεύδομαι lie, tell lies **[13F]**
ψευδῶς falsely **[2C]**
ψηφίζομαι vote **[10E]**
ψήφισμα (ψηφισματ-), τό decree (3b) **[12D]**

ψῆφος, ἡ vote, voting-pebble (2a) **[9H]**
ψῡχή ἡ soul, life (1a) **[17C]**

Ω

ὠ- augment (*if not under* ὠ- *look under* ὀ-)
ὤ what . . .! (+ gen.) **[4D]**
ὦ O (+voc./nom.) (*addressing someone*) **[1B]**
ὧδε thus, as follows **[18E]**
ὠθέω push, shove **[12A]**
ὠλόμην aor. of ὄλλῡμαι
ᾤμην impf. of οἶμαι
ὦμος, ὁ shoulder (2a) **[20G]**
ὤν οὖσα ὄν (ὀντ-) part. of εἰμί **[87]**
ὦν = οὖν **[19C]**
†ὠνέομαι (πρια-) buy **[16C]**
*ὡς how! **[1C, 5C-D]**; as **[6A]**; that **[7B]**
  (+acc.) towards, to the house of **[12F]**
  (+fut. part.) in order to **[13B]**
  (+sup.) as – as possible **[16C]**
  (+subj./opt.)= ἵνα in order to/that **[20C]**
ὧς thus, so **[20A]**
ὥσπερ like, as **[2D]**
*ὥστε so that, with the result that, consequently
  (+inf./indic.) **[16C]**

List of proper names

Most names of people(s) and all names of places will be found in the running
vocabularies where they occur. The names which recur several times and are
not repeated in the running vocabularies are listed here for convenience of
reference.

Ἄδμητ-ος, ὁ Admetos (2a) (husband of Alkestis)
Ἄδρηστ-ος, ὁ Adrastos (2a) ('Unable to escape'; member of the Phrygian royal
  family and suppliant of Croesus)
Ἀθήν-η|-ᾱ, ἡ Athene (1a/b) (goddess of craftsmanship and protectress of
  Odysseus)
Ἀλκίνο-ος, ὁ Alkinoos (2a) (king of the Phaiakians and father of Nausikaa)
Ἀμφί-θε-ος, ὁ Amphitheos (2a) ('God on both sides'; goes to Sparta to get
  Dikaiopolis' private peace-treaty)
Ἀπολλόδωρ-ος, ὁ Apollodoros (2a) (prosecutor of Neaira and Stephanos; friend
  of Aristarkhos)
Ἀπόλλων (Ἀπολλων-), ὁ Apollo (3a: but voc. usu. Ἄπολλον; acc. Ἀπόλλω)
  (god of prophecy, with oracular shrine at Delphi)

Ἀρίσταρχ-ος, ὁ Aristarkhos (2a) (friend of Apollodoros, narrator of his legal troubles at the hands of Theophemos and Euergos)

Ἀφροδῑτ-η, ἡ Aphrodite (1a) (goddess of love; used often as synonym for sexual pleasure)

Βδελυκλέων (Βδελυκλεων-), ὁ Bdelykleon (3a) ('Loathe-Kleon'; son of Philokleon)

Δικαιόπολις, ὁ Dikaiopolis (3e) ('Just citizen'; Attic farmer in search of peace)

Διονῡσόδωρ-ος, ὁ Dionysodoros (2a) (sophist, brother of Euthydemos)

Ἐπιμηθ-εύς, ὁ Epimetheus (3g) ('Aftersight'; brother of Prometheus)

Ἑρμ-ῆς, ὁ Hermes (Id) (Zeus' messenger)

Εὐεργίδ-ης, ὁ Euergides (1d) (experienced dikast)

Εὔεργ-ος, ὁ Euergos (2a) (brother of Theophemos and his helper in seizing Aristarkhos' goods)

Εὐθύδημ-ος, ὁ Euthydemos (2a) (sophist, brother of Dionysodoros)

Θεογέν-ης, ὁ Theogenes (3d) (*basileus archon* and for a short time husband of Phano)

Θεόφημ-ος, ὁ Theophemos (2a) (enemy of Aristarkhos and responsible for the seizure of his goods)

Ἰλῑσ-ός, ὁ river Ilisos (2a) (see map, *Text*, p. 19)

Κῑνησί-ᾱς, ὁ Kinesias (1d) ('Sexually active'; husband of Myrrhine)

Κλεινί-ᾱς, ὁ Kleinias (1d) (a young friend of Socrates)

Κλεονῑκ-η, ἡ Kleonike (1a) (friend and fellow-conspirator of Lysistrata)

Κροῖσ-ος, ὁ Croesus (2a) (king of Lydia) (see map, *Text*, p. 157)

Κωμί-ᾱς, ὁ Komias (1d) (experienced dikast)

Λάβης (Λαβητ-), ὁ Labes (3a) ('Grabber'; dog indicted on a charge of stealing cheese)

Λῡδ-οί, οἱ Lydians (2a) (Croesus' people) (see map, *Text*, p. 157)

Λυσί-ᾱς, ὁ Lysias (1d) (the famous orator, lover of Metaneira)

Λῡσιστράτ-η, ἡ Lysistrata (1a) ('Destroyer of the army'; prime-mover of the women's sex-strike)

Μετάνειρ-α, ἡ Metaneira (1b) (a slave and prostitute in Nikarete's brothel, loved by Lysias)

Μυρρίν-η, ἡ Myrrhine (1a) (friend of Lysistrata and wife of Kinesias)

Μῡσ-οί, οἱ Mysians (2a) (see map, *Text*, p. 157)

Ναυσικά-ᾱ, ἡ Nausikaa (1b) (unmarried daughter of Alkinoos, king of the Phaiakians)

Νέαιρ-α, ἡ Neaira (1b) ('wife' of Stephanos; indicted by Apollodoros for living with Stephanos as his wife and pretending that her children were citizens)

Νῑκαρέτ-η, ἡ Nikarete (1a) (brothel-keeper; former owner of Neaira)

Ξανθί-ᾱς, ὁ Xanthias (1d) (slave of Bdelykleon)

Ὀδυ(σ)σ-εύς, ὁ Odysseus (3g) (cunning Greek hero, who wandered for ten years after the Trojan War before finally returning to Ithaka, his kingdom)

Ὅμηρ-ος, ὁ Homer (2a) (epic poet, author of the *Iliad* and the *Odyssey*)

Πεισ-έταιρ-ος, ὁ Peisetairos (2a) ('Persuade-friend'; friend of Dikaiopolis; plans to leave Athens with Euelpides)

Περικλ-ῆς, ὁ Pericles (3d: uncontr.) (political leader in Athens during the mid-fifth century)

Προμηθ-εύς, ὁ Prometheus (3g) ('Foresight'; brother of Epimetheus)

Πῶλ-ος, ὁ Polos (2a) (a rower on board a trireme)

Στέφαν-ος, ὁ Stephanos (2a) ('husband' of Neaira; indicted by Apollodoros for living with a foreigner as his wife and trying to pass off her children as citizens)

Στρεψιάδ-ης, ὁ Strepsiades (1d) ('Twist and turn'; debt-ridden farmer, father of Pheidippides)

Στρῡμόδωρ-ος, ὁ Strymodoros (2a) (inexperienced dikast)

Σωσί-ᾱς, ὁ Sosias (1d) (slave of Bdelykleon)

Φαίηκ-ες, οἱ Phaiakians (3a) (Alkinoos' people)

Φαν-ώ, ἡ Phano (acc. Φαν-ώ; gen. Φαν-οῦς; dat. Φαν-οῖ) (daughter of Neaira; married to Phrastor, then Theogenes)

Φειδιππίδ-ης, ὁ Pheidippides (1d) ('Son of Pheidon and horse'; chariot-racing, horse-mad son of Strepsiades)

Φιλοκλέων (Φιλοκλεων-), ὁ Philokleon (3a) ('Love-Kleon'; jury-service-loving father of Bdelykleon)

Φράστωρ (Φραστορ-), ὁ Phrastor (3a) (for a time husband of Phano)

Φρῡνίων (Φρῡνιων-), ὁ Phrynion (3a) (former lover of Neaira, from whom Stephanos rescued her)

Χαιρεφῶν (Χαιρεφωντ-), ὁ Khairephon (3a) (good friend of Socrates)